# THE END OF WOKE

# ANDREW DOYLE

# THE END OF WOKE

**How the Culture War Went Too Far and
What to Expect from the Counter-Revolution**

CONSTABLE

CONSTABLE

First published in Great Britain in 2025 by Constable

1 3 5 7 9 10 8 6 4 2

A CIP catalogue record for this book
is available from the British Library.

ISBN: 978-1-40872-396-8 (hardback)
ISBN: 978-1-40872-397-5 (trade paperback)

Typeset in Goudy Old Style by SX Composing DTP, Rayleigh, Essex
Printed and bound in Great Britain by Clays Ltd, Elcograf S.p.A.

Papers used by Constable are from well-managed forests
and other responsible sources.

Constable
An imprint of
Little, Brown Book Group
Carmelite House
50 Victoria Embankment
London EC4Y 0DZ

The authorised representative
in the EEA is
Hachette Ireland
8 Castlecourt Centre, Dublin 15,
D15 XTP3, Ireland
(email: info@hbgi.ie)

An Hachette UK Company
www.hachette.co.uk

www.littlebrown.co.uk

*For Edward McLaughlin*

*1909 – 1987*

'There are two solutions. One of them is the Nazi solution. If you don't like people, kill them, banish them, segregate them, and then strut up and down proclaiming that you are the salt of the earth. The other way is much less thrilling, but it is on the whole the way of the democracies, and I prefer it. If you don't like people, put up with them as well you can. Don't try to love them: you can't, you'll only strain yourself. But try to tolerate them. On the basis of that tolerance a civilised future may be built.'

E. M. Forster, *Two Cheers for Democracy*

# Contents

# PROLOGUE

# The Reckoning

---

It was an extraordinary scene. Donald Trump, recently re-elected as president of the United States, found himself surrounded by women and girls in the East Room of the White House. The date was 5 February 2025, and Trump was signing an executive order entitled 'Keeping Men Out of Women's Sports'. As the president took to his desk and prepared his pen, he invited his all-female audience to draw closer. 'Secret service is worried about them?' he joked. 'If we have to worry about them we have big problems.' There was laughter, applause, a hubbub of palpable relief that an egregious social injustice was on the cusp of being corrected. Photographers captured the moment in a flurry of snapping shutters. Would this be the image that marked the beginning of our post-woke era, the first phase of sobering up for a once drunken world?

The significance of this event could not be dismissed as a mere publicity stunt. Here was one of the most controversial Republican presidents in history, a man who had been accused repeatedly of misogyny, nevertheless enacting the most pro-feminist directive since

Richard Nixon signed Title IX of the Education Amendments in June 1972, a measure that prohibited sex-based discrimination in federally funded educational institutions. The culture war of our times has often been misinterpreted as a conflict between left and right but, as I shall argue, these designations are hangovers from the French Revolution, ill-suited to today's complex ideological skirmishes. The sudden rise in the early 2010s of Critical Social Justice – that sprawling, complex and disparate movement known colloquially as 'woke' – has meant that the terms 'left' and 'right' have lost much of their utility. Definitions of 'woke' are as varied as can be imagined, but it is best understood as a cultural revolution that seeks equity according to group identity by authoritarian means. Yet for all its institutional clout, this ideology has never enjoyed popular support. Estimates by More in Common, a nonprofit organisation committed to the promotion of social cohesion, suggest that at its height the woke movement was endorsed by approximately eight per cent of the population of both America and the United Kingdom. As such, its power could only ever be sustained through misdirection and imposition.

This is why Trump's executive order received such an overwhelmingly positive reception from across the political spectrum. A poll by NPR and Ipsos in 2022 showed that 63 per cent of Americans did not approve of men who identify as female competing in women's sports. By January 2025, a poll by the *New York Times* and Ipsos revealed that this figure has risen to 79 per cent. Even among Democrat voters, a significant majority (67 per cent) supported the principle of keeping men out of the female category. For such a divisive figure, Trump had somehow found a unifying cause. The author J. K. Rowling echoed the feeling of many Democrat voters when she posted on social media a photograph of Trump signing the executive order and wrote: 'Congratulations to every single person on the left who's been campaigning to destroy women's and girls' rights. Without you, there'd be no images like this.' It was not so much that Trump had suddenly rebranded the Republican Party as liberal, but that Democratic leaders had embraced the politics of illiberalism. Evangelists of the woke movement had seized disproportionate power in a relatively short time precisely because their aims had been so widely misapprehended. They had dissembled and played endless word games to coax unsuspecting progressives into backing regressive causes. So while it felt almost oneiric to witness a Republican president upholding the ideals once championed by the left, this was simply a reminder that our liberal consensus still prevailed in spite of the best efforts of culture warriors. We have far more in common than the extreme identitarians on both the left and the right would have us believe. To our shame, we have allowed the most brattish and irrational voices to dictate the terms of debate.

The culture war, in other words, is the politics of infantilism writ large. This has been borne out by my own experiences. When I announced in May 2021 that I was working on a book about the origins of the social justice movement and how it fosters aggressive and childish behaviour, some activists immediately suggested that they would acquire copies only to burn them. One said that he intended to kick it under the bookshop shelf 'so that it could rot in darkness'. A left-wing website called *Byline Times* even claimed that I was waging 'a perpetual battle against social justice – fighting against a contrived present world of aggressive "woke snowflakes" in order to return to an imagined past'. This was news to me given that my book was a defence of liberal values, a critique of intolerance, and it explicitly reproached those who resort to the 'snowflake' slur. I particularly enjoyed the suggestion that I had conjured enemies into existence in order to fight them. It takes some chutzpah to make such a claim of a book you haven't actually read.

It would seem that the title alone – *The New Puritans: How the Religion of Social Justice Captured the Western World* – was enough to stir the ire of these culture warriors. In a sense, this is unsurprising. One of the key aspects of the woke movement is that its adherents treat all challenges as a form of heresy that must be quashed. For all the relish with which they smear their detractors as 'bigots', they forget that the principal definition of the word – 'a person who is utterly intolerant of any differing creed, belief or opinion' – applies most accurately to themselves.

That book was intended to be my final word on the subject, and yet since its publication in 2022 the culture war has developed in surprising and significant ways. In *The New Puritans* I traced the origins of Critical Social Justice and explored its various metamorphoses and ultimate cultural ascendency. Now we find ourselves entering a new phase of the culture war, one in which the woke ideology is being tamed and will soon relinquish its chokehold on the Western world. The Black Lives Matter protests and riots of the summer of 2020 had propelled the movement into overdrive. The countersigns of virtue were now firmly established: taking the knee, demolishing 'problematic' statues and historical landmarks, waving the rainbow 'Progress Pride' flag, declaring pronouns, wearing masks even where there was scant risk of infection, hounding dissenters through a retributive system known as 'cancel culture'. Big tech was cracking down on free speech, governments were ramping up legislation to punish citizens for thought crimes, universities were promoting dogma rather than the pursuit of knowledge, and all of this was ostensibly happening in the name of progress. Something had gone very wrong; authoritarianism was winning.

In repackaging such instincts as 'progressive', the woke had destabilised an ongoing liberal project that had been making tremendous headway since the civil rights movements of the 1960s. They supported draconian speech codes and suppression of their political opponents. They modified school curricula so that children were taught new pseudo-religious creeds, including the belief that all white children are complicit in racial supremacy and that biological sex is a kind of fiction. Having secured bureaucratic, managerial and political dominance in both the public and private sector, they attempted to re-engineer society so that we might achieve equality of outcome rather than equality of opportunity. They preached their belief that society operates according to invisible power structures that perpetuate inequality, and that these can only be redressed through a fanatical emphasis on group identity and the recognition that – in the words of activist Ibram X. Kendi, author of *How to Be an Antiracist* (2019) – 'The only remedy to past discrimination is present discrimination.' As I have argued many times, the closest synonym for what we now call 'woke' is 'anti-liberal'.

Culture wars never die, but they do evolve. The power of the woke movement is now perishing as quickly as it was birthed, and we find ourselves treading unfamiliar terrain. Its hegemony in the arts, the media, law enforcement, education and the corporate world is still intact, but no longer seems unassailable. Trump's slew of executive orders in January 2025 was not limited to the matter of sports. He signed orders to recognise that 'women are biologically female, and men are biologically male', to put an end to prisoners being accommodated according to 'identity' rather than sex, and to prevent federal agencies from supporting 'the so-called "transition" of a child from one sex to another'. Although these orders go some way to reinstating protections for the rights of vulnerable people, the method was troubling for those of a liberal disposition. Executive orders were originally intended to be memoranda from the president to officials in the executive branch of government, but in recent years they have been used as a shortcut to implement policy changes at breakneck speed. Like the president's right to pardon convicted criminals, this procedure has a certain monarchical quality to it, which accounts for Trump's previous quip about being a 'dictator' on 'day one'. That said, executive orders have been adopted with increasing frequency by Republican and Democratic presidents alike. Both parties have been happy to take advantage of a system that permits the president to sidestep Congress and act unilaterally.

Those of us who have opposed the power of the woke movement on liberal grounds will have mixed feelings about the prospect of its demise being partly actuated by illiberal means. We will be concerned about Trump's misjudged choice of language, such as his high-handed statement that 'He who saves his Country does not violate any Law', a sentiment that would surely be echoed by any autocrat in history. At the same time, the pushback against Trump's executive orders has been similarly troubling, with unelected judges in Democrat-run districts – what Press Secretary Karoline Leavitt described as 'judicial activists' – quickly applying temporary blocks to specific executive orders that threatened to undermine the woke orthodoxy. This was predictable, since many of these directives were the antithesis of those signed by President Joe Biden. On his first day in office in January 2021, for instance, Biden had issued an executive order 'Preventing and Combating Discrimination on the Basis of Gender Identity or Sexual Orientation' which insisted that identity rather than sex should be the determining factor when it comes to sports, toilet facilities and other aspects of life traditionally divided into male and female. Similarly, Trump's order aimed at 'Ending Radical and Wasteful Government DEI Programs and Preferencing' was a direct countermand of Biden's order 'Advancing Racial Equity and Support for Underserved Communities Through the Federal Government'. Although Biden had secured the nomination as leader of his party as the 'non-woke' candidate, his first few days in office made it clear that this was an agenda that he would vigorously pursue.

By contrast, Trump's mandate was to dismantle the woke apparatus put into place by his predecessor, most notably its commitment to Diversity, Equity and Inclusion (DEI). Under Trump, meritocracy and colour-blindness were to be reinstated, and the new fashionable form of racial discrimination was to be jettisoned. The impact was felt almost instantaneously. Federal workers from the DEI industry were placed on administrative leave, websites and social media accounts were modified to reflect the new policies, and contracts related to DEI work were scotched. The shockwaves radiated beyond the machinery of the state and out into the corporate world. Even before Trump's inauguration, Mark Zuckerberg, CEO of Meta, announced that he was terminating the company's DEI programmes, with an internal memo explicitly recognising that 'the legal and policy landscape surrounding diversity, equity and inclusion efforts in the United States is changing'. Other companies – including giants such as McDonald's, Walmart, Ford, Amazon and Google – quickly followed suit and scaled back their DEI commitments and goals. For all the incessant declarations of the 'values' of corporations and their capitalist shareholders, few were surprised to see such ethical considerations subordinated to the acquisition of money. Fidelity to DEI was sustainable right up until the point when infidelity became more profitable.

These relentless salvos against the woke movement culminated in the establishment of Trump's 'Department of Government Efficiency' (DOGE) – spearheaded by entrepreneur Elon Musk – which stripped back the $124 billion of annual federal spending on DEI initiatives. This was Musk's *glasnost* to Trump's *perestroika*, a shift from bureaucracy to transparency that shattered the carapace of the fallen regime. As a result, the public were suddenly barraged with news stories about how taxpayers' money had been gratuitously wasted on woke projects. Most notably, it was revealed that the United States Agency for International Development (USAID) had been funding causes overseas that seemed more proselytising than humanitarian. While even the most jingoistic of patriots might appreciate the moral justification for USAID's contributions to landmine-clearance, disease prevention, and aid for refugees displaced in war – all of which were curbed under the new administration's policies – there would be meagre support for its ideological boondoggling. For instance, $2 million had been earmarked to subsidise pottery classes and promotion in Morocco. A further $2 million had been awarded to *Asociación Lambda*, a Guatemalan LGBTQ+ rights organisation, to 'strengthen trans-led organizations to deliver gender-affirming health care, advocate for improved quality and access to services, and provide economic empowerment opportunities'. A grant of $13 million went to the nonprofit organisation Sesame Workshop to fund a version of *Sesame Street* in Iraq (*Ahlan*

*Simsim Iraq*) which would focus on the promotion of 'inclusion, mutual respect, and understanding across ethnic, religious, and sectarian groups'. The nature of much of the expenditure meant that the relevant aspects of Trump's speech to the joint session of Congress in March 2025 had the quality of a stand-up comedy routine.

> Just listen to some of the appalling waste we have already identified: $22 billion from HHS to provide free housing and cars for illegal aliens, $45 million for diversity, equity and inclusion scholarships in Burma, $40 million to improve the social and economic inclusion of sedentary migrants. Nobody knows what that is. $8 million to promote LGBTQ+ in the African nation of Lesotho, which nobody has ever heard of, $60 million for indigenous peoples and Afro-Colombian empowerment in Central America. $60 million. $8 million for making mice transgender.

Those in charge of USAID had jeopardised its credibility and humanitarian work through this pursuit of what journalist Andrew Sullivan described as the 'pet ideological projects' of 'our enlightened elites'. It is a reminder of one of the key lessons of this culture war: when any given organisation is ideologically captured, it ceases to function effectively and becomes primarily a mechanism for the propagation of the creed.

The victory of Donald Trump over Kamala Harris in the presidential election of November 2024 is already being celebrated as the moment that woke died, the final reckoning of this short-lived paradigm shift, but it was a symptom rather than a cause. Certainly there is no doubt that in throwing its support behind Trump, the electorate was rejecting an ideology that had been imposed from the top down against their wishes. Woke was never a belief-system sincerely held by any significant numbers; it was a set of rules and mantras adopted out of fear by a subdued population. By steamrolling over this ideology in his first few weeks in office, Trump was fulfilling a promise that had been articulated throughout his campaign. This was incontrovertible proof that culture war issues can win and lose elections; even many of those who despised Trump voted for him as a means to resist the careening juggernaut of wokeness. In its post-election analysis, the *New York Times* singled out a Republican advertisement which drew attention to Harris's statement that all prison inmates identifying as transgender ought to have access to surgery. The tagline was: 'Kamala is for they/them. President Trump is for you'. Although the writers of the article considered this a 'seemingly obscure topic', they were forced to admit its success. Even Trump's aides had been astonished at the campaign's popularity. According to the political action committee Future Forward, a group established to support the Democratic Party, this advertisement triggered a 2.7-point shift in favour of Trump among those who saw it. Inevitably, the *New York Times* misclassified the message as 'anti-trans', a ploy guaranteed to exacerbate the very resentment that made the slogan so effective in the first place. They had forgotten, or never knew, that trans activism in its current form is essentially authoritarian, because it seeks to foist a belief-system onto a population that does not share it.

The death rattles of the woke ideology have become so audible that they can no longer be gainsaid. Leftists politicians such as Democratic representative Alexandria Ocasio-Cortez and the former US secretary of transportation Pete Buttigieg have quietly removed the pronouns from their social media profiles. Multiple sporting bodies have barred men who identify as women from competing in female categories. Gay rights groups are rejecting the forced teaming with divisive LGBTQIA+ campaigns. The Supreme Court of the United Kingdom has ruled that 'sex' means 'biological sex' for the purposes of equality law, meaning that men who identify as women have no legal right to enter women-only spaces; the *Telegraph* ran with the front-page headline 'Trans women are not women'. Puberty blockers for the treatment of gender dysphoria in children have been banned indefinitely in the United Kingdom. This followed on from one of the most transformational developments in the culture wars: the *Independent Review of Gender Identity Services for Children and Young People* – typically known as the

Cass Review – commissioned by the National Health Service (NHS) in 2020 and carried out by leading paediatrician Dame Hilary Cass, which was published in April 2024 (see Chapter 7). At last, the public had confirmation that there is a paucity of evidence for the efficacy of puberty blockers, and the reverberations are still being felt. Major medical bodies worldwide had been treating young patients on the basis of a superstitious and pseudo-scientific belief in 'gender identity' and unquestioningly practising the 'gender-affirming' model of healthcare (by which therapeutic treatment for gender dysphoria is rejected in favour of an automatic reinforcement that the patient has been 'born in the wrong body' and requires medical intervention). The goal of the Cass Review had been to elucidate the truth; it ended up being a wrecking ball to the delicate *piñata* of the new fundamentalism.

Statistical analysis of polling data by the *Economist* found that support for woke causes began to grow in 2015, peaked in 2021, and has been steadily declining ever since. Black Lives Matter is now a largely discredited movement. Although not centralised, many of its key figureheads have been exposed as fraudulent. Having raised over $90 million in the wake of the death of George Floyd, by May 2023 the Black Lives Matter Global Network Foundation was facing bankruptcy. One of its co-founders, Patrisse Cullors, was found to have spent $3.2 million on luxury homes, although she claimed these were private funds. Its tax filing of May 2022 revealed expenditure on luxury properties to the tune of $12 million, with significant sums paid to Cullors's relatives for security services. After the massacre of civilians in southern Israel by Hamas on 7 October 2023, a Black Lives Matter affiliated organisation in Chicago posted 'I stand with Palestine' on social media along with an image of one of the terrorists who had committed the atrocity, identifiable due to the paraglider used in the attack. Anti-Israel protests across the Western world broke out, but the explicitly antisemitic tenor of some of the participants changed the nature of the debate. Palestine had become a compulsory talking point for the woke, but it appeared that racism was baked into the ideology.

A seemingly frivolous but perhaps equally revealing moment occurred when the car company Jaguar released a new advertisement campaign in November 2024. A short commercial showcased a number of flamboyant epicene models posing against a minimalist but colourful backdrop, with syntactically inelegant slogans appearing periodically on the screen, such as 'live vivid' and 'delete ordinary'. No vehicles were featured, and it looked very much as though Jaguar was more interested in promoting the doctrine of DEI rather than selling cars. Inevitably, the company's sales soon plummeted, but the significance was in the broader reaction. Like many woke initiatives, the concept was rooted in conformism masquerading as radicalism. A few diehard activists praised the company's new direction, but the effort seemed forced; whimpers rather than cheers, the faintest borborygmi of an ageing beast. The overriding impression was one of fatigue. An advertisement that would have been standard fare in 2020 suddenly felt very dated.

So is woke truly at an end? Gentle reader, if you will indulge me, I would ask that you take a moment to envisage your author in sackcloth and sandals, staff in hand, standing upon a hillock to declare my prophecy: 'the end of woke is nigh'. It is both melodramatic and almost certainly accurate. The influence of woke still lingers, of course, and the ideology will doubtless find a way to mutate and resurrect in some other guise. In addition, we are already seeing the rise of an 'anti-woke' contingent that may fill the vacuum. In seeking to re-establish the importance of freedom and liberal values, some leading figures of this predominately right-leaning counter-movement have now reached the conclusion that the only effective response to 'wokery' is a different kind of authoritarianism. As the saying has it, they hope to fight fire with fire, and as such have earned themselves the much-contested label of 'the woke right'. Those of us who have taken a stance against the excesses of the illiberal left would be advised to be vigilant about the possibility of a backlash that will only guarantee the continuation of this culture war. We should be striving to return to a time when absurdities were treated with the indifference they deserve, and the shrill demands of a handful of ideologues were drowned out by the steady chorus of reason.

This present volume is intended to reflect these developments, and to show that the authoritarian impulse at the heart of wokeness is replicated wherever human beings succumb to ideological thinking. The culture war has been needlessly prolonged due to this common insistence that it can be reduced to a matter of party politics. As I shall propose, far from blaming the left for this ongoing societal upheaval, we must acknowledge that culture warriors exist across the political spectrum. This has never been a matter of left or right, but rather what John Stuart Mill in 1859 called the 'struggle between Liberty and Authority'. My concern is how we reached this period of competing narratives and regressive tribal politics, where we might go next, and how we should learn from the recent past to guide us through the imminent future. It is an argument for the cooling of temperature, the detribalisation of politics, the acknowledgement that no group has all the answers. It is a reminder that we have as much to learn from our critics as they might learn from us, that there is a kernel of truth even in the most grievous falsehood, and that our agency is diminished if we insist on reciting someone else's script.

Some of the arguments in this book might resonate, others will doubtless infuriate. The urge to dismiss perspectives that do not precisely align with our own is instinctive, but ultimately self-destructive. How you respond to this book will be a test of its thesis. This, I suppose, is a sly way of absolving myself of all responsibility if you do not enjoy it. A cynic might say that I have forged a career from the very ideology I so despise, and yet I would like nothing more than my commentary from the last five years to become obsolete. I am writing these words now in the sincere hope that we will soon reach the point where nobody will want to read them. If all goes to plan, the book you are holding in your hands will be little more than a historical curiosity. It might make a decent doorstop.

# 1

# Culture Warriors

## The Curse of Titania McGrath

The culture war is a story of imaginary hate. It has the quality of a nightmare, propelled by fear of the non-existent. Every reputable recent survey into attitudes towards minorities plainly reveals that the Western world has never been more tolerant. Neo-fascism is in terminal decline and its adherents have long been consigned to the penumbra of society. Yet somehow, between the early 2010s and the mid 2020s, an entire industry was concocted on the flimsy basis that ours is an irredeemably bigoted era with stormtroopers goose-stepping in every shadow. Perhaps the radical intersectional activist Titania McGrath summarised it best when she boasted that the definition of the word 'Nazi' had been successfully broadened to include anyone vaguely to the right of Karl Marx. 'Although this is a great victory for the progressive cause', she wrote, 'it does mean that there are now more Nazis living in modern Britain than even existed in 1930s Germany.'

Titania McGrath is not real. I created her on Twitter in early 2018 to satirise an increasingly common brood of po-faced puritans who spend most of their time pontificating on social media, that digital crèche in which grown adults toss their half-baked opinions around like pies in the famous scene from *Bugsy Malone* (1976). I wanted to ridicule this irredeemably collectivist outlook, one that interprets any and all disagreement as evidence of evil, and values human beings for their race, gender and sexuality above their qualities as individuals. I had decided from the outset that Titania would be a slam poet, which would give me the opportunity to write some deliberately excruciating verse with unsubtle pious messaging. She would be 'hay-racial', meaning that her ethnic identity would fluctuate depending on the pollen count. She would have a ruthless, almost sociopathic quality which would mirror the hypocrisies of those fire-snorting acolytes of Critical Social Justice. She would represent everything about this powerful ideology that has regalvanised racial division and legitimised bullying. She would take aim at the nuclear family, claiming that 'future generations will thank us if we successfully eliminate heterosexuality'. She would insist that the only way to prevent the rise of fascism was to empower the police to arrest people for their words and thoughts. As she wrote, 'we shall only achieve true diversity in our society when everyone thinks in exactly the same way as me'.

It was Titania who dragged me into this maddening culture war. Suddenly I was following the example of Randle Patrick McMurphy in *One Flew Over the Cuckoo's Nest* (1962), voluntarily immersing myself in a world of lunatics. When I was eventually 'outed' as the Dr Frankenstein to this online monster, I found myself writing articles and books on this subject, talking endlessly on podcasts, and hosting a weekly television show on GB News with a particular focus on woke issues. Prior to these developments, I had been perfectly content muddling along as a writer and comedian, with no aspirations whatsoever to venture into political commentary. Titania's fame soared after she received what Twitter called a 'permanent suspension', a semantic contradiction which really meant that she had been banned for mocking the 'wrong' subjects. At the time, the ideological position of the executives at Twitter – and their dystopically named 'Trust and

Safety Council' – was very much in lockstep with the woke movement. In the end, the ban only lasted for twenty-four hours, and Titania's follower count exploded on her return. It was a manifestation of the 'Streisand effect', whereby censorship draws attention to the very thing it seeks to suppress. Yet Titania's experience of being locked out of her Twitter account for a day had left its scars. She immediately published an article entitled: 'I now understand how Nelson Mandela felt'.

Not everyone appreciated the joke. I was deluged by torrents of online venom and even direct threats of violence, which struck me as a needlessly histrionic form of comedy criticism. If these little Titanias had really hoped to disprove my point about their ferocity and intolerance, perhaps screaming abuse at a total stranger was not the optimal method. It is of course entirely natural to feel displeasure when one's worldview is being derided. I still retain some sympathy for the journalist who suggested that copies of Titania's first book would be given to every person in Hell, and that 'lampooning the language of social justice is a cheap shot'. This critic was not the target audience; she was the target. If I were absorbed in an ideology that mistrusts humour and perceives that jokes have the potential to 'normalise hate', I would doubtless be similarly vexed by anyone who had the temerity to mock it. But that's the trouble with religious convictions. However important they seem to our sense of personal identity, there is no guarantee that our icons will be protected from desecration by unbelievers. When Titania performed her live stage show in London's West End in 2020 – played brilliantly by the actor Alice Marshall – she was awarded five stars in the right-leaning *Daily Mail* and one star in the left-leaning *Guardian*, which neatly encapsulated how her fans and detractors tended to divide along political lines. The *Guardian*'s critic even asked the question: 'what are we laughing at?' To which the only answer that springs to mind is: 'you'.

Titania, like the culture war itself, was incredibly polarising. She was popular among those who had grown tired of this cruel and self-aggrandising ideology comprising of zealots who enjoyed the support of major corporations and yet still maintained that they were 'anti-establishment'. On the other hand, those who were the subject of the satire tended not to be amused. Many took to social media to proclaim their indifference to Titania by compulsively tweeting about her. They were of course entitled to loathe the character, to claim they have a psychic insight into my motivations, and, above all, to find it desperately unfunny. As Titania points out, 'If you find yourself laughing at comedy, it probably isn't sufficiently progressive.' Others bewailed it as a 'one joke' account, somehow misunderstanding that her monomania was precisely the point; she was a representation of activists who have a singular obsession and can only see the world through the narrowest of prisms.

One of the most common criticisms I faced was that I was attacking a straw man, and that no one like Titania existed either online or in the real world. Yet virtually every tweet she posted was taken seriously by respondents on Twitter. If she was so unrealistic, why did the customer service department at the NatWest bank reply in earnest when Titania complained that it was inciting violence against vegans? Why did Liz Wheeler, host of *Tipping Point* on One American News Network, invite Titania on to her show to discuss the problem of transphobia? After the 2024 United States election, Titania immediately took to X to write: 'I just fired my immigrant housekeeper because even though I'd educated her about the evils of Donald Trump she still voted for him. There is no place for racism in my house.' If this was so unfeasible, why did the Republican Senator Ted Cruz repost it along with the question: 'Is this possibly real?' In December 2021, the French magazine *Le Point* reported that one of Titania's aphorisms had been retweeted approvingly by Rokhaya Diallo, France's most renowned social justice activist. In January 2019, Titania promoted her debut book *Woke: A Guide to Social Justice* by tweeting: 'I have written the most important book of 2019. Do not buy it for my sake, but for the sake of humanity.' *Private Eye*, the United Kingdom's leading satirical magazine, duly quoted her in their 'Pseuds Corner', a regular feature that ridicules the most pretentious statements made in any given week.

*Portrait of Titania McGrath by Lisa Graves.*

They added a mocking cartoon, not realising that the woman they had quoted was a fictional creation. An email from the *Private Eye* offices to Titania's publisher confirmed that they had 'printed a quote from her book in error (misunderstanding the satire)' and that its editor, Ian Hislop, 'wanted to hold his hands up'. It is curious indeed when a satirical magazine is satirising a satirical character because they don't realise that she's satirical.

As I have explained more times than I care to remember, the driving force behind Titania was my contempt for bullies. Far from being an exercise in 'punching down' – the most common accusation from critics – the target was the mostly bourgeois woke authoritarians who patronise and demean minorities while claiming to defend them. Moreover, she was an attempt to expose the inherent contradictions of a movement that had gulled so many genuinely liberal people into supporting causes that they would typically oppose. Consider the example of actor Kathy Burke, who in March 2022 wrote on Twitter: 'I love being "woke". It's much nicer than being an ignorant fucking twat.' In her Channel 4 documentary *Kathy Burke: Growing Up* (2023), she further argued that 'woke' simply refers to people who are neither racist nor homophobic, which would surely mean that the overwhelming majority of us would happily embrace the term. Thinking along similar lines, former Conservative prime minister Theresa May has declared herself to be 'woke and proud'. In her memoir *The Abuse of Power* (2023), May cites the standard definition of 'woke' as 'alert to racial or social discrimination and injustice'. 'On that basis,' she writes, 'who would not want to be woke?' But for those who have been on the receiving end of harassment and intimidation by activists who self-define as 'woke', it is clear this issue is not so straightforward. Do the likes of Burke and May genuinely support the widespread censorship of debate? Do they support the mutilation and sterilisation of children for being gender nonconforming? Do they support treating individuals according to the colour of their skin rather than the content of their character? Do they support the erosion of women's rights and the shaming of gay people for their sexual orientation? As I shall show, these beliefs are at the core of what it now means to be 'woke', but it seems unlikely that either Burke or May would endorse any of these reactionary ideas.

This is entirely typical of those who weigh into the culture war without first attempting to grapple with the implications. Veteran human rights campaigner Peter Tatchell has consistently championed the notion of 'gender identity' – the most anti-gay ideology in living memory (see Chapter 7) – yet still thinks that his activism is pro-gay. The novelist Joyce Carol Oates has complained that Donald Trump's executive order protecting women in sports proves that the 'right wing is now stronger' and that too many people are 'roused to rage by transgender issues that affect virtually no one'. Yet a report by the United Nations revealed that 600 female athletes have lost at least 890 medals to men identifying into their category. In prisons, over 30 per cent of female inmates have been sexually abused and almost 60 per cent subjected to domestic violence; yet these women are now expected to share facilities with men. And all of this is before we get to the problem of rape crisis centres that have been open to males, the institutional medicalisation of predominately gay adolescents, and the confounding implications of the widespread denial of reality by those in authority (see Chapter 6). Far from affecting 'virtually no one', this issue affects virtually everyone.

Woke is gradually drawing to an end because the public is finally realising that its aims are not accurately reflected in the language of its proponents. Claims to be 'anti-racist' are all very well, until one realises that 'anti-racism' in its current form is a racially divisive endeavour. The language of activism is often intended to obfuscate rather than clarify. For instance, a poll carried out by Survation in August 2023 on behalf of Murray Blackburn Mackenzie, an Edinburgh-based policy analysis group, found that 40 per cent of respondents misunderstood the phrase 'trans woman' as referring to an individual who was born female but now identifies as male. This has not prevented the media class from adopting this confusing language in its reporting. The result has been that a significant proportion of the public ends up supporting ideas that are in direct opposition to its values.

This problem has been exacerbated by collusion between western governments and big tech to censor online speech, a sinister development that I shall explore in Chapter 5. In addition, activists have devised increasingly duplicitous schemes to smuggle their demands into legislation without the kind of scrutiny that would see them unravel. For instance, a report by the law firm Dentons called 'Only adults? Good practices in legal gender recognition for youth' – written in collaboration with the Thomson Reuters Foundation and the International Lesbian, Gay, Bisexual, Transgender, Queer & Intersex Youth and Student Organisation (IGLYO) – suggests ways in which activists can affect changes in the law through clandestine means. The aim is to enable children to change their legal gender without parental consent. One recommendation for campaigners is to 'Get ahead of the government agenda', which involves publishing proposed legislation before the government has the opportunity to do so. Another is to 'Tie your campaign to more popular reform'. The report offers the example of Ireland, Denmark and Norway, where unpopular reforms based on gender recognition were hitched to 'more popular reforms such as marriage equality'. In other words, those who thought they were voting for the right to same-sex marriage had been conned into supporting an unrelated cause.

Perhaps the most disturbing recommendation in the Dentons report is that campaigners 'Avoid excessive press coverage and exposure'. As the report explains, gender ideology has been built into law most successfully in countries where public understanding of the issues has been limited. Journalist James Kirkup's summary of the report for the *Spectator* is damning in its candour:

> A major international law firm has helped write a lobbying manual for people who want to change the law to prevent parents having the final say about significant changes in the status of their own children. That manual advises those lobbying for that change to hide their plans behind a 'veil' and to make sure that neither the media nor the wider public know much about the changes affecting children that they are seeking to make. Because if the public find out about those changes, they might well object to them.

It is a masterpiece of elitist Machiavellianism that would put Titania McGrath to shame.

## Distractions

As this phase of the culture war trundles on towards its terminus, there are hordes of denialists at hand to reassure us that it was only ever a figment of our collective imagination. 'There's no actual "culture war", is there?', writes LBC talk-show host and culture warrior James O'Brien. 'It's just a new way of describing disagreements between people who hate racism and discrimination and people who love it.' Labour Member of Parliament Ben Bradshaw warns us that we need 'to resist the Tory culture war', as though it had been concocted by the very party that presided over its worst excesses. Then there are those who claim that the culture war is a mere 'distraction', a baby rattle for the lower orders, the modern equivalent of the bread and circuses of Ancient Rome. Writing in the *Scotsman*, journalist Joyce McMillian claims that the Scottish National Party's gender recognition reform bill is 'being used as a culture-war distraction'. *The Times* columnist Matthew Parris insists that the 'Why-Oh-Why War with Woke' is 'not a real culture war', and if we 'stop thinking about it, stop talking about it, it will finally go away'. Wishful thinking only explains so much. An ungenerous interpretation would be that all this talk of 'distraction' is a ploy to minimise the significance of the culture war, an approach likely to appeal to those who would prefer to see it prolonged. Perhaps the better explanation is that culture warriors have been very successful in misleading the public when it comes to their methods and objectives. The claim that the culture war is a 'distraction' is, in other words, a distraction.

The strategy is not unique to the left. In June 2024, the former Conservative Member of Parliament Dehenna Davison participated in a debate on BBC's *Newsnight* regarding her party's attempts to clarify the Equality Act to ensure that women's rights were protected in law. Cabinet minister Kemi Badenoch had pointed out that it was necessary to make clear that the term 'sex' in the Equality Act did not incorporate 'gender identity', since the uncertainty was being exploited by those who insisted that men who identified as women ought not to be excluded from women-only spaces and services. When Davison was asked whether she welcomed Badenoch's intervention, she replied: 'I don't at all. I think regrettably the debate around trans issues right now seems to be used as some kind of political football for this mythical culture war that the Conservative party seems to be fighting.' This will come as a surprise to the disabled women who have been smeared as bigots for requesting female carers, or the female prisoners who are terrified of being accommodated with convicted rapists, or the victims of sexual assault being turned away from rape crisis centres because they feel uncomfortable speaking to a male counsellor. The Tory Reform Group seemed to approve of Davison's position, posting on X: 'The Conservative Party has to think very carefully about the type of campaign it wants to run, and the longer term impact of stoking culture wars. It is clear that voters are rejecting the politics of division. We must not run on "wedge issues" for a narrow core voter base alone.' Few will be convinced that the rights of 51 per cent of the population qualifies as a 'wedge issue'.

Former Labour strategist Alastair Campbell was quick to offer his contribution: 'I'm sure the world of trade and business will take note that the actual Secretary of State for Trade and Business has decided that the biggest issue on her agenda on her first big election outing is the weaponisation of trans rights.' As J. K. Rowling pointed out, Campbell seemed to be unaware that Badenoch was also the Minister for Women and Equalities, so it was hardly a stretch to suppose that women's rights and the Equality Act fell within her remit. As Rowling put it: 'Thanks once again for highlighting Labour's complacency and indifference towards the rights of half the electorate.' It is remarkable that so many well-meaning politicos have inadvertently implied that the rights of women simply do not matter. And while it is always prudent to take people at their word, the Himalayan quantity of evidence at this point makes it difficult to believe that anyone seriously maintains that the culture war is 'mythical'. The charitable explanation is that Davison, Campbell and their ilk are simply ignorant of some of the most significant cultural developments over the past decade, from the fallout of the Black Lives Matter protests to the Scottish Hate Crime Bill to the campaigns of harassment against gender-critical feminists. Rather than accusing such commentators of dishonesty, we should not rule out the possibility that they generally avoid reading newspapers, watching television programmes, or speaking to anyone with an interest in current affairs.

The most common insinuation about those of us who criticise the culture war is that we are actively promoting it. No doubt there are a handful of commentators who have cynically exploited these controversies to forge a career as 'anti-woke' campaigners. But the suggestion that challenging wokeness is a universally self-serving enterprise is not only wrongheaded, it can often function as a ploy to delegitimise the liberal opposition by conflating it with the regressive old guard. With such widespread mistrust, how is the liberal-minded observer supposed to refute the anti-liberalism of culture warriors without being automatically branded as a 'culture warrior' himself?

It largely comes down to how the culture war ought to be defined. Many who are watching from the sidelines perceive it as a conflict between the zealots of the social justice movement and reactionaries who rail against 'snowflakes'. The combatants in both factions appear to be extremely vocal but few in number, and most spectators are left bewildered as to how such sound and fury can signify so little. Yet beneath all the pabulum about schoolchildren self-identifying as cats and disputes over whether Lego is heteronormative, there is an ongoing civilisational struggle between liberty and authority. It is the difference between unlettered tabloid columnists and John Stuart Mill. It is to the advantage of those who wish to deny the existence of the culture war to conflate the two so that legitimate criticisms of authoritarian overreach or cancel culture can be dismissed as the frenzied boilerplate of the 'PC gone mad brigade'. These tactics should not prevent genuine liberals from resisting those who seek to diminish our freedoms, and if that makes us antagonists in the culture war, then so be it.

This is not to deny the frivolity of much culture war discourse. It is, of course, eminently sensible to shrug off bitter screeds about vegan sausage rolls or reports of young people tweeting about how old sitcoms are 'problematic', that ubiquitous buzzword that has much the same effect as a harpy's talons scraping along a blackboard. All conceivable opinions are available on social media if one searches long enough. Just as the devil can cite scripture for his purpose, so too a lazy journalist can quote the hordes of Facebook to confect some juicy clickbait. But these kinds of trivialities are often symptomatic of a much deeper cultural malaise. We may laugh at the University of Nottingham's decision to apply a 'trigger warning' to Geoffrey Chaucer's *Canterbury Tales* (c. 1400), informing students that it contains potentially offensive 'expressions of Christian faith', or Sheffield University's scheme to pay students £9.34 an hour to spy on their coevals and report them for 'microaggressions', but the proliferation of such measures is an authentic concern. It points to an increasingly infantilising tendency in higher education, one that accepts the dubious premise that words can be a form of violence and that adults require protection from ugly ideas. Worse still, it is related to growing demands that certain forms of speech must be curtailed by the state. In July 2023, for instance, a poll by *Newsweek* found that 44 per cent of Americans between the ages of 25 and 34 believe that 'misgendering' should result in criminal prosecution. Such developments are anything but a distraction. The 'woke left' promote the postmodernist belief that knowledge is a construct of power perpetuated oppressively through language, and therefore censorship by the state, big tech or mob pressure is fully justified. The 'woke right' take the view that censorship of obscenity or degeneracy is necessary to strengthen the moral core of society. Neither outcome will satisfy liberals.

When James Davison Hunter popularised the term 'culture war' in his book *Culture Wars: The Struggle to Define America* (1991), he was describing tensions between religious and secular trends as well as alternative visions of the role of the family in society. He was using the term in its established sense, where any given 'culture war' has clearly demarcated and opposing goals, such as the conflict between Catholicism and secularism in the *Kulturkampf* of late nineteenth-century Germany. Hunter's application of the term mapped neatly onto accepted distinctions of right versus left in American politics.

Our present-day understanding of a 'culture war' is still predominately interpreted through this lens, but it is not so simple. The goals are certainly oppositional, but the terms are vaguely defined and often muddied further through obfuscation. The toxicity of the debates might testify to the frustration of participants in a conflict that they do not understand.

So why do so many of the key figures in this culture war deny that they are waging it? In part, this strategy is a means by which the defence of liberal values can be dismissed. In particular, the claim that it is a kind of 'distraction' amounts to an elaborate form of whataboutism. Contemporary critics of John Stuart Mill might well have argued that in writing *On Liberty* (1859) he was allowing himself to be distracted from more pressing causes. Why wasn't he writing about social reform, for instance, or the Franco-Austrian war? Why, for that matter, was George Orwell so concerned with events in the Soviet Union at a time when apartheid was being implemented in South Africa? Similarly, while some economists ask why we are discussing climate change during a cost-of-living crisis, an environmentalist might well ask why we are discussing the cost-of-living crisis in the midst of climate change. The extent to which we are being 'distracted' is very much dependent on our individual priorities.

That is not to suggest that there are not important issues that are being neglected. Journalist Matthew Syed has observed the curious lack of interest in the possibility that we are facing self-annihilation due to our rapidly advancing technology. As he points out, in an age when the full sequence of the Spanish flu can be uploaded online and reconstructed in a laboratory, 'how long before it is possible for a solitary fanatic to design and release a pathogen capable of killing millions, perhaps billions?' And why, Syed asks, aren't world leaders devoting time and money to confronting these existential threats? He writes persuasively, and I certainly share his concerns, but I part company when it comes to his diagnosis of our culture war as 'a form of Freudian displacement', that 'the woke and anti-woke need each other to engage in their piffling spats as a diversion from realities they both find too psychologically threatening to confront'. Syed is right that there are some who specialise in the inconsequential, but there are many more who are undertaking in earnest the crucial task of halting the ongoing erosion of our freedoms. While living under authoritarian conditions might well be preferable to no existence at all, surely we can address these threats to humanity while at the same time advancing the case for social liberalism?

The liberal approach to redressing injustices is often dismissed as 'anti-woke'. In *The Counterweight Handbook* (2024), an indispensable guide for employees facing ideological impositions in the workplace, author Helen Pluckrose laments that she is often characterised as an 'anti-woke campaigner' because it is not so cumbersome as 'advocate of liberal approaches to social justice and critic of Critical approaches to social justice who nevertheless wants everyone to be free to hold and express whatever views they have (including woke ones) provided they don't impose them on anybody else'. Needless to say, this is also an accurate summary of my own position.

In fact, ideas that have been so crassly reduced to 'anti-woke' have a long and illustrious history. We might look to Mary Wollstonecraft, Frederick Douglass, Mahatma Gandhi, Martin Luther King, Jr., Sojourner Truth and many others who understood that freedom of speech and individual liberties were fundamental to human progress. Identity politics in its current form is diametrically opposed to the ideals of these civilisational heroes. While many of today's culture warriors promote polarising narratives of incompatible group identities, the proponents of universal liberalism – as embodied in the movements for black emancipation, second-wave feminism and gay rights – have always advanced individual rights in the context of our shared humanity. Far from being a distraction, then, our culture war cuts to the heart of what kind of society we wish to inhabit. While it continues to be misapprehended as a conflict between left and right, those of us who are urging vigilance when it comes to the preservation of our freedoms will continue to be mistrusted and maligned. The likes of Matthew Parris are free to assert that ignoring the agents of authoritarianism will make them 'go away', but I am not aware of any historical precedents that support this view. When it comes to the culture war, apathy is tantamount to surrender.

## Beginnings

During my early adult life, I followed the expected gravitation towards left-wing politics, a feature of youth as inevitable as acne and a super-charged ego. As a small child I had admired the Conservative prime minister Margaret Thatcher, but that was probably more to do with her immaculate perm and enviable handbags. I was soon assured by my friends and teachers that she was a hellhound in human form, an escapee from Pandemonium who had clawed her way through the ogres and cambions of the Tory party to emerge triumphantly as leader. I was thenceforth 'left-wing'; not because I had given it any real thought, but rather that it was the fashionable way to be. It was as compulsory as having to pretend to be interested in football to avoid being beaten up.

Yet there was something instinctive about my political leanings that cannot be explained away simply by peer pressure. Even as a stripling in primary school, I always believed that the mark of a civilised society is how it treats its most vulnerable. Anti-gay comments were ubiquitous, of course, as one would expect from a convent school in the 1980s, but racism baffled me. As I grew up, my economic instincts veered leftwards. Proportionate taxation made a great deal of sense to me, and I was proud that we supported the underprivileged by means of our welfare state. Above all, from an early age I harboured a suspicion of authority, and in particular those strange giants knowns as 'teachers', who wielded power in their cumbersome, red-faced way. All children loathe injustice above all things; the cry of 'that's not fair' is the most common refrain of the playground. On one occasion, at the age of four,

I was beaten with a shoe by our headmistress, Sister Hilda, as a punishment for breaking a window. It's a vivid memory that has never faded, probably because it was painful and humiliating in equal measure. I suppose the intention was to teach me to control my temper, but all it did was leave me with a lifelong mistrust of nuns.

It could be argued that my dedication to liberalism is one of those unexamined instincts that we retain throughout our lives. Yet nothing I have read or heard since childhood has persuaded me that the liberal approach is not the most just and effective engine of a civilised society. Moreover, as I have argued, the conflict between liberty and authority has become a far more effective framework by which to interpret the culture wars than the dichotomy of left and right. These political designations date from the National Assembly established in the aftermath of the French Revolution. Members who felt that the power of the king ought to be circumscribed sat to the left of the assembly's president, those who did not sat to the right. The historian Marcel Gauchet has outlined the subsequent 'long drawn-out process that lasted more than three quarters of a century', but by the beginning of the twentieth century the association of the 'right' with traditional values and the 'left' with progressive reform was firmly established. The rise of the woke movement and its concomitant anti-woke equivalent has destabilised these terms to the point of irrelevance. Many people whose socialist credentials could not be more well established have been dismissed as 'right-wing', 'far right' or 'fascist' simply for insisting on the importance of evidence-led analysis and free speech. We are all swamped in the accretions of this ideology irrespective of whether we come from the left or the right, or accept its tenets or not. One's position on gender self-identification, structural racism, the efficacy of the lockdowns, environmentalism, or any of the other culture war topics, is now commonly deemed a marker of where one is situated on the political spectrum. Opposition to gender self-identification in law, for instance, is deemed 'right-wing', in spite of the fact that it was a Conservative prime minister, Theresa May, who promised to introduce legislation that would enable such a policy. For all the Conservative Party's much-vaunted 'war on woke', its members have been in charge for the entire period of its ascendency.

These circumstances have birthed some strange alliances. Many left-wing feminists are now writing for right-wing publications. Lifelong Labour voter and women's rights campaigner Julie Bindel has hit back at critics who claim that she has betrayed the leftist cause by writing for the right-leaning *Daily Mail*. In July 2021, she wrote on Twitter: 'Instead of asking me, "Why are you writing for the *Mail*" ask why the *Guardian* won't publish this stuff?' (Appended to the post was a link to her article about a female prisoner who was sexually assaulted by a male inmate.) This phenomenon is not restricted to the sphere of journalism. In Parliament, cross-party alliances on some of these issues occur with greater frequency. During her period as a sitting Labour MP, Rosie Duffield's views on the dangers of gender identity ideology were far closer to that of many of her Conservative opponents than the majority of her own party. Whereas it was once possible to agree on how 'left' and 'right' were defined, such unanimity no longer exists.

That culture warriors were seeking to sabotage our liberal consensus during the woke era is now beyond doubt. Many of their enterprises seemed needlessly carping and divisive. After the Brexit referendum of June 2016 was broadly misinterpreted as evidence of widespread racism (see Chapter 2), a campaign began in which enlightened members of the public were invited to show solidarity with ethnic minorities by wearing safety pins, usually on lapels or somewhere similarly prominent. The display was an example of what came to be known as 'virtue signalling', and was roundly mocked, even by those who supported the cause. After Donald Trump's victory a few months later, there was an attempt to replicate the trend in America, and the response was likewise contemptuous. Activist Christopher Keelty wrote a piece for the *Huffington Post* entitled 'Dear white people, your safety pins are embarrassing', and offered numerous other suggestions of how to be 'a better ally'. Although himself white, Keelty could not see racial groups as anything other than homogenous monoliths of identical tendencies and collective responsibilities. 'Let me explain something, white people,' he wrote, with all the certainty and dogmatism we have come to expect from identitarian homilists. 'We just fucked up. Bad. We elected a racist demagogue who has promised to do serious harm to almost every person who isn't a straight white male, and whose rhetoric has already stirred up hate crimes nationwide.' That many ethnic minority individuals supported Trump and many white people opposed him seemed to escape his notice. With the death of woke, virtue signalling through the medium of safety pins might strike us as outlandish. But at the height of the movement's power, it was fairly typical.

For instance, in 2018, the Evelina Children's Hospital in London implemented the NHS 'rainbow badge' scheme, by which staff who wished to show their support for 'LGBT+' patients could be more visible. By 2019, the scheme had been rolled out to 61 per cent of NHS trusts. Of course, very few of those who wore the badges will have done so out of a genuine faith in genderism. Rather than acting as a symbol of solidarity, it was more likely to be an apotropaic gesture to keep angry activists at bay. Surely our default assumption must be that medical staff are not homophobic or prepared to discriminate on the basis of how patients choose to identify? In the same way, why should one feel compelled to wear a safety pin to communicate a positive attitude towards other racial groups? The depletion of trust during the culture war had resulted in an unfounded generalised expectation that tolerance was an aberration rather than the norm. This would explain why the search engine Google began adding notes to results for restaurants in late 2024 to specify whether they were 'LGBTQ+ friendly'. It is difficult to imagine any business turning away potential customers on the basis of their sexual orientation, so the necessity for these details seemed highly dubious. From a restaurateur's point of view, surely the only discriminating factor is whether or not you can afford to pay for your meal.

Stories of this kind are often branded as 'woke', but the term is highly contentious. Those who regularly use the word – as a form of self-identification, a pejorative, or simply as a means to describe a belief-system – tend to do so without consideration of the multiple ways in which it is interpreted. Take the opinion piece that appeared in the *Guardian* in April 2024 under the headline '"Woke" isn't dead – it's entered the mainstream. No wonder the right is furious'. Its author, Gaby Hinsliff, showed no sign of having attempted to understand the various meanings of the term or how it has mutated over the years. The comprehensive Cass Review into gender identity services in England published in April 2024 offers a case in point (see Chapter 7). Hinsliff understands in some vague way that the lack of evidence of 'gender medicine' and the sterilisation of healthy children, outlined in detail in this landmark review, has come about due to the rise of the woke ideology. Yet her understanding of the term means that she ends up conflating this grotesque medical scandal with the closure of vegan restaurants and the declining popularity of oat milk. This is precisely the kind of semantic confusion that the professional blusterers at the *Guardian* are usually so eager to criticise.

Hinsliff defines woke as 'the broader push for social, racial and environmental justice', but misses an important qualification. To this formulation, it would be accurate to add the words: 'by authoritarian means'. To take one example, let's consider the woke response to the phenomenon of 'cultural appropriation', the adoption of traditional elements of another culture without respect for their original significance. In August 2020, there was a backlash against the singer Adele for wearing her hair in Bantu knots around the time of the Notting Hill Carnival (suspended that year due to Covid-19 restrictions). Many critics felt that, as a white woman, Adele had no right to emulate African cultural hairstyles and was guilty of 'blackfishing'. One writer for *Glamour* magazine argued that white artists 'need to understand the historical context and sensitivities around this topic and culture'. This kind of criticism does not in itself qualify as 'woke' because, although it shares an emphasis on the policing of racial differences, it lacks the authoritarian aspect.

Compare this to poet and teacher Jaspreet Kaur's passionate arguments against cultural appropriation in her book *Brown Girl Like Me* (2022), in which a 'top-down approach' to social change is proffered:

> One of the problems with tackling cultural appropriation is there is a lack of legal framework to address when cultural appropriation takes place, especially by multinational corporations and businesses, which leaves communities without guidance or protection. There are laws against speeding, drug use and littering, and we know that these things are next to impossible to enforce. Yet the fact that these laws exist reinforces the idea that society disapproves of these activities, and they act as a deterrent. If cultural appropriation was recognised as similarly harmful, the law would at least attempt to assign rights and set guidelines for behaviour.

The key distinction between the liberal and the woke case for social justice is that the former agitates for change through discussion, debate and protest, while the latter seeks changes to the law in order to enforce a particular worldview. Let's take another example from left-wing commentator Laurie Penny:

> I am done pretending that the good intentions of white patriarchy are more important than the consequences enacted on the bodies of others. Good intentions aren't the issue here. Feel free to be as racist as you like in the privacy of your own heart, if you can live with yourself, but not – and this is very important – in the privacy of your own house.

It is refreshing to read such an explicit rejection of the principle of free speech, given that most of those who oppose it are rarely so candid. The journalist Carlos Maza has been similarly forthcoming, arguing that free speech 'was, and is, an unmitigated disaster . . . every piece of evidence points to the fact that we need really aggressive government regulation of speech platforms'. The liberal response to racism and other forms of prejudice is to challenge robustly, not to censor. The woke take a different view.

For all that the woke movement has attracted bullies who are able to machinate beneath a mask of virtue, I do not doubt that many of these activists are well intentioned and genuinely believe that they are fighting for a better world. I too would like to see an end to racism and injustice, but I do not for one moment imagine it is a realistic aim given the imperfectability of human nature, and nor do I suppose that the erosion of free speech and liberal values is the best way to attempt it. On the contrary, the only successful and provable method of curbing racism and other forms of injustice has been the liberal approach. Sadly, this is the very method that the woke have been so determined to scupper. To put it simply, woke social justice and liberal social justice have always been diametrically opposed.

In the pursuit of truth and the settling of disputes, the liberal system offers the most effective means of sifting through the wheat and the chaff. The author and journalist Jonathan Rauch has suggested five answers to the question of 'how to sort true beliefs from the "lunatic" ones'. These are:

The Fundamentalist Principle: Those who know the truth should decide who is right.

The Simple Egalitarian Principle: All sincere persons' beliefs have equal claims to respect.

The Radical Egalitarian Principle: Like the simple egalitarian principle, but the beliefs of persons in historically oppressed classes or groups get special consideration.

The Humanitarian Principle: Any of the above, but with the condition that the first priority be to cause no hurt.

The Liberal Principle: Checking of each by each through public criticism is the only legitimate way to decide who is right.

As Rauch argues, 'the last principle is the only one which is acceptable', and yet it is the authoritarian solution that is becoming more main-stream. The recent hate speech law in Scotland, the proposed equivalent in Ireland which very nearly passed through Parliament, and the last Conservative government's various efforts to curb peaceful protest, all point to a disturbing trend (see Chapter 5). In February 2022, the Canadian prime minister Justin Trudeau imposed draconian measures on truckers who were peacefully protesting against the cross-border vaccine mandate between Canada and the United States which was having a detrimental impact on their livelihoods. Under the aegis of the Emergencies Act, never previously used, Trudeau ordered a police crackdown and even froze the bank accounts of some of those participating in what became known as the 'Freedom Convoy'. A court later ruled that such an abuse of power was unjustified, but the overt nature of Trudeau's authoritarian approach was startling. One Canadian Liberal Member of Parliament, Ya'ara Saks, even claimed that the truckers honking their horns in support of the cause were communicating a clandestine fascist signal, and that 'Honk Honk' was a code for 'Heil Hitler'.

All of this, of course, came about because many decent people were hoodwinked into believing that wokeness was – to recall Hinsliff's definition – simply a 'broader push for social, racial and environmental justice', rather than an essentially authoritarian philosophy. Given that the stakes could hardly be higher, we do require accessible terminology to describe the fundamental aspects of this ideology that wreaked so much havoc on the Western world and from which we are only now recovering. The common formulation of 'woke left' is not wholly satisfactory because to conflate 'woke' and 'left-wing' is misleading. Of course, the origins of the movement lie in the theories of the Frankfurt School and the Marxian theorists responsible for the 'cultural turn', that moment when group identity superseded class as the defining feature of revolutionary struggle. I have outlined this history at length in my book *The New Puritans* and will not repeat myself here. Suffice to say that although the woke ideology has certainly been promoted and enforced by those who identify as left-wing, and although the philosophical origins of the movement can be traced to leftist thinkers, its rejection of class consciousness and its essentially capitalistic timbre make it difficult to describe as 'left-wing' in any meaningful sense. Its practitioners' weapon of choice, what we colloquially refer to as 'cancel culture', mostly preys upon those without the financial means to protect themselves. Wealthy individuals cannot be 'cancelled', which means that woke activists disproportionately end up attacking the poor. Moreover, in disputes over DEI initiatives in the workplace, or the imposition of 'unconscious bias' training, woke operatives invariably side with corporate bodies over individual workers. The impact of the woke movement, in other words, has been the empowerment of the richest in society. We might fudge the matter by designating the woke as 'left-wing capitalists', but this is certainly not the revolution anticipated by Marx and Engels. As such, my use of 'woke left' will specifically relate to self-identified leftists who perceive the tenets of Critical Social Justice to be an inherent corollary of their value system, while acknowledging that the shorthand is far from ideal.

The list of victims of cancel culture is endless, but a handful of examples will be sufficient to make the point.

- In June 2019, BBC Books removed the writer Gareth Roberts from a *Dr Who* short story anthology because he expressed his view that the trans activist movement reinforces demoded gender stereotypes.

- In December 2021, choreographer Rosie Kay was compelled to resign from her own dance company after an investigation process that began because she expressed her gender-critical views at a gathering with dancers at her own home. Although she had cooked a meal and invited the company to her house, some of those present took it upon themselves to report her to the board.

- In 2018, barrister Allison Bailey, a lesbian with a long history of gay activism, raised concerns about her chambers' decision to join Stonewall's Diversity Champions Programme due to its uncritical stance on gender self-identification. As a result, she was labelled as 'transphobic' by Garden Court Chambers, which publicly announced that Bailey was under investigation. Bailey later won a court case for discrimination.

- In 2018, the children's author Rachel Rooney published a book called *My Body is Me!*, which challenged sexist stereotypes and promoted a positive self-image for children. It was branded 'transphobic' and Rooney was subjected to a campaign of harassment by figures in the publishing industry. Some book-shops capitulated to activists and stopped stocking her work, and her publisher told her to stop expressing her opinions on the subject.

- In June 2023, it was reported that Sybil Ruth, an editor at Cornerstones literary consultancy, was dropped because of her gender-critical views. Following an employment tribunal, she received an apology and substantial damages.

- In October 2023, Newcastle United fan Linzi Smith was banned from the football club's stadium for three seasons for her belief that sex is immutable and that men should not have access to women's changing rooms or compete in women's sports. In addition to her ban, she was investigated by a secret unit at the Premier League, who created a dossier on what they described as their 'target'. They attempted to find her home address, assessed photographs from her social media accounts, and even downloaded images in which Smith could be seen walking her dog.

- In 2021, the actor James Dreyfus was dropped from the audio range of *Dr Who* stories for signing a letter to Stonewall – the foremost LGBT charity in Great Britain – calling for an open and respectful debate on the subject of gender identity ideology and its impact on the rights of women and gay people. The company not only dropped him, but erased his episodes from a compilation in which he was meant to be featured.

- In April 2021, trainee psychotherapist James Esses was ousted from his master's course at the Metanoia Institute in London, and removed as a counsellor for the youth charity Childline, after he created an online petition against the proposed ban on 'trans conversion therapy' which may have seen the criminalisation of therapists treating children for gender dysphoria. The Metanoia Institute eventually apologised and admitted that it had violated its own internal appeal policies by expelling him without a hearing.

- In November 2021, social worker Rachel Meade was sanctioned by her employer Social Work England because of gender-critical posts she had shared and liked on Facebook. This led to her being suspended on charges of gross misconduct by Westminster City Council. Meade later won her claim for discrimination against her employer and the judge ruled that the disciplinary procedure amounted to harassment.

We have grown accustomed to associating cancel culture with the left, but that does not mean that the same tactics are not employed by the right. After the attempted assassination of Donald Trump and the murder of retired fire chief Corey Comperatore at a rally in Butler, Pennsylvania in July 2024, there were the inevitable gloating comments from political partisans. Some expressed what appeared to be genuine irritation that the gunman had missed his target, while the less imaginative repeated the identical joke: 'Make America Aim Again'. For such activists, confidence in their own compassion seems to bear an inverse relationship to their capacity for empathy. Elon Musk, who had acquired Twitter in October 2022 for $44 billion and later rebranded the platform as X, was inundated with complaints about these kinds of posts. Many were from Republican users demanding censorship, and Musk felt obliged to respond:

> We have recently received many requests to suspend or otherwise impact accounts on the left.

> However, X is a free speech platform that aspires to give equal voice to all, within the bounds of the law.

> This is what we will do.

The existence of right-wing cancel culture became apparent when an employee at the retail chain Home Depot was filmed at work by a stranger questioning her about a recent Facebook post regarding the assassination attempt. She had written: 'To [sic] bad they weren't a better shooter!!!!!' The video went viral and she was fired. Her words may express an ugly flippancy about the sanctity of human life, but they do not come close to the threshold for incitement to violence. This is likely a worker on a minimum wage and not somebody who can afford to be unemployed, let alone endure the ongoing stigma of such a targeted online campaign. Her detractors might just have easily responded with criticism, or blocked her account, or simply ignored her. There's a very good reason why the singer Nick Cave described cancel culture as 'mercy's antithesis'.

As emotions are running high, the need to lash out is understandable but unjustifiable. It seems grossly unfair to penalise people for mistakes that would in usual circumstances be almost instantly forgotten. The gravamen of these complaints seems to be that no company would wish to associate with 'that kind of person', and so by revealing their true natures they have surrendered their right to be employed. This is to reduce humanity to the woke's preferred template of Good versus Evil. It is simply not the case that we exist as players in some elaborate cosmic morality play, where good people say good things and bad people say bad things. It is perfectly possible that the woman fired from Home Depot might later have regretted her words, perhaps written unthinkingly in the heat of the moment. Even if she hadn't, is public shaming really the answer?

Those calling for cancellations might want to ask themselves a simple question. If all the private messages they had ever sent were suddenly uploaded online for everyone to see, would they be happy with that? Are they really so pure that no statement they have made in the past could be weaponised against them? A famous Nazarene once put it this way: 'Let him who is without sin cast the first stone'. In one of the more high-profile cases, the actor and musician Jack Black announced the cancellation of his Tenacious D tour after fellow band member Kyle Gass made a joke about the assassination attempt at a show in Sydney. While blowing out the candles of a birthday cake on stage, he made the wish: 'Don't miss Trump next time'. Black later wrote on Instagram that he 'would never condone hate speech or encourage political violence in any form'. Yet even those who consistently and explicitly take joy in the suffering and deaths of their political opponents have the right to free speech. It seems unlikely, however, that Gass falls into this category. It is far more plausible that he was simply indulging in a tasteless joke.

The amorphous term 'woke' has proved to be an effective shorthand because, once someone is so described, it is not difficult to outline their views on all subjects relating to politics and culture. This set of beliefs, disparate and yet connected, has become known colloquially as 'the omni-cause'. It explains why Greta Thunberg, a kind of modern version of the child saints of medieval Christendom, was able to shift from environmental activism to anti-Israel campaigning so seamlessly. It is why there is no need to ask someone wearing a 'Progress Pride' lanyard whether they support 'taking the knee' for Black Lives Matter. Extinction Rebellion co-founder Stuart Basden has argued that his movement 'isn't about the climate', but is concerned with overturning white supremacy, the patriarchy, Eurocentrism, heteronormativity and class hierarchy. Or, as another activist insists: 'Environmental justice is the intersection of both social justice and environmentalism, where the inequity in environmental degradation is also considered'. Endorsement of any of these causes implies support for the others and, although there are doubtless exceptions, they are remarkably rare. It would take an unprecedented surge of independent spirit for the true believer to break his programming.

## The Woke Left

For those who self-identify as being 'on the right side of history', there is a sense that Western civilisation itself is a cancer that must be destroyed. It has been built on heteronormative, white-supremacist and cis-patriarchal power structures that perpetuate injustice and bolster the elites. This fundamental precept of the omni-cause explains activists' hostility to the arts, a point that many have noticed but few find comprehensible. To take one example of many, in October 2022 members of environmental campaign group Just Stop Oil entered the National Gallery in London and doused Vincent van Gogh's *Sunflowers* in tomato soup. The two young women who vandalised the painting knew that the footage would go viral, and that commentators like me would mention them in our books. While they were being filmed, one of the activists posed a rhetorical question: 'Are you more concerned about the protection of a painting or the protection of our planet and people?' Her accent was plummy and clipped. No great shock there; we have grown accustomed to being hectored about oppression by the most privileged in society. Such events bring to mind one of the few extant fragments of work by the Ancient Greek dramatist Menander. In a scene from *The Apparition*, a slave berates his youthful master. 'You are too well-off,' he says, 'your whole life is sleep. What is wrong with you is that you have no genuine troubles, so you need an imaginary cure. You had better take up religion.' He might have been speaking to virtually all young people who turn to wokism in their search for meaning.

Attacks on art have such a visceral effect because we understand that they represent a repudiation of human civilisation. For intersectional activists, art and literature are merely further manifestations of the will to power. We have seen this in recent trends in criticism, by which art is judged on the basis of whether or not it is sufficiently intersectional or diverse. Faced with a piece as monumental as Pablo Picasso's *Guernica* (1937), could these activists see anything other than the labour of a misogynist who mistreated his wives and mistresses, a tribute to oppressive patriarchal systems of control? Consider the lack of scruples of the activist who smeared cake on to Leonardo da Vinci's *Mona Lisa* in the Louvre in May 2022. 'Think of the planet!' he cried. 'There are people who are destroying the planet!' One witness reported that the *Mona Lisa* vandal had attempted to break the protective glass in an effort to damage the painting itself. We are dealing with a catastrophising mindset that sees art as little more than a futile hobby, a distraction from the greater mission. The activists at the National Gallery said as much themselves. To them, *Sunflowers* is just 'a painting'.

Those who are sympathetic to Just Stop Oil's cause were quick to defend these actions, and to note that the painting sustained no damage due to its glass covering. 'Spilling soup on glass isn't a major offence,' one person tweeted. 'Personally it moved me,' said another. 'I thought, hell, I really hope humans can see this painting in a thousand years' time. They won't if civilisation is destroyed by floods.' The gut-churning impact of the sight of a desecrated masterpiece is precisely the point. The activists intend to unsettle, and in most cases they succeed. Damage has thus far been limited, precisely because the targets tend to be the most famous works which are therefore shielded, but the same cannot be said for many of our greatest treasures. How long before an activist sets fire to a Titian, or carves political slogans into a Botticelli with a penknife? If you think that such philistinism is beyond them, you have not understood the soullessness of their creed. The destruction of art is always an authoritarian act, which is perhaps why it is so appealing to present-day activists who see the values of Western civilisation as essentially toxic. I have no doubt that the foot-soldiers of the Taliban who demolished the Buddha statues of Bamiyan in March 2001 felt much the same way.

While devotees to the omni-cause disdain Western culture, they are enamoured by Diversity, Equity and Inclusion (DEI), a decidedly Western industry that rakes in $8 billion annually. So pervasive is this doctrine that even the universities of Oxford and Cambridge announced in January 2025 a move away from 'traditional' examinations towards a 'more diverse and inclusive range of assessments' that may have the effect of boosting the grades of students from minority racial backgrounds. The new policies include open-book examinations and take-home papers. The *Telegraph* reported that this initiative has come about 'as universities face pressure to close the gap between the number of firsts and 2:1 degrees given to white, middle-class students compared with other groups'. While it is true that ethnic minorities are far more likely to come from poorer backgrounds, this does not explain why working-class people are deemed incapable of performing as well as their peers. Those educated in private schools do enjoy a huge advantage, but this is a problem that can be addressed through improvements to the education system and the admissions process. Applying different standards to students according to their skin colour helps precisely no one. It leaves racial minorities in a lamentable situation whereby there is now widespread suspicion that their achievements have only come about due to preferential treatment. This degrades their talents and accomplishments, all of which would be unimpeachable in a purely meritocratic system. One can only imagine how racial minority students will react to being patronised in this way.

These kinds of racialised policies are often strangely inconsistent. They rarely apply to Asian Pacific students who are considered to be 'white-adjacent' because of their disproportionate rates of success. For example, in November 2020, the North Thurston Public School in Washington published its 'equity report' in which Asian Americans were disqualified from the category of 'students of color'. In doing so, they were making the racist implication that academic achievement is a specifically white trait. Of course, if Asian students were to be included, the narrative of systemic racism would be more difficult to maintain. At Ivy League universities, Asian applicants have faced routine discrimination insofar as they have been expected to attain higher test scores to qualify. The *Guardian* has described these as 'race-conscious admissions' intended 'to raise the number of Black, Hispanic and other underrepresented minority students at selective US higher education colleges and universities'. Activists who have decried 'systemic racism' even in cases where there is no evidence of its existence nonetheless seem perfectly content to cheer on an authentically and verifiably racist system. In June 2023, the United States Supreme Court ruled that such policies were unconstitutional and effectively put 'race-conscious' criteria to an end, another sure step on the pathway to the end of woke.

At the heart of the DEI industry is the belief that all inequalities of outcome are evidence of systemic racism. The activist Ibram X. Kendi has explicitly argued that 'racial inequality is evidence of racist policy' and has called for an amendment to the United States constitution to enshrine this belief. This contention is rooted in faith rather than evidence; hence his reference to racism as America's 'original sin'. The term 'equity' so closely resembles 'equality' that many have been duped by DEI experts into supposing them to be synonymous. In truth, 'equity' necessitates treating people unequally in order to equalise identity-based outcomes. It is therefore the precise opposite of 'equality', just as 'diversity' actually means 'political homogeneity' and 'inclusion' means 'exclusion of non-conformists'. As I have argued many times before, the culture war is really about language and who gets to control the meaning of words. The prevalence of DEI did not come about because it is the best system, but rather because its practitioners use slippery terminology that operates as a Trojan Horse, sneaking in regressive ideas under the cover of progressivism.

These beliefs are rooted in the notion of victimhood and oppression, and so statistics that deviate from inconvenient truths must be disregarded. This explains why the Labour government promised to implement a Race Equality Act, unveiled in February 2024, to ensure that those from ethnic minorities are entitled to 'full right to equal pay', somehow not realising that this has been enshrined in law since 1965. As Conservative Party leader Kemi Badenoch has pointed out, 'Labour's proposed new race law will set people against each other and see millions wasted on pointless red tape. It is obviously already illegal to pay someone less because of their race. The new law would be a bonanza for dodgy, activist lawyers.' Labour is taking its lead from critical theories of race in assuming that all disparities in outcome are evidence of systemic racism. This position was challenged in the report by the Commission on Race and Ethnic Disparities, published in March 2021, which found that there was no evidence whatsoever that the legal and educational systems of the United Kingdom were rigged against minorities. Activists were so furious that the facts went against their narrative that the commission's chairman, Tony Sewell, was compared to Joseph Goebbels and the Ku Klux Klan. These privileged and predominately white woke activists apparently have little patience for black people who do not know their place.

The woke left's fixation with race has led to some markedly retrograde outcomes. For instance, activists at SOAS (formerly the School of Oriental and African Studies) in London have demanded that the discipline of Philosophy be 'decolonised' to reduce the influence of dead white men such as Socrates, Plato and Aristotle. Those who are obsessed with identity can apparently see little else. Kathryn Yusoff, a professor of Geology at Queen Mary University in London, has argued in her book *Geologic Life* (2024) that the study of rocks is 'riven by systemic racism', and that 'black, brown, and indigenous subjects' have 'an intimacy with the earth that is unknown to the structural position of whiteness'. Does this grievance, seemingly intellectualised into existence from the flimsiest gossamer, bear any comparison to genuinely racist systems such as the segregation that existed in the Antebellum South?

Similarly tenuous claims about systemic racism have been made about the oppressive quality of the British countryside. In its 2024 report on 'racism relating to climate change, environment, and rural affairs', the Welsh government concluded that certain racial groups 'face barriers created by exclusions and racism preventing them from fully participating in "environmental" activities'. In testimony presented to Parliament, the charity group Wildlife and Countryside Link asserted that the countryside was 'dominated by white people' and influenced by 'racist colonial legacies'. A report by Climate Cymru BAME, published on the government's website in November 2024, highlighted the 'barriers faced by minority ethnic people when visiting green spaces' and recommended the creation of 'dog-free areas' in parks on the basis that some ethnic minorities are troubled by the animals. This story seemed almost designed to agitate the tabloids, and inevitably there were numerous articles of the 'PC gone mad' variety. In truth, the Welsh government did not act upon this recommendation. As I have argued, this kind of media pantomime enables supporters of woke authoritarianism to dismiss legitimate concerns as reactionary. The issue here is not a frivolous debate about whether dogs are bigots, but the fact that a government is subscribing to an ideology whose key goals are racial division and the curbing of free speech. While the clowns are dancing in the circus, the ringmaster is reaping the rewards.

We saw this scenario recur throughout the era of woke, with media outlets luxuriating in asinine stories while failing to address the underlying cultural significance. For instance, a sightseeing guide issued by Transport for London maintained that gardens are racist and full of 'problematic plant life', with wisteria specifically cited as having colonial roots. The guide singled out Myatt's Field Park, named after nineteenth-century rhubarb producer Joseph Myatt. Its authors explained that although rhubarb is not racist in and of itself, its popularity as an ingredient in desserts had increased due to the importation of sugar and, since sugar is associated with the slave trade, rhubarb is therefore racist-adjacent. Ellie Harrison, a presenter of the BBC's environmental television show *Countryfile*, found herself in similarly agonised contortions over this kind of media-friendly crackpottery. 'In asking whether the countryside is racist,' she wrote, 'then yes it is; but asking if it's more racist than anywhere else – maybe, maybe not.' An article appeared in the *Guardian* soon after that was more conclusive, insisting that 'the British countryside remains a distinctly white and often intimidating place for BAME communities'. A piece in the *Metro* echoed this sentiment, claiming that the countryside was 'shaped by colonialism' and therefore is 'unwelcoming to people of colour'. As evidence of the article's central thesis, it was accompanied by a cartoon illustration of three white people scowling at a black woman while standing in a meadow. One may as well sketch a shiny goblet and claim it as evidence of the discovery of the Holy Grail.

It's a neat strategy. This kind of coverage effectively goads the tabloids into outrage, which enables the woke left to then claim that the right are getting upset about nonsense such as racist gardens, even though the origin of the story was theirs. Yet when something as innocuous as the countryside can be weaponised for identitarian politics, it is surely unreasonable to expect journalists not to take the bait. In 2023, Kew Gardens launched its 'Queer Nature' project, a celebration of diversity in art, plants and fungi, which sought to draw connections between plants and LGBTQ+ communities. It sounds like the sort of story I would invent for satirical purposes, but when quizzed on the purpose of the project by a member of the public, the official Kew Gardens account on X responded by asserting that 'plants and flowers have often been associated with queer identities, both positively and negatively, and this will be explored in the Queer Nature festival by amplifying queer voices through art, allowing for new conversations'. Another post explained that 'while the basic system of reproduction in lots of plants involves the fusion of male and female gametes, some individual plants do not neatly fit into binaries'. While it is true that most flowering plants are hermaphrodites, it should be noted – for those who have missed it – that human beings are not plants.

So why all the infantile attempts at activism? The answer lies in the organisation's 'Equality, Diversity and Inclusion Delivery Plan'. One of Kew's EDI 'strategy pillars' includes the seeking of accreditation by outside activist groups, including Stonewall. This is the ideological rot that should have been exposed while the online right were moaning about gay flowers. The dominance of activists in every nook of life, no matter how mundane, also explains recent campaigns by the National Trust, the United Kingdom's foremost charity committed to the preservation of stately homes and other historical properties. In recent years, the organisation has been making a sustained effort to pass judgement on the former owners of these properties, alerting visitors to putative connections with the slave trade, or the oppression of the 'LGBT community'. Is it a coincidence that members of the National Trust are mostly 'small-c' conservative? The upkeep of these aristocratic mansions and sprawling country parks is an essentially conservative enterprise; the National Trust is meant to preserve the past for the benefit of the present. That it has become infected with intersectional identity politics feels, once again, like a form of deliberate provocation.

The examples of ideological capture at the National Trust are myriad. A few years ago, volunteers at Ickworth in Suffolk were requested to wear rainbow-themed clothing and make-up as part of their Pride celebrations, and it was suggested that they wear body and face paints to display their commitment to LGBT rights. In 2017, staff at Felbrigg Hall in Norfolk were told to wear rainbow badges and lanyards to commemorate the fiftieth anniversary of the decriminalisation of homosexuality. In the wake of the death of George Floyd, the Trust commissioned a report outlining the connections that some of the properties had to the slave trade and colonialism. They established the 'Colonial Countryside' project, described as 'a child-led writing and history project exploring the African, Caribbean and Indian connections at 11 of our properties'. This was launched in consultation with Dr Corinne Fowler at the University of Leicester, a professor of Postcolonial Literature in the English department. The historian David Starkey asked the pertinent question: 'how on earth, in what seems a staggering example of managerial incompetence, did the National Trust come to hire a non-historian to do a job that only an historian could do?' The answer is that ideology had triumphed over credibility. Where the original owners of houses were slave traders, it makes complete sense that those biographical details would be included on the various visitor information boards. Yet the overemphasis on the slave trade in recent National Trust initiatives is patently political. As Starkey notes, the charity's own report found that only somewhere between 5 and 10 per cent of the properties can be connected with the slave trade. Such low figures hardly justify the continual haranguing of visitors.

This desperate scrabbling for clandestine racism is an insult to those who have experienced genuine oppression on the basis of skin colour. When reading of racist rhubarb and the alleged barriers that black people face when walking down country lanes, it is instructive to remind ourselves of why Martin Luther King, Jr. had been willing to face imprisonment for his non-violent campaigns. In his *Letter from Birmingham Jail* (1963), he outlined the grotesque segregation of the era.

> Perhaps it is easy for those who have never felt the stinging darts of segregation to say, 'Wait.' But when you have seen vicious mobs lynch your mothers and fathers at will and drown your sisters and brothers at whim; when you have seen hate filled policemen curse, kick and even kill your black brothers and sisters; when you see the vast majority of your twenty million Negro brothers smothering in an airtight cage of poverty in the midst of an affluent society; when you suddenly find your tongue twisted and your speech stammering as you seek to explain to your six year old daughter why she can't go to the public amusement park that has just been advertised on television, and see tears welling up in her eyes when she is told that Funtown is closed to colored children . . . then you will understand why we find it difficult to wait.

The triumph of social liberalism is evident in the multiple studies that show how Western societies are the most tolerant and diverse to have ever existed. It is no coincidence that all the major civil rights movements have traditionally been underpinned by a commitment to free speech and liberal ideals. King's insistence on non-violence might not resonate with many of those who claim to be his successors, but his approach should remain the model for genuine progressives.

One of the chief signals of the end of woke is the confidence with which major corporate figures are now rejecting it. The movement has not solely been propelled through politics, but through the corporate sphere, a phenomenon explored thoroughly in Vivek Ramaswamy's book *Woke, Inc.: Inside the Social Justice Scam* (2021). Yet we now see evidence that the inexorable spread of DEI across the Western world is potentially being reversed. In June 2024, the Artificial Intelligence company Scale launched a new policy to ensure that its employees would be selected on the basis of their talents and qualifications rather than their race, gender and sexuality. Scale's CEO, Alexandr Wang, explained that – rather than adopt DEI policies – the company would henceforth favour MEI, which stands for Merit, Excellence, and Intelligence. He explained the thinking behind the new scheme in a post on social media.

> There is a mistaken belief that meritocracy somehow conflicts with diversity. I strongly disagree. No group has a monopoly on excellence. A hiring process based on merit will naturally yield a variety of backgrounds, perspectives, and ideas. Achieving this requires casting a wide net for talent and then objectively selecting the best, without bias in any direction. We will not pick winners and losers based on someone being the 'right' or 'wrong' race, gender, and so on. It should be needless to say, and yet it needs saying: doing so would be racist and sexist, not to mention illegal. Upholding meritocracy is good for business and is the right thing to do.

One can almost hear influential 'whiteness experts' such as Robin DiAngelo, author of *White Fragility* (2018), honking in fury at this blatant implementation of good old-fashioned liberal values. Surely the only way to defeat racism and homophobia is to treat ethnic and sexual minorities as incapable of high achievement and in need of a leg-up from their betters?

It is instructive to compare the reactions to Wang's initiative from major figures in the corporate world with those of woke activists. Wang was praised ardently by Tobias Lütke (CEO of Shopify), Palmer Luckey (founder of Oculus VR) and Elon Musk. By contrast, here were some of the responses on Instagram:

> You're 'disrupting' current hard-fought standards you don't like, by reverting to a system rooted in bias and inequality that asks less of you as a hiring manager and as a leader.
>
> *Dan Couch (He/Him)*

Curious to see how hiring processes can effectively (and objectively) measure one's 'merit', 'excellence', and 'intelligence', all of which are very subjective terms.

*Cole Gawin (He/Him)*

What is merit and how do we measure it?

*Rio Cruz Morales (They/Them)*

This sounds a lot like excuse making for casting off DEI principles.

*R.C. Rondero De Mosier (He/Him)*

The pronouns, of course, are part of a hieratic ritual to signify membership of the cult, and so we should not be surprised to see these sentiments mirroring each other so closely. What Wang is proposing builds equality into the hiring system and, contrary to these complaints, it is entirely possible to measure merit objectively. This, after all, is the purpose of academic assessment. The arguments against merit can only be sustained if one presupposes that systemic inequalities are ingrained within society, that all of these relate to the concept of group identity, and that adjustments have to be made accordingly to guarantee equality of outcome.

That the workplace has become so politicised is also, of course, why cancel culture has been able to wreak such mayhem. In September 2020, I posted on Twitter a proposed six-part pledge for business owners to tackle this problem.

1. We will never discipline or fire members of staff on the basis of pressure from online activists.

2. We have no interest in our employees' political opinions, and how they choose to express themselves outside the workplace is no business of ours.

3. We will not probe into our employees' thoughts with 'unconscious bias training', or force them to undertake workshops that presuppose the existence of 'systemic injustice'.

4. We will never make statements of fealty to any given cause, political or ideological, or claim to promote certain 'values'. Our aim is to make a profit, not to preach to our customers.

5. We will not tolerate the public shaming of employees if they cause offence, either through a joke or poor phrasing, and will instead seek to resolve internally any disputes that naturally occur when human beings work together.

6. We reject the current predominance of identity politics and will simply treat everyone equally (staff and customers alike) irrespective of their race, gender, sexuality, or any other immutable characteristic.

Fanciful stuff, obviously. I was later informed that at least one manager had adopted my suggestions, and it would be interesting to hear, all these years later, how this worked out. Perhaps as DEI continues to wither, such proposals might no longer seem so exotic.

While 'the omni-cause' is an enjoyably barbed label, 'woke' as a descriptive term is perhaps more apt. It need not bear pejorative connotations and, given that so many activists and thinkers have embraced the word for themselves, it seems like a courtesy to refer to them as such. Those who claim that 'woke' was invented by the right as a 'snarl-word' simply do not know their own history. It is not an ideal term because, as surveys have repeatedly shown, there is no broad agreement on a definition. For instance, a YouGov poll in 2021 found that only 59 per cent of respondents understood the word, with only a third of this contingent claiming it as an accurate reflection of their own views. Yet we do require a shorthand to encapsulate this diffuse and Byzantine ideology. It is the new state religion, the creed of the establishment, but without accurately describing it we have no means of holding it to account.

I present for your consideration the following two options. In describing this dominant movement of the culture wars, we might adopt the following formulation:

An ideology underpinned by the postmodernist notion that our understanding of reality is produced in the context of linguistic and cultural frameworks, that knowledge is a construct of power wielded oppressively through language, and therefore censorship and other authoritarian measures are necessary to reshape society, with an intersectional focus that rejects the traditional Marxist prioritisation of class and economic disparities in favour of a conceptualisation of group identity as the prism through which all analysis must be filtered, with a particular emphasis on a form of standpoint epistemology that asserts there are multiple 'ways of knowing' and that the 'lived experience' of the marginalised must take precedence over empirical or scientific methodology – which are merely tools of the oppressor class – all of which is predicated upon the Foucauldian notion that society operates on the basis of invisible power structures, and that denials of such structures are evidence of their existence (as anyone who would deny them is likely to be benefiting from the privileges they afford) and that there must therefore be a cultural revolution in order to guarantee equality of outcome rather than equality of opportunity, one that will ultimately achieve the wholesale obliteration of 'whiteness', 'patriarchy' and 'cis-heteronormativity', in which the parameters of thought and speech are limited to the propagation of the cause, and in which all activities of all branches of the media, the arts and the state must be directed towards that end.

Or we could just say 'woke'.

## The Woke Right

The pendulum theory would have it that history is cyclical, and that as one movement rises against its antithesis it produces the necessary momentum for the process to be reversed. In this sense, one could suggest that the triumph of liberalism in the West since the various civil rights campaigns of the 1960s has created the conditions for its own demise. The gradually developing liberal consensus can be said to have reached its peak around the turn of the century. During that goldilocks period, most people of my generation concurred that racism and other forms of discrimination based on immutable characteristics were unacceptable. We agreed that the most vulnerable in society required support, even when we might have disagreed on how best that support should be provided. Right and left were generally in concord when it comes to the inherent value of human life, and that freedom of speech was the bedrock of our democracy.

Yet no one could have anticipated that the pendulum would swing back from an unexpected direction. For all its efforts, it was not the reactionary right that successfully overthrew the liberal consensus, it was the rise of Critical Social Justice which, in turn, produced its own resistance from traditionalists and conservatives. It's as though the pendulum had fractured and reproduced itself. So while we still have the eternal back-and-forth of liberty and authority, the latter now consists of a subsidiary struggle between left and right, working against each other but also simultaneously swinging back against the liberal norms that we have worked so hard to establish. In other words, we have two oppositional forces that we might colloquially call 'woke' and 'anti-woke' that, for all their differences, are united in their contempt for liberalism. These are enemies who do not realise that they are fighting on the same side.

The difficulties that we have seen when it comes to the evolution and various redefinitions of the word 'woke' are inevitably compounded by the development of the 'anti-woke'. If we cannot agree on the meaning of the term itself, how can we even begin to define its opposite? We are entering a new front in the culture war, in which a significant contingent of those who oppose wokeness do so by manifesting similar traits. It is for this reason that 'anti-woke', a term that I would argue approximates 'liberal', cannot suffice. Some commentators have attempted to resolve this issue through a new formulation: 'the woke right'. By this, they do not mean to allude to the phenomenon of Critical Social Justice inveigling itself into traditionally right-wing arenas of influence, although this is certainly how the term was first used. To take one example, in May 2022, Kathy Barnette, a candidate in the Republican Senate primary election in Pennsylvania, described her opponents in her own party as the 'woke right' on the grounds that they were too progressive.

Like all entries in the culture war lexicon, the meaning of the term 'woke right' has evolved rapidly. Konstantin Kisin, co-host of the *Triggernometry* podcast, has adopted the phrase to refer to those who identify as right wing, but whose tactics mirror those of the woke left. 'Every retardation has an equal and opposite retardation,' he writes. 'The deranged worldview of the woke left, along with its disregard for truth, hatred of the West and falsification of history, is now being replicated on the right.' The author James Lindsay has defined it in similar terms, as 'a victimhood-based identity politics' whose 'victim groups are whites, Christians, men, and straight people'. He argues that the movement is 'roughly intersectional' insofar as it is obsessed with identity politics and a grievance relating to anti-white racism. 'Like their counterparts on the Woke Left,' Lindsay writes, 'the Woke Right have accepted as fact that there's a conspiracy against people like them and that their only real hope is to lean into the identity grouping and advocate for collective power under that heading.' In these terms, the 'woke right' is a kind of ideological doppelgänger, whose members exhibit the same precisionist and absolutist tendencies of their leftist counterparts. Andrew Torba, CEO of right-wing social media platform Gab, seems to embody this notion in his open endorsement of identity politics.

The classical liberal ideal of a society where people interact purely based on individual merit, free from any group identity considerations, might sound appealing in theory; however, in practice, it's only truly possible in a homogeneous society. In a society where the majority of people share the same race, culture, and values identity politics would be irrelevant because there would be no competing identity groups, but rather competing individuals and ideas. However, in a multi-cultural multi-ethnic society like ours, tribal identity politics is inevitable. Different identity groups will always strive to protect and promote their own interests. This is common sense and White people are starting to wake up to this reality and realize that if they don't advocate for themselves no one else will.

It is noteworthy that Torba capitalises the word 'white'. This is an echo of the convention among the disciples of Critical Social Justice to capitalise 'black'. It would seem that the woke right and woke left share not only their strategies, but also an analogous style guide.

Writing for *The Critic*, Connor Tomlinson has quibbled with the use of the term 'woke right' on largely tactical grounds, given that it is 'ill-defined' and 'self-contradictory'. He believes that these commentators' usage of the term can be summarised as 'adopting contrarian opinions to mainstream narratives, and adopting identity politics in a defensive posture against the progressive attack on the history, culture, and statehood of the peoples of the US and Europe'. Tomlinson is insistent that where anti-white racism exists it ought to be exposed, and rejects the label 'woke right' as 'an attempt by yesterday's Left to tone police, gatekeep, and redefine the Right'. This is reminiscent of complaints by intersectional activists that the term 'woke' has been deployed as a slur to keep their worst excesses in check. YouTuber Benjamin Boyce has likewise decried the term 'woke right' on the grounds that it is 'a political weapon' akin to 'racist', 'climate denier' or 'transphobe'. For Boyce, there is 'too much conflation between tactics and beliefs when "woke right" is used. And there are too many people being assigned that term, with very little similarity other than loose crosstalk between them.' Boyce is correct to note that the features often identified with the 'woke right' are not proscriptive in the manner of a set of doctrines in a religion. The phenomenon of antisemitism, while not uncommon among the dissident right, is not necessarily a defining feature. There are those, for instance, who take great exception to the antisemitism one finds among 'Groypers' – an online cult of trolls and white nationalists – but who nonetheless believe that white men are an oppressed identity class and that liberalism is to blame.

And yet the conviction among the dissident right that Western society is unregenerable is a close cousin of the view on the identitarian left that the West is an oppressive tyranny that must be destroyed. When conservative commentator Tucker Carlson interviewed the podcaster Darryl Cooper, it was Cooper's claim that Winston Churchill was the true villain of the Second World War that generated the most controversy. On social media, Cooper had previously posted an image of Hitler's occupation of Paris alongside one of drag queens performing a parody of the Last Supper at the opening ceremony of the 2024 Paris Olympics, and claimed that the former scenario was 'infinitely preferable in every way'. This sense that the Western elites have engineered society for the benefit of 'degenerates' might help explain the impulse of the handful of extremists who posit that the West would have been better served by a victory for the Third Reich. Similarly, at an event at Churchill College, Cambridge in February 2021, a panel of left-wing activist academics chaired by Priyamvada Gopal, a professor of Postcolonial Studies, sought to frame Churchill as an irredeemable racist. One panellist, Kehinde Andrews, branded Churchill the 'perfect embodiment of white supremacy' who helmed an empire that was 'far worse than the Nazis'. Cooper and Andrews are approaching their analysis from completely opposing political worldviews, and yet they have somehow arrived at an identical conclusion with regard to the singular evil of Churchill.

Perhaps it would be helpful, then, to summarise the key characteristics of the movement that has come to be known as the 'woke right', while acknowledging that those to whom it pertains do not necessarily embrace the term.

### Group identity

A tendency to perceive humanity through the lens of identity categories such as race, sex, sexual orientation and class. In the woke movement, economic inequality is often sidelined in intersectional considerations, but for the woke right it has become a key concern given the palpable hostility towards working-class communities.

### The politics of resentment

Just as intersectional politics has given rise to what is colloquially known as the 'oppression Olympics', those on the woke right perceive themselves to be subject to open discrimination in a system that works against their interests. The Diversity, Equity and Inclusion (DEI) industry has led to cases in which white people have been explicitly excluded. For example, in June 2021 it was reported that a BBC trainee production management assistant position was advertised as 'only open to black, Asian and ethnically diverse candidates'.

### Anti-liberalism

The woke left and the woke right share a conviction that liberalism has failed, and that it should therefore be abandoned altogether. The liberal fealty to free speech is mistrusted by the woke right, and in some cases censorship is advocated in order to curb the excesses of wokeness. Calls to ban certain forms of protests and repeal same-sex marriage fall into this category.

### The denial of truth

The rejection of objective truth in favour of unevidenced claims is common to both the woke left and the woke right. In the case of the former, this manifests in the concepts of 'lived experience' and 'standpoint epistemology' (the notion that there exist multiple 'ways of knowing' and that those who are oppressed benefit from a more accurate insight into reality). For the latter, it takes the form of assumptions about global conspiracies that are asserted as true based on instinct and wild theorising rather than proof. It is telling that members of both factions describe themselves as uniquely 'awake'.

## Antisemitism

A key overlap between the woke left and woke right is a tendency towards antisemitism. Jews are perceived as holding disproportionate institutional power, and are often scapegoated for broader societal problems.

## Disdain for the West

A sense in which the elites in the West have conspired against the people has become palpable on the dissident right. Misinformation and a lack of government transparency during the Covid-19 pandemic, the imposition of wildly unpopular 'progressive' social policies, and repeated attempts to undermine the democratic process, have contributed to a narrative that the West is irreparably broken.

## Purity spirals

The movement is characterised by an intolerance of alternative views and an expectation of moral purity. Dissenters are often subjected to online 'dogpiling', or being otherwise slandered and publicly shamed. Liberals who have advocated for multiculturalism are seen as responsible for the ongoing degradation of society. The concept of religious freedom is seen as particularly deleterious given Islamist opposition to democratic values and free speech. Sexual freedom is likewise rejected in favour of traditionalist monogamous family units.

## The new theism

The sense of a failed liberal system has given rise to a belief that humankind cannot function without a guiding and overarching belief-system, and that given the Judeo-Christian foundations of the West, a reinstated Christian theocracy would be preferable to the current status quo. While many have embraced Christianity out of authentically revelatory experiences, others on the woke right have performatively adopted the trappings of faith as an identity category for pragmatic and political reasons. This form of Christianity is unrelated to the belief in God but is rather a conscious effort to restore a unifying ethical framework to the West.

Observable similarities between the woke left and the woke right are to be expected. A 2020 study in the journal *Heliyon* sought to establish any kind of connection between what are known as the 'Dark Triad' (DT) personality traits – Machiavellianism, narcissism and psychopathy – and left or right affiliations. The sample consisted of over five hundred subjects from a broad range of ages, ethnicities and political views. The researchers, Jordan Mossa and Peter J. O'Connor, focused on three extremes commonly found in culture war discourse: 'White Identitarianism' (WI), 'Political Correctness-Authoritarianism' (PCA), and 'Political Correctness-Liberalism' (PCL). The study found evidence that even politically disparate groups share a belief that restrictions on freedom are necessary to achieve their goals.

> In conclusion, our study indicates that an emerging set of main-stream political attitudes – most notably PCA, WI, are largely being adopted by individuals high in the DT and entitlement. Individuals high in authoritarianism – regardless of whether they hold politically correct or right-wing views – tend to score highly on DT and entitlement. Such individuals therefore are statistically more likely than average to be higher in psychopathy, narcissism, Machiavellianism and entitlement.

In his analysis of the study for *Quillette*, Zaid Jilani echoes the sense in which these findings intuitively ring true: 'Notwithstanding their diametrically opposed political postures, both hard Left and hard Right seem disproportionately populated by individuals who are impelled to control others' behavior, and draw attention to themselves.'

But is this connection between anti-social personality traits and authoritarianism most effectively summarised through the use of the terms 'woke left' and 'woke right'? These erroneously imply that the culture war is a matter of long-established political designations which, as we have seen, is far from the case. If the woke left are not left-wing in any serious sense, the same problem must apply to the woke right. Just as traditional leftism does not seek to demonise the working class and empower corporations against them, traditional conservatism does not characterise itself as a reaction against illiberalism. Debates about personal responsibility, property ownership, the welfare state or the value of laissez-faire economics and free-market capitalism rarely feature in the skirmishes of culture warriors. With this in mind, it is easy to see how the term 'woke right' can be misleading.

Classifications such as 'woke left' and 'woke right' will always be imprecise and subject to variations. Yet it is surely advantageous to agree on some shorthand by which to refer to certain ideological tendencies, while acknowledging that these are trends rather than fixed tenets of an identifiable and cohesive movement. 'Woke right' has its limitations, but it also has the advantage of effectively communicating the key principles. Above all, it makes complete sense when one understands that the core belief of wokeness is that its ideological dogma should be imposed on society by force and coercion, rather than persuasion and consensus. Authoritarianism is not specific to any political cause. It is a natural impulse in humanity that we must learn to resist.

# 2

# The Before Times

---

## 'This Is All Your Fault, McLaughlin'

Derry, Northern Ireland, 1939. My grandfather, Edward McLaughlin (known as 'Ted'), has volunteered to join the British Army. He is marching out of the city with other recruits, all wearing the uniform of the hated British state. Some of Ted's friends consider his actions a betrayal. As a Catholic he should be fighting the crown, not joining its forces. One of his friends follows at his heels as he marches. 'McLaughlin,' he shouts, 'you ought to be ashamed of yourself.' Ted replies: 'The Nazis aren't going to stop in England. If they are not defeated they will march into Derry. Catch yourself on and join up.'

The extent of my grandfather's courage cannot be overstated. Not only was he volunteering to participate in a bloody conflict, but he also knew that in doing so he would become a kind of pariah at home. Ever since the partition of Ireland in 1921, Derry has always had a Catholic majority. When he was thirteen, Ted had watched his father being beaten by British soldiers who had raided their house during the night. The next morning he sought out some local Irish Republican Army (IRA) members and signed up to the Fianna Éireann, the youth wing of the paramilitary movement. For a man with this background to join the British Army was far from trivial.

Principles of course count for nothing if they cannot override personal convenience. This kind of moral stance has always been rare, and is surely rarer still in the Western world today. The rise of social media appears to have elevated entitlement and narcissism to the status of virtues. The ideals of self-sacrifice and stoicism are incoherent in a society in which clout is secured through victimhood and grievances have become a kind of currency. When C. S. Lewis delivered his lecture 'The Weight of Glory' at the Church of St Mary the Virgin in Oxford in 1941 he was able to assert that most people would consider unselfishness to be the ultimate virtue. The same could not be said with any confidence today.

Our culture war could only have arisen in the context of immense privilege. My generation and those that have followed have not endured the hardship of a global conflict, and it is very easy to deride our own nation if we have never been called upon to defend it. Many of today's activists believe that they are bravely standing up against tyranny, but there can be no comparison between the generation that fought the Nazis and the culture warriors who think they have achieved something by getting a supermarket worker fired for 'misgendering' someone on social media. While my grandfather's generation put their lives at risk to resist authoritarianism, many of today's young adults are calling for their own liberties to be restricted. This baffling volte-face has arisen for a number of reasons, not least that the threat has taken a more opaque form. There is little ambiguity in a murderous tyrant who seeks to consolidate his power through conquest and subjugation, but what happens when authoritarianism disguises itself as benevolence and accrues power so gradually that it becomes almost imperceptible?

A couple of years after my grandfather signed up, he was stationed with British troops in North Africa. During one battle, his regiment was bombarded by artillery shells and he was forced to take cover. He jumped into a crater which had been left after an explosion. He then

*My grandfather, Edward McLaughlin, in 1941.*

heard a voice mutter: 'This is all your fault, McLaughlin.' It was the same man who had harangued him on his march out of Derry back in 1939. Something about my grandfather's words that day had prompted this man to rethink, and he eventually joined up in the struggle against Hitler.

Ted would tell this story because of the extraordinary nature of the coincidence, but there is far more to it than that. The bravery of my grandfather's generation represents the apotheosis of a principle that we could all do well to emulate. That is to say, we ought not to refrain from the morally correct course of action simply because it is the more difficult choice. No one group has all the answers, and sometimes it is necessary to take 'our own side' to task. As I will show, it is naïvely utopian to suppose that the authoritarian instinct in humankind can ever be eliminated. Irrespective of our views – political, ideological, religious or otherwise – the struggle for liberty and against authoritarianism is one that many of us would support. It will take a collective effort to cultivate a more open-minded political climate, one which reverses our apparent trajectory towards a Manichean future of heroes and villains.

## The Rip Van Winkle Effect

Some of my most vivid memories of my time as an undergraduate student involve late-night conversations with housemates, all of us inebriated and excitable, in the tumbledown spider-ridden house we shared on the outskirts of Aberystwyth. The property was poorly insulated and often cold, and so we would congregate in the kitchen and fire up all four hobs on the stove until the room was swelling in a haze of toxic heat. Our gas bills were included in the rent, and so this was far more cost-effective than feeding coins into an electricity meter that seemed permanently ravenous.

And sometimes these nocturnal symposia would become as torrid as the air we were breathing. I recall one evening in particular when a visitor had taken umbrage at some comment on Welsh nationalism. Before long the drunken discussion had morphed into an argument, slurred salvos flew back and forth through the cigarette smoke, and there seemed to be no possibility of compromise. And when we all woke the next morning – or rather, afternoon – there remained not the faintest aftertaste of bitterness. There was no suggestion that the profound disagreements within the group would sully our friendship. We probably went for a jacket potato.

This was typical of the time. Friends could take opposing views on contentious topics without fear of ostracism. Is this even possible any more? Recently I spent some time crunching through my smartphone to delete the numbers of former friends. So many have taken the view that by consistently defending free speech and liberal values, and by choosing to satirise the left as well as the right, I have somehow violated the tribe's sacred creed. All of this is fairly depressing, but it does free up one's social calendar. Whenever I tell the friends that remain of those who have departed, the typical response is that these turncoats could not have been friends to begin with, and that their behaviour has simply exposed their true nature. In this, they are echoing Seneca: *'Qui amicus esse coepit, quia expedit, et desinet, quia expedit'* ('He who begins to be your friend because it is expedient will also cease because it is expedient'). The emotional impact of disappointment, the realisation that those we thought we knew were merely play-acting for our affections, is an unmooring experience. It threw Hamlet into melancholy, after all.

How have we reached this point? In their book *How to Have Impossible Conversations* (2019), Peter Boghossian and James Lindsay address this growing factionalism.

> In a disagreement, people frequently assume their partners' intentions and motivations are worse than they are. Many people, for example, assume conservatives are racist, liberals aren't patriotic, Republicans don't care about poor people, or Democrats are weak on national defense. They then go on to assume that these perceived shortcomings motivate beliefs and arguments. This is usually false.

This now common tendency must surely be partly ascribed to the rise of the ideology of Critical Social Justice and its consolidation of power through the detection and elimination of heresy. It has established a new trend of intolerance and, with its insistence on a Disneyfied 'Good versus Evil' vision of humanity, it has guaranteed that a significant proportion of people now resolve their political disputes through 'ghosting'; that is to say, by ending relationships abruptly and ceasing all communications. In a survey for the Centre for Policy Studies in 2021, pollster Frank Luntz found that '29 per cent of Britons have stopped talking to someone because of something political they said, and 22 per cent have had someone stop talking to them'. Whereas once we might have relished debate among friends and understood it to be a sign of a healthy relationship, there has since been an escalation of purity spirals.

I have heard a number of commentators refer wistfully to the 'Before Times', those years when a robust challenge to one's point of view did not result in the termination of a friendship. As the end of woke approaches, we are well placed to reflect on these recent years of intellectual suffocation in which the marketplace of ideas was treated with suspicion and tribes were formed according to sclerotic political affiliations. The deranging impact was only accentuated by the unreasonable demands that we were expected to support. During the woke era, we were encouraged to declare that human beings could change sex when we knew they could not, and were urged to accept the re-racialisation of society as somehow progressive. From time to time, most of us noticed that we had grown accustomed to this everyday lunacy. We found ourselves reading one of those bizarre but suddenly commonplace headlines – such as 'Is classical music racist?', 'The whiteness of *Toy Story 4*' and 'This new health minister thinks you can identity as a llama' – and were suddenly reminded that such preposterous notions would not have been entertained only a short while ago. The madness was part-authentic, part-performative. Very few people accepted such premises, but there were plenty who were prepared to assert them to be true, possibly as a means to elevate their status. Flagrant absurdities had become high-status opinions.

Perhaps a little thought experiment will help us to put the rise and fall of the woke hegemony into perspective. Try to imagine yourself as you were in the year 2000. What would have been your reaction had someone told you that just two decades later British police would be keeping a record of thousands of citizens deemed guilty of 'non-crime hate incidents' (see Chapter 5)? Or that free speech would be dismissed in the press as a right-wing talking point? Or that a school district in

Canada would be burning thousands of books because the contents are offensive to modern sensibilities, and that they would refer to this as a 'flame purification ceremony'? What if this person had told you that by the 2020s major corporations would be paying visiting speakers to berate their staff for their 'white privilege', and telling them they should 'try to be less white'? Or that activists would be demanding that statues of Winston Churchill, Mahatma Gandhi and even slavery abolitionists like Thomas Henry Huxley should be torn down, and that such appeals would be taken seriously by the establishment? Or that some of the world's leading experts on race relations would be claiming that the ideal of colour-blindness, so beautifully expressed in Martin Luther's King Jr.'s 'I have a dream' speech, was actually racist, and that in promoting this dream King was upholding white supremacy? Or that one of the most prestigious schools in London would be segregating its pupils by skin colour for after-school activities?

Or what if you had been told that in a little over twenty years' time, the BBC would be broadcasting a film aimed at children asserting that there are over a hundred genders, and that teachers throughout the country would be doing the same? Or that politicians would stumble and stutter when asked 'what is a woman?' and be unable to answer the question? Or that 'woman' itself would become a dirty word and that some would favour the neologism 'womxn'? Or that companies, charities, media outlets and even some factions of the NHS would be using alternatives like 'menstruators', 'people who bleed' and 'individuals with a cervix'? Or that rapists would be identifying as female and being moved to women's prisons where they would commit further sexual assaults? Or that healthy teenage girls would be encouraged by health professionals to undergo double mastectomies, and that young effeminate boys would be told that they are actually girls and that they should be put on medication to halt puberty? Or that reputable medical journals would be denying biological reality, claiming that sex isn't binary at all, but that it's a spectrum? Or that women would be fired from their jobs and subjected to threats of death and rape for saying that biological sex is real?

We might call this 'the Rip Van Winkle effect'. In Washington Irving's story, his character falls asleep in a drunken stupor and remains unconscious for twenty years, missing the entirety of the American Revolution. Had we fallen asleep in 2000, would we recognise the prevailing values of our culture twenty years later? If nothing else, this thought experiment highlights the breathtaking rapidity of these societal changes. Few of us would deny that all the claims outlined above would have been dismissed as laughable at the turn of the millennium. No sane person would have conceded that any of these outcomes were possible in a free and liberal society. And yet here we are.

Somehow, those who have raised concerns about these radical and destructive changes have been accused of 'starting a culture war'. This outright inversion of observable truth is known as 'gaslighting', and has become a common tactic of culture warriors. During the woke era, their ideology was dominant in all major corporate and public institutions. They determined the creative and conceptual trajectory of the arts, the media and education. To have achieved such a widescale coup and simultaneously deny that it happened is a form of audacity so extreme that not even the ruling party in George Orwell's *Nineteen Eighty-Four* (1949) would have dared to attempt it. The political scientist Timur Kuran has coined the phrase 'preference falsification' for the phenomenon of those whose privately held opinions differ from those that are publicly expressed, either for reputational enhancement or due to perceived social pressures. Virtually everyone agrees that men cannot be lesbians, but in the woke regime to declare this truth openly carried a potential cost. In the Before Times, we could rely on our senses to accurately interpret the world around us. But in the midst of the culture wars, we were expected to lie about what we saw, or ignore aspects that contradicted the ideological narrative of the ruling class.

There are precedents for this. In his fascinating book *It's Only a Joke Comrade!* (2018), historian Jonathan Waterlow draws on documents from the Soviet era in order to analyse the ways in which citizens would use humour as a means to adapt to their oppressive conditions.

He describes their sense of living in two realities at once: that of their authentic daily lives, and the version of society approved by the regime. He calls this 'crosshatching', drawing from China Miéville's novel, *The City & the City* (2009):

> The novel's conceit is to have two different cities exist topographically in the same place, but which remain culturally, linguistically and socially separate. More importantly, the citizens of each place must learn to 'unsee' and act as though the other one doesn't exist, or face dire consequences from enforcement agents. In most areas, architecture, signposts and other cues made it clear to which city they belonged, but in others – the crosshatched areas – things were unclear and mixed; they seemed to belong to two cultures at once.

Waterlow adapts this metaphor to the Soviet state's demands that its citizens 'unsee' aspects of the world that contradict the propaganda, pointing out that 'even if many pretended to do so, contemporaries were really living in the crosshatching of ideology and daily experience'.

Although the woke had not threatened non-conformists with incarceration in gulags, for a time we were nonetheless existing in this sort of crosshatched world. Many of us kept our opinions to ourselves for fear of repercussions, even if those opinions happened to be shared by the vast majority of the population. In the Before Times, we could be confident in expressing our scepticism about fashionable but insubstantial ideas; in the woke era, we found it safer just to nod along. The end of woke will entail a return to the sanity of the Before Times, a far preferable state than remaining forever locked in an ideological cage. An effective means to overcome this 'crosshatching', this continual need to balance reality against the official narrative, will be found once we have regained the courage to speak our minds and dare to disagree. We need to move beyond these self-imposed echo chambers, and we can start by maintaining friendships with those whose worldview is not simply a mirror image of our own.

## The Legacy of Brexit

The turning point in Shakespeare's *Othello* (c. 1604) occurs precisely midway through the play, during the third scene of the third act. Iago's continual insinuations that Desdemona has committed adultery are finally corroding Othello's faith in his wife. The fatal strike occurs when Iago tells Othello that he has seen Cassio – the alleged paramour – wiping his beard with Desdemona's handkerchief. Othello's reaction is an unbridled detonation.

> O that the slave had forty thousand lives!
> One is too poor, too weak for my revenge.
> Now do I see 'tis true. Look here, Iago.
> All my fond love thus do I blow to heaven – 'tis gone.
> Arise, black vengeance, from the hollow hell.
> Yield up, O love, thy crown and hearted throne
> To tyrannous hate! Swell, bosom, with thy fraught,
> For 'tis of aspics' tongues.

From this moment, Othello's fate is fully charted. His mind has been curdled and his transformation from dignified and respected general to volatile and uxoricidal madman is complete and irreversible. He is now seeing the world through a blood-soaked lens of rage, and not even Desdemona's final desperate appeals to his reason and love can rescue him from these delusions.

This sudden shift into insanity might serve as a metaphor for the way in which the United Kingdom seemed to detach from reality in the aftermath of the 2016 referendum on the country's membership of the European Union (EU). Like Othello, we seemed to pivot from one state to another, from dignity to mania, in a matter of moments. One referendum had been all that was required to send us spiralling into a whole new world of unforgiving and unthinking venom. A bleak fantasy had replaced the truth. The Before Times were officially over.

The result was close, with 52 per cent voting to leave and 48 per cent to remain. Brexit divided families and friends with an efficiency unprecedented since the Irish Civil War, a historical catastrophe that saw siblings in the same households take up arms against each other. We should be thankful that very few Brits in 2016 had access to guns, but the extent of the animosity was comparably volatile. This dispute over a neoliberal trading bloc had become a proxy for the perennial battle of the forces of light and darkness, with combatants on each side determining that the others were the authentic villains. It was as though we had been transported into a landscape devised by J. R. R. Tolkien, only with fewer orcs.

The hysteria took me by surprise. My opposition to Britain's membership of the European Union was identical to that of prominent leftists such as Tony Benn or Barbara Castle. I maintained, and still do, that those in power ought to be accountable to the electorate, and I consider it undemocratic to outsource lawmaking capabilities to an unelected body. These are standard left-wing views; indeed, the 1983 Labour Party manifesto included a pledge to leave the European Economic Community, the precursor to the European Union, within a period of five years. Former Labour leader Jeremy Corbyn had spent most of his lifetime in politics opposing our membership of this body, so that when he campaigned against Brexit in the run-up to the referendum he only did so reluctantly. 'I'm not a huge fan of the European Union,' Corbyn said during an interview on Channel 4's *The Last Leg*, describing his support as a 'practical decision'. The host Adam Hills then asked him directly, in terms of a one to ten scale, how passionate he was about remaining in the EU. Corbyn said his enthusiasm could be rated around 'seven' or 'seven and a half'. If 'Remainers' were looking for a stirring call to arms in the manner of Henry V at Agincourt, they would have been sorely disappointed.

For many comedians, Brexit provided an endless source of material. Soon after the referendum, jokes on the comedy circuit at the expense of Leave voters became commonplace to the point of vapidity. The gags in question tended to be based on the fallacy that those who opposed the EU were stupid, racist or 'low-information'. I recall one comedian friend approaching me in a green room and asking whether it was true that I had supported the Leave campaign. At this time, I was one of only four or five stand-ups on the circuit who had openly voted in favour of Brexit, but I was still taken aback when he said: 'How could you do that? I thought you were meant to be intelligent.' It still strikes me as bizarre that so many were prepared to smear 17.4 million of their fellow citizens in this way, and all in the name of tolerance. One would have thought that comedians of all people would have some appreciation of irony.

I have always respected those who voted Remain and their many sound reasons for it. I would never assume that their disagreement originated in ignorance or stupidity or malevolence. For my part, it was simply that I could not reconcile my belief in democracy with our membership of the EU. I felt that it took a specifically bourgeois form of doublethink to pronounce oneself left-wing and in the same breath to cheer on centre-right technocrats such as Jean-Claude Juncker, Guy Verhofstadt, Michel Barnier and Donald Tusk, to claim to be subversive but to wholeheartedly support the establishment and the prolongation of the status quo, to consider oneself progressive whilst simultaneously endorsing a pro-corporate, neoliberal, protectionist, bureaucratic bloc with scant respect for democratic principles. That, to me, was the biggest joke of all.

Perhaps my choice was wrongheaded, but it had not been taken lightly. I was certainly naïve to assume that differences of opinion were still permissible on the comedy circuit, and that society more broadly had retained the necessary maturity to accept that not all citizens hold identical views. I was not the only one to have noticed that the most zealous champions for the EU in the wake of the referendum had previously regarded it with indifference at best. During one particularly heated argument with a celebrity comedian who was denouncing the evils of Brexit voters in the manner of Henry II railing against turbulent priests, I asked him to name any of the members of the European Commission, the EU's executive branch responsible for proposing and implementing new laws. He had never heard of it. It was remarkable to see a man spin himself into a dervish of indignation over something he knew precisely nothing about.

Many people on all sides of the debate had apparently surrendered their rationality, and yet I do not believe that Brexit alone could have actuated this generalised shift into the parochial and clannish thinking that still dominates today's political discourse. There was the election of Donald Trump in the same year, of course, but this was just one event in a broader concatenation. Had the British public voted to leave the EU in the 1990s, there would probably have been a mass shrugging of shoulders and a resigned acceptance of what we call the 'loser's consent'. After all, a democracy can only function if its members understand that collective decisions cannot always go their way. A few months after the EU referendum I was having a conversation with a Labour backbencher and former member of Ed Miliband's shadow cabinet who, although a fierce opponent of Brexit, considered the idea that Parliament might overturn the result to be an impossibility. As far as she was concerned, no MP would seriously countenance such a grossly undemocratic course of action. But in the following three years there was a general change of outlook, one fostered by the unending repetition of lies, which enabled MPs to disregard the referendum result with a clear conscience.

It is known as the 'illusory truth effect', one that has become a defining feature of today's culture war. We had been assured that two plus two equals five for so long that the rules of arithmetic no longer seemed to apply. We were told that those who voted for Brexit had no idea what they were voting for, even though there were months of debate on the subject and the population had never been more politically energised. We were told that the electorate did not understand that leaving the EU would involve leaving the Single Market, even though the ramifications of leaving the Single Market were a continual feature of the numerous televised debates. We were told that the referendum was advisory, even though no leading campaigner on either side of the argument ever remotely suggested such a thing before the result. We were told that the Leave vote was based on widespread xenophobia, even though studies repeatedly confirm that the UK is one of the least xenophobic countries in the world. We were told that Brexit supporters were slaves to nostalgia who yearned for a colonial past, even though nobody seemed to have actually met any of these supposedly ubiquitous colonialists. And ultimately, of course, we were told on a daily basis that thwarting this monumental democratic mandate would somehow be in the best interests of democracy, and that the attempt to enact the result of a national referendum was some kind of 'coup'. Only in the midst of the woke era could such doublethink be possible and, looking back, it is difficult to comprehend how any politician succumbed to it.

When it comes to democracy, it is essential that we strive for consistent principles, even when we do not take pleasure in the outcome. The philosopher Roger Scruton called this a 'pre-political loyalty', by which we resolve the common problem of living under a government for which most of the electorate did not vote. We respect our fellow citizens even when they do not vote our way, because 'the government is not "mine" or "yours" but "ours"'. The electorate is bound together, in other words, by the first-person plural. Hence the famous preamble to the US constitution: 'We the people...' How is this compatible with the various placards one sees in the aftermath of elections: 'Not My President' or 'Not My Prime Minister'? The more one considers the implications of this sentiment, the more sinister it seems. It means that we no longer accept the democratic contract and, more worryingly, that we yearn for something else.

The end of woke will involve the restoration of the value of democracy as an imperfect system for an imperfect society. One thinks of that phrase often attributed to Winston Churchill: 'democracy is the worst form of government, except for all the others'. I tend to agree with E. M. Forster's view that democracy 'is less hateful than other contemporary forms of government, and to that extent it deserves our support'. The alternative, after all, must be a kind of tyranny, and while a benevolent dictatorship is theoretically possible, history teaches us that to advance such a solution is rarely a risk worth taking. Confucius envisaged a supremely ethical individual as the ideal leader, one whose example would encourage his subjects to act according to their particular roles in society. Yet this kind of noocracy – government by the wise – would presuppose a dutiful citizenry and an incorruptible ruler. A despot might well do wonders for society, right up until the point at which his ego becomes inflated with overfeeding. Let us not forget that Caligula was lauded by the Roman population at first, with Philo describing the early period of his reign as a 'golden age'. Later, he developed a taste for torture, rape and incest, and would execute anyone who mentioned goats because he resented being reminded of his excessive body hair.

With its archaic 'first past the post' method of selecting MPs, our democracy is as flawed as any other in the Western world. In the 2015 General Election, for instance, the United Kingdom Independence Party (UKIP) secured 3.9 million votes but won only one seat in the House of Commons. By contrast, the 1.5 million votes for the Scottish National Party (SNP) resulted in fifty-six seats. Under proportional representation, UKIP would have ended up with eighty-three MPs. Similarly, in the 2024 general election, the Reform party won approximately four million votes which translated to only five seats in Parliament. This equates to 14 per cent of the vote share and only 1 per cent of the seats. If, like me, you have never voted for UKIP or Reform, it is difficult to resist the temptation to justify such an undemocratic system on the grounds that it ensured the failure of parties we do not support. At the time, we heard many commentators resorting to a combination of casuistry and self-deception to claim that it was somehow in the interests of the demos to prevent its wishes from being realised. How often have we heard smaller parties belittled as irrelevant or 'populist'? In the case of UKIP, Conservative leader David Cameron famously referred to their supporters as 'fruitcakes', 'loonies' and 'closet racists'. This last accusation sounds very much like the kind of amateur telepathy one hears from those who habitually accuse their political opponents of 'dog-whistling'.

Even if it were the case that the electorate was merely some kind of 'basket of deplorables' – to borrow Hillary Clinton's self-destructive utterance – this would not warrant the high-handed dismissal of their wishes. One thing is certain: the current system is not working. A 'trust in government' survey by the Office for National Statistics in 2023 revealed that Parliament and the political parties were the least trusted of all public institutions (trusted by 24 per cent and 12 per cent of the population, respectively). This is the natural consequence of a rise of a technocratic approach to governance, a preponderance of careerists rather than truly vocational members of Parliament, and a paternalistic attitude from our representatives towards those who have put them in power.

These are combustible times, with many of us now joining that growing tribe of the 'politically homeless'. The failings of both of our major parties are not going to be remedied by the electorate lurching from one government to the other, a kind of see-saw that swings according to desperation and fatigue. Events of recent years have disclosed an unappealing truth: many of the political class no longer believe in democracy. After Clinton lost the 2016 United States election, she went on to claim that Trump was an 'illegitimate president' and warned future candidates: 'You can run the best campaign, you can even become the nominee, and you can have the election stolen from you.' And after his loss to Joe Biden in 2020, Trump repeatedly claimed that he had won and even urged the Georgia Secretary of State Brad Raffensperger to 'find 11,780 votes' to overturn the result. Neither left nor right has a monopoly on the condition of soreloserhip.

The same was evidently true in the United Kingdom of the post-Brexit years, with MPs on both sides of the House brazenly attempting to subvert the result of the largest mandate in political history. The ignorant oiks had voted the 'wrong way' and had to be stopped. This is why Brexit ultimately became less about our membership of the European Union, and more about restoring the electorate's faith in representative democracy. For MPs to be finding loopholes and reinterpreting the constitution for partisan ends was a breach of trust that many members of the public soon grew to resent. There was an urgent need at the time for Remain and Leave voters to find common ground, a reassertion of the need to maintain our pre-political loyalty to each other, to remember that, in the words of British socialist Tony Benn, parliamentary democracy is based 'not upon the sovereignty of Parliament, but upon the sovereignty of the People'.

Rather than reflect on why the public voted the way they did, many politicians instead sought to game the system and work around the wishes of the people. Former deputy prime minister Nick Clegg wrote a book called *How to Stop Brexit* (2017); it might as well have been called *How to Stop Democracy*. Political philosopher Jason Brennan was more explicit in his aims, arguing in his book *Against Democracy* (2016) that voters are too fickle, ill-informed and easily manipulated to be entrusted with major decisions.

> Most of my fellow citizens are incompetent, ignorant, irrational, and morally unreasonable about politics. Despite that, they hold political power over me . . . I should not have to tolerate that. Just as it would be wrong to force me to go under the knife of an incompetent surgeon or sail with an incompetent ship captain, it seems wrong to force me to submit to the decisions of incompetent voters.

Brennan favours an epistocracy, rule of the knowledgeable, a notion reminiscent of Plato's ideal of the 'philosopher king'. Patrick J. Deneen has seized upon this attitude as proof that the end point of liberalism is the demolition of democracy, that the 'growing divide between the claims of democracy and the absence of popular control' is inevitable in a liberal system because the demos will always be thwarted, irrespective of how it votes. He cites libertarian thinkers such as Bryan Caplan, Jeffrey Friedman and Damon Root, who claim that 'when democracy threatens the substantive commitments of liberalism – which they maintain will be unavoidably the case, since uneducated and uninformed voters are illiberal – it might be better simply to consider ways to jettison democracy'. The class snobbery of many anti-Brexit commentators has not dissipated. As late as January 2025, Will Dunn, business editor of the *New Statesman*, was bewailing the 'body of voters' who had 'briefly left Wetherspoons to rewrite our geopolitical and economic status'.

The rejection of democracy invariably entails a specifically aristocratic conceptualisation of power. Like Brennan, Plato was concerned that the average man is too capricious to prioritise the salient matters of the day, that his self-interest would override his concern for society. This is a criticism often levelled at modern-day liberalism, to which we will later return. This is how Socrates puts it in Plato's *Republic* (c. 375 BC).

> Day after day he gratifies the pleasures as they come – now fluting down the primrose path of wine, now given over to teetotalism and banting; one day in hard training, the next slacking and idling, and the third playing the philosopher. Often he will take to politics, leap to his feet and do or say whatever comes into his head; or he conceives an admiration for a general, and his interests are in war; or for a man of business, and straightway that is his line. He knows no order or necessity in life; but he calls life as he conceives it pleasant and free and divinely blessed, and is ever faithful to it.

Like Strepsiades in Aristophanes's *The Clouds* (423 BC), Socrates's 'democratic man' has the tendency to agree with whoever spoke last. The Platonist sees freedom as a dangerous weapon when extended beyond the ruling class, which is why Plato in the *Republic* envisages a future in which married couples of especial beauty and intelligence would be depended upon to produce the next generation of leaders. His fears were later echoed by his student Aristotle, who drew no distinction between ochlocracy – mob rule – and democracy.

In his *Thoughts on Parliamentary Reform* (1859), John Stuart Mill went so far as to advance the concept of 'plural voting', whereby those with a greater stake in society, who 'could afford a reasonable presumption of superior knowledge and cultivation', are accorded multiple votes.

> If every ordinary unskilled labourer had one vote, a skilled labourer, whose occupation requires an exercised mind and a knowledge of some of the laws of external nature, ought to have two. A foreman, or superintendent of labour, whose occupation requires something more of general culture, and some moral as well as intellectual qualities, should perhaps have three. A farmer, manufacturer, or trader, who requires a still larger range of ideas and knowledge, and the power of guiding and attending to a great number of various operations at once, should have three or four. A member of any profession requiring a long, accurate, and systematic mental cultivation, a lawyer, a physician or surgeon, a clergyman of any denomination, a literary man, an artist, a public functionary (or, at all events, a member of every intellectual profession at the threshold of which there is a satisfactory examination test) ought to have five or six. A graduate of any university, or a person freely elected a member of any learned society, is entitled to at least as many.

It should be noted that Mill later modified his elitist view in response to criticism from his peers, and it is difficult to reconcile these comments with his staunch defence of individual liberty and his support for female suffrage. But the concept of plural voting has gained a troubling degree of traction. Back in 1935, the president of the American Political Science Association, Walter J. Shepard, made the case that tests ought to be implemented to ensure that voters were sufficiently informed.

'The dogma of universal suffrage', he wrote, 'must give way to a system of educational and other tests which will exclude the ignorant, the uninformed, and the anti-social elements which hitherto have so frequently controlled elections.' While it is true that, by definition, approximately half the public will have a below average intelligence quotient, it would be the bold commentator in present-day Western society to suggest a threshold in IQ tests as a prerequisite for voting rights. Yet the obsession with identity has led to similarly discriminatory electoral propositions from the disciples of Critical Social Justice. In an article for the *Nation*, law scholar Brandon Hasbrouck has explicitly called for 'vote reparations' to redress structural racism, a system by which ballots cast by black Americans would count twice.

On balance, it seems clear that the power of the electorate is essential for monitoring signs of corruption within any given government. Politicians ought to fear the voters and their ability to dispense with their services. Tony Benn was fond of asking five key questions regarding democracy.

What power have you got?

Where did you get it from?

In whose interests do you use it?

To whom are you accountable?

How do we get rid of you?

This final question strikes at the heart of what it means to live in a society free from tyranny. In a democracy, those in political authority are servants of the people, and may be ousted at their collective whim.

Perhaps the future of British politics in a post-woke era lies with the smaller parties that might effectively elevate the voices of the demos rather than strategise to see them stifled. This will require a system of proportional representation, and it is not in the interests of either side to countenance such an eventuality. No major party will actively implement the conditions for its own demise, meaning that the nature of the problem works against its own solution. It has been said that our 'first past the post' (FPTP) system protects us from the ineffectual and volatile nature of coalition governments, and one might point to Italy as a cautionary tale. But Germany, Finland and the Netherlands have an effective track record of proportional representation, and there is no reason to think it would not be preferable to the instability we have experienced under our two-party system. Ultimately, it looks as though we are going to be stuck in this infuriating cycle, this back and forth from left to right, for the foreseeable future. Like Sisyphus, we'll just have to keep on rolling that rock up the hill until someone finds a way to break it apart.

In the meantime, it is worth considering how the two-party systems of the United Kingdom, the United States and Canada might serve to bolster the sense of voters being presented with a moral binary. Is it possible that the very concept of left versus right has encouraged us to think in terms of Good versus Evil? Is this why so many commentators will make any and all excuses for the faults of 'their own side', having settled into a comforting narrative that their gang can do no wrong?

## Lessons from Orwell

In my ongoing quest to avoid the clatter and smog of modern life, I often take long rambles in the countryside near my home in Hertfordshire. Barely an hour from my doorstep is the tiny village of Wallington, and during the lockdown period of the coronavirus pandemic I developed the habit of walking there and back, specifically to a few cottages on the junction of Kits Lane and 'The Street'. I must have taken this route on dozens of occasions, and yet somehow I missed the significance of one particular thatched cottage on the corner. This was the former home of one of my favourite writers, George Orwell.

So much for my powers of observation. The little property where Orwell wrote *Animal Farm* (1945) is adorned with a red plaque erected by Hertfordshire County Council, declaring that he lived here in the decade preceding the Second World War. Further exploration of the village would have revealed the presence of Manor Farm, a name that will be familiar to anyone who has read his famous 'fairy story'. And it doesn't take a sleuth to make the connection between Wallington and the 'Willingdon' of the book. The village has barely changed since Orwell's time here. The population has doubled, but that brings it to a mere one hundred and fifty. You can still visit the old church of St Mary's where Orwell married his first wife Eileen. The cottage itself,

*George Orwell's cottage in Wallington, Hertfordshire, as it appears today.*

known as 'The Stores', is well preserved, and one can see why the
beanpole that was Orwell was prone to banging his head on its low
front door and ceilings. To return to Wallington today is to immerse
oneself in this most productive period of Orwell's life. Meandering
along the dusty network of lanes, it's perhaps a little too easy to
romanticise the lifestyle, although most writers crave isolation and it is
clear that Orwell would have found it here. It was along one of these
lanes that Orwell saw that small boy leading a carthorse, the image that
inspired *Animal Farm*. What would happen, Orwell thought to himself,
if the beast were to exercise its superior brawn and turn on its master?

During the woke era, I found myself returning to *Animal Farm* to
make sense of it all. The original intentions of the woke revolutionaries
were doubtless good. They were dismayed at the fact that racial
injustice endures in our society, in spite of laws to prevent it. They
were alarmed by the ways in which the rise of social media had
enabled unpleasant individuals to express their hateful views to an
unlimited audience. They were concerned about what they perceived
to be an escalation in prejudice against people on the basis of
immutable characteristics. Human nature being what it is, the story
didn't end there. Like the pigs in *Animal Farm*, these noble intentions
were soon scuppered by an innate tendency to see them imposed by
authoritarian methods.

As I have argued, the end of woke could mean that this cycle is
repeated via the growing intolerance on the right. Although Orwell
had Stalin in mind for his pig Napoleon and Soviet Russia for his
Manor Farm, it is a fable that could be tailored to the birth of any similar movement. We must be watchful, he seems to be saying, of the
essentially authoritarian impulse in humanity. In other words, however
noble our intentions, human nature ensures that our innate piggish-
ness will eventually emerge. Shakespeare knew this too, which is why
he repeatedly shows us that even the most benevolent of men are corruptible once they secure power. Furthermore, Orwell is adamant that
those with the necessary temperament to push for revolution are also

often themselves hungry for clout and prestige, and so their corruption becomes all the more inevitable.

*Animal Farm* had been rejected by four publishers in relatively quick succession after Orwell had finished the work in February 1944. Victor Gollancz, who had published his other novels, could not agree to see an anti-Stalinist work in print at a time when the Soviet Union was such a key ally against the Axis forces. After Jonathan Cape agreed in principle to publish the novel, he was dissuaded by a contact at the Ministry of Information who ominously said that such a move would be 'highly ill-advised'. When Cape offered feedback suggesting that 'it would be less offensive if the predominant caste in the fable were not pigs', Orwell simply wrote next to it: 'Balls'.

The poet T. S. Eliot, in his role as a director at the publishing firm Faber & Faber, was the next to reject the manuscript. It was only when Orwell sent it to Secker & Warburg that the novel was approved, although it did not appear until a few months after the war had ended in August 1945. Orwell's willingness to criticise a wartime ally is the reason why even to this day he is despised by certain figures on the left. Into this category we would place the journalist Benjamin Norton, who described Orwell as a 'vile man' and in 2016 wrote a petulant hit piece which dismissed him as 'the worst kind of reactionary turncoat'. Then there are the weaker postmodernist critics, whose banal method of analysis consists of putting dead authors on trial for their moral shortcomings, teasing out the homophobia, sexism and racism of any given text. In his latest biography of Orwell, D. J. Taylor likens this breed of critic to 'a small child trying to bring down an elephant with a pea-shooter'.

It was while living in Wallington that Orwell perfected the style that secured his place among Britain's greatest essayists. Although *Animal Farm* and *Nineteen Eighty-Four* are the keystones of Orwell's legacy, I find that his essays surpass his fiction both in terms of their flair and their intellectual heft. In these punchy tracts, more often quoted than read in full, one senses a great thinker testing his own theses, forever fluctuating, refining his views in the very act of writing.

The essays span the last two decades of his life, offering us the most direct possible insight into this unique mind. A few early essays recount his formative years and how his opposition to imperialism developed during his time as a police officer in Burma. Later, there are vivid reflections on his role in the Spanish Civil War, a foray into anti-fascism that formed the basis of his memoir *Homage to Catalonia* (1938). During his time as a volunteer for the Workers' Party of Marxist Unification (POUM) militia, Orwell was shot in the throat, an injury that would weaken his voice permanently. But in his essays, his voice remains as strong as ever.

One yearns for more writers to emulate the clarity of Orwell's prose. Our present-day culture wars are characterised by evasions and euphemism, with activists continually redefining terms and denying that they are doing so. We have seen epithets such as 'racist' and 'misogynist' so promiscuously applied that they have been rendered almost meaningless. A series of 'phobias' have emerged – 'transphobe', 'homophobe', 'Islamophobe' – pathologising differences of opinion rather than identifying authentic instances of fear or hatred. Orwell was particularly alert to this kind of rhetorical chicanery. His mistrust of obscurantism in writing is why he would have had no patience with the arcane style favoured in academic circles today, particularly among those of a postmodernist bent. Deliberate lack of clarity to give the impression of substance, sometimes snobbishly defended as a form of safeguarding of advanced discourse, is simply bad writing, and Orwell loathed it as much as the use of clichés and what he described as 'ready-made phrases'. It is one of the reasons his own prose style is so effervescent.

Orwell's disquisitions on literature are among his most rewarding. 'All art is propaganda,' he declares in his extended piece on Charles Dickens (1940). This conviction, flawed as it is, accounts for his determination to focus less on Dickens's literary merits and more on his class consciousness, which is found wanting. Even better is Orwell's rebuttal to Tolstoy's strangely literal-minded reading of Shakespeare

– 'Lear, Tolstoy and the Fool' (1947) – which is so rhetorically deft that it seems to settle the matter for good. Another impressive essay, 'Inside the Whale' (1940), opens with a glowing assessment of Henry Miller's *Tropic of Cancer* (1935) but soon broadens its range to cover many contemporary novelists and their approach to social commentary. The title is a reference to Miller's remarks on the biblical tale of Jonah, suggesting that life inside the whale has much to recommend it. Orwell puts it this way:

> For the fact is that being inside a whale is a very comfortable, cosy, homelike thought. The historical Jonah, if he can be so called, was glad enough to escape, but in imagination, in day-dream, countless people have envied him. It is, of course, quite obvious why. The whale's belly is simply a womb big enough for an adult. There you are, in the dark, cushioned space that exactly fits you, with yards of blubber between yourself and reality, able to keep up an attitude of the completest indifference, no matter *what* happens.

He invites us to imagine that the whale is transparent, and so writers of Miller's ilk may snuggle contentedly within, observing without interacting, recording snapshots of the world as it bounces by. This kind of inaction is anathema to Orwell, whose every written word seems to be driving towards the enactment of social change.

Orwell's essays often serve as a cudgel to batter his detractors. He dislikes homosexuals, or those 'fashionable pansies', who lack the masculine vigour to take up arms in defence of their country. Some of the best essays are unexpected diversions from politics. There's the evocative account of his favourite pub, 'The Moon Under Water' (1946), its décor and clientele described in affectionate detail, and only later revealed as a fabrication of our author's imagination. 'A Nice Cup of Tea' (1946) is a simple guide to the successful brewing of this quintessentially English drink. All of which is quite the contrast to the grisly experience of 'Shooting an Elephant' (1936). One of Orwell's most unpleasant duties as a police officer was to kill an elephant that was rampaging through a Burmese town, although it has often been claimed that his story was embellished as a form of commentary on the horrors of colonialism. His narration is propelled by a sense of guilt at the injustices of the regime he is compelled to serve, but also by his anger towards the local bureaucrats who sustain it. The honesty is often brutal:

> With one part of my mind I thought of the British Raj as an unbreakable tyranny, as something clamped down, in saecula saeculorum, upon the will of prostrate peoples; with another part I thought that the greatest joy in the world would be to drive a bayonet into a Buddhist priest's guts.

Yet Orwell's humanity is always evident. In 'A Hanging' (1931), it is the smallest gesture of the condemned man that stirs Orwell into an appreciation of what it means to obliterate a perfectly healthy human life. 'When I saw the prisoner step aside to avoid the puddle', he writes, 'I saw the mystery, the unspeakable wrongness, of cutting a life short when it is in full tide.'

By contrast, Orwell is at his worst when he is snide or cruel. As he recalls bisecting a wasp with a knife while it is eating the jam on his plate, one cannot help but feel repulsed. 'He paid no attention,' he writes, 'merely went on with his meal, while a tiny stream of jam trickled out of his severed oesophagus. Only when he tried to fly away did he grasp the dreadful thing that had happened to him.' The telling of it seems almost gleeful, although of course the anecdote is in the service of a deeper point; in this case, modern man's obliviousness to the amputation of his own soul. One could be forgiven for supposing that the metaphor occurred to Orwell before the killing of the wasp itself. So often he deliberately seeks out experiences as subject-matter for his essays, most notably in 'The Spike' (1931), which describes his night in a foetid London workhouse, and 'Clink' (1932), an account of when Orwell deliberately got drunk in order to experience arrest and imprisonment.

Such excursions, familiar to those who have read Orwell's books *Down and Out in Paris and London* (1933) and *The Road to Wigan Pier* (1937), have been criticised as examples of 'poverty tourism', a case of an Eton-educated man romanticising the working class. Taylor argues that Orwell was a self-mythologiser, and 'spent much of his time projecting visions of himself that he thought compatible with the kind of person he imagined himself to be'. Although Taylor makes a strong case, surely this criticism could be applied to almost anyone.

The culture wars have reignited Orwell's relevance in a manner that no optimist could have anticipated. The phrases he coined in *Nineteen Eighty-Four* have become staples of popular culture and political analysis. When we hear the term 'Big Brother', we think of state authoritarianism, or possibly the reality television show in which we were once treated to the spectacle of the socialist politician George Galloway on all fours impersonating a cat at the feet of the actress Rula Lenska. *Room 101* is the title of a popular television show in which celebrities chat about their *bêtes noires*, but we also know it from Orwell as the place where our greatest fears are reified. The torture of Winston Smith in Room 101 is one of the most disquieting passages of *Nineteen Eighty-Four*, although it was apparently named after the room in which Orwell attended editorial meetings while working at the BBC's Eastern Service. Similarly, phrases such as 'memory hole', 'Newspeak', 'thought-crime' and 'doublethink' are routinely deployed by commentators as they try to make sense of the revisionist and authoritarian tendencies of the woke movement. When *The Times* reported that Scottish police were recording male rapists as female if they so identified, J. K. Rowling tweeted her criticism by adding a final line to the motto of Oceania: 'War is Peace. Freedom is Slavery. Ignorance is Strength. The Penised Individual Who Raped You is a Woman.' The sense of drifting into an Orwellian society is so palpable that a meme has been created and circulated by the online right, urging us to 'Make Orwell Fiction Again'.

Orwell may have become the go-to author for right-leaning commentators seeking a rhetorical shorthand, but this is not to say that he is a natural bedfellow. As Christopher Hitchens has argued, the 'body-snatching of Orwell' should 'not be attempted by any known faction', least of all by the political right. Orwell's fundamentally left-wing values remained consistent throughout his life, but they were underpinned by a traditionalism and a love of his country that today might be called socially conservative, a perspective most exemplarily conveyed in his essay 'The Lion and the Unicorn' (1941). When *Nineteen Eighty-Four* was characterised as an attack on the Labour government, Orwell issued a statement emphasising that he was a supporter of the party, and that his novel was 'a show-up of the perversions to which a centralized economy is liable and which have already been partly realized in Communism and Fascism'. Totalitarianism, he said, '*if not fought against*, could triumph anywhere'. If it were possible to encapsulate his oeuvre into one sentence, this could be a serious contender.

This point recurs throughout Orwell's writing. In his review of the British political scientist Harold Laski's *Reflections on the Revolution of Our Time* (1943), Orwell censured the author for his 'unwillingness to admit that Socialism has totalitarian possibilities'. The publisher Fred Warburg saw *Nineteen Eighty-Four* as marking a 'final breach between Orwell and socialism, not the socialism of equality and human brotherhood, which Orwell clearly no longer expects of socialist parties, but the socialism of Marxism and the managerial revolution'. And despite the inevitability that *Animal Farm* would be weaponised by the right, Orwell did not falter when it came to this much-needed rebuke of Stalinist tyranny. As Hitchens noted, for Orwell 'there was always the hope that socialists could be for freedom, even if socialism itself had bureaucratic and authoritarian tendencies'.

And still the body-snatching continues. Many of those who like to cite Orwell in defence of their position are often guilty of sidestepping the inconvenient aspects of his writing. While claiming him as their mascot, they are illustrating precisely the closed-mindedness that he excoriated so vehemently. When sales of *Nineteen Eighty-Four* soared almost tenfold after Donald Trump's election in 2016, it is probable that many left-leaning readers were seeking a better understanding of a commander-in-chief whose relationship with the truth is erratic. One wonders if the novel's contents might instead have encouraged them to reflect upon their own worst excesses. In particular, activists' demands for the renaming of streets, the demolition of historical landmarks and the sanitisation of fiction by 'sensitivity readers' invariably bring to mind the words of Winston Smith: 'Every record has been destroyed or falsified, every book has been rewritten, every picture has been repainted, every statue and street and building has been renamed, every date has been altered. And that process is continuing day by day and minute by minute. History has stopped.'

That both the right and the left can claim Orwell for 'their side' should tell us something about the shared tendency towards authoritarianism that is the subject of this book. As a writer, he has always been difficult to pin down politically, which is troubling to those for whom 'left versus right' is an inflexible and convenient dualism. While Orwell's body of work stands as a warning against cleaving to one's own ideological group irrespective of the circumstances, today's commentators cling limpet-like to their political clans, making excuses for their party's faults and interpreting every oppositional statement in the most negative light. In essays such as 'Notes on Nationalism' (1945), Orwell exposes how this 'with us or against us' mindset results in the outsourcing of individual agency. He is nervous about the tendency to assume 'that whole blocks of millions or tens of millions of people can be confidently labelled "good" or "bad"', and he cautions against 'the habit of identifying oneself with a single nation or unit, placing it beyond good and evil and recognising no other duty than that of advancing its interests'. In 'Writers and Leviathan' (1948), he posits that to 'yield subjectively, not merely to a party machine, but even to a group ideology, is to destroy yourself as a writer'. If we situate ourselves too dogmatically within the confines of a specific party, he argues, we are no longer thinking for ourselves but parroting a script.

Orwell admitted his misgivings about criticising his 'own side' but had the courage to do so anyway. In a discussion about *Animal Farm*, he had remarked to the philosopher A. J. Ayer that he was concerned that the book could be advantageous to British conservatives. Ultimately, however, he was guided by the consistency of his principles, and rejected entirely concerns which were often summarised in the common phrase 'playing into the hands of'. He described it as 'a sort of charm or incantation to silence uncomfortable truths. When you are told that by saying this, that or the other you are "playing into the hands of" some sinister enemy, you know that it is your duty to shut up immediately.' And while he acknowledged that it was 'difficult to attack one party to a dispute without temporarily helping the other', he understood that in refraining from criticising our allies we only weaken our cause. He gives the example of writing 'anything truthful about the London slums' only 'to hear it repeated on Nazi radio a week later'. As he puts it, 'what, then, are you expected to do? Pretend there are no slums?' Providing ammunition to the enemy is sometimes required in the pursuit of truth. This is why Socrates in the *Republic* cautions against the misconception of Simonides and Polemarchus that 'justice is to help your friends and harm your enemies'.

A recent example will further illustrate the point. During the course of Joe Biden's term as president of the United States, it became increasingly obvious that he was in a state of cognitive decline. After Biden's speech at the White House Conference on Hunger, Nutrition and Health in September 2022, in which he asked whether the recently deceased congresswoman Jackie Walorski was in the audience, the press should have been more rigorous in demanding to see his medical assessments. These kinds of instances, frequent as they were, cannot be dismissed as mere 'gaffes'. The press were in dereliction of duty, quite plainly because they did not want to risk providing ammunition to the Republicans and securing another victory for Trump. Yet it was precisely this failure of the left to draw attention to its own failings, this fear of 'playing into the hands of' their opponents, that helped usher Trump back into power.

The problem is a familiar one. One of the most common complaints we hear from those who take umbrage at even justifiable criticisms of their own group is that we should not be engaging in 'bothsidesing'. There are certainly cases where equivocation is unmerited. For instance, there has been much suggestion that there is hostile rhetoric on 'both sides' of the gender debate. While it is true that abusive language is not the singular prerogative of one side or the other, threats of violence and rape only ever emerge from trans activist groups and rarely, if at all, from gender-critical feminists. Yet to point out, as Orwell did, that authoritarianism is not specific to any one political affiliation is not an example of needless 'bothsidesing'. When we think only in terms of the demands and aims of the tribe, we are not thinking at all. Those who have convinced themselves that 'my side can do no wrong' are suffering from a delusion.

In the pessimism of his pre-war essays, Orwell imagines that 'we are moving into an age of totalitarian dictatorships' and that 'in the remaining years of free speech' there will be no authors actively seeking to improve society. His own work, by contrast, is what he would term 'constructive', profoundly moral, and purposefully crafted in the hope of actuating real-world change. While other writers resigned themselves to a life inside the whale, Orwell was determined to cut his way out. We have now reached the point in the culture war that Orwell would have recognised, where the revolutionaries have become the tyrants they sought to resist. The illiberal left and the woke right share that quality of the pigs in the farmhouse at the end of *Animal Farm*, being observed by the other animals through the window. 'The creatures outside looked from pig to man, and from man to pig, and from pig to man again: but already it was impossible to say which was which.'

# 3

# The Authoritarian Impulse

## 'Et Tu, Brute?'

When Orson Welles stabbed the actor Joseph Holland, he did so in front of hundreds of witnesses. Welles had been playing Brutus in his adaptation of Shakespeare's *Julius Caesar* (c. 1599) at the Mercury Theatre in New York, and had insisted on using a real knife in the assassination scene because he felt that the fake rubber ones did not properly catch the light. Welles was nothing if not a perfectionist.

Holland was playing Caesar, and was presumably horrified when, in that fateful performance on 6 April 1938, Welles misjudged his aim and stabbed him through the arm and chest, severing an artery near his heart. As the consummate professional, Holland uttered his final line – 'Et tu, Brute? Then fall, Caesar' – before collapsing in a pool of his own blood. The scene continued for another fifteen minutes until the blackout, at which point Holland was rushed to a hospital. He barely survived.

The incident is recounted in the memoir of the show's producer, John Houseman. Apparently Holland 'was admired and blamed for lying quite still for almost fifteen minutes while bleeding to death'. This kind of fortitude is perhaps apt, given that the entire production had been intended as an attack on the notion of human weakness. Welles was convinced that the rising fascist threat in Europe was being enabled by feeble men, those who clung fast to the notions of liberalism, and whose tolerance would be their own undoing. This is why in his version of *Julius Caesar*, subtitled *Death of a Dictator*, the role of Caesar was explicitly depicted as Benito Mussolini, with fascist rallies presented on stage. Welles felt that liberalism was for cowards. So too, apparently, were fake knives.

Increasingly, many of today's prominent thinkers are coming round to Welles's view, particularly those on the right flank of politics who have been voluble in their prognostications about the end point of 'wokeness'. Whereas threats to liberty in the past have always arisen from totalitarian dictatorships – most notably the Soviet Union, Nazi Germany, Imperial Japan, and the fascist regimes of interwar Europe – today it is liberal governments that are imposing restrictions on their own freedoms. That there are no rulebooks to consult is the major appeal of liberalism to those of a freethinking disposition, but it is also the source of its instability. The authoritarian has no need to engage with his detractors; he can simply have them eliminated. By contrast,

*Orson Welles's production of* Julius Caesar *at the Mercury Theatre, New York (1938)*

the liberal must find a way to coexist with those who would like to see his freedoms quashed, to somehow reconcile himself to the multiplicity of human outlooks and their inherent incommensurability. But how can you run a marketplace of ideas while there are hooligans trying to overturn the tables?

And this is liberalism's major flaw, according to its critics. They contend that liberal civilisation, in which freedom of speech and thought are taken for granted, is a thing of the past. They maintain that our belief in progress is naïve, and that when tested against the ineluctable reality of human nature it is exposed as deficient. We in the West presume that democracy and freedom are the natural states of humankind, but the enduring appeal of totalitarianism would suggest otherwise. In particular, the rising threat from China and Russia – two societies in which liberalism has never triumphed – might imply that if we hold true to our liberal values, we will be ill-prepared for any onslaught. In her essay 'Why I am now a Christian', academic and writer Ayaan Hirsi Ali echoes this view:

> Western civilisation is under threat from three different but related forces: the resurgence of great-power authoritarianism and expansionism in the forms of the Chinese Communist Party and Vladimir Putin's Russia; the rise of global Islamism, which threatens to mobilise a vast population against the West; and the viral spread of woke ideology, which is eating into the moral fibre of the next generation.

Many commentators have gone further, claiming that the only solution to the authoritarian excesses of the modern left, Islamic fundamentalism, and expansionist foreign powers, is to impose other kinds of restrictions. Liberalism has been seen as an enervating force, and has been blamed for cultivating the circumstances in which infantile protesters can bring university campuses to a halt, and activists can call for modifications to the First Amendment so that speech they find offensive is no longer protected. It is claimed that the West is cannibalising itself through a surfeit of tolerance.

This misgiving, a sense that we are softened to our detriment through compassion, is common to liberal systems. In 1946, E. M. Forster claimed that the experience of being raised in 'the fag-end of Victorian liberalism' had conditioned him to view the world through a distorting lens, blinding him to the realities of economic inequality and the exploitation of the poor. So while the era of his youth seemed to embody the ideals of social liberalism, that it 'practised benevolence and philanthropy, was humane and intellectually curious, upheld free speech, had little colour-prejudice, believed that individuals are and should be different, and entertained a sincere faith in the progress of society', it was ultimately 'imperfect'. A similar outlook is proposed by Patrick J. Deneen in his books *Why Liberalism Failed* (2018) and *Regime Change: Towards a Postliberal Future* (2023). According to Deneen, liberalism is an essentially elitist project, applied with the best of intentions but nonetheless contributing to the ruination of society. 'Today's widespread yearning for a strong leader,' Deneen writes, 'one with the will to take back popular control over liberalism's forms of bureaucratized government and globalized economy, comes after decades of liberal dismantling of cultural norms and political habits essential to self-governance.' Deneen does not accept that we are creatures who naturally thrive under conditions of freedom.

This essential vulnerability of liberalism is always tested in moments of crisis. Governments enact emergency powers when at war because short-term authoritarianism seems preferable to the alternative. But even in peacetime, liberalism is always susceptible to changing trends within the nation state. What happens, for instance, when the majority of any given population reject the liberal values upon which their society is based? What if a government has implemented reckless migration policies that grant citizenship to those who do not recognise the value of individual freedoms? In such circumstances, the principle of democracy could be its own undoing. This is precisely why so many in the anti-woke camp believe that liberty is overrated. They contend that multiculturalism has resulted in communities being isolated and living parallel lives, with little effort at assimilation. They argue that the liberal values that we all once took for granted cannot function in a society where a significant proportion reject them. There have been calls for censorship and even deportations for those who oppose the core values of the West, but the attempt to impose liberalism by force is incoherent.

Writers such as Louise Perry have argued that the sexual revolution was the catalyst to our civilisational decline, and that too much freedom had a toxic effect on our culture. In his book *The Age of Entitlement* (2020), Christopher Caldwell outlines how the well-intentioned reforms of the 1960s, with an emphasis on justice and humanity, ultimately had the opposite effect. At the same time, we have seen some gender-critical feminists – traditionally opposed to 'wokeness' – proposing new limitations of human freedom in the sphere of male and female relations. As the rise of gender self-identification threatens women's spaces, some voices in the feminist movement are calling for bans on cross-dressing and for rigidly policed codes of gendered behaviour. Is it the case, then, that even liberals are prone to reneging on the concept of liberty when faced with the more unpleasant realities of human nature? Since the pogrom in Israel on 7 October 2023 by Hamas terrorists and the subsequent war in the Middle East, we have seen a kind of prolonged acid test of the West's commitment to liberalism. Although pro-Palestine marches on the streets of the United Kingdom and elsewhere have been conducted mostly by peaceful, well-intentioned individuals, we have also seen a disturbing rise in antisemitism and open calls for 'jihad' and 'intifada'; a baffling alliance between woke activists and militant jihadists. Middle-class *bien pensants* have been asserting that mass murder requires 'context', and a group calling itself 'Queers for Palestine' has come to prominence, in spite of the brutal oppression of gay people in the Arab world. Protesters at some of the marches have been seen holding placards that celebrate the slaughter, rape and kidnapping of Israeli civilians, and an official advisor to the Met police was filmed leading a chant of 'from the river to the sea', a phrase widely interpreted as a call to eliminate Jews from the state of Israel.

There are other signs that liberalism in the West is crumbling. In April 2024, protesters took to the streets of Hamburg to call for an Islamic caliphate which would entail the imposition of sharia law and the curbing of freedom of speech along religious lines. This would be to replicate the reality of many Islamic states, in which blasphemy and apostasy are punishable by death, and criticism of the government is likewise dangerous. In Iran, the 'morality police' ensure that women do not violate codes of dress and decency (the killing of Mahsa Amini in September 2022, a young woman who was detained by the morality police for not wearing her hijab in the approved manner, sparked a series of protests and civil unrest). By definition, our notion of liberty in the West is incompatible with sharia law, or the diktats of any theocratic state. Many in the 'anti-woke' movement have taken all this for proof that multiculturalism has failed, and that recent events have represented the final straw that broke the back of liberalism. Hate speech laws must now be strengthened, certain protests ought to be banned and we must no longer tolerate the intolerant.

For instance, Republican senator Tom Cotton called for those who express support for Hamas to be deported from the United States, and Donald Trump campaigned partly on the fulfilment of this pledge. In October 2023, French president Emmanuel Macron outlawed pro-Palestine rallies on the grounds of maintaining public order, although his decree was largely ignored. The next month, a pro-Palestinian protest was scheduled in London for Armistice Day, which generated precisely the kind of outrage that the organisers surely intended. The Metropolitan Police commissioner was under pressure to ban the marches from those who would typically defend the right to free expression. Prime Minister Rishi Sunak stopped short of a ban, but called on the Metropolitan Police to make 'robust use' of its powers to prevent the Remembrance events being disrupted. In this, he was out of kilter with the majority of the country: only 18 per cent believed that the marches 'should be allowed to go ahead'.

In all of this, it has been dispiriting to see our commitment to Enlightenment values being assaulted on multiple fronts. There are theocratic extremists who oppose free speech and would happily see blasphemers and apostates executed. There are Western activists intoxicated by the moonshine of intersectional identity politics calling for censorship and other restrictions. And now, we have those who once considered themselves to be 'liberal' pronouncing that there should be limitations to freedom of speech and assembly. Even those who have previously decried cancel culture appear to be relishing its impact on their opponents. A lecture at Liverpool Hope University by Professor Avi Shlaim, a critic of Israel, was cancelled out of concern for the 'safety and well-being' of students. Michael Eisen, a geneticist at the University of California, Berkeley, was fired as editor-in-chief of *eLife* magazine for sharing a satirical article from *The Onion* which took a pro-Palestine stance. Eisen, some have pointed out, had previously questioned whether cancellation really exists, but while a degree of *Schadenfreude* is understandable, it is hardly helpful. Inevitably, one thinks of Karl Popper's famous paradox that 'in the name of tolerance', we should claim 'the right not to tolerate the intolerant'. This is often invoked by activists to defend censorship of their opponents, but Popper's formulation is usually decontextualised and misread. One sentence in particular is often omitted, in which he emphasises that so long as public opinion and rational argument can 'keep them in check', suppression of intolerant views would be 'most unwise'. Protesters who take to the streets to celebrate murder fall into this category because they are self-discrediting. They are impervious to reason, but their sentiments are so essentially rebarbative that there is no risk of public opinion shifting in their favour.

But if liberalism is so delicate and continually under threat, why bother with it at all? In short: because it works. Liberalism has enjoyed a long and successful history in the Western world. It has seen advances in civil rights, equality law, tolerance and social cohesion. For all the claims by identitarian activists that the West is a racist hellhole, few living in the era of Jim Crow could have conceived of the advances we have since made. Yet while liberalism has a proven track record of success, it is not the norm. Very few nation states, either globally or historically, embrace the principles of freedom of speech, individual autonomy and equal rights for all. We are fortunate to have reached a consensus that human liberty is a force for good, even at a time when that consensus is under threat. Of course it is only natural that our patience wears thin when we see people openly supporting the demolition of our civilisation and showing utter contempt for our shared values and history, but this is a right that must be preserved. Taking action against direct incitement to violence is one thing, but compromising on our key values is another. If we renege on our liberal principles at the very moment when they are most imperilled, we risk undermining the very foundations upon which our civilisation is built.

## Fingers and Tongues

In an early episode of the HBO television series *Game of Thrones*, the minstrel Marillion is hauled before King Joffrey for performing a song in a local tavern that satirises the death of the king's father. He is forced to sing the offending ditty at court and, having done so, Joffrey fixes him with one of his habitual glowers and asks: 'Which do you favour: your fingers or your tongue?' After some stammering, the poor minstrel replies that every man needs hands. 'Good!' says Joffrey. 'Tongue it is!' The scene ends much as you'd imagine.

Tyrants have often thrived on the illusion of choice. This can take many forms. It could be rigged elections that generate a pretence of democracy. It could be social policy that maintains citizens' dependence on the state. In virtually all tyrannies, criticism of the government is permitted so long as one is willing to surrender one's freedom or right to existence. Like Joffrey's fingers-or-tongue dilemma, it's really not much of a choice at all.

Joffrey's cruelty makes for exhilarating television only because it strikes us as so outlandish. We forget that in most societies throughout history it would not occur to anyone to question the whims of the monarch, irrespective of how unreasonable they might be. Liberal democracy is not the norm; it is an ideal that can only be attained through decades of turmoil and self-sacrifice from freethinkers who are willing to risk everything for future generations of strangers. Such people are exceedingly rare, guided by principle above all other considerations.

And yet, if we've learnt nothing else from history, we must surely know by now that authoritarianism has an enduring appeal. Something in the human instinct is drawn to the notion of simply making obstacles disappear – through censorship, suppression, or sometimes more drastic means – which is why we so often see double standards applied when it comes to free speech. As I argued in my book *Free Speech and Why It Matters* (2021), the preservation of our own liberties depends on our support for the liberties of those we despise. It is my contention that the project of social liberalism is the best, and perhaps the only, antidote to the authoritarian impulse. At this moment of woke's demise, we should restate the case for liberalism as the most effective strategy for an as yet uncertain future. However, the term 'liberal' is subject to a multiplicity of definitions, and so my contention will require some preliminary clarifications.

Straw man arguments have become the default characteristic of political discourse. Too often, we are debating imaginary versions of our opponents, attributing views to them that they do not hold, or interpreting their positions in the most ungenerous possible way. Increasingly, the concept of liberalism is taking a battering from across the political spectrum, and it seems as though in many cases the source of the animosity might be definitional rather than conceptual. In America the term 'liberal' has become synonymous with the left, whereas in Australia the Liberal Party leans towards the right. Some of those who identify as liberal have promoted – in the name of wokeness – some of the most illiberal policies in living memory, from calling for laws to restrict freedom of speech to championing the erosion of women's rights to single-sex spaces. If those who claim the term 'liberal' for themselves are embodying its opposite, we can be sure that the confusion is widespread.

The first thing to say about liberalism is that there has never really been any unanimously agreed definition, which is why it is incumbent on those of us who defend its values to be clear about precisely what it is we are defending. Liberal thinkers often hold incompatible views, and the most common forms – classical liberalism, social liberalism, economic liberalism and neoliberalism – cannot be readily consolidated into one harmonious belief-system. The more utilitarian aspects of social liberalism, for instance, with their emphasis on collective responsibility for the vulnerable and the underprivileged, are inconsistent with neoliberalism and its prioritisation of free-market capitalism. In his book *The Once and Future Liberal* (2017), Mark Lilla uses the term 'identity liberalism' to denote the form of evangelism now known as 'wokeness'. Such a worldview is about as far away from classical liberal values as can be imagined.

We often hear that we live in a 'liberal' society, but what precisely does this mean? Are we to suppose that one form of liberalism has triumphed over all the others? Or do we simply mean that we have reached a broad consensus on the principles of democracy and freedom of speech? Or maybe we are suggesting that we have elevated the needs and desires of the individual above all other considerations. In a pre-Enlightenment era, we might consider this type of liberalism to be an uncomfortably spinous prospect, given that it centres the rights of human beings over the will of God. Certainly, many prominent religious groups find liberalism to be inherently antithetical to the tenets of their faith. The political philosopher John Gray has defined liberalism in terms of four pillars:

> It is *individualist*, in that it asserts the moral primacy of the person against the claims of any social collectivity; *egalitarian*, inasmuch as it confers on all men the same moral status and denies the relevance to legal or political order of differences in moral worth among human beings; *universalist*, affirming the moral unity of the human species and according a secondary importance to specific historic associations and cultural forms; and *meliorist* in its affirmation of the corrigibility and improvability of all social institutions and political arrangements.

While Gray identifies these features as transcending the 'vast internal variety and complexity' of competing forms of liberalism, his outline neglects the strong current of social responsibility that runs through much of traditional liberal discourse. My own understanding of liberalism is perhaps best summarised in John Stuart Mill's maxim in *On Liberty* (1859): 'the individual is not accountable to society for his actions, in so far as these concern the interests of no person but himself'. That is to say, a free society depends upon the right of each citizen to retain his or her autonomy. Yet all branches of liberal thought – from the conservative liberalism of Friedrich Hayek to the social liberalism of John Rawls – share an understanding that the rule of law is paramount. Individual autonomy cannot be preserved if the state is unable to maintain the peace and impartially resolve the natural conflicts of human existence. This is why Mill is keen to stress that 'for such actions as are prejudicial to the interests of others, the individual is accountable and may be subjected either to social or to legal punishments'. Liberalism, then, is not some kind of anarchic free-for-all, but a means to ensure that individual freedom can flourish on the condition that the rights of others are not impaired.

It is for this reason that I consider the great civil rights luminaries of the 1960s and 1970s to be the chief catalysts of the brand of liberalism that we have since enjoyed, the very achievements that were so continually undermined during the woke era in the name of 'social justice'. Woke activists maintain that the persistence of racism, misogyny and other forms of bigotry is evidence of the failure of the liberal project. But this is to misunderstand the nature of liberalism and its recognition that humankind is imperfectible. The civil rights campaigners instigated a chain of thinking that is ongoing, one that tackles injustice as and when it arises, rather than assuming it can be eradicated wholesale. Just as figures on the woke left often claim to be upholding liberal values, those on the woke right have been known to assert that wokeness is a direct consequence of liberalism. But when commentators on both sides of this debate claim that 'wokeness' and 'liberalism' are synonymous, they are attempting to dovetail two irreconcilable modes of thought. Wokeness is not an extension of liberalism; it is its opposite.

To my mind, the key principles of liberalism are as follows:

- individual autonomy
- social responsibility
- freedom of speech, assembly, association, belief and conscience
- civil rights and social progress
- meritocracy
- rationality
- democracy and accountability for those in power
- equality before the law

As I have noted, there will be points of disagreement here. An economic liberal would insist on small government and unfettered competition in the market. A social liberal would insist on the prioritisation of the welfare state. So while it would be fair to accuse me of selecting a specific brand of liberalism, this same accusation could be levelled at any liberal in history. The form of liberalism that I have outlined here offers a means to resolve potential conflicts between the desires of the individual and the needs of society. This is why, for liberalism to be effective, the rule of law must be robust and free from tyrannical influence. Recent commentators who have argued that liberalism has failed, and that an alternative approach is long overdue, neglect to take into account that most Western governments reject some or all of the principles outlined above. The United Kingdom is supposedly a liberal country, but we have hate speech laws that criminalise those who cause offence, and successive governments have been hostile to press freedom and the right to peacefully protest. In a truly liberal society, there would be no such exceptions.

In this, I am skirting dangerously close to the view that 'real liberalism has never been tried', a variation of the typical fallacy of leftists who claim that all the failed socialist states of history were 'socialist' only in name. And yet I cannot help but be reminded of the words of Christopher Hitchens:

> Find a society that's adopted the teachings of Spinoza, Voltaire, Galileo, Einstein, Thomas Paine, Thomas Jefferson and gone down the pits – as a result of doing that – into famine and war and dictatorship and torture and repression. That's the experiment I would like to run.

While we have developed a liberal consensus in the West when it comes to human rights, we have only partially cultivated freedom of speech and thought and innovation within the rule of law. There have always been caveats, ideals half attempted. Our challenge as human beings with incompatible goals and incommensurable values is to find a way to live together. Liberalism, as defined above, surely offers us the best possibility of achieving this aim.

This does not mean that the rule of law might not be unjust and open to challenge. Martin Luther King, Jr.'s *Letter from Birmingham Jail* (1963) is often cited by Black Lives Matter activists to counter the view that its author was a liberal in the traditional sense, and to suggest that he would have approved of the riots that took place in the summer of 2020. This sort of misinterpretation is striking, given what King so clearly tells us. Having distinguished between just and unjust laws, he proposes a wholly liberal methodology to tackle the latter.

> In no sense do I advocate evading or defying the law, as would the rabid segregationist. That would lead to anarchy. One who breaks an unjust law must do so openly, lovingly, and with a willingness to accept the penalty. I submit that an individual who breaks a law that conscience tells him is unjust, and willingly accepts the penalty of imprisonment in order to arouse the conscience of the community over its injustice, is in reality expressing the highest respect for law.

King's conceptualisation of non-violent civil disobedience is hardly the most apt template for the looting of shops and the shooting of police officers in the name of social justice.

When it comes to the worst overindulgences of the woke movement, it is not liberalism that is to blame but rather a failure to maintain its principles. The examples I have given – such as those who have called for the banning of protests only when they oppose the cause – suggests that our principles are not always fixed, and there is a human tendency to make exceptions so long as our enemies are the only ones affected. We would do well to guard against these natural inconsistencies. We should keep in mind that to live in a country where liberty is constitutionally enshrined is a global and historical anomaly. Only in a free society could we begin to take our freedoms for granted in this way. Too many of us simply assume that we will always be able to speak and act as we wish within the rule of law, and so the privilege has been all but forgotten. Complacency is one of our greatest enemies.

This observation brings to mind a speech delivered by the novelist David Foster Wallace at Kenyon College in Ohio in 2005. He opened with the following story, which could be read as a parable or a joke depending on your point of view:

> There are these two young fish swimming along, and they happen to meet an older fish swimming the other way, who nods at them and says, 'Morning, boys. How's the water?' And the two young fish swim on for a bit, and then eventually one of them looks over at the other and goes, 'What the hell is water?'

We have grown so accustomed to the conditions of a liberal democracy that its benefits have become invisible to us. Had we lived in a feudal society in which our very existence is conditional on deference to the elites, we might better appreciate why our freedoms are so precious. Although today many of us feel politically lost and powerless to effect change, we retain the collective ability to depose our rulers if they fail in their obligations. We have a free press that can hold the government to account. Our freedom to criticise our leaders has been facilitated by our incredible good fortune to have been born in the digital age.

And yet many of us cannot see it. Why else would self-proclaimed 'left-wingers' act as cheerleaders for censorship by major corporations? Why would so-called 'progressives' demand that freedom of the press be limited? Why would politicians on all sides of the spectrum insist that democratic elections or referendums are 'illegitimate' if the outcome does not go their way? These are the fish who do not notice that they are swimming. The radical proposals of John Locke and John Stuart Mill have won out so completely that we no longer realise that they need to be continually defended. This is why we must be particularly vigilant when it comes to those who pay lip service to liberal values while seeking their demolition. As the end of woke brings with it new forms of tyranny obscured within a carapace of righteousness, we should resist the temptation to resort to their tactics. Replacing one form of authoritarianism with another is no kind of solution at all. We should not be put in the position where we can choose to keep our fingers at the expense of our tongue.

## The New Colossus

A bare-breasted woman is charging into battle, a musket fixed with a bayonet in one hand, the French tricolour defiantly held high in the other. She is leading a group of armed citizens over a barricade, trampling over the dead towards victory. It is a diverse and motley militia; a gentleman in a top hat and coat armed with a rifle, a tatterdemalion labourer brandishing a sabre, a young boy with a pistol in each small hand. It is a spirited and heroic charge towards immortality, citizens fired with the fuel of freedom. Framed against the backdrop of the rising white smoke, the semi-naked woman leading the charge is a godlike figure. Our eyes are drawn up from the darkness of the rubble and death to her lofty, transfigured presence. She is leading us as much as the men who follow in her wake.

The painting is *Liberty Leading the People* by Eugène Delacroix, a dynamic commemoration of the July Revolution in Paris in which King Charles X was overthrown. It was first exhibited at the Paris Salon in 1830, and serves as a reminder of how the very concept of liberty was once perceived as profoundly radical. When the design for New York's iconic statue of *Liberty Enlightening the World* was first revealed, many were sceptical. The work was not only intended to mark the centennial of American independence, but also as a paean to the principle of liberty itself. The thirteenth amendment to the constitution which finally abolished slavery had been ratified in 1865, the same year in which the

Liberty Leading the People *(1830) by Eugène Delacroix*

historian Édouard de Laboulaye first mooted the idea of this commemorative colossus which would be gifted to the United States by the people of France. Yet Lady Liberty's embodiment would differ significantly from Delacroix's famous depiction. Instead, the neoclassical design by sculptor Frédéric Auguste Bartholdi, executed by Gustave Eiffel, saw this variation of the goddess Libertas standing majestically in contrapposto, holding a blazing torch as a beacon of freedom. Instead of piles of corpses, her pedestal would be a granite block with Doric portals. The original torch design was gilded to harness the sunlight for an illusion of radiance, and in 1886 portholes were cut into the base so that it could be illuminated from within. Located on Bedloe's Island – later Liberty Island – in New York Harbour, it would represent a powerful statement to immigrants as they drew near to their new home. Liberty was no longer a revolutionary force, but one of hope and hospitality.

It is easy to be cynical about such a powerful image; it is perhaps too 'on the nose' for British sensibilities. I understand E. M. Forster's feeling when he wrote: 'I do not take the Statue of Liberty in New York harbour as seriously as she takes herself', but I am not persuaded that bold and radical ideas are best served by subtlety. Even the most jaded among us can appreciate the appeal of 'The New Colossus', the sonnet by poet Emma Lazarus which was penned to raise funds for the construction of the statue's pedestal. It can be seen today engraved on a bronze plaque in the pedestal's museum.

> Not like the brazen giant of Greek fame,
> With conquering limbs astride from land to land;
> Here at our sea-washed, sunset gates shall stand
> A mighty woman with a torch, whose flame
> Is the imprisoned lightning, and her name
> Mother of Exiles. From her beacon-hand
> Glows world-wide welcome; her mild eyes command
> The air-bridged harbor that twin cities frame.
> 'Keep, ancient lands, your storied pomp!' cries she
> With silent lips. 'Give me your tired, your poor,
> Your huddled masses yearning to breathe free,
> The wretched refuse of your teeming shore.
> Send these, the homeless, tempest-tost to me,
> I lift my lamp beside the golden door!'

It took little more than a century for this once controversial ideal to achieve a consensus in the Western world. In 1989, the political scientist Francis Fukuyama published his landmark essay 'The End of History?', in which he proclaimed 'an unabashed victory of economic and political liberalism'. He argued that the 'triumph of the West' was 'evident first of all in the total exhaustion of viable systematic alternatives to Western liberalism'. The competing ideologies of the twentieth century – fascism and communism – had fallen as absolutely

*Statue of Liberty, New York.*

as monarchic rule, and only liberal democracy had secured a consensus
in the West so that it constituted the 'end point of mankind's ideological
evolution'. In this, Fukuyama was promoting a vision of liberalism by
which the needs of the individual and those of society had found the
most effective means of reconciliation within the restrictive properties
of human nature.

This balancing act between the citizen and the state is sustained
through the rule of law, which is why liberalism has often been interpreted as a theory of justice. The most well-known proponent of this
view is the philosopher John Rawls, who identifies three key strands of
a 'liberal political conception of justice' as 'a list of equal basic rights

and liberties, a priority for those freedoms, and an assurance that all members of society have adequate all-purpose means to make use of these rights and liberties'. Without the scaffolding of the state and a commitment to egalitarianism, individual liberties are meaningless. This interdependence lies at the heart of all debates about liberalism from its earliest inception. The need for strong governance to curb the anarchic aspects of human nature was addressed at length by the philosopher Thomas Hobbes in his *Leviathan* (1651). He argued that societies are formed as a mechanism to overcome our oppressive 'natural condition'; most readers will be familiar with his famous maxim that the 'life of man' is 'solitary, poore, nasty, brutish, and short'. This concept is typically known as the 'state of nature', and describes humankind in its pre-civilisational age.

Hobbes contended that we accept certain limitations on our liberty in a social contract which works to the mutual advantage of both the ruling class and their subjects. These ideas anticipated those of the philosopher and physician John Locke, whose insistence that we are born with natural rights became a cornerstone of liberal thought. His *Second Treatise of Government* (1689) has become known as a key foundational document in the history of liberalism. In Chapter II, he outlines what he means by the 'state of nature'.

> To understand political power right, and derive it from its original, we must consider what state all men are naturally in, and that is, a *state of perfect freedom* to order their actions, and dispose of their possessions and persons, as they think fit, within the bounds of the law of nature, without asking leave, or depending upon the will of any other man.
>
> A *state* also *equality*, wherein all the power and jurisdiction is reciprocal, no one having more than another: there being nothing more evident, than that creatures of the same species and rank, promiscuously born to all the same advantages of nature, and the use of the same faculties, should also be equal one amongst another without subordination or subjection, unless the lord and master of

them all should, by any manifest declaration of his will, set one above another, and confer on him, by an evident and clear appointment, an undoubted right to dominion and sovereignty.

Locke deviated from Hobbes's pessimistic view of our inherently 'brutish' condition, favouring instead the view that human beings are naturally cooperative, equal and autonomous. His plea for religious freedom in A *Letter Concerning Toleration* (1689) was in accordance with this sense of the necessity for the retention of individual conscience and belief. We see a further development of this view in *The Social Contract* (1762) by the philosopher Jean-Jacques Rousseau, who shared the conviction that a government was sustained only by the consent of its people, while acknowledging the inevitable conflicts that might arise between individual desires and the 'general will'. This is a conflict that liberal thinkers to this day are forever seeking to resolve.

Critics of liberalism often judge its origins to be hopelessly sanguine, a perception of the human race occupying an idyllic fairyland in which noble instincts and good intentions are the norm. While the likes of Hobbes saw civilisation as a means to tame our feral state of nature, Rousseau saw this pre-civilisational condition as morally neutral. We are born neither good nor bad, he proposed, acting according to our corporeal needs in a free world with an innate sense of compassion and empathy towards our fellow man. Rousseau's treatise *Émile* (1762) outlines his contention that humankind may be socialised organically due to its natural impulses rather than through the rigidities of formal education. This notion is perhaps best encapsulated in William Blake's poem 'The School-Boy' (1789), in which the classroom is analogised to a cage.

> How can the bird that is born for joy,
> Sit in a cage and sing?
> How can a child, when fears annoy,
> But droop his tender wing,
> And forget his youthful spring?

Wordsworth too saw the child as the best philosopher. The implication is that humankind in its pre-political condition is essentially free, equal and autonomous, and that what we call 'civilisation' is achieved only through our submission to the law or the impositions of oppressive hierarchies. As Locke would have it, we exchange certain aspects of our natural liberties for the security of broader freedoms.

While these ideas were formative to the early liberal thinkers, they have little to do with the notion of liberalism as understood in the modern world. We are not solitary creatures like the boy of Blake's poem, but dependent on the organisation of functional collectives in order to survive. We recognise that life is unfair, which is why we promote meritocracy as the ideal means to satisfy the ambitious and status-seeking impulse that is our evolutionary inheritance. Rather than adopting a Pollyannish view of freedom as the innate quality of humankind, most liberals see it as an aberration that we must struggle to maintain. In other words, liberty does not come naturally to us, which is why the principle must be defended anew in each successive generation.

Civilisation, then, is the gloss we apply to a scabrous reality. When we think of the zenith of English literary culture, the drama of the Elizabethan period as embodied in Shakespeare, we cannot entirely blot out the brutality of the age that produced him. It is harmless enough to indulge in time-travelling fantasies, to imagine the privilege of huddling with the groundlings in the Globe, to be among the first ever to witness those sublime theatrical moments: Portia in her boyish garb discoursing so poignantly on the quality of mercy, the reconciliation of King Lear and the only daughter who loves him, Antony's soldiers marvelling at the subterranean music reverberating on the eve of the battle. But what then happens if we sustain the fantasy too long? In those exquisite moments of pathos, when even this drunken rabble are mesmerised into silence, we might catch distant howls from beyond the timber walls. Something profane is intruding on the sacred. A little further along the riverbank, at a place called the Beargarden, our neighbours are experiencing a different kind of show. For there is Harry Hunks, the ageing brown bear, chained to a post while men whip his back until his fur is matted with blood. The cries and shrieks of women tell us that Sackerson is loose again, a bear so famous that he is namechecked in *The Merry Wives of Windsor*. And there too is a terrified ape, tied to a horse and set upon by ravenous hounds, while the audience hollers in frenzied delight to see the flesh of this simian rider and his steed torn away. It was only a few minutes' walk from the Globe to the Beargarden, but in civilisational terms the distance was vast.

A vision of liberalism that acknowledges what Hobbes understood as the brutish heart of humankind is not one that is recognised by many of its most vocal opponents. The authoritarian impulse is one that is restrained by civilisation, which is why the liberal insists on socialisation through education and a fair application of the rule of law as a safety net for when that process has failed. Yet liberals are accused of promoting a quixotic view of human nature, of building theories on brittle assumptions. In other words, those of us who still defend liberal values find ourselves attacked for principles that we do not hold. Liberalism has come to be synonymous with progressivism, not because it favours a teleological view of history by which progress is inevitable, but rather that its origins lie in the need to tackle exploitation, whether that be from feudal systems, monarchies, institutionalised religion, or any other ideological framework or manifestation of instinctive human cruelty. Its focus on individual rights is not a negation of social responsibility, but a corollary of it. When Locke urges readers to dispense with leaders who subject them to a 'train of abuses', it is not because he envisages a moral free-for-all in which every fleeting desire, however sordid or self-centred, is satisfied. It is because in a cohesive society the general will can only be sustained where there is harmony between the needs of the citizens and those of the state. If the natural rights of humankind are self-evident, as the likes of Locke and Mill presuppose, then the very existence of government needs to be continually justified and tested so that it might effectively serve its function. When we speak of 'holding power to account', this is what we mean.

In Patrick J. Deneen's *Why Liberalism Failed*, perhaps the most cogent polemic against the naïvety of modern-day liberals, we are reminded that those who participate in these debates cannot evade these definitional quagmires. The rhetorical architecture of the book is established in its title. Just as Roger Scruton's *England: An Elegy* (2000) condenses the crux of the argument in the title itself (with the added device of writing of England throughout in the past tense), Deneen establishes that liberalism has perished before his case has even been launched. John Gray achieves a similar effect with the subtitle of his book *The New Leviathans: Thoughts After Liberalism* (2023), in which he asserts that 'liberal civilization has passed away'. Deneen insists that liberalism is as much an ideology as communism or fascism, and that its tenets establish the conditions for its own inevitable demise. That is to say, 'Liberalism has failed because liberalism has succeeded.' He sees the marriage of majority rule and individual aspirations as inherently paradoxical, claiming that an operational democracy requires 'shared social practices and commitments that arise from thick communities, not a random collection of unconnected selves entering and exiting an election booth'.

Liberalism has always been a tricky prospect, cherishing personal autonomy and freedom of speech up to the point where our behaviour encroaches on the rights of others. To ideologues it is a poison, because it rejects their insistence that we ought to follow a preordained set of rules. This is why Deneen's contention that liberalism is itself an ideology is unconvincing. He argues that it ranks alongside fascism and communism as one of 'the modern world's three great competitor political ideologies', and insists that its danger lies in its pretence to neutrality. At the risk of repeating the point that Deneen is at pains to refute, I take the view that liberalism represents a wholesale repudiation of ideological thinking, because it refuses to accept oversimplified interpretations of reality, or to outsource our decision-making capacities to an already established creed. This is why there are liberals on the left, the right, and everywhere in between. Liberalism is not an ideology, but the absence of an ideology. It would be akin to classifying atheism as a faith, a common tactic that I have never found persuasive. By definition, an ideology demands conformity; liberalism, by contrast, cannot exist within conformist structures.

Deneen begins from the premise that liberalism is essentially utopian, that it stakes its claim to legitimacy on the grounds that it can fix all society's ailments. Yet the project of liberalism is ongoing and entails an appreciation of humankind's fallibility. The etymology of 'utopia' is from the Greek *ou topos*, meaning 'no place'; it is an imaginary idyll that cannot be reified. While communists yearn to bring an equal society into being, and fascists seek total submission to the state, the liberal recognises the inherent plurality of human nature and the inevitable conflicts that must ensue. Our follies, flaws, prejudices and other innate complexities are not problems to be solved, but inherent aspects of our being. The liberal does not claim that these negative traits can be eliminated, but promotes a social contract by which we voluntarily subordinate our selfish desires in the service of our community. Injustice, then, is not something that can be flattened out of existence, but rather an inevitable feature of humanity that we must resist as best we can as and when it arises. We do not seek to remake the world according to our values, but to cultivate the optimal circumstances for cooperation and coexistence. Progress is possible, but not inevitable.

The form of liberalism that Deneen criticises is one underpinned by two foundational assumptions: 'anthropological individualism and the voluntarist conception of choice' and 'human separation from and opposition to nature'. He sees it as a development away from the ancient Christian tradition of liberty by which we are called to a state of rational self-governance. He may be right that there are those who call themselves liberals who seek a primordial state of anarchy, but this is to reject the principle of social responsibility that is embedded in present-day liberal discourse. To borrow a formulation from Socrates, the majority of liberals may necessarily be rascals, but this is not the fault of liberalism. I will return shortly to this key distinction between liberty and licence, but it is worth noting here that Deneen sees the development from the former to the latter as the self-sabotaging element in today's mode of liberal thought. He outlines the contradiction of securing individual autonomy that can only be maintained through a comprehensive expansion of the state. If our animal natures are not tempered by 'all forms of associations and relationships, from family to church, from schools to village and community', then the subsequent freefall will require the fail-safe of positive law.

The terminus of Deneen's understanding of the liberal system, then, is a kind of self-indulgent chaos, one that leads to the contradictory outcome of individual freedom and oppressive state control.

> In this world, gratitude to the past and obligations to the future are replaced by a nearly universal pursuit of immediate gratification: culture, rather than imparting the wisdom and experience of the past so as to cultivate virtues of self-restraint and civility, becomes synonymous with hedonic titillation, visceral crudeness, and distraction, all oriented toward promoting consumption, appetite, and detachment. As a result, superficially self-maximizing, socially destructive behaviors begin to dominate society.

So we are back with Hobbes, with his insistence that the composition of the body politic is one of individual passions contained by the state. Deneen quotes Hobbes's remark about the solipsistic presuppositions of the liberal mindset, that human creatures are 'from the earth like mushrooms and grown up without any obligation to each other', but this is neither true in terms of our evolutionary history or our current way of life. This interpretation of liberalism as a form of rootlessness, with no obligations to country or community, is wholly disconnected from the worldview of liberalism as I conceive it. Plato has Socrates remind us that 'no one of us is sufficient for himself, but each is in need of many things'. We rely on our communities and the various roles fulfilled within them according to each member's individual gifts. While Plato's *Republic* is built on authoritarian principles, the necessity for communal living is a conviction that liberals generally share. So while Deneen's criticisms are specifically focused and valid, we must ensure that we do not carelessly envelop all forms of liberalism into his critique. This would be a disservice to both Deneen's analysis and our own.

Put simply, the title of Deneen's book – *Why Liberalism Failed* – might be more accurately (albeit inelegantly) rendered *Why a Perverted Form of Liberalism Failed*. Deneen's argument is not wrong, so long as the reader accepts as definitive the specific version of liberalism that he denounces, with its 'relentless emphasis upon private over public things, self-interest over civic spirit, and aggregation of individual opinion over common good'. His view is that a fealty to liberalism invariably results in a new form of oppression to replace the old, what Deneen describes as a 'liberlocratic despotism'. He sees the sanctification of 'diversity' and 'personal identity', promoted in recent years by the apparatchiks of Critical Social Justice, as 'sewn into the deepest fabric of the liberal project'. In truth, the obsession with group identity as a means to reinterpret power structures, along with the concomitant insistence on censorship as a means to redress the imbalances, is as severe a betrayal of liberalism as can be envisaged. Of course, there is nothing new in this debate over terminology. We have already seen that the term 'liberalism' encapsulates many, often contradictory, points of view.

Ultimately, Deneen suggests that we have two options. 'We can either elect a future of self-limitation born of the practice and experience of self-governance in local communities, or we can back inexorably into a future in which extreme license coexists with extreme oppression.' My chief objection to Deneen's dichotomy is the assumption that the former would entail a renunciation of liberalism rather than an enactment of its key values. To better explain what these might be, it is worth returning to one of the most historically salient figures in the history of liberal thought.

## The Three-Dimensional Liberal

For John Milton, death was not the end of his troubles. He spent his final years blind and disgraced, in continual fear of execution by the state. As a fervent republican who had written tracts defending regicide, the restoration of the monarchy in 1660 left his legacy in a precarious position. The author of *Paradise Lost* (1667), the greatest epic poem in English since *The Faerie Queene* (1590), might have anticipated a burial in Westminster Abbey alongside other literary luminaries such as Edmund Spenser and Geoffrey Chaucer. As it transpired, Milton's controversial political history meant that he was interred in the humbler environs of St Giles Cripplegate. To make matters worse, a little over a century later his corpse was exhumed and mutilated. Likely inspired by the anti-republican fervour that followed the French Revolution, Milton's resurrectionists tore away pieces of his jawbone, his teeth, and his remaining locks of hair, possibly selling them on as souvenirs. The poet William Cowper was so outraged that he wrote 'Stanzas on the late indecent liberties taken with the remains of the great Milton'. To say that these vandals were 'taking liberties' is something of an understatement.

St Giles Cripplegate is a small Gothic church, one of the few medieval places of worship lucky enough to survive both the Great Fire of London and the Blitz. It is located at the heart of the Barbican Estate, whose charmless brutalist architecture makes for quite the incongruous backdrop. Few people visit the church today, even though John Bunyan was a parishioner, Oliver Cromwell was married here, and Shakespeare lived just around the corner at Silver Street. It is one of the city's many overlooked gems. When I was teaching English Literature at the City of London School for Girls, one of the key texts on the curriculum was Milton's *Paradise Lost*. Given its author was buried less than thirty metres from my classroom, I would take my students to the church to see for themselves the nondescript plaque on the floor by the altar which simply reads: 'Near this spot was buried John Milton author of *Paradise Lost* born 1608 – died 1674'. This is a striking contrast to the elaborate marble memorial in Westminster Abbey erected in 1737, with a likeness of the poet sculpted by John Michael Rysbrack.

Milton was a freethinker whose worldview was grounded in reason above all else. As a religious man, he had no time for those who deviated from God's truth, and yet in his own way his worldview was profoundly heretical. Consider the opening to *Paradise Lost* in which he expresses his intention to 'justify the ways of God to men'. The audacity of this motive is only matched in his confidence in declaring it, and it testified to his firm conviction that we can and must think for ourselves. Many of Milton's ideas were groundbreaking. At a time when the divine right of kings was rarely contested, he considered it unreasonable that a man should be monarch on the basis of an accident of birth. He believed in meritocracy, which is partly what drew him to Cromwell. In spite of his puritanical strain, he was at odds with conventional doctrine in his eschewal of the Calvinist notion of predestination. For Milton, free will was an essential aspect of our humanity. The fall of man depicted in *Paradise Lost* is meaningless unless Adam and Eve have chosen freely to partake of the forbidden fruit. In Book III, God explicitly declares to Jesus that he has bestowed free will upon his creation and that mankind is culpable if he strays from the path: 'I made him just and right, / Sufficient to have stood, though free to fall'. Adam's mistake was to exercise that freedom, condemning us all to exist in a postlapsarian state.

Milton presents Adam and Eve, then, not as mere marionettes enacting some preordained cosmic pantomime, but as individual agents. This is why the archangel Raphael is sent by God to explain that obedience to their maker must be a matter of choice.

> God made thee perfect, not immutable;
> And good he made thee, but to persevere
> He left it in thy power – ordained thy will
> By nature free, not over-ruled by fate
> Inextricable, or strict necessity;
> Our voluntary service he requires,
> Not our necessitated; such with him
> Finds no acceptance, nor can find, for how
> Can hearts not free be tried whether they serve
> Willing or no, who will but what they must
> By destiny, and can no other choose?

It could barely be clearer than that. It is Adam's uxoriousness and fear of separation from Eve that motivates him to eat the fruit from the Tree of Knowledge at her request. It is an irrational decision, given that he understands fully the consequences of his actions. In Book XII, the archangel Michael elucidates this interconnection of liberty and reason: 'Since thy original lapse, true liberty / Is lost, which always with right reason dwells / Twinned, and from her hath no dividual being'. Milton's conceptualisation of 'liberty', therefore, differs significantly from ours. His was a specifically Christian ideal, predicated on this notion of virtuous self-regulation. He was at pains to distinguish between what he called 'licence', the freedom to do whatever one desires, and 'liberty', by which the faithful man is called to purge those passions and temptations that enslave the soul. Licence, Milton contends, is no freedom at all, but an indulgence that amounts to a form of self-imposed tyranny. Milton believes in the laws of nature and the laws of God, and that these are accessible through a process of reason.

When Milton wrote his tract 'The Doctrine and Discipline of Divorce' (1643), he was alarmed at some of the backlash from his peers.

His argument for the legal dissolution of the conjugal state was not, as some interpreted it, a selfish plea for sexual licentiousness. While he might be accused of intellectualising a position that would benefit men such as himself who were experiencing troubled marriages, Milton made a powerful case that once companionship and concordance were absent in a partnership, the institution no longer served its function. His position was not some kind of forerunner of the 'free love' movement of the 1960s. Rather, his defence of divorce was grounded in the belief that in certain circumstances it might have spiritual and societal advantages. As a devout puritan, Milton took issue with the misinterpretations, and addressed them in a sonnet.

> I did but prompt the age to quit their clogs
>> By the known rules of ancient liberty,
>> When straight a barbarous noise environs me
>> Of owls and cuckoos, asses, apes and dogs:
> As when those hinds that were transform'd to frogs
>> Rail'd at Latona's twin-born progeny
>> Which after held the sun and moon in fee.
>> But this is got by casting pearl to hogs,
> That bawl for freedom in their senseless mood,
>> And still revolt when truth would set them free.
>> Licence they mean when they cry liberty;
> For who loves that, must first be wise and good.
>> But from that mark how far they rove we see,
>> For all this waste of wealth and loss of blood.

An identical philosophy underpins Milton's *Areopagitica* (1644), a tract written in response to the Licensing Order of June 1643 which demanded that all printed texts should be approved by a censor before publication. 'Give me the liberty', he writes, 'to know, to utter, and to argue freely according to conscience, above all liberties'. Since Milton has it that we are not guided by divine providence, but rather individual agents with responsibility and choice, the act of censorship deprives us of our right to determine for ourselves how best to conduct our lives. He makes the case that censorship might begin with good intentions, but that subjective judgement will always blur the line between the heretical and the distasteful. As he puts it in *Areopagitica*, censors do not 'stay in matters heretical' but 'any subject that is not to their palate'.

This is surely an unanswerable argument against the validity of 'hate speech' laws, a point to which we will return in Chapter 5. Those responsible for such misguided legislation ought to read their Milton. Their intentions may be compassionate, but the dangers of limiting the scope of individual conscience should be clear by now. Besides, how can we be sure that the person making the decision about what constitutes 'hate' is not wrong? As the Roman poet Juvenal asks in his *Satires*: who watches the watchmen (*'quis custodiet ipsos custodes'*)? The authority of the censor presupposes a kind of omniscience. 'How shall the licencers themselves be confided in,' writes Milton, 'unless we can confer upon them, or they assume to themselves above all others in the land, the grace of infallibility and uncorruptedness?' Mill made a similar point in *On Liberty*. 'All silencing of discussion', he wrote, 'is an assumption of infallibility'.

Milton reminds us to retain our trust in humanity's capacity for reason. We have convinced ourselves that we exist in an age of 'fake news', but the concept is hardly unprecedented. Milton saw the struggle between Truth and Falsehood as perpetual, and envisaged them as antagonists on a battlefield. 'Let her and Falsehood grapple; who ever knew Truth put to the worse, in a free and open encounter?' It isn't so much that 'fake news' is unique to the digital age, but rather that we appear to have lost our faith in our ability to make the stronger case. It is Milton's contention that we are far better placed to know and overcome evil if we are acquainted with its essence, and censorship deprives us of this opportunity. The silencing of speech, he maintains, is tantamount to a betrayal of the human spirit. This is why he reserves particular scorn for the destruction of books. During the Bishops' Ban of 1599, satirical works were seized and burned in public. To Milton, this is akin to a form of homicide, 'whereof the execution ends not in the slaying of an elemental life, but strikes at that ethereal and fifth essence, the breath of reason itself'. The man who destroys a book, he tells us, 'slays an immortality rather than a life'.

Yet Milton leaves himself wide open to accusations of hypocrisy. *Areopagitica* is a counterblast against licensers and the way in which they stymie the possibility of individual choice, but Milton was to become a censor for the Commonwealth five years after its publication. He was an elitist whose emphasis on liberty certainly did not extend to Catholics. His final written work, the polemical tract *Of True Religion* (1673), railed against the 'growth of popery' and exhorted the public to 'beware the growth of this Romish weed'. While this may strike us as inconsistent, to Milton it was the logical progression of his principles. Milton perceived the Catholic Church to be a weapon against freedom, a belief that was surely consolidated by his tour of Europe in the late 1630s. Milton claimed to have met the ageing Galileo Galilei (1564–1642) in Florence, who at the time was under house arrest by the Inquisition; he had fallen foul of the 'hate speech' laws of the Holy See.

To what extent might Milton inform an understanding of liberalism as wokeness perishes and we emerge from the present culture war? If we take the view that human beings are essentially rational creatures, and that their capacity for reason is enabled through a process of socialisation that depends upon education, community and tradition, and that this quality encourages self-regulation in accordance with a broader social contract maintained through public consensus and the rule of law, are we not already firmly within the ambit of Milton's philosophy? This is a species of liberalism that most closely resembles the great liberal thinkers of the twentieth century and beyond.

Let us consider the example of Martin Luther King, Jr., whose commitment to this form of liberalism is evident throughout his writings. In particular, we might look to his speech 'The three dimensions of a complete life', delivered at the New Covenant Baptist Church in

Chicago on 9 April 1967. In this spectacular address, King proposes that the fulfilling existence ought to be measured by its length, breadth and height.

> Now the length of life as we shall use it here is the inward concern for one's own welfare. In other words, it is that inward concern that causes one to push forward, to achieve his own goals and ambitions. The breadth of life as we shall use it here is the outward concern for the welfare of others. And the height of life is the upward reach for God. Now you got to have all three of these to have a complete life.

For me, this metaphor encapsulates the spirit of social liberalism. There is the freedom of conscience and belief and self-governance in the length, the social responsibility to other people and the community at large in the breadth, and the need to strive towards a higher purpose in the height. This third aspect need not be spiritual, but could incorporate what even atheists might accept today as a 'higher truth', borne out in our traditions, myths, philosophies and, above all, artistic achievements. A life without purpose is self-evidently intolerable, and while some find this in their faith in God, and others might turn to their families or community, it is also to be found in the glimpses of the numinous we experience through great art and literature. The 'height' of a complete life, then, is akin to Milton's view that the laws of nature and God might be discovered through the human capacity for reason. To seek the length but not the breadth is to find licence. To seek the breadth but not the length is to find self-abnegation. To seek the length and breadth but not the height is to deny ourselves the avenue to the transcendent which is the hallmark of a complete life. For liberty to mean anything at all, it surely must take on all three dimensions.

Locke's view of liberty was similarly three-dimensional. It is not solely that individual freedom is a natural right, but that our reason 'teaches all mankind, who will but consult it, that being all equal and independent, no one ought to harm another in his life, health, liberty, or possessions'. The third dimension aligns with his conviction that a higher 'law of nature' governs our 'state of nature'. This is a world away from the form of liberalism that Deneen decries. The idea that we should 'consume without limits' – that is to say, attend only to the length of a complete life – was, according to Deneen, the cause of the economic crisis of 2008. 'Our appetite justified consumption,' he writes. 'Our want was sufficient for our satiation. The result was not merely literal obesity but moral obesity – a lack of self-governance of our appetites ultimately forced us on a starvation diet.' By contrast, the liberalism of the 'three Johns' – Milton, Locke and Mill – as well as that of Martin Luther King, Jr., implores us to strive towards virtuous self-rule in tandem with a concern for all humanity. It bears similarities to the liberal organicism of the economist J. A. Hobson, who reminds us that a body can only function when all its component parts are working in tandem; that is to say, social responsibility and an alertness to the needs of others are essentially liberal goals because individual autonomy cannot flourish without them.

Hobson regards society as 'a moral rational organism in the sense that it has a common psychic life, character, and purpose, which are not to be resolved into the life, character, and purpose of its individual members'. Where some critics might perceive this as antithetical to liberalism as it is traditionally understood, Hobson explains that the liberal perception of the relationship between the individual and society has evolved.

> Liberalism is now formally committed to a task which certainly involves a new conception of the State in its relation to the individual life and to private enterprise. That conception is not Socialism, in any accredited meaning of that term, though implying a considerable amount of increased public ownership and control of industry. From the standpoint which best presents its continuity with earlier Liberalism, it appears as a fuller appreciation and

realisation of individual liberty contained in the provision of equal opportunities for self-development. But to this individual standpoint must be joined a just apprehension of the social, viz., the insistence that these claims or rights of self-development be adjusted to the sovereignty of social welfare.

A meaningful education is the key to this cooperative process, because freedom is inauthentic unless built upon a secure foundation. We may fail along the way, or choose to deviate from social norms but, as with Adam in *Paradise Lost*, the choice is securely our own.

Deneen notes that Alexis de Tocqueville's understanding of liberty was aligned with Milton's Christian tradition. His *Democracy in America* (1835) draws attention to the puritan origins of the founding fathers' conception of democratic values, citing the reference in the puritan minister Cotton Mather's *Magnalia Christi Americana* (1702) to a liberty that approximates to the behaviour of those who 'do what they list', as opposed to the Miltonic view of liberty as rational self-governance. One thinks of the moral vacuum espoused by the occultist Aleister Crowley in his injunction: 'Do what thou wilt shall be the whole of the law'. Alternatively, we might think of the novelist Norman Douglas, whose entire way of life was predicated on the fulfilment of his own pleasures irrespective of the cost to others. 'The business of life is to enjoy oneself,' Douglas writes in *How About Europe?* (1929), 'everything else is a mockery'. In *We Who Wrestle with God* (2024), Jordan B. Peterson describes this as 'the elevation of narrow self-will to the highest conceivable place, in the guise of ultimate freedom'. He argues that it amounts to 'the presumption of subjective omniscience, omnipresence, and omnipotence', the conviction that one has 'the capacity to determine the very definition of right and wrong, valuable and contemptible, good and evil'. This is not liberty at all, but licence.

For those of us who are dismayed at the rejection of liberalism from both the right and the left, the ongoing confusion of liberty and licence is a seemingly perennial obstacle. For a truly free society, we must strive towards a reconceptualisation of liberalism as a way of life that can flourish only on the foundations installed through effective socialisation, rigorous educational values, a just legal system, and a shared social contract formed on the basis of consensus rather than top-down imposition. Naysayers will deny that this qualifies as liberalism at all, but theirs is a myopic view that fails to observe a debate that has been raging for centuries. When we cry for liberty, they mistake it for licence. To put it simply: freedom can only exist when its conditions have been successfully cultivated.

## The Primacy of Education

We are often lawbreakers in our dreams. In that unconscious realm we can be the worst of human beings, participating in deeds that we would never contemplate in waking life. In Plato's *Republic*, Socrates proposes that this dichotomy between our real-world conduct and the anarchy of the oneiric state is evidence of the impact of the civilising process. While speaking of the 'unnecessary pleasures and desires', the often unlawful impulses that are 'probably innate in everyone', Socrates suggests that in dreams they find an outlet.

> When the rest of the soul, the reasoning, gentle, and ruling part of it, is asleep, then the bestial and savage part, when it has had its fill of food or wine, begins to leap about, pushes sleep aside, and tries to go and satisfy its instincts. You know how in such a state it will dare everything, as though it were freed and released from all shame or discernment. It does not shrink from attempting incestual intercourse, in its dream, with a mother or with any man or god or beast. It is ready for any deed of blood, and there is no unhallowed food it will not eat. In a word, it falls short of no extreme of folly or shamelessness.

Socrates acknowledges that a quiet sleep is more likely to those of sound mind and body, but that the 'lawless class of desires exists in every man, even in those of us who have every appearance of being decent people' and that these proclivities are 'revealed in dreams'.

In other words, the innate brutishness of our state of nature is sublimated through the process of effective education and socialisation. This is the Nietzschean conflict of the Apollonian and the Dionysian, the tug-of-war between the transcendent and the decadent, the ethereal and the corporeal, the ordered and the chaotic, as outlined in *The Birth of Tragedy* (1872). Camille Paglia builds upon Nietzsche's foundation in her book, *Sexual Personae* (1990), which draws upon a broad sweep of the historical, cultural and artistic achievements of the Western world to support the view that paganism was not defeated, but 'still flourishes in art, eroticism, astrology, and pop culture'. She invokes Freud's characterisation of the unconscious as a 'daemonic realm', and echoes Plato in her conviction that 'at night we descend to the dream world where nature reigns, where there is no law but sex, cruelty and metamorphosis'. While instinct is amoral, civilisation offers us the framework within which to cooperate and thrive. Contrary to the claims of Critical Social Justice, by which Western society produces inequality and systems of power that enable crimes against the most vulnerable, our civilisation is our armour against such violations. It protects us from rape, murder and other infringements on our human rights. So while today's woke activists claim that injustice is generated by the inherently oppressive quality of our cultural norms, it would be more accurate to say that whenever such outrages occur, it is a sign that the civilisational process has failed.

The liberal understands this. As we have seen, liberals recognise that our essential nature and the societies we construct are imperfectible, even while they embrace the meliorist principle that progress through human endeavour is both achievable and desirable. We accept that the cultivation of a social contract that bestows us with rights and upholds the sanctity of human life is an everlasting project. We are constantly at war with the chthonian, the authoritarian impulse that drives us one way while our ideals and rationality drive us another. Pornography is an aperture through which we glimpse our animal origins, what Paglia calls 'nature's daemonic heart, those eternal forces at work beneath and beyond social convention'. As Plato puts it in the *Republic*, there is no desire more excessive, more intense and more maddening than sexual pleasure. The formalisation of sex through the customs of courtship and marriage is a containment measure; it declaws an otherwise bloodlustful beast. D. H. Lawrence's efforts to dignify the sexual act in *Lady Chatterley's Lover* (1928) could never have worked because the instinct behind it is precisely what the process of civilisation pushes against. The novelist Compton Mackenzie understood this all too well, which is why he pointed out to Lawrence that 'except to the two people who are indulging in it the sexual act is a comic operation'. It can be dangerous to succumb to our most elemental desires, but it can also make us the objects of ridicule.

As I have argued, the process of socialisation through an effective educational system is key to adult autonomy and the development of our capacity to reason. As Roger Scruton writes, human beings can be 'freely choosing individuals, but only when set in the social context that makes them so'. Education is our gravity; it settles us. The gradual formation of the social contract through consensus has little chance of success where learning standards are allowed to plummet. This is not simply about protecting ourselves from the hardwired instincts that predispose us to violence and sexual misconduct, it is the means by which we establish the bedrock upon which artistic, philosophical and scientific achievements become possible. This is why education should be the chief priority for all governments, because the consequence of inadequate socialisation is philistinism. Rousseau's assumption that our natural state is essentially good, and that sin and vice are the consequences of societal corruption, is unpersuasive. William Blake's idealised schoolboy from his *Songs of Experience* is a sentimental fiction, and so too is his remark: 'There is no use in education, I hold it wrong. It is the great Sin. It is eating of the tree of Knowledge of Good and Evil.'

Where failed states will have the kind of corrupting influence on the young that Rousseau warns us against, a society that embraces liberalism will have the opposite effect. The creation of universities was a key development in the history of the liberal project; now there were institutions in which learning was not simply a matter of passive reception, but also critical evaluation. This radical notion, that education was foundational to individual liberty, was advanced by philosophers of the Enlightenment such as Johann Gottfried von Herder. They understood that closed systems of thought are the enemies of intellectual development. Naturally, there have always been debates and conflicts regarding the form that education should take. To return to Plato's *Republic*, Socrates takes the view that gymnastics and music should be paramount to the educational process. And while we would of course reject the essentially authoritarian template of Socrates's ideal state, a holistic approach to education that nourishes both the body and the mind is doubtless worth emulating.

In *The New Puritans*, I made the case that critical thinking ought to be embedded in all aspects of school curricula as a means to sever the bridles of ideology. The dominance of Critical Social Justice in the national curricula of the United Kingdom, an incongruous importation from niche strands of American academia, has meant that pupils are herded into these narrow interpretative trammels. We can see this in the bizarre proposition that accurate written English is a sign of white supremacy. Proponents include Pran Patel, a prominent campaigner for 'decolonisation of the curriculum', who has said: 'The more I think about it the more I believe teaching standard English is racist.' In May 2019, the charity Youth Music called for pupils to be taught about the work of the rapper Stormzy instead of Mozart. It is both wrongheaded and patronising to assume that young black pupils are inherently incapable of appreciating classical music, but nevertheless such regressive notions have been allowed to prevail. As a former teacher,

I understand the temptation to assert one's own politics to the captive audience of the classroom. But when it comes to contentious issues, it is important for teachers to take the impartial approach. This is not only a matter of professional ethics, but one of adherence to the law. Section 406 of the Education Act 1996 prohibits 'the promotion of partisan political views in the teaching of any subject'. This applies not only to political belief-systems such as Marxism, but also ideological frameworks such as Critical Race Theory and gender identity ideology.

It is unsurprising that activists who are convinced that language causes real-world 'harm' should be troubled by the reading habits of children. In May 2022, the Centre for Teaching and Learning at the University of Cambridge suggested that Laura Ingalls Wilder's *Little House on the Prairie* series (1932–43) ought to come with 'content notes', a substitute phrase for 'trigger warnings' given that the word 'trigger' connotes violence and could therefore induce trauma. This fear that children might be morally corrupted by 'problematic' literature explains the deluge of 'progressive' children's books on the market during the woke era: just as children are deemed so malleable that they might transform into bigots if they read outdated work, it is assumed that they can be steered in the 'correct' way if their reading materials are layered with messaging that reinforces the creed of social justice. Indoctrination of the young is always a temptation for those whose ideas would not withstand adult scrutiny. This trend arguably began in 2016, with *Good Night Stories for Rebel Girls* by Elena Favilli and Francesca Cavallo. Thereafter, the tone of such books became more strident, and highly dubious ideological positions were being represented as uncontested truths. In October 2021, the *Daily Mail* undertook a survey of the woke children's books on display at a number of branches of Waterstones in the United Kingdom and Barnes & Noble in the United States. The results were as depressing as they were hilarious. Among the more prominent texts were *Antiracist Baby* (2020) by Ibram X. Kendi, *Woke Baby* (2018) by Mahogany L. Browne, *The Black Friend: On Being a Better White Person* (2020) by Frederick Joseph, and *Gender Swapped*

*Fairy Tales* (2020) by Karrie Fransman and Jonathan Plackett. According to the *Daily Mail*'s report, Titania McGrath's *My First Little Book of Intersectional Activism* (2020) was also featured in these displays. It described the appearance of this outlier as 'awkward'.

The task of distinguishing satire from reality has become more onerous in recent years. What is the satirist to do when the Arizona Department of Education is releasing an 'equity' toolkit which claims that even babies as young as three months old are capable of racial prejudice? In Titania's book for children, she claims that obstetricians choose the sex of babies by flipping a coin. Theresa Thorn earnestly makes a similar claim in *It Feels Good to Be Yourself: A Book About Gender Identity* (2019). Next to an illustration of a newborn baby, she writes: 'See, when you were born, you couldn't tell people who you were or how you felt. They looked at you and made a guess. Maybe they got it right, maybe they got it wrong.' In the context of such propaganda, it is more readily comprehensible that at one leading British secondary school one in every fifteen pupils identifies as transgender or non-binary. Some of these children may be suffering from a form of gender dysphoria, but most will find such confusions resolved through the natural process of puberty. Yet this has not prevented the Council for the Curriculum, Examinations and Assessment in Northern Ireland from releasing an online LGBT guidance for primary schools, which initially included a passage asserting that 'transgender young people become aware that their assigned birth sex is different from their gender identity between the ages of three and five'. After campaigners pointed out that there was no basis for this claim, the statement was excised. To offer a further example, we might consider the anonymous article in *Business Insider* in September 2021 which bore the extraordinary headline: 'My toddler came out as trans at age 4. He's so much happier now'. It would take quite the leap of faith to suppose that adult influence has not played a role here. As trans-identifying YouTuber Blaire White said: 'A transgender 4 year old is like a vegan cat. We all know who's making the lifestyle choices.'

Few parents have grasped the significance of these developments, largely because these attempts at indoctrination have been couched in progressive terminology. One exception is in Wales, where the government was sued in 2022 by more than five thousand parents and grandparents over their decision to make compulsory the teaching of gender identity to children as young as three. The government had apparently adopted Stonewall's misinterpretation of the Equality Act, and accordingly substituted 'gender identity' for 'gender reassignment' in its Equality and Diversity Policy. In addition to legal challenges, mockery has proven an effective defence. Take the controversy surrounding the success of *Daily Wire* host Matt Walsh's book for children, *Johnny the Walrus* (2022). It tells the story of Johnny, a boy who enjoys pretending to be a walrus by using spoons as tusks. The online community mobilises and tells him that he must choose between either being a walrus or being a human, and that he cannot be both. In response to the book, hysterical staff at Amazon held a meeting to discuss the 'trauma' the book had caused. Executives were even heard strategising about how to demote the title on their website to limit potential sales.

Reducing schools to factories of ideology is to invert their purpose. It is no coincidence that universities are currently facing a crisis of free speech, with a minority of activists wielding disproportionate power and resisting all efforts to improve diversity of opinion on campus. These are the latest cohort to have been educated in the secondary school system, and it would appear that they have been coached in the value of authoritarianism. In the most comprehensive recent survey of academics, the University and Colleges Union found that 56 per cent of its members believed that freedom of speech in higher education was in decline and that 'self-censorship is very common'. In European Union countries, 19.1 per cent of respondents admitted to censoring themselves at work, as compared to 35.5 per cent of teaching staff in the United Kingdom. The report outlined how 'many staff have had their academic freedom abrogated and thereby been subjected to cruel and degrading treatment by their peers, on account of their academic views', and that the practice of self-censorship was the major factor in preventing 'the incidence of bullying, psychology pressure and other unconscionable behaviour from being even higher'. The conclusion was harrowing: 'Self-censorship at this level appears to make a mockery of any pretence by universities of being paragons of free speech and that of being advocates of unhindered discourse in the pursuit of knowledge and academic freedom.' In his book *Bad Education* (2025), Matt Goodwin argues that this is common knowledge among lecturers, but that there exists a 'secret code of silence' – which he compares to the Mafia concept of *omertá* – by which 'no matter how glaringly obvious the crisis becomes, no matter how visibly these once great institutions are failing our young people, you just never, ever tell people on the outside'. Although woke is in decline, this fear of speaking out means that its influence persists in the bolthole of higher education.

An unspoken maxim looms over the free speech crisis in our universities: it is only ever denied by those whose views fall in line with the current orthodoxy. There exists an activist contingent within academic circles that has become so adept at intimidating colleagues into silence that they have created what Eric Kaufmann, a professor of Politics at the University of Buckingham, has described as 'an increasingly monocultural higher education ecosystem'. While right-wing scholars are those most likely to self-censor, left-wing academics are also increasingly at risk, notably those who are sceptical about activists' demands that the highly contested belief in 'gender identity' (see Chapter 6) ought to supersede biological sex in matters of public policy. As far back as 2011, writer and feminist campaigner Julie Bindel was officially 'No Platformed' by the National Union of Students (NUS), when delegates at the LGBT conference passed a motion called 'This conference believes Julie Bindle [sic] is vile'. In the following decade, a number of other leading academics would join the list of undesirables, among them Linda Bellos, Selina Todd, Kathleen Stock and Jo Phoenix.

In *Welcome to the Woke Trials* (2021), Julie Burchill neatly encapsulates the problem of universities in the post-Covid era.

> Places which had once been about helping young people to grow into adults seemed now intent on turning back time, Benjamin Button style, so that students went in as young people and came out as monstrous toddlers, the perfect breeding ground for a temper-tantrum masquerading as a crusade.

I am reminded of Richard Brome's play *The Antipodes* (1640), which depicts a chaotic topsy-turvy society where children are able to discipline their parents and send them back to school. At Colorado State University in January 2022, a sign was spotted which read: 'If you (or someone you know) are affected by a free speech event on campus, here are some resources...' These included hotlines that enabled brittle students to contact university authorities so that these fiendish free speech advocates might be investigated. All of this is suggestive of a broader failure in the education system. Perhaps counter-intuitively, the conservation of freedom for an adult population depends upon greater restrictions in childhood, and yet many so-called 'educators' would rather furnish them with a coat of cotton wool instead of a hornbook. This is why I have often felt a tinge of envy towards my parents' generation, who were schooled before the advent of GCSEs and the grade inflation that so consistently rewards mediocrity. I barely revised for my end-of-school examinations, still managed to achieve a respectable set of results, and emerged knowing very little. The far more demanding O-level system of previous decades meant that intelligence was not enough. This is why older people are often able to recite whole poems from memory or the dates of the kings and queens of England, while the rest of us are having to resort to an online search engine.

In April 2023, I visited the Michaela Community School in north-west London, an institution established in 2014 that seeks to restore these lost educational principles. As a state-funded 'free' school, it is able to set its own curriculum and operate independently from the local authority. For those of us who grew up after the 1970s, the regime at Michaela under Katharine Birbalsingh – often referred to in the media as 'Britain's strictest headmistress' – immediately strikes us as unusual. Pupils are not permitted to talk to each other in the corridors as they move from one class to another. They cannot chat during lessons, but are expected to be attentive to the teacher and eager to be involved in answering questions. They are punished with detentions for seemingly trivial infractions such as failing to complete homework or even neglecting to bring their pen to school. Smartphones are not permitted. The school is perceived by its critics as an 'abomination', a 'gulag' and a miniature 'North Korea'. Birbalsingh herself has been characterised as 'scary' and a 'dragon woman'. An article in the *New Statesman* posed the question: 'Is Britain's Strictest Headmistress a visionary or a tyrant?'

Yet these rules have not been imposed arbitrarily. The silence in the corridors significantly reduces the risk of bullying. By taking a firm stance on the smaller details such as missed deadlines and forgotten stationery, more serious misdemeanours are far less likely to occur. For all the claims that the system is oppressive and cruel, the children evidently relish it. I spoke to numerous pupils who testified to the impact that Michaela was having on their education and general happiness. One boy told me that he had been moved from another school where misbehaviour was common and his peers continually talked among themselves in class rather than getting on with work. 'I used to be congratulated just for getting homework done on time,' he said. 'But that should be normal.' At Michaela, high expectations are set and pupils invariably strive to reach them. Contrary to the received wisdom of our times, most children crave discipline and structure, and are relieved when it is provided. Moreover, the system works. Michaela is ranked as the United Kingdom's top school when it comes to raising attainment, even though its intake is overwhelmingly from working-class and disadvantaged families and a quarter of the pupils qualify for free school meals. Its pupils are able to receive an education of the highest standard, and most leave with grades that exceed those of most private schools. For helping to raise children out of poverty, Birbalsingh is monstered in many quarters of the media and the political class.

One could argue that the regimented nature of the lessons does not afford sufficient opportunity for creativity to flourish. Yet it is precisely this approach to education that has produced some of the most indispensable artists in history. William Shakespeare's grammar school education, for instance, was one of endless graft, rote-learning, and an unremitting focus on the classics. There is a good reason why Jaques in *As You Like It* (c. 1599) describes 'the whining schoolboy with his satchel / And shining morning face, creeping like snail / Unwillingly to school'. Shakespeare was instructed in Latin, and would have encountered the canonical works of Ovid, Horace, Virgil, Cicero, Quintilian and Sallust. It was this rigorous education that explains not only the frequency of literary allusions in his plays, but the sheer abundancy of his art. He had been introduced in his most formative years to some of the most significant works in the history of human accomplishment. He was undeniably an innovator, but it was precisely this bank of knowledge, locked into his mind from an early age, that enabled his genius to thrive.

While this kind of highly disciplined education may not best serve every single young individual, from a utilitarian perspective that prioritises the greatest good for the greatest number it would appear to be the optimal approach. If the reader will forgive the bucolic sentimentality, we might analogise the process of education as a garden, with its borders and edging, its fences and enclosures, its terraces and patios. Without these configurative features in place, and a gardener to tend the plant life, the weeds would soon run riot and all potential for beauty and harmony would be lost. Similarly, creative accomplishments are enabled and enhanced through structure and the bedrock of knowledge. With the advent of the internet, today's pupils have access to more of the world's information and historical records than ever before. Yet this has reduced the capacity for the younger generation to think independently without the assistance of a computer. They know where to find information, but do not retain it themselves. Peter Boghossian and James Lindsay have dubbed this the 'Unread Library Effect'. They describe our tendency to 'think we possess the information in the books because we have access to them, but we don't have the knowledge because we've never read the books, much less studied them in depth'. We cannot think for ourselves if we are borrowing our insights from others. It is a form of cerebral indigestion.

This has partly come about due to a general devaluation of knowledge for its own sake. I recall very little about my history lessons at school, although I do have fond memories of an enjoyable project in which we were tasked to produce a diary as though we were one of the communist soldiers on the 'long march' (October 1934 to October 1935) from their base in south-eastern China to the province of Shaanxi in the north-west. It was an imaginative exercise which urged us to empathise with the tribulations of those who struggled on limited resources to cross many mountain ranges in treacherous conditions. For all that, the project did not instil in my memory details about the context of the march, or even its subsequent impact. This focus on human emotion and individual plight is all very well, but I would have been far better served had I been set a series of rote-learning exercises about the key figures and dates from Chinese history.

A grounding in historical knowledge is the engine to the moving vehicle of intellect and imagination. Furthermore, it connects us to the past in order that we might avoid errors in the present. A commonality of ideological groups is that they claim to have all the answers, and that previous generations and cultures are to be condemned outright for their unenlightened ways. A classical education offers its recipients untold advantages, and ensures that the handful of geniuses who emerge every generation have the necessary skills to realise their potential. It is sobering to ruminate on the possibility of great minds stifled by an education that did not nourish their abilities. Had Shakespeare been born in different circumstances, perhaps to a family that could not afford to send him to grammar school, humankind would have been deprived of *Hamlet, Macbeth, King Lear* and all the other masterworks from writers who followed in his wake. If each individual has a maximum potential, education is the means by which we reach it. Understood in those terms, society has an obligation to foster the conditions within which self-actualisation may be assured. In a civilised society, in other words, a sound education is a birthright.

The principle does not apply solely to the creative arts. Compton Mackenzie was convinced that the abolition of the study of Greek and Latin in the curriculum was a disaster for the broader health of the nation. He felt that this example of modernisation 'begot a notion that the past did not matter', that it severed the thread of transhistorical human experience. For Mackenzie, in other words, writing and speaking and thinking in these supposedly dead languages fostered this sense of kinship with our ancestors. In 1903, as a student at Magdalen College, Oxford, he wrote an article in which he jested that the abolition of compulsory Greek in schools would herald 'the end of the British empire'. Sixty years later, he became convinced that his attempt at undergraduate humour had turned out to be prescient, and that the policy would eventually lead to 'the decline and fall of western civilisation'. He feared that without a grounding in the classics, the trivial was becoming more highly valued than the indispensable, and that the education system was 'encouraging human nature to achieve the Insect State'.

At the risk of writing something that might be quoted as an example of the old-fashioned human beings who are blind to the splendour of glorious technology I doubt if a century hence much imaginative literature will be written or read. The fact that more books are published than ever before does not mean that people are reading more; it means that publishers are manufacturing more books to keep up with growing lust for quantity instead of quality. But I must dismount from my hobby-horse...

While we might baulk at sharing such a dire prognostication, Mackenzie is correct that a knowledge of the classics is a gift that we ought not to withhold from younger generations. If we do not learn about the past, we are at risk of forgetting it.

Matthew Arnold captures this timeless interconnectivity in his poem 'Dover Beach' (1867). As the narrator listens to the tide surging back and forth, he senses that 'eternal note of sadness', audible to all men in all aeons.

> Sophocles long ago
> Heard it on the Ægean, and it brought
> Into his mind the turbid ebb and flow
> Of human misery; we
> Find also in the sound a thought,
> Hearing it by this distant northern sea.

While we tend towards feelings of isolation, our consciousness of the past reminds us that human experience is cyclical, that there is nothing we feel now that has not been felt before. A rigorous education, therefore, is the indispensable prerequisite to the maintenance of the social contract; it fosters empathy, knowledge and, above all, humility. The efforts of activists to demolish our civilisation suggests a failure of that process. As an adult whose vocation is writing creatively, I rely on my storehouse of reading as a stimulus to my own imagination, and I find myself continually catching up on the opportunities I missed as a child to read widely. I was not sufficiently disciplined, and I am now paying the price. Life is finite, books are countless, and I would have appreciated the head start.

# 4

# Heresies

---

## Burning Books

The most idiosyncratic book-burning I ever witnessed was during an early episode of *Till Death Us Do Part*, a BBC sitcom which ran between 1965 and 1975. In an episode broadcast on 27 February 1967 called 'Alf's Dilemma', our hero – the cantankerous and bigoted white working-class patriarch Alf Garnett – is seen in his living room reading a copy of *Cleaning Up TV: From Protest to Participation* (1967) by the campaigner Mary Whitehouse. He is berated by his progressive daughter Rita (Una Stubbs) and her socialist husband Mike (Anthony Booth) for reading the book, while he launches a spirited defence. 'That woman is concerned for the moral welfare of your country, in't she. The moral fibre that's being rotted away via corrupt television.' After Alf develops a stomach bug, Rita and Mike take the opportunity to claim that Whitehouse's book is probably contaminated and therefore must be burned in the fireplace. The climax is semi-ritualistic. 'He said paper breeds disease,' exclaims Rita. 'He's touched it, so we've got to burn it.' She takes the coal tongs and drops the book into the fire. 'Burn his clothes!' shouts Mike. 'Burn sulphur candles . . . Unclean!'

It seems unlikely that Johnny Speight, the show's creator and writer, had read the book that he was so eager to incinerate. It seems amusing enough for Mike to complain that if Whitehouse had her way, 'all you'd get on television is Pinky and Perky and bloody Noddy'. Little did he realise that, in the very book Garnett is reading, Whitehouse argues that the callous behaviour of these puppet pigs 'could be the origin of the cruelty some find it hard to understand of juvenile delinquents towards the elderly and helpless'. That being said, Speight made no secret of his loathing for Whitehouse. During an appearance on the BBC's programme *The World at One*, he had referred to Whitehouse and members of her organisation – the National Viewers' and Listeners' Association (NVALA) – as 'Fascists' who 'were hypocritically conceal-ing their Fascism under the cloak of a moral campaign' and who 'held racialist views and were like the killers of Christ'. On today's digital scrapheap of social media there are rarely consequences for this kind of defamation, but this was not the case in 1960s Britain. After Whitehouse launched a libel case, Speight and the BBC were forced to pay damages and issue an apology for the allegation: 'The BBC and Mr Speight have made it clear that they at no time intended this meaning which they agree is wholly inapplicable to Mrs Whitehouse and her associates.'

Given the historical connotations of book-burning, one would have thought that Speight might be more circumspect when it came to accusations of fascism. The ceremonial burning of books in Germany and Austria in the 1930s has ensured that the act will always have a uniquely disquieting and visceral charge. The trans activists who have burned J. K. Rowling's books and posted the footage online have chosen this form of protest for good reason. The potency of the image of a burning book is why the most memorable chapter in Mervyn Peake's novel *Titus Groan* (1946) is when the villain Steerpike sets fire to the library of his master Sepulchrave, the seventy-sixth Earl of Groan. It is a gesture designed to disavow the very heights of human achievement, and to hurl his victim into a spiral of despair. The stratagem works: Sepulchrave goes mad and is eventually eaten by owls.

These stakes are exponentially raised when it comes to the question of Islam. Towards the end of Christopher Marlowe's play *Tamburlaine Part Two* (c. 1587), our marauding anti-hero burns a copy of the Koran, along with other Islamic books, as a kind of audacious test. 'Now, Mahomet,' he cries, 'if thou have any power, come down thyself and work a miracle.' Two scenes later, he is dead. We might see this as a cautionary tale for our times. After all, it isn't only Turco-Mongol conquerors who find themselves punished for Koran-burning. We might look to the murder of anti-Islam campaigner Salwan Momika, an Iraqi man who had been awaiting a verdict in Sweden for the crime of 'agitation against an ethnic or national group'. Momika had publicly burned a number of copies of the Koran during the summer of 2023. He was shot dead during a live stream on TikTok at his home in the city of Södertälje in January 2025. There were suggestions that the assassination may have involved a foreign power. Salwan Najem, another Iraqi refugee, was later given a suspended sentence and fined for his role in the burnings. The judge, Göran Lundahl, issued a bone-chilling closing statement which effectively endorsed Islamic blasphemy codes. 'There is a great deal of scope within the framework of freedom of expression to be critical of a religion in a factual and valid debate,' he said. 'At the same time, expressing one's opinion about religion does not give one a free pass to do or say anything without risking offending the group that holds that belief.' The phrasing was a variation of that craven platitude: 'I believe in freedom of speech, *but* . . .'

Other victim-blamers had been predictably vocal. Within hours of the news of Momika's murder, television personality Bushra Shaikh posted the following on X: 'Some of you may disagree but the public desecration of any holy book should be viewed as a hate crime and the offender should face consequences.' She later clarified that by 'face consequences' she was not supporting murder, but rather the principle that the 'government decides on the punishment'. Of course, Shaikh's logic defeats itself. Her post has been widely interpreted as hate-filled and authoritarian. Does this mean that, if the government were to designate the public advocacy of blasphemy laws a 'hate crime', she would be content to be prosecuted? Those who endorse authoritarianism, in other words, are laying a trap for themselves. If we look to the state to punish our detractors, where does that leave us when the values of those in power no longer align with our own? Momika had been blamed for the riots and the international diplomatic rows that ensued following his campaigns, but the peaceful protester is not responsible for those who break the law in response.

We never seem to learn that appeasement of religious extremists only makes them stronger. That Momika was on trial in the first place suggests that Sweden's commitment to freedom of expression had been subordinated to the creed of multiculturalism. According to the BBC, following Momika's campaigns in 2023 the Swedish government had 'pledged to explore legal means of abolishing protests that involve burning texts in certain circumstances'. In December 2023, the Danish Parliament voted to ban the desecration of all religious texts following a spate of protests in which copies of the Koran had been destroyed. Inevitably, the new law was couched as a safety measure. This burning of the book, claimed Justice Minister Peter Hummelgaard, 'harms Denmark and Danish interests, and risks harming the security of Danes abroad and here at home'. He had a point. Even unconfirmed accusations of Koran-desecration can be sufficient to prompt extremist violence. In 2015, after being accused of defiling the 'holy book', Farkhunda Malikzada was beaten to death by a ferocious mob in Afghanistan while bystanders, including police officers, did nothing to intervene. Many filmed the brutal murder on their phones and the footage was widely shared on social media. In early 2022, a mentally unstable man called Mushtaq Rajput was similarly accused, then tied to a tree and stoned to death in Pakistan. In January 2023, it was reported that Koran-burning protester Javad Rouhi was tortured so severely in an Iranian prison that he could no longer speak or walk. He was sentenced to death for apostasy and later died in prison under suspicious circumstances.

But while we might anticipate that the desecration of the Koran would be proscribed in Islamic theocracies, it is troubling to see similar laws being passed in secular nations such as Denmark. The government had not been so faint-hearted when faced with similar problems in 2005. After cartoons of the Prophet Mohammed were published in the Danish newspaper *Jyllands-Posten*, a global campaign from Indonesia to Bosnia demanded that the Danish authorities take action. The government stood firm and the judicial complaint against the newspaper was dismissed. In a free society this is the only justifiable response, albeit one that takes considerable courage. The American neuroscientist Sam Harris has pointed out that there is an oddity in the fact that so many Muslims do not appear to be alarmed that 'their community is so uniquely combustible'. In a civilised and pluralistic society, the burning of a sacred book might provoke a variety of responses – anger, disbelief, or just a rolling of the eyeballs – but it should never lead to violence. Back when the satirical website *The Onion* still retained the last of its teeth, it satirised this 'unique combustibility' through the depiction of a graphic sexual foursome between Moses, Jesus, Ganesha and Buddha. The headline said it all: 'No One Murdered Because Of This Image'.

Most of us appreciate the emotive power and historical overtones of the image of a burning book. We have all seen the famous footage from 10 May 1933, when students and Nazi soldiers threw books onto a pyre in the public square in Berlin while members of the Hitler Youth marched in celebration. This was philistinism in its purest form, and one is struck by the suspicion that they would have happily substituted the books for the authors themselves. As Heinrich Heine famously wrote: 'Where they burn books, they will in the end burn people too.' Yet there is an important distinction to be drawn between the acts of the Nazis and protests by the likes of Salwan Momika. We might take the view that Momika's method of protest was insensitive or provocative, but in a free society such behaviour is a matter of individual conscience. Momika's copies of the Koran belonged to him, and he was free to dispose of them as he wished. The Nazis, by contrast, had raided libraries, universities and other private collections to harvest works by political dissidents, sexologists, 'degenerate' artists and any others deemed to be 'un-German'. Books by political writers such as Karl Marx, Bertolt Brecht and Rosa Luxemburg were publicly incinerated, along with fictional works by the likes of Thomas Mann, Franz Kafka, Victor Hugo, Oscar Wilde and James Joyce. This was an authoritarian act designed to eliminate whole branches of thought. This is not to be conflated with an individual who chooses to vandalise his or her own property as a form of peaceful protest.

The burning of books, then, falls into the category of an emotive anti-liberal act that must be defended according to the principles of liberalism, and to reinstate blasphemy laws by specifying that religious books deserve special protections is fundamentally retrograde. In November 2024, the Labour MP for Birmingham Hall Green and Moseley, Tahir Ali, said the following at Prime Minister's Questions:

> November marks Islamophobia Awareness Month. Last year, the United Nations Human Rights Council adopted a resolution condemning the desecration of religious texts, including the Koran, despite opposition from the previous Government. Acts of such mindless desecration only serve to fuel division and hatred within our society. Will the Prime Minister commit to introducing measures to prohibit the desecration of all religious texts and the prophets of the Abrahamic religions?

Rather than take the opportunity to reassert the primacy of free speech, including the right to criticise and mock religious belief, Prime Minister Kier Starmer instead dodged the question. 'I agree that desecration is awful and should be condemned across the House,' he said. 'We are, as I said before, committed to tackling all forms of hatred and division, including Islamophobia in all its forms.' He might have simply informed Ali that we no longer live in a society which is subject to medieval canon law. A copy of that year's calendar would have done the trick.

Freedom of expression remains the keystone of our civilisation, and if that means a few hotheads and miniature Tamburlaines might burn their copies of the Koran, then so be it. In the weeks following Momika's murder, a man was arrested in Manchester for burning the Koran in solidarity with the victim. Greater Manchester Police was so proud of enforcing Islamic blasphemy codes that its official account on X posted a gloating statement in which the suspect's name and date of birth were published. This doxxing was deeply irresponsible, and placed a target squarely on his back for any psychopathic zealots who might wish to take vengeance for their bruised feelings. There was also a gratuitous image of a pair of handcuffed wrists with the word 'charged' splashed across it, like the cover of some tasteless tabloid. They may as well have written: 'We got 'im, lads! Death to the kaffir!' A fortnight later, another man burned his Koran outside the Turkish consulate in London. His protest was abruptly interrupted when he was assaulted by a knife-wielding man. Both the aggressor and the victim were charged.

It is unfortunate that the woke era has brought us to the point where Islam must be ringfenced from scorn, whether due to fear of violent repercussions or a misguided and patronising effort to promote 'social justice'. Many will be astonished to learn that blasphemy laws were only fully abolished in England and Wales in 2008, with the passing of the Criminal Justice and Immigration Act. In Scotland, blasphemy was decriminalised in the Hate Crime and Public Order Act of 2021, which came into effect in April 2024. Unfortunately, this particular piece of legislation smuggled in a new blasphemy code to replace the old, a point to which we will return in Chapter 9. The last successful prosecution for blasphemy was in 1977, when Mary Whitehouse brought a private prosecution against Gay News and its editor Denis Lemon for publishing a poem called 'The Love That Dares to Speak Its Name', which depicted an explicit sexual encounter between Jesus Christ and a Roman centurion.

After the guilty verdict, both *Gay News* and Lemon were fined, and the latter received a suspended sentence of nine months. The poem was embarrassingly poor, but it should go without saying that there is no need for criminal prosecution when literary critics are available and in need of work.

The authoritarian impulse in humankind has always meant that blasphemy laws are an inevitability in one form or another. In Ireland, such laws were weaponised as recently as 2017 against the actor and writer Stephen Fry. Police had decided to launch an investigation into remarks that Fry had made during a televised interview for RTÉ in early 2015. During the course of the programme Fry expressed the view that if God exists he must be 'utterly, utterly evil', 'totally selfish', and 'quite clearly a maniac'. 'Why', Fry asked, 'should I respect a capricious, mean-minded, stupid God who creates a world which is so full of injustice and pain?' That the Christian God is 'capricious' and 'mean-minded' has some biblical justification. In the Second Book of Samuel, we are told that God killed the Israelite Uzzah for accidentally touching the Ark of the Covenant after a pesky ox stumbled and knocked him aside. In the Second Book of Kings, we see God unleashing two wild bears to mutilate and kill forty-two children for the crime of mocking a bald man. Given this track record, I'm astounded that Fry wasn't struck down then and there on national television. If nothing else, this does at least prove that God has developed a greater degree of restraint.

The Irish authorities eventually settled on taking the matter no further, which meant that we were deprived of the entertainment value of seeing the Gardaí attempting to prove in court not only that God existed, but that he was mightily grumpy about the whole affair. Such a public farce would have probably seen the repeal of Section 36 of the 2009 Defamation Act, which included an amendment concerning 'publication or utterance of blasphemous matter', and stipulated that anyone found guilty will be 'liable upon conviction on indictment to a fine not exceeding €25,000'. Ireland is the only developed Western nation to have created new blasphemy laws since the beginning of the twenty-first century, but these were ultimately repealed in January 2020 after a constitutional referendum. It is tempting to wonder whether the anonymous individual who reported Fry to the police only did so to demonstrate the preposterousness of such a law existing on the statute books in the first place. The complainant made assurances that he was not personally offended, that he 'believed that the comments made by Fry on RTÉ were criminal blasphemy' and that he was merely doing his 'civic duty'. The man was clearly either bored, mad, or trying to make a point.

God can look after himself, so there is really no need for us to create laws on his behalf. Even so, the demand for the reintroduction of blasphemy codes is remarkably widespread. When the Olympic gymnast Louis Smith was filmed making jokes about Islam, he was subjected to a barrage of criticism in the media and was banned for two months by British Gymnastics. Mohammed Shafiq, chief executive of the Ramadhan Foundation, called for Smith to apologise unreservedly and declared: 'Our faith is not to be mocked.' With the gradual reintroduction of blasphemy laws in various European countries, the likes of Smith are far more likely to face criminal prosecutions. In Hamburg, activist and blogger Michael Stürzenberger was found guilty of inciting racial hatred and sentenced to six months in prison for his harsh criticisms of Islam. On appeal, his sentence was reduced to a fine. After his conviction, Stürzenberger was stabbed in a terrorist attack by a former refugee from Afghanistan which left one police officer dead. His experiences have prompted many commentors to conclude, in the words of writer Sabine Beppler-Spahl, that 'the German elites regard criticism of Islam as an act of right-wing extremism that needs to be censored'.

During a pre-debate discussion for the Fixed Point Foundation with mathematician John Lennox in March 2009, the journalist Christopher Hitchens issued a prescient warning:

This is very urgent business, ladies and gentlemen, I beseech you. Resist it while you still can, and before the right to complain is taken away from you, which will be the next thing. You will be told you can't complain because you are Islamophobic. The term is already being introduced into the culture as if it was an accusation of race hatred, for example, or bigotry, whereas it's only the objection to the preachings of a very extreme and absolutist religion. Watch out for these symptoms. They're not just symptoms of surrender. Very often ecumenically offered to you by men of god in other robes, Christian and Jewish and smarmy ecumenical. These are the ones who will hold open the gates for the barbarians. The barbarians never take a city until someone holds the gates open for them. And it's your own preachers who will do it for you and your own multicultural authorities who will do it for you. Resist it while you can.

When I was interviewed by Andrew Gold for his podcast *Heretics* in November 2024, the monetisation platform Patreon swiftly deleted the video. We had been discussing the topic of free speech, and yet because Gold had quoted from Hitchens's comments above, the interview was censored on the grounds that we had engaged in 'hate speech'. This kind of reaction to the defence of liberal values in the face of spurious charges of 'Islamophobia' lends credence to Hitchens's entire point. 'Resist it while you can' indeed, because there are powerful forces who will attempt to smother the slightest whimper of dissent.

It is likely that Hitchens's phrase 'men of god in other robes' was an allusion to Rowan Williams, the former Archbishop of Canterbury, who claimed that sharia law in the United Kingdom was 'unavoidable'. During a lecture at the Royal Courts of Justice in February 2008, Williams argued that sharia law would help members of the Muslim community who felt alienated from the British legal system to overcome the 'stark alternatives of cultural loyalty or state loyalty'. In a sense, this was a candid admission that multiculturalism creates parallel societies, something that its critics have long known. Whereas true liberals support a multiracial society with shared cultural values, multiculturalists promote a system that leads to incompatible groups living disparate lives. As citizens of a secular democracy, we naturally incline in favour of freedom of belief and worship and condemn those who seek to suppress it. And yet those of us who maintain that the belief-system of Islam is essentially wrong, that the veiling of women is rooted in misogyny, and that no religious icon should be exempt from ridicule, are often dismissed with the 'Islamophobia' slur. This is to conflate the actions of bigots and criminals with those who are simply exercising their right to criticise ideas. Worse still, this is a form of linguistic sleight-of-hand that the government of the United Kingdom is only too happy to mimic in its policy-making.

In February 2025, for instance, Deputy Prime Minister Angela Rayner revealed her plans for the establishment of a sixteen-member council on 'Islamophobia' which could lay the groundwork for the future implementation of yet another vaguely defined term on the statute books. The chair was named as Dominic Grieve, the former Conservative attorney general, who wrote the foreword to the report by the All-Party Parliamentary Group (APPG) in November 2018 which made the incoherent claim that 'Islamophobia is rooted in racism and is a type of racism that targets expressions of Muslimness or perceived Muslimness'. The inelegance of the phrase is unconscionable enough, but the conflation of religion and racism makes no sense whatsoever. There are over two billion Muslims in the world, and they belong to multiple ethnicities. To criticise Islam is to criticise an idea, not a racial demographic. If we wish to live in a free society, that means we must retain the right to reject or embrace ideologies as we see fit. We would not outlaw 'Islamophobia' any more than we should 'Christianophobia', 'Marxistophobia' or 'Freemarketcapitalismophobia'. If the APPG's definition were to be applied in law, there is little doubt that mocking or decrying Islam could be criminalised along with attacks on mosques and Muslims. Given that assault and vandalism are already illegal, what exactly would be the purpose of this redefinition other than to suppress freedom of speech? A phrase such as 'anti-Muslim prejudice' would be more accurate and less open to weaponisation, but to criminalise prejudice would be to criminalise human nature. One may as well outlaw lust.

The conflation of race and belief is, of course, a strategic means to silence dissent. Most of us in the West have reached the consensus that racism is an intolerable evil, and so by making criticism of Islam akin to racial hatred, we implicitly render such criticism beyond the scope of acceptability. This is perhaps why so many intersectional campaigners are silent on the treatment of women in Islamic theocracies. While Western 'progressives' are claiming that the veil is empowering, courageous women in Iran are throwing off these oppressive garments and dancing in the streets. This is in spite of the risks of imprisonment and violence by the 'morality police'. As I noted in Chapter 2, the term 'Islamophobia', like many other 'phobias', is an attempt to pathologise perfectly legitimate points of view. As a tactic, it's about as sophisticated as saying: 'Oh, don't pay any attention to him. He's a nutcase.'

The term 'Islamophobia' apparently dates back as early as 1910, when it appeared in the French form *islamophobie* in an essay by Alain Quellien, and was popularised in the 1970s by Iranian Islamic fundamentalists. Like all ideologues, they understood that cultural revolutions are best achieved through the control of language. All factions in the culture war are prone to sloganeering and the deployment of thought-terminating clichés to circumvent the necessity for debate, such as 'the right side of history' or 'God made Adam and Eve, not Adam and Steve'. The propagation of the term 'Islamophobia' works in much the same way. It prevents open discussion about Islamic beliefs by stigmatising those who participate.

We saw this explicitly when the European Court of Human Rights agreed with a court in Austria that criticism of the Prophet Mohammed was 'beyond the permissible limits of an objective debate'. As Qanta Ahmed pointed out in the *Spectator*, this was offensive to Muslims because it infantilised them by implying they should be treated like children who are prone to violent tantrums when insulted. In criminalising the denigration of Islam, the government of the United Kingdom would effectively be asserting that Muslims are second-class citizens who need to be protected from the realities of life in a pluralistic society. Would this not be a violation of its own principle? Might not the implementation of a law against 'Islamophobia' itself be an act of Islamophobia? These are dizzying possibilities that remind us that the state should never attempt to control the speech or thoughts of its citizens. Islam's disciples are not entitled to a life free from offence. Anti-Muslim hatred and prejudice exist and ought to be criticised, but they are not the same as the mockery or denunciation of a religious creed.

## The Iron Mullah

In his novel, *Shalimar the Clown* (2005), Salman Rushdie traces the deterioration of Kashmir from an idyll where Muslims and Hindus could live together in peace and cooperation to a country ravaged by conflict. This descent is signalled early in the story with the arrival of a character called the Iron Mullah, a blood-and-thunder preacher with 'skin the colour of rusting metal'. We think his name is metaphorical, but the Iron Mullah has risen from the scrapheaps of the Indian army, the junkyards of weaponry and tanks that have been left to decay. When he arrives, he removes his turban and raps his knuckles against his head so that the locals can hear the metallic clang. It's Rushdie's way of portraying the idea that it was the actions of the Indian army that gave rise to the appeal of Islamic extremism in Kashmir. Soon after the appearance of the Iron Mullah, a local Muslim man challenges him.

'Be off with you. We don't want any trouble, and you, standing here in the middle of our little town and yelling your head off about the punishments of hell – you look like trouble to me.' 'There are big infidels,' replied the stranger calmly, 'who deny God and his Prophet; and then there are little infidels like you, in whose belly the heat of faith has long since cooled, who mistake tolerance for virtue and harmony for peace.'

For the likes of the Iron Mullah, moderate peaceful Islam is just another form of heresy. He soon has a mosque built in which he preaches from a pulpit made of scrap metal, old bits of radiator and 'bent fenders spearing upwards like horns'. He is a frightening and ridiculous figure, but everyone is too intimidated to laugh. *Shalimar the Clown* was published in 2005, sixteen years after the fatwa issued by the Ayatollah Khomeini of Iran drove its author into hiding. Religious intolerance is something that Rushdie has had to live with for most of his life. Whereas extremists cannot reason and therefore resort to violence, Rushdie's power has always been in his words. His depiction of Kashmir's degeneration from an ecumenical paradise to a sectarian warzone is heart-rending and ranks among his best writing.

The fatwa had been a reaction to Rushdie's novel *The Satanic Verses* (1988), and specifically a subplot that imaginatively reinterpreted the founding stories of Islam. After the death sentence was pronounced, one would have hoped for a unified front on behalf of one of our finest writers. Instead, much of the literary and political establishment abandoned or even censured him. Crime novelist John le Carré stated that 'there is no law in life or nature that says great religions may be insulted with impunity' and that 'there is no absolute standard of free speech in any society'. On the Australian television show *Hypotheticals*, the singer Yusuf Islam, formerly known as Cat Stevens, strongly implied that he would have no objections to Rushdie being burned alive. The host Geoffrey Robertson asked Islam whether he would consider attending a demonstration where an effigy of Rushdie was to be burned. Islam's response was: 'I would have hoped that it'd be the real thing.' That a work of fiction such as *The Satanic Verses* could not even be published today gives us some indication of the extent to which we have forsaken the principle of free speech.

The evil spectre of the Iron Mullah was resurrected in August 2022, when an Islamist fanatic attempted to murder Rushdie at an event in New York, leaving him struggling for his life in hospital with multiple stab wounds. Although there was widespread condemnation, the silence from certain quarters was curious to say the least. In particular, most would have anticipated some kind of response from the Royal Society of Literature (RSL), founded in 1820 and devoted to representing the leading literary figures in the United Kingdom. In February 2024, fellows of the RSL finally came forward to criticise the charity's leadership for not being forthcoming on condemning the atrocity. The RSL's former president, Dame Marina Warner, revealed that its leadership had refused to issue a statement in support of Rushdie's right to free expression because to do so 'might give offence'. Apparently the feelings of knife-wielding maniacs and their apologists must be prioritised over those they gouge. The RSL's thinking on the subject was then outlined in a piece for the *Guardian* by its president, Bernardine Evaristo:

> Finally, to the matter of 'freedom of speech'. There's no question that the current leadership believe in this. However, the society has a remit to be a voice for literature, not to present itself as 'the voice' of its 700 fellows, surely a dangerous and untenable concept. It cannot take sides in writers' controversies and issues, but must remain impartial.

The best response to this glib effort at evasion came from Rushdie himself. 'Just wondering if the Royal Society of Literature is "impartial" about attempted murder . . . ? (Asking for a friend.)' Apparently, remaining 'impartial' means not issuing statements of support for authors when there are attempts to cancel them both figuratively and literally. When activists hounded the poet Kate Clanchy with spurious allegations of racism and ableism in her award-winning memoir *Some Kids I Taught and What They Taught Me* (2019), the RSL were mute. 'They would not make a stand about the attacks on Clanchy,' said Warner, or mount any kind of defence 'for all writers facing these social media attacks'.

In recent years, we have seen attempts by activists of many stripes to conflate language and violence, to claim that offensive words can cause the equivalent of physical harm. By this kind of twisted logic, bloody repercussions against authors and artists can be deemed a form of self-defence. A survey of American students in 2017 found that 30 per cent of respondents agreed with the statement: 'If someone is using hate speech or making racially charged comments, physical violence can be justified to prevent this person from espousing their hateful views.' Of course, the RSL is not responsible for assaults against authors, but it does have a duty to offer vocal support to the principle of artistic freedom, particularly when so many are tacitly blaming Rushdie for writing his novel in the first place. The bitter reality is that terrorism works, especially when so many governments across the Western world are seemingly willing to take a chisel to our bedrock of liberal values. This has been encouraged, in part, by an alliance of two very different forms of authoritarianism: ultra-conservative Islamic dogma and the ideology of the woke. The latter has always claimed that causing offence is no different from physical brutality, and the former has been quick to adopt the same tactics.

As a result, we have permitted a climate of intimidation to develop which enforces blasphemy laws against Islam in an unwritten form. How many stagings of *Tamburlaine* in our time would include the scene in which the Koran is destroyed? Even as far back as 2005, director David Farr added books from other religions to the on-stage pyre in his production at the Barbican. He claimed that this was an artistic decision, but others accused him of tempering Marlowe's play for Islamic sensibilities. In March 2023, a fourteen-year-old autistic boy was suspended from his school in Wakefield, reported to the police, and received death threats after he accidentally dropped a copy of the Koran on the floor, causing some of the pages to be scuffed. He might not have committed a crime, but the authorities behaved as though he had. The same unwritten laws are evident from the plain truth that few would be brave enough to publish cartoons of the Prophet Mohammed after the massacre at the offices of French satirical magazine *Charlie Hebdo* in 2015. Five years later, the schoolteacher Samuel Paty was beheaded on the streets of Paris after allegations that he had showed the offending images during a lesson. Rumours that he had ordered Muslim pupils to leave the classroom were based on lies spread by one schoolgirl who was not present and was attempting to avoid punishment from her parents after being suspended for poor behaviour.

It is sadly inevitable that such severe allegations would be uncritically trusted, even when the source was a child with a grudge. In Stalin's Russia, children were known to inform on their parents, a betrayal that would sometimes result in death by firing squad. During the Chinese Cultural Revolution, innocent mothers and fathers were executed after their children had overheard them criticising Chairman Mao. In the 1980s, Nicolae Ceaușescu blackmailed thousands of Romanian children to spy on their families and teachers. Closer to home, at the Batley Grammar School in West Yorkshire in March 2021, pupils attempted to film their teacher on their phones in order to see him denounced. It had been a Religious Studies lesson on blasphemy, and cartoons of the Prophet Mohammed had been shown. Given that these same images had been the catalyst for the massacre at the *Charlie Hebdo* offices and the beheading of Paty, they could not have been more relevant to the subject of the lesson, but this was not sufficient to save the teacher. Some of the pupils were offended, and so his fate was sealed.

One is reluctant to blame the young in such instances. Like the thirteen-year-old Briony Tallis in Ian McEwan's novel *Atonement* (2001), children generally cannot grasp the implications of turning informer on an innocent man. After the complaints, the teacher at

Batley Grammar was suspended, and his name was published by a group called Muslim Action Forum along with false accusations that he had incited hatred against the Islamic community. Protesters gathered outside the school demanding that he be fired. After anonymous death threats were issued, the teacher retreated from public life and went into hiding. What does it say about our society that a man is threatened with murder simply for doing his job, while his employers, his union, and the police fail to adequately defend him? Why were those sending the death threats not tracked down and arrested? Why were there no counter-demonstrations against the religious zealots who gathered outside the school? Why did the headmaster not issue a statement to the effect that this is a free society, and those who are offended by cartoons have no right to censor others for the sake of their own feelings?

Inevitably, the mob at Batley Grammar borrowed from the modish lexicon of Critical Social Justice in an effort to achieve their goals. Spokesmen – and they were all men – appealed to the 'safety and well-being' of the pupils in the face of the 'threatening and provocative' conduct of the teacher, and the need for the school to observe its 'duty of safeguarding'. Similarly, the Muslim Council of Britain criticised the school for not maintaining an 'inclusive space'. This was a sinister alliance of religious fundamentalism and 'safetyism', a term coined by journalist Pamela Paresky to denote the elevation of emotional 'safety' to a sacred value. When activists say 'this person makes me feel unsafe', they are effectively saying 'I don't agree with this person and I want them to be censored.' Depressingly, this tactic generally works. Event organisers, school authorities, and employers feel obliged to act because they are gulled into believing that this is an issue relating to their legal duty of care. But disagreement and causing offence are not a threat to anyone's safety, and we need to stop pandering to anyone who claims otherwise.

A striking example of this strategy occurred in April 2024 at the National Conservatism Conference in Brussels. Emir Kir, a local mayor, dispatched the police to disrupt the gathering on the grounds that the attendees – including leader of the Reform Party Nigel Farage, and former Home Secretary Suella Braverman – were 'far right', and that he had taken this action 'to guarantee public safety'. But did he really suppose that these politicians exercising their right to free speech were a threat to anyone? Was Farage likely to run amok with a truncheon, or was Braverman going to erupt in a frenzy and start nibbling immigrants? We all know that 'far right' is generally used by the woke as a smear rather than an accurate political description. But even if we take the mayor's claims at face value – that he was genuinely concerned that right-leaning figures gathering to discuss politics could grease the slippery slope to widespread public radicalisation – it takes an acute kind of cognitive dissonance to maintain that ordering the police to crack down on freedom of assembly is the best antidote to fascism.

Virtually every tyrant in history has invoked 'public safety' to justify suppression, so perhaps the sinister misuse of language by the likes of Kir is a deliberate form of goading. When Twitter set up its 'Trust and Safety Council' to limit the scope of permissible opinions on its platform, was it consciously echoing the 'Committee of Public Safety' of the Reign of Terror during the French Revolution? Was it channelling the spirit of Robespierre who presided over this *de facto* executive cabinet to impose the *'une volonté une'* ('one single will') that he felt was required to keep his rivals in check? The same linguistic oleaginousness was evident when the academic and writer Alka Sehgal Cuthbert was 'No Platformed' from the 'Rethinking Education' conference in September 2023. Although she was the only ethnic minority individual on the panel, some claimed that her opposition to Critical Race Theory made them feel 'unsafe'. Having dropped Alka from the bill, they were able to go ahead with an all-white panel in the name of diversity.

The most revealing aspect of the case at Batley Grammar School was the collective failure of the authorities to support the teacher against the demands of theocrats. It is yet another instance of those who claim to be defending the dignity of Muslims by treating them as irascible children. In March 2024, a report by Dame Sara Khan was published by the government, which delved into the problem of cancel culture and censorship by the mob. The Batley Grammar School incident was specifically mentioned as an example of how not to react in these circumstances. Khan spoke to the teacher as part of the consultation for her report, and he revealed that the ordeal left him feeling suicidal and that he had been 'thrown under the bus' by school authorities. Rather than accept the criticism, the Batley Multi Academy Trust responded by claiming that they had fulfilled their responsibility and that Khan's report contained 'inaccuracies'. They did not indicate what these 'inaccuracies' might be. It is notoriously difficult to be specific when one is attempting to promote an imaginary narrative.

Khan's report makes for grim reading. According to her survey, 85 per cent of the public are aware of the existence of freedom-restricting harassment in the United Kingdom, and 76 per cent have self-censored to avoid such treatment at the hands of angry mobs, either online or in the real world. Those of us who have been paying attention will already know that we are living in a climate of conformity, and that cancel culture is very real, in spite of the continual denials from commentators whose opinions happen to fall within the ever-narrowing Overton Window. For instance, in October 2022, the comedian and BBC presenter Graham Norton suggested that a better term for cancel culture would be 'accountability'. But is it really fair to harass, defame and ruin people's lives simply for expressing commonly held opinions? What exactly are they being held accountable for?

Khan recommended that the government tackle this growing problem through the establishment of 'an independent, impartial Office for Social Cohesion and Democratic Resilience (OSCDR)'. While the intention is sound, it might be better simply to urge those in authority – whether they be in the police, the schools or the trade unions – to regrow their spines and stand up for the principle of free speech. We might also ask them to consider treating Muslims in precisely the same way as everybody else, rather than patronisingly assuming that they require a parallel system of law and ethics. It is surely a soft form of bigotry to regard a particular contingent among our citizenry to be singularly prone to violence. A further recommendation in Khan's report is that schools should be ringfenced with 'a buffer zone of 150m'. This would prevent protests from occurring 'with the possible exception of pickets relating to industrial action by school staff'. Although there is much to admire in this effort to tackle the problem, those of a liberal disposition will remain unconvinced that further restrictions against protests are the answer. So often in history we have seen the behaviour of unreconstructed mobs used as justification for authoritarian impositions. Once such legislation is passed, there can be no guarantees that it will not be exploited in the future for purposes well beyond its original scope. One obvious example is the 'Battle of Cable Street' on 4 October 1936, the moment when demonstrators intercepted Oswald Mosely's 'blackshirts' at their march in the East End of London. It was the Labour Party that campaigned most assiduously for public order legislation to stop further uprisings by the far right, but these very same laws have since mostly been invoked to crack down on left-wing activism, most notably the arrests of striking miners during the Thatcher years.

The right to peaceful protest is a fundamental aspect of living in a free society, and while I do not agree with the cause espoused by the groups who gathered outside Batley Grammar, they were not breaking the law. There were no calls for violence or threats, just weak and unconvincing appeals to the 'safety' of the Muslim community, in spite of the fact that the only person who had experienced any authentic physical danger from the showing of the cartoon was the teacher himself. The protests outside the school were never the problem; it was the lily-livered response from the authorities. The Batley Grammar debacle should serve as a reminder that we must be steadfast when it comes to the application of the law and the equal treatment of all citizens. No mob should be entitled to the 'heckler's veto', to decide where the limits of freedom of speech are to be drawn. Capitulation might seem like a tempting short-term solution but, as we have seen, the long-term consequences are invariably dire.

The story of Batley Grammar shows that we are still living under the shadow of the Rushdie affair, and our failure to take a firm and uncompromising stance when it mattered most. It should never have been difficult to reach an immediate consensus that violence is not an appropriate reaction to a novel, or that one of the most acclaimed authors of our time should be granted the same privilege of free speech as everyone else. It is doubtless the case that very few of the swivel-eyed demagogues who condemned *The Satanic Verses* had actually read it. This was never really about people reading a book and finding its contents offensive, it was about philistines who had not read the book and chose to be offended anyway because some Iron Mullah had demanded they should be. When it comes to freedom of expression, we all need to be a little braver. We need to remind those who complain about works of fiction that their offence is their own business. They do not get to dictate the reading habits of other people, or to decide which cartoons should or should not be drawn, or which ideas should or should not be ridiculed or critiqued. How often must we fail these tests before the fabric of society is irreparably torn? In his memoir *Joseph Anton* (2012) – the pseudonym adopted during his time under police protection – Rushdie includes the following letter to a reader:

> Thank you for your kind words about my work. May I make the elementary point that the freedom to write is closely related to the freedom to read, and not have your reading selected, vetted and censored for you by any priesthood or Outraged Community? Since when was a work of art defined by the people who didn't like it? The value of art lies in the love it engenders, not the hatred. It's love that makes books last. Please keep reading.

This is sound advice. We need to keep reading, speaking and think-ing, in spite of those Iron Mullahs of the world who would compel us to stop.

## A Cautionary Tale

It's not often I get invited to a palace. True, the ornate seventeenth-century Van der Nootska Palatset in Stockholm is relatively small, but as a venue for a book launch it certainly beats a conference room in a Travelodge. The event took place in October 2023, and I had been invited to dinner and drinks to mark the translation of three of my books into Swedish by Nopolar Publishing, a new company that specialises in heterodox writing. The palace was built in 1674 and, thanks to the renovations in the late nineteenth century, retains much of its original charm. In the hour before the dinner, I was able to mingle with some of the attendees. One of them informed me that the palace was haunted by a mermaid. This supernatural creature refrained from making an appearance, which was admittedly something of a disappointment.

During the course of the evening, I found myself speaking to a number of residents of Stockholm about local politics. These were mostly middle-class liberals, and so it was mildly surprising that many of them seemed keen to discuss the question of mass immigration. I don't recall every aspect of every conversation that night, but one remark from a soft-spoken woman has stayed with me. She expressed the view that Swedish people tended to take liberalism for granted, and that they had assumed newcomers would be eager to adopt the values of the nation that had welcomed them. Now many feared that this was warm-hearted naïvety, and that the government had not done enough to ensure widespread integration. She closed by muttering in a plaintive tone: 'we got it wrong'.

Sweden now serves as a kind of cautionary tale for other European countries. According to its national police chief, the rapid surge in migration over the past decade has led to an 'unprecedented' rise in gang warfare between those who do not respect the rule of law. Yet the woman's comments about the general liberal approach of the population is borne out by the statistics. In 2007, the Pew Research Center found that Sweden had the second highest level of social trust among the forty-seven countries included in the survey. 78 per cent of respondents agreed with the statement that 'most people in this society are trustworthy', the highest figure in all of Europe. Over many years Sweden has cultivated its image as an activist nation, a 'moral superpower' as political scientist Lars Trägårdh termed it, with an international foreign policy that favoured left-wing and revolutionary causes. This accounts for the popular assumption that refugees would adapt to the Swedish way of life. Theirs seemed to be the kind of rose-tinted worldview that mirrored Rousseau's conception of the innate sense of liberty and equality in humankind's 'state of nature'.

Innocence has been obliterated by experience. Citizens without a shred of racial prejudice are now alarmed by gang violence and grenade attacks in the suburbs, enclaves of immigrants living in isolation from Swedish culture and traditions, and the spread of Islamic extremism. I remember being astonished when a friend of mine, the Swedish stand-up comedian Tobias Persson, expressed his exasperation in a private message in September 2022. He wrote:

> We have had daily shootings for years now. People who are horrified now have done *nothing* about shootings, honour killings, kids getting robbed, we've had big middle eastern clan-fighting in the streets (50–70 people kicking each other in the head) and stuff like this ... and the progressive woke people just pretend that it's business as usual. Of course I hate populism and right-wing parties but no one else *dares* to tackle reality ...

Matters have only worsened since then, and the election of a right-leaning coalition government in September 2022 suggests that public patience is wearing thin. Nima Gholam Ali Pour, an Iranian-born politician for the *Sverigedemokraterna* (Sweden Democrats), has said that 'Sweden has had very difficult problems with immigration in recent years', with 'areas that are 90 per cent immigrants who don't accept Swedish values and where ethnic Swedes have had to move out'. In spite of once boasting a crime rate significantly lower than most of its European neighbours, Sweden is now known as 'the gun-crime capital of the continent, fuelled by violent gangs disproportionately made up of first-generation migrants who control the nation's illicit drug and prostitution trades'. With the exception of Mexico, Sweden has the highest incidence of grenade and bomb attacks in any nation not at war. This former high-trust society is at peril, and it is clear that this extraordinary experiment in multiculturalism has been a failure. While woke is in retreat in many Western nations, for Sweden it may be too late.

We can trace all this back to the country's so-called 'special period' from 2015 to 2018, during which refugees were admitted at unprecedented rates. The writer Malcom Kyeyune has described this as 'Sweden's cultural revolution', and argues that the shocking image of the Syrian boy Alan Kurdi – washed up on the shore of Turkey having perished during the attempted crossing – fostered a climate in which anyone who opposed unlimited immigration was branded a 'racist' or 'too self-interested to heed the humanitarian clarion call'. Subsequently, the country's collision with reality has forced even progressive commentators to accept that these immigration policies have led to an exponential rise in crime rates and an enhanced risk of violence to native Swedes. Kyeyune notes that the cruelty of immigrant gangs has even birthed a new term, *förnedringsrån*, to describe robberies that are carried out in such a way as to maximise the potential humiliation and injury to the victim.

Racists have been quick to capitalise on the disintegration of Swedish cultural life as proof that certain ethnicities are more prone to violence and anti-social behaviour. The insistence on cultural relativism – the conviction that there can be no absolute truths in morality given the diverse nature of human societies – has provided ammunition to reactionaries and race essentialists. Many countries do not record crime by the national origin of the perpetrators for fear of stoking racism, but those that do reveal a clear trend. It is indisputable, for instance, that immigrants from Muslim-majority 'Menapt' countries (Middle East, North Africa, Pakistan and Turkey) are wildly overrepresented in crime statistics. If we do not wish to provide succour to white nationalists, we surely need to acknowledge this reality and address the cultural differences that are the source of the problem. A man born in Pakistan is no more innately predisposed to rape than a man born in Scotland, but a culture that devalues women to the extent that they are subjected to extreme human rights violations – such as flogging or being stoned to death for 'sexual impropriety' – is far more likely to produce rapists. This should not be a controversial point.

In September 2024, there was widespread outrage when future leader of the Conservative Party, Kemi Badenoch, penned an article for the *Telegraph* in which she denied that 'all cultures are equally valid'.

> Culture is more than cuisine or clothes. It's also customs which may be at odds with British values. We cannot be naïve and assume immigrants will automatically abandon ancestral ethnic hostilities at the border, or that all cultures are equally valid. They are not. I am struck for example, by the number of recent immigrants to the UK who hate Israel. That sentiment has no place here.

With depressing predictability, these remarks prompted many to decry Badenoch as a 'fascist', a 'racist', an 'extremist', and all those other epithets that have been denuded of any significance through continual misuse. One wonders what cultural relativists would make of the Aztecs. If they could travel back in time, how might they console the bawling infants who were being sacrificed to Tlaloc, the god of rain and earthly fertility? 'Stop complaining,' they would probably say, 'this is just your culture.'

The folly of cultural relativism is usually tied to a loathing of Western imperialism and a reluctance to criticise any nation that has faced historical mistreatment at its hands. To pass judgement on cultures that our ancestors may have subdued is seen as a manifestation of a superiority complex, a sour vestige of Empire and the paternalistic assumption that our civilisation is best. The condemnation of unfamiliar cultural mores is thereby perceived as an extension of colonial oppression. It is of course true that ethnical mores fluctuate according to time and place, but this does not mean that we should not be able to measure one cultural norm against another. True inclusivity and equality means holding everyone to the same standards. If we decide that all morality is relative, then the very notion of Right and Wrong becomes redundant. We may as well abandon the concept of a moral compass altogether. Even if one were to argue that universal human rights is a Western construct, that does not mean the principle ought to be jettisoned. Activists who are seemingly obsessed with the United Kingdom's past complicity in the slave trade clearly have no trouble in condemning that particular culture, alien as it is to our own. It is therefore incoherent for them to claim that cultures where slavery is still practised today are not also deserving of censure.

In many ways, of course, Badenoch's critics already tacitly accept that our culture has advantages over others. When they fall ill, do they book an appointment with their general practitioner, or do they contact a soothsayer in Tanzania who might analyse their dreams for the presence of demons and prescribe a broth of rare plants and herbs? After Mahatma Gandhi's wife was diagnosed with pneumonia, he refused to allow her the shot of penicillin which would have saved her life. Tellingly, his mistrust of Western medicine seemed to evaporate when he himself caught malaria and allowed doctors to treat him with quinine. When it comes to science, medicine and technology, in other words, we all accept that some cultures are more advanced than others. Why should the same principle not apply to ethics? I am perfectly comfortable in asserting that our culture is morally superior to those that treat women as second-class citizens, or murder people for being gay, or mutilate the genitals of children, or force young girls into marriage, or call for the genocide of Jews. That self-declared 'progressives' would consider this to be a reactionary position shows the extent to which they have lost their way.

I am not suggesting that human beings should be valued according to the norms of their culture. Had we been born a few centuries ago, we would have doubtless supported many things that we now abhor. Similarly, if we were raised in an Islamic theocracy, we would almost certainly end up holding very different views about human rights or free speech or democracy. A recognition that we are all products of our upbringing and tradition does not mean that we should dispense with the notion of moral appraisal altogether, or make excuses for societies in which abhorrent crimes have become normalised. This is not to imply that our foreign policy ought to be based on the project of 'civilising' other nations, or that there are not cultural practices of our own that are worthy of criticism. However, we can surely all agree that basic human rights should not be restricted to those who are fortunate enough to live in liberal democracies. Nor is it acceptable that governments that deny such rights to their citizens should escape scrutiny on the grounds of cultural differences. We have reached a consensus in the West that all human life is precious, irrespective of immutable characteristics. For all our failings, we should consider ourselves lucky that we have progressed beyond the days of child labour, slavery and the criminalisation of homosexuality. To ignore human rights abuses abroad is to take a high-handed and superior position as 'betters' to an 'uncivilised' other. Badenoch's critics are not only morally confused, but also fail to understand that hers is the genuinely progressive stance.

This is why a realistic assessment of criminal trends according to cultural origin is necessary, while at the same time we should acknowledge that the results may be exploited by those with a nefarious agenda. The journalist Michael Murphy addressed this problem in a piece for the *Telegraph* in May 2024. He cited data from the Danish government which shows that although non-Western immigrants constitute only 9 per cent of the population, they account for 25 per cent of convictions for violent crime. He went on to outline that this trend is replicated in other Nordic countries.

> In Denmark and Sweden, immigrants are twice as likely to commit violent crime as the native populations. The pattern becomes even starker with certain types of crime: in Sweden, from 2013–17, immigrants were three times more likely to be registered as a suspect for assault than the native population – which grows to four times for robbery, and five times for rape.

While there may be many reasons to explain such egregious disparities, an open discussion about the problem is long overdue. Yet for years the British government claimed that it did not record such data, a head-in-the-sand admission that would only satisfy the most dogged of party apparatchiks. This struthious approach to societal malaise, one adopted by successive Conservative and Labour governments, effectively stymied the potential for any serious analysis. It was not until January 2025 that crime league tables according to nationality were released for the first time in the United Kingdom. Data from the police forces, the Home Office and the Office for National Statistics had been analysed by the Centre for Migration Control. The results were startling. We now know that foreign nationals are three times more likely to be arrested for sexual offences, and twice as likely for all other crimes. This presents a challenge to those of us who believe in liberal values. We might factor in relative poverty as contributing to the rates, but this in itself cannot possibly account for the excessive disproportionality. Our history of supporting those fleeing from war or oppression is something we should cherish, but at the same time citizenship should be contingent on successful integration. Nobody is suggesting that immigrants ought to dispense with their own beliefs or practices, but it does mean that they must adapt to the rule of law of the host nation.

Well-intentioned progressive commentators who attempt to overlook the crime data relating to nationality are doing their cause no favours. When police in the north of England failed to enforce the law against predominately Pakistani rape gangs for fear of being branded 'racist', they were not only complicit in the sexual assault of thousands of children, but they also gave a publicity boost to those on the far right who were sounding the alarm. The public were first alerted to the scandal with the revelations about mass child sex abuse in the English town of Rotherham in 2010, before it became clear that similar gangs were operating in Rochdale and Telford. A report by Professor Alexis Jay in 2022 eventually determined that more than 1,400 young girls were raped and abused by what became known as the 'grooming gangs', comprising mostly of men of Pakistani heritage, in the period between 1997 and 2013. The report noted that several members of council staff 'described their nervousness about identifying the ethnic origins of perpetrators for fear of being thought as racist; others remembered clear direction from their managers not to do so'. A further inquiry into similar crimes in Telford found that police did not adequately investigate those accused of child sexual exploitation because they felt it would be 'too politically incorrect'.

Some of the stories are blood-curdling. Andrew Norfolk, a reporter for *The Times*, described one occasion when police discovered a thirteen-year-old girl, inebriated and mostly naked, in the company of seven Pakistani men. Instead of questioning the adults, the police arrested the girl for being drunk and disorderly. Politicians and media commentators were more concerned with maintaining the fantasy that multiculturalism has been a success, rather than taking seriously their obligation to safeguard children. When Julie Bindel – the first journalist to investigate the grooming gangs – tried to publish her findings, she faced resistance 'because some editors feared an accusation of racism'.

After a renewed outcry in January 2025, the Labour government showed itself incapable of making amends. Prime Minister Keir Starmer stated that politicians demanding a full-scale inquiry into these failings were jumping 'on a bandwagon of the far right'. This acute form of tone-deafness would, in any sound political climate, be cause for immediate resignation. While it is true that racists will be quick to weaponise the criminal behaviour of a minority, there is nothing remotely 'far right' in taking an interest in the well-being of children and wishing to see those who abuse them held to account. This was never an issue of left or right, but a simple matter of right and wrong. Political tribalism and a callow fear of societal division had led to an unforgivable failure of safeguarding and justice. As I have argued, an essential aspect of liberalism is that all citizens must be equally subject to the rule of law, irrespective of their race, sex or creed. Far from revealing liberalism's weakness, the rape gangs scandal showed what happens when its principles are not applied. There is little doubt that multiculturalism, in its current form, is an essentially anti-liberal philosophy.

Even as far back as 2010, German Chancellor Angela Merkel was asserting that multiculturalism had 'utterly failed', which makes her later policy of unchecked immigration even more bewildering. Too often 'multiculturalism' is mistaken for 'multiracialism', when the two could not be more different. A multiracial society is one in which people of all races are able to coexist together in peace and cooperation as equal citizens under the law. A multicultural society is one in which people are encouraged to ghettoise themselves according to national or cultural identity. Multiculturalism has been a catastrophe not only for social cohesion but also for individual agency. In 2016, when Prime Minister David Cameron announced a £20 million fund for English lessons for the 22 per cent of Muslim women in the United Kingdom who could not speak the language, he was accused of 'stigmatising' a marginalised group. In truth, he was doing the opposite. Women in Islamic communities are disproportionately impacted by the failed multicultural system, because encouraging parallel societies only benefits the most powerful within them.

At time of writing there are eighty-five sharia courts – known euphemistically as 'councils' – operating in Britain. Many of them were established in 1982 with the formation of the Islamic Sharia Council of Great Britain and Northern Ireland, a registered charity which oversees marriage and divorce proceedings. *The Times* reports that Britain is now the 'Western capital' for sharia courts, 'with men able to end their marriages by saying "divorce" three times'. As many human rights campaigners have pointed out, the existence of sharia courts effectively relegates women to second-class citizens. According to Diana Nammi, founder of the Iranian & Kurdish Women's Rights Organisation, in these courts women have 'half the worth of men . . . In some cases, imams forced women to withdraw their court orders and go back to their husbands. They are mediating but they don't consider violence as a reason for divorce. Some don't think rape happens within marriage: it's a woman's duty to be ready any time.' An app for Muslim men, approved by British sharia courts, includes the option to select one to four wives and accords daughters half the inheritance value of sums received by sons. While defenders of sharia courts insist that they have no legal standing, the fact remains that women from ultra-conservative religious families have no choice but to defer to their decisions. That such a parallel system exists at all in a supposedly secular nation would strongly suggest that our 'two-tier society' is not a myth. Religious belief has been subsumed into an identity category and treated as though it were an immutable characteristic worthy of protection. This is why, as Rakib Ehsan has pointed out, we should also be concerned about the existence of 'rabbinical courts, such as the London Beth Din, which refers to itself as "one of Europe's premier halachic authorities" – overseeing marriages, divorces, and conversions, as well as resolving British commercial disputes in a manner consistent with Jewish law'. When it comes to preserving a liberal democracy, consistency is key.

The creed of multiculturalism has made it difficult to discuss the impact of unfettered immigration, and for good reason. The genuine far right – not those who are merely smeared as 'far right' for the slightest deviation from the woke orthodoxy – has always opposed immigration on the basis of racial prejudice and ethno-jingoism. Yet there are authentically liberal concerns to be raised about the problem of political Islam and how all discussions are stifled through accusations of 'Islamophobia'. The cautionary tale of Sweden – a country of liberals scuppered by their own naïvety – shows what can happen when an essentially anti-democratic ideology is allowed to flourish within a society that otherwise depends upon democratic norms. Racists are able to capitalise on the silence of the browbeaten, which in turn generates the false impression that only they are willing to grapple with the issue. As a result, non-racist critics of calamitous immigration policies are inclined to keep quiet for the sake of an easy life. It's a vicious circle that guarantees that nothing is ever done for the minorities – women and gay people especially – whose protection is contingent on the preservation of a liberal system.

It was not an Iron Mullah that caused the problems in Sweden, but the ingenuousness of bighearted progressives. While Rushdie's *Shalimar the Clown* explores the mercilessly destructive power of fundamentalist religion, we might look to a much older novel to help illuminate the troubles of our time, and in particular the perverted form of liberalism that ensures its own undoing. I am thinking of G. K. Chesterton's *The Flying Inn* (1914), a whimsical tale about a future Islamic England. With today's proliferation of sharia courts and the government's determination to criminalise blasphemy against Islam by legislative stealth, one might call Chesterton's novel prescient. Yet when it was published at the tail end of the Edwardian era, its premise was seen as too absurdist to have any such pretensions. 'It might well be called "What Might Have Been"', noted the publisher's blurb, 'for it was sketched out before the legend of the Invincible Turk was broken'. Chesterton's satire, in other words, does not genuinely anticipate western susceptibility to Islamic doctrine, a case of a weaker force submitting to the strong, but rather the folly of liberals whose principles are so inconsistently upheld that they ultimately self-destruct.

The key figure in the novel is Lord Ivywood, a politician who becomes enamoured of Misysra Ammon, an Islamic cleric who styles himself as the 'Prophet of the Moon'. Ivywood is an exemplar of the zealotry of the progressive reformer, a prototype of the virtue signaller, one who 'did not care for dogs' but 'cared for the Cause of Dogs'. He first introduces Ammon at a private event at the 'Society of Simple Souls', where he is able to preach his creed to the gullible *bons vivants* of the upper middle class. The collective thrill of the crowd is pure orientalism, and they are easily mesmerised by Ivywood's panegyrics. Inevitably, Ivywood's submission to Islam is framed in syncretic terms; not so much surrender as a beautiful fusion. 'The East and the West are one,' Ivywood says. 'The East is no longer East nor the West West; for a small isthmus has been broken, and the Atlantic and Pacific are a single sea.' Islam, he claims, is the 'religion of progress', a phrase that anticipates today's oft-echoed slogan of Islam as the 'religion of peace'. This kind of doublespeak is ubiquitous among those activists who routinely strive to force the square peg of Islamic doctrine into the round hole of woke politics. This is exemplified by articles such as 'Prophet Muhammed was an intersectional feminist' in *Muslim Girl* magazine, a piece that includes the inane claim that the founder of the religion 'wanted to generate as much inclusivity as possible'. In similarly convoluted terms, Ammon in *The Flying Inn* argues that there is nothing more feminist than a harem. 'What is the common objection our worthy enemies make against our polygamy?' he asks. 'That it is disdainful of the womanhood. But how can this be so, my friends, when it allows the womanhood to be present in so large numbers?'

Today's readers will recognise Chesterton's depiction of the tendency of liberal politicians to kowtow to the demands of Islamic clerics in a bid to avoid causing offence. At one point, Ivywood explains that he has tabled the 'Ballot Paper Amendment Act' in Parliament to allow citizens to vote with a mark resembling a crescent rather than the traditional cross.

> If we are to give Moslem Britain representative government, we must not make the mistake we made about the Hindoos and military organization—which led to the Mutiny. We must not ask them to make a cross on their ballot papers; for though it seems a small thing, it may offend them. So I brought in a little bill to make it optional between the old-fashioned cross and an upward curved mark that might stand for a crescent—and as it's rather easier to make, I believe it will be generally adopted.

Just as the Muslim protesters at the Batley Grammar School appropriated the woke language of safetyism, the Prophet of the Moon soon learns to exploit Ivywood's rhetoric for the promotion of his belief-system. 'The Cause progress! Everywhere it progress!' he cries. 'The hygienic curve of the crescent will soon superimpose himself for your plus sign.' Even the game of 'Noughts and Crosses' is soon to be supplanted by 'Noughts and Crescents'.

For all that, the main plot of The Flying Inn revolves around the innkeeper Humphrey Pump and the Irish sailor Captain Patrick Dalroy, who take it upon themselves to sell alcohol in spite of the new Islamic prohibitions in England. They find a loophole in the law that permits them to conduct their business so long as they first erect an official inn sign. And so we follow the pair as they dash from location to location, with their barrel of rum and a wheel of cheese on a donkey's back, planting their portable sign wherever refreshment is needed. Like all farce, the implausibility is the point, and much of Chesterton's satire retains its relevance today. There is the continual excuse-making for the most regressive aspects of political Islam, the word games and historical revisionism as a means of ideological manipulation, and the tendency among the most privileged to rally around causes that are antagonistic to their interests. Ivywood seems like every affluent western liberal who eagerly stokes the incineration of his own society out of some desperate psychological need for a purpose. The key moment comes when Ivywood is asked: 'Do you think you made the world, that you should make it over again so easily?' 'The world was made badly,' Ivywood replies, 'and I *will* make it over again'. This could serve as a fitting epitaph for any of today's woke activists.

*The Flying Inn* ends with a sequence that strikes a discordantly ominous note. The women who have followed Ivywood suddenly realise that they are being collected for a harem. One aristocrat, Joan Brett, now understands that the true nature of the Islamic project was being introduced to England by stealth and deception. She explains to the other women that Ivywood believes in 'doing things slowly' and that he is probably 'getting us accustomed to living like this, so that it may be the less shock when he goes further – steeping us in the atmosphere before he actually introduces . . . the institution'. The final showdown comes when we discover that Ivywood has all along been concealing and preparing an Islamic army to conquer the country by force. As dusk approaches, Joan spies the torchlit warriors emerging in the grounds of Ivywood's estate.

> There flew the green standard of that great faith and strong civilization which has so often almost entered the great cities of the West; which long encircled Vienna, which was barely barred from Paris; but which had never before been seen in arms on the soil of England. At one end of the line stood Phillip Ivywood, in a uniform of his own special creation, a compromise between the Sepoy and Turkish uniform. The compromise worked more and more wildly in Joan's mind. If any impression remained it was merely that England had conquered India: and Turkey had conquered England.

This seems to be the realisation of what Dalroy had previously described as the 'four acts' of 'the great destiny of Empire': 'Victory over barbarians. Employment of barbarians. Alliance with barbarians. Conquest by barbarians.' Those who maintain that the West is committing suicide through its tolerance of the intolerant will find much to support their view in Chesterton's story. Yet its essentially farcical nature means that it lacks the proleptic power of the likes of Orwell's *Nineteen Eighty-Four*. Its caricatured rendering of Islam has all the subtlety of an acetylene blast. To better appreciate the recklessness of the gullible liberal, we might turn from *The Flying Inn* to another novel, one that has likewise slipped into the abyss of obscurity.

## Sweetness and Light

Anthony Burgess's early book *The Worm and the Ring* (1961) did not enjoy the kind of longevity its author had envisaged. The story was based on Burgess's time as a schoolmaster at Banbury Grammar School in the early 1950s. He had modelled some of the characters on real-life colleagues, and when one of them recognised herself in the portrayal of Alice, the headmaster's secretary, she threatened to sue. The book was withdrawn by the publishers and pulped. It has never been reprinted in its unexpurgated form and copies of the original edition are scarce.

The headmaster in the novel is Mr Woolton, whose authority is fatally undermined by his permissive predisposition. He prides himself on being one of the last of the liberal humanists, believing in 'Sweetness and light, the core of good which slept in all men, waiting to be awakened and revealed by time'. When the disconsolate English teacher Miss Fry complains to Mr Woolton about her unruly class, he suggests that she send the worst offenders to his office.

> 'But they just laugh.' She had taken a small, very clean handkerchief from her sleeve and was trying to stop the tears, ineffectually, like dabbing a new razor-cut.

'I'll hit them harder next time.' (But he knew he wouldn't; he hated the cane.) 'They won't laugh again.'

'They say it doesn't hurt. They're not frightened.'

It was true: it didn't hurt because it wasn't really meant to hurt. That rod in the corner was a fossil. He would much rather talk to the miscreant, make him see sweet liberal reason. They would, however, just listen sullenly: 'Yessir. Yessir.' And then quiet laughter in the corridor as they went off, having missed a whole period of PT.

I recognise Woolton's combination of pomposity and naïvety in a former employer of mine at a private school. This headmaster was so convinced in the merits of positive reinforcement that he was oblivious to the cynicism of many of the pupils. One of my tutees was known as the most wayward and underachieving boy in the school. On one occasion, the headmaster had called him in for a discussion about his lack of progress, and later reported back to me that the boy had simply stood there and smirked while he was being rebuked. 'The poor lad has a natural expression that looks like he's not taking anything seriously.' Such was his faith in the essential piety of youth that this amiably doltish man had no idea that he was being openly derided.

Woolton could be seen as an embodiment of Friedrich Nietzsche's comment in *Beyond Good and Evil* (1886): 'There is a point in the history of society when it becomes so pathologically soft and tender that among other things it sides even with those who harm it, criminals, and does this quite seriously and honestly.' The Chinese even have a word – *baizuo* (白左) – to describe these milksop white Western liberals whose generous nature leaves them open to exploitation. With the end of woke, there is a growing sense in which Western weakness, a certain dearth of masculine vigour, was responsible for its manifestation. George Orwell certainly took the view that a nation without strength would be soon overpowered by others willing to make the tough decisions. He explicitly defended the aerial bombardment of civilians as one of the war's ghastly inevitabilities, a fierce and uncivilised act in the service of future civilisation. When faced with the unique evil of Nazism, in other words, a limited war was not an option.

> You cannot be objective about an aerial torpedo. And the horror we feel of these things has led to this conclusion: if someone drops a bomb on your mother, go and drop two bombs on his mother. The only apparent alternatives are to smash dwelling houses to powder, blow out human entrails and burn holes in children with thermite, or to be enslaved by people who are more ready to do these things than you are yourself; as yet no one has suggested a practicable way out.

The tragic necessity for brutality in war is the extreme point of the principle explored by Burgess in *The Worm and the Ring*. Whereas Ivywood in *The Flying Inn* shows liberalism at its most naïve, elsewhere it has been depicted as too soft, too feminine, and insufficiently robust to tackle the challenge of those who reject its principles. In Shakespeare's *Troilus and Cressida* (c. 1601), for instance, Hector dies unarmed in an ambush because of his ingenuous faith that the codes of honour in battle would be observed by his foe. His fate could be said to represent the way in which liberalism is perceived by its critics, an ideal that shatters as it collides with the reality of human nature. While we extend the olive branch, our enemies beat us to death with it.

This criticism is especially germane when it comes to the question of immigration. The argument follows that if we permit an unmanageable influx from countries where free speech and individual liberty are not only undervalued, but actively disdained, the liberal approach is doomed to fail. We have a tradition of offering asylum for those in need, and we typically take a compassionate view towards foreigners seeking a more prosperous life. At the same time, there must be a degree of societal consensus for the ethos of any nation to survive at all. For where such a consensus is jeopardised, either through mass immigration or radical domestic political movements, the temptation to dispense with liberal values is inevitable. If we tolerate the intolerable, are we not at risk of following Woolton's example, of allowing ourselves to be exploited out of a guileless conviction that our generosity will be reciprocated? In Europe, we have seen Islamic clerics calling openly for sharia law and the upending of our liberal system. Patience is running short, and there is a burgeoning sense that those who do not value our culture ought to be forced to leave. But to call for the deportation of citizens who actively seek the demolition of our culture is to surrender our principles to the very people who oppose them. It is to resign oneself to authoritarianism in a perverse effort to defeat it.

How, then, might we address the problems that have attended mass migration at a rate that has prevented effective assimilation and has led to the erosion of the liberal consensus and the social contract? The escalating frequency of terrorist threats in Western countries is undeniably connected to these failures. In the United Kingdom, this has become most visible in the 'two-tier' policing strategies that have become all too obvious, as well as ongoing denials from the authorities that such problems exist at all. This lack of honesty has exacerbated frustrations from a public that has been expected to ignore observable reality in the name of political correctness. In December 2024, Surrey Police issued the following statement: 'Whilst you are out and about at events across Surrey in the festive period, you may see some armed police presence. We appreciate that this can be an alarming sight, which is why we wanted to take the time to reassure you that these are part of routine foot patrols to deter serious criminality and not in response to any particular threat.' In November 2024, Manchester City Centre Police had posted a similar statement, reassuring the public that the 'heightened police presence' at Christmas markets was simply 'to keep you all safe'. It is not difficult to detect the unsaid words screaming through this mealy-mouthed boilerplate.

There is something undeniably incongruous about the sight of happy-go-lucky police officers patrolling with lethal weapons at

Christmas as though it were the most unremarkable thing in the world. This represents a radical shift in recent years by which we have grown accustomed to public events requiring a perimeter of what some sarcastically call 'diversity barriers'. These huge steel bollards are designed to prevent a repeat of the appalling atrocity in Nice in July 2016, when a Tunisian jihadist ploughed through crowds of families on Bastille Day in a truck, killing eighty-six and injuring a further four hundred and thirty-four. For the police to claim that there is no 'particular threat' is unlikely to be believed by anyone with a memory more far-reaching than your average goldfish. There are many wholesome images we associate with the season of goodwill: trees bedecked with tinsel and baubles, elves distributing candy canes and enticingly wrapped gifts, Mariah Carey frolicking in the snow with that corpulent fellow in a fake beard. It is quite the development to add to that list anti-terror crash-barriers and armed police at festive markets. Is this the 'new normal'? Has the very concept of the high-trust society depleted to such an extent that a visit to Santa's grotto must now be supervised by uniformed men with machine guns? London Mayor Sadiq Khan famously claimed that terrorist attacks are simply 'part and parcel of living in a big city'. He may not have said it with a shrug, but a shrug was most definitely implied.

It is true of course that terrorists have always targeted the major metropolises. I have had the dubious pleasure of walking past the very spot in the subterranean passageways below Parliament where Guy Fawkes was apprehended in November 1605 while preparing his deadly explosives. I am old enough to remember the bombing of the gay pub the Admiral Duncan in London, and the various IRA atrocities in the city in the last decades of the twentieth century. And I will never forget attempting to check in at the airport for my flight to New York on 11 September 2001, only to be told that a plane had collided with the World Trade Center. I had assumed it was an accident involving a light aircraft and naïvely asked the question: 'Is there going to be much of a delay?'

Yet it is quite the stretch to suppose that these appalling acts of violence mean that we should downplay the threat of Islamist extremism. Nobody is suggesting that our major cities were once utopian oases of tranquillity and love, or that occasional outbreaks of violence are not inevitable wherever large numbers of human beings choose to dwell. The point is that we have a responsibility to prevent such incidents as best we can, and that means first acknowledging the nature of the problem. There is a very good reason why 75 per cent of MI5's counter-terrorism work is specifically related to Islamist threats. Many of these are directed towards children and other vulnerable targets by religious fanatics who believe that there is no higher cause than murdering innocent people as they go about their daily lives. We would never forgive our intelligence services if their bosses suddenly declared that they needn't bother any more on the grounds that terrorism is just 'part and parcel of living in a big city'.

Our social contract in this country has been cultivated over many generations. It has never been perfect, because there will always exist those who hold scant regard for the rights of their fellow citizens. The high-trust society will ever be precarious, but without it our lives would be continually plagued with anxiety and fear. In the face of even deadly risks, it is surely worth preserving. Yet in our larger cities, the values of the high-trust society seem to be in irreversible decline. How many of us would intervene if we were to witness an aggressive altercation between strangers on a street? Rising knife crime means that we could be injured or killed for doing the right thing, and so increasingly people are unwilling to take the chance. In some districts in the United States, thefts under $950 have been reduced to misdemeanours, which has prompted shop owners to protect even low-cost goods behind locked plexiglass. When I last visited New York, I was flabbergasted to find that an act as straightforward as buying a bottle of shampoo required a member of staff to fetch a key.

There has been a consensus among social scientists for many years that high-trust societies produce better results. A report by the Pew

Global Attitudes Project has noted that 'societies where people tend to trust each other' enjoy 'stronger democracies, richer economies, better health, and they suffer less often from any number of social ills'. The survey concluded that 'in countries where people generally trust one another, there are fewer worries about crime or corrupt political leaders'. And yet we seem to have glided into this new reality where automatic firearms are a standard feature of Christmas markets, theft is too common to prosecute, and strangers will not support each other in moments of peril. All of this suggests that our mutual trust has been supplanted by fear. While threats to public safety are undeniably real, these new and undesirable circumstances appear to have been meekly accepted as somehow inevitable rather than as symptoms of a broader failure of multicultural policy.

Fear is burgeoning on multiple fronts. On the one hand, members of the public are growing wary of the risks that attend the breakdown of the high-trust society, but are simultaneously frightened of articulating their concerns in case they are perceived as racist. This has left a lacuna for the far right to position itself as the only release valve for these mounting pressures. Calls for mass deportations are now extending into traditionally conservative discourse, and so the boundary between the right and the far right is in certain cases fast becoming indistinct. With hindsight, we might consider how our present circumstances would have been different had citizenship been more prudently bestowed. In November 2024, a video of the assault of a ninety-one-year-old woman at Sollentuna Station near Stockholm went viral. Her attacker, Syrian asylum seeker Karam Kanjo, was seen grabbing the victim and dragging her down a flight of stairs before pulling away her necklace. The judge in the subsequent trial described the incident as 'life-threatening' and sentenced the perpetrator to five and a half years in jail and forced him to pay damages. The shocking aspect of this story extends beyond the violence itself, given that Kanjo had been granted entry into Sweden in 2015 and had committed at least nineteen crimes since then. He had previously been incarcerated for rape in 2021 and later released on parole. His defence had included a plea that if deported he would be 'subjected to torture or inhumane treatment' in his home country. Our sympathy for a rapist and would-be killer of old women is inevitably limited.

It is instructive to consider how such a dangerous criminal could be permitted to reside in a country whose laws he had so flagrantly disregarded. It suggests an institutionalised gullibility, a refusal to accept that those who are hostile to the liberal social contract are unwilling to modify their conduct and beliefs accordingly. That is to say, the policy of mass migration from countries where liberal values are seen as a form of sacrilege has precluded any serious possibility of new citizens adapting to a Western way of life. The inevitable ghettoisation leaves little incentive for cultural assimilation, and the host nation is forced to adapt to the beliefs of immigrant communities rather than the other way round. This has a detrimental impact on minority groups who have struggled for decades by liberal means to achieve equal rights. The intersectional mindset that has conflated criticism of Islam with racism locates its followers at the very summit of the category of the oppressed, meaning that to denounce prevailing cultural practices in Muslim-majority countries is deemed unacceptable. This is why media outlets in thrall to the ideology of Critical Social Justice were slow to report the mass sexual assaults committed by immigrants at a New Year's Eve event in Cologne in 2015. After more than eight hundred and twenty women complained that they had been assaulted, the organisers of the *Kölner Karneval* (Cologne Carnival) in February 2016 issued pamphlets to inform migrants that raping women was unacceptable in German society. Matters have only worsened in the intervening years. In November 2024, Berlin's chief of police Barbara Slowik issued a warning that gay and Jewish people should be circumspect in how they present themselves in districts with large Arab populations. 'There are areas of the city,' she said, 'we need to be perfectly honest here, where I would advise people who wear a kippah or are openly gay to be more careful.' One would have thought that in

Berlin of all places, the idea that Jews and homosexuals are now encouraged to make themselves invisible to avoid violent repercussions would be cause for alarm.

This holding of migrants to lower moral standards is regressive in the extreme, a dehumanising and racist attitude that implies that they cannot possibly act in accordance with the law because 'they don't know any better'. Examples of this patronising mentality are plentiful. In April 2016, a Norwegian man who was raped by a migrant said that he felt 'a strong sense of guilt and responsibility' when his attacker was subsequently deported. 'I was the reason why he should not be left in Norway,' he said, 'but rather to face a very uncertain future in Somalia. He had already served his sentence in prison. Should he now be punished again? And this time much harder?' Some would argue that this is an instance of the liberal outlook taken to its most extreme conclusions. Yet the reductive classification of human society into distinct groups of oppressor and oppressed according to group identity, and the assumption that individuals who commit crimes should be treated differently according to their subset, is a markedly illiberal approach. A similar case saw a British Muslim spared jail after raping a thirteen-year-old girl due to his indoctrination at a madrassa. Having claimed that his religious upbringing had left him unaware that the rape of children was illegal, and that 'women are no more worthy than a lollipop that has been dropped on the ground', the judge suspended his sentence, saying that it was 'quite clear' that the rapist was 'very naïve and immature when it comes to sexual matters'.

The problem is more widespread than many would care to admit. An extensive poll for the Channel 4 documentary *What British Muslims Think* in 2016 found that 23 per cent supported the prospect of sharia law in the United Kingdom, 39 per cent believed that wives should always be obedient to husbands, 31 per cent agreed that bigamy was acceptable, 47 per cent said that gay people should never be allowed to teach in schools, and 52 per cent thought that homosexuality ought to be against the law. The show's presenter, anti-racism campaigner Trevor Phillips, was lambasted for describing the findings as 'extremely worrying', and was eventually suspended from the Labour Party after allegations of 'Islamophobia' for raising concerns about Pakistani grooming gangs and the need for a more 'muscular' approach to integration. When a majority of any given demographic take the view that gay people's sex lives should be a police matter, it is quite the stretch to claim this as an exemplar of successful cultural assimilation. Ultimately, the failure to criticise and oppose the anti-liberal norms within immigrant communities is a form of paternalism that prioritises the needs of their most reactionary factions. Sharia law may be an ambition for ultra-conservative theocrats, but many female and gay Muslims will not find it such an appealing prospect. For years we have been appeasing these minorities within minorities, small groups of extremists that by no means represent the average British Muslim. Perversely, the creed of woke 'tolerance' has resulted in excuse-making for homophobic, misogynistic and antisemitic practices and attitudes. To feel sympathy for rapists on the grounds of cultural difference must be the epitome of what Michael Gerson, a speechwriter for President George W. Bush, once described as 'the soft bigotry of low expectations'.

At the same time, there has been a marked tendency for commentators in the British media to overlook or minimise evidence of rising antisemitism. During the year following the pogrom of 7 October 2023 in Israel, there were over 5,500 antisemitic incidents recorded, three times more than the previous year. Many of us in the West have grown complacent, assuming that the horrors of the Holocaust would prevent this ancient prejudice from re-emerging. But as the conflict between Israel and Hamas escalated, few of us could be in any doubt that antisemitism had once again goose-stepped into the spotlight. Of course, criticism of the Israeli government and its military strategy is entirely legitimate; it is practised after all by many of the country's own citizens. So too is our profound concern for the innocents of Gaza and the many thousands of non-combatants who have lost their lives in the war.

But there is no denying the explicit anti-Jewish hatred that has accompanied these discussions in certain quarters.

The day after Hamas committed its atrocity, British citizens were filmed celebrating on the streets of London, openly supporting a terrorist group whose charter explicitly calls for the extermination of Jews and blames them for both world wars and the Russian and French revolutions. Jubilant Hamas supporters on the streets of Sydney cried out 'Fuck the Jews', and a banner in New York City declared 'Long live 7 October'. After Israel won the Eurovision Song Contest in May 2024, there was a slew of openly anti-Jewish reactions online. Underneath a link to an article I had written about the contest, a former Oxford academic posted an image of Eden Golan, the Israeli entry, with bloodstains photoshopped onto her dress. She went on to dismiss the victims of the 7 October pogrom as 'silly ravers' and to blame the massacre on the Israel Defense Forces. In that same month, vandals daubed the Shoah memorial in Paris with handprints of red paint. One of the perpetrators defended his actions as 'just hooliganism', but it is difficult to see how the desecration of the memory of Holocaust victims could possibly be explained away as anything other than racial hatred.

Brendan O'Neill analyses many such examples in his book *After the Pogrom* (2024), and explains how intersectional theory has cultivated the conditions for such reactions.

> This is one of the most ruinous ideologies of the post-class left. It holds that the multiple forms of discrimination a group faces combine, overlap and 'intersect' to give rise to an entirely distinct experience of suffering that people from outside the group are unlikely to be able to understand. So where a Muslim woman, say, faces many 'intersecting' forms of discrimination – on the basis of her skin colour, her sex, her religious beliefs, her veil – a Jewish man experiences very few. He's white, he's male, he's probably cishet – he's *fine*.

We have seen how intersectionality in its current form operates on the basis of hierarchical classifications according to group identity. Antisemitic sentiment is forgiven and even encouraged due to this ideological taxonomy of Jewishness as a feature of the oppressor class. This explains, but not does excuse, the many protests at universities openly supporting Hamas, or even praising its acts of barbarism. A poll in May 2024 found that 63 per cent of the students then campaigning at universities in the United States had at least some sympathy for Hamas. There were reports on campus of overtly antisemitic statements, and Jews being harassed. At Columbia University, one protester cried out 'We are Hamas', while another shouted at a group of Jewish students: 'The 7 October is about to be every fucking day for you. You ready?' These are the very people who have spent the last few years calling anyone who dissents even slightly from their worldview a 'fascist', and yet they are blind to actual fascism when it emerges within their own ranks. Refracted through the lens of intersectional oppression, a complex conflict in the Middle East had been reduced to Muslims versus Jews, or Oppressed versus Oppressor respectively.

Antisemitism has assumed myriad and outlandish forms over the centuries. In England, Jews were deported in 1290 only to be readmitted in 1656. In the interim years, only those who had converted to Christianity were allowed to remain; specifically, they were able to reside at the *Domus Conversorum* in London, established by Henry III in 1232. Anti-Jewish sentiments were reignited by a plot to poison Elizabeth I in 1594, which was blamed on the queen's physician Roderigo Lopes, a Portuguese man of Jewish ancestry who was executed for treason. This is the context in which the forced conversion of Shylock at the end of Shakespeare's *The Merchant of Venice* (c. 1597) ought to be understood. Unpleasant myths about Jews have abounded throughout history, some of which still linger in Islamic regimes and the darker crannies of the internet, where neo-Nazis gather to wallow in their bile. The poisoning of wells by Jews was thought to have initiated the Black Death epidemic in 1348. This notion was still pervasive by the time Christopher Marlowe wrote his play *The Jew of Malta* in 1589. Consider Barabas's mass extermination of an entire convent of nuns by means of 'a precious powder', or his boastful claim: 'Sometimes I go about and poison wells'. The hate-filled fantasies didn't end there. The seventeenth-century preacher Thomas Calvert speculated that male Jews menstruated and murdered Christian infants to replenish their blood. In a 1656 pamphlet addressing the question of readmission, the puritan polemicist William Prynne stated that 'the Jews almost every year crucify one child, to the injury and contumely of Jesus'.

Those who have been paying attention will have noticed new forms of these blood libels recurring online since the pogrom, with many activists claiming that Israel is specifically targeting children in the conflict. For whatever reason, many opponents of the war cannot resist veering into antisemitic tropes. The unique savagery of the Holocaust shows us that human civilisation might at any point collapse into the abyss. In Anthony Burgess's novel *Earthly Powers* (1980), the narrator Ken Toomey witnesses the immediate aftermath at Buchenwald, what he describes as the 'lowest point in human history'. His newfound sense of humankind's capacity for evil leads him to conclude that we cannot possibly have been created by God. This is the essence of despair.

The writer and illustrator Mervyn Peake was one of the first to see Bergen-Belsen after its liberation by allied forces. He visited the camp as a war artist, and what he saw there haunted him forever. His final novel *Titus Alone* (1959) is a fragmentary and bleak affair, a consequence partly of his degenerative illness, but also of his psychological need to reckon with the evil he had glimpsed. It appears in the novel in the form of the 'factory', an infernal place of shadows and death, where identical faces stare out of countless windows and macabre scientific experiments are conducted within its walls. One of Peake's sketches from Belsen depicts a young girl, looking directly at the artist as she lies dying from consumption. As he drew the girl, Peake was overwhelmed with a sense of helplessness and self-reproach. In the final stanza of

*Mervyn Peake's drawing of a girl dying of consumption
at Belsen (1945).*

his poem 'The Consumptive. Belsen 1945', he tried to make sense of
his feelings:

> Her agony slides through me: am I glass
> That grief can find no grip
> Save for a moment when the quivering lip
> And the coughing weaker than the broken wing
> That, fluttering, shakes the life from a small bird
> Caught me as in a nightmare? Nightmares pass;
> The image blurs and the quick razor-edge
> Of anger dulls, and pity dulls. O God,
> That grief so glibly slides! The little badge

On either cheek was gathered from her blood:
Those coughs were her last words. They had no weight
Save that through them was made articulate
Earth's desolation on the alien bed.
Though I be glass, it shall not be betrayed,
That last weak cough of her small, trembling head.

As Peake sketches the girl, he struggles with the sheer futility of it all. He is troubled that his pity is fleeting; that even in the moment he is too focused on his task and not on the human being who lies dying before him. But is this really a lack of empathy, or a natural human reaction to the knowledge that there is nothing he can do to remedy the cruelties of the world?

The evil of the Holocaust serves as a reminder of what can happen when the core tenets of liberalism are abandoned and fascism prevails. We cannot afford to be complacent while antisemitism is on the rise and supposed progressives are cheering on those who openly wish to eliminate an entire race of people. If nothing else, we should do our uttermost to ensure that the lessons of history are not forgotten.

# 5

# The Death of Liberty

## Black Ants or Red Ants

I have before me a copy of a rare book from 1942 called *Calvary*. It is a snapshot of a volatile time; a collection of pencil drawings by an anonymous artist, known here only as 'Peregrine'. The images are harrowing; powerful expressionist renditions of some of the worst moments of war. The human figures are often presented with indistinct outlines, softly blended against darker backgrounds in a dreamlike chiaroscuro. In 'Shadow of the Bomber', we are observing a gathering of men from below, our attention directed to the aeroplane passing over like an angel of death. Some of the figures are twisted into impossible forms and poses, as though we are anticipating the moment when their sense of reality will be obliterated in a sudden shock of fire and blood. In 'Rotterdam, 1940', we see a family attending to a father on a stretcher against a backdrop of a building engulfed in flames. 'Delirium' is a noisy image: a man with glazed eyes on his hospital bed, holding an arm above his head as though to repel the grinding machinery and smoke that dances around him. 'Brotherhood' shows a soldier carrying a wounded compatriot through an imploding cloud of destruction. In 'Sirens', a young girl stares upwards in terror during an air raid, her toy doll like a small smiling corpse discarded to the floor. Elsewhere, in 'Quo Vadis, Domine?' two burly men are seen hewing through the base of Christ's cross with a crosscut saw.

'Peregrine' is Imre Hofbauer, a Hungarian artist whose satirical drawings against Hitler meant that he eventually was forced to flee to London. Although the images in *Calvary* depict various locations, they were all inspired and informed by his time volunteering for the London Fire Brigade during the Blitz. The collection is supplemented with an essay by the novelist Compton Mackenzie and another by his wife, Faith Compton Mackenzie. In the former, Mackenzie sketches out the background to these drawings and, in doing so, provides a fascinating insight into how humankind repeatedly fails to detect the early signs of totalitarianism. In particular, he acknowledges the absolutist tendencies of the left while blaming the right for convincing itself 'that Hitler was the defence of Europe against Communism' and so leaving it too late to tackle the rising threat. He anticipates what has come to be known as the 'horseshoe theory' which sees the spectrum of left to right as curved rather than linear, so that the far left and far right almost meet. 'The seat of the trouble', he writes, 'was that confused thinking which led to the failure to recognise that Fascism and National Socialism were only different expressions of the same basic evolutionary drive as inspired Communism. Black ants or red ants, they are both ants. The initials of Liberté, Egalité and Fraternité provide the first three letters for the Left, and T stands for Totalitarianism.'

In an especially baleful passage, Mackenzie recounts the moment he first saw a swastika in September 1932, painted on a rickety fence in the city of Danzig (now Gdańsk) in Poland. Unfamiliar with the symbol, Mackenzie nonetheless 'apprehended something of its vitality, and in that apprehension was caught by a faint malaise about the future'. It was merest instinct, but it struck him as 'black and poisonous-seeming as a tarantula'. He compares it to the tendency of henbane and deadly nightshade to emerge 'unaccountably from the rubble of collapsed buildings'. Similarly, in these squalid environs, the swastika 'seemed to have been hatched from decay and collapse'.

> Yet we should not look upon it so much as an evil as a misdirected activity. It is a cancer not a destructive bacillus. It arises from an honest effort to achieve regeneration; but even as the cells of the human body, by seeking to restore themselves, succeed only in destroying the rest of the body, so too must the triumphant swastika destroy Europe, and lead the body of Western man along a path in which his soul must shrivel.

The horrors of Nazi Germany strike us in hindsight as unfathomable acts perpetrated by evil men, monsters disguised in military uniforms with horns discreetly concealed under visored caps, and hooves stuffed into jackboots. Yet the truth is far more disturbing, and it plays out at regular intervals throughout human history. This is the endlessly recycled story of men who commit atrocities under the delusion that they are doing good. If the world could conveniently be divided into Good and Evil, authoritarianism would be more readily anticipated and prevented. This is why we must be comprehensive in our vigilance; if we focus our attentions too steadily in one direction, we can be certain that the threat will emerge from an unscrutinised source.

Vigilance, however, does not mean that we ought to confuse the seeds of authoritarianism with the brutalities of totalitarianism. The point is rather that we recognise and curb the potential for tyranny in all political movements. This is to be preferred to the hysterical finger-pointing and thundering cries of 'fascist!' which appear to dominate today's discourse. Of course, there is nothing new in the use of 'Fascism' as a catch-all smear. Even during the Second World War, George Orwell was complaining that the word was subject to multiple definitions. In his column for *Tribune* on 24 March 1944, Orwell argued that the word had been rendered 'entirely meaningless' through misapplication:

I have heard it applied to farmers, shopkeepers, Social Credit, corporal punishment, fox-hunting, bull-fighting, the 1922 Committee, the 1941 Committee, Kipling, Gandhi, Chiang Kai-Shek, homosexuality, Priestley's broadcasts, Youth Hostels, astrology, women, dogs and I do not know what else . . . By 'Fascism' they mean, roughly speaking, something cruel, unscrupulous, arrogant, obscurantist, anti-liberal and anti-working-class. Except for the relatively small number of Fascist sympathizers, almost any English person would accept 'bully' as a synonym for 'Fascist'. That is about as near to a definition as this much-abused word has come.

Orwell recognised that there is some 'kind of buried meaning here', insofar as there are clear differences between 'the regimes called Fascist and those called democratic', but his eventual conclusion was that people ought to 'use the word with a certain amount of circumspection and not, as is usually done, degrade it to the level of a swearword'. He returns to the topic in his essay 'Politics and the English Language' (1946), in which he notes that the word 'fascism' has 'now no meaning except in so far as it signifies "something not desirable"'. The importance of mutually agreed definitions desperately needs to be restated today. The comparison of mainstream viewpoints to an ideology that instigated mass atrocities in the past century is unhelpful and historically illiterate. If anyone is unclear about what fascism actually means, he or she could do a lot worse than spend some time looking at Hofbauer's illustrations.

To restore some kind of clarity, it might be worth returning to the definition provided by that grisly father of fascism, Benito Mussolini. We know that one of his key implementations had been the 'corporate state', which is to say that the economy would be managed by workers and their employers as relatively autonomous bodies of political representation. These 'corporations', more akin to early guilds than the modern commercial companies of today, operated in tandem with the government but were always subordinate to it. This was in line with the common Fascist refrain '*tutto nello Stato, niente al di fuori dello Stato, nulla contro lo Stato*', which translates as 'everything within the state, nothing outside the state, nothing against the state'. 'At its fullest development,' writes historian Robert O. Paxton, 'fascism redrew the frontiers between private and public, sharply diminishing what had once been untouchably private.' The most significant aspects of Mussolini's conceptualisation of fascism were embodied in an essay he wrote in 1927 in collaboration with the philosopher Giovanni Gentile called '*La dottrina del fascismo*' ('The Doctrine of Fascism'), eventually published in 1932 as part of the *Enciclopedia Italiana*. The essay advances the key principles that one would expect, most notably that the interests of the individual should only be taken into account when they 'coincide with those of the State', which must have 'absolute primacy'. According to Mussolini, fascism demands that the citizen develops his mind and body for the betterment of the nation, that he prioritises education and intellectual pursuits – the artistic, the religious and the scientific – as much as his physical prowess. This is a specifically spiritual worldview, represented through the Ancient Roman symbol of the *fasces*, the bundle of sticks bound together to connote strength through unity.

Fascism, says Mussolini, is the repudiation of three key ideas: socialism, democracy and liberalism. He explicitly opposes liberalism as an ideology which has 'exhausted its historical function', and further rejects Marxian Socialism with its assumption that the class struggle can explain all aspects of human history. With the needs of the individual subordinated to those of the collective, democracy as traditionally understood is unnecessary, since the principle of 'quality rather than quantity' suggests that 'the conscience and will of the few, if not, indeed, of one' must ultimately serve as 'the conscience and the will of the mass'. We are back with Plato's absolutist notion of the 'philosopher king'.

Democracy is represented by Mussolini as a kind of myth, in which the masses are conned into thinking that they have any sovereignty at all, while clandestine forces are busy exercising their power. He claims that fascism is forward-thinking, but at the same time insists that it rebuffs the utopian dream that a perfect society is at all achievable. While he acknowledges the importance of tradition, he insists that 'history does not travel backwards'. That is to say, fascism 'preserves what may be described as "the acquired facts" of history; it rejects all else'. According to Mussolini, fascism satisfies a fundamental human need for authority and the ordered life, hence the sacralisation of the state and the absolutism it entails. 'If liberalism spells individualism,' he writes, 'Fascism spells government'. His ideology is explicitly impe-rialistic, seeing in 'the tendency of nations to expand' a 'manifestation of their vitality'. He maintains that pacifism is a decadent abhorrence, that war is not only necessary but desirable because it 'keys up all human energies to their maximum tension and sets the seal of nobility on those peoples who have the courage to face it'.

We can already see where these broad principles simultaneously dovetail and depart from National Socialism. Hitler's emphasis on racial purity and his pseudo-pagan and utopian concept of the destiny of the Fatherland seems barely compatible with Mussolini's worldview. 'Fascism' has become a protean term, with as many varying definitions as can be imagined, which is why it can be applied to just about anybody. If all it takes to justify the epithet 'fascist' is a concurrence with a few elements of Mussolini's manifesto, then the word could be used to describe any of today's mainstream political movements. Similarly, if we take as our benchmark the key features of most fascist regimes – the violent suppression of opposition, a hostility to democracy and due process, restrictions on free speech and freedom of assembly, extreme nationalism and worship of the state, and a hyper-racialised conceptualisation of society – we see that there is some overlap with all major parties in the Western world. The goal is to rip out the weeds of authoritarianism as and when they sprout, always remembering that no field is immune.

According to Mackenzie, Hitler was too often dismissed as a

clownish figure early in his ascendency. He relates some gossip, current at the time among political circles, that at the Munich Conference in September 1938, Mussolini had taken Chamberlain to one side and 'whispered in English to leave Hitler to him because he knew how to manage him'. Hitler's tantrums were already well known, but were taken to be a sign of his unseriousness as a leader. Mackenzie recalls that the general mood among the public before the war was that Hitler and Mussolini were 'a pair of buffoons', who were openly laughed at by British cinema audiences when they appeared in the newsreels.

> Both men are good actors, but Mussolini, with a longer professional experience, had learnt how to stand up in a car and give the Roman salute while the car was moving. Hitler had not acquired the trick of balance. Every time he stood up impressively to salute the crowd the car would jerk forward and the funny little man would stagger and nearly fall back on the seat.

Mackenzie concludes that 'it was a mistake to laugh at that little man', who had seemed to the British public to resemble 'an anxious lavatory-attendant at a railway terminus'. By the time Hitler instigated the war, he had learned to feign a more statesmanlike demeanour.

Perhaps it is this lesson from history that accounts for much of what we call 'Trump Derangement Syndrome', the fear that the buffoonish and gaffe-prone Donald Trump might one day develop into a grave threat to civilisation. In Salman Rushdie's novel, *The Golden House* (2017), Trump appears to be represented in the form of 'The Joker', a crazed billionaire who seizes power through a wave of populism and initiates the country's descent into chaos. During a discussion about the book at the London Literature Festival, Rushdie explained that he had not named Trump explicitly because he wanted to keep his name out of the novel. 'I thought it would pollute it in some way, and so I thought, in a deck of playing cards there's only two cards that are unusual to play. One of them is the Trump, and the other is the Joker.'

Where Rushdie was pessimistic, some commentators in the build-up to the 2024 election were outright histrionic. At a rally in support of Democratic presidential candidate Kamala Harris on the night before the polls opened, the television chat-show host Oprah Winfrey suggested to the assembled crowds that a Trump victory would spell the end of democracy itself. 'If we don't show up tomorrow,' she said, 'it is entirely possible that we will not have the opportunity to ever cast a ballot again.' In an appearance on CNN, Democratic Representative Debbie Dingall claimed that Trump was planning to 'start internment camps' for Muslims and the Arab-American community. 'You may have to visit me in one,' she said, suggesting that Trump's political opponents would also be incarcerated. These are unserious comments, and so it followed naturally that the election cycle should collapse into a battle of memes. Trump's now infamous reference to migrants allegedly eating cats and dogs in Springfield, Ohio, was remixed into dance tracks and shared more widely than any campaign statement. Harris's team played their part in the circus too, embracing the 'Brat' identity bestowed upon their candidate by the popular singer Charli XCX.

The steer into accusations of 'fascism' is an altogether less risible development. It was perhaps epitomised after Donald Trump held a rally at Madison Square Garden on 27 October 2024, an event that appeared to have the effect of tipping the left-wing commentariat over the precipice. MSNBC's Jonathan Capehart described the proceedings as 'particularly chilling, because in 1939, more than 20,000 supporters of a different fascist leader, Adolf Hitler, packed the Garden for a so-called pro-America rally'. His coverage of the event was spliced with footage from an actual Nazi rally from 1939, but he neglected to mention that this had taken place in an entirely different building, since the venue for Trump's rally had not been constructed until 1968. Capehart was positively priapic with the conviction that he was witnessing a rerun of a scene from *Triumph of the Will* (1935), and so he wasn't about to let any trifling 'facts' dampen the sheer drama of it all.

Such galloping imbecility from the mainstream media raises the question of why Democratic voters do not find it more offensive. Evidently, the reporters at MSNBC are under the impression that their viewers know nothing whatsoever about history and will be swayed by this kind of propaganda. We are assured that Trump's event was populated with Nazis of all stripes. 'Donald Trump's got this big rally going at Madison Square Garden,' vice presidential candidate Tim Walz said at an event in Nevada. 'There's a direct parallel to a big rally that happened in the mid-1930s at Madison Square Garden.' The Nazis in attendance at Trump's event were highly unconventional: there were black Nazis, Hispanic Nazis, Indian Nazis, gay Nazis, and even Jewish Nazis flying their Star of David flags (strangely absent at Nuremberg). There was a broad range of ethnicities among the speakers too, so at the very least MSNBC and Tim Walz should have admitted that, when it comes to white supremacist gatherings, this was one of the most diverse.

Given Trump's propensity for blunders and outrageous remarks, it is curious that his critics feel the need to venture into the marsh of self-discrediting hyperbole. Overwrought and spasmodic claims of Trump's supposed 'fascism' only weaken all other criticisms that might be levelled against him. An especially vivid example took place in June 2017, when New York City's Public Theater staged an open-air production of *Julius Caesar* in Central Park in which the titular role was portrayed as Trump. The theatrical spectacle of the sitting president being murdered in broad daylight stirred outrage in conservative circles, and was even seen as an example of direct incitement to violence. This kind of depiction of Trump as a dangerous tyrant has become commonplace. The cover of the June 2024 edition of the *New Republic* featured a composite image of Hitler and Trump along with the title 'American fascism: what it would look like'. In the United Kingdom, Labour MP David Lammy wrote an article for *Time* magazine asserting that 'Trump is not only a woman-hating, neo-Nazi-sympathizing sociopath' but 'also a profound threat to the international order that has been the foundation of Western progress for so long'. After Lammy was appointed as Foreign Secretary, he quickly reversed his position and posted a warm message to congratulate the new president elect on X, saying that he was 'looking forward' to working with him in the future. Assuming that Lammy's opinions of Trump have not significantly altered, we can only interpret this volte-face in two ways: either his accusations or his congratulations were insincere. After all, if Lammy genuinely believed that Trump was the modern-day equivalent of Hitler, to congratulate him would be grotesque.

All of this tells us that these charges of 'fascism' are more opportunistic than authentic. They fall squarely into what has become known as 'Godwin's Law', which suggests that the longer an online discussion continues, the greater the likelihood that a comparison with the Nazis or Hitler will occur. The man who invented the law, Mike Godwin, had been objecting to the infantilism of online political discourse, but in an article for the *Washington Post* in December 2023, he attempted to carve out an exception in an opinion piece entitled 'Yes, it's okay to compare Trump to Hitler. Don't let me stop you'. It seems that even Godwin is susceptible to Godwin's Law. Such tactics are appealing to all sides, particular when egos are bruised and retaliation is the only balm. During a town hall event in Pennsylvania, Kamala Harris was directly asked whether she considered Trump to be a fascist. Her answer was 'Yes, I do'. She later clarified her view by saying that voters would not welcome 'a president of the United States who admires dictators and is a fascist'. For his part, Trump referred to Harris as a 'fascist' on multiple occasions during his campaign, and even called her a 'Marxist, communist, fascist, socialist'.

This normalisation of such language is symptomatic of a form of hysteria, a nation divided into two factions who simply cannot see the world beyond their own specific phantasmagoria, driving themselves insane within the confines of their echo chambers. We might suppose that the reading of a few history books might help them to break out, except there are plenty of educated people who are likewise susceptible to this collective fantasy. To lower the temperature of this debate, it would surely be prudent to remind ourselves that fascism was a very specific, and uniquely evil, ideological movement of the twentieth century. To casually conflate the various forms of mainstream authoritarianism we see today with the devastation of the Second World War is a tremendous insult to those who have lived through genuinely fascistic regimes. It is also recklessly misleading. The assassination attempts on Donald Trump show plainly what can happen if you convince a significant part of the population that Hitler has been reincarnated and is running for office.

The problem isn't restricted to Trump. Today, accusations of fascism are levelled against those who don't believe males should compete in women's sports, or those who support free speech even for the most objectionable people. This is called 'concept creep', where generally understood terms have their definitions gradually expanded. Labour MEP Julie Ward, for instance, explicitly called Brexit a 'fascist coup'. Paul Mason wrote a whole book called *How to Stop Fascism* (2021), in which he revealed that he doesn't know what 'fascism' means. Laurie Penny mimicked this folly in her book *Sexual Revolution: Modern Fascism and the Feminist Fightback* (2022). The academic Judith Butler argued that gender-critical feminism represents 'one of the dominant strains of fascism in our time'. Labour MP Claudia Webbe claimed that the government's decision to privatise Channel 4 was 'the seedbed of fascism'. It is one thing for internet trolls to promiscuously hurl these terms about like crockery at a Greek wedding, but when politicians join the crackbrained chorus, we ought to take note.

Such definitional slippage is why figures on both sides in the United States election of 2024 felt comfortable in deploying the 'fascist' smear. But given the criteria outlined in Mussolini's essay, which candidate more closely fitted the bill? Trump, for instance, is quite plainly far more nationalistic than Kamala Harris, and he has an erratic record when it comes to free speech. He had been quoted as saying that 'it's very possible' that 'the president's wife and the former secretary of state' could be thrown in jail if he were to win the election. And yet we heard this kind of bluster in his previous claims that he would prosecute his former rival Hillary Clinton, all of which came to nothing. Trump's behaviour on 6 January 2021, when he denied that he had lost the election and groups of his supporters marched on the Capitol, was foolhardy and irresponsible. The Democrats, on the other hand, have actively supported the manipulation of the law to see Trump convicted in court, so they are in no position to complain about 'threats to democracy'. Moreover, Trump's insistence on tax cuts and deregulation is incompatible with the corporatism of Mussolini, whereas Biden had subjected businesses to increased government bureaucracy. As for racial politics, the Democrats have openly endorsed DEI and Critical Race Theory, divisive policies that risk reversing many of the gains of the civil rights luminaries of the past.

As we have seen, any attempts to outline the illiberal qualities of major figures on the left and right of politics often provoke accusations of 'bothsidesing'. But when people dismiss arguments relating to 'both sides' they are attempting to undermine a truth that we would all be advised to heed. Yes, 'both sides' are engaging in the politics of infantilism, resorting to smears and lies to achieve their goals. Yes, 'both sides' are disregarding the true meaning of 'fascism' to score cheap points against their opponents. And yes, 'both sides' are capable of reneging on their commitment to free speech. With commentators doomed to wade indefinitely in these linguistic swamps, surely it would be wiser for them to avoid the term 'fascist' altogether and consign it to the history books. Their energies would be more productively expended on holding power to account, which would mean exposing the various new forms of state overreach as and when they emerge. Above all, they would do well to remember that neither left nor right has a monopoly on the tendency towards authoritarianism.

## Thought Police

In discussions around the demise of woke, one often hears references to the 'deep state'. It sounds like the most conspiratorial of phrases, evoking images of masked men in wine-red cloaks, blazing torches in hand, gathered around a large pentagram chalked onto the floor of a subterranean crypt. Perhaps they have secret handshakes, or coded expressions to signify allyship. It is probable that they sacrifice adolescent wombats to appease the spirits of the Styx.

Like much of the lexicon of today's culture wars, the phrase 'deep state' is one whose definition is subject to wild disagreement. There are some who believe there exists a clandestine Satanic cohort of powerful men for whom the world's leaders are the merest sock-puppets, appointed by them and directed at will. Everything that goes wrong has been deliberately planned and executed, and everything that goes right is a 'psy-op' to distract the gullible masses from the true objectives. As with most conspiratorial thinking, it isn't long before the Jews are blamed, but even without the antisemitic elements there is a sense that evil as a force has manifested on earth through the networks of the rich and powerful. Sometimes these theories cluster around the World Economic Forum (WEF) and its exclusive gatherings at Davos, but while the world's super-rich no doubt enjoy disproportionate influence on various governments, that does not mean that they are appointing the rulers who will do their bidding and plotting to cull the world's population and force us all to eat insects. I recently saw a viral video which claimed that Jonathan Yeo's portrait of King Charles III was communicating satanic symbolism, because if you excise certain segments of the painting, invert and reposition them, you can just make out the image of the demonic caprine deity of Baphomet. You may have to squint your eyes a bit, but it's definitely there.

A more viable understanding of the 'deep state' is the way in which culture warriors now exert considerable control within our institutions – including, crucially, the civil service – which means their worldview will inform major policy decisions irrespective of which party is at the helm. We might be able to vote a particular government out of office, but we cannot do anything about the sundry quangos and publicly funded bodies who are in the grip of this ideology. The impact of the deep state can be severe. An investigation by the *Daily Wire* revealed that after the state of Florida was struck by Hurricane Milton in October 2024, a supervisor at the Federal Emergency Management Agency (FEMA) instructed relief workers to 'avoid homes advertising Trump' as a form of 'best practice'. As a result, households in need of help that happened to display pro-Trump insignia were neglected. The supervisor responsible was later suspended, but this was an example of a remarkably common phenomenon: the bureaucrat who ignores instructions from above to satisfy his own creed. This is what Elon Musk meant by the 'radical-left shadow government' that was being exposed in the early part of Trump's second term.

This is by no means a recent development. Bureaucrats of one form or another have always wielded power disproportionate to their public accountability. When the novelist Anthony Burgess appeared on the American talk show *Firing Line* in December 1972, he outlined a similar phenomenon to the host William F. Buckley Jr.

> The people who rule any state in whatever part of the world are anonymous people. We do not imagine for instance that the British state is run by the elected representatives of the people. There is a parliament, there's an executive, but behind all these there is a civil service which is totally anonymous, there are economic experts from Hungary who were behind the failed Wilsonian revolution of socialist England a few years ago, there are scientists, there are research workers, there are pundits of various kinds who occasionally produce books . . . there are forces which never achieve the incarnation of a name, never appear on television, never appear in the press, are not subject to a cult, say as the president or the vice president is, and yet are conceivably running the country.

Little has changed. Over the past few years, *Telegraph* journalist Steven Edginton has written a series of exposés about how the woke ideology has infected the civil service, the Ministry of Defence, and other government departments in the United Kingdom. Leaked internal documents have detailed compulsory training sessions on gender ideology and racial equity, and provided evidence of staff who were obstructive in the execution of their duties. Whistleblowers at Whitehall revealed that they were bullied into silence if they opposed the 'Maoist-style cultural revolution that has swept through government departments'. One anonymous civil servant wrote an article exposing what he called a 'culture of defiance' in what has become known as 'the blob' of activists working within and against the system. On the issue of immigration, his colleagues at Whitehall were 'viewing their role as being part of the resistance to what they see as a radical Right-wing Government', and 'overruling the instructions of ministers and thereby their democratic mandates'.

Yet when it comes to threats to liberty, nothing exceeds the antics of the College of Policing, the body responsible for law enforcement training in England and Wales and the originators of the infamous 'non-crime hate incident' (NCHI). This sinister phenomenon was introduced in 2014 without a direct government mandate. Police officers have been trained to believe that their role is to monitor the speech and thought of citizens in line with the tenets of Critical Social Justice, which means that they have been operating as the woke movement's *de facto* paramilitary wing. Officers are under an ethical obligation to act without fear or favour, but by recording and investigating 'non-crime' they are engaging in behaviour that represents the precise opposite of their purpose. It would be the equivalent of a doctor who limits his attention to the vigorous and the healthy.

Some elucidation is required. Once a complaint has been made against an individual, a 'non-crime hate incident' is recorded against his or her name irrespective of any evidence of hateful intent. The person so branded will not be informed, but it could appear on checks

by the Disclosure and Barring Service (DBS), a compulsory requirement for those applying for jobs with vulnerable people, such as
teachers or healthcare workers. As such, the recording of NCHIs can
directly impede employment prospects without the candidate ever
knowing why. Since there is no evidential threshold to be met for
whether an incident was motivated by hate, the system of NCHIs gives
a green light to any person with a grudge to exact revenge on anyone
at all. From the perspective of the police, the ostensible purpose is to
keep track of 'hate' on the presumption that it might escalate into
criminality. This concept is reminiscent of the short story 'The
Minority Report' (1956), in which science-fiction author Philip K. Dick
coined the phrase 'pre-crime'. Not even the most pessimistic of dystopian writers could have anticipated that in twenty-first century Britain
the police would be actively engaged in the auditing of our private
thoughts and emotions.

The recording of 'non-crime', as with many of these authoritarian
developments, stems from good intentions. After the racially motivated
murder in 1993 of Stephen Lawrence, a black teenager from south-east
London, a subsequent report by Sir William MacPherson in February
1999 found that racism within the police force meant that there were
widespread failings in the investigation of crimes of this nature. The
report recommended that the definition of a 'racist incident' should be
'any incident which is perceived to be racist by the victim or any other
person', thereby enforcing the notion that perception was to be
prioritised. The report further stated that 'crimes and non-crimes' of a
racist nature 'must be reported, recorded and investigated with equal
commitment'. In 2005, the Association of Chief Police Officers, in
conjunction with the Home Office, published a belated response
in the form of its 'Good Practice and Tactical Guidance' which drew a
clear distinction between a 'hate crime' and a 'hate incident'. But it
wasn't until 2014 that the College of Policing decided on its own
initiative that the policy of recording 'non-crime hate incidents' should
be rolled out across forces in England and Wales. From then on, an

offensive tweet or insult could be classified as a 'hate incident' if a complainant perceived it to have been motivated by hatred against one of the 'protected characteristics' which are listed on the websites of the Crown Prosecution Service and the College of Policing: race, religion, sexual orientation, transgender identity and disability. This list is notably different to the 'protected characteristics' in the Equality Act, which also includes sex, but specifies 'gender reassignment' rather than 'transgender identity'. In other words, the law enforcement agencies have been using a revised list of their own making. This explains why threats against women for standing up for single-sex spaces tend to be ignored, but people have been rigorously investigated for 'misgendering'.

The existence of 'non-crime hate incidents' is one prominent example of how the interpretation of the culture war as a simple clash of left versus right is misguided. The origin of the practice coincides with the coalition government of the Conservatives and the Liberal Democrats, led by David Cameron and Nick Clegg respectively. In spite of demands for their discontinuation by successive Home Secretaries, and a ruling from the High Court that they are 'plainly an interference with freedom of expression', NCHIs persisted throughout the years of Conservative rule. The judge, Mr Justice Julian Knowles, could not have been clearer in his condemnation: 'In this country we have never had a Cheka, a Gestapo or a Stasi. We have never lived in an Orwellian society.'

This is wishful thinking. The College of Policing's flagrant disregard for direct instructions from the Home Office reveals the extent to which it has been ideologically captured. Activists have exerted undue influence and have even reached positions of power. In 2013, Alex Marshall, chief executive of the College of Policing, received the top award from Stonewall, the campaign group that is more responsible than any for the infusion of genderism into the lifeblood of our political culture. Marshall became 'LGBT envoy' to the government, and it was only one year into his tenure that 'non-crime hate incidents' were introduced. Although this is not proof of causality, there can be no doubt that there exists a clear relationship between activism and law enforcement. One former detective told me that for twenty-five years, policing has 'been pulled around, by the nose, by self-appointed community leaders and fringe political groups'. Police officers, in other words, are being trained to defy the government and the courts in order to fulfil the decrees of the high priests of wokeness.

Analysis by the Free Speech Union has estimated that approximately a quarter of a million NCHIs have been recorded by police since the policy was inaugurated, an average of sixty-five per day. Freedom of information requests by *The Times* gathered information from forty-five of the forty-eight police forces in the United Kingdom and revealed that in excess of 13,200 'hate incidents' were recorded between June 2023 and June 2024. The range of recorded NCHIs reads like something from the pen of Edward Lear. A man in Bedfordshire was slapped with a non-crime hate incident for whistling the theme tune from *Bob the Builder* at his neighbour, which for some reason was interpreted as racist. Other examples include a disputed line call in a tennis match, a dog defecating on someone's lawn, a man saying that he was campaigning for Brexit, and even children's playground insults. *The Times* has revealed that NCHIs have been recorded against a pair of secondary school girls who said that a peer smelt 'like fish', as well as a nine-year-old child who referred to a classmate as a 'retard'. The lawyer Sarah Phillimore was recorded as having committed a non-crime hate incident when she posted a satirical tweet which featured a picture of her puppy along with the caption 'my dog will call me a Nazi for cheese'.

Politicians have even been targeted in this way. In December 2023, it was reported that Rachel Maclean, deputy chair of the Conservative Party, had reposted a statement on X which referred to Green Party candidate Melissa Poulton as 'a man who wears a wig and calls himself a proud lesbian'. This happened to be a statement of fact, but this didn't stop the West Mercia Police recording it as an instance of 'non-crime'.

In 2017, the then Home Secretary Amber Rudd had an NCHI recorded against her because she referred to 'migrant workers' in a speech at the Tory party conference. In March 2024, Scottish Conservative MSP Murdo Fraser initiated legal action against the police after discovering that the force had recorded an NCHI against him for an online post regarding the SNP's policies on gender self-identification. Fraser had written: 'Choosing to identify as "non-binary" is as valid as choosing to identify as a cat. I'm not sure Governments should be spending time on action plans for either.' Only the most dogged ideologue could have seen this as anything other than a reasonable position to take. At moments like these, it is difficult to decide whether we should be more disturbed by the police involvement, or the fact that so many lack the necessary historical knowledge to see where it leads.

### Zersetzung

Franz Kafka's *The Trial* (c. 1914) opens with the novel's protagonist, Josef K., being arrested early in the morning by two officers of the law. When he asks them to explain their reasons, one of the men tells him: 'It's not our job to tell you that. Go into your room and wait. The proceedings have now been started and you will learn everything in good time.' He never finds out, of course. Even after the story's abrupt and haunting dénouement, the reader is none the wiser as to why any of this has occurred. And so it is hardly surprising that *Telegraph* columnist Allison Pearson described it as 'Kafkaesque' that she was visited by two police officers on the morning of Remembrance Sunday in November 2024. Standing on her doorstep in her dressing gown and slippers, she was informed that she had been accused of 'stirring up racial hatred' by means of an unspecified social media post from a year before. Her account of the discussion that followed could have been lifted directly from *The Trial* itself:

'What did this post I wrote that offended someone say?' I asked. The constable said he wasn't allowed to tell me that.

'So what's the name of the person who made the complaint against me?'

He wasn't allowed to tell me that either, he said.

'You can't give me my accuser's name?'

'It's not "the accuser",' the PC said, looking down at his notes. 'They're called "the victim".'

Ah, right. 'OK, you're here to accuse me of causing offence but I'm not allowed to know what it is. Nor can I be told whom I'm being accused by? How am I supposed to defend myself, then?'

The term 'Kafkaesque', like 'Orwellian', has become something of a cliché, precisely the kind of writing that Orwell continually urged us to avoid. But what else are we to call it? Although Allison Pearson was initially under the impression that she had been accused of a 'non-crime hate incident', she was later told that she was being investigated for criminal activity under Section 17 of the Public Order Act 1986. This surely makes it even more sinister that she was not given any details of the alleged crime. Note also the menacing correction of the officer who insisted that the 'accuser' should be referred to as the 'victim'. This is a legacy of Keir Starmer's time as Director of Public Prosecutions and his determination that all accusers ought to be automatically believed. Perhaps he hadn't heard of Salem.

It should have been possible by now for the government to put a stop to this intolerable state of affairs, to pass a law that makes the recording of non-crime hate incidents unambiguously illegal, but it has neither the confidence nor the will. In *The New Puritans*, I predicted that police would soon stop this illiberal and unethical practice, but I had not counted on the authoritarianism of the Labour government that was voted into office on 4 July 2024. One of the first acts of the new Education Secretary, Bridget Phillipson, was to scotch the Higher Education (Freedom of Speech) Act, just one day before Parliament went into recess, presumably to avoid debating the matter openly. Few further details were provided, other than her awareness of 'concerns that the Act would be burdensome on providers and on the OfS [Office for Students]'. This was an act that had been many years in the making, subject to endless debates in both houses and, ultimately, cross-party approval in May 2023. That Phillipson was happy to jettison it without any consultation was an act of political vandalism that nobody anticipated. The Higher Education Act involved the creation of a 'free speech tsar' at the Office for Students, a role fulfilled by Professor Arif Ahmed, a philosopher and former fellow at Gonville and Caius College, Cambridge. Initially, part of Ahmed's job was to design a 'free speech complaints scheme', whereby universities that fail in their responsibilities could be fined. There was also a 'statutory tort' provision, which would have enabled academics who had lost their jobs for exercising their right to free speech to sue their universities. However, peers in the House of Lords attempted to see this aspect of the bill ditched and, after it was reinstated by the Commons, a watered-down version was passed.

Only a few weeks before the act was interrupted by the Labour government, the new Culture Secretary Lisa Nandy was declaring that the 'era of culture wars is over'. If the doublespeak was not bad enough, the Home Secretary Yvette Cooper soon after reversed the Conservative Party's pledge to limit the recording of NCHIs. Labour had resurrected this absurd policy just on the verge of its expiration. Cooper argued that the Conservative government's efforts to curb investigations into 'non-crime' were, according to a report in *The Times*, 'preventing police from monitoring and identifying tensions and threats to Jewish and Muslim communities that may escalate into violence'. No evidence for this claim was forthcoming. Potential terrorists were already on intelligence watchlists, and those branded as 'non-criminals' are typically those who are unlikely to break the law. What Cooper could never admit is that the recording of NCHIs is simply a chilling means to control the parameters of acceptable opinion through state coercion. We already know that before the Conservative government modified the guidelines, NCHIs were being recorded against anyone accused of 'hostility towards religion, race or transgender identity'. Given that 'hostility' is now commonly deployed as a synonym for 'criticism' or 'disagreement', we cannot possibly reach any helpful conclusions from these records. For instance, those who take issue with Critical Race Theory could be accused of 'hostility towards race', even though such concerns are typically based on a belief that people should not be judged by the colour of their skin. Similarly, those who maintain that men should not be in women's prisons are routinely smeared as 'transphobic', even though their motivation is to preserve important safeguarding measures. How many of these legitimate points of view have been recorded as 'non-crime'? Due to a lack of transparency in the system, we will probably never know.

Gavin Stephens, chair of the National Police Chiefs' Council (NPCC), explicitly outlined the rationale in the system at a summit in November 2024. 'Hate left unaddressed,' he said, 'whether that's propagated online or in person, has real world consequences.' This theory can be traced to a single book, *The Nature of Prejudice* (1954) by psychologist Gordon Allport, in which a five-point scale – which later became known as the 'pyramid of hate' – purports to demonstrate how even 'biased attitudes' can escalate into genocide.

| | |
|---|---|
| 5 | GENOCIDE |
| 4 | BIAS-MOTIVATED VIOLENCE |
| 3 | SYSTEMIC DISCRIMINATION |
| 2 | ACTS OF BIAS AND DISCRIMINATION |
| 1 | BIASED ATTITUDES |

The pyramid is a variation of Allport's scale, which ran from antilocution (the discussion of prejudices), to avoidance (withdrawal from proximity to the disliked group), to discrimination (the practice of excluding the group from certain opportunities and rights in society), to physical attack, and finally to extermination. Allport summarises his hypothesis as follows:

> This five-point scale is not mathematically constructed, but it serves to call attention to the enormous range of activities that may issue from prejudiced attitudes and beliefs. While many people would never move from antilocution to avoidance; or from avoidance to active discrimination, or higher on the scale, still it is true that activity on one level makes transition to a more intense level easier. It was Hitler's antilocution that led Germans to avoid their Jewish neighbors and erstwhile friends. This preparation made it easier to enact the Nürnberg laws of discrimination which, in turn, made the subsequent burning of synagogues and street attacks upon Jews seem natural. The final step in the macabre progression was the ovens at Auschwitz.

Toby Young, founder of the Free Speech Union, has pointed out that today this scale is applied unevenly as a result of unofficial 'two-tier policing' strategies. Since Muslims are ranked highly on the intersectional hierarchy as an oppressed class, whereas Jews are seen as white-adjacent and therefore oppressors, an ideologically captured police force does not see them as equivalents on their pyramid of hate. Why, asks Young, 'do the police and the Crown Prosecution Service apply Allport's model . . . to Islamophobia but not to antisemitism?' Given the unmitigated barbarity of the Holocaust, and the fact that Allport had based his research on interviews with Jewish survivors, this application of the principle seems perverse in the extreme.

Ultimately, it would appear that the purpose of 'non-crime hate incidents' is intimidatory. As lawyer Sarah Phillimore has noted:

> The recording of malicious and ideologically motivated com-plaints of 'hate' provide the police with zero useful operational

information, even assuming they can ever get round to analysing them. This is about 'Zersetzung' – the Stasi technique of psycho-logical degradation, to make us afraid, to make us our own jailers and our own censors. Cheaper that way than prison or bullets.

It may be that the end of woke will entail the abolition of the College of Policing and its replacement with a service that observes the law rather than the demands of activists. And surely the electorate will soon begin to wake up to the authoritarianism that is hardwired into the DNA of its own government. We are now firmly in the age of thoughtcrime anticipated by George Orwell. If those in charge do not understand the importance of liberty, the people will have to remind them, ideally through the ballot box. The alternative is too horrendous to contemplate.

## The War Against Hate

In October 2021, I appeared on a panel at the Conservative party conference in Manchester. It was an ideal opportunity to draw attention to the government's failure to protect free speech and address some of those who were directly responsible. I specifically took aim at the Police, Crime, Sentencing and Courts Bill, which would empower officers to crack down on peaceful protests if they caused 'serious annoyance' or were 'too loud'. I also criticised the Online Safety Bill, formerly known as the Online Harms Bill, in which 'legal but harmful' speech would be outlawed. I pointed out that these terms of emotional 'safety' were directly lifted from the playbook of Critical Social Justice, and that far from waging a 'war on woke', the Conservatives were actively promoting it. 'I wanted to talk about this here at the conference,' I said, 'because I've never seen an MP stand up in Parliament and make the case for repealing the laws that we currently have that criminalise hate speech. I'd like to see someone have the guts to do that.' Disappointingly, during the audience questions afterwards, no attendee was willing to take me to task or defend the government's position on this matter. I would have relished the opportunity for the debate.

Neither major political party in the United Kingdom appears to take seriously the preservation of free speech. They are united in the belief that 'hatred', nebulous term as it is, can be eradicated through legislation. This hubristic notion that human nature can be fundamentally altered through the stroke of a pen is not restricted to a particular political viewpoint, and it is striking that so little thought has been exercised in the formation of laws and guidelines against so-called 'hate speech'. This problem was exacerbated in the summer of 2024, when anti-immigrant riots broke out throughout cities in the United Kingdom. On 29 July, seventeen-year-old Axel Rudakubana attacked a group of children participating in a dance and yoga workshop in Southport. He stabbed and killed three and injured ten others. Rumours soon circulated online suggesting that the perpetrator was an asylum-seeker; in truth, he was a British citizen born of Rwandan immigrants. After the trial, in which Rudakubana pleaded guilty and was sentenced to a minimum of fifty-two years in prison, it was revealed that the techniques used in the attack were drawn directly from an al-Qaeda training manual he had downloaded from the internet, although the materials found in his possession suggested a more generalised obsession with anti-white hatred and genocide. The Labour prime minister Keir Starmer blamed the civil unrest that followed on the 'far right', and doubtless much of it was fuelled by opportunism from those quarters. There were openly racist attacks. A hotel in Rotherham housing migrants was set on fire while rioters shouted 'smash the pakis', and mosques were assailed with bottles and bricks. This was white identity politics at its most repugnant. As editor of *Spiked* Tom Slater remarked, the culprits had 'presented two-tier policing not as an affront to law and order and blind justice, but as an expression of white male British victimhood'.

At the same time, there was also a strong element of collective anger from non-racists at the failures of the authorities to take seriously the issue of mass migration and its impact on crime. Previous atrocities had laid the groundwork for the riots. An independent inquiry into the bombing of the Manchester Arena by Islamic terrorist Salman Abedi in May 2017, in which twenty-two people were murdered, found that there were multiple 'missed opportunities' to intercept the killer. Although the presence of a lone male with a rucksack at this concert was deemed suspicious, a member of the security personnel admitted that he failed to question Abedi because 'he was fearful of being branded a racist and would be in trouble if he got it wrong'. This fear had arisen in the context of a climate in which to even address the potential problems caused by mass migration is to invite accusations of bigotry and hatred. While the violence of the summer riots could never be justified, and all those responsible for criminal activities fully deserved to be prosecuted, it would be foolish not to acknowledge that tensions had been intensified by a stubborn refusal among the media and political class to acknowledge legitimate concerns. Open conversations about key issues had been stymied, and yet in the wake of the riots the Labour Party doubled down by applying pressure to the judiciary to impose harsh jail terms for offensive comments online, while pledging to increase internet censorship in the future. Instead of treating the cancer in society, the government had chosen to give the carcinogens a boost.

In other words, the riots had provided all the pretence necessary for the Labour government to crack down further on free speech. This displacement activity was hardly unprecedented. The murder of Conservative MP Sir David Amess by an Islamic terrorist in October 2021 had precisely nothing to do with social media, and yet politicians immediately exploited the atrocity to argue that his death was evidence of the need to curtail speech online. Even after the trial of Rudakubana, there was a slew of preposterous articles about how he had purchased his knife from Amazon, as though this was the chief cause of the attack. Starmer pivoted to a discussion about greater control on the sales of knives and the need for stronger internet censorship.

While most of those prosecuted in the aftermath of the riots had committed acts of violence or vandalism, some of the cases were related solely to offensive speech. For example, Jordan Parlour was sentenced to twenty months for inciting racial hatred. After the Southport attack, he had posted the following message on Facebook: 'Every man and his dog should be smashing the fuck out of Britannia Hotel'. That such sentiments are reprehensible hardly needs to be stated. One of the major fallacies in the free speech debates is the assumption that those who are upholding someone's right to make objectionable statements are thereby endorsing what they have said. On the contrary, we need to support free speech even for those we despise, because once we have diluted the principle the consequences will affect us all. When it comes to incitement to violence, sensitivities are naturally high, but this is all the more reason why we need to initiate a sensible discussion. At present, we seem to be allowing our emotions to overcome our reason. Parlour's words were unconscionable, but even if his intention had been to incite violence there is precisely no evidence that he was successful. It is one thing to point out that there are keyboard warriors cheering on needless brutality, but it is quite another to assert a causal link between the two. This is a hypothesis that should be tested, not merely asserted, and this is especially the case if this hypothesis is to be the justification for public prosecutions.

Lucy Connolly, a mother and childminder, was sentenced to thirty-one months in prison in October 2024 for writing: 'Mass deportation now, set fire to all the fucking hotels full of the bastards for all I care, while you're at it take the treacherous government politicians with them. I feel physically sick knowing what these families will now have to endure. If that makes me racist, so be it.' Connolly deleted the post within three hours, but this was not sufficient to prevent the police taking action. Again, the assumption that there is a causal relationship between these kinds of comments on the internet and real-world harm has no basis in reality. Over six decades of research into media effects theories has proven that the public does not act on cue to suggestions or demands from the media. In his book *Mass Communication* (2011), Ralph E. Hanson describes the efforts of researchers in the period after the Second World War who were seeking to determine whether 'opinion and behavioural changes' might be actuated by media messaging, that viewers would be 'passive targets who would be hit or injected with the message, which, like a vaccine, would affect people in similar ways'. No correlation could be found and, according to Hanson, 'in the 1940s and 1950s researchers sometimes doubted whether media messages had any effect on individuals at all'. Rather, the studies have shown that there are numerous mediating factors to take into account, not least that 'audience members perceive and interpret these messages selectively according to individual differences'. In other words, those who act violently in response to other people's suggestions are already predisposed to do so and have not suddenly surrendered their individual agency.

Connolly was found guilty of 'distributing material with the intention of stirring up racial hatred', and yet in stating that 'it is a strength of our society that it is both diverse and inclusive' the judge revealed that his ruling was political in nature. It followed on from Prime Minister Keir Starmer's suggestion that judges ought to mete out the harshest sentences to set an example, which is why so many of the jail terms at this time seemed so draconian. Worse still, defendants were being advised to plead guilty to avoid being on remand indefinitely, and so apologists for this kind of state overreach were able to claim that justice had been served. During a television interview in August, Starmer said: 'I'm now expecting substantive sentencing before the end of this week, that should send a very powerful message to anybody involved, either directly or online.' Although the separation of powers is not so strictly enforced in the United Kingdom as the United States, this incident suggested that the government was disregarding judicial independence and leaning on the scales of justice. Moreover, the crime was elevated to 'category A' on the grounds that Connolly had intended to 'incite serious violence', a proposition that seems highly unlikely but was nevertheless asserted as justification for the length of the sentence. 'When you published those words, you were well aware how volatile the situation was,' the judge had said. 'That volatility led to serious disorder where mindless violence was used.' Quite so. And yet surely it should be the perpetrators of violence who are punished, not those who simply lash out on social media. In my view, the judge was mitigating the responsibility of the criminals by outsourcing it to Connolly, who committed no acts of violence and burned no hotels.

In order to limit the potential for state persecution of speech and thought in the United Kingdom, it would be prudent to implement an equivalent to the United States' threshold for incitement to violence known as the 'Brandenburg Test'. This was established by the Supreme Court in 1969, when the conviction of Ku Klux Klan leader Clarence Brandenburg for promoting violence was overturned. Following that precedent, the relevant test is that the speech in question must be deliberately aimed at inciting violence, likely to do so, and that any impact should be imminent. The case of Connolly does not qualify.

To his credit, Boris Johnson was one of the few politicians who criticised the judgement. 'What she said was vile, truly horrible,' he wrote in his column for the *Daily Mail*. 'She certainly deserved to be punished, perhaps with a fine or community service. But she is a mother of a young child, with no previous criminal record, and I can see no evidence that her disgusting remark – which she deleted within three hours – was intended to be seriously acted upon.' In this, Johnson was half-right and half-wrong. While he is correct to say that there is no evidence that her remark incited others to commit violence, I do not share his view that she should have faced criminal prosecution. Although few would support the content of her post, the consequences of empowering the government to punish its citizens for speech are too grave. That is to say, the issue is far more significant than Connolly, Parlour, or any of the other individuals who received excessively punitive jail terms during this period. For all our shared revulsion at the posts, we should ask ourselves which we consider to be more of a threat: a handful of people encouraging each other to commit violent crimes, or a state that seeks to regulate human emotion and imprison citizens on the basis of what they choose to say.

In his book *Censored* (2016), Paul Coleman helpfully gathers all of the existing legislation on 'hate speech' from across Europe and, in doing so, reveals that no two governments are able to agree on its meaning. The European Court of Human Rights has admitted that there 'is no universally accepted definition of the expression "hate speech"' and a manual published by UNESCO in 2015 agreed that 'the possibility of reaching a universally shared definition seems unlikely'. When it comes to the statute books, one would have thought that precision and detail would be of paramount importance. Hatred, like any emotion, cannot be legislated out of existence. Will we be seeing laws against envious speech on the statute books? And what about codes against wrath or pride? As for 'hate crimes', there is no need for mind-reading in order to determine the appropriate punishment. If I am physically assaulted, it makes little difference to me if my assailant was motivated by homophobia. I would prefer the sentence to reflect the crime itself, not to be moderated according to speculations about the perpetrator's private thoughts. The state should have absolutely no licence to probe inside our heads, any more than employers should insist on compulsory 'unconscious bias training' which, as studies show, is not only completely ineffective but can actually heighten bias in the workplace. In a free society, we are entitled to think and feel as we see fit. And so long as that does not interfere with the liberties of others, that includes the right to hate.

A plethora of activist publications have been busy promoting the myth that 'hate crime' is continually surging. Whenever crime statistics are published, ideologues leap upon the findings to promote their view that further restrictions on speech are necessary as a prophylactic measure. To take one example of hundreds, an article in the *Metro* published in June 2024 claimed that there had been a 462 per cent increase in homophobic hate crime and a 1,426 per cent increase in transphobic hate crime since 2012. The source for these remarkable figures was the House of Commons Hate Crime Statistics report. If true, it would seem to confirm activists' claims that the country is an anti-LGBTQIA+ cesspit. The truth is not so melodramatic. The supposed escalation of hate crimes in the United Kingdom can be accounted for by the way in which they are now recorded. Police actively trawl for complaints, inviting citizens to report offensive comments or any action – criminal or otherwise – that the 'victim' perceives to have been motivated by prejudice. No evidence of hatred is required for it to be recorded as such, other than the assumption of the complainant. Journalist Fraser Myers has described the result of these policies as a 'dangerous feedback loop':

> As more resources are piled into 'raising awareness' and investigating hate crime, the police end up with more reports. The rise in reporting then feeds into yet more demands for awareness-raising and more resources to tackle hate crime. All the while, the police insist that the true scale of hate crime remains hidden.

With such methodology in place, it is inevitable that the statistics will rise, and this is entirely in line with the College of Policing's belief that a drop in hate crime figures would not be acceptable. Its operational guidance specifies that 'targets that see success as reducing hate crime are not appropriate'. By the admission of the Home Office, 'increases in police-recorded hate crime in recent years have been driven by improvements in crime recording and a better identification of what constitutes a hate crime'. In other words, there is no hate crime epidemic at all. It is simply that the definitions have expanded.

Rather than rely on the Home Office statistics, we would be better turning to a source that has been insulated from ideological corruption.

The Crime Survey for England and Wales has not adopted the new police methods of recording, and shows that between 2008 and 2020 the number of hate crimes fell by 38 per cent. The disparity between the reality and the narrative could not be more stark. This is pure opportunism, untethered to empirical truth, similar to the continual claims that the 'trans community' is the most abused and marginalised. As writer and feminist campaigner Madison Smith has shown, those who identify as trans are among the safest demographic in Europe. Her analysis of the statistics reveals that 'the average adult in England and Wales has a one-in-100,000 chance of being murdered in a given year whereas the average trans person has a one-in-200,000 to one-in-500,000 chance of being murdered in the UK over the course of a year'. When Edinburgh City Council unfurled a flag over the city chambers in November 2024 to honour 'Transgender Day of Remembrance', it claimed to be doing so 'to remember people who have lost their lives in acts of transgender violence'. Given the exceptionally low rates of these kinds of crimes, the necessity for this gesture was unclear. The only Scottish individual included in the official list of those being commemorated was Andrew Burns, who had claimed a female identity and renamed himself Tiffany Scott following a string of convictions. This was sufficient to see his transfer to a female prison approved by the Scottish government, even though he had stalked a thirteen-year-old girl and was known as 'one of the most menacing people' inside the prison system and an 'unmanageable risk to public safety'. His death had nothing whatsoever to do with his pretensions to a trans identity, yet the flag was nonetheless raised in his honour above the city chambers.

Those who are sceptical of gender identity ideology are particularly susceptible to the misapplication of hate speech laws, and there is no way of knowing which other beliefs will eventually be criminalised. Once a state has outlawed 'hatred' and failed to define it, the law becomes a cudgel to beat anyone who holds heterodox points of view. Who is to say that a future government might not deem it 'hateful' to criticise its policies? What starts with the depletion of free speech ends with the criminalisation of opposition. As one who has received my fair share of online abuse, I understand that free speech has its downsides. But I choose to ignore those of the childish and hateful ilk rather than call for them to be censored. The price we pay for living in a free society is that obnoxious people are going to say obnoxious things. But their right to do so is precisely the same right that allows us to take them to task. If we attempt to silence even our most abusive critics, we are essentially surrendering our principles at their behest.

With the notable exception of the United States, the trajectory of laws around the western world is clear. The French government currently permits the prosecution of citizens for 'public insults' based on religion, race, ethnicity or national origin. In Germany, paragraph 103 of the criminal code insists that 'whosoever insults a foreign head of state or an accredited diplomat in Germany . . . shall be liable to imprisonment of up to three years or a fine'. In Finland, 'agitation against a minority group' is a crime under the criminal code, which is why politician Päivi Räsänen was prosecuted for posting a Bible verse on Twitter that was perceived to be homophobic. In March 2024, the Canadian government proposed a law that would give judges the ability to put a citizen under house arrest if they thought they *might* commit hate crimes in the future. It is known as Bill C-63, and would allow citizens to file complaints if they see any examples of online 'hate speech', leading to a potential $20,000 fine for those found guilty.

In Ireland, the Criminal Justice (Incitement to Violence of Hatred and Hate Offences) Bill represented one of the most severe forms of hate speech legislation yet produced. It was eventually quashed after various protests and a long campaign by free speech advocates, but it is chilling to consider how close it came to becoming law. In June 2023, the Irish Green Party Senator Pauline O'Reilly made no effort to disguise the authoritarian nature of the proposed bill. 'We are restricting freedom,' she said, 'but we're doing it for the common good.' Hasn't every tyrant in history made an identical claim? In her speech, O'Reilly invoked the notion of 'safety' to justify state censorship. 'If your views on other people's identities go to make their lives unsafe, insecure and cause them such deep discomfort that they cannot live in peace,' she said, 'then I believe it is our job as legislators to restrict those freedoms.' The Irish hate speech bill went further than most of its equivalents in other European countries. It was to give the state the right to prosecute those who cause offence under the catch-all of 'inciting hatred', and those found guilty could have faced up to five years in prison. Even more worryingly, a citizen could have been jailed for two years simply for possessing offensive material. In the proposed bill, 'hatred' was defined as 'hatred against a person or a group of persons in the State or elsewhere on account of their protected characteristics or any one of those characteristics'. Given that the Irish authorities were happy to implement legislation that depended on the circular definition of 'hatred' as 'hatred', we must be wary of further attempts to gift a rubber stamp to any future tyrannical government that wishes to suppress dissent.

## Tremors

The earthquake that struck Pompeii in 62 AD was devastating. Houses were toppled, streets torn apart, and over two thousand people killed. The locals assumed that this was the whim of some intemperate god, rebuilt the city, and got on with their lives. But this was just the prelude. Seventeen years later, Vesuvius erupted and the city was swallowed in a deluge of volcanic ash.

It is all too easy to miss the early warnings of an impending disaster. Today's culture wars are often interpreted as the symptoms of an ephemeral fad. Most can feel the tremors – restrictions on liberty, public shaming of those with unfashionable views, regressive identity politics masquerading as 'progress' – but there is a widespread sense that if we ignore the problems, they will simply disappear. But what if these rumblings presage something far worse to come? What if the end of woke is just the beginning of our troubles? What if the next phase of the culture war is even more devastating for free speech than the last? What if, like the people of Pompeii, we are at risk of civilisational collapse but are misinterpreting the signs?

Further tremors have reverberated recently courtesy of what has become known as the 'censorship-industrial complex'. The term is a derivative of the 'military-industrial complex', which describes the allegedly close relationship between defence contractors and the government, popularised after its inclusion in President Dwight D. Eisenhower's farewell address in January 1961. The various laws and policies enacted by the government to control speech are only likely to spiral as more citizens begin to understand the extent to which our liberties are being jeopardised by those in power. A new era of state censorship is potentially looming, with governments across the globe convincing themselves that all societal ills could be cured if only the speech of citizens was more carefully regulated. In these dying days of woke, a conflict is brewing between Europe and the United States, with the former clinging to the ideological shackles of the recent past as the latter seeks an unfettered future. It has the qualities of a novel by Henry James for the digital age, with the distinctions between the old world and the new brought into sharp focus. These were further highlighted by the United States vice president J. D. Vance in his speech at the Munich Security Conference in February 2025.

> When I look at Europe today, it's sometimes not so clear what happened to some of the cold war's winners. I look to Brussels, where EU Commission commissars warned citizens that they intend to shut down social media during times of civil unrest: the moment they spot what they've judged to be 'hateful content'. Or to this very country where police have carried out raids against citizens suspected of posting anti-feminist comments online as part of 'combating misogyny' on the internet.

Vance was blistering about the tendency of many European leaders to disregard the wishes of voters on the subjects of migration and free expression. 'If you're running in fear of your own voters,' he said, 'there is nothing America can do for you.' The speech was received with the predictable degree of indignation, with the German defence minister Boris Pistorius huffily dismissing it as 'not acceptable'. That censors do not enjoy being criticised should surprise precisely no one.

According to many members of the political class, the solution to the problem of a public that will not accept these fabricated narratives is censorship. In May 2024, the unelected president of the European Commission – Ursula von der Leyen – announced her intention to create a 'European Democracy Shield' to protect EU citizens from online 'disinformation'. Speaking at the Copenhagen Democracy Summit, she compared free speech to a virus:

> As technology evolves we need to build up societal immunity around information manipulation. Because research has shown that pre-bunking is much more successful than debunking. Pre-bunking is basically the opposite of debunking. In short, prevention is preferable to cure. Perhaps if you think of information manipulation as a virus. Instead of treating an infection, once it has taken hold, that is debunking. It is much better to vaccinate so that the body is inoculated. Pre-bunking is the same approach.

As a new synonym for 'censorship', 'pre-bunking' must surely rival 'pre-crime', 'thoughtcrime' and 'public safety' for the most unnerving entries in the dystopian lexicon. Naturally, social media is the key battleground. Activists, journalists and politicians have repeatedly called for restrictions to online platforms. In August 2024, Facebook CEO Mark Zuckerberg wrote a letter to Jim Jordan, the head of the judiciary committee at the House of Representatives, in which he admitted that 'senior officials from the Biden administration, including the White House, repeatedly pressured our teams for months to censor certain

Covid-19 content, including humour and satire, and expressed a lot of frustration with our teams when we didn't agree'. Elon Musk's free speech policies on X, and his refusal to censor at the whims of politicians, has prompted some to call on the police to intervene. In a piece written by Robert Reich, a former labour secretary under the Clinton administration, we had the following: 'Regulators around the world should threaten Musk with arrest if he doesn't stop disseminating lies and hate on X.' Jonathan Freedland wrote a piece in the *Guardian* entitled 'You know who else should be on trial for the UK's far-right riots? Elon Musk'. In August 2024, journalist Paul Mason demanded that the government 'enact the full Online Safety Act now' and summon the executives of X in the United Kingdom 'to explain why their CEO is personally boosting hate speech, incitement and disinformation – and pull the plug on the service until this stops'. Similarly, Edward Luce, Associate Editor of the *Financial Times*, has railed against 'Elon Musk's menace to democracy' and accused him of attempting 'to stoke racial conflict and civil breakdown'.

What has become known as 'Musk Derangement Syndrome' began in earnest when the entrepreneur first acquired Twitter in October 2022. In *The Atlantic*, Charlie Warzel wrote that 'there is, both inside and outside the company, an apocalyptic feel to the ordeal'. *Washington Post* columnist Taylor Lorenz went further, likening the platform's new ownership to the opening of the 'gates of hell'. The award for the most harrumphing and melodramatic response has to go to *The Independent*, which ran with: 'RIP Twitter, 2006-2022: Dead at the hands of Elon Musk'. In this article, the author describes Musk as a 'right-wing radical' and claims that his takeover of Twitter 'will bring nothing but the demise of democracy'. One must have a heart of stone to read it without laughing.

As Musk would agree, it is right to criticise one of the most powerful men on the planet in the most unflinching terms. The diagnosis of 'Musk Derangement Syndrome' has often been used as a cynical means of undermining anyone who takes issue with his conduct or opinions. And yet the examples provided here are so unrooted in reality that the

MDS label seems appropriate, if somewhat inelegant. As for Musk's other critics, they are correct to point out that it is far from ideal for billionaires to wield too much power over public discourse, but why did they not complain when Jeff Bezos, the left-leaning CEO of Amazon, bought the *Washington Post*? Might it be that their concern is more ideological than principled? We shall leave this mystery to one side so we might hear from Musk himself, who has offered the following explanation:

> The reason I acquired Twitter is because it is important to the future of civilisation to have a common digital town square, where a wide range of beliefs can be debated in a healthy manner, without resorting to violence.

These words make plain the impulse behind the hostile reaction. Prior to Musk's intervention, Twitter had been enacting policies that censored those points of view that deviated from those held by its executives. It had deliberately vague 'terms of service' that meant it could delete accounts without having to provide any justification. This is why feminists who believe that acknowledging the reality of biological sex is crucial for women's rights often found themselves thrown off the platform.

The pre-Musk Twitter had also purged satirical accounts that mocked the ideological worldview of its staff. *The Babylon Bee* was locked out for a satirical tweet in which the trans-identified US Assistant Secretary of Health Rachel Levine was named 'Man of the Year'; it was one of the many comedic accounts reinstated when Musk bought the platform. Within hours of his arrival at Twitter, Musk had fired a number of top executives, including Vijaya Gadde, who was head of legal, policy and trust. It was Gadde who made the decision to delete the account of President Donald Trump in January 2021. Musk also released the 'Twitter Files' in December 2022 – via a select group of journalists and writers including Matt Taibbi, Bari Weiss and Michael Shellenberger – which exposed collusion between Twitter and the state to see certain viewpoints censored. It also revealed details of how the company had suppressed an article by the *New York Post* in the run up to the 2020 election. Hunter Biden, son of Joe, had left his laptop to be repaired at a computer shop and had not returned to collect it. The contents of the hard drive were leaked to the *New York Post*, and were found to contain materials which suggested that Joe Biden may have been involved in his son's various dealings with foreign businessmen. This was potentially catastrophic for Biden's presidential campaign, and so Twitter locked the *New York Post* out of its account and prevented any user from sharing the article, even in the form of private messages. Twitter claimed that this action was necessary because the story might have been using 'hacked material', but that was pure speculation and turned out to be false. The 'Twitter Files' released by Musk revealed that not only did senior staff at Twitter understand that they had no grounds to censor the story, but that they were routinely suppressing tweets on the instructions of politicians. Both the Trump and Biden campaign teams were contacting the company to have tweets erased at their bidding but, as the staff were overwhelmingly in support of the Democrats, it meant that posts critical of Biden were the most commonly deleted. In one leaked email, a Twitter executive listed tweets that had been flagged and chillingly responded: 'handled these'.

The end of woke must entail a restoration of the indispensability of truth, and a renewed trust in the public to cope with misinformation themselves rather than appealing to authorities for greater censorship. There have been some positive signs. In January 2025, Mark Zuckerberg announced that Meta – the parent company of Facebook and Instagram – would be dispensing with politically partisan 'fact-checkers' who had exploited their roles to enforce the orthodoxy. The extent of their collective hubris was such that they genuinely seemed to believe it was their job to police the opinions of the world. To further redress this bias, Zuckerberg pledged that he would be moving the Meta headquarters from California to Texas, and lifting restrictions on contentious topics.

This course-correction is long overdue. For too long, the richest people in the world have enjoyed their plutocratic privilege of imposing their beliefs on everyone else. Donald Trump's executive order – 'Restoring Freedom of Speech and Ending Federal Censorship' – was candid in its intention to tackle this problem:

> Over the last 4 years, the previous administration trampled free speech rights by censoring Americans' speech on online platforms, often by exerting substantial coercive pressure on third parties, such as social media companies, to moderate, deplatform, or otherwise suppress speech that the Federal Government did not approve. Under the guise of combatting 'misinformation,' 'disinformation,' and 'malinformation,' the Federal Government infringed on the constitutionally protected speech rights of American citizens across the United States in a manner that advanced the Government's preferred narrative about significant matters of public debate. Government censorship of speech is intolerable in a free society.

The fear of the written word is one that we have seen before. The development of the printing press in Europe in the Middle Ages generated a kind of hysteria among the elites. Virtually overnight, the plebeians were able to read about world events unmediated by those in power. In 1501, Pope Alexander VI threatened to excommunicate those who printed texts without the permission of the church. For obvious reasons, the dissemination of knowledge is a significant threat to those whose authority depends on keeping the masses uninformed. When content moderators, government officials, or 'fact-checkers' refer to 'misinformation', they typically mean information that challenges the narrative they wish to promote. It is based on a contempt for the people; many world leaders simply do not trust their citizens to think critically. This is why so many politicians blamed 'Russian bots' for Brexit, as though the electorate comprised of mindless drones who act on cue to commands issued on social media.

Rarely do these politicians stop to consider the plausibility of their position. Yes, there are some who are happy to submit to authority and whose opinions seem to derive from prejudice or fashion rather than individual reflection. But most people are perfectly capable of thinking for themselves, and would rather not be herded one way or the other. Besides, why would we trust Silicon Valley tech giants – those whose stated goal is the accumulation of as much money as possible – to determine the scope of acceptable viewpoints? Is there anyone who genuinely believes that true objectivity is possible when it comes to content moderation? The online space offers an ideal forum for bad ideas to be tested with better information and analysis. Moreover, it is unfeasible to attempt to eliminate falsehoods from human discourse. All of us are wrong about many things at any given time, and it is only through discussion and debate that we are able to edge closer to the truth.

The tremors of authoritarianism have reverberated most aggressively with the renewed attacks on the First Amendment to the United States Constitution, perhaps the final bastion of free speech in the West. In the run-up to the election of 2024, the public saw evidence that neither the Democratic nor Republican parties observed a firm commitment to the principle. In October, Donald Trump called for the federal government to withdraw the broadcasting licence of CBS News – even though no such licence exists – because of its misleading editing of an interview with Kamala Harris. As president elect in 2016 and during his campaign in 2024, Trump asserted that those who burn the national flag ought to be imprisoned for a year. At a rally in Texas in 2016, he threatened to 'open up the libel laws' to make it easier to sue his critics. The Democratic Party fared no better. During the vice-presidential debate on 1 October 2024, the Democratic candidate Tim Walz interjected to claim that 'hate speech' is excluded from First Amendment protections. The remark was so fleeting that it was not even included in the official CBS News transcript, but it was perhaps the most significant moment of the evening. In the previous month, former Secretary of State John Kerry had argued that when it comes to 'disinformation', the 'First Amendment stands as a major block to be able to just, you know, hammer it out of existence'.

The First Amendment codifies a 'negative liberty', not a licence for certain behaviour but rather a protection from government interference.

> Congress shall make no law respecting an establishment of religion, or prohibiting the free exercise thereof; or abridging the freedom of speech, or of the press; or the right of the people peaceably to assemble, and to petition the Government for a redress of grievances.

Challenges to the First Amendment began in earnest with the emergence of the woke movement. In March 2018, an article appeared on the website of the American Civil Liberties Union (ACLU) which noted that by this point it was 'common' for leftist activists 'to call for lower legal protections for speech'. The writer concluded that such calls were misguided, describing the First Amendment as 'our most powerful tool to keep the government from regulating the conversations that spark change in the world'. But other activists took a different view from the ACLU. In 2018, two early proponents of Critical Race Theory, Richard Delgado and Jean Stefancic, republished their 1997 book *Must We Defend Nazis?: Hate Speech, Pornography, and the New First Amendment*. This version of the book was modified according to the shift in activists' demands, and the subtitle was now *Why the First Amendment Should Not Protect Hate Speech and White Supremacy*. In that same year, activist and legal scholar Justin Hansford argued in the *Yale Law Journal Forum* that, when it comes to race, the 'marketplace of ideas' does not apply. 'When ideas on race that would disrupt the racial hierarchy of white over Black emerge,' he wrote, 'the First Amendment is disproportionately applied to trample that dissent.'

The woke faithful have always taken a pro-censorship stance, but by 2018 the First Amendment was clearly identified as the key obstacle to their aims. This was developed further in *The Cult of the Constitution* (2019), in which legal scholar Mary Anne Franks took aim at 'First Amendment fundamentalism'. An entire chapter was devoted to what Franks calls 'the cult of free speech'. In October 2019, former editor of *Time* magazine Richard Stengel continued this disturbing trend with an article for the *Washington Post* entitled 'Why America needs a hate speech law'. Stengel rehashed the typical concerns about 'false narratives' and 'lies', as though any kind of speech regulator could possibly be immune from deceptive or misleading behaviour. He also repeated the 'direct effects theory' which posits that people act on cue from social media posts, even though such notions have been fully discredited. The First Amendment, Stengel argued, 'should not protect hateful speech that can cause violence by one group against another. In an age when everyone has a megaphone, that seems like a design flaw.'

A snobbish mistrust of the masses lies at the heart of the opposition to the First Amendment, a feature that we can trace to the Frankfurt School and the French postmodernists of the 1960s, two groups that have substantially influenced the philosophy behind wokeness. According to this view, popular culture has created a society of unthinking clones. What Herbert Marcuse described as the 'one-dimensional man' is therefore irredeemably blind to his own persecution and reacts mechanically according to decrees from above. It is maintained that 'hate speech' has the power to rile up one group against another, even though the evidence for this claim is scant. The history of censorship plainly reveals that it does not have the desired effect, because bad ideas that are driven underground tend to fester and multiply. Furthermore, laws against offensive speech soon become expanded to incorporate any viewpoints that are not approved by those in power. Any attempt to carve out exceptions to the First Amendment for 'hate speech' will inevitably embolden the state to curb freedom of expression at will. The wholly subjective notion of 'hate' means that this will be tantamount to a censor's charter, a means by which political opposition can be stifled with the backing of the constitution. As more and more political figures are willing to openly question the validity of the First Amendment, the threat to free speech in the West is now palpable. The tremors are becoming more frequent, and we ignore them at our peril.

# 6

# Gender Wars

## Mannish Women and Womanish Men

'A man in his natural perfection is fierce, hardy, strong in opinion, covetous of glory, desirous of knowledge, appetiting by generation to bring forth his semblable. The good nature of a woman is to be mild, timorous, tractable, benign, of sure remembrance, and shamefast.' These words were written by the diplomat Sir Thomas Elyot in 1531 but, with a little tinkering, they could pass for the kind of rigid assertions currently gaining traction among a handful of prominent conservative commentators. Social media influencer Andrew Tate, for instance, has gained an immense online following for promoting conventional roles for men and women, equating male success to wealth, physical strength, and a duty to dominate a timorous and tractable wife. Tate might well be trolling – some have claimed that he is committed to playing an elaborate character – but his position nonetheless reflects a growing trend of those who hold such views in earnest. It is no coincidence that these ideas are enjoying a resurgence at the very same time that certain left-leaning activists are doing their utmost to advance a social constructionist view of both sex and gender.

The result has been a curious theoretical alliance between gender ideologues – those for whom outmoded stereotypes are taken to signify an authentic self – and traditionalists who similarly feel that male and female behaviour ought to be strictly defined.

That Elyot's ideas about men and women do not seem out of place in today's gender wars is a striking reminder that we have been here before. Debates about gender were common in early seventeenth-century England, due to a combination of the rise of puritanism, concerns over cross-dressing, and the accession of King James I who would openly kiss his boyfriends at court. The puritans were particularly exercised over the influence of the theatre, perceiving it as a decadent distraction from the worship of God and liable to corrupt the soul; William Prynne had condemned the theatre as the 'chief delight of the Devil' in his *Histrio-Mastix* (1633). England was unusual in banning women from the stage – most European countries did not have such prohibitions – and Prynne dismissed actresses as 'notorious whores'. He saw the male actors in women's attire as 'an inducement to Sodomy', an affront to scripture and natural law.

Inevitably, these anxieties found their way into the work of dramatists. In John Fletcher's *Love's Cure* (c. 1612), the boy Lucio is raised as a girl in order to protect him from becoming the victim of a vendetta between feuding families. Lucio's manner of speech approaches what we would now call 'high camp', and one cannot help but imagine a young Kenneth Williams in the role. Here Lucio is complaining to the family servant Bobadilla:

> Go fetch my work: this Ruffe was not well starch'd,
> So tell the maid, 't has too much blew in it,
> And look you that the Partridge and the Pullen
> Have clean meat, and fresh water, or my Mother
> Is like to hear on't.

An exasperated Bobadilla exclaims to the audience: 'Oh good St Jaques help me: was there ever such an Hermaphrodite heard of?' The premise of Fletcher's comedy is that having been socialised as female, Lucio cannot help but embody stereotypically feminine traits. Eventually, Lucio learns how to fight and his inherent masculinity is restored through marriage. Just as the homoerotic relationship between Antonio and Sebastian in Shakespeare's *Twelfth Night* (c. 1602) is contained by the eventual marriage of the latter to Olivia, Fletcher is free to explore gendered dissidence so long as it is 'cured' by the end of the play.

This desire to ensure that sexual orientation and gendered behaviour is aligned with biological sex is similarly prominent in today's culture wars. Battle lines have been drawn in which gender non-conformity in youth, a reliable predictor of homosexuality in adult life, is being interpreted as a problem to be rectified by medical intervention. The ascent of gender identity ideology has meant that the achievements of feminists and gay rights activists over the last fifty years have been temporarily reversed. Heteronormative expectations and stereotypes are back in fashion, and young people who do not naturally fulfil these roles appear to be the casualties. I am reminded of an anonymous pamphlet from the late Jacobean era called *Hic-Mulier: Or, The Man-Woman* (1620), which likewise sees gender non-conformity as something to be fixed. Women who cross-dress and embody masculine tropes are described as 'an infection that emulates the plague'. A form of reply came in a subsequent publication entitled *Haec-Vir; Or, The Womanish-Man* (1620), in which a feminine man and a masculine woman discuss their respective conditions. The pamphlet takes the form of a dialogue, and their ultimate resolution is to swap their identities. Haec-Vir declares: 'We will here change our attires, as we have chang'd our minds, and with our attires, our names. I will no more be *Haec-Vir*, but *Hic Vir*, nor you *Hic-Mulier*, but *I Iaec Mulier*: from henceforth deformity shall pack to Hell: and if at any time he hide himself upon the earth, yet it shall be with contempt and disgrace.'

Ours is clearly not the first culture to develop an obsession with gender roles and how they might be subverted, although it is perhaps

*Illustration from Haec-Vir; Or, The Womanish-Man (1620).*

the first to entertain the notion that sex itself is a kind of fiction. 'It's not correct that there is such a thing as biological sex,' claims Dr Nicholas Matte of the Sexual Diversity Studies programme at the University of Toronto. For Amia Srinivasan, Professor of Social and Political Theory at the University of Oxford, sex is 'a cultural thing posing as a natural one', or 'gender in disguise'. Such faddish ideas have trickled from the most obscure niches of academia into mainstream thought, which is why *Forbes* magazine could publish an article entitled 'The myth of biological sex', in which the author breezily asserts 'there is no one parameter that makes a person biologically male or female'. Developmental biologists will be unsurprised to learn that the word 'gamete' does not appear once in the article.

It is significant that activists who insist that stereotypes of male and female behaviour are suggestive of an innate 'gender identity' should also seek to deny the reality of sexual dimorphism. Both positions are based on faith rather than evidence. The view that sex is a 'spectrum' has even infiltrated major academic literature, including the prestigious *New England Journal of Medicine*. Arguably, such pseudo-scientific notions have much in common with medical discourses of the early modern period, derived in part from the theories of Galen, who saw women as defective men, a mere diversification from what the historian and sexologist Thomas Laqueur has described as the 'one canonical body'. These ideas had the advantage of establishing sex as inherently hierarchal, meaning that patriarchy was not so much a philosophical proposition as a condition of natural law. According to the prevailing view of the time, men's genitals were external because they had been forced out by their innate heat. As Helkiah Crooke, court physician to King James I, asserted in his *Mikrokosmographia* (1615), women's genitals 'remain within, because their dull and sluggish heat is not sufficient to thrust them out'. There is even an essay by Michel de Montaigne from 1574 ('On the power of the imagination'), in which he describes a young woman called Marie Germain whose genitals one day emerge from her body as she takes a particularly masculine stride. That activists are returning to this notion of sex as a spectrum is a sure sign that their movement is fundamentally regressive. Such outright denial of reality is only ever likely to exacerbate the kind of biological essentialism of conservatives who demand that boys and girls behave in their 'natural' way. Nor is it persuasive to insist, in accordance with a minority of feminists, that gender is entirely socially constructed. The truth, of course, lies somewhere in between.

The inescapable reality of sexual dimorphism means that it is a natural target for those of an authoritarian mindset who seek to exert control on how we see the world. As a strategy of dominance, there is little difference in forcing people to declare that there are more than two sexes, or that sex does not exist, or that it operates as a spectrum, and demanding that they chant 'two plus two equals five'. In Orwell's *Nineteen Eighty-Four*, Winston Smith writes in his diary: 'Freedom is the freedom to say that two plus two make four. If that is granted, all else follows.' After the prolonged torture in Room 101, his worldview has been inverted, and he finds himself unconsciously tracing the equation '2+2=5' in the dust on a table. The process of compelled thought begins with compelled speech, and compelled speech begins with gentle coercion. 'Why not add your pronouns to your email signature?' 'Why not announce your pronouns at the beginning of meetings?' 'Why not encourage your staff members to ask for pronouns in day-to-day conversation?' After all, it's just about being compassionate and creating a more 'inclusive' work environment. Surely only an unreconstructed bigot would object to that?

It's this kind of skewed reasoning that led to the firing of Fran Itkoff, a 90-year-old volunteer for the National Multiple Sclerosis Society, who simply expressed confusion when faced with a request that she add pronouns to her emails. 'I had seen it on a couple of letters that had come in after the person's name', Itkoff said in an interview, 'but I didn't know what it meant'. It is to be expected that a nonagenarian would be befuddled by this strange new quasi-religious ritual, so rapidly has the practice taken hold. This didn't stop the National MS Society from turning its back on Itkoff, a volunteer whose commitment to the charity dated back six decades. For committing heresy against the Holy Creed of DEI, Itkoff was immediately sacrificed. The statement issued by the National MS Society claimed that her query about pronouns was 'viewed as not aligning with our policy of inclusion'. Declaring pronouns makes little sense in any case, given that they are used in place of a name when talking *about* someone, not *to* someone. Besides, human beings are perfectly capable of determining someone's sex without being told, usually instantaneously.

When Ramsay Bolton in *Game of Thrones* insists that his captive Theon Greyjoy adopts the name 'Reek', it is not simply a method to shape his new identity as his slave. For all the many violations that tyrants can commit against their subjects – imposing restrictions on their movement, impeding their living conditions, and even taking their lives – freedom of thought is not so easily defeated. A man on the rack may privately despise his torturers, all the while praising their munificence and pleading for release. The ultimate power of the ruling party in Orwell's *Nineteen Eighty-Four* is only achieved once they have burrowed into Winston's mind and rearranged his thoughts. Compelled speech is the route to this kind of domination, and the more maddening the process, the more likely it is to succeed. The invention of neo-pronouns such as 'xe', 'xem' and 'xyr' falls into the category. So too does the insistence that 'they' and 'them' should be normalised as singular pronouns, when they have only ever been used as such when the sex of an individual is unknown. A phrase such as 'I wonder who left their keys here?' causes no confusion at all because the sentence automatically conveys the uncertainty. Such colloquial exceptions aside, 'they' is simply not used as a singular pronoun among the general population. It is far too unwieldy and impracticable for members of the public to willingly adapt their speech patterns. The mainstream media, beholden as it is to the new dogma, has nonetheless wholeheartedly embraced this initiative in various style guides. Most of the articles that adhere to this creed end up being both syntactically and stylistically incoherent. Take the following excerpt from a review in the *Atlantic* of Judith Butler's book *Who's Afraid of Gender?* (2024):

> In essence, Butler accuses gender-crits of 'phantasmatic' anxieties. They dismiss, with that invocation of a 'phantasm,' apprehension about the presence of trans women in women's single-sex spaces . . .

At first glance, 'they' could appear to be referring to the 'gender-crits', but in this case it refers to Butler. A reader unfamiliar with the subject will inevitably find this confusing. Throughout the article, one is forced to reset one's reading instincts – cultivated through a lifetime of universally shared linguistic conventions – and, even though the meaning eventually becomes clear, the prose is irredeemably maladroit. In other words, those who accept these new rules must first surrender their capacity to write well.

While identitarian activists exult in dismissing Shakespeare as an irrelevant dead white male, they are happy to invoke him to support their attempts to impose their own modifications to the English language. In almost all articles on the singular 'they', one will find a reference somewhere to Shakespeare. 'For decades, transgender rights advocates have noted that literary giants Emily Dickinson, William Shakespeare, William Wordsworth, and Geoffrey Chaucer all used singular they in their writing', claims one writer for the *Los Angeles Times*. 'Shakespeare used the singular they, and so should you', claims another on the *Medium* website. In the *Washington Post*, a professor of English writes that 'Shakespeare and Austen both used singular "they" . . . just as many English speakers do now'. It is difficult to see how this argument is in any way compelling. Nobody is claiming that language does not evolve. The point is rather that the singular 'they' has not caught on in modern usage, in spite of activists' demands that it should.

In any case, this common claim is simply false. If it is true that Shakespeare frequently refers to individuals by a plural pronoun, why are there so few examples? A cursory scan of the innumerable articles on the subject reveals that only one instance is generally cited. As the *Los Angeles Times* puts it: 'In "Hamlet," Shakespeare used "them" in reference to the word mother: "'Tis meet that some more audience than a mother – Since nature makes them partial – should o'erhear the speech"'. This is an instance of synesis, or notional agreement, where the strict grammatical rules are suspended for semantic clarity. It is not the case that Polonius, the speaker of this line, is here referring to one individual as 'they', as he is clearly talking about all mothers and their inherent biases towards their offspring. Having trawled the various articles on this topic, the only examples that are ever actually provided of Shakespeare using the singular 'they' are similar cases of notional agreement. For instance: 'God send every one their heart's desire!' from *Much Ado About Nothing* (c. 1598), or 'There's not a man I meet but doth salute me / As if I were their well-acquainted friend' from *The Comedy of Errors* (c. 1594). Shakespeare is referring to multiple hearts and multiple men, and it is quite the stretch to assert that he is here promoting the validity of non-binary identities.

Those who take umbrage at the natural evolution of language are wasting their energy. Yet in the case of 'they' and 'them' as singular, there has been no such evolution at all, only an attempt to impose by coercion a new set of diktats. Even those who gleefully refer to individuals as 'they' soon trip themselves up, because there is a good reason why the English language has developed with readily differentiated singular and plural terms. Gender ideologues and their elitist allies are free to speak the language as they see fit, but they have little chance of imposing their foibles on the rest of us. Even in these final days of the woke movement, they continue to insist with all the aggression they can muster that sex has been superseded by 'gender identity', but this does not improve its chances of being accepted as true. For most of us, announcing pronouns makes about as much sense as declaring the colour of our aura.

To ask for pronouns in the workplace, in other words, is the equivalent of suggesting that employees pledge fealty to a deity they do not worship. It is a kind of test, a way to ensure that the tenets of Critical Social Justice are being observed. Spinoza argued that for any man to 'be compelled to speak only according to the dictates of the supreme power' is a violation of his 'indefeasible natural right' to be 'the master of his own thoughts'. While the declaration of pronouns remains a purely voluntary matter, it is fair to say that no one's free speech is being violated. But the consequences for non-compliance in the workplace are becoming increasingly severe. Members of staff are passed over for promotion, smeared as bigots and 'transphobes', and eventually shunned and isolated. And once you agree to make statements in favour of a belief-system you do not hold, you are surrendering your agency to those who will exploit it.

There have been similar efforts to impose 'cis' on a public that has no need to adopt it in everyday usage. This is in spite of the fact that many people consider the term to be a slur. 'Cis' is a Latin prefix meaning 'on the same side as' – as opposed to 'trans' meaning 'on the opposite side as' – which has long been applied in scientific disciplines. However, 'cisgender' and 'transgender' are neologisms, whose popularity has exploded in recent years only in niche activist circles. The term 'cis' has a specifically political function: to normalise the very concept of 'gender identity' and to suggest that those who are happy with their biological sex need to be defined *against* something. But of course if one accepts that there are only two sexes, then any further qualifications become redundant. Whereas the creation of the terms 'heterosexual' and 'homosexual' in late nineteenth-century medical discourse helped to reinforce the fact that being same-sex attracted is a natural, albeit less common, phenomenon, there is nothing innate about the ideological belief in 'gender'. It would be like dividing humankind into 'Marxists' and 'non-Marxists'. The only purpose in doing so would be to promote the idea that Marxism is the natural default.

Let's consider a hypothetical analogy. Imagine that a profoundly religious man refers to an atheist as a 'heretic'. Is this intended as a slur? Possibly. One can imagine the term 'Heretic!' being screamed by a zealot as a form of angry reproach, much like John Cleese's Pharisee in *Monty Python's Life of Brian* (1979) who shouts 'Blasphemer!' at the man who dares to utter the name of Jehovah. But in most cases the term 'heretic' is used by a believer to describe a non-believer, if not always dispassionately. The online world has many of its own Pharisees, who do indeed scream 'Cis!' as a kind of slur. When one hears activists complaining about 'cis lesbians' who refuse to include men in their dating pools, the tone is clearly spiteful. But we also see it used by those who consider it to be merely descriptive and are baffled by the idea that it could cause offence. The problem is that the word 'cis' is only intelligible in the context of the faith. Does an atheist accept the designation of 'heretic', given that he does not believe in the religion he is meant to be denying? For that matter, isn't the term 'atheist' questionable on the grounds that it assumes there is a debate to be had over the existence of God in the first place? There is no word for those who disbelieve in unicorns or fairies, so for someone who does not believe in God, the very term 'atheist' is redundant.

The standard definition of 'cisgender' is that it refers to 'people whose gender identity corresponds with their sex assigned at birth'. This is unsatisfactory mostly because it is based on an obvious factual error: sex is never 'assigned at birth', it is observed, usually before birth. But the definition also neglects the point that very few people believe in a 'gender identity' in the first place, so the term 'cisgender' is only comprehensible when attributed to one of the faithful. No educational, governmental or media establishment ought to be insisting on terminology that has its roots in a quasi-religious belief-system. We should object to its use in the workplace for the same reason that we object to the insistence that we announce our pronouns in emails, or that before business meetings we should declare our faith in Christ, Mohammed, Jehovah, Baal, or Pomona the ancient Roman goddess of plenty. Of course, the attempts to normalise 'cis' in everyday language have generally failed. Even today, most people do not know what it means, and struggle to understand the point when it is explained. It is the same reason why the concept of the 'thetan' is unlikely to become mainstream; very few will be cajoled into believing that we have extra-terrestrial spirits inside our bodies that can only be ablated by selling one's soul to the Church of Scientology.

Many of the demands of gender activists, linguistic or otherwise, are habitually couched in tones of faux-benevolence, but we have seen how this group has a particular tendency to viciousness and bullying. Its members carry with them the inquisitorial spleen of the elect. 'Be kind . . . or else' is not a maxim to which any of us should be willing to capitulate, and there is incontrovertible evidence that violence has become normalised within the movement. In March 2023, women's rights campaigner Kellie-Jay Keen (aka Posie Parker) was physically assaulted at an event in Auckland, New Zealand. Keen has run numerous protests around the world under the banner of 'Let Women Speak' because she takes the view that women who have attempted to raise concerns about their sex-based rights are often silenced. In an effort to disprove her arguments, large groups of angry men have frequently turned up to prevent her from speaking. Evidently such groups are not well attuned to irony.

In the run-up to the event in Auckland, the partisan mainstream media had been busy smearing Keen as efficiently as they could. Most disgracefully, the national media outlet Newshub – which disbanded in July 2024 – had even gone so far as to falsely accuse Keen of being a white supremacist. The dishonest contortions were something to behold. The editors at Newshub had taken a freeze-frame from an interview with Keen at the moment that she was adjusting the zip on her top. They had pixellated her hand, and then pretended that she was making the 'OK' symbol that some believe is a cipher for 'white power'. Those who had seen the original interview without the blurred effect knew that this claim was false. In that same interview Keen had defended the speech rights of Māori women which, as commentator and podcaster Stephen Knight pointed out, would have been 'an odd flex for someone intending to signal to their white supremacist supporters'. There can be little doubt that Newshub had intentionally attempted to mislead its viewers, especially given its further claim that neo-Nazis had attended the Let Women Speak event in Melbourne, Australia, just days before. While it is true that such groups were present, as the Australian Jewish Council noted these were thugs who 'saw an opportunity to hijack the event for their own publicity'. In fact, the neo-Nazis had been clashing with Socialist Alliance, a supposedly anti-fascist group that nonetheless seemed to be more concerned with shutting down a women's gathering than confronting the actual fascists. This gate-crashing had provided the opportunity for Newshub and other media outlets to conflate the neo-Nazis with the women, falsely claiming that they were allies. Had they reflected for even one eyeblink, they would have remembered that fascists are not renowned for their profound concerns over women's safeguarding.

The activists masquerading as journalists had done their job, and the temperature was duly raised. There was no police presence at the Let Women Speak event in Auckland, and so a baying mob quickly gathered; viral footage circulated of these mostly male activists pushing, shoving and screaming abuse at Keen. Were it not for the courage of the stewards, she might have been seriously injured or killed. One trans-identified observer boasted that he 'got turned on today watching the fear in Posie Parkers [*sic*] eyes. She actually was fearing for her life.' During the chaos, a young activist punched a seventy-one-year-old woman in the face, resulting in a concussion and bruising. This was violence unleashed under the pretence of compassion. Even so, we are continually assured that these activists are 'marginalised' and 'vulnerable'. If this is true, why do they enjoy the support of all major corporations and public institutions? Why are they able to call on the police to arrest those who refuse to comply with their speech codes? Why are they tolerated and even celebrated when they harass and physically assault women who are gathering peacefully to express their views?

It is incontestable that the majority of trans-identified people are appalled by such conduct. I have often heard transsexuals complain that the antics of these activists have made their lives much worse, and that these so-called 'allies' are doing far more harm than good. How does it help anyone to smear J. K. Rowling as a 'transphobe' and send her so many death and rape threats that she has remarked she could 'paper the house with them'? Hundreds of screenshots of violent threats against women campaigning for their rights have been collated on the 'Terf is a Slur' website. The acronym 'TERF' stands for 'Trans Exclusionary Radical Feminist', and has become an abusive term for women's rights campaigners, equivalent to 'whore' or 'witch'. Some typical examples from this website include:

Any trans allies at Pride London right now need to step the fuck up and take out the TERF trash. Get in their faces. Make them afraid. Debate never works so fuck them up.

If you're a TERF, you can get fucked with the business end of the barbed-wire baseball bat.

Stab a TERF today! Remember to twist the knife and then remove it.

Just to clarify, and I cannot stress this enough, no TERF deserves teeth. Punch any you see as hard as you can. I say this because talking to them absolutely will not work.

If these campaigners sincerely hope to persuade us that they are women, acting like drunk blokes with anger management issues is hardly a sensible approach.

The history books are full of instances in which groups have been vilified as subhuman to justify appalling atrocities. The acronym 'TERF' is a shorthand to connote a bestial status, a kind of incantation that disobliges activists from treating their targets as human beings. By their rationale, a TERF is a cockroach, and cockroaches can be crushed. Steven Shaviro, an academic at Wayne State University in Detroit, posted the following on his Facebook page: 'So here is what I think about free speech on campus. Although I do not advocate violating federal and state criminal codes, I think it is far more admirable to kill a racist, homophobic, or transphobic speaker than it is to shout them down.' The pernicious and inhumane tenor of the culture wars has meant that we have grown accustomed to such opinions, even from professors working in higher education. Leaving aside our obvious objections to murder in any circumstances, Shaviro also fails to take into account that virtually everyone who is branded a racist, homophobe or transphobe in the current climate is nothing of the kind. In that context, surely it is unwise to claim that murdering them is 'admirable'.

The bone and muscle of liberalism is the belief in freedom of speech. This means that we are able to assault our opponents verbally but not physically. Offensive speech is not violence; it represents its precise negation. It means that the speaker has chosen to attack ideas rather than bodies. The insistence from activists that 'words are violence' is a dangerous inversion of the truth, one that can encourage the view that bloodshed is an acceptable form of debate. Political violence is an oxymoron. It is an essentially authoritarian phenomenon. In his attempted assassination of Donald Trump in July 2024, Thomas Crooks sought not only to deprive another human being of his life, but also to deprive voters of their right to choose. Tony Benn was correct to describe all war as 'a failure of diplomacy', and this description is similarly apt for the actions of any would-be Gavrilo Princip taking history into his own hands.

Has the woke movement nudged us into a new world in which political violence is the norm? At the 'London Trans+ Pride' march in July 2023, an ex-convict who identifies as a woman took to the stage and proclaimed: 'I was going to come here and be really fluffy, be really nice and be really lovely and queer and gay. Nah, if you see a TERF, punch them in the fucking face.' The words would have been bad enough, but the reaction of the audience was surely the most disturbing aspect. If violent rhetoric hasn't been habitualised in this movement, why would the crowd cheer upon hearing these words? Surely the overwhelming majority of sensible adults would have reacted with stunned silence, or removed this unhinged individual from the platform before he could harm their cause any further? Virtually all trans activist protests involve some kind of demonstration of aggression, whether that be placards bearing phrases such as 'Kill J. K. Rowling' or 'Punch TERFs' or actual instances of physical hostility. Such rhetoric is now so commonplace that two SNP politicians were photographed next to an activist holding a placard with the slogan 'Decapitate TERFs', along with an image of a guillotine, and they didn't even notice.

It is surely about time that mainstream commentators condemned such tactics rather than pretending this is simply a civil rights movement like any other. Instead, reporters persist in claiming that women's rights is a Trojan Horse for fascism. This misapprehension was made explicit in a cartoon by Rod Emmerson in the *New Zealand Herald* in which Kellie-Jay Keen was depicted as a large wooden horse surrounded by neo-Nazis. It was clear that Emmerson did not understand the concept of the Trojan Horse; I doubt very much the Greeks would have made it into the city of Troy if they had been standing *outside* the structure. Such quibbles aside, surely the Trojan Horse metaphor would be far more apposite for individuals who claim to be compassionate, are convinced of their own archangelic perfection, and yet routinely send threats of death and rape to anyone who challenges their worldview. The genderist movement is often presented as saccharine and kittenish, garlanded with glitter and rainbow flags and 'Love Wins' hashtags. But, like the Trojan Horse, there are plenty of angry men inside waiting to commit bloody carnage.

## The Drag Revolution

During the woke era, the gender wars became the key means by which power was exerted and the authoritarian impulse unleashed. Whereas the establishment once sought to curb transgressive gender expressions, it suddenly sought to celebrate and even impose their normalisation. Those who failed to applaud such transgressions were stigmatised as bigots and punished. Whereas gender fluidity had once represented a challenge to those in power, it had now become the authoritarians' chief weapon. Paradoxically, to transgress was to conform.

How else might one account for the enthusiasm for 'Drag Queen Story Hour', in which drag queens visited schools, libraries and other council venues to read to young children? This bizarre subgenre has been championed by celebrities and politicians in an effort to pose as progressive. In July 2022, the MP for Walthamstow, Stella Creasy, tweeted about taking her infant son to a show in which a drag queen called Greta Tude 'put so much energy into story telling and entertaining local children'. Her colleague Nadia Whittome replied, describing the event as 'so wholesome'. But do fans of drag, a longstanding form of adult entertainment, really crave a wholesome version? The appeal of the art form is that it revels in sexual dissidence, as the American drag queen Kitty Demure has pointed out:

> I have no idea why you want drag queens to read books to your children . . . Would you want a stripper or a porn star to influence your child? It makes no sense at all. A drag queen performs in a nightclub for adults. There is a lot of filth that goes on, a lot of sexual stuff that goes on, and backstage there's a lot of nudity and sex and drugs. Okay? So I don't think this is an avenue that you would want your child to explore.

Anyone whose familiarity with drag extends beyond sanitised television acts such as Hinge and Bracket will know that this assessment is accurate. One Easter Sunday, many years ago, some friends and I attended a showcase of performances in a network of dank subterranean vaults called *Visions of Excess*. The event was self-consciously avant-garde, and many of the artists were drag queens who were exploring the more subversive aspects of their craft. This involved a great deal of screaming, bloodletting and carnal brouhaha. At one point I wandered into a chamber in which two naked performers were engaged in full penetrative sex. Around them a cluster of middle-class hipsters had formed, pensively observing them as though they were connoisseurs contemplating a sculpture by Henry Moore.

It is curious to consider how the taming of drag as an art form has enabled it to be weaponised in the culture war. The sexual element of drag is impossible to deny. Even the more tepid drag queens tend to interlace their performances with suggestive gestures, provocative quips and the occasional slut-drop. That is not to say that drag queens cannot theoretically adapt to a younger audience. It's perfectly possible for performers of 'Drag Queen Story Hour' to read aloud to children without all the eroticised preening and pouting that we have come to expect from them. But why would any self-respecting drag artist want to do it? There is something deeply mystifying about drag queens who choose to anaesthetise their art in order to regale infants with tales of teddy bears and picnics. It is not so much disturbing as dull.

While many drag queens are happy to tone it down, others have made little effort to modify their raunchy style for the underage. It may be that only a handful of performers fall into this category, but all it takes is a few viral videos for parents' worst fears to be confirmed. One widely shared clip showed a drag show at a club in Dallas attended by children with the words 'It's Not Gonna Lick Itself!' presented in large neon lettering on the upstage wall. It is hardly puritanical to point out that, while performers have every right to express themselves in this way, children ought not to be in attendance. In July 2021, Redbridge Council in London commissioned an event at a local library which featured an actor dressed as a bare-bottomed monkey with a large fake penis attached to his crotch. In April 2022, *The Family Sex Show* – devised by Bristol-based theatre company ThisEgg – was cancelled after parents discovered that it featured full-frontal nudity and content about masturbation, despite being aimed at children as young as five. Such creative decisions have often been interpreted as sinister and paedophilic in intention, but it is more likely that the creed established by decades of sex education, in which it is asserted that children should be exposed to graphic details at an early age, has taken hold. Protestations from concerned parents have been dismissed as old-fashioned, but there is nothing prudish about objecting to five-year-olds being urged to 'try sexual practices' with their 'sexual parts', as the website of *The Family Sex Show* suggested. Nor is age-appropriate curation to be confused with censorship.

All this explains why drag performers are struggling to convince parents their intentions are benign. Inevitably, many critics have raised safeguarding concerns. In July 2022, protesters disrupted a Drag Queen Story Hour event at a library in Reading, chanting 'paedophile' and accusing the performer of 'child grooming'. Such accusations are, of course, unfounded and unhelpful. Yet they also speak to the emotive nature of this debate, in which some reckless artists refuse to observe boundaries around children, and others who are more responsible pay the reputational price. To defuse these tensions, some library staff have been trained to refer to drag queens as 'pantomime dames', as though the two were in any way synonymous. This is misleading, and possibly insulting to the acts, as it strips away the political history of the genre and enervates its impact. There is more to drag than cross-dressing; it is a satirical commentary on gender roles and heterosexual norms, a means to stretch the ambit of decorum. If drag is not transgressive, it ceases to be drag.

It is difficult to escape the feeling that all of this is consciously goading, a way to provoke those who are perceived as conservative and reactionary and to increase the 'visibility' of the LGBTQ+ movement. Stonewall tweeted a claim that 'research suggests that children as young as two recognise their trans identity'. It's hardly surprising, then, that Drag Queen Story Hour is being interpreted as an extension of Queer Theory propaganda. The organisers of one drag library tour claimed that they wanted to 'show the world that being different is not a bad thing, and by providing imaginative role models for children to look up to, we can change the world book by book!' While it is not uncommon for children's stories to convey a moral message, it does seem strange that so many drag queens are keen to undertake a pedagogic role that, in contrast to their typically bacchanalian late-night productions, must seem somewhat insipid. Drag delights in the smashing of taboos. There are many genres and art forms that can be sanitised for a younger audience, but drag has at its heart a lascivious energy, a 'fuck you' attitude to societal norms. If you strip away all that to make it age-appropriate, what is left? Just a man in a dress. And Widow Twankey already has that covered.

But while we are right to criticise the activist takeover of drag as an art form, we need to be vigilant against censorial reactions. The handful of right-wing commentators who have called for outright bans on drag shows are displaying an instinct every bit as authoritarian as those who insist on the indoctrination of children into niche belief-systems. In March 2025, it was reported that drag performances had been banned at Texas A&M University, a move that was described by the Foundation for Individual Rights and Expression (FIRE) as 'a clear violation of the First Amendment'. While preventing children from being exposed to adult entertainment is not an example of censorship, the ideological co-opting of drag will likely continue to prompt a form of pushback that seeks to quell artistic expression. Some performers have been so insistent about politicising the art form – and pretending that drag queens should be considered as a protected characteristic in law – that it was inevitable that their detractors would eventually politicise their response. Feminists have made a valid point that drag has long been seen as an excuse for men to mock and fetishise what it means to be female, even comparing it to black-and-white minstrel shows, but to extend such criticisms to calls for outright bans is not compatible with the values of a free society.

The backlash to the opening ceremony of the Paris Olympics in July 2024 provided a snapshot of how conservatives are losing patience with performances that explore gender ambiguity. The most controversial moment was a drag reimagining of Leonardo da Vinci's *The Last Supper* (c. 1495), a kitsch parody that seemed engineered to provoke Christians. There were false claims that one of the performers had exposed his genitals, a misperception caused by an unfortunate tear in his tights which revealed a patch of skin at the top of his leg. The conservative activist group Judicial Watch filed a complaint to the Federal Communications Commission, believing that the broadcaster had broken guidelines on obscenity and indecency. Once the error had been realised, many campaigners persisted with their anger at what they deemed to be the blasphemous nature of the ceremony. While there is every justification for criticising the value of a performance which deliberately seeks to antagonise, particularly given the fact that the Olympic Games is conceived as a unifying event, the outrage seemed overblown. After unconvincingly claiming that the parody of *The Last Supper* was unintentional, the organising committee was eventually forced into an apology. A more insightful criticism came from writer Gareth Roberts, who emphasised the banality of the piece rather than its potential to cause offence. 'This is the kind of phoney rebellion that was already embarrassing on stage at the Royal Vauxhall Tavern in 1994,' he wrote, 'but at least was confined safely to bad gay pubs'.

The performers had mocked one faith in order to promote another of their own. There is a religiosity to the woke obsession with drag which has become inescapable. In one of those surreal moments reliably vomited up by the culture war, a Protestant church in Dallas, Texas, hosted a celebratory service to bless a muster of drag queens. The video of the event that went viral in September 2023 surely qualifies as the pinnacle of the sanctification of drag. Around a dozen men in lavish gowns and gargoylish make-up were seen perched on the altar, as the congregation were led in a liturgical prayer, a strange blend of pseudo-religious cant and social justice boilerplate.

> We celebrate this divine diversity, and commit to lifting up the voices of the LGBTQ+ community and creating spaces where everyone can thrive . . . We honour their strength and we pledge to be allies to the drag community, recognising their full humanity and their incredible contributions to our world. We embrace radical inclusivity and work to dismantle systems of oppression. We will fight against all forms of hate, prejudice and intolerance, and work to build a world that affirms and celebrates every person's unique identity and gifts.

The compulsory buzzwords were all present – 'diversity', 'spaces', 'allies', 'community', 'inclusivity', 'oppression', 'hate', 'prejudice', 'intolerance', 'identity' – that ugly poetry of the moment that will age and perish as swiftly as any gastrotrich. Details of the drag queens' 'incredible contributions to our world' that justified such public exaltation were not provided, but one assumes that it had something to do with lip-synching to Donna Summer.

## The Sexed Soul

The sheer rapidity of the profileration of genderism has been bewildering. In July 2022, I was the master of ceremonies for an event held at the House of Lords in support of freedom of expression arranged by public relations group Riverside Advisory. The first speaker I introduced to the platform was the future leader of the Conservative Party, Kemi Badenoch. At one point, she directly addressed the common misapprehension that free speech is 'a cover for bigoted middle-aged white men to spout politically incorrect nonsense'. When Badenoch pointed out that she was neither middle-aged, white, nor a man, a heckler shouted: 'Are you sure?' Without missing a beat, Badenoch replied: 'I'm sure. I am a woman and I know what a woman is.' This was greeted by cheers and applause, particularly from the strong contingent of left-wing feminists who were present. This kind of effusive response to a statement of the obvious would have made little sense to a time-travelling observer from the early 2000s. The Rip Van Winkle effect strikes again.

The concept of 'gender identity' is highly contested, and yet it has been the engine of a woke revolution in public health policies and school curricula, as well as guidelines for the civil service, law enforcement agencies, academia, the army, the judiciary and the corporate world. In November 2024, it was reported that the Labour government had instructed all its departments to modify its official language to use the phrase 'LGBT+' rather than 'LGBT'. The '+' is intended to reflect those whose 'gender identity' falls outside of the standard binary of male and female. Such is the power of this movement that it can even pressurise governments into altering the way they speak.

Also in November 2024, the Supreme Court of the United Kingdom initiated its hearing on how 'sex' ought to be defined in the Equality Act 2010. This act was penned during the Before Times, and so it would never have occurred to its authors that 'woman' could be interpreted as anything other than 'adult human female'. This case with the Supreme Court was raised by the campaign group For Women Scotland as a challenge to the Scottish government's contention that the word 'sex' in the Equality Act incorporates men who identify as female and hold a Gender Recognition Certificate. The philosopher Kathleen Stock described the hearing as a 'surreal experience' in an article for *The Times*.

> It was glorious to hear the ghosts of arguments first dreamt up by teenagers on Tumblr hitting daylight. 'If I may, I'll come back to that after lunch,' was a frequent response of the increasingly demoralised-looking lawyer, probed by judges in the morning session. At one point, questioned on how the presence of males who looked like males but were categorised as 'women' might affect discrimination claims by fellow women in the workplace, she spoke for a bamboozled nation and declared she would have to consult a flow chart.

Those who hold fast to the old adage of the law being an ass could find no better instantiation of their view than the spectacle of the country's top judges gathering to decide how the word 'woman' ought to be defined. This is not to suggest that clarity in the law is unnecessary, but the fact that we have even reached this moment is the stuff of satire. It has the quality of the interminable Jarndyce and Jarndyce case in Dickens's *Bleak House* (1852), a protracted and pointless legal exercise that could only ever occur in a society in which bureaucracy is valued above common sense.

The story of Sall Grover, the founder of women's app Giggle, is similarly confounding. Her decision to exclude men from the app led to a prolonged legal battle in Australia in which the judge eventually ruled that 'sex is changeable', an utterance that flies in the face not only of common sense but also of incontestable biological facts. The law might well seek to upend reality, but that does not make it true. The story began in 2020 when Grover, a former Hollywood screenwriter, established Giggle and introduced facial recognition software to ensure that men could not participate. The software was not foolproof; a man who identifies as a woman and calls himself 'Roxanne Tickle' was somehow accepted, and when the mistake was noticed he was barred from the app. Affronted at being denied access to a women's only space, Tickle took Grover to court, claiming discrimination. Judge Robert Bromwich at the Federal Court of Australia eventually ruled that this was indeed an instance of indirect discrimination (as opposed to direct discrimination, as it was not proven that Tickle's 'gender identity' was the discriminating factor). A women-only app, by definition, will discriminate on the basis of sex, but the law in Australia insists that 'gender identity' is a protected characteristic due to amendments to the Sex Discrimination Act passed by the federal Parliament under the Labour government in 2013. Fast forward eleven years, and a judge had determined that one man's belief that he has a gendered soul should automatically grant him the right to access women's only spaces. Tickle was awarded $10,000 and Grover instructed to pay his legal costs. The precedent is disturbing. If a man can successfully take legal action for being denied access to a women's service, this effectively means that single-sex spaces for women can no longer exist. The Australian judiciary has decided that it is illegal for women to organise in their own interests. It is no easy feat to explain the contortions of logic on display here.

The ramifications of wholesale policy changes on the basis of 'gender identity' have been severe. We have seen rapists in women's prisons, men in women's sports, male patients accommodated on female hospital wards, children medicalised, and citizens arrested for failing to conform to the new diktats. The executive order signed by Donald Trump in January 2025 to recognise that there are only two sexes could only make sense in the heady mania of our culture war. It has only been in recent years that politicians have struggled to define the word 'woman'; with the death of woke they will doubtless feel confident enough to do so again. As for 'gender identity', not even its most ardent defenders can attempt a definition. Former Labour Member of Parliament Jacqui Smith – now the Rt Hon the Baroness Smith of Malvern and the government spokesperson for equalities – was asked to define the term in the House of Lords in November 2024.

> Lord Lucas (Con): My Lords, do the Government have a working definition of gender and gender identity and, if so, could they share it with the House?

> Baroness Smith of Malvern (Lab): The noble Lord would be well advised to look at the Equality Act, for example. I have to say that this would be a better debate if we spent more time worrying about how we provide services and account for people's needs, and less about how we catch our political opponents out.

> Lord Markham (Con): As a previous Health Minister, I know that there is a serious health reason to have a proper understanding of the answer to the question of when a woman is a woman and needs to have treatment based on her sex. Please: this is a serious question that deserves a serious answer.

> Baroness Smith of Malvern (Lab): I agree – a woman is an adult female, and her biological sex may well determine what services she needs from the NHS. That is why it is important that, in statistics that are used both in the census and more broadly by our public

services, we have a consistent and an agreed approach to that. That is what I have been talking about up to this point. Frankly, I was taking this seriously, and I hope that others around the House will as well.

But was Smith really taking this seriously at all? Although she was brave enough to acknowledge that a 'woman' is an 'adult female', a strangely controversial statement in our time, she certainly did not vouchsafe a direct answer. Not a bat's squeak of a definition of 'gender identity' was attempted here, which can only lead us to assume that Smith did not have one.

In February 2024, a debate had taken place in the House of Lords on the Conversion Therapy Prohibition (Sexual Orientation and Gender Identity) Bill being championed by the Liberal Democrats. Baroness Claire Fox was particularly strong on the point of 'gender identity' and how the proposed legislation failed to define it. 'It is, at best, a contested concept,' she said. 'I appreciate that a precise, fixed definition might be tricky, when this particular identity can cover over one hundred to three hundred genders: transgender, gender fluid, genderqueer, gender-variant, genderless and non-binary.' Were it not for the inherent austerity of the House of Lords, Fox might well have added the identity category of 'genderfuck', defined on *LGBTQIA+ Wiki* as 'a gender identity and/or gender expression where gendered expectations are deliberately played with to combine gender-specific signals'. Make of that what you will.

All of this raises an obvious question. If no one knows what 'gender identity' means, why is it the basis of any government policy at all, let alone the wellspring of an entire branch of so-called 'medicine'? To put this into context, here are some of the definitions of 'gender identity' proffered by the world's leading medical institutions. In comparing these definitions, the reader will be struck by the similarity of the language used by each group, almost as though a set script has been distributed and ventriloquised.

Gender identity is a way to describe a person's innate sense of their own gender, whether male, female, or non-binary, which may not correspond to the sex registered at birth.

*National Health Service (NHS)*

Gender identity is a person's intrinsic sense of being male, female, or an alternative gender. This internalized sense of gender is not necessarily visible to others and may differ from the gender role traditionally associated with a person's sex assigned at birth.

*World Professional Association of Transgender*
*Health (WPATH)*

Gender identity refers to a person's deeply felt, inherent sense of being a boy, a man, or male; a girl, a woman, or female; or an alternative gender (e.g., genderqueer, gender nonbinary, gender neutral) that may or may not correspond to a person's sex assigned at birth.

*American Psychological Association (APA)*

Gender identity is defined as a person's deeply felt internal and individual experience of gender, which may or may not correspond with the sex assigned at birth, including the personal sense of the body and other expressions of gender, including dress, speech, and mannerisms.

*World Health Organisation (WHO)*

Activist groups have likewise suggested definitions that fall broadly in line with these nebulous and periphrastic efforts.

Gender identity reflects a deeply felt and experienced sense of one's own gender, which can include being male, female, a blend of both, or neither, and it may correspond to or differ from the sex assigned at birth.

*United Nations (UN)*

Gender identity is one's internal, deeply held sense of their gender. For transgender people, their sex assigned at birth and their own internal sense of gender identity are not the same.

*Human Rights Campaign (HRC)*

Gender identity is the personal sense of one's own gender. Gender identity can correlate with a person's assigned sex at birth or can differ from it. Gender expression typically reflects a person's gender identity.

*Mayo Clinic*

A person's innate sense of their own gender, whether male, female or something else, which may or may not correspond to the sex assigned at birth.

*Stonewall*

Gender identity is a person's internal, deeply held sense of their gender. For transgender people, their own internal gender identity does not match the sex they were assigned at birth.

*Gay & Lesbian Alliance Against Defamation (GLAAD)*

All of this is simply jargon ladled out of the postmodernist stockpot. In addition to the obvious similarities of the formulae, note how all these definitions are circular in nature. Gender is gender. Which is to say, it means nothing at all.

So perhaps we can turn to individual commentators and campaigners to have a crack at this most thorny of definitions. Psychiatrist Jack Turban defines 'gender identity' as one's 'sense of identity in relationship to masculinity and femininity'. He further argues that this falls into three categories: 'the hard to put into words feeling of it', 'your relationship to gender roles and expectations' and 'your relationship with your primary and secondary sex characteristics'. On my GB News show *Free Speech Nation*, barrister and trans campaigner Robin Moira White described 'gender identity' as 'an essence of male or female'. Trans activist Julia Serano veers close to agreement, having coined the term 'subconscious sex' to approximate the 'inexplicable self-understanding of what sex/gender one should be'. 'Gender identity', then, is that which is claimed once an individual determines what their 'subconscious sex' might be. A close approximation to this concept is encapsulated by what Helen Joyce has described as 'something like a sexed soul' within a discrepant body. Or, as evolutionary biologist Colin Wright bluntly puts it, 'that internally felt soul-like quality that supposedly transcends such superficial physical indicia as gonads and genitalia'.

Judith Butler, that doyenne of Queer Theory, rejects the notion of an innate gender identity entirely. In prose like overcooked porridge, she explains that she sees it as 'performative'.

> In other words, acts, gestures, and desire produce the effect of an internal core or substance, but produce this *on the surface* of the body, through the play of signifying absences that suggest, but never reveal, the organizing principle of identity as a cause. Such acts, gestures, enactments, generally construed, are *performative* in the sense that the essence or identity that they otherwise purport to express are *fabrications* manufactured and sustained through corporeal signs and other discursive means. That the gendered body is performative suggests that it has no ontological status apart from the various acts which constitute its reality. This also suggests that if that reality is fabricated as an interior essence, that very interiority is an effect and function of a decidedly public and social discourse, the public regulation of fantasy through the surface politics of the body, the gender border control that differentiates inner from outer, and so institutes the 'integrity' of the subject. In other words, acts and gestures, articulated and enacted desires create the illusion of an interior and organizing gender core, an illusion discursively maintained for the purposes of the regulation of sexuality within the obligatory frame of reproductive heterosexuality.

For Butler, the concept of 'gender' need not be defined even when talking incessantly about it. In her book *Who's Afraid of Gender?* (2024), she claims that gender 'has to remain relatively wild in relation to all those who claim to possess its correct definition'. This is only a helpful strategy to those who wish to indulge in vacuous theorising in lieu of judicious analysis. At least Butler's logorrhoea somehow makes one more favourably inclined to the dizzyingly circular definitions favoured by every major medical institution in the Western world. Alternatively, we could turn to Titania McGrath, whose definition is about as comprehensible as any other. 'Gender identity', she tells us, is simply 'the immutable yet totally fluid feeling that one is male or female or neither or both based on conceptions of masculinity or femininity that are natural and innate but also social constructs that don't actually exist'.

The mainstreaming of 'gender identity' has generated confusion around how the concept of 'gender' was originally understood within feminist discourse. As Julie Bindel observes in her book *Feminism for Women* (2021), what was once 'a theoretical tool to describe the social construction of femininity and masculinity', those 'fabricated identities and sex stereotypes' that women's rights campaigners sought to dismantle, feminists are now expected 'to forfeit the term, or to concede that it means the opposite – a biological phenomenon which determines our assumed identity'. This refocus of gender as a matter of biology has further entailed the invention of the notion of the 'trans child'. 'Protect Trans Kids' is one of the many shibboleths you will see frequently displayed at protests by genderists. At demonstrations outside the US Supreme Court in the case of *US v. Skrmetti* – the American Civil Liberties Union's challenge to the state of Tennessee's ban on 'gender-affirming care' in late 2024 – even young children were photographed holding placards bearing the phrase. But if adults cannot understand what 'trans kids' means, how can the children who it ostensibly describes?

The concept of the 'trans child' has become an essential tool in gender activism. In order to justify reorganising society according to 'gender identity' rather than sex – and thereby admitting men who identify as women into female-only spaces – it must first be determined that the concept of a 'gender identity' is real. And if there is such a thing as a sexed soul that is misaligned with our body, it must surely be present from the moment of conception. As such, being 'trans' is not a decision one makes in adult life, but an innate quality that exists at all ages. In December 2024, J. K. Rowling posted the following statement on X:

> There are no trans kids. No child is 'born in the wrong body'. There are only adults like you, prepared to sacrifice the health of minors to bolster your belief in an ideology that will end up wreaking more harm than lobotomies and false memory syndrome combined.

The subsequent firestorm was unavoidable. Even the most sensible of comments on this topic is liable to whip up a frenzy of indignation. This in itself is proof of the absurdity of the proposition. If the concept of a sexed soul were legitimate, measured debate and discussion would be adequate to persuade the undecided. But given the weakness of the claim, threats, insults and tantrums become the default tactic.

The term 'trans' has been muddied in recent years by insisting that it is an abbreviation of 'transgender'. Previously, it had denoted 'transsexual', a term that specifically relates to those who have undertaken surgery or other medical interventions to appear as the opposite sex. The lexical shift to 'transgender' implies that the existence of a 'gender identity' is incontestable, and that we each have that 'essence of male or female'. No evidence for the existence of this essence has, as yet, been produced. Transgenderism, then, is best understood as a form of self-identification, a way to classify oneself with a concordant set of behaviours, tastes and dress codes, much like 'goth' or 'punk'.

Given that no human being has ever changed from male to female or vice versa, the term 'trans' must therefore refer to a process undertaken to more closely resemble the opposite sex. There are two methods by which this can be achieved. Firstly, there is the transvestic approach, by which attire, accessories and behaviour are adopted according to sex stereotypes. For example, a man might wear a frock, high-heeled shoes, lipstick and a long wig, tilt his head coquettishly, and generally behave in a caricatured manner of a woman. Cross-dressers rely on sex stereotypes for effect; whereas many women routinely wear jeans and a T-shirt and no make-up at all, a man who did this would be unremarkable and not identifiably 'trans'. The other approach is surgical intervention. For men who wish to appear as women this can include: orchiectomy (removal of the testicles), vaginoplasty (removal and reshaping of the male genitals to create a faux-vagina), breast augmentation, facial plastic surgery, tracheal shave (reduction of Adam's apple), vocal surgery to raise pitch, hair removal and hair transplants. For women who wish to appear as men, this can include: mastectomy (removal of breasts), pectoral implants, hysterectomy, vaginectomy and phalloplasty (the removal of the vagina and creation of a faux-penis), and body contouring. The process of vaginoplasty would seem to offer a reification of a misogynistic myth, dating back to classical antiquity, that the vagina is simply an inverted form of the male genitalia. The sixteenth-century French writer Guillaume Bouchet put it bluntly: 'La matrice de la femme n'est que la bourse et verge renversée de l'homme' ('the matrix of the woman is nothing but the scrotum and penis of the man inverted').

Whereas any adult surely must retain the right to dress as he or she chooses, the ethical validity of such surgical procedures is disputable. If a patient desperately desires to have an arm amputated, should this wish automatically be carried out, or does the doctor not have a professional responsibility to 'first do no harm'? Whereas psychotherapeutic treatment strikes us as the most appropriate course of action, many individuals who identify as trans argue that 'gender reassignment' surgery is a psychological necessity. Irrespective of where one stands on that debate, it should be clear that no child can possibly give informed consent to any of these procedures. By these terms, if 'trans child' approximates to 'transsexual child', then such a thing cannot right-fully exist.

However, if we decide that 'trans child' means 'transgender child', then we are in the realm of a philosophical or pseudo-religious faith. It is certainly possible for children to believe that they have gendered souls which do not align with their bodies, but such an esoteric view has not developed from a mature process of reflection and analysis. This is the same reason why evolutionary biologist Richard Dawkins objects to the concept of a 'Christian child' or a 'Muslim child'. In such cases, invariably we are using a shorthand for 'a child of Christian parents' or 'a child of Muslim parents'. Children are simply ill-equipped to have grappled with complex theological belief-systems and weighed up whether they accept them as valid or not. Moreover, the term 'transgender child' points to a highly specific principle within a broader ethos. Given that it refers to the notion of a soul in the wrong body, it is more closely akin to the idea of a 'possessed child' rather than a 'Christian child'. Again, it is unfeasible to suppose that an infant could possibly have interrogated these beliefs with any degree of intellectual rigour. The main difference is that trans activists are lauded by the media and political class, whereas exorcists are given a wide berth.

As such, whichever way one looks at it, the very concept of the 'trans child' is incoherent. It makes sense to speak of 'trans people' because it is an effective shorthand for 'people who call themselves trans' or 'people who believe they were born in the wrong body', or 'people who, out of psychological desire or necessity, present in accordance with the stereotypes of the opposite sex'. For the same reason, we can describe someone as a 'Catholic' without sharing his or her faith in transubstantiation. But the term 'trans child' is predicated on the notion that it is possible for a child to comprehend a belief-system that even adults struggle to explain. To use the phrase at all is to participate in the indoctrination. So while anyone has the right to refer to 'trans children', we have the right to tell them why such a phenomenon does not exist. It is a political construct masquerading as a medical one.

## Social Contagions

One of my shortest-lived jobs was as a teacher at a school for girls near Sloane Square in London in 2012. I resigned after only a few weeks because the headmistress had objected to my inclusion of a novel in my sixth-form teaching which featured a gay character. I was told in private by the Head of English, in hushed and fearful tones, that she had also demanded that Oscar Wilde be removed from the curriculum. I did not object to her beliefs, or even that she had ghostwritten a book which described homosexuality as a 'disgust to God', but it did strike me as unprofessional that she could not prevent her own personal prejudices from dictating her policy decisions. In my resignation letter, I explained that I wasn't prepared to work at a school which fostered such antediluvian attitudes. I stayed on to finish the term, but was delighted when I eventually made my escape.

But the most disturbing aspect of my time at the school was when I learned that many of the girls were engaged in what can only be described as competitive starvation. During lunch duties, I was warned to keep watch for anyone taking just a single lettuce leaf from the salad bar. If I saw any pupil doing so, I was told I must immediately intercept her and demand that she return and fill her plate. By contrast, at my first teaching job at a co-ed boarding school, skin-cutting had been the fashion. We even had a visiting expert telling us how to encourage these pupils to hold ice cubes in their hands until they felt shooting pains as a substitute for the razor. I remember at the time thinking that this wasn't the best advice, but I was too green to raise an objection. Besides, this speaker had spent a considerable part of the session reminiscing about a shepherd she had once counselled who had, over the course of many months on the hillside, used a sharp wire to whittle his penis so that it eventually became forked. To this day, I am none the wiser as to the purpose of this anecdote.

The shift from cutting to starvation was striking. At the former school, pupils were not refraining from food, and at the latter there were very few who were injuring themselves with blades. It was almost as though only one form of self-harm could predominate at any given time. And when a small group started doing it, the trend spread with remarkable speed. Such social contagions are especially common among teenage girls, as numerous historical precedents can show. The Salem witch trials of the late seventeenth century were caused by a group of girls who had seen demons in the shadows and members of their own community signing pacts with the Devil. The medieval 'glass delusion', mentioned by John Locke in *An Essay Concerning Human Understanding* (1689), resulted in many people being convinced that they were 'made of glass' and had 'used the caution necessary to preserve such brittle bodies'. Then there were the various 'dancing plagues' of the Middle Ages, which seemed to impact young women in particular; in Strasbourg in 1518, a group of people inexplicably 'danced themselves to death'. In the late nineteenth century, there were multiple outbreaks in Europe of schoolgirls who would involuntarily shake their hands whenever they performed writing exercises. And when I visited Sweden in October 2023, I was told about a local village where, during the medieval period, the girls all inexplicably began to limp. It is perfectly clear that the latest social contagion to take hold in the Western world is that of girls identifying out of their femaleness, through claims that they are either trans or 'non-binary'. Whereas in 2012, there were only two-hundred and fifty referrals (mostly boys) to the NHS's Gender Identity Development Service (GIDS), by 2021 the figure had risen to more than five thousand (mostly female) patients. Gender activists like to claim that this is simply the consequence of more people 'coming out' as society becomes more tolerant, and simultaneously insist that there has never been a worse time to be trans. Consistency is not their strong suit.

*The Salem witch trials of 1692, lithograph by George H. Walker (1892).*

There are no easy answers as to the explosion of this latest fad, but surely the proliferation of social media has something to do with it. Platforms such as TikTok are replete with activists explaining to teenagers that their feelings of confusion are probably evidence that they have been 'born in the wrong body', cuckooed at birth into an alien nest. For pubescent girls who are uncomfortable with their physiological changes, as well as sudden unwanted male sexual attention, the prospect of identifying out of womanhood is an emotional salve. These online pedlars have some snake oil to sell. And while a limping epidemic in a medieval village would be unlikely to travel very far, social contagions cannot be so confined in the digital age. Much of this is reminiscent of the recovered memory hysteria of the late twentieth century, when therapist cranks promoted the idea that most victims of sexual abuse had repressed their traumatic memories from childhood. It led to numerous cases of people imagining that they had been abused by parents and other family members, and many lives were ruined as a result. One of the key texts in this movement was

*The Courage to Heal* (1988) by Ellen Bass and Laura Davis, which made the astonishing and unevidenced claim that 'if you are unable to remember any specific instances . . . but still have a feeling that something abusive happened to you, it probably did'.

A common feature of social contagions is that they depend upon the elevation of intuition over material reality. Just as innocent family members were accused of sexual abuse because of 'feelings' teased out by unscrupulous therapists, many girls are now being urged by online influencers to trust the evidence of their emotions and accept a misalignment between their body and their gendered soul. We are not talking here about the handful of children who suffer from gender dysphoria, but rather healthy children who have been swept up in a temporary craze. Activists have been quick to reject the entire notion of 'social contagion' as a 'transphobic talking point', but the evidence for it is now indisputable. The review into paediatric 'gender medicine' by Dame Hilary Cass, published in April 2024, cautioned against schools practising the 'social transitioning' – the practice of allowing children to dress as the opposite sex and be referred to by different names and pronouns – on the grounds that such an approach may consolidate a child's psychological conceptualisation of herself or himself as a member of the opposite sex. Cass had noted that 'those who had socially transitioned at an earlier age and/or prior to being seen in clinic were more likely to proceed to a medical pathway'.

Some social contagions are more damaging than others. Whereas limping and dancing and trembling can be overcome, the lifelong impact of puberty blockers, cross-sex hormones and surgery will not be so transient. The concept of a 'non-binary' identity is arguably less harmful given that it does not generally lead to medical intervention. However, it is based on the same unevidenced belief in the notion of a gendered – or, in this case, agendered – essence which is not replicated in the anatomy. The new craze for 'non-binary' identities was evinced at the final of the Eurovision Song Contest held in the city of Malmö in Sweden in May 2024. The trophy went to Switzerland's Nemo, a man in a skirt who identifies as neither male nor female. The United Kingdom's entry was sung by Olly Alexander, who calls himself 'gay and queer and non-binary' but magnanimously accepts the pronouns 'he' and 'him'. And then there was the 'queer' and 'non-binary' Irish entry by Bambie Thug, a woman who came sixth in the competition but first in the award for the sorest of losers. Having being beaten by Israel, whose very presence in the competition was a source of outrage for Thug, she had the following to say:

> I'm so proud of Nemo winning. I'm so proud that all of us are in the top ten that have been fighting for this shit behind the scenes because it has been so hard and it's been so horrible for us. And I'm so proud of us. And I just want to say, we are what the Eurovision is. The EBU [European Broadcasting Union] is not what the Eurovision is. Fuck the EBU. I don't even care anymore. Fuck them. The thing that makes this is the contestants, the community behind it, the love and the power and the support of all of us is what is making change. And the world has spoken. The queers are coming. Non-binaries for the fucking win.

One might argue that all of this is simply an extension of the high-campery of old. Thug certainly looks pantomimic, with her Christmas-cracker devil horns, and the layers of makeup piled on to what used to be a face. But what were once the glittery fripperies of gay culture have been hijacked by the acolytes of genderism, a movement that has appropriated this whimsical sheen to advance its authoritarian goals. When Thug cries out 'Non-binaries for the fucking win!', the connotations are a little more sinister than the teenage trends of yesteryear.

'Non-binary', then, is a reactionary concept dressed up in the guise of progressivism. Most of those who identify as 'non-binary' are embracing, rather than rejecting, sex stereotypes. They claim to feel neither sufficiently masculine nor feminine, which is simply another way of reinforcing what it means to be male or female. One of the common mantras intoned by activist groups is that 'non-binary identities are valid'. They are not referring to the standard definition of 'valid' as an argument that has 'a sound basis in logic or fact'; after all, there are only two human sexes and no third gamete. Rather, in the activist lexicon to be 'valid' is an acknowledgement of the legitimacy of personal feelings, or 'individual truths', a close cousin of the notion of 'lived experience'. We are assured that 'non-binary people have always existed', a form of historical revisionism intended to shame anyone who refuses to dance along to the circus march of our times. Gareth Roberts points out the folly of such declarations in his book *Gay Shame* (2024), and how they are 'throwing back into the unknowable past something that was literally invented on Tumblr in 2011'. To be 'non-binary' is a modish form of self-identification with an added authoritarian twist. Whereas those who called themselves 'teddy boys' in the 1960s did not impose their identity on others, the classification of 'non-binary' now comes with a demand that others pretend this form of self-identity is something innate. To be born 'non-binary' is about as feasible as being born an 'emo', and I have yet to hear of a case of a baby emerging from the womb in ripped skinny jeans and black eyeliner. There is no serious comparison to be made between the historical persecution of homosexuals and experiencing some pushback when you demand that others refer to you as 'they' or 'them'. Coming out as gay in 1970 increased the risk of being violently assaulted; coming out as 'non-binary' today only increases one's chances of being employed at the BBC.

## The War on Women

It's time for a horror story.

In a suburb of New York, police discover various dismembered body parts. An adult female torso has been left in a shopping trolley. A few blocks north, they find a leg. Once the police have identified their suspect, an eighty-three-year-old woman, they uncover a human head and saw-blades in her apartment. On further investigation, it turns out that this is no novice. Sixty years prior to these latest atrocities, this octogenarian had been jailed for murdering one woman and convicted of manslaughter for stabbing another.

This lurid story strikes us as too unbelievable to be true. Very few women are serial killers, and fewer still target other women. And yet precisely these details were outlined in a report on the *BBC News* website in March 2022. It was only towards the end of the article that a key piece of information was added. The perpetrator, one Harvey Marcelin, had 'recently identified as a woman'.

We should have seen that twist coming. At no point did this ring true as a female crime. So why did this BBC journalist only mention the biological sex of the murderer as a casual aside towards the very end of its account, as though she were writing an Agatha Christie novel rather than a report about a real event? Many of us have noticed with weary regularity the way in which journalists pretend that male criminals are women if they so identify. In February 2024, the *Guardian* ran an article with the headline: 'Cat-killing woman guilty of murdering man as he walked home in Oxford'. This was the heinous story of a trans-identified male who had killed, dissected and mangled the corpse of a cat in an electric blender before going on to strangle and drown a stranger. Yet throughout the article the journalist insisted that this psychopath was female. Many were outraged at this misrepresentation. One of the *Guardian*'s own writers, Louise Tickle, wrote a letter to the editor Katharine Viner to say that she could not continue working for the publication until it was 'able to demonstrate that its reporters, editors and management understand what constitutes a fact, and stops deceiving its readers'. But the *Guardian* is not the only media outlet routinely engaging in this kind of disinformation. In December 2023, a shocking story appeared on the *BBC News* website about a predatory woman who had directed a man to abuse a four-year-old child. At no point did the article reveal that the criminal was a man, but instead referred to him throughout with 'she/her' pronouns. Only the photograph of the culprit conveyed the truth.

One of the key misunderstandings about this widespread media deception is that it has been mandated by either the law or press regulators, but there is absolutely no legal or professional obligation for journalists to misstate the sex of a criminal. There is therefore no justification whatsoever for headlines such as 'Ex-soldier exposed her penis and used wheelie bin as sex toy in public' in the Metro, or 'Woman jailed over cocaine-fuelled sex with dog in disgusting incident' in the Mirror, when all sentient readers will be aware that these crimes were committed by men. If we believed the mainstream media, we would be under the misapprehension that there had been an inexplicable and exponential rise in the numbers of women perpetrating acts of violence and sexual assault. In reality, there are currently 84,000 men in British prison as compared with just 3,500 women and, according to the most recent census data, men are one hundred times more likely than women to be convicted sex offenders.

A generous interpretation of this sudden abundance of disinformation might be that reporters are merely following the language used by the police. However, the guidance is muddled at best and practice is inconsistent across the country. A Freedom of Information request by the group Keep Prisons Single Sex found that of the twenty-four police forces who replied, fifteen said they record suspects by 'gender identity' and just two on the basis of biological sex. When a suspect identifies as non-binary, many police forces record the sex as 'indeterminate' or 'non-specified' even though 'non-binary' does not exist as a category in English law. In other words, the police appear to be making it up as they go along, resulting in the widespread skewing of crime statistics. The most obvious and straightforward solution is to record suspects and criminals by biological sex and, in those rare cases where a criminal or suspect claims to possess a 'gender identity', include this as an additional detail. If we must record the metaphysical beliefs of criminals, then we should at least not conflate them with the significant facts of the case. Under the present system of improvisation and inconsistency, we have no way of knowing how many of these 'female rapists' are actually men. Moreover, we need to prevent male criminals from exploiting the religion of genderism as a loophole to be moved to women's prisons. The double rapist Adam Graham famously sought to be housed in the female estate by wearing an unconvincing wig and calling himself 'Isla Bryson'. He was temporarily accommodated in a female prison while the Scottish government conducted a risk assessment. What kind of 'risk assessment' does a double rapist require? Is not the conviction for sexual assault sufficient for the government to know that he is a threat to women? So absurd was this situation that, when it came to light, it arguably contributed to the fall of First Minister Nicola Sturgeon.

It could be argued that media professionals are merely observing style guides established by ideologically biased authorities. When the Independent Press Standards Organisation (IPSO) published its 'Guidance on researching and reporting stories involving transgender individuals' in October 2016, it had only consulted with trans activist groups. Inevitably, the advice was contorted accordingly. Rather than compel 'preferred pronouns', IPSO asked a question of reporters: 'If known, have you used the pronouns the individual uses to describe themselves in your story?' At the same time, it asked: 'Have you taken care not to publish inaccurate or misleading information?' The implications behind these two questions appear to be contradictory. Yet in framing the advice in this way, IPSO has avoided taking a dogmatic stance on the issue. In other words, reporting a criminal's 'gender identity' but not his sex is by no means compulsory, but is rather a conscious choice taken by media outlets. The same is true of televised journalism; Ofcom (the regulatory body for broadcasting in the United Kingdom) does not mandate using 'preferred pronouns' for criminals. There is absolutely no requirement for the media to engage in some ridiculous charade to spare the feelings of rapists, paedophiles and murderers. That reporters continue to do so is confusing, unethical and frankly embarrassing.

Feminists who have raised concerns about the impact of media disinformation on the matter of sex and gender have frequently faced the iron fortress of 'no debate'. This was a strategy popularised by Stonewall, a charity created to campaign for the rights of gay people that transitioned in 2015 into a lobby group for the promotion of gender identity ideology. After an open letter in the *Sunday Times* in October 2018 petitioned Stonewall to 'acknowledge that there are a range of valid viewpoints around sex, gender and transgender politics' and to 'commit to fostering an atmosphere of respectful debate', many of the signatories – including several trans-identified individuals – were demonised both in the press and online. Apparently 'respectful debate' was simply not an option.

There are two categories of people who refuse to debate. The first are those who fear they might lose, and the second are those who feel it is unnecessary. In the latter category you will find every sort of authoritarian who has ever lived. No tyrant has ever called for a serious debate; they have simply imposed their wishes. Stonewall and other trans activist groups fall into both categories. Their tactics have always been essentially authoritarian, which is why they support the censorship and even criminalisation of their opponents. But they are also quite plainly aware that their belief-system will dissolve under the sunlight of scrutiny. When it comes to the controversial topic of men identifying their way into women's spaces – such as prisons, toilets, hospital accommodation and rape crisis centres – this 'no debate' strategy has not ultimately been successful. In response, some activists have moved on to the even more authoritarian rallying cry of 'shut up'.

In an interview with the *Sunday Times*, for instance, the broadcaster Sandi Toksvig had the following to say in response to the interviewer's question about women's fears that their right to single-sex spaces is being eroded:

I don't get this. I'm in my 45th year in showbusiness, travelling the country touring. I've been to every service-station toilet in the country. Every one has a sign up saying male cleaners in attendance. I don't recall anybody saying, 'We need to group up against these male cleaners.' Why would someone dress as a woman when they could just pick up a cleaning cloth? If it really bothers you there's a toilet some place else. Go there. Shut up. Let's join together and fight stuff that actually needs fighting. Why are they talking about this when women in Afghanistan are not allowed to sing or to look a man in the face? Who is benefiting from all this? The patriarchy.

Leaving aside the palpable nonsense about male cleaners who, unlike sexual predators, announce their presence with a sign precisely so that women can avoid them as they are working, the most astonishing aspect of Toksvig's position is her assertion that those who oppose her should 'shut up' simply because she made no effort to understand their arguments. As an inelegant but effective parental strategy, 'shut up' works when deployed against squalling infants because they are incapable of reason; there is little point in inviting a child to debate whether screaming about sweets at the checkout of Tesco is anti-social and unbecoming. But the view that women ought to be entitled to single-sex spaces has an entirely rational basis, one that has been outlined endlessly with great care by numerous intelligent commentators. Can it be that Toksvig has not listened to any of them?

The statistics should settle the matter: 91 per cent of the victims of rape and sexual assault are women; 98 per cent of those prosecuted for rape and sexual assault are men. There is no evidence whatsoever that men who identify as women are any less likely to commit sexual crimes. While it is true that incidents of women being attacked in public toilets are thankfully rare, research by the *Sunday Times* has proven that 'almost 90 per cent of reported sexual assaults, harassment and voyeurism in swimming pool and sports-centre changing rooms happen in unisex facilities'. In County Loudoun, Virginia, a teenage girl was sexually assaulted at her high school in the toilets by a boy in a skirt. It has been alleged that the school attempted to cover it up, being more interested in 'trans rights' than girls' safety, and the family later sued for compensation. It would seem that single-sex spaces exist for a reason.

The emerging concept of 'gender self-identification', and the elision of 'transsexual' and 'transgender', has meant that the parameters of the discussion have rapidly shifted. The overwhelming majority of those who identify as 'trans' have undergone no surgery at all, which has resulted in fully intact males using women's services. According to the theory of self-identification, one need only declare oneself to be female for it alchemically to be so. For the sake of the Sandi Toksvigs of this world, it is worth being explicit on this point. There is no reason to believe that trans-identifying people have an innate predisposition towards sexual predation. However, there is clear evidence that male rapists are identifying as female in order to gain access to their services. Data regarding prison populations from the Ministry of Justice in 2020 showed that there were 76 sex offenders out of 129 trans-identifying males (58.9 per cent), 125 sex offenders out of 3,812 women (3.3 per cent) and 13,234 sex offenders out of 78,781 men (16.8 per cent). In December 2023, the Ministry of Justice released a fresh report which showed that out of the 245 male prisoners who were legally recognised as female, 151 (62 per cent) had committed at least one sexual offence. This is in keeping with the 2021 United Kingdom census figures, which show that one in every 585 trans-identifying males in England and Wales are convicted sex offenders. That compares to one in every 2,750 men and one in every 243,000 women. Anyone who denies that self-identification is being exploited by sex criminals is effectively making the claim that trans people are inherently more predatory.

Yet in March 2022, Shona Robison, the SNP's Cabinet Secretary for Social Justice, said in Parliament that 'there is no evidence that predatory and abusive men have ever had to pretend to be anything else to carry out abusive and predatory behaviour'. Is it possible that she had never heard of the countless incidents of male predators who fall precisely into this category? One could mention Harvey Glatman, the serial killer who posed as a photographer to lure women with the promise of securing them a modelling career. Or the 'hillside stranglers' of Los Angeles, Angelo Buono and Kenneth Bianchi, who pretended to be undercover police officers to entrap their victims. Or the policeman killer of Sarah Everard, who pretended to be arresting her for breaching Covid restrictions. Robison's claim was almost Herculean in its inaccuracy.

Robison was making the comment as part of a debate about reform to the Gender Recognition Act (GRA) and the SNP's proposed bill that would have permitted trans-identifying individuals to change the sex marker on their birth certificates without medical evidence of gender dysphoria. Feminist campaigners had warned that this could open up loopholes for men to identify as women and gain access to female-only spaces. It was notable that the bill referred to 'gender' on two hundred and forty-four occasions, but did not use the word 'sex' once. It was clear that Robison did not understand the principles of safeguarding. When adults applying for teaching roles are requested to undertake a police disclosure check, that is not to suggest that people interested in a career in teaching are inherently abusive, it is because without such checks abusers could exploit the system. When convicted rapist Stephen Wood changed his name to Karen White and was moved to a female prison, he went on to sexually assault two inmates. As the writer Debbie Hayton pointed out, 'safeguarding weaknesses attract those looking for safeguarding weaknesses. And the SNP's bill introduces them.'

Rosie Duffield, the former Labour Member of Parliament for Canterbury, has been raising these safeguarding concerns for many years, and was diabolised in her own party for her troubles. In September 2021, she announced that she had withdrawn from the Labour party conference in Brighton due to threats she had received for her gender-critical views. After her resignation in September 2024, Duffield continued to be attacked by her former colleagues. Nadia Whittome, the Labour representative for Nottingham East, falsely accused Duffield of making a political career 'out of dehumanising one of the most marginalised groups in society'. She added that 'Labour should have withdrawn the whip long ago' and thereby silenced this pesky termagant for good. It will surprise no one to learn that Whittome had previously boasted that when in government her party would implement gender self-identification with 'no ifs, no buts' and 'resist calls to exclude trans women from women's spaces'. Those who support accommodating prisoners according to gender identity rather than sex should answer one simple question: how many rapes are acceptable for this policy to be maintained?

When it comes to the issue of men in women's sports, the priority comes down to a combination of fairness and safety. The controversy over Imane Khelif of Algeria, who won the gold medal in the women's welterweight boxing category at the 2024 Olympic Games in Paris, has brought the debate to the fore. Khelif had been previously disqualified from the Women's World Boxing Championships in India in March 2023, along with Taiwan's Lin Yu-ting, when tests by the International Boxing Association (IBA) 'conclusively' revealed XY chromosomes. Italy's Angela Carini had to withdraw from her fight with Khelif at the Olympic Games after just forty-six seconds, and later said that she had never experienced such a powerful punch and had feared for her life. The matter has yet to be resolved, with Khelif refusing to take further tests and critics arguing that this is a likely case of DSD (Differences in Sex Development), a rare intersex condition by which it is possible for a man to believe himself to be female until the onset of puberty. So why would the International Olympic Committee decree that it is perfectly acceptable to put female boxers at risk by forcing them to fight against men?

It is utterly exhausting to point out that this is completely unfair, recklessly dangerous, and should never have been allowed to happen. Activists and their supporters in the media often engage in elaborate casuistry in an attempt to complicate what is actually a straightforward matter. Modifications to hormones will never eliminate the inherent advantage that men incur through the process of male puberty, whether that be in regard to muscle mass, bone density, heart and lung size, longer limbs, greater height and other factors. For those in any doubt, Helen Joyce provides specific statistics in her book *Trans: When Ideology Meets Reality* (2021).

> The average adult man has 41 percent more non-fat body mass (blood, bones, muscles and so on) than the average woman, 50 percent more muscle mass in his legs and 75 percent more in his arms. His legs are 65 percent stronger, and his upper body is 90 percent stronger. The overwhelming upper-body advantage is nowhere near accounted for by differences in size – as can be seen in weightlifting competitions, where competitors are banded by weight, and the male world champion in each category lifts around 30 percent more than the female one.

In April 2017, the Dallas under-15 boys football club beat the women's national team 5–2 in a friendly game. This was not because these teenage boys were enjoying a streak of luck or the women were hung-over; it was because one team comprised of males and the other of females. It really is that simple.

During an appearance on *Late Night with David Letterman* in 2013, tennis superstar Serena Williams explained that 'men's tennis and women's tennis are completely, almost, two separate sports', and that if she were to play against Andy Murray she 'would lose 6–0, 6–0 in five to six minutes, maybe ten minutes'. For all the endless testimonies from female athletes who have patiently explained why competing with men is unfair, many sporting authorities seem determined not to listen. The physical dangers are most troubling of all. Introducing a male into an all-girls' rugby team carries obvious risks of injury. Fallon Fox, a male martial arts fighter who identifies as female, has boasted about fracturing a woman's skull during a competition. 'I enjoyed it,' he wrote on Twitter. 'See, I love smacking up Terfs in the cage who talk transphobic nonsense. It's bliss!'

It has always been understood that the existence of women's sports enables them to compete and to win. Female participation was introduced to the Olympics for the first time at the Paris games in 1900, where women were able to take part in tennis, sailing, croquet, equestrianism and golf. Now the authorities at the Olympics seem to think that all-female categories are not worth preserving. Female runners devote years to intense training to reduce their timings by a matter of fractions of seconds. All of this can be obliterated in an instant once a male is included. When I spoke to long-distance runner Mara Yamauchi about this topic, she explained to me that any women who speak up about the injustice of it all tend to be demonised, harassed and subjected to threats. This has even happened to tennis legend Martina Navratilova, who has been a trailblazer for minority rights. This is par for the course for militant trans activists, who surely know that their belief-system cannot be sustained by argument or persuasion. They are asking the world to accept the impossible, and so bullying is their only option.

With more and more high-profile cases of men winning women's sporting accolades, one would have thought that this debate would be easily won. There was the case of Lia Thomas, the male swimmer who won gold in the 500-yard freestyle at the 2022 NCAA Division I Women's Swimming and Diving Championship. In July 2024, male cyclists were part of teams that won gold, silver and bronze at the elite women's Madison at Washington's Marymoor Grand Prix. The sight of three hulking men on the winner's podium caused an outcry, but surprisingly there are some female athletes who appear to support the destruction of their own sports. The Belgian judo fighter Charline Van Snick, who won a bronze medal at the 2012 Summer Olympics, has compared her experience of homophobia at the games with transgender rights, saying that when it comes to trans athletes 'we have a long way to go'. But chickens who demand a fox-inclusive coop shouldn't be surprised when they get eaten.

So many sporting authorities seem determined to pretend that biology is not a factor when it comes to competition, and that 'gender identity' is more important than the size and shape and strength of human bodies. But if there is one space that we can all agree must require single-sex provisions, it should be a rape crisis centre. In what world would a man, however he identifies, be convinced that a refuge for women who have been sexually assaulted is the place for him? It's the kind of notion that back in the Before Times nobody would have believed was possible. Yet from 2021 until 2024, the Edinburgh Rape Crisis Centre was run by a trans-identified male called Mridul Wadhwa. That he did not hold a Gender Recognition Certificate (GRC) ought to be beside the point. It should go without saying that victims of rape are individuals at their most vulnerable, and it is entirely reasonable that they would expect not to be in the vicinity of men in the aftermath of such a horrific experience, irrespective of how they might identify. The fact that Wadhwa applied for the post in the first place tells us a great deal about the entitlement that drives the genderist movement, and the fact that he was appointed reveals the extent of its power. It is remarkable that until J. K. Rowling established Beira's Place in Edinburgh, there were no women-only centres for rape victims in Scotland.

As the woke movement perishes, there will be fewer women smeared as bigots for defending their spaces, or being forced to defend their rights in court. A series of landmark cases are hastening an end to these kinds of injustices. In October 2024, the Health Secretary Wes Streeting met with five nurses who were concerned that they were being compelled to undress in front of male colleagues who identified as female. One such colleague had allegedly 'stared at their breasts' and lingered in the changing room 'longer than necessary'. This group – who became known in the media as the 'Darlington Five' – had previously complained to their employers at the Darlington Memorial Hospital, only to be rebuked for their intolerance. Twenty-six nurses had raised objections and were eventually informed by the ward manager that they should be 'more inclusive', 'broaden their mindset' and 'be re-educated'. One of the Darlington Five had been sexually abused as a child, and was nonetheless branded a bigot for feeling unsettled when a man in her changing room repeatedly asked her: 'Are you getting changed yet?'

February 2025 saw the employment tribunal of Sandie Peggie, a nurse at the Victoria Hospital in Kirkcaldy in Scotland who was suspended for 'harassment' when she complained about the presence of a man, Dr Beth Upton, in the female changing room. Few would disagree that nurses absolutely require changing facilities as part of the job. In this specific instance, Peggie had been menstruating and so asked Upton to leave, an action that was interpreted as 'bullying'. Quite rightly, Peggie took legal action against her employers. Upton's sense of entitlement throughout the tribunal was as palpable as his devotion to his ideology. In spite of being a doctor, he claimed that male and female have 'no defined and agreed meaning in science', and that the term 'biological sex' was a 'nebulous dog whistle'. He repeatedly claimed that he was simply seeking 'respect', as though inveigling himself into his female colleagues' private spaces should be deserving of any courtesy. Not content with accusing Peggie of 'harassment', he also claimed that he had been victimised by the judge and the entire proceedings. Upton asserted that he had 'been treated horribly, this tribunal has been harassment. Not just for me but for all trans people in the country, just trying to be themselves.'

And this, of course, is where the essential authoritarianism of the trans movement becomes manifest. In a liberal society, we are able to dress as we like, call ourselves whatever we like and request that others do the same. We cannot force compliance when it comes to our private speech codes, nor can we intrude on the rights of others. Upton is free to call himself a woman, to change his name to 'Beth', and to ask others to address him as such. He is not entitled to their acquiescence, and nor is he entitled to assert his own desires at the expense of women's rights. Even when Peggie revealed that she had been molested by a male doctor as a girl, Upton dismissed this aspect of her experience by saying that 'someone's trauma doesn't justify bad behaviour towards colleagues'. This wild reversal of victim and aggressor, this determination to bully and claim to be bullied, tells us everything about the unfettered narcissism at the heart of gender identity ideology. When the *Scottish Daily Express* reported on this case, and referred to Upton as a man, the editor was reported to the police for 'intentional and gratuitous misgendering and deadnaming'.

Thankfully, there are signs that our society still retains a few scraps of sanity and the ability to break its way out of this asylum. Many women who have been hounded out of their jobs or been discriminated against due to their recognition of biological reality have been vindicated in the courts, including Maya Forstater, Jo Phoenix, Allison Bailey, Denise Fahmy and Rachel Meade. In May 2024, the judgement was handed down in the constructive dismissal case of Roz Adams, a former support counsellor at the Edinburgh Rape Crisis Centre. Although never opposing the rights of trans-identified people, Adams had always understood that the reality of biological sex is paramount when it comes to supporting those who have suffered violence at the hands of men. Having discovered that the management team at the centre favoured the ideological view that sex isn't real, and that 'gender identity' is all that matters, Adams had raised some entirely reasonable concerns. In particular, she had suggested that victims of rape ought to be given clear information regarding the sex of their counsellors. After all, what would happen if a victim were to ask for female-only support? According to the management, in such a scenario they were to be reassured that there were no men working there. This created problems when one victim specifically asked Adams to reveal the sex of a 'non-binary' counsellor, and she asked her managers whether she should respond according to biological sex or 'gender identity'. That Adams sought clarity on this issue was all it took to see a disciplinary procedure launched against her.

In the findings of the tribunal, it was revealed that the Edinburgh Rape Crisis Centre refused to refer victims who sought single-sex services to Beira's Place, which would strongly suggest that their ideology matters more than the people supposedly in their care. The judgement could not have been more damning. The disciplinary process against Adams was described as 'completely spurious' and 'deeply flawed' and 'unfortunately a classic of its kind, somewhat reminiscent of the work of Franz Kafka'. In all of this, we should remind ourselves how little the general public have ever supported the revolutionary goals of genderism. A report by Sex Matters – *Women's Services: A Sector Silenced* – shows that 84 per cent of British people say that women who have been the victims of rape, sexual assault or domestic violence should have access to female-only services. The only surprise in these statistics is that the figure is not higher.

The woke hegemony has enabled activists like Mridul Wadhwa, former head of the Edinburgh Rape Crisis Centre, to make important decisions that fly directly against popular consensus. On his appearance on *The Guilty Feminist* podcast in August 2021, Wadhwa was asked about those victims of sexual crimes who would rather not be in the company of men, trans-identified or otherwise.

> Sexual violence happens to bigoted people as well. And so, you know, it is not a discerning crime. But these spaces are also for you. But if you bring unacceptable beliefs that are discriminatory in nature, we will begin to work with you on your journey of recovery from trauma. But please also expect to be challenged on your prejudices.

He went on to say that these women should 'reframe' their trauma and develop 'a more positive relationship with it'. In other words, all must defer to the ideology of Wadhwa and his fellow activists, and if this means smearing a few rape victims as 'bigots', then so be it. Such is the nuclear-strength arrogance of those who subscribe to this quasi-religious worldview that they are willing to denounce and shame innocent people even when they are at their most traumatised. Surely the Edinburgh Rape Crisis Centre case must be seen as the moment when gender identity ideology 'jumped the shark'. It is impossible to conceive how it could get any worse – or, as the judgement put it, more Kafkaesque – than female victims being turned away from a support centre because they do not wish to be counselled by men.

Naturally, the war on women soon developed into an attack on the concept of motherhood. In February 2021, it was reported that Brighton and Sussex University Hospitals Trust had introduced terms such as 'chestfeeding' and 'birthing parent' into its professional lexicon. As always, such measures were intended to be 'inclusive', but ended up making a lot of women feel very excluded indeed. By this point, we had grown accustomed to these kinds of grimly misogynistic euphemisms. The media company CNN has referred to women as 'individuals with a cervix'. In promoting their sanitary products, Tampax has opted for 'people who bleed' while Kotex has settled for 'menstruators'. New language guides by Healthline and Jo's Cervical Cancer Trust rebranded vaginas as 'front holes' and 'bonus holes' respectively. All of this is dispiritingly reminiscent of when Titania McGrath suggested that women ought to be referred to as 'bipedal gestation units'.

In February 2024, a letter from the University of Sussex Hospitals Trust emerged claiming that men who take drugs after transitional surgery are able to produce milk 'comparable to that produced following the birth of a baby'. It would seem that the principle of inclusivity has gone so far that even the NHS was willing to disregard concerns over the safety of newborn infants. In its coverage, the BBC interviewed one Kate Luxion, introduced as a research fellow at University College London and a 'lactation consultant trainee'. On the UCL website, Luxion is described as a 'non-binary/genderqueer postgraduate researcher' with a focus 'on LGBTQ+ reproductive health and parenting'. In other words, a more accurate description for Luxion's role would have simply been 'activist'. During the interview Luxion was able to state, unchallenged, that drug-induced milk from trans-identified males was 'at least, if not higher, quality' than breast milk from mothers. She claimed to be citing a recent study, but no specific details were forthcoming.

In order to develop milk-producing glands, a man would need to take the hormone progestin in combination with a drug such as domperidone to stimulate lactation. The manufacturer of domperidone – whose brand name is Motilium – has warned against this 'because of possible side effects to a baby's heart' and that it 'should be used during breastfeeding only if your physician considers this clearly necessary'. Even if the risk is slight, why would anyone prioritise the feelings of a trans-identified male over the safety of a baby? Many men throughout history have fetishised the experience of motherhood, but up until now they have not been accommodated in mainstream culture. One thinks of the 'molly houses' of the eighteenth century, sex clubs in which cross-dressing men were known to perform birthing ceremonies with wooden babies. These days there are online chat rooms devoted to men who delight in feigning pregnancies and posting videos of their imagined experiences of 'menstrual cramps'. Liberals may have no issue with fetishistic behaviour that does not encroach on anyone else's rights, but when babies are being put at risk, this clearly crosses that line.

Unfortunately, this was not the first case of its kind. In July 2023, it was reported that a research team of sociologists, funded to the tune of half a million pounds by a subsidiary of UK Research and Innovation – a non-departmental public body of the British government – had recommended changes to NHS guidelines. They argued that mothers who identified as male should continue to take testosterone during pregnancy because their sense of gender identity ought to be prioritised over 'normal foetal outcomes'. In a document that has to be read to be believed, these activists cautioned against 'offspring-focused treatment approaches'. By their logic, birth defects are only considered a problem because of 'normative' prejudices.

What's more, to be overly concerned with the health of the baby was apparently deemed a form of transphobia:

> These approaches reinscribe binarized notions of sex, resulting in social control in their attempts to safeguard against non-normative potential future outcomes for offspring.
>
> These offspring-focused risk-avoidance strategies and approaches are, we argue, part of the gendered precautionary labour of pregnancy and pregnancy care itself, and not without potentially harmful consequences for trans people.

If the British taxpayer is funding activists without medical qualifications to make such dangerous suggestions, is it really that astonishing to see the NHS prioritising the desires of trans-identified individuals over their children?

In April 2025, what may transpire to be the pivotal battle in the gender wars was finally won. In the case brought to the Supreme Court by For Women Scotland, it was ruled that the term 'sex' in the Equality Act 2010 refers to biological sex, and that women's single-sex spaces must exclude even those men who hold a Gender Recognition Certificate. The highest court in the United Kingdom had determined that reality still matters. After years of sophistry and word games from activists, the rights of women were belatedly being upheld in spite of the inevitable accusations that the ruling was 'transphobic'. This clarified that the various schools, prisons, hospitals, charities and businesses that had been permitting anyone who self-identified as female to gain access to women's accommodation, toilets and changing facilities were not acting in accordance with the law. The United Kingdom has often been described as 'TERF island', and it is undeniable that the tenacity of these women's rights campaigners has shifted the balance of power in the gender wars on a global scale. Could this decisive victory prove to be the final agonal moment of the era of woke?

# 7

# Woke Homophobia

## The Gay Plague

'All of my friends are dead.' It was said in his customary matter-of-fact tone, without the slightest hint of self-pity. This was Robin Robbins, one of my doctoral supervisors at Oxford, who would often discuss his pre-academic life and what it was like to be a gay man during the worst of the Aids crisis. That he had survived at all struck him as incredible. In those early days, the sense of an angel of death targeting a particular community seemed like the realisation of a nightmare. When it first emerged in the United States it was known as GRID (gay-related immune deficiency). An article appeared in the *New York Times* on 3 July 1981 with the ominous headline: 'Rare cancer seen in 41 homosexuals'. Some called it the 'gay plague'. Confusion turned into widespread panic, not limited to the gay community. The first time I heard of the disease was during a physical education lesson at primary school. Such was the general ignorance that our teacher warned us not to borrow each other's plimsolls or we might catch Aids. Some time later I saw the government's public health advertisement on the television; I remember little about it except the large tombstone with the dreaded four-letter acronym as an epitaph. A headline in the *Sun* declared that 'perverts are to blame for the killer plague'. A writer for the *Daily Express* likewise held 'those who choose unnatural methods of self-gratification' responsible for the disease, and letters to the editor followed suit. One reader called for the incarceration of homosexuals. 'Burning is too good for them,' wrote another. 'Bury them in a pit and pour on quicklime.' Someone had been reading his Dante.

It was sadly inevitable that the Aids crisis would exacerbate this ancient prejudice. In the decades since the virus was identified, there has been a sea-change in attitudes. Whereas the government's campaign set out to frighten people with the message 'it's a deadly disease and there's no known cure', an advertisement by the Terrence Higgins Trust released in October 2023 reminds people that those diagnosed with HIV 'can live a healthy, happy life just like anyone else'. Much of the stigma has dissipated, and the same is true of homosexuality itself. One could say that while the Aids crisis exacerbated the hatred and mistrust against an already beleaguered community, it also spurred activists onto the pathway to normalisation. Whereas the pursuit of a gay lifestyle was romanticised – or demonised – as a dance of Eros and Thanatos, a way to ensure that one remained beyond the scope of civilised society, today the very notion of being oriented towards one's own sex is largely perceived as unremarkable. Those who bleat about their oppression as gay people in a climate of widespread tolerance are luxuriating in a kind of perverse nostalgia for a reality they could never comprehend.

For those who lived through it, the Aids crisis was a moment when the concept of a 'gay community' actually meant something. Lesbians were instrumental in providing support for their gay brothers, and amid the loss there was a sense of greater solidarity. It brings to mind a production of Larry Kramer's *The Normal Heart* (1985) that I saw in New York in 2004. The audience mostly comprised older gay men, and Kramer was among them. Afterwards, people were visibly shaken from watching the worst of their past so unflinchingly dramatised. One man approached Kramer and, through his sobs, I heard him simply say: 'Thank you.' Kramer has been credited as a kind of Cassandra figure, one who had warned that the hedonism of gay life in the late seventies would lead to trouble. His novel *Faggots* (1978) was loathed by conservatives for its graphic depiction of the sexual free-for-alls of New York's bathhouse culture, but it was also mistrusted by the gay community for its moralising implications. Its lead character is on an impossible quest to find meaningful love in a world of fleeting sexual encounters. Kramer was criticising what he saw as a sybaritic and morally vacuous culture, and the sense of an impending reckoning has led to the novel being interpreted as predicting the outbreak of Aids.

When the crisis exploded, Kramer was one of those calling on gay men to exercise sexual temperance, and to shut the bathhouses until the virus could be contained. For this he was accused of being a puritan and a traitor to the gay lifestyle. His play *The Normal Heart* is set around this time, and in one furious monologue, a character rails against a Kramer-type figure for trying to make gay men feel ashamed of their own liberation. As for the ultra-religious, Aids was seen as a righteous punishment from God. Many had been appalled at the promiscuity of the gay scene. Male sexuality has always been contained to a degree by the institution of marriage, but gay men had been forced to exist on the periphery. There was no need to abide by sexual mores, because the rules had clearly not been written with them in mind. In other words, sex became an integral aspect of their own defiance against the society that had shunned them.

It always seemed a catch-22. Gay men were loathed for their sexual licentiousness, and at the same time excluded from the very ethical framework that would, to a degree, offer some kind of incentive against it. In his 1982 lecture, 'Rediscovering gay history', the historian John Boswell addressed this fundamental contradiction and argued for the need for a gay archetype or moral aspiration. He pointed out that when a straight man cheated on his wife, he at least knew that he was falling short of society's expectations. But the same could not be said for gay men:

> I think that part of the reason for the ambivalence of the intellectual establishment in the United States is that they can't tell when they read a book like Edmund White's *States of Desire* [1980], whether the life of casual promiscuity it depicts represents a homosexual *ideal* or the failure of an ideal. Are they reading about what gay people should do, what they do, or both, or neither? So they don't know how to fit it into their usual critical apparatus. They don't understand what would be a departure from homosexual ethics because they don't know what homosexual ethics would be. And neither do we.

Boswell was right that this ambivalence existed within and without the gay community. When William Friedkin's film *Cruising* was released in 1980, the most vehement opposition came from gay campaigners who feared that it would depict them as being inherently deviant. And yet the movie had been shot in the leather bars of New York City, and the real-life sex acts that were filmed were hardly atypical. This subculture was by no means reflective of gay society as a whole, but it certainly existed.

Perhaps it could be said that the activists who sought to ban *Cruising* won out in the end. Their implicit goal was that gay people could be brought under the aegis of heterosexual respectability; that they could, in other words, live as conventionally as everybody else. It made sense, therefore, that it was a Conservative government in the United Kingdom that eventually legalised same-sex marriage. It would appear that we have seen the cultivation in the Western world of the kind of shared ethical ideals that Boswell seemed to crave. Gay monogamy is no longer seen as an oxymoron. Yet many gay rights groups opposed same-sex marriage, seeing it as a means to control gay people, to bring them within the same heteronormative yoke that dominated the rest of society. This debate echoed those of *The Normal Heart*, where there was a fear of an attempt to 'civilise' those who had found freedom in occupying a realm outside social convention. To be gay was to be different, and for many this was a source of pride. An older gay man once told me that sex was far more exhilarating when it was illegal. It meant that even the most casual sexual encounter was a little act of rebellion.

But even as tolerance has increased, anti-gay feeling has not gone away. The Aids crisis galvanised such prejudices, and of course religious fundamentalists have always opposed those who they deem to be acting against the wishes of their various gods. Today, these prejudices are resurfacing through the obsession with gender identity, an ideology that shames gay people for not being attracted to members of the opposite sex, and has been responsible for the government-funded medicalisation of gay youth. As we shall see, in many ways, this is a 'progressive' rehash of Section 28 of the Local Government Act 1988 and its prohibition in schools against the 'promotion' or 'acceptability of homosexuality as a pretended family relationship'.

At the same time, we have seen a surge in anti-gay sentiment among the 'anti-woke' commentariat. A poll by Ipsos in June 2024 found that support for gay marriage has been steadily declining since 2021, from 59 per cent to 51 per cent in just three years. In February 2025, it was reported that at least five states – Michigan, Idaho, Montana, North Dakota and South Dakota – were seeking to overturn the 2015 Supreme Court ruling in *Obergefell v. Hodges* which had made it legal for same-sex couples to marry. Open declarations of anger towards gay people are now common online, and the kind of commonplace anti-gay rhetoric of the 1980s, declaiming gay men as 'faggots' and 'degenerates' has returned. A cascade of factors has almost certainly contributed to the backlash. The excesses of gender ideologues – with hypersexualised 'family-friendly' drag shows and the promotion of age-inappropriate teaching materials – have been interpreted as being an extension of the gay rights lobby, although their goals are antithetical. There has been an effort to embrace the core values of Christianity as an identity rather than a faith category, leading to more overt denunciations of same-sex love on biblical grounds. Among the gender-critical fringe, we have seen a renewed conviction that male sexuality is inherently toxic and largely to blame for the efforts to dismantle women's rights in the name of 'transgenderism'. Gay men are therefore seen as uniquely culpable as the ultimate instantiation of the male libido.

Whereas at the time of the Aids crisis, gay people largely had to contend with hostility from the Christian right, it is now emerging from multiple fronts. For instance, the effort to appease radical Islamism has led to a strange myopia from self-proclaimed 'progressives' when it comes to gay rights abuses in Muslim-majority countries. The campaign group 'Queers for Palestine' represents the apotheosis of this phenomenon, but when a Channel 4 poll revealed that a majority of British Muslims agreed that homosexuality ought to be criminalised, the *Guardian* immediately published a piece in which a number of Muslims were interviewed on the subject. Naturally, all dismissed the findings rather than engage with the problem they identified. The piece was even credited as being co-authored by 'Guardian readers', as though to emphasise the sense of solidarity in rejecting the statistics outright.

Many conservatives have always opposed same-sex relations on moral or religious grounds, but the notion of gender self-identification has been far more effective when it comes to dismantling gay spaces. If 'homosexuality' is based on gender rather than sex, then it is possible for a man to be a lesbian. He may have been born male – or 'assigned male at birth', to borrow the voguish parlance – but his 'gender identity' is female and this should be the salient factor when it comes to sexual orientation. This explains why, as of September 2023, Australia's Human Rights Commission prohibits lesbians from holding women-only events on the grounds that they discriminate against men who identify as female. Lesbian dating apps are now replete with men who claim to be women, many fully bearded and bepenised. Likewise, sex clubs for gay men now routinely admit women who have had their breasts removed and believe themselves to be male. CliniQ, a clinic at King's College Hospital funded in part by the NHS, even produced a leaflet called *Cruising: A Trans Guy's Guide to the Gay Sex Scene*, encouraging women to deceive men into sexual activity in gay saunas. It approvingly quoted a woman boasting that she enjoyed 'giving head and experimenting in public without others having to see what's under my towel', an act that is known in law as 'sex by deception'. Those familiar with Shakespeare's *Measure for Measure* (c. 1604) and *All's Well That Ends Well* (c. 1605), in which female characters conceal their identities to trick men into sleeping with them, might know it as the 'bed trick'. And while it is considered acceptable for women to sexually assault gay men, the hook-up app Grindr prohibits its gay male users from filtering out women. As the company's website puts it:

> When designing gender settings on Grindr, it was important to us to not further perpetuate discrimination and harm for the trans and non-binary community. For this reason, we allow filtering based on gender – you can specify that you want to see men or women – but this will include *all men* or *all women*, because trans men are men and trans women are women.

What Grindr calls 'discrimination', most of us call homosexuality. It is disorientating to see a company that has made a fortune from gay men's libidos now shaming its customers for being gay.

While many trans campaigners consider themselves supportive of gay rights, overt homophobia is nonetheless often tolerated and encouraged within their circles. Whereas we have always been accustomed to this kind of thing from the far right (one recalls the British National Party leader Nick Griffin's remark on the BBC's *Question Time* in October 2009 about how he finds the sight of two men kissing 'really creepy'), nowadays the most objectionable anti-gay comments are to be heard from gender ideologues. The significant difference is that the word 'cis' has been added to the homophobe's lexicon. Some examples:

Cis gay men are a disease.

Cis gay men are truly some of the most grotesque creatures to burden this earth.

I hate cis gay people with a burning passion.

If you're a cis gay man and your sexuality revolves around you not liking female genitalia I hope you die and I will spit on your grave.

Cis gays don't deserve rights.

There's so many reasons to hate gay people, most specifically white gays, but there's never a reason to be a transphobe.

It's time to normalise homophobia.

Of course, any bile can be found on the internet, but these kinds of phrases are remarkably commonplace among online genderist communities. Many thousands of examples had been collated on Google Photos under the title 'Woke homophobia: anti-gay hatred & boxer ceiling abuse from trans activists & gender-identity ideologues'. The site was taken down in 2023, presumably because it violated Google's policy on hate speech, or perhaps because it revealed the toxicity of the ideology the company has spent so long promoting. Many activists claim that 'genital preferences are transphobic', or that sexual orientation based on biological sex is a form of 'trauma'. The idea that homosexuality is a sickness was one of the first homophobic tropes I encountered as a child. Now it is being rebranded as progressive.

Consider a recent post on X by Stephen Whittle, OBE, a professor of Equalities Law at Manchester Metropolitan University. In a reply to LGB Alliance's co-founder Bev Jackson, Whittle took issue with the notion that 'love is all about genitals', an argument that Jackson has never made. Having dismissed this straw man as 'a very hetero/homo-normative perspective', Whittle then claimed that 'a lot of gay men can't resist a young furry ftm [female-to-male] cub'. While it is true that there are some bisexuals who identify as gay, it is simply not the case that homosexual men 'can't resist' certain kinds of women. As Jackson rightly noted in her response, this is rank homophobia, 'disturbed and disturbing on every level'. Yet it has been expressed by an individual who has been described as a 'hero for LGBTQ+ equality'.

When it comes to the question of gay spaces, then, there is a shared antipathy from the 'woke' and the 'anti-woke' alike. After one man posted online his view that the presence of women in his local gay sauna was defeating the purpose, he was bombarded not only from the Christian right, but also from women's rights campaigners. The editor-in-chief of one feminist website commented that she was 'glad their virus exchange party was interrupted' and that 'male sexuality without the natural throttle of a female counterpoint is genuinely disturbed'. Previously, she had claimed that: 'When not restricted by society, family, female sexuality, morality, etc . . . male sexuality will naturally deviate towards the obscene.' We are seeing here a return to what author and philosopher Christina Hoff Sommers has called 'fainting couch feminism', a kind of throwback to the Victorian perception of women as dainty, timid and prudish. Author Joanna Williams calls this 'victim feminism', by which 'moral beatification' is achieved in a culture where victimhood equates to power. This 'damsel in distress' form of women's liberation has recast the very notion of sexuality as oppressive and, according to political commentator Ella Whelan, has helped to 'feed the idea that women are vulnerable creatures in need of protection from public life'. Of course, the ubiquity of male violence against women makes this widespread distrust understandable; men are simply far more likely to be predators. As feminist luminary Germaine Greer puts it, 'Women in search of romance are coming to grief at the hands of men who are after conquest'. While these trends make safeguarding measures on the basis of sex essential, they are no excuse for lazy collectivist judgements about men and women. No individual bears any responsibility for the conduct of others who happen to fall within his or her demographic. This is the universalist view of the genuine liberal.

Male homosexuality, although for obvious reasons less threatening to women's safety, is nonetheless seen as the most unregulated and baleful manifestation of the masculine libido. Helen Pluckrose has theorised that the specific hostility towards gay men is an extension of the radical misandry which 'has always had a presence in the feminist movement' but at the same time has 'always been opposed by other feminists'. She continues:

> But why would misandry cause this subset of feminists to engage in virulent homophobia? Even if men were all violent, domineering sexual predators perpetuating a misogynistic rape culture to satisfy their own depraved sexual appetites, surely the men we'd have to worry about least are those whose appetite for sex with women is non-existent? My observation of this odd phenomenon suggests that this is related to a strong streak of puritanical opposition to male sexuality as something dark and inherently dangerous alongside a belief in the gentle purity of female sexuality.

Pluckrose is rightly focusing on elements within groups, and avoids the trap of identitarian collectivism. But she is also correct to note the 'sizeable contingent of old-fashioned extreme authoritarian social conservatives' who have been attracted to the gender-critical movement in recent years. If male sexuality is a force for evil, the thinking goes, it is only compounded when women are removed from the equation. An alternative anti-gay stance was taken by the Redstockings, a radical feminist group formed in 1969, who perceived male homosexuality as a 'rejection of women and therefore completely objectionable'.

The instinctive disgust that many people feel towards those who do not share their own sexual inclinations is seemingly hardwired, and so what we call 'homophobia' will always emerge in one way or another in a majority heterosexual culture. As a child of the eighties and nineties, I remember well that homosexuals were fair game in the mainstream media. One columnist in the *Daily Star* railed against 'Wooftahs, pooftahs, nancy boys, queers, lezzies – the perverts whose moral sin is to so abuse the delightful word "gay" as to render it unfit for human consumption'. After the death of the singer Freddie Mercury, sympathy in the *Mail on Sunday* was limited. 'If you treat as a hero a man who died because of his own sordid sexual perversions,' columnist John Junor cautioned, 'aren't you infinitely more likely to persuade some of the gullible young to follow in his example?' Writing for the *Daily Mirror*, Joe Haines declared that 'Mercury died from a disease whose main victims in the Western world are homosexuals. For his kind, Aids is a form of suicide.' Peter McKay in the *London Evening Standard* was even more abrupt: 'Freddie's life was consumed with sodomy. He died from it.'

I happened to come out in a much less hostile climate. In the early 2000s, we were enjoying a kind of Goldilocks moment, neither too hot nor too cold. We weren't generally on the receiving end of homophobic slurs, but nor were we patronised by well-meaning progressives. My memory of this time was that no one particularly cared. To be gay was no longer defined solely by the sexual act, and that for one man to fall in love with another was widely considered to be an unexceptional fact of life. Today's culture war has turned back the clock, and an alliance of woke and anti-woke groups, along with a faction of neo-Victorian feminists, has regenerated a hostility that many of us mistakenly assumed had faded away. Aggressively anti-gay sentiments from the woke right and the woke left are shared with apparent glee, and even those who claim to be supportive of sexual minorities are exacerbating the problem through their ignorance of the issues. A viral TikTok video from June 2024 featured transgender influencer Kelly Cadigan explaining to gay men why they should transition to female and that 'maybe being gay is an outdated concept'. Trans-identified author Juno Dawson has claimed that 'a lot of gay men are gay men as a consolation prize, because they couldn't be women'. In April 2022, an online influencer called Davey Wavey uploaded his attempt at gay conversion therapy in a video entitled 'How To Eat Pussy – For Gay Men'. Nancy Kelley, former CEO of Stonewall, compared women who were not interested in trans-identified males to 'sexual racists'. With friends like these, who needs homophobes?

## The Myths of Stonewall

If you visit Greenwich Village in New York, the sense of non-conformism seems built into the topography. Whereas the streets of Manhattan are largely a perpendicular affair, those of the Village vary in width and intersect in unpredictable ways. The New York grid plan of 1817 had been opposed by the local residents, as the author Anna Alice Chapin explained a century later:

> Greenwich will not straighten its streets nor conventionalise its views. Its intellectual conclusions will always be just as unexpected as the squares and street angles that one stumbles on head first. Its habit of life will be just as weirdly individual as its tangled blocks. It asks nothing better than to be let alone. It does not welcome tourists, though it is hospitality itself to wayfarers seeking an open door. It is the Village, and it will never, never, no *never* be anything else – the Village of the streets that wouldn't be straight!

It is as though the seeds of resistance had been sown in the neighbourhood long before the riots at the Stonewall Inn.

The protests that erupted at that small gay bar in the early hours of 28 June 1969 represent a turning point in the history of civil rights. While the riots themselves may not have directly resulted in societal change, the activism that they inspired in the subsequent years made a lasting difference. The events of those nights have been widely misrepresented and subjected to crude historical revisionism, from assertions that the uprising was a reaction to the death of Judy Garland to false claims that trans-identified people were at the forefront. For those who have seen the photographs of young gay men leading the charge, this will seem confusing. This seedy bar in the heart of Greenwich Village had become a fulcrum for dispossessed and destitute homosexuals, many of them teenagers. At the time of the riots, animosity towards gay people was the norm. Traditionalists opposed same-sex desire for the same reason they always have, seeing it as against the natural law. Progressives saw it as a mental illness, which meant they generally treated those afflicted with pity rather than scorn. Gay sex was illegal in all states except Illinois. These circumstances meant that young gay people often found themselves homeless having been disowned by their families. Many of those who fought at the riots had gravitated to the Village in the hope of finding others like themselves.

The history of the Stonewall Inn dates back to 1930, when two former stables at 51 and 53 Christopher Street became the premises for a new tearoom called 'Bonnie's Stone Wall'. It is likely that the proprietor – we assume it was a woman called Bonnie – had taken the name from Mary Casal's gay memoir *The Stone Wall* which had been published that year. In his definitive study, *Stonewall: The Riots That Sparked the Gay Revolution* (2004), David Carter surmises that Bonnie had thereby been sending 'a coded message to lesbians that they would be welcomed there'. Over the decades the name evolved: it became 'Bonnie's Stonewall Inn' in the 1940s, then the 'Stonewall Inn Restaurant' in the 1960s, and only after a fire did it rise from the ashes in 1967 as the gay bar known as the 'Stonewall Inn'. By this point, it was owned by the mafia. Under the watchful eye of 'Fat Tony', the bar operated in the guise of a private club to evade the city's liquor licence laws. There was no running water, so the bartenders would rinse glasses from the sinks filled in advance of each night's shift, a practice which on one occasion resulted in an outbreak of hepatitis. Ultimately, it was the mafia's monopoly on the city's gay bars, and the police who saw them as easy targets, that stirred the frustrations that would eventually explode on that blisteringly hot summer night in June 1969.

Given that so many activists are determined to distort the history of the Stonewall riots as one in which trans people bravely stood up to the police on behalf of their gay brethren – fitting in to their revisionist narrative that gay people owe their rights to the trans community – it is worth setting the record straight. Very few trans individuals were even counted among the Stonewall clientele, let alone became involved in the uprising. Carter offers the following overview:

> Perhaps the most accurate way to characterize the Stonewall Inn in terms of what we currently call transgender identity is that while there was a lot of gender transgression going on there, this was largely a reflection of the male homosexual world of the time, that most men who went there were conventionally masculine, but that there was a considerable minority of men there who ran the gamut from men effeminate in their mannerisms, to scare or flame queens, to a few transvestites and some transsexuals.

As for the riots themselves, Carter has this to say:

> My research for this history demonstrates that if we wish to name the group most responsible for the success of the riots, it is the young, homeless homosexuals, and, contrary to the usual characterizations of those on the rebellion's front lines, most were Caucasian; few were Latino; almost none were transvestites or transsexuals; most were effeminate; and a fair number came from middle-class families.

The truth of the historical records is rather inconvenient for revisionist activists. As late as February 2025, MSNBC's Rachel Maddow was insisting that the Stonewall uprising was 'a riot by trans people', and the *Guardian* was making the similarly fraudulent claim that the riots were 'led by trans women of color' and that a black trans woman called Marsha P. Johnson 'threw the first brick'. While the *Guardian* has a deserved reputation for prioritising ideological expedience over truth, it is surprising to see such a comprehensively debunked myth restated so brazenly. By his own admission, Johnson was a drag queen who did not identify as female and was not even present when the riots began; even his adopted surname was a *double entendre* that referred to the male appendage. Johnson was certainly an active participant at Stonewall, but to claim him as a 'leader' of the uprising requires a total disregard for the facts. In a parliamentary debate in March 2024, Conservative MP Alicia Kearns claimed that 'it was trans people who stood with gay people at Stonewall; it was trans people who fought alongside them for LGB rights'. To find an

*Demonstrators at the Stonewall Inn in June 1969.*

authentic instance of trans activists involving themselves in these kinds of riots, one would have to go back even further, to the disturbances at Compton's Cafeteria in San Francisco in August 1966. In that case, it is very clear that the trans participants were fighting in their own interests, not in an effort to promote the rights of homosexuals. Compton's was just around the corner from the office of the first surgeon in US history to offer sex-reassignment operations, and so of course the trans-identifying population was predominant.

By contrast, the Stonewall riots were very much an event that centred on the gay community. The police unit responsible for tackling that night's disturbances, led by Deputy Inspector Seymour Pine, intended to arrest any men wearing women's clothing; transvestism was a criminal offence at the time. If any post-operative transsexuals were caught, they would not have been subject to prosecution. That the Stonewall riots were so specifically centred around gay men meant that even when subjected to violence and intimidation, many of the participants retained that waspish sense of humour which is so characteristic of what some have called 'the gay sensibility'. Carter relates how when patrons were being ejected from the bar in the initial raid, some of them would make provocative gestures to the police. 'As one young man swished by the detective posted at the door, he tossed the classic come-on line at him: "Hello there, fella!"' And as employees of the bar were carted into police vans, the crowds started singing mischievous camp variations on the civil rights anthem 'We Shall Overcome'.

Local residents Craig Rodwell and Fred Sargeant had been walking down Christopher Street in the early hours of 28 June, and passed by at the moment when the crowds were forming outside the Stonewall Inn. There were rumours that the police were keeping customers inside and physically assaulting them, and so whenever the police would open the door they would be forced back by the pebbles and coins thrown by the crowd. 'The police were waiting for something,' recalled Sargeant in one interview. 'We didn't know what they were waiting for. As it turned out they were waiting for paddy wagons, and they were waiting for back-up.' He recalled the moment that he saw a black butch lesbian, later putatively identified as Stormé DeLarverie, fighting back as police attempted to arrest her. Her now famous cry of 'Why don't you guys do something?' is considered the catalyst to the riots that ensued. The police had seen nothing like this before, and were uncertain how to tackle gangs largely comprising of gay street youths, along with some drag queens and other effeminate men.

Howard Smith, columnist for the *Village Voice*, had found himself trapped inside the venue with police, and afterwards wrote that 'the sound filtering in' did not 'suggest dancing faggots any more' but more 'like a powerful rage bent on vendetta'. Carter describes how when the riot police approached in formation, they were shocked to see the protesters make a formation of their own. 'Suddenly the gay street youths linked their arms around one another,' writes Carter, 'and kicked Rockette style as they sang their old reprise'.

> *We are the Stonewall Girls,*
> *We wear our hair in curls.*
> *We wear no underwear:*
> *We show our pubic hairs.*

What followed was a continual game of cat-and-mouse, with the rioters taunting the police and then scarpering down the streets they knew so well. This 'kick-line routine' was played out repeatedly, while the dancing rioters teased the police by calling them 'the girls in blue' and 'Lily Law'. As some set fire to trash cans and kicked and punched, a few brave souls humiliated their oppressors with synchronised dance.

The protests continued for five days, only coming to an end on 3 July. They were the inevitable consequence of gay people who had lost patience. They were sick of being the targets of casual violence and abuse, not just by the police, but by society at large. They were sick of living in the shadows, having to rely on mafia thugs who despised them to run their bars. They were sick of the endless police entrapment and surveillance, and the raids on their gatherings on the flimsiest of pretexts. The Stonewall riots, what the *Village Voice* had sneeringly described as the 'Great Faggot Rebellion', turned out to be the Rubicon that the gay community had finally summoned the courage to cross. Those kick-dancing street queens certainly had the last laugh.

Yet the riots were not so significant as the transformative activism that followed in their wake. The author and gay activist Randy Wicker once criticised the uprising by saying that 'rocks through windows don't open doors'. So while the Stonewall riots were a spur to action, the endless arguments about 'who threw the first brick?' have obscured the truth that gay equality was achieved by the activists who persisted in the aftermath, harnessing that energy and changing the world for ever. Perhaps a more important milestone was the march organised by a handful of campaigners a year after Stonewall. Craig Rodwell's idea had been to make this a yearly commemoration that would supersede the 'Annual Reminder' picket events that he had been holding every Independence Day in Philadelphia since 1965. It would be known as the 'Christopher Street Liberation Day' – later retrospectively rebranded as the first New York 'Pride' march – and it was orchestrated chiefly by Rodwell, Fred Sargeant, Linda Rhodes and Ellen Broidy.

The march took place on 28 June 1970, and it was an audacious display. Police hostility to gay people was rife, the local media were overwhelmingly unsympathetic, and there were fears of violent repercussions from observers. The day passed off peacefully, perhaps because of a general sense of astonishment that thousands of gay people would assemble so openly. Jonathan Black wrote in the *Village Voice* that 'no one could quite believe it, eyes rolled back in heads, Sunday tourists traded incredulous looks, wondrous faces poked out of air-conditioned cars'. At the head of the march, Fred Sargeant carried a bullhorn and called out instructions to the marchers as they made their way from the West Village to Central Park.

Half a century later, and Pride has transformed from an important act of resistance into a month-long orgy of corporate veneration and virtue signalling, teeming with heterosexuals desperate to slink their way into an oppressed group with the help of gender ideology. 'Progress Pride' flags flutter from every high-street store. This relatively new design – a kaleidoscopic eyesore that has replaced the traditional six-stripe Pride flag – is emblazoned on schools, universities, hospitals, civic buildings. In June 2024, in the city of Arlington in Texas, the 'family-friendly' Pride event included displays of dildos, half-naked drag queens and human dogs in bondage gear, all co-sponsored by Lockheed Martin, the world's largest producer of armaments. In Regent Street in London, scores of 'Progress Pride' flags are draped with regimental precision and symmetry throughout this hallowed month; one cannot evade the impression that the nation's capital has been temporarily taken over by the paramilitary wing of the Care Bears. In addition, numerous pedestrian crossings have been repainted with the 'Progress Pride' motif, even though disability rights campaigners have repeatedly pointed out that the rainbow colours cause huge problems for the partially sighted and their guide dogs. Police horses also find walking across the coloured stripes confusing and disturbing, so the animals have undergone special training to overcome their fears. Apparently it is essential to address the rampant homophobia within the equine community.

This mania for flags means that other designs have been created to represent the innumerable sexualities and genders that we've only just heard of but that have apparently always existed. There are flags to signify people who identify as non-binary, polyamorous, polysexual, agender, genderfluid, genderqueer, neutrois, two-spirit and many more. There are flags for pansexuals (those who are attracted to all sexual identities), somnisexuals (those who are only attracted to people in their dreams), parasexuals (those who don't feel sexual attraction but will have sex for reproductive purposes) and, most bewildering of all, quoisexuals, who do not identify with any labels at all. Quoisexuals are so fiercely independent that they consider labels to be just for conformists, but for some reason they still need their own flag. Of course, the majority of these flags are really about sexual proclivities, rather than sexual orientation. When Alfred Kinsey published his famous reports into human sexuality in the 1940s and 1950s, readers were shocked at the sheer range of behaviours. And given that no two people have precisely the same tastes, isn't the logical end point to assign everyone his or her own flag? That's a lot of fabric.

The original Pride flag was designed by the American artist Gilbert Baker in 1978. It a was a simple rainbow with eight stripes, later whittled down to six. This is the flag with which we all became familiar, symbolising joy, hope, harmony and equal rights for gay people. That flag is rarely seen these days. The shift began in 2017, when the 'Office of LGBT Affairs' in Philadelphia added black and brown stripes to include racial minorities, a bizarre modification given that the rainbow had represented everybody, regardless of race. With the floodgates now open, activists decided that unless they were specifically included on the flag, they were not welcome. When a pink, blue and white chevron representing trans people was added in 2018 by the activist Daniel Quasar, the 'Progress Pride' flag was born. Other additions have been attempted, with 'sexual health and well-being advocate' Jason Domino adding a red umbrella in 2020 to symbolise the plight of sex workers across the globe. The following year, 'equality speaker' Valentino Vecchietti ('she/they') added the 'intersex symbol', a purple circle on a yellow background, to represent the tiny minority who are born with ambiguous sex characteristics. Not to be outdone, in 2022 Microsoft created a garish monstrosity of forty different variations on the Pride flag. Thankfully, this insane headache-inducing patchwork has failed to catch on.

Needless to say, these groups actually have very little in common with one another. The all-inclusive rainbow flag, which worked perfectly well as a symbol of unity for decades, has been distorted by campaigners determined to cram it with as many new symbols and colours as possible to promote their own idiosyncratic and decidedly niche causes. What might the thousands who turned out on that summer day in New York in 1970 make of this distorted version of Pride? Those gay men and lesbians who risked social ostracism and physical violence to gather in public have little in common with this unsettling facsimile. Consider the strange evolution of the term 'queer'. Many homosexuals see this as an anti-gay slur, associating the term with the practice of 'queer-bashing'. But now, many young heterosexuals are identifying themselves into this category as a means to claim the high status that accompanies victimhood. The singer Dannii Minogue, a lifelong heterosexual, recently 'came out' as 'queer'. To many of those who have been the victims of homophobic invective and violence, it was galling to see a straight woman embracing this term of abuse as a fashion accessory. It was not long before she backtracked in a post on Instagram. 'I was not making an announcement that I'm a lesbian or queer,' she explained. 'I'm straight and in a long-term hetero relationship.' When Michaela Kennedy-Cuomo – daughter of the former governor of New York, Andrew Cuomo – announced that she was 'demisexual', few realised that the definition of this term is one who only feels sexually attracted to someone if they have an emotional bond. Cuomo had effectively 'come out' as an old-fashioned heterosexual.

With such semantic lubricity, identity politics is akin to the ouroboros that eats itself out of existence. As the writer Julie Burchill put it, terms such as 'queer' are 'just noises masquerading as words, like a small child deciding to bark and demanding to be accepted as a dog'. A study by the Arizona Christian University, which surveyed six hundred people between the ages of 18 and 37, found that of those in the lower age bracket (18 to 24), 39 per cent identified as 'LGBT'. Given the vast majority identifying as such consider themselves to be 'trans', 'non-binary' and 'queer', this means it is statistically certain that gay people are now the minority in this coalition. The oppression of homosexuals is an incontestable fact, but straight people with kinks have generally been left alone. Just because a majority rebrands itself as a minority, that does not make it oppressed. Little wonder that gay people are increasingly rejecting the 'LGBTQIA+' label entirely. The early pioneers of gay rights didn't risk so much for their movement to be usurped by fetishistic heterosexuals with a martyr complex.

It would be interesting to see polling data on how many gay people support Pride in its new 'trans-inclusive' incarnation. One recent poll on X asked a simple question: 'Do you want Pride anymore?' And although 93.5 per cent of the 490 respondents replied in the negative, social media polls are notoriously useless and we would be unwise to draw any conclusions from them. Still, it is surely significant that this poll was reposted by Fred Sargeant, and that his answer was a resounding 'No'. That the man who led the first Pride march, bull-horn in hand, should now reject the annual event that he co-created because of its embrace of gender ideology is hardly trivial. Nor is it trivial that while handing out pamphlets critical of the trans move-ment at a Pride event in Vermont in 2022, Sargeant was physically attacked by trans activists.

He is not alone. Many gay people have expressed dismay at the metamorphosis of Pride and feel that it no longer represents them. This can be confusing for those who have not been paying attention to its ongoing political evolution, but there is a very good reason why groups of gay men and lesbians are now holding alternative Pride rallies. In August 2022, police in Cardiff insisted that lesbians leave a Pride parade because their banners, proclaiming that 'lesbians don't like penises' and 'trans activism erases lesbians', were causing consternation. When gay people are being escorted away from Pride marches by the police, we can safely say that the movement has fallen.

Some might argue that the LGBTQIA+ explosion is an example of what happens when liberalism goes unchecked, that it is the natural consequence of an excess of tolerance and the rise of identity politics. Yet while identity politics in its current intersectional form has proven to be deeply illiberal and regressive, there have been sound reasons throughout history for people with shared characteristics to organise and resist. Unlike the various campaigns for imaginary victimhood that dominate today's woke causes, being openly gay in the 1970s came at a huge cost. At the time of the first Pride parade, homosexuality was not only criminal, but discrimination against gay people was permitted in services and employment. This is a world away from the exaggerated or factitious grievances of the DEI industry today. Now that gay people have complete equal rights under the law, the protest element of Pride has been appropriated by those with an apparent craving for oppression. Asexual activists, for instance, have taken centre stage at certain Pride events, even though nobody in the history of humankind has ever been burned at the stake for not wanting to have sex. One such activist, Yasmin Benoit, posted an image of herself marching at Pride along with the following statement: 'Asexual people deserve equal rights. We deserve legal recognition. We deserve protection. Thank you Stonewall for allowing me to march with you again at Pride in London today and for helping me to bring about this change.' Writer and podcaster Stephen Knight asked the obvious questions: 'in what ways are asexual people being denied equal rights? Which legal protections are they lacking? What specific "change" is Benoit attempting to bring about, other than an increase in her own profile?' It has never been the case that those who identify as asexual are facing discrimination; it's that nobody cares about what they don't get up to in the bedroom. But of course, for those of a narcissistic temperament, there can be nothing more devastating than being ignored.

Far from being a collective gesture of unity, Pride is now widely interpreted as a celebration of homophobia, a promotional circus for an ideology that seeks to eliminate gay people from their own history. Although trans-identified individuals were rarely seen at activist meetings and events in the early decades of the gay movement, revisionists are now insisting that gay people owe their rights to the hard work of trans campaigners. Fred Sargeant has been much vilified for exposing the truth of what took place in these early years of the gay rights movement, and he is now a thorn in the side of activists whose worldview depends on a narrative that runs contrary to the truth. Recently he posted online a link to the Digital Transgender archive on the Third International Conference on Transgender Law and Employment Policy, which explicitly outlines how gay and trans movements in the twentieth century were completely separate. The conflation of the LGB and T is an invention as recent as 2015. As the document explains, while the gay rights movement in the US began in the 1920s, 'the existence of a transgendered community that seeks reforms did not come into existence until the 1990s'. Bev Jackson was a co-founder of the Gay Liberation Front and was present at the first ever gay rights protest in the United Kingdom on 27 November 1970 in Highbury Fields, London. 'I recall the expressions of revulsion on the faces of the people lining the streets to watch us,' she recalls. 'That was certainly scary. But we held our heads high.' She has pointed out that transsexuals were never part of the early campaigns, and has criticised the anachronistic application of the initialism 'LGBT' to this period. Another founding member of the Gay Liberation Front, Stuart Feather, has recounted in his book, *Blowing the Lid* (2016), how transsexuals later attempted to hijack the movement. Rather than today's forced teaming of the LGB and the T, the attitude of the early gay rights activists was 'to encourage transsexuals and transvestites to make their own revolution'.

The historical revisionism doesn't end at Stonewall. Activists have attempted to claim that certain gay historical figures were mistaking their true trans identity for homosexuality. Just as Mormon priests have been known to baptise the dead and thereby convert them unwillingly to their cause, trans activists have been busy harvesting the annals of history for potential recruits. Those falsely claimed as trans include Louisa May Alcott, George Eliot, Dr James Barry and Radclyffe Hall. People who were gay and gender nonconforming are particularly vulnerable to this kind of retrospective 'transing'. It is very convenient for activists that the dead cannot complain.

The most obvious example of how gay rights have been threatened by gender identity ideology is that young gay people are now disproportionately at risk of surgical 'correction'. Homosexuality, in other words, is being treated as gender dysphoria. While we are right to be mistrustful of accusations of various 'phobias', which can be used as a rhetorical technique to discourage disagreement, in this case it has some merit. If medicalising people for being same-sex attracted doesn't qualify as homophobic, I'm not sure that anything does. In other words, Pride and its accoutrements have come to represent an ideology that seeks not only to erase the foundations of gay rights, but also to re-conceptualise same-sex attraction as a condition that requires medical treatment. When police officers decorate their cars with the Pride colours, when NHS workers display the rainbow lanyard, when schools decorate their halls with bunting in solidarity, they are almost certainly doing so with the noble intention of promoting equal rights. But they are also inadvertently bolstering a movement whose end goal is the eradication of homosexuality.

The corporate world has failed to take any of this into account as it embraces the new flags and the multiple identities they represent. In 2019, Budweiser released nine novelty cups in the colours of different groups, including bisexuals, demisexuals and asexuals. This ostensible gesture of solidarity was, of course, just a cynical ploy to sell beer. During Pride month, we invariably see major corporations such as YouTube, Mercedes-Benz, Unilever and BMW updating their social media profiles with the 'Progress Pride' colours. It has not escaped the attention of gay rights groups that they do not do the same for their outlets in the Middle East. Flying a rainbow flag in Saudi Arabia, where being gay carries the death penalty, might actually be a gesture worth making. In 2022, the official FIFA Twitter account posted a statement of 'celebration for the LGBTQIA+ community', claiming that it was 'working to ensure the FIFA World Cup Qatar 2022 will be a celebration of unity and diversity'. This will provide little consolation to the people of Qatar who have been locked in jail, sentenced to being lashed in public, or who live under the threat of the death penalty simply for being same-sex attracted. While it might seem inclusive to fly these bright and colourful flags, they are simply providing a glossy sheen to a much darker reality.

This is not to deny that the 'Progress Pride' flag and all it represents has been embraced by many gay people. It is clearly the case that a majority have not realised the extent to which the flag has been hijacked for a cause that actively works against their interests. The situation has hardly been helped by prominent celebrities, often now referred to as 'Vichy gays', who continue to cheer on these sinister developments, feeding the beast that wishes to devour them. Homosexuals are not immune to the condition of useful idiocy. But given that Pride has become so divisive, and given that so many lesbians, bisexuals and gay men now consider it to be an essentially hostile enterprise, it would be prudent for corporations and government bodies to stop pretending that there is a consensus on this issue. Ignorance is no longer an excuse. By flying the 'Progress Pride' flag, they are taking a side in a highly contentious cultural debate, one that alienates as many gay people as it attracts.

## The New Gay Conversion Therapy

In April 2023, the Conservative government of the United Kingdom issued guidance on how schools should accommodate trans-identified pupils, and specified that sex must take precedence over identity. The cries of horror were shrill and sustained. A common refrain from activists was that these measures were 'this generation's Section 28'. But this was to get it precisely backwards. Gay rights were secured on the recognition that a minority of the population are same-sex attracted. In dismantling the very notion of sex and substituting it for this nebulous concept of 'gender identity', activists and their disciples in Parliament were reversing this process. The widespread homophobia of the 1980s, epitomised by Section 28, was based on the notion that homosexuality was unnatural, dangerous and ought to be corrected. Present-day gender identity ideology perceives homosexuality as evidence of misalignment between soul and body. In other words, it seeks to 'fix' gay people so that they fit into a heterosexual framework. It is no coincidence that so many 'detransitioners' – those who are pressured into transitioning and later regret it – are gay people who were simply struggling with their sexuality. Genderism is the true successor to Section 28.

To grow up gay in the 2020s, in other words, is a far riskier prospect than during the time of Section 28 in the 1980s. Although during my time at school to be openly gay would have been to invite violent assaults, at least we did not have to contend with teachers, politicians and other figures in authority telling us that we required surgical correction. Nor were the organisations established to fight for gay rights working against us. The situation today is so confusing that we now have mainstream celebrities such as the musician Billy Bragg effectively campaigning against gay rights without realising it. It is only fair to assume that he is not homophobic, and yet he spends much of his time on social media assiduously promoting a movement whose objective is the elimination of homosexuality. Bragg's 1991 song 'Sexuality' included the lyric: 'Just because you're gay, I won't turn you away'. Perhaps a more appropriate version would be: 'Just because you're gay, I'll have you surgically corrected in order to better conform to stereotypical heterosexual paradigms', although it wouldn't scan or rhyme.

Consider the attempt to sabotage the annual LGB Alliance conference at the Queen Elizabeth II centre in Westminster in October 2024, when teenage activists unleashed thousands of crickets into the auditorium. The inconvenience was only temporary. The crowd simply relocated to another room and the event went on as before. Yet to release bags of insects into a gathering of homosexuals is the kind of tactic we might once have seen from neo-Nazis and extreme religious fundamentalists. The symbolism of the crickets was, of course, deliberate. It was an attempt to dehumanise those in attendance, to suggest that they were akin to parasites, vermin, spreaders of disease, a common trope of those who seek to demonise minorities. Just because those responsible now claim to be 'progressive' does not alter the implication. These are the new reactionaries, espousing a particularly toxic form of anti-gay ideology because it has the approval of the corporate, media, political and managerial class. Homophobia never went away, it just took on a fresh guise.

The perpetrators were children, and so it would be unwise to speculate too much on their motives. It is likely they were being manipulated by the group that has claimed responsibility, calling itself 'Trans Kids Deserve Better'. As Bev Jackson, co-founder of LGB Alliance, said to me in an interview on *Free Speech Nation*:

> Trans kids do deserve better. They deserve better than to be told lies that they might have been born in the wrong body. They deserve better than to be told that these hormones and surgeries that they are clamouring for will somehow solve all their problems. Many are on the autism spectrum. Many are struggling with their sexual orientation. We know that. They deserve better than to be told that we hate them. And they deserve better than to be labelled trans when they're going through all the turbulence of adolescence, when your feelings about yourself are in constant flux.

Irrespective of the intentions of the teenagers involved in the sabotaging of the LGB Alliance conference, this was anti-gay activism. To attack a group of lesbian, gay and bisexual people who have assembled to discuss the ongoing threats to their civil rights could hardly be defined in any other way. Likewise, to refer to groups such as LGB Alliance as 'anti-trans', 'transphobic' or 'hateful' – as activist media outlets such as the *Metro* and the *Guardian* have been known to do – is also an anti-gay strategy. In order to address a problem, one needs to label it accurately; gender ideologues are, by definition, anti-gay. They are campaigning to force their pseudo-religious belief-system onto the rest of society, one that claims that same-sex attraction is a myth, and that a mysterious spiritual sense of 'gender' is the defining feature of homosexuality. Even if they have convinced themselves that they are 'pro-trans' and 'compassionate' and 'progressive', the implementation of their demands would be a catastrophe for gay rights.

This key point has often proved difficult to effectively communicate, largely because of the language games that have become so central to the culture war. Many of the disputes over the past decade are destined to remain unresolved because there are few shared definitions among competing parties. We are left with armies of straw men thrashing about on an imaginary battlefield, while most of us look on in a state of catatonia. The recent debates over 'conversion therapy' are a case in point. At a Labour Party event in Parliament in January 2024, Keir Starmer pledged to 'implement a full, trans-inclusive, ban on all forms of conversion therapy'. His initiative was in concordance with popular sentiment. A YouGov poll in April 2022 revealed that 65 per cent of voters believe that 'gay conversion therapy' ought to be banned and 62 per cent feel the same about 'trans conversion therapy'. This would suggest that most voters do not recognise the difference between the two, a natural consequence of a climate in which discussion of sensitive issues is routinely stymied by both the browbeaters and the browbeaten. Yet when we move beyond the messy definitional details, we find that the phrase 'conversion therapy' is only coherent when applied to sexual orientation rather than gender identity. The consequence of this semantic ambiguity means that most people do not understand that in order to oppose gay conversion therapy, one must be opposed to a ban on 'trans conversion therapy'.

This will require some explanation. When we hear the phrase 'conversion therapy', most of our minds leap to a variety of horrific practices. In America, Christian fundamentalists have established programmes to address the 'problem' of homosexuality. One might argue that these attempts to 'pray the gay away' are at least a step forward from the brain surgery, castration and electric shock treatment favoured by scientific practitioners in the twentieth century. One thinks of the American psychiatrist Dr Robert Galbraith Heath, whose team implanted electrodes into the brains of patients, which were then stimulated while the victims were shown heterosexual pornography. Heath claimed to have successfully converted a gay man, and wrote a paper with his colleague Charles E. Moan called 'Septal stimulation for the initiation of heterosexual behavior in a homosexual male'. This was happening in England too. In 2014, I performed in a show called *Outings* at the Edinburgh Festival Fringe, in which we dramatised verbatim testimonies of real-life coming-out stories. One of the scenes had been submitted by a Liverpudlian man who, as a teenager in the 1960s, was referred by doctors to an institution where he was forced to look at pictures of naked men while drinking to excess and being injected with substances that caused him to vomit. These medical practitioners also applied electrodes to his penis. Needless to say, it didn't work.

Another form of conversion therapy is the 'corrective rape' of lesbians to 'cure' them of homosexual tendencies. One victim, Simphiwe Thandeka, was interviewed by the *New York Times* in July 2013 as part of a piece about the 'epidemic of corrective rape' in South Africa. A tomboy in youth and a lesbian in adult life, Simphiwe was raped on three occasions by an uncle who then paid a friend to rape her multiple times and take her as a wife. She was left pregnant by this man and HIV positive from her uncle. Her mother and grandmother encouraged her to keep it a secret, saying that it was a 'family matter' and 'not to be spoken of again'. Such practices are, of course, already illegal in the UK, so why are there so many calls for bans on 'conversion therapy', even from members of the Conservative Party? We have seen Labour politicians holding placards calling for this 'trans-inclusive ban' even before Starmer confirmed that this was the official Labour position. But what precisely does it mean?

In her book *Time to Think* (2023), Hannah Barnes quotes figures from the Gender Identity Development Service (GIDS) from 2012, in which it was revealed that between 80 and 90 per cent of adolescents who had been referred to the Tavistock paediatric gender clinic were same-sex attracted. This has been confirmed in the Cass Review – published in April 2024 after four years of painstaking research by the leading paediatrician, Dame Hilary Cass – which found that 89 per cent of girls and 81 per cent of boys referred to GIDS were either homosexual or bisexual. We have known for a long time that there is a strong correlation between gender non-conformity in youth and being gay in adult life. Members of the staff at the Tavistock itself joked that 'soon there would be no gay people left' and whistleblowers revealed that homophobia was endemic. In other words, children who are likely to grow up gay are being 'fixed' by medical practitioners to better conform with gendered stereotypes. The NHS had been practising gay conversion therapy in plain sight.

Starmer's proposed 'trans-inclusive ban' on conversion therapy is therefore based on a misunderstanding. It conflates the state-sanctioned torture of gay people in the past with the important work of paediatricians who support children that are struggling with their feelings. Moreover, Barnes's research shows that the Tavistock clinic 'ignored evidence that 97.5 per cent of children seeking sex changes had autism, depression or other problems that might have explained their unhappiness'. With only 2 per cent of the country's children suffering from an Autistic Spectrum Disorder (ASD), why did 35 per cent of referrals to the Tavistock fit into this category? In almost all instances, children who are prescribed puberty blockers go on to cross-sex hormones, which in some cases lead to irreversible surgery. The Manhattan Institute found evidence that between 2017 and 2023 around 6,000 girls under the age of eighteen had undergone double mastectomies, although the true figure could be much higher. Shockingly, at least fifty of these children were under twelve and a half years old. We are dealing overwhelmingly here with gay and autistic children, fast-tracked onto a one-way route to sterilisation.

The Scottish government had already charged down this regressive path via its consultation on 'banning conversion practices'. As Dennis Kavanagh – the director of the Gay Men's Network – has shown in his overview of the consultation, the SNP sought to introduce a 'new criminal offence which imposes liability for practices that seek to change or suppress a person's sexuality or gender identity'. This risked the criminalisation of medical practitioners who did not automatically take the 'gender-affirming' approach, by which children who say they are 'in the wrong body' must be instantaneously believed and fast-tracked to medicalisation. This law could have seen parents referred to social services if they failed to support the 'social transitioning' of their children, which had already been recognised as 'not a neutral act' in the interim Cass Review, one that could risk exacerbating feelings of gender dysphoria that in most cases will naturally resolve themselves through puberty.

In June of 2023, the NHS responded to Cass's findings by announcing that puberty blockers would be limited to children on clinical trials. Following similar reviews, Finland, Sweden and Norway also implemented restrictions. One case study had revealed the depletion of longitudinal IQ scores in an eleven-year-old boy treated for gender dysphoria. Another peer-reviewed study in the journal *Endocrine Connections* concluded that puberty blockers present risks to the healthy development of bones. In February 2024, the equalities minister Kemi Badenoch wrote to the Commons Women and Equalities Select Committee about her discussions with former clinicians at the Tavistock. Her conclusion was that so-called 'gender-affirming care' amounted to 'conversion therapy for gay kids'. Crucially, she cited a survey of detransitioners in which 23 per cent of respondents attributed their decisions to seek treatment to experiences of homophobia. Badenoch quoted a gender clinic in Germany:

> It must be understood that early hormone therapy may interfere with the patient's development as a homosexual. This may not be in the interest of patients who, as a result of hormone therapy, can no longer have the decisive experiences that enable them to establish a homosexual identity.

Starmer's Labour Party, therefore, was officially supporting gay conversion therapy in the form of a ban on 'trans conversion therapy'. A charitable interpretation is that the inherent semantic confusions had meant that Starmer and his colleagues simply did not understand the issues behind these dangerously anti-gay proposals. Homosexuality was removed from the World Health Organisation's list of psychiatric disorders in 1993, and we can be sure that this future prime minster did not sincerely believe that gay people required medical treatment for their sexual orientation. Once again, the distorting power of language had played a key role.

It is sobering to consider that the promotion of sex reassignment to 'heterosexualise' gay people on the NHS bears similarities to the situation in Iran. Given that Iranian citizens can be executed for homosexuality, they are often pressurised into surgery to present as heterosexual. A report by the BBC noted that, although this is not official state policy, Ayatollah Khomeini – founder of the Islamic Republic of Iran – had issued a fatwa to permit the practice. One interviewee recalls how her short hair would attract the attention of police officers who would say: 'Why are you like this? Go and change your gender.' When the government of Pakistan announced that it would be offering financial support for transitional surgery in January 2020, PinkNews reported approvingly. 'Pakistan just said trans rights,' declared the reporter, seemingly oblivious to the anti-gay reasoning behind the decision. There is surely no more apt illustration of the topsyturvyism of our era than this alliance between LGBT activism in the West and the mullahs of the Islamic world.

## The Cass Review and the WPATH Files

The ideological march through the medical institutions had been brisk and unexpected. The findings of the Cass Review confirmed that there was insufficient evidence for the efficacy of 'gender-affirming' care in the treatment of minors, and yet it had quickly become the default approach endorsed by experts worldwide. Cass explicitly noted how the fear of standing up to ideologues resulted in a situation in which 'attempts to improve the evidence base have been thwarted by a lack of cooperation from the adult gender services'. The risks of puberty blockers are now clear, and Cass notes that there is no evidence to justify them. Most crucially, we now know that the common assertion that puberty blockers and cross-sex hormones reduce the risk of suicide is completely false.

In spite of resistance from activists and the institutions they have successfully captured, the ramifications of Cass's meticulous study have been immense and have supercharged the demise of woke. For years, those who have sounded the alarm over the dangers of 'gender-affirming' paediatric treatment have been monstered as 'bigots', 'hateful', 'transphobic' and even 'fascist'. Now their concerns have been entirely vindicated, and those most responsible for the monstering have been desperately attempting to slither their way out of accepting responsibility. Take Stonewall, the charity most culpable for spreading this toxic ideology. In a statement posted on X, it appeared to endorse the review's findings, even quoting approvingly Dr Cass's plea 'to remember the children and young people trying to live their lives and the families, carers and clinicians doing their best to support them'. What can one say about such serpentine sleight of tongue? Perhaps the actor James Dreyfus put it best: 'The absolute fucking nerve of these people'.

Lauren Stoner, CEO of disgraced youth trans charity Mermaids, was another in the running for the Brass Neck Award, appearing on *Sky News* to claim that 'we're not medical experts, we don't advocate for any pathway'. Mermaids made the same claim in 2023 in the tribunal it initiated in a failed attempt to strip LGB Alliance of its charitable status. Yet in leaked emails it was discovered to have given advice to the Gender Identity Development Service (GIDS) at the Tavistock Clinic. Most notably, Mermaids had offered support in the drafting of an NHS service specification, including details on how '[puberty] blockers will now be considered for any children under 12'. Mermaids was later subjected to a probe by the Charity Commission which found that, although there was 'no evidence of misconduct', it had been 'mismanaged'. The investigation was launched after the *Telegraph* discovered that the charity had provided breast binders for children without parental consent, devices which can result in broken ribs and breathing difficulties. The Mermaids website had previously claimed that 'puberty blockers are an internationally recognised safe, reversible healthcare option', even at a time when there was mounting evidence of the dangers of these drugs.

During Stoner's interview for *Sky News*, she was also quick to remind viewers that Mermaids has 'been supporting trans young people and their families for nearly thirty years'. What she neglected to mention is that until the arrival of former CEO Susie Green (a mother who accompanied her sixteen-year-old son to Thailand on his birthday to have castration surgery), Mermaids actually offered sensible advice to parents of children who were struggling with their gender. A leaflet produced by the charity in 2000 was more in line with the 'watchful waiting' approach favoured by many paediatric therapists. 'Gender-identity disorders in infancy, childhood and adolescence are complex and have varied causes,' it said, before stating that 'in the majority of cases the eventual outcome will be homosexuality or bisexuality but often there will be a heterosexual outcome as some gender issues can be caused by a bereavement, a dysfunctional family life, or (rarely) by abuse. Only a small proportion of cases will result in a transsexual outcome.' That even Mermaids once held this position shows the extent to which gender identity ideology drives well-intentioned people away from the truth. It also serves as a reminder of just how swiftly this belief-system has taken hold.

Both Mermaids and Stonewall were mentioned by Tavistock whistleblower Dr David Bell as being chiefly to blame for the current climate of making 'people afraid even of listening to another view'. To this we might add groups such as Gendered Intelligence, the LGBT Foundation and the online *PinkNews*, which has published defamatory pieces about those who have objected to the rise of this ideology. These groups, while claiming to advocate for LGBT rights, have tried to intimidate into silence anyone raising questions about the irreversible surgical malpractice that has left many young people sterile and eliminated their sexual function. Then there were the private practices that, before the government's comprehensive ban, had worked around the NHS's proscription of puberty blockers. On the day that the Cass Review was published, Dr Aidan Kelly from private clinic Gender Plus had even appeared on a podcast by Novara Media to argue that the evidence demanded by Cass is neither deliverable nor desirable. Host Michael Walker seemed to think that the figure of approximately a thousand patients prescribed puberty blockers in ten years was too low to merit concern, and that 'some of these issues have been politicised to a degree that they don't need to be'. One wonders how many instances of testicular atrophy, increased risk of cancer, osteoporosis or impaired brain development in healthy children should be considered acceptable? Why were we even countenancing ruining young people's lives through the unevidenced and experimental medicalisation of problems that almost certainly required a psychotherapeutic approach? In the overwhelming majority of these cases feelings of gender discomfort are resolved during puberty, so why had we been blocking the cure?

Novara Media had planted its own ideological flag in December 2021, when it published an article offering advice on how to deceive medical professionals in order to be prescribed opposite sex hormones. 'I'm not suggesting you tell any especially big fibs,' the author had said, 'but maybe finesse your story into one that's likely to be received with the least amount of confusion (and bear that in mind with the psychiatrists too) . . . You're not here to make friends, you're here to get hormones. Don't feel bad about it.' This kind of duplicity had been widespread. In discussing her review, Dr Cass had revealed to the *British Medical Journal* that children have been 'coached on what to say and what not to say' in order to be prescribed puberty blockers. 'They're told not to say they're unsure about their sexuality, not to say they've been abused, because it's so high stakes at that point.' We also know that those who have suffered abuse were disproportionately represented among these patients. One study cited in the final Cass report shows that at least one in five children referred to gender services had suffered sexual or physical abuse. In other words, rather than experiencing some kind of esoteric mismatch between body and gendered soul, most of these young people were simply gay or troubled. And yet they were being coached to lie about their actual problems to satisfy the expectations of ideologues. These people had an agenda, and if a few children had to suffer, then so be it.

One of the reasons why this has been allowed to happen is that so many have been duped into accepting that this quasi-religion has some basis in science. This is largely down to the influence of WPATH (World Professional Association of Transgender Health), a body established in 1979 in the United States that is recognised as the leading global authority in the field and has relentlessly pushed for the normalisation of the 'gender-affirming' approach. Its 'Standards of Care' have formed the basis of policies throughout the Western world, including in the NHS, and they are explicitly critiqued in the Cass Review for their lack of 'developmental rigour'. In March 2024, an explosive series of leaked files from within the organisation should have seen the credibility of WPATH irreparably shattered. Whistleblowers had provided author and journalist Michael Shellenberger with videos and messages from the WPATH internal chat system, which suggested that the health professionals involved in recommending 'gender-affirming' healthcare were aware that it was not scientifically or medically sound. A full report was subsequently written by journalist Mia Hughes for the Environmental Progress think-tank. The title was as chilling as its contents: *The WPATH Files: Pseudoscientific Surgical and Hormonal Experiments on Children, Adolescents, and Vulnerable Adults.* Yet the scandal went largely unreported. Where there should have been a media murmuration, there were just murmurs.

Some of the leaked internal messages were astonishing in their disregard for basic medical and ethical standards. For all that paediatric gender specialists have publicly stated that there is a consensus in favour of the 'affirmative' model, that it is evidence-based, and that it is safer than a psychotherapeutic alternative, their private conversations seemed to suggest otherwise. There were messages proving that surgeons and therapists were aware that a significant proportion of young people referred to gender clinicians suffered from mental health problems. Some specialists associated with WPATH were proceeding with treatment in the knowledge that no consent had been secured from either the children or those directly responsible for their well-being. They had also withheld from patients details of potentially lifelong complications, or continued down this path knowing that the children could not understand the implications. But then, how could a pre-pubescent or even adolescent child fully grasp the concepts of lifelong sterility or loss of sexual function? As one author of the WPATH 'Standards of Care' acknowledged in a leaked message:

> It's out of their developmental range to understand the extent to which some of these medical interventions are impacting them . . . They'll say they understand, but then they'll say something else that makes you think, oh, they didn't really understand that they are going to have facial hair, right?

Another endocrinologist admitted that 'we're often explaining these sorts of things to people who haven't even had biology in high school yet'. These were the very patients who had been approved for potentially irreversible procedures. The unethical aspect of this approach has not escaped many within the medical profession. The psychiatrist Dr Az Hakeem has pointed out that puberty blockers amount to a form of chemical castration. 'We watch a film about Alan Turing and feel sorry for him and say how can we possibly have done this,' he says, 'but we're doing the same thing to our children'.

Even when mental health conditions were severe (the WPATH Files include references to schizophrenia and dissociative identity disorder) patients had been allowed to 'consent' to surgical procedures. Consider the following example, in which a nurse had contacted a leading member of WPATH to raise concerns about an adult patient with PTSD, major depressive disorder, observed dissociations, and schizoid typical traits. Could such a person possibly consent to treatment? According to one of the authors of WPATH's 'Standards of Care', the answer was a resounding 'yes'. 'I'm missing why you are perplexed,' he said. 'The mere presence of psychiatric illness should not block a person's ability to start hormones if they have persistent gender dysphoria, capacity to consent, and the benefits of starting hormones outweigh the risks. So why the internal struggle as to the "right thing to do?"' Treatments discussed in the leaked files include the removal of genitals, mastectomies, 'minimal-depth vaginoplasties (vulvoplasties), phallus-preserving vaginoplasties, and nullification procedures'. A gender therapist in California spoke of intervening 'on behalf of people who have been diagnosed with major depressive disorder, cPTSD [complex Post-Traumatic Stress Disorder], homeless, and got at least an orchiectomy' (removal of the testicles). Those who have raised questions about such extreme procedures have been accused of 'gatekeeping'. Even those who have later regretted their surgery have had their concerns trivialised. A Canadian endocrinologist is quoted in the WPATH Files acknowledging evidence from Dutch researchers of post-transitional regret, but says 'it's there, and I don't think any of that surprises us'. The files make clear that specialists are aware of the risks, but that they simply accept them as inevitable. One doctor is quoted as saying: 'It would be great if every patient could be perfectly cleared prior to every surgical intervention, but at the end of the day it is a risk/benefit decision.'

The 'gender-affirming' approach favoured by clinics across the Western world has now been thoroughly debunked. Even before the publication of the WPATH Files, there had been an open letter in July 2023 to the *Wall Street Journal* penned by twenty-one leading experts in paediatric gender treatment to oppose the view that gender-affirming care is best for children.

> Every systematic review of evidence to date, including one published in the *Journal of the Endocrine Society*, has found the evidence for mental-health benefits of hormonal interventions for minors to be of low or very low certainty. By contrast, the risks are significant and include sterility, lifelong dependence on medication and the anguish of regret. For this reason, more and more European countries and international professional organizations now recommend psychotherapy rather than hormones and surgeries as the first line of treatment for gender-dysphoric youth.

Most significantly, these experts pointed out that there was no secure evidence that puberty blockers reduced the risk of suicidal ideation. In February 2024, this was confirmed in a study published in the *British Medical Journal*, based on a group of Finnish adolescents who were being treated for gender dysphoria between 1996 and 2019. This was a key development, because for years activists had been threatening parents with a kind of twisted ultimatum: 'Do you want a happy little girl or a dead little boy?'

So why had experts at WPATH taken a different view, in spite of their awareness of serious side effects and potentially fatal outcomes of the treatment they were espousing? The answer lies in one word:

ideology. The new religion of gender identity is entirely faith-based, and so evidence that exposes its inherent dangers is dismissed outright by believers, even those with medical qualifications. The impact of all this was summarised by Mia Hughes in her report, in which she argued that WPATH had violated its ethical responsibilities: 'While there is a place in medicine for risky experiments, these can only be justified if there is a reliable, objective diagnosis, no other treatment options are available, and the outcome for a patient or patient group is dire. However, contrary to WPATH's claims, the best available evidence suggests that gender medicine does not fall into this category.'

Version 8 of WPATH's 'Standards of Care', released in December 2021, contains a chapter in which 'eunuch' is proffered as a legitimate gender identity that requires surgical actualisation. WPATH offers the following definition: 'Eunuch individuals are those assigned male at birth (AMAB) and wish to eliminate masculine physical features, masculine genitals, or genital functioning'. In its statement of recommendations, it concludes: 'We recommend health care professionals and other users of the Standards of Care 8th guidelines should apply the recommendations in ways that meet the needs of eunuch individuals.' The earlier draft version, uploaded in 2022 to NHS Scotland's official website, not only included this chapter on 'eunuchs', but also a direct acknowledgement and link to a fetish website called the 'Eunuch Archives'. Painstaking investigative research by Genevieve Gluck at *Reduxx* magazine revealed that nearly half of the pornographic stories featured on this site depicted fantasies about the castration of children. Some of these stories 'contain violent sexualized depictions of children with stunted puberty being raped by doctors'. Having accessed a password-protected subpage of the Eunuch Archive, Gluck was able to read more than three thousand stories about the sexual abuse of minors, which included 'themes such as Nazi doctors castrating children, baby boys being fed milk with estrogen in order to be violently sex trafficked as adolescents, and pedophilic fantasies of children who have been castrated to halt their puberty, "freezing" them in a childlike state'. She also revealed that the word 'minor' was 'a specially curated tag that users could select to easily access stories specifically featuring children'.

The connections between members of WPATH and this website, and the appearance of the link itself in the official 'Standards of Care', should be sufficient to discredit an organisation that is endorsing puberty blockers for children. That this story was not picked up widely in the mainstream media tells us a great deal about the lengths to which the establishment will go to protect the proponents of this ideology. This is not to suggest that WPATH endorses child castration for the sexual titillation of adults, but it is clear that some individuals within the medical establishment have a personal fetishistic incentive to promote 'gender-affirming care' to minors. Even without this repugnant aspect of the story, the fact that WPATH explicitly encourages doctors to castrate patients who believe they have an innate 'eunuch identity' is surely a violation of the Hippocratic Oath.

The revelations of the WPATH files and the research by *Reduxx* should have heralded the end of 'gender-affirming' care, but the ideology is so deeply embedded in all our major institutions that it was always going to take a lot more to see it uprooted. Politicians on both sides of the House have been complicit in the spread of genderism and its destructive consequences. When former Conservative Party leader Liz Truss tabled a debate on her Health and Equality Acts (Amendment) Bill in March 2024, a motion which raised concerns about the social transitioning of children in schools and how private companies are evading the NHS ban on puberty blockers, Labour and Conservative MPs spent four hours filibustering about ferrets in order to prevent the discussion. Their ignorance of this ideology has made them its most valuable defenders.

Now that woke is dying and we are moving into a new phase of the culture war, we should not expect many of these people to admit that they were mistaken. The psychological consequences of accepting that one has been complicit in gay conversion therapy and the medicalisation of healthy children is perhaps too much for many to bear. Since the Cass Review was published, Scottish Green MSP Maggie Chapman – a woman who has criticised biology textbooks in schools for stating that sex is binary and who has suggested that children as young as eight should be able to transition – has already decried its contents. 'Trans Healthcare is vital to protecting and supporting the rights and lives of trans people,' she posted on X, adding that her party 'will oppose any moves to increase the age of accessing gender-affirming care to 25'. Of course, the Cass Review makes no such recommendations. Rather, it says that 'NHS England should establish follow-through services for 17- to 25-year-olds at each of the regional centres, either by extending the range of the regional children and young people's service or through linked services, to ensure continuity of care and support at a potentially vulnerable stage in their journey.' This kind of moderate caution is certainly commendable, given that the adult brain is not fully developed until around the age of twenty-five. Regrettably, it is too late for some. One detransitioner took to social media to lament: 'Had the recommendations from the Cass Review been implemented when I transitioned, in particular the recommendation of waiting until the age of 25, I would never have transitioned. I grew out of gender dysphoria by the age of 22, but had my genitals amputated by then.'

The pseudo-science of 'gender-affirming care' is seemingly perishing, albeit slowly. In May 2024, the then Health Secretary Victoria Atkins used emergency powers to ban puberty blockers in the United Kingdom, and this was ratified by the new Health Secretary Wes Streeting in December. Unscrupulous private health clinics that were profiting from the prescription of these drugs had been trying to find legal loopholes to continue even after the NHS had banned the treatment in March, but Streeting's announcement made clear that all such loopholes would finally be closed. Some ill-informed politicians were not happy with Streeting's statement. Labour MP Kate Osborne declared that she was 'hugely disappointed' and claimed that 'the restrictions on puberty blockers remove the clinical expertise from medical decision making'. Of course, the precise opposite was the case. The Green Party representative for Brighton Pavilion, Siân Berry, went even further, asking: 'Does he understand that this is, at heart, discriminatory?' Streeting's response summarised what should have been asserted many years ago, that such claims from ideologues like Berry demonstrate 'why we should listen to clinicians, not politicians'.

Undoing the influence of such pseudo-science was always going to be a long and arduous process. The ideas are too entrenched, which explains why even the Cass Review has adopted some of the language of the ideology, such as 'cisgender', or references to sex as 'assigned at birth'. Besides, too much is at stake for individuals who have promoted these beliefs. Soon after the publication of the review, commentators such as LBC talk-show host James O'Brien were blaming the 'toxicity' of those who have tried to warn people of the dangers over the last decade. We can expect similar revisionist attempts from others who have failed to speak out, and no doubt 'the culture war' will be blamed by those most responsible for waging it. Whatever the outcome, we need to ensure that children are never again sacrificed on the altar of ideology.

# 8

# Strangled Muses

## The New Morality

Mary Whitehouse was an unlikely prostitute. She had left her job as an art teacher in 1964 to focus her energies on campaigns against the lax morality of television broadcasting. Soon after, Whitehouse was horrified to read an interview with the satirist Ned Sherrin in which he had commented on her resignation: 'What puzzles me is – what sort of job was she doing that kept her busy at the hour of the night when we're going on the air? I suppose that she must have been on the streets.' Whitehouse sued and was awarded £500 in damages.

Whitehouse has often been mischaracterised. The folk devil persists; a humourless, puritanical, matronly figure in her pearl necklace, round-rimmed spectacles, and a perm like a pristine cauliflower. No doubt she played up to the impression she had created, but rewatching old interviews with Whitehouse is an enlightening experience. During a debate on the film *Rambo* in an edition of *Daytime* in 1985, it seems as though the host, Sarah Kennedy, has deliberately tried to flummox Mrs Whitehouse by parading before her a series of shirtless, muscular, oiled young men, dressed in the scant attire of Sylvester Stallone's anti-hero. Rather than take offence, Whitehouse chats to the lads amiably, while filmmaker Michael Winner attempts to deflate her with his sneering barbs.

For from embodying the terrifying hydra of the media's collective imagination, Whitehouse was amiable, polite, and unflinching in the face of even the most robust criticism. She was courageous too, facing threats of violence as a matter of routine. On one occasion, two police officers visited her home in Wolverhampton to warn her that thugs were on their way from London to attack her. She retains a curious relevance to today's culture wars in a number of ways. Her unshakeable and unevidenced belief that television has a corrupting influence on the masses informed her entire 'Clean-Up TV' campaign. In this respect, her views were identical to those of the priestlings of Critical Social Justice who, in spite of all the research, insist that 'problematic' depictions in popular culture have a toxic effect on the population. When I interviewed the comedian and actor Ricky Gervais for the *Spectator*, he drew this very comparison. 'The new puritans aren't sixty-year-old women in twinsets and pearls,' he said, 'the Christian right trying to make us turn off our televisions because they don't like it. It's a younger crowd with trendy haircuts, who you'd think would have left-leaning liberal sensibilities, who have invented this new term "hate speech".'

The irony is inescapable. As a God-fearing conservative, Whitehouse ostensibly represents everything that the identitarian left oppose, and yet they have embraced the core aspect of her philosophy in order to justify their calls for censorship. Yet the comparison is not so straightforward. While Whitehouse's censorial instincts seem to mirror precisely those of today's woke activists, in another respect she bears similarities with those who fall into the anti-woke category. For most of the 1960s, Whitehouse was hornlocked with the then director general of the BBC, Sir Hugh Greene. During his tenure, Greene had been adamant that the BBC should promote progressive values that were nevertheless unpopular with the majority of the public. This paternalistic approach to broadcasting was akin to the spooning of bitter medicine to a recalcitrant toddler. We see precisely the same scenario playing out today, with the BBC propagandising for a niche and elitist ideological movement while ignoring complaints from those who pay the licence fee.

As the state broadcaster, the BBC has a kind of constitution in the form of its Royal Charter, by which it is required to maintain due impartiality in its news reporting and when it comes to controversial subjects. In holding politicians from the left and the right to account, accusations of bias are always likely to occur. For every critic who claims that the BBC is inherently left-leaning, there is another who insists that it skews to the right. A few notable lapses aside, the BBC generally maintains its political impartiality in its news programming, but any pretence to ideological impartiality is entirely absent. The organisation's systemic fealty to woke ideology has become undeniable. In August 2020, BBC staff were instructed to take a day's paid leave to 'educate' themselves on diversity, inclusion and Critical Race Theory. Kerris Bright, chief customer officer and member of the BBC Executive Committee, provided a list of resources for staff, including texts on 'Whiteness', 'The End of Policing' and 'The Urgency of Intersectionality'. Such extreme bias from the state broadcaster explains why so many viewers no longer trust its reporting. Anecdotal reports from within the BBC have suggested that an ongoing internal struggle to rectify the problem is currently taking place, with activist staff members wielding significant and disproportionate control. Whitehouse complained about an almost identical phenomenon. 'I can only guess at possible explanations', she wrote in 1967, 'as to why the BBC appears to have given an opportunity to a small but powerful minority in Broadcasting House to use the BBC as a vehicle for their own propaganda'.

Some of the BBC's output is wildly and uncritically ideological in nature. One need only consider its educational film *Identity*

– *Understanding Sexual and Gender Identities*, aimed at nine- to twelve-year-olds, which claimed that there are 'over 100 gender identities'. Omissions in the BBC's reporting are equally telling. It has not once mentioned the revelations of the WPATH Files, one of the biggest medical controversies in living memory. Yet in the twenty-four hours after the scandal broke, the BBC news website did report on apparently urgent stories such as 'University of Essex campus cat honoured with statue', 'Recycling bins shake-up for Highland households', 'Winchester park-and-ride buses to run on vegetable oil' and 'More beavers released in Cairngorms National Park'. Rather than inform the public about a global authority in medicine sanctioning the experimental treatment and irreversible surgery on children who were unable to consent, the BBC instead opted to focus on beavers and recycling bins.

Even when news broke that staff in the office of Rachel Levine, the assistant secretary for health at the Department of Health of the Biden administration, allegedly put pressure on WPATH and pushed for the removal of trans surgery age restrictions, the BBC failed to cover the story. The White House had considered the news sufficiently important to put out a statement, but apparently not even this measure merited BBC coverage. On my weekly show *Free Speech Nation* on GB News, I was able to produce a two-hour special on the WPATH Files which covered all aspects of the scandal and featured interviews with leading clinicians and journalists with specialist knowledge of 'gender-affirming care'. So why could the public broadcaster not do the same? Over a period of a month in early 2024, I emailed the BBC press office on five occasions to ask why it had neglected to cover the WPATH Files. Even after the release of the Cass Review and its explicit criticism of the influence of WPATH on the NHS, the BBC refused to respond to my enquiries. Finally, in April 2024, a reply was sent: 'News items are chosen by the news editors of the day based on a number of factors.' While this did not even begin to answer my question, it did prove that the press office would rather take an evasive approach than face a challenge about the organisation's ideological bias. To make sure, I contacted the press office again in June to ask why there had still been complete silence on this major story. The reply? 'News items are chosen by the news editors of the day based on a number of factors.' No indication was given whether this was the same automaton that had previously replied, or another with identical programming.

All of this is reminiscent of the 'no debate' approach adopted by Stonewall since around 2015. The *Nolan Investigates* podcast for the BBC in 2021 revealed that Stonewall had a huge influence on the corporation's policy, in spite of former CEO of Stonewall Nancy Kelley's claim that the charity didn't have 'any real influence' at all. If further proof of bias were needed, it was generously provided in April 2024 when a journalist whistleblower at the BBC penned an article for the *Spectator* under the pseudonym Charlie Walsham. His insights were as damning as they were predictable.

> Regrettably, I believe there is a straight line between the BBC's capitulation to extreme trans rights ideologues and the disturbing findings in Dr Hilary Cass's 388-page report. Crucially, what Dr Cass has exposed was only able to happen because of a skewed and distorted national conversation around the issue of sex and gender, a narrative aided by the nation's broadcaster. Dissenting voices have been marginalised, castigated, cancelled, silenced.

The article went on to provide a litany of examples of how the BBC has covered up stories or silenced those within the organisation who wish to expose the truth. In a follow-up piece in May, Walsham wrote about how, since he blew the whistle, BBC employees were trying to identify him and get him fired. This antagonism to dissent, so characteristic of the practitioners of cancel culture, of course proved why it was so important for Walsham to remain anonymous in the first place.

The culture war has left the BBC burdened with its woke martinets. One BBC insider told me that their power is mostly wielded through LGBT staff networks, which consistently attempt to influence the decisions of editors, partly through intimidation. Furthermore, the BBC has infused the ideology into its system, with an 'Identity Unit' supplying correspondents to appear on programmes and gathering news on behalf of the channel. There is also a full-time 'Gender Identity Correspondent'. Given that this is a belief-system shared by a minority of the population, one wonders why the corporation has not also employed a 'Transubstantiation Correspondent'. For a long while, controllers at the BBC have been pledging to make cuts so that the institution can be more efficient. At the same time, it squanders taxpayer money on pandering to this regressive movement. By eliminating the Identity Unit, the BBC could simultaneously fulfil two of its objectives: save money and reduce its bias.

The challenge that those of us of a liberal disposition now face when confronting the ideological capture of the BBC is, therefore, not dissimilar to the situation in which Mary Whitehouse and her associates found themselves during their campaign. Our goals are, prima facie, in total opposition. Whitehouse sought to 'clean up TV', to pressurise the corporation to deodorise its output on the grounds that it had a deleterious societal impact. Today's liberal believes that artistic freedom is paramount, and that calls for censorship are invariably wrongheaded and, moreover, does not accept the specious premise that popular culture creates real-world violence. And yet both factions share concerns about the BBC pursuing an ideological direction in the face of disapproval from the population. Whitehouse, like today's liberals, does not accept the patronising assumption that the public needs to be cattle-prodded into a certain way of thinking.

The comparison only goes so far. Whitehouse, after all, was a cattle-prodder of a different kind. This is why she was able to use the BBC's own mission statements against it. The first director general, John Reith, had famously declared that the role of the state broadcaster would be to 'inform, educate and entertain', but in addition to this noble goal there was a patrician conviction that television might reshape society for the better. It was not for nothing that in its first decade the BBC commissioned the sculptor Eric Gill to create a likeness of Prospero and his sprite Ariel from Shakespeare's *The Tempest* (c. 1611) over the main entrance of Broadcasting House in London. As servant to the magician Prospero, one of Ariel's roles is to transmit his music throughout the island. The reader will recall Caliban's extraordinary speech.

> Be not afeard. The isle is full of noises,
> Sounds, and sweet airs, that give delight and hurt not.
> Sometimes a thousand twangling instruments
> Will hum about mine ears, and sometime voices
> That if I then had waked after long sleep
> Will make me sleep again; and then in dreaming
> The clouds methought would open and show riches
> Ready to drop upon me, that when I waked
> I cried to dream again.

If Prospero is the BBC, then Ariel is the wireless service. Gill himself found the subject matter of his statue gimmicky. 'Very clever of the BBC to hit on the idea,' he said. 'Ariel and Aerial. Ha! Ha! And the BBC kidding itself, in the approved manner of all big organisations (British or foreign, public or private), that it represents all that is good and noble and disinterested.' This disdain for his patron led Gill to privately modify the commission so that he was not merely sculpting 'a clever old magician' and his 'silly fairy'. 'I took it upon me to portray God the Father and God the Son,' he said. 'For even if that were not Shakespeare's meaning, it ought to be the BBC's.' When a vandal took a hammer and chisel to Gill's statue in May 2023 – a protest against the artist's history of sexual abuse and incest – he had no idea that his iconoclasm was of a religious nature, and that he had been desecrating an image of God and his son. The outrage at Gill's crimes has been compounded by the belief that the statue depicts a naked child. Ariel was actually modelled on the then twenty-seven-year-old actor Leslie French. In 1933, the author R. W. Hallows claimed that the resemblance was questionable: 'Mr French is much better looking, though, and his legs really aren't a bit like that.'

In a sense, Whitehouse shared this view that the BBC occupied a godlike role, benevolently shepherding the masses. That her view of the state broadcaster's role should be identical to that of the BBC itself is made clear by her choice to borrow the Latin inscription in the lobby of Broadcasting House for the epigraph to her book. It is translated as follows:

> This Temple of the Arts and Muses is dedicated to Almighty God by the first Governors of Broadcasting House in the year 1931, Sir John Reith being director general. It is their prayer that good seed sown may bring forth a good harvest, that all things hostile to peace and purity may be banished from this house, and that the people, inclining their ear to whatsoever things are beautiful and honest and of good report, may tread the path of wisdom and uprightness.

In paraphrasing the passage from Philippians (chapter 4, verse 8), the BBC was asserting that its vocation was a holy one. Whitehouse was merely using its own words as a cudgel with which to beat it, emphasising how much it had strayed from its original purpose. She described the progressive stance of the state broadcaster in the 1960s as 'the New Morality', but instead of championing an impartial BBC, she called for its ideology to be replaced with hers. This was an unashamedly Christian mission, as reflected in the manifesto she produced for her campaign in tandem with her friend, the vicar's wife Norah Buckland.

1. We women of Britain believe in a Christian way of life.

2. We want it for our children and country.

3. We deplore present-day attempts to belittle or destroy it, and in particular we object to the propaganda of disbelief, doubt and dirt that the BBC projects into millions of homes through the television screen.

4. Crime, violence, illegitimacy and venereal disease are steadily increasing, yet the BBC employs people whose ideas and advice pander to the lowest in human nature and accompany this with a stream of suggestive and erotic plays which present promiscuity, infidelity and drinking as normal and inevitable.

5. We call upon the BBC for a radical change of policy and demand programmes which build character instead of destroying it, which encourage and sustain faith in God and bring Him back to the heart of our family and national life.

A conflict was brewing between two alternative ideologies – the Christian and the progressive – and each party was determined to impose its own vision upon the public. Today's liberal critics of the BBC do not take this kind of authoritarian approach. They seek impartiality from the state broadcaster, not the substitution of one belief-system for another in the form of televised propaganda.

One wonders what Whitehouse would have made of an episode of the daytime soap opera *Doctors* entitled 'Furryland', broadcast on BBC One in November 2023, in which the tropes of a typical gay coming-out story are applied to a character, Ethan, who wants to dress up as a teddy bear for sexual gratification. There is even an intolerant grandfather who censures Ethan for his perversion, but is eventually placated and is even seen sharing a drink with a group of young people dressed as animals in a 'furry' bar. While this was almost certainly intended to promote a niche fetish that activists have attempted to rebrand as the innate characteristic of an oppressed group, it came across as a satire against gay people and their often troublesome experiences of revealing their sexual orientation to close family members. The show serves as an example of how the BBC, in its current captured manifestation, tends to double down against complaints from viewers regarding its unceasing propaganda. Rather than take these criticisms seriously, it indulges in ever more ideological output in what is doubtless a deliberate act of needling. Whitehouse's experiences were comparable. She described the BBC as voluntarily locking itself into a 'trial of strength with its viewers', being 'determined to answer criticism by producing programmes even more likely to affront the good taste of the country'. So while Whitehouse's conflicts with the BBC are similar to the broadcaster's resistance to its anti-woke critics today, the comparison is frustrated by the fact that the BBC now appears to agree with Whitehouse that television can have a morally corrupting influence on the public. This goes to show that history is not so much a linear thread as a cat's cradle.

Whitehouse has been much maligned as a prude and a philistine, and yet in addition to her former role as an art teacher, she had also led classes on sex education. Her group, the National Viewers' and Listeners' Association (NVALA), was branded by Richard Hoggart, a member of the BBC's General Advisory Council in the 1960s, as the 'new populists'. Often she has been smeared as a bigot and a reactionary with contempt for marginalised groups but, like the woke activists of today, she repeatedly expressed concerns at how ethnic and sexual minorities might be detrimentally impacted by their representation on television. For example, she complained about John Hopkins's *Fable*, a play broadcast on BBC One in January 1965, which depicted a parallel version of the United Kingdom in which black people ruled over a white underclass and even dispatched them to concentration camps. 'So helpful to the solving of our colour problems,' she mused sardonically. Whitehouse likewise took umbrage at Hopkins's play *Horror of Darkness*, broadcast in March of that same year, because of the suicide of a gay character. 'This was a most powerful play,' she wrote, 'but what was the likely effect on the thousands of homosexuals who must have seen it?'

Whitehouse sincerely believed that society was being irreparably damaged by the form that popular culture was taking. When describing television, she said that its 'power is absolute', and that 'all broadcasting is propaganda: the question is for what?' In this, she was in alignment with the thinkers of the Frankfurt School, those radical left-wing academics who came to prominence in the United States in the 1960s, and whose work retains a great deal of influence in the Critical Social Justice movement. Comparisons between Whitehouse and woke activists are not without merit: both mistrust popular culture and its impact on the public, both believe in a directly causal relationship between words and violence, and both would like to see their values foisted on society by those in power. However, the prominent strand of sadism that exists within wokeness would have been anathema to Whitehouse. Although many woke campaigners are motivated by genuine compassion, they are also subject to manipulation from bad actors who can piggyback on the movement to find an outlet for their sadistic desire to bully others. Whitehouse had no time for cruelty. She was an empathetic human being who was motivated, above all, by a praiseworthy desire to protect the innocence of children. Yet while it is right to restrict viewing material for the very young, adults in a free society must be able to make decisions for themselves. This was a distinction that Whitehouse often failed to draw clearly. It would be accurate and fair to describe her as a well-intentioned authoritarian.

For instance, Whitehouse quoted approvingly an article in the *Universe* which argued that 'people who make freedom a fetish are dangerous'. One of the chapters in her book *Cleaning Up TV* is entitled 'Fetish of Freedom'. In this, she was in lockstep with today's left-wing activists who insist that there can be 'no debate', and that the preservation of free speech is a threat to social cohesion. Labour MP Nadia Whittome has exemplified this view by writing that 'we must not fetishise "debate" as though debate is itself an innocuous, neutral act'. But debate is not, and never has been, a fetish. It is the cornerstone of democracy, the mechanism of progress, the way in which we refine our ideas and change our minds. Those who brand debate a 'fetish' are making the case for authoritarianism, however much they claim to be upholding progressive values.

Whitehouse's claims that she was not in favour of censorship were never convincing. Although she was a great believer in open discussion with her detractors, and would never seek to have them silenced, she took a different line on artistic freedom. In her book *Whatever Happened to Sex?* (1977), Whitehouse scoffs at those who are concerned about what happens when those in authority are permitted to limit the scope of artistic expression.

> Well, one really has to be careful here, doesn't one? For this raises the spectre of a fate worse than death – censorship. To even whisper the word is to fly in the face of 'libertarian' orthodoxy – the most heartless and aggressive philosophy since Fascism. It is to risk knocking the smirk off the face of the moneygrubbers – and when the smirk goes they can look very nasty indeed.

For all her claims not to be advocating outright censorship, Whitehouse intimates that this is simply because that power could never be bestowed upon her.

> We repeat, we are not for censorship, although if it were the only way of preventing the gradual erosion of our Christian values and the character of the nation, we would not hesitate to call for control over certain influences which confuse liberty with licence and flout at will the conscience of millions. But we ourselves neither have the opportunity nor the power to exercise such control.

In other words, she would censor if she could. Certainly, her successful private prosecution against Gay News for blasphemy (see Chapter 4) is not the act of one who believes in creative liberty.

Whitehouse's brand of authoritarianism was not restricted to appeals to censorship; she also wanted to proselytise. She believed that the BBC had a 'responsibility to raise the level of public taste', and that television programmes ought therefore to promote her favoured values. 'Marital faithfulness' and 'toughness of moral fibre' were fundamental to the 'national welfare' and, she argued, made for 'exciting drama and discussion'. She was supportive of a statement given in the House of Commons in January 1966 by the MP for Ilford North, Tom Iremonger. While accepting the BBC's decision to repeat its broadcast of Up the Junction, a show that Whitehouse found offensive, he urged the corporation 'to affirm and proclaim through its other programmes the undoubted danger and evil of fornication, adultery and sodomy, not in stale and implausible terms of fire and brimstone, but rather in terms of modern insight into the deepest needs and fullest potential of the human personality'. Iremonger concluded by calling on the BBC 'fully to exploit every opportunity, including its wilting satirical programmes, to uphold and extol the institution of Christian and all other formally constituted and loyally maintained monogamous marriages'. Given the content of this speech, the aptronym 'Iremonger' must surely lend some credence to the theory of nominative determinism.

The question of whether Mary Whitehouse was correct about the decline of civilisation in the United Kingdom is moot and entirely a matter of subjective opinion. It may be that she was right to detect trends of declining empathy, the erosion of the social contract, the inchmeal demolition of the high-trust society, the rise of anti-social behaviour, and the lack of stability that comes when the nuclear family is no longer valued as an ideal. Yet it is a matter of intuition rather than evidence that would lead us to suppose that all of this has come about due to television and film. Whitehouse remains relevant as an icon for those who seek to curb artistic freedom for the good of society. Such people will always be with us, but they will appear in a variety of guises. One day they might be rainbow-robed gender ideologues with 'they/them' pronouns calling for comedy shows to be censored, but the next they could be Christian conservatives seeking to ban books that offend the followers of Jesus Christ. The ideology may be different, but the authoritarian impulse remains the same.

## Pearl-Clutchers and Puritans

It is no great revelation that authoritarians instinctively mistrust the power of books. These bothersome little items represent all that the ideologue most despises: independent thinking, artistic freedom, the unlimited dissemination of fresh ideas and heresies. When William Tyndale persisted with his English translation of the Bible, he was depriving the religious clerisy of their exclusive authority to interpret the word of God. He paid for it with his life.

Woke activists are invariably attracted to careers that empower them as custodians of language, knowledge and history. This is why so many galleries now feature little explanatory plaques next to various works lamenting the moral shortcomings of the artists. This is why staff at online dictionaries are modifying definitions to promote their own political aims rather than to reflect the common usage of words. This is why curators at museums are apologising for exhibits, or cancelling them altogether. This is why activist librarians and booksellers are concealing items from the public rather than facilitating access for minds more intellectually curious than their own. In October 2023, Human Resources staff at the library service in Calderdale Council were caught hiding gender-critical books such as *Irreversible Damage* (2020) by Abigail Shrier, *Trans* (2021) by Helen Joyce and *Material Girls* (2021) by Kathleen Stock. When asked whether other books had been similarly restricted, the council replied that the only precedent was a copy of Adolf Hitler's *Mein Kampf* (1925). One seller at a branch of Waterstones bookshop in Brighton was so offended by the work of journalist Douglas Murray that she boasted online that she would 'go back to hiding this cunt's books in the storeroom'. This member of staff was apparently unfamiliar with the existence of a phenomenon known as 'the internet' where books can be freely ordered without devious little pink-haired gremlins getting in the way.

With any luck, the end of woke will mean that books will no longer be treated with suspicion. In February 2024, the Surrey school district in Vancouver decided to remove a number of books from curricula in order to protect the mental health of students. These included: *Of Mice and Men* (1937) by John Steinbeck, *To Kill a Mockingbird* (1960) by Harper Lee, *In the Heat of the Night* (1965) by John Ball, and *The Absolutely True Diary of a Part-Time Indian* (2007) by Sherman Alexie. Many would have supposed that the anti-racist message of *To Kill a Mockingbird* would be sufficient for it to qualify as a progressive mainstay, but not according to Ritinder Matthew, a spokesperson for the school district, who said: 'We did a comprehensive review of these resources that determined that the merits of these novels do not outweigh the potential trauma and harm they may cause to some students.' Would it be impudent to suggest politely that if pupils are 'traumatised' by novels that expose the follies of racism, then their teachers might be failing in their pedagogic duties?

Children are generally sharper than these worrywarts suppose. During my time as a teacher, I quickly learned that even younger pupils are capable of understanding that societal values vary over time. Outdated racial stereotypes in the ludic romps of Dr Seuss may require a degree of contextualisation, but there was no sane reason for the author's estate to withdraw a number of his titles from sale altogether. The activist infiltration of libraries, museums, schools, the arts, the media and the publishing industry needs to be seen in the context of a broader scheme to police the limitations of acceptable thought, one that is key to all authoritarian movements. This is why the Catholic Church created its *Index Librorum Prohibitorum*, a catalogue of forbidden books that was continually updated for four centuries until 1948. Writing in March 1992, the horror novelist Stephen King addressed the issue of certain school libraries removing offensive books from their shelves. He had the following to say to pupils:

> Do not argue with them; do not protest; do not organize or attend rallies to have the books put back on their shelves. Don't waste your time or your energy. Instead, hustle down to your public library, where these frightened people's reach must fall short in a democracy, or to your local bookstore, and get a copy of what has been banned. Read it carefully and discover what it is your elders don't want you to know.

A few decades on, and the woke were to usher in a thumb-sucking cry-baby culture in which adults were no longer trusted to read 'problematic' books and were coddled by those whose capacity for critical thinking had been stunted by ideology.

That said, the arts have forever been in the crosshairs of the authoritarians. Plato famously banished poets from his *Republic* on the grounds that education ought to be entrusted to the guardians in society, not to those who peddle in artifice. In the 'ancient quarrel between philosophy and poetry', philosophy must win out, and so Socrates insists that 'we should expel poetry from the city'. The artist deals in imitation, not reality itself, and so he is dabbling in 'a form of amusement and not a serious occupation'. Like many of Plato's texts, he is reacting against Homer and his idealisation of the heroic man, one which once served as the exemplar in the teaching of boys. He is explicitly concerned about the influence of storytelling on the young and its capacity to corrupt.

Our first duty then, it seems, is to set a watch over the makers of stories, to select every beautiful story they make, and reject any that are not beautiful. Then we shall persuade nurses and mothers to tell those selected stories to the children. Thus will they shape their souls with stories far more than they can shape their bodies with their hands. But we shall have to throw away most of the stories they tell now.

The notion that children are unable to distinguish truth from fiction, or that stories must, as Socrates would have it, 'teach virtue in the fairest way', is a reasonable summary of Mary Whitehouse's guiding principle. Whether she would have approved of Athenian culture – with its propagation of slavery, pederasty and pornographic pottery – is quite another matter.

Although woke is elsewhere coming to an end, the sentinels of the arts are pigheadedly grasping to their treasured beliefs. We are living in conformist times, and inexplicably those in the creative arts have turned out to be the most conformist of all. Nowhere is this more evident than the theatre industry, where wrongthink is outlawed and artistic freedom is subordinated to the promotion of identity politics. This has affected all aspects of commissioning, casting and production, which means that modern-day theatregoers are compelled to tolerate its influence. The signs are manifold: there's the tick-box casting to fulfil identity quotas rather than to serve the integrity of the show, the rainbow lanyards worn by ushers, the little sermons in the programmes by directors who think their job is to educate the masses in social justice. A theatrophile friend once remarked to me that so long as the preaching only amounts to one fifth of the show's content, he is willing to accept it. I suppose it's like going for dinner in an especially pious household, and having to put up with a long-winded prayer before a delicious meal.

In April 2022, I went to see *Diary of a Somebody*, John Lahr's 1986 adaptation of Joe Orton's diaries, at the Seven Dials Playhouse in

London. The theatre had lately rebranded the men's and women's toilets as 'gender neutral', meaning that punters of both sexes were invited to play a little game if they wished to relieve themselves. The two doors now bore identical labels, but one led to a cramped and pungent cubbyhole with urinals next to the sinks, whereas the other led to a spacious and relatively luxurious area complete with individual cubicles. It was like a variation on the old 'Monty Hall Problem'. Audience members had to pick a door and take their chances, and those who guessed wisely were rewarded with a more pleasant experience. Minutes before the show was due to begin, there was a suitably Ortonesque moment. A flustered woman emerged from one of these doors exclaiming angrily that there were 'men pissing in front of everyone'. One cannot help but wonder who Orton's targets might be in the context of today's culture wars. Would it be the kind of woman who was clearly upset at having to wash her hands in full view of male genitalia, or would it be the authorities at the theatre who expected her to do so and would presumably brand her a 'transphobe' or a 'bigot' should she complain?

Woke reactionaries have effectively ironed out the genuine subversives from within the theatre world, because the likes of Orton holding them up to ridicule is not a prospect that the authoritarian can stomach. If their role model is not Mary Whitehouse, it is most definitely Mrs Edna Welthorpe, the alter ego of Orton who would write to the press and to theatres in the late sixties to complain about his own plays. One of her most excoriating letters was published in the *Telegraph*, and concerned the new production of Orton's *Entertaining Mr Sloane* (1964).

> I myself was nauseated by this endless parade of mental and physical perversion. And to be told that such a disgusting piece of filth now passes for humour! Today's young playwrights take it upon themselves to flaunt their contempt for ordinary decent people. I hope that the ordinary decent people of this country will shortly strike back!

When an audience member wrote a letter of complaint to the Criterion Theatre about Orton's *Loot* (1965), Welthorpe responded directly, claiming that she was an employee at the theatre and that the letter had been passed to her for filing. 'Please, please, as a fellow Christian, let me applaud your design in writing to the Lord Chamberlain,' she wrote. 'This truly horrible play shouldn't contaminate our streets.'

With all their talk of how libraries ought to be 'decolonised', their pruning of supposedly offensive comedy shows on streaming services, and their attacks on 'outdated' representations in art and literature, many of today's woke activists are the very reincarnation of Mrs Edna Welthorpe. This is why Orton enjoyed a huge advantage over the satirists of our time. While he was lauded for deflating the pretensions of the establishment and breaking taboos, writers who do so today are likely to be chastised by critics and the doyens of the industry for failing to toe the line. That Orton should assume a persona to fulminate against his own plays was simply his way of broadening the scope of his satirical work from the stage to the real world. He was obsessed with the sham gentility of a society that was, to his mind, essentially rotten. Orton loved to shock, perhaps because he was seemingly incapable of being shocked by anything. In his plays, he was able to take a hacksaw to those figures of authority he so despised, be they doctors, police officers, or any other breed of moralising hypocrite. But the hoax letters served a different purpose. They mocked their targets through the pretence of sympathy, effectively encouraging more of the kind of behaviour that his farces sought to lampoon.

This technique is the precursor to what we now call 'trolling'. The term is often misused as a synonym for malicious and bullying online behaviour but, as traditionally understood, trolling is the art of coaxing people into a reaction. Motivations vary from troll to troll. For some, it is simply a matter of revelling in the gullibility of strangers. For others, the intention is to expose the vices and shortcomings of those in power. Jonathan Swift was an early exponent of this kind of trolling in the creation of his alter ego Isaac Bickerstaff, who wrote pamphlets which predicted, and then announced, the death of the astrologer John Partridge. Swift resented Partridge because of his attacks on the Church, and must have been immensely gratified that Bickerstaff's announcement had been taken on trust by so many. It is said that Partridge was thereafter continually having to fend off queries about his uncanny resemblance to a dead man.

Of course, many hoaxers are driven purely by self-interest. When, in 1806, Mary Bateman used concentrated vinegar to write 'Christ is coming' onto her chicken's eggs, and then charged members of the community to visit her 'Prophet Hen of Leeds', it is unlikely that she intended to make any kind of satirical point. Yet one might argue that even in hoaxes of this kind there is some societal insight to be gleaned, however inadvertently. Mary Toft managed to destroy the reputations of a number of prominent surgeons who, in 1726, believed that she had given birth to rabbits. One of the king's doctors, Nathaniel St André, was so convinced that he published *A Short Narrative of an Extraordinary Delivery of Rabbets* (1727). William Hogarth immortalised Toft in his *Cunicularii: or the Wise Men of Godlimon in Consultation* (1726), which depicts her in labour, surrounded by learned men of the medical profession, while multiple rabbits roam at their feet. If Toft was no satirist, she at least inspired some of the best of her age.

Perhaps the most celebrated instance of satirical hoaxing in recent years was Chris Morris's television series *Brass Eye* (1997), which took aim at celebrity and media culture by inviting public figures to join campaigns against entirely fabricated social justice causes. In one episode, celebrities such as Bernard Manning, Rolf Harris and Noel Edmonds were enlisted to warn against the dangers of 'cake', a fictitious drug that, as Manning dutifully informed viewers, caused one girl to vomit out her own pelvis. In another episode, newsreader Nick Owen expounded on the dangers of 'heavy electricity' which, due to the effect of 'sodomised electrons' was 'regularly flattening cattle in Sri Lanka'. Then there was the radio DJ Neil Fox, who was tricked into making this astonishing claim: 'Genetically, paedophiles

William Hogarth, *Cunicularii: or the Wise Men of Godlimon
in Consultation* (1726).

have more genes in common with crabs than they do with you and
me. Now, that is scientific fact. There's no real evidence for it, but it
is scientific fact.' Many of those duped by Morris were seemingly
happy to read aloud any hogwash from an autocue in return for
television exposure and the impression that they were on the right
side of history. Such hoaxes could potentially be even more effective
in today's climate, with so many soft-witted influencers eager to
endorse fashionable but illiberal notions of 'social justice' they barely
understand. But, unlike the days of *Brass Eye*, the jesters are now in
lockstep with these establishment lines, and so the most pertinent
sources for satire are generally left untapped. They are, as Morris puts
it, more interested in 'doing some kind of exotic display for the court'
than exposing the follies of the powerful.

It is perhaps inevitable, then, that one of the most impressive
hoaxes of recent years has come from outside the comedy industry.

THE END OF WOKE

In October 2018, it was revealed that James Lindsay, Peter Boghossian and Helen Pluckrose had spent a year writing and submitting bogus academic papers to various journals in order to show how certain branches of the humanities were now routinely prioritising ideological goals over the pursuit of truth and knowledge. By the time the hoax was exposed, seven of their twenty articles had been accepted for publication, and a further seven were in the process of review. As a work of satire, this project was an undoubted success. It provided evidence of what many had long suspected: that nonsensical ideas could thrive within the academy so long as they were camouflaged in vogueish argot. One paper purported to be a study of the sexual activity of dogs in urban parks, and used this phoney data to draw conclusions about contemporary 'rape culture'. Another argued that white male students ought to be chained to the floor during lessons as a form of reparation for slavery. Most audacious of all was the article based entirely on a chapter of Hitler's *Mein Kampf*, rewritten in the language of intersectional feminist theory. That all of these articles were accepted for publication in peer-reviewed journals should have alerted academics to a troubling strain of corruption and fraudulence in their field. They should have resolved to rectify the problem, but instead chose to demonise and smear the hoaxers who had exposed it. When satirists hit on uncomfortable truths, they are rarely thanked for their efforts.

As for Joe Orton, it was arguably his time in prison that consolidated this desire to provoke, and that appears to have been the driving motivation in both his life and his work. Orton and his partner Kenneth Halliwell served six months in jail for defacing books at Islington Library. The pair would add semi-pornographic images to dust jackets, or rewrite the blurbs in the hope of shocking unsuspecting readers. Orton later claimed that prison 'crystallised' his sense of 'something rotten somewhere', and that 'the old whore society really lifted up her skirts and the stench was pretty foul'. For Orton, nothing was more satisfying than exasperating the pearl-clutchers of his day.

As he noted in his diary when revising his farce *What the Butler Saw* (1969), 'sex is the only way to infuriate them. Much more fucking and they'll be screaming hysterics in next to no time.' There are no likeable characters in *What the Butler Saw*; Orton sees humanity as a parade of degraded creatures, slaves to baser instincts, whose only value rests in being figures of fun for us to pruriently observe. The title invites us to imagine a butler taking a moment from his duties to peer into one of those seaside peepshow machines, popular in Edwardian England; this is what his 'betters' get up to behind closed doors. Through his treatment of themes such as police brutality, institutionalised abuse, incest and necrophilia, Orton strips away the patina of respectable society. Whether one finds this cynical or not, it is undeniably funny.

Are any of today's playwrights exhibiting this kind of dissident glee? Consider the responses to the West End revival of Jez Butterworth's award-winning *Jerusalem* (2009) in April 2022. Playwright Bea Roberts was ambivalent on whether the new production was a good idea.

> Should the play be revived? I'm not sure. I read the script again recently and there's a lot that feels dated: the laddish chat about 'birds' and the racial references – will they change those or at least acknowledge them? I understand it's a safe bet for producers, this big, much-loved hit – and I loved it too. But at a time when theatre is grappling with questions of diversity and representation after Black Lives Matter, and when we're seeing the rise of nationalism post-Brexit, doing a play about defending homeland and Englishness seems ill-judged.

Roberts is not alone in her belief that it is the responsibility of the dramatist to reinforce modish and ephemeral trends. It seems unlikely that a work as genuinely subversive as *What the Butler Saw* would ever be commissioned by a major theatre in the current climate. Early drafts would require a thorough going-over by a 'sensitivity reader', and doubtless a director with concerns about how theatrical productions ought to send the 'correct message' would mangle whatever glimmers of genius remained.

I'm exaggerating, but only slightly. I have spoken to actors who have found that valuable rehearsal time is often now occupied with interrogating the morality behind the texts, and how the first session invariably commences with each cast member declaring their preferred pronouns. Many avid theatregoers have been turned off because so many productions feel more like sermons than works of art. Critics in the mainstream press are now regularly assessing drama on the putative morality of the piece, or whether or not they approve of the way in which characters are represented. The star-rating review system has always been fatuous, but it is especially so if marks are docked for insufficiently diverse casting. In Orton's day, the Lord Chamberlain would ensure that potentially subversive material would not make it to the stage. Today, theatrical practitioners have taken on that role for themselves, embodying the kind of prissy moralisers that Orton took such pleasure in skewering. It is for this reason that choreographer Rosie Kay and arts producer Denise Fahmy established 'Freedom in the Arts', a project specifically aimed at tackling groupthink. It is to be hoped that initiatives of this kind attract the degree of support necessary to rescue the arts from this self-constructed oubliette.

This is a perennial phenomenon. The puritans of Shakespeare's day enjoyed a similar degree of institutional clout, although of course they opposed the very existence of the public theatres and sought their permanent closure. Paradoxically, the new puritans working in today's theatres share this censorial and anti-artistic mindset, but are working within the industry and claim to be its bastions. For Shakespeare, the puritans represented the most persistent threat to his livelihood, with the obvious exception of the plague. As far as these zealots were concerned, the theatre was a realm of 'Adulterers, Adulteresses, Whoremasters, Whores, Bawdes, Panders, Ruffians, Roarers, Drunkards, Prodigals, Cheaters, idle, infamous, base, prophane, and godlesse persons'. These were the words of the polemicist William Prynne from his *Histrio-Mastix* (1633). He was eventually to get his way in 1642 when the puritan-led Parliament shut the theatres down. When the ban was lifted on the accession of Charles II, older plays had to be dusted off to satisfy the public's appetite for drama. It was Shakespeare's work that proved to be the most popular, establishing a trend that has never waned. Of course, many recent major productions have minced Shakespeare's work into the kind of bland pulp craved by the regressive tastemakers of our time. Today's audiences are seeing a vague shadow of these masterworks through a narrow and uninspiring prism. How strange, then, that the values of Mary Whitehouse, a woman despised by many in the arts world, should have set them such an example. They have become the unwitting disciples of their own folk devil.

It goes without saying that Shakespeare's body of work is not enlivened by forcing it into the iron maiden of identity politics. In his drama we find ourselves unmolested by ideology. We know nothing of Shakespeare's opinions on matters of politics or religion, and attempting to glean any suggestions from his writing is futile. I think A. L. Rowse put it best when he pointed out that Shakespeare 'saw through everybody equally'. Neither prince nor pauper escapes his sceptical gaze. Even in *Henry V* (1599), written at a time when England was gripped in a patriotic fervour, Shakespeare ensures that our hero remains morally ambiguous. When Laurence Olivier made his government-funded nationalistic film adaptation during the Second World War, he was compelled to excise the moment where Henry at Agincourt orders the French prisoners to be killed. For this paragon of Englishness to behave so ruthlessly would have derailed the jingoism of the endeavour. Shakespeare, in other words, cannot satisfy our desire for a kindergarten world of Goodies and Baddies. Yet this is precisely the world imagined by the high priests of Critical Social Justice, those killjoys who have invaded the theatre industry and seek to deprive us of our cakes and ale.

The two major companies responsible for producing Shakespeare's works – the Royal Shakespeare Company and the Globe in London

– are now seemingly beholden to the tenets of wokeness. The Globe regularly holds 'Anti-Racist Shakespeare' webinars which assemble 'scholars and artists of colour from a wide variety of backgrounds to examine Shakespeare's plays through the lens of race and social justice'. It sounds like a kind of punishment, but apparently there are some who attend such sessions voluntarily. In August 2022, the Globe staged a new play called I, Joan, which presented Joan of Arc as 'non-binary', on the basis that she was powerful, independent and wore armour. Presumably a female Joan of Arc would have been too busy knitting, gossiping and shopping for shoes to fight the English. To accompany the production, an activist academic called Kit Heyam was invited to write an essay in which it was claimed that Queen Elizabeth I could have been 'non-binary' for similar reasons. She was even assigned they/them pronouns. According to Heyam, Elizabeth I 'described themself regularly in speeches as "king", "queen" and "prince", choosing strategically to emphasise their female identity or their male monarchical role at different points'. One thinks of the queen's famous speech to the troops at Tilbury: 'I know I have the body of a weak and feeble woman, but I have the heart and stomach of a king.' For the literal-minded, this wasn't a declaration of strength against an imperial threat but a coming-out party.

The artistic decline of the Globe Theatre has been ongoing for some years now. When Michelle Terry took on the role of artistic director in 2018, she made it clear that diversity and inclusivity were her priorities. She said to Time Out that 'this binary way of looking at gender, looking at the world, has reached a tipping point', and that she intended to mount 'a gender-blind, race-blind, disability-blind production' of Hamlet (c. 1600). That show didn't go well. As one critic waspishly mused: 'To leave or not to leave: that is the question.' In 2021, the Globe Theatre produced a new 'woke reimagining' of Romeo and Juliet (c. 1595), in which the drama was reinterpreted as a comment on mental health. The lovers' obsession for each other was presented as some kind of mental disorder, with statistics about depression among teenagers projected onto a screen above the stage. The suicides at the end were explained away in similar terms. Never has tragedy been so tedious.

A collection of essays called *White People in Shakespeare* (2023) could only have been produced by this most banal of fads. The editor laments the 'fact of Shakespeare's global, representational power' existing 'in tandem with a global white cultural supremacy'. As one librarian explained, many educators are now 'coming to the conclusion that it's time for Shakespeare to be set aside or de-emphasized to make room for modern, diverse, and inclusive voices'. The Shakespeare Birthplace Trust, the charity in charge of various properties connected with the great playwright, announced in March 2025 that it was 'decolonising' its collection to 'create a more inclusive museum experience'. Apparently, some of its artefacts and archive materials may include 'language or depictions that are racist, sexist, homophobic, or otherwise harmful'. While there is nothing wrong with examining the ways in which Shakespeare may have been appropriated throughout history by racists or colonisers hoping to justify their worldviews, attempts to 'decolonise' his corpus are fruitless and facile. Those who once sought to elevate Shakespeare as a moral exemplar for Englishness have much in common with the woke activists of today. Both groups seek to curtail and contort his art to promote their own particular ideology. Colonisers and decolonisers are equally ill-equipped to appreciate his genius. *The Two Gentlemen of Verona* (c. 1591) will always be preferable to *The Two Transwomen of Brighton and Hove* because the universal human themes of love, friendship and infidelity are far more exhilarating than tokenistic identity politics. To read Shakespeare through the restrictive lens of today's fashionable beliefs is to denude his work of its vitality and abundance. It would be like visiting the Sistine Chapel and only looking at the floor.

Yet it is not simply the messaging of an artist's work that riles the sensibilities of activists, but his or her perceived moral impurity. Take the novelist Virginia Woolf, whose statue in Tavistock Square in Bloomsbury, London, was erected in 2004. Those who scan the adjacent QR code on their smartphones might expect to learn more about Woolf's novels *Mrs Dalloway* (1925) or *To the Lighthouse* (1927), or her relationship with Vita Sackville-West, or her key position in the Bloomsbury Set, that coterie of artists and intellectuals that included E. M. Forster, John Maynard Keynes and Lytton Strachey. Instead, the code directs the visitor to details about Woolf's 'imperialist attitudes and offensive opinions' and her 'challenging, offensive comments and descriptions of race, class and ability which we would find unacceptable today'. One wonders what the person responsible for these judgemental remarks has ever accomplished, if anything at all. In the maelstrom of the culture war, mediocrities have been able to position themselves as superior to the geniuses of the past. It's a profoundly depressing prospect, redolent of Turgenev's metaphor: 'when a gale is blowing the lower branches of a tree can touch the top ones'.

The best approach to writers of genius is humility, but this quality seems to be on the decline. We see evidence of this in the self-importance of those who have rewritten books by P. G. Wodehouse, Ian Fleming, Agatha Christie and Roald Dahl. It should go without saying that Wodehouse's prose cannot be improved, least of all by know-nothing activists who have greased their way into the publishing industry. These self-important purists do not possess the singular wit of Dahl, whose works for children remain unsurpassed. When Dahl's children's novel *The Witches* (1983) was republished by Puffin in 2022, some of the bowdlerisations gutted the original phrases of their waspish mirth and added a moralistic dimension. For instance, where Dahl had written 'You can't go round pulling the hair of every lady you meet, even if she *is* wearing gloves. Just you try it and see what happens', his censor had interpolated as follows: 'Besides, there are plenty of other reasons why women might wear wigs and there is certainly nothing wrong with that'. Elsewhere, 'great flock of ladies' became 'great group of ladies', 'maid' became 'cleaner', 'him' because 'them' and 'his' became 'its'. Other phrases were removed entirely, such as 'immensely fat', 'rather pretty young lady' and 'we could round them all up and put them in the meat-grinder'.

As with Dahl's work, those looking to read Ian Fleming's James Bond novels would be advised to seek out second-hand copies, given that the series has also recently been republished in sanitised form. Naturally, these books include sentiments that are considered unacceptable by today's standards. 'All women love semi-rape' is an incendiary sentence – in this case, it's by the female narrator of *The Spy Who Loved Me* (1962) – but are readers genuinely all that corruptible? Besides, it's not as though the cynical and ruthless Bond, with his licence to kill, is even meant to be a likeable character. In that regard he's reminiscent of the hero of George MacDonald Fraser's *Flashman* (1969), a character based on the bully from *Tom Brown's School Days* (1857) by Thomas Hughes. Flashman is a violent boorish rapist, but the novels are still entertaining because most of us are not reading them for moral instruction.

This is not to imply that art cannot be didactic. *Tom Brown's School Days* is an undeniably pedagogic novel but a fine one nonetheless. Doubtless the reader will recall the death of Jo in *Bleak House* (1852), where Charles Dickens halts the narrative to lecture the wealthy reader on the plight of the poor.

> Dead, your Majesty. Dead, my lords and gentlemen. Dead, Right Reverends and Wrong Reverends of every order. Dead, men and women, born with Heavenly compassion in your hearts. And dying thus around us every day.

The novel momentarily turns into a homily and, although the book remains one of his best, this is its least effective moment. The expectation that fiction ought to reflect the morally laudable aspects of our civilisation is an intellectual and creative cul-de-sac. In exploring the gamut of human experience, writers will often feel compelled to recreate the grotesque, the uncomfortable, the outrageous, the downright evil. Who ever supposed that works of fiction should restrict themselves to rose-tinted idealisations of human existence? Imagine *Macbeth* (c. 1606) without the regicide, or *King Lear* (c. 1605) without the eye-gouging, or *Titus Andronicus* (c. 1592) without the cannibalism. Would Dante's *Divine Comedy* (c. 1321) retain its power if some 'sensitivity reader' excised the *Inferno*?

Most of these changes have come about due to outdated depictions of racial and sexual minorities. In her novel *Between the Acts* (1941), Woolf writes: 'Down among the bushes she worked like a nigger'. Had we been born into an upper middle-class family in London in 1882, we would doubtless find this sentence utterly unremarkable. It would take a reader with the intellect of a boiled turnip not to understand that times change and ethical standards along with them. The author of the QR code's text informs us that Woolf was 'someone who was a product of imperialist attitudes of the time', but one is left wondering how she could possibly have been otherwise. I cannot help but notice that much of this disapprobation of the past is selectively applied. Why do we not hear of activists calling for the 'cancellation' of Karl Marx? Wouldn't the following excerpt from a letter to Friedrich Engels be sufficient to see him condemned?

> The Jewish Nigger Lassalle, who fortunately departs at the end of this week, has luckily again lost 5,000 taler in a fraudulent speculation . . . It is now completely clear to me that he, as is proved by his cranial formation and [curly] hair – descends from the Negroes who had joined Moses' exodus from Egypt (assuming his mother or grandmother on the paternal side had not interbred with a nigger). Now this union of Judaism and Germanism with a basic Negro substance must produce a peculiar product. The obtrusiveness of the fellow is also Nigger-like.

If those pointing the accusatory fingers into the past were sincere, surely these statements by their spiritual leader could not possibly be overlooked? Why is there no QR code on the bronze bust of Marx on his tomb in Highgate cemetery, one which offers visitors the chance to read about his appalling racism?

The double standards make sense when one considers that the arts have always been a target for those of a postmodernist activist mindset. From the attacks on popular culture by the Frankfurt School to the post-Foucauldian critique of the nexus of language and control, art has been crudely reduced to a series of elaborate power-grabs. None of this is really about the past at all, but rather the ideological obsessions of the present. Nobody requires a QR code or a 'contextualising' plaque to understand that racism and homophobia are unpleasant, or that our ancestors held different views about the world than we do. And to assume positions of moral superiority over those who happened to be born in previous eras is equally facile. If we must have QR codes added to statues and other historical landmarks, perhaps they could simply offer that well-known opening line from L. P. Hartley's novel *The Go-Between* (1953): 'The past is a foreign country: they do things differently there.'

## Pedicabo Ego Vos et Irrumabo

There's nothing worse than a puritanical postman. When James Joyce's *Ulysses* was being serialised between 1918 and 1920 by the *Little Review*, an American literary journal edited by Margaret Anderson and Jane Heap, it was the postal authorities that intervened to prevent its distribution. Copies were seized and burned, and after the book's thirteenth chapter ('Nausicaa') was published – in which Leopold Bloom masturbates as he watches three girls on Sandymount Strand – the New York Society for the Suppression of Vice decided to get involved. The ensuing trial would see Anderson and Heap convicted for obscenity and the serialisation of *Ulysses* discontinued, perhaps the most famous overreaction to an orgasm since God killed Onan.

By modern standards, Joyce's imaginative elision of Bloom's ejaculation on the beach with a nearby firework display seems euphemistic rather than obscene:

And then a rocket sprang and bang shot blind blank and O! then the Roman candle burst and it was like a sigh of O! and everyone cried O! O! in raptures and it gushed out of it a stream of rain gold hair threads and they shed and ah! they were all greeny dewy stars falling with golden, O so lovely! O so soft, sweet, soft!

In the early twentieth century, however, it was predictable that such imagery would stir the ire of the censors. Ezra Pound, the man most responsible for persuading the editors of the *Little Review* to publish the novel, acknowledged the risk in a letter to Joyce: 'I suppose we'll be damn well suppressed if we print the text as it stands. *But* it is damn well worth it.' The trial took place a little over a century ago and, inevitably, our conception of 'obscenity' has shifted beyond recognition. Today, woke moralists are calling for censorship of artistic works that offend their sensibilities, but in the post-woke era we are likely to see such demands recur from the traditionalist right. The comedian and broadcaster Nick Dixon has already addressed this re-emergence of the conservative censorial instinct in relation to the arts. In reviewing Bret Easton Ellis's novel *The Shards* (2023), Dixon acknowledged that he was hesitant to recommend the book to his predominately right-leaning readership due to its graphic depictions of sex and violence. 'This is a concern I haven't really felt before,' he writes, 'but I suspect it is something that will increasingly become an issue as a divide emerges on the right between those who are inherently conservative and those who are simply rebelling against the prevailing culture.' While Dixon rejects the 'perceived degeneracy' of the 'cultural sludge' of the woke era, he cautions against slipping 'into the philistinism sometimes associated with the right'. The end of woke will doubtless generate fresh debates about the limitations of the arts and, as ever, obscenity will be the flashpoint.

*Ulysses* is just one of many examples of literary works that have got the hackles of the pious rippling with displeasure. In his book *Bound and Gagged* (2000), Alan Travis discusses the British state's 'Blue Book', a catalogue compiled by the Home Office in the 1950s, and issued secretly to the police, which marked for destruction over four thousand 'obscene' works. Of course, the very notion of obscenity is as hopelessly subjective as taste in music or sense of humour. As Anthony Burgess put it in a lecture to the Malta Library Association in June 1970: 'What is an obscene thing? It is a thing which corrupts. What is a thing which corrupts? It is an obscene thing. The argument is circular.' That the threshold for obscenity ought to be self-evident accounts for the sheer bewilderment of the judge and chief prosecutor in the 1960 trial against Penguin Books – the publisher of a new edition of D. H. Lawrence's *Lady Chatterley's Lover* (1928) – at the jury's disposition to acquit. Lawrence had an obsessive interest in sex, but one that was more intellectual than prurient. During a conversation about Greek philosophy while strolling in the famous piazza on the island of Capri in 1919, Lawrence turned to his fellow novelist Compton Mackenzie and declared 'What we have to learn is to think here' while pointing at the buttons on his fly. Lawrence believed that the Etruscans had successfully learned to think with their genitals, and that other civilisations ought to follow suit. It was a kind of sacred creed, based on his notion that sex needed to be perceived as a vital aspect of human experience, not to be degraded to the level of titillation or pornography.

During a later walk with Mackenzie, this time along a cliff on the south side of the island, Lawrence complained that his ongoing failure to climax simultaneously with his wife was a sign that the marriage was 'imperfect'. The nearest he had ever experienced to a 'perfect love', he said, was at the age of sixteen 'with a young coal miner'. This moment in Capri was probably the genesis for *Lady Chatterley's Lover*. Lawrence had been complaining about *Ulysses*, which, he felt, was 'muck' that was 'more disgusting than Casanova'. He resolved then and there to 'show that it can be done without muck'. *Lady Chatterley's Lover* was his attempt to 'make the sex relations valid and precious'. Reading it now, the sexual passages have an almost reverential air.

He dropped the shirt and stood still, looking towards her. The sun through the low window sent in a beam that lit up his thighs and slim belly, and the erect phallus rising darkish and hot-looking from the little cloud of vivid gold-red hair. She was startled and afraid.

'How strange!' she said slowly. 'How strange he stands there! So big! and so dark and cock-sure! Is he like that?'

The man looked down the front of his slender white body, and laughed. Between the slim breasts the hair was dark, almost black. But at the root of the belly, where the phallus rose thick and arching, it was gold-red, vivid in a little cloud.

During the court case in 1960, the defence barrister was to describe language of this kind as 'dirt for dirt's sake', an assessment that could not possibly have been further from Lawrence's intention. Much was made during the trial of prosecutor Mervyn Griffith-Jones's opening statement, in which he asked the jury to consider whether the novel was something they would 'wish your wife or your servants to read'. The defence understood something that Griffith-Jones could not: that this was a trial about incommensurable social values. For a certain class of citizen, Lawrence's novel was an unambiguous attack on British morality. This did not square with the lived reality of a population on the cusp of a sexual revolution.

For Griffith-Jones, the appearance of the word 'fuck' in the pages of a book surely disqualified it from the possibility of literary merit. What he would have made of François Rabelais's description of Pope Calixtus as a 'cunt barber' is anyone's guess. How might he have even begun to decipher the graphic depiction of the sexual assault of an unconscious girl in Hubert Selby, Jr.'s *Last Exit to Brooklyn* (1964)? The unpunctuated flurry of violence, recalling in style if not substance the final chapter of *Ulysses*, serves as a powerful condemnation of an envenomed society.

. . . and the kids who were watching and waiting to take a turn took out their disappointment on Tralala and tore her clothes to small scraps put out a few cigarettes on her nipples pissed on her jerkedoff on her jammed a broomstick up her snatch then bored they left her lying amongst the broken bottles rusty cans and rubble of the lot and Jack and Fred and Ruthy and Annie stumbled into a cab still laughing and they leaned toward the window as they passed the lot and got a good look at Tralala lying naked covered with blood urine and semen and a small blot forming on the seat between her legs as blood seeped from her crotch . . .

The mistaken assumption that the reader is meant to be titillated by this depiction, or that it has the capacity to morally corrupt, is precisely why the book was arraigned under the Obscene Publications Act in 1966 and copies ordered to be destroyed. Those unfamiliar with literary history are often blind to the ways in which shock has been an important tool for writers. It can be didactic, as in the case of Selby, or subversive in the sense of Mikhail Bakhtin's concept of carnival, by which social norms and hierarchies are upended; transgressive performance as a healthy counterpunch to the powerful. In Chaucer's *Canterbury Tales* (c. 1400), for instance, 'The Miller's Tale' is offered as a direct response to that of the Knight, which is why the elevated courtly style gives way to phrases such as 'prively he caughte hire by the queynte'. In *Twelfth Night* (1601), Shakespeare mocks the puritanical Malvolio by having him inadvertently spell out the word 'cunt' while examining the handwriting of a forged love letter: 'these be her very C's, her U's and her T's' (the 'n' of 'cunt' marked with the word 'and': a commonplace abbreviation). The imagery is made explicit, of course, by the deliberately gratuitous line 'and thus makes she her great P's'. We might also cite Hamlet's anatomical punning:

Hamlet    Lady, shall I lie in your lap?

Ophelia   No, my lord.

Hamlet   I mean my head upon your lap?

Ophelia   Ay, my lord.

Hamlet   Do you think I meant country matters?

Ophelia   I think nothing, my lord.

Hamlet   That's a fair thought to lie between maids' legs.

Ophelia   What is, my lord?

Hamlet   No thing.

If obscenity has the imprimatur of the bard, might this not give even the staunchest of smut-sniffers pause for thought?

Obscenity laws do little more than codify a sense of disgust, an experience that we all share to some degree but that cannot possibly be universalised. It was not until the Obscene Publications Act of 1857 and the trial of *Regina v. Hicklin* eleven years later that the legal test of obscenity was established as whether media has the potential 'to deprave and corrupt', an amorphous formulation if ever there was one. The Hicklin test was retained in the Obscene Publications Act 1959, legislation that remains on the statute books to this day. But just as thousands are arrested in the UK every year for 'grossly offensive' statements under the Communications Act 2003, the way in which material might 'deprave and corrupt' has never been satisfactorily explained. During the so-called 'video nasties' panic of the 1980s, films such as *Driller Killer* (1979), *Cannibal Holocaust* (1980) and *The Evil Dead* (1981) were seized on the grounds that they – in the words of the Director of Public Prosecutions – had the capacity 'to deprave and corrupt, or make morally bad, a significant proportion of the likely audience'. No evidence for this assertion was ever forthcoming. Like the pornography restrictions brought in by the UK government in 2014 – which included bans on the depiction of various consensual adult activities such as 'caning', 'humiliation' and 'facesitting' – the benchmark for what might 'deprave and corrupt' is probably best paraphrased as 'things we don't like'. These are standards that cannot be applied with any degree of consistency, particularly when it comes to literature. Is it obscene, for instance, to write that Egyptian men have members the size of donkeys, and ejaculate violently like wild stallions? And, if so, should the Book of Ezekiel be excised from the Bible?

The very concept of obscenity – whether it emerges from the woke left or the woke right – seems to be based on a distrust of the masses, an elitism that would prefer the bawdy talk to be confined to the smoking rooms of private members' clubs. We see this mentality in the early editions of the Roman and Greek classics, in which offensive phrases were sanitised or redacted in translation. For instance, in Charles Stuttaford's 1912 edition of the poems of Catullus, the line 'Pedicabo ego vos et irrumabo' – 'I will bugger you and fuck your face' – is rendered into English as 'I will give you proofs of my virility'. 'I think most people will agree with me that many of the poems of Catullus are not fit to be put into English,' writes Stuttaford in his preface. 'Manners have changed, and no longer do we charge people, from whom we happen to differ in opinion, with perversion of the sexual instinct, either in jest or in anger.' In the 1921 edition of the Loeb Classical Library, F. W. Cornish substitutes the entire line for an ellipsis. This kind of academic paternalism is reminiscent of the technique deployed by television streaming services in the woke era, silently omitting offensive scenes from old comedy shows without alerting the viewer.

While it may seem contradictory to be worried about the Great Unwashed being exposed to a little more dirt, such is the chief concern of those who set themselves up as the public arbiters of good taste. When the British Board of Film Classification decreed that *The Exorcist* (1973) was unsuitable for home viewing, they were acting *in loco parentis* over the entire nation, implying that they were able to stomach imagery that would corrupt lesser mortals. Similarly, *Lady Chatterley's Lover* was not so menacing when it existed solely in limited Italian and French editions, or in its expurgated form. It was only when

Penguin Books decided to publish the full version in 1960, over thirty years after it was written, that the ruling classes saw it as an existential threat to the foundations of societal respectability.

This is what prompted Norman Douglas to publish his book *Some Limericks* in November 1928, five months after the Italian publisher Pino Orioli had brought out *Lady Chatterley's Lover*. Douglas felt that Lawrence had usurped the aristocrat's privilege of lewd indulgence, and had democratised a subculture in which – to quote Douglas's biographer Mark Holloway – 'gentlemen of discretion' could 'be relied upon to keep their filth in its proper place'. To take a typical example:

> There was an old fellow of Brest,
> Who sucked off his wife with a zest.
>     Despite her great yowls
>     He sucked out her bowels,
> And spat them all over her chest.

Obscene? No doubt. But the puerility is offset by the book's pseudo-scholarly annotations and, in any case, Douglas had explicitly written this work for the 'Dirty-Minded *Elect*'. He had rushed through the publication of *Some Limericks* having read Lawrence's novel in draft form, feeling that its impact would be lessened if the taboos had already been broken.

The implications are somewhat paradoxical. While censorship is an affront to artistic freedom, obscenity as a literary device loses its potency where there are few boundaries of social decorum. So perhaps we need the Mervyn Griffith-Joneses and the Mary Whitehouses and the activists wrapped in their 'Progress Pride' flags as much as we need those artists who are willing to provoke them. In many ways, obscenity is the great test of our commitment to freedom, and our determination to resist the authoritarian impulse. A society that permits artistic liberty, and accepts that offence is subjective and cannot be obviated by the state and its laws, is one that is authentically free. We all share an instinctive understanding of disgust, and so censorship offends us less if it is directed towards material that we find objectionable. At the same time, we should be aware that tabloid outrage over books and movies is often no more sophisticated than those early critics of *Ulysses* who failed to see any distinction between Joyce's masterpiece and the kind of vulgar scribblings one finds on a toilet wall. Disgust has the effect of destabilising our critical faculties; like rage or sexual arousal, it actuates our passion at the expense of our reason. Just because we find an artist's work obscene does not mean it lacks value. We would do well to remember this even as we recoil.

## A Plague of Literal-Mindedness

One of Compton Mackenzie's more curious pastimes was to scour newspapers for various examples of where the term 'literally' had been misused. In 1928, he wrote a letter to the *Evening Standard* in which he noted some of his favourites, including the journalist who had claimed that a criminal 'as a matter of fact had literally gone to pieces after his arrest'. Soon after Mackenzie's letter was published, he was inundated with examples that had been spotted by readers elsewhere. One letter came from the future Home Secretary, Sir Herbert Samuel, also an avid collector of 'literallys'. These included:

> He is literally here, there and everywhere.
> *Daily News*

> He was born, literally, with printer's ink in his veins, and was an outstanding character in the field of local journalism.
> *Farmworker Journal*

To this day I see his face exactly as I saw it then – stricken and defiant, blazing with an anger that seemed literally volcanic.

J. A. Spender, *Life, Journalism and Politics*, vol. 1

The monster's death in an avalanche on the Jura mountains is noisy enough to literally bring down the house.

Review of a production of *Frankenstein* in the
Manchester Guardian

If this last example did literally happen, one wonders how many members of the audience perished in the accident? Mackenzie remarked that this was a particularly satisfying 'literally' because it had clearly been dropped in to avoid a split infinitive. Or perhaps I am being literal-minded in assuming that 'literally' ought to be understood literally. After all, the Merriam-Webster online dictionary has recently added a new definition of the word. The original meaning is still there – 'in a literal sense or manner' – but there is also now a secondary definition: 'In effect: virtually – used in an exaggerated way to emphasize a statement or description that is not literally true or possible.' So apparently these days 'literally' can literally mean 'figuratively'.

Mackenzie and Herbert were collecting 'literallys' almost a century ago, but I doubt that they could possibly keep up in today's culture war. How often have we heard activists claiming that their political opponents are 'literally Hitler', even though only Hitler was literally Hitler. Or how about the claim that 'words are literal violence' or that anyone who is willing to publicly admit that human beings cannot change sex is an 'actual fascist'? Those who speak in this way are not simply demonstrating their cognitive shortcomings, they are also butchering the language. (That's a metaphor, by the way; I do not mean to imply that anyone has been hacking away at a copy of the dictionary with a meat cleaver.)

We have seen that the determination to censor offensive speech, particularly when it comes to the arts, is often times a reflexive response to a sense of disgust. But the existence of obscenity laws has always been a manifestation of literal-mindedness. Our reactions to the arts can be visceral, but this sense can be heightened if we assume that the artist himself is promoting immorality through its very depiction. Mary Whitehouse had this literal-minded tendency, but no more so than today's pompous, semi-sniggering puritans. In the publishing industry, an entire new profession has been invented for the congenitally literal-minded in the form of 'sensitivity readers'. These envious hobgoblins pore over authors' manuscripts and demand, should any aspect carry the potential to be taken as an affront. In an article written for *UnHerd* in February 2022, the poet Kate Clanchy shared some of the recommendations from sensitivity readers who had assessed her memoir and, in doing so, provided an insight into the sheer priggishness and precisionism of the entire process.

> I should not use 'disfigure' of a landscape (infraction level 3, as presumably comparing bings – spoil heaps – to boils might be harmful to acne sufferers). Nor should I use 'handicap' in its ordinary sense of 'impede' (infraction level 2, serious); and I should prefer the acronym 'SEN' to its origin phrase, special educational needs, because it is more inclusive (infraction level 2).

They could not see the metaphor in the term 'disfigure', only an ableist slur. Other sensitivity readers of Clanchy's book decreed that 'paragraphs, sub-sections and even entire chapters should be revised'. What these professional fussbudgets lack in artistic vision, they more than make up for in sanctimony. Their task is to excise the yeast and leave only the dough.

Cartoonists at the French satirical magazine *Charlie Hebdo* are accustomed to this kind of literal-mindedness from its critics. In June 2017, the front cover featured an image of the then British prime minister Theresa May holding her own decapitated head in her hands. The cartoon alluded to a terrorist attack at London Bridge, in which a van was driven into pedestrians before its three occupants went on a stabbing spree. Rather than understand the point about May's multicultural policies, the editors of the *Metro* saw fit to publish an article under the headline: 'Charlie Hebdo beheads Theresa May and mocks London Bridge terror victims'. It is sadly necessary to point out that the cartoonists had neither ridiculed victims of terrorism nor decapitated any prime ministers. And it isn't only sub-literate hacks at the *Metro* who are prone to such misreadings; it is a problem that also plagues the intelligentsia. In April 2015, thirty-five respected members of PEN International, including writers such as Joyce Carol Oates and Junot Díaz, signed an open letter to protest the 'courage award' given to *Charlie Hebdo* in the wake of the horrific massacre by Islamist philistines. These authors claimed that the magazine had mocked a 'section of the French population that is already marginalized, embattled and victimized'. This was, of course, to misidentify the target. The cartoonists weren't 'punching down' at the Muslim minority, but rather 'punching up' at the authoritarianism of institutionalised religion.

Literal-mindedness is bad enough, but the pretence of literal-mindedness is surely even worse. Politicos seem to be especially culpable in this regard, a point that was clearly demonstrated in March 2024, when Donald Trump made remarks at a campaign rally in Ohio. He had been talking about attempts by Chinese car companies to avoid paying tariffs, particularly by means of the recent construction of factories in Mexico. In words aimed at the president of China, Xi Jinping, Trump said that he would impose a 'hundred per cent tariff on every single car'. He continued: 'You're not going to be able to sell those cars, if I get elected. Now, if I don't get elected, it's going to be a bloodbath for the whole . . . that's going to be the least of it. It's going to be a bloodbath for the country. That'll be the least of it. But they're not going to sell those cars.' This 'bloodbath' for the car industry was misreported in the most astonishingly dishonest way. 'Donald Trump warns of a "bloodbath" in US if he isn't elected as president again', ran one typical headline in the *Independent*. 'Trump says country faces "bloodbath" if Biden wins in November', ran another in *Politico*. While it was perfectly clear that Trump was using a common metaphor, one that politicians and commentators of all stripes have deployed in many different contexts before, the mainstream media reacted as though Trump had authentically called for violent uprisings should his opponent win. A similar situation arose when prominent reporters and politicians were asserting that Trump had said he wanted to execute former United States Representative Liz Cheney by firing squad. His actual words were: 'Let's put her with a rifle, standing there with nine barrels shooting at her. Okay? Let's see how she feels about it, you know, when the guns are trained on her face. You know they're all war hawks when they're sitting in Washington in a nice building saying, "Oh, gee, well, let's send, let's send 10,000 troops right into the mouth of the enemy".' Quite plainly, Trump was making the point – one not altogether convincing – that Cheney's attitude to overseas military intervention would be different if she were facing the gunfire herself. One can challenge the point without completely deceiving the public about its substance.

Given the certainty that the deception would almost instantaneously become apparent, these reporters were inadvertently bolstering Trump's support. Much of his appeal has been based on the narrative that there are shadowy forces working against him in the 'deep state' and the mass media. Every time prominent news outlets are caught lying about him, it supports the very worldview that he has been espousing. We have been here so often before that it's impossible that lessons haven't been learned by now. We know that bluebottles will continually collide with windows, never considering that there might be a preferable route, but one would expect more from sentient human beings. We might recall that bizarre moment in January 2017 when many members of the media class claimed that Trump had hired a group of Russian prostitutes to urinate on the hotel bed once occupied by Barack and Michelle Obama. This was scarcely credible for all sorts of reasons, not least that Trump could never have devised a form of revenge so avant-garde.

In the United Kingdom, we routinely experience our own 'bloodbath' moments, where politicians and media commentators appear to exercise an almost wilful ignorance of the basic concepts of metaphor and hyperbole. Consider, for instance, a tweet posted by Robert Rowland, a Brexit Party MEP, in July 2019: 'We are behind all our fisherman [*sic*] and the restoration of sovereignty over our waters. 200 miles of exclusion zone with any foreign fishing vessel given the same treatment as the Belgrano!' The *Guardian* took this literally, reporting that Rowland had 'called for' the vessels to be sunk. Likewise, the *Independent* claimed that Rowland had 'called for the Royal Navy to sink EU fishing vessels'. The Liberal Democrat MEP Chris Davies claimed to feel 'sick to the stomach' after hearing that Rowland was 'calling for fishermen from another nation to die in our waters'. In all of this, it is difficult to discern between those who genuinely believe the worst of their opponents, and those who are merely feigning ignorance out of sheer opportunism.

But for sheer asininity, nothing could match the efforts of commentators who claimed that Elon Musk had made Nazi salutes at Trump's inauguration rally in January 2025. 'Elon Musk appears to make back-to-back fascist salutes at inauguration rally' exclaimed the *Guardian*, delirious with glee that Trump's most powerful ally had just publicly endorsed Hitler live at his inauguration. The Anti-Defamation League quickly put out a sensible statement in an effort to subdue all the frenzied mutual masturbation of the literal-minded:

> It seems that Elon Musk made an awkward gesture in a moment of enthusiasm, not a Nazi salute, but again, we appreciate that people are on edge. In this moment, all sides should give one another a bit of grace, perhaps even the benefit of the doubt, and take a breath.

The very idea that Musk, as a clandestine fascist, would inadvertently reveal his evil scheme during one of the most watched televised events of the year stretches credulity well beyond its limits. Nobody believed it, of course. Or, if they did, they should be supervised at all times, especially around cutlery. That goes for Rex Huppke at USA *Today*, who wrote a piece entitled 'Elon Musk's "odd-looking" salute sure looked like a "Sieg heil" to me'. Perhaps he's telling the truth. I once thought I saw the face of David Hasselhoff in my spinach frittata, and yet I'm pretty sure that would have been the old pareidolia playing tricks on me again. If I were as literal-minded as Huppke, I'd probably assume that The Hoff had actually found a way to invade my breakfast and urgently call an exorcist.

It is telling that not once in his piece does Huppke mention the context for the admittedly ill-advised gesture. Musk had said to the audience, 'My heart goes out to you', which is why he struck his heart and mimed throwing it out to the crowd. This key sentence was edited out of the clip shared widely by his detractors, the very same people who are distressed by Musk's failure to crack down on 'disinformation'. Naturally, Democratic politicians were quick to exploit the situation as much as the press. Jerry Nadler, Representative for the 12th District of New York, jumped on to X to post his verdict:

> I never imagined we would see the day when what appears to be a Heil Hitler salute would be made behind the Presidential seal. This abhorrent gesture has no place in our society and belongs in the darkest chapters of human history. I urge all of my colleagues to unite in condemning this hateful gesture for what it is: antisemitism.

These tactics are no longer working. This kind of literal-mindedness, either feigned or real, is increasingly insufficient to sway the public in these final days of woke. Most people are now wary of the narratives spun by the mainstream media. They are also aware that Nazis generally do not pay visits to Auschwitz to learn about the horrors of the Holocaust and lay wreaths at Jewish memorial services, as Musk did in January 2024.

As a teacher, I was always careful when making jokes with the younger pupils, because they had a tendency to take them at face value. On reflection, I cannot help but wonder whether the sheer ubiquity of literal-mindedness suggests a culture that has retreated into a state of infancy. Another moment from Mackenzie's autobiography may help to illustrate the point. On a ship to Bombay, a fellow passenger told him an anecdote about a mother who had castigated her child by saying 'If you're not good I'll throw you out of the port-hole'. But mark the sequel: 'She then left the child in charge of a small older brother, and he *did* throw the kid out of the port-hole, presuming that to be the right way to deal with bad behaviour.' Children are apt to be literal-minded because they have underdeveloped brains and have not yet fully experienced the process of socialisation. As adults, we have no such excuse.

# 9

# Sacred Cows

---

### The Front Line

Stop me if you've heard this one. A man's wife divorces him and shacks up with his boss. Soon after, a friend suggests that he should remarry. 'What for?' he asks. 'Are you looking for a wife as well?'

It may not be the funniest joke, but that's because it's an anecdote from *The Lives of the Caesars* (c. 121) by the Ancient Roman historian Suetonius. The comedian in this case was a senator called Aelius Lamia, whose wife had left him for the Emperor Domitian. For making this casual quip, Domitian had Lamia put to death. Now that's a bad review.

As the art form most associated with the breaking of taboos and with the telling of uncomfortable truths, comedy is a natural front line for the free speech battles. This is why so many stand-ups have found themselves drawn into the culture war. The American comedian Bridget Phetasy, for example, has now created a successful podcast covering issues relating to culture and politics, and has aptly described herself as 'the accidental pundit'. 'Everything became political', Phetasy reflected in one interview, 'and comedians ended up in punditry whether they wanted to be there or not. Because you either spoke The Approved Message and got work in Hollywood or did your job as a comedian and called out the ridiculousness wherever you saw it – which often meant striking out on your own.' The arts were always likely to be a major casualty of the new puritanism because inspiration cannot thrive in conditions of conformity. For many in the creative industries, resisting this trend in the woke era became a matter of obligation.

While activists continue to insist that words are akin to landmines, and that their feelings must be protected at all costs, comedy clubs will be considered hotbeds of heresy. For some years now, there has been an undeniable strain of groupthink among those in positions of power: promoters, commissioners, critics and even some performers. This tediously pharisaic approach to the art form has revealed that the comedy industry is seemingly dominated by those who are simply not comedy-literate. We find ourselves in that strange situation envisaged by John Cleese: 'People without a sense of humour should not be allowed to decide what people with a sense of humour are allowed to laugh at. It would be like allowing colour-blind people to decide which colours should be on a colour chart.' Acts who conform to the new creed have been rewarded, while those who refuse to do so have been shunned. It hasn't taken much for up-and-coming comics to realise that it is more profitable to be seen to convey what Phetasy calls 'The Approved Message', rather than to develop their craft in innovative and individual ways. The impulse to serve Mammon rather than the Muses has enervated the comedy scene, and self-censorship is now the norm.

In early 2020, comedians Matt Lucas and David Walliams announced that they were hoping to resurrect *Little Britain*, a television comedy series known for its caricatures of minorities, but they admitted that they would now 'do it differently because it's a different time'. Such deference to the prevailing orthodoxies was not sufficient to satisfy the custodians of 'social justice', always watchful for potential future transgressions. The *Guardian* produced two hit pieces in quick succession to bewail the return of this 'problematic' show, with Zoe Williams complaining that 'the way minorities are demonised in Britain is no laughing matter' and Barbara Ellen arguing that it was 'too late' for the 'bad boys of repulsive comedy' to 'clean up their act'. When previous series of *Little Britain* were deleted from streaming services including Netflix and BBC iPlayer in the wake of the Black Lives Matter protests, one writer for *Glamour* magazine applauded the decision on the grounds that this brand of humour is 'dangerous' and that we should be 'leaving behind an era we should all be ashamed of'. This is a religion in which the possibility of repentance is notably absent.

Comedians in the digital era have been compelled to work within a climate where social media can catalyse a flurry of competing storms. Offence is a contemporary form of currency, and declarations of virtue are deemed an adequate substitute for virtuous acts. Jokes that violate the creed can therefore see stand-ups aggressively denounced, a phenomenon that is fatally counter-productive to the craft. It is not even as though live performance is beyond the reach of these tinpot tyrants. At the Edinburgh Festival Fringe in August 2022, comedian and magician Jerry Sadowitz had his show cancelled after the first night by the Pleasance Theatre Trust. In an incredible feat of doublespeak, Anthony Alderson, director of the Pleasance, claimed that although he 'champions freedom of speech' and does 'not censor comedians' material' he had nonetheless cancelled this show because it 'is not acceptable and does not align with our values'. There is much to criticise in Alderson's statement, not least his high-handed claim that 'this type of material has no place on the festival'. To put this into context, this is how I opened my review of Sadowitz's live show for *ScotsGay* magazine in 2008:

> Jerry Sadowitz is a nasty piece of work. His venomous tirade is relentless, consisting of unabashed racism, homophobia, misogyny, antisemitism, xenophobia, and every other kind of prejudice known to humankind. If it exists, he hates it. The man is a monster. He's also one of the best showmen on the Edinburgh Fringe.

I described his performance as 'an explosion of hate on stage', but noted that the effect was both prurient and deliriously funny. That Sadowitz's unending bile is often interspersed with adroitly executed magic tricks makes his routines all the more compelling. When critics quote his jokes out of context, it's easy to see why so many are offended. But when it comes to performers like Sadowitz, context is everything.

So why is it that a show explicitly marketed at adults who enjoy controversial comedy would need to be cancelled? The Pleasance Theatre Trust issued a further statement claiming that 'opinions such as those displayed on stage by Sadowitz are not acceptable', thereby revealing how little it understands about the essential theatricality of stand-up. Are 'jokes' and 'opinions' now synonymous? To take stand-up at face value, and attempt to apply moral guidelines to a theatrical performance, is to misapprehend the experience. Denouncing Sadowitz's onstage persona as racist, sexist or homophobic makes about as much sense as condemning Macbeth for his ruthless ambition. Moreover, the cancellation of shows fosters an atmosphere in which artistic risk-taking is disincentivised. Following the Sadowitz controversy, comedy critic Kate Copstick described the atmosphere at the festival in grim terms.

> In all my years of covering the Fringe, there has never been a more joy-stranglingly censorious August. Councillor Moira Knox in her heyday seems like a libertine now, in comparison to today's recrea-tionally offended. When the blood-chilling phrase 'unacceptable and does not align with our values' is bandied about, and by a venue like the Pleasance, then it is time to fear for the freedom of our funny. The point of a Fringe is that it does not align with anything. But now the corporate hairdressers have taken over the salon. And they have a style book.

It is frustrating to see the curtailing of artistic freedom simply because a handful of critics cannot comprehend the notion of an onstage persona and its function in stand-up. Jokes are not literal expressions of a comedian's perspective. We need not worry about whether or not the chicken who crossed the road was free range, because the chicken does not exist.

We have reached a point where the arts have been demeaned by a myopic fixation on language and power relations. To give just one example, after the knife attack on Salman Rushdie in August 2022, the tax lawyer and online activist Jolyon Maugham responded by saying that, when it comes to free speech, one should 'engage with relative power. Who has a platform to speak – and for what purpose do they use it, to challenge or to embed power?' This is the basic formulation to which all artistic expression is now reduced. Seen through this lens, when Sadowitz screams racial slurs, he is not doing so as part of an unhinged comedic persona, but is perpetuating power structures that maintain his privilege. That he is Jewish doesn't seem to matter because, as comedian and writer David Baddiel has argued, Jews don't count.

While 'regime comedians' – those who diligently toe the establishment line – continue to claim that no performers are being censored, the list of shows cancelled following activist pressure continues to grow. One of the earliest cases was that of Dapper Laughs – the stereotypically laddish character created by Daniel O'Reilly – whose ITV television series *Dapper Laughs: On the Pull* was axed in 2014 following a campaign. Forty-four comedians had signed an open letter to condemn ITV for providing a platform for 'sexist narratives' which 'encourage street harassment, rape culture and normalise misogyny'. O'Reilly later said that the entire affair had struck him as classist: 'Big-name, well-connected comedians said worse but got a pass – right background, right accent, right connections. No issue. Me? Working-class, rough-edged from a council estate and sounding too dumb to be able to create characters, be satirical or write jokes was easy to destroy.'

Since then, there have been numerous examples of cancelled comics. In January 2019, Leo Kearse's show *Right Wing Comedian* was cancelled at the Perth Fringe in Australia after accusations of 'transphobia', even though material for the show had been co-written by the trans person he was dating at the time. Alistair Williams was banned from YouTube and blacklisted from most major comedy clubs in the United Kingdom after a routine he performed in April 2019 which mocked those who had attempted to overturn the result of the Brexit referendum. In February 2022, Mary Bourke was removed from a line-up at a comedy club in Brighton following complaints from audience members that her material made them feel 'unsafe'. In April 2023, Raurie Williams (aka 'NoHun') had his tour cancelled for pointing out that men cannot get pregnant. In February 2023, Samantha Pressdee's show at the Leicester Comedy Festival was cancelled after she had written an article in defence of women's single-sex spaces. There were two cancellations on the same day in March 2024, when Lewis Schaffer was pulled from a charity benefit gig in London on the grounds that his material was offensive to the LGBTQ+ community, and Scott Capurro had his booking cancelled at a Dublin comedy club after he refused to censor his material on Israel and Palestine. After a performance in a London club two months later, Capurro was reported to the police for homophobia, which must have come as a surprise to his husband. In July 2023, Roy 'Chubby' Brown's show at the Strathpeffer Pavilion in Scotland was cancelled following a 'public outcry'. Frazer Mackenzie, the CEO of the trust that runs the venue, stated that the event had been a 'booking misjudgement' and that the venue had 'been approached by members of the community expressing real concerns regarding the language and material associated with this individual's show'. At each step on this road to Pandemonium, regime comedians have remained silent, as though it is of no concern to them that their craft is being subjected to continual battering. To claim that there is no problem with censorship in comedy is easy enough if your views are naturally in lockstep with the prevailing orthodoxies of the time, but it does suggest a degree of solipsism. The energy it must take to studiously ignore the continual stream of reported cases of artists being cancelled would be sufficient to keep the Large Hadron Collider running indefinitely.

The frenzied climate of the culture war has made it very difficult to engage in a sensible discussion about the nature of controversial comedy without being accused of some kind of latent bigotry. This became clear when the comedian Andrew Lawrence was dropped by his agent and had his tour cancelled following a furore over jokes that he had posted on Twitter after the final of the UEFA European Football Championship in July 2021. The day after the England team's defeat, Lawrence tweeted a joke about Marcus Rashford, one of the three players who missed the crucial penalties at the end of the game. 'All that time Rashford spent virtue signalling,' Lawrence wrote, 'he could have been practising penalties.' Rashford had been the figurehead of a highly successful campaign to end child food poverty, and was universally acclaimed as a result. Lawrence was therefore fulfilling the traditional role of comedians: to take a bolt-gun to our sacred cows. When it became apparent that many of Lawrence's followers on Twitter had interpreted the joke as racist because Rashford is of Afro-Caribbean descent, he took the joke further. 'All I'm saying is, the white guys scored,' he wrote, and followed this with the even more provocative: 'I can see that this has offended a lot of people, and I'm sorry that black guys are bad at penalties.' It is understandable that many people unfamiliar with Lawrence might interpret these remarks as racist, but a moment's reflection would have been advisable here.

Was it the case that Lawrence, a well-renowned and critically acclaimed comedian, was making the bizarre and obviously outrageous claim that black people are innately bad at football? Or was he doing something else? Lawrence is one of those comics who delight in testing the limits of his audience's tolerance; his onstage persona transgresses the social contract as a matter of routine. Like all the best stand-up, it's an essentially theatrical performance. In this case, Lawrence had attempted a joke about how Rashford should have spent more time practising. Then came his doubling-down, his remark that white people are somehow innately better at penalties. His critics have interpreted this as an authentic expression of his feelings on the subject. Stand-up afficionados will have seen this kind of scenario play out in clubs on numerous occasions: a heckler takes a joke at face value, makes an accusation of bigotry, and so the comedian decides to then embody what it is the heckler thinks that he or she has seen. It's a kind of role-playing to ridicule the blockheadedness of the initial misinterpretation.

All of which is bound to be lost on social media, where generosity of interpretation is in short supply. For comedians of this kind, the sensitivity is the point. One thinks of the likes of Sam Kinison or Andy Kaufman, those clowns whose transgressions were often considered abominable but were a necessary corrective to the pretentions of polite society. In breaking boundaries, such performers remind us why we have boundaries in the first place. Lenny Bruce was convicted in court for a stand-up routine and was sentenced to four months in a work-house. It was not for nothing that he pointed out 'if you can't say "fuck", you can't say "fuck the government"'. Comedy has always been a means

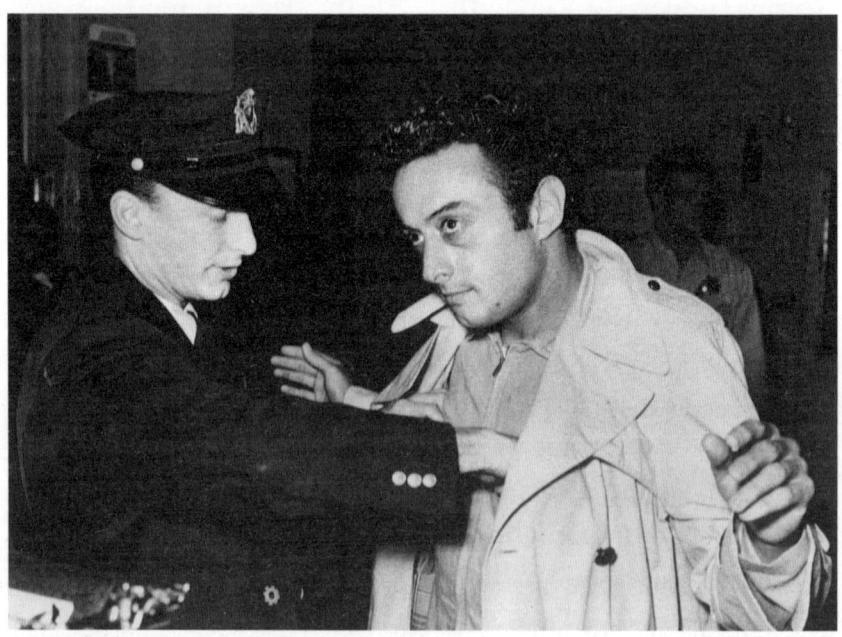

*Comedian Lenny Bruce arrested at the Jazz Workshop, San Francisco, on 4 October 1961.*

to reckon with power but, in doing so, its practitioners take risks. As actor and comedian Rob Schneider points out in his book *You Can Do It!* (2024): 'Stand-up comedians are held accountable for not just everything they say, but for other people's interpretations of what they said.'

In recent years, controversial comedians have been dismissed as 'edgelords', but this is to fail to distinguish between those who are able to stir outrage as a deft comedic tool, and those who use shock tactics in lieu of talent. Lawrence is an undeniably gifted comic whose success has depended on his dissident instincts. Those who read his offending tweets as a baffling attempt at career suicide did so only because they do not share his compulsion towards misrule. Comics with this kind of instinct are invariably attracted to the topics that they are told are 'off-limits'. In such circumstances, destroying a comedian's livelihood and cancelling his gigs seems less like constructive criticism and more like revenge.

### Policing Punchlines

The toxicity of cancel culture has been enhanced lately by the weaponisation of the law. In February 2022, a media firestorm ensued after a segment from comedian Jimmy Carr's Netflix special *His Dark Material* went viral. There were calls for Carr to be prosecuted, with social media users directly alerting the police to the clip. Culture Secretary Nadine Dorries subsequently said that new laws put into place via the Media Bill could criminalise jokes of this kind that appear on streaming services. A spokesperson for Prime Minister Boris Johnson echoed her response, saying that he was looking into 'toughening measures for social media and streaming platforms which don't tackle harmful content on their platforms'. SNP Councillor Julie McKenzie called for Carr to be 'prosecuted' along with 'his applauding audience'.

THE END OF WOKE

What sin might Carr have committed to justify being throttled by the arm of the law? No stand-up material is well served by being quoted in print, but defending the joke will require that context:

> When people talk about the Holocaust, they talk about the tragedy and horror of six million Jewish lives being lost to the Nazi war machine. But they never mention the thousands of Gypsies that were killed by the Nazis. No one ever wants to talk about that, because no one ever wants to talk about the positives.

The complaints revealed more about the literal-mindedness of Carr's detractors than the show itself. Reality television star Paddy Doherty asserted that it 'wasn't a joke', and Dorries described the joke as 'not comedy'. Such claims require assessment. Carr is a comedian. The clip was taken from a comedy show in which an audience is heard laughing uproariously at the line in question. All the signs would suggest that there is at the very least a comedic element to this scenario. If Doherty and Dorries are correct, then we must accept the premise that Carr, having cultivated a huge following and a successful career in comedy, had suddenly made the extraordinary decision to openly support mass genocide, and to do so by means of a stand-up special on Netflix. It's a bold move.

While it is entirely understandable that many would take offence, this does not justify the claim that the joke should be taken literally. Anyone is free to criticise the material either on grounds of taste or quality, but to argue that it does not qualify as comedy is simply false. A joke does not suddenly morph into a literal statement simply because an audience member does not approve of its content. The key question is not whether the joke is funny, or morally justifiable, but whether we support the introduction of legislation to curb artistic freedom. Rather than call for censorship, there is a proven solution to the problem of feeling offended by a comedian's work: don't buy a ticket. Instead, we find ourselves in this deranging new world where activists, commentators, and even politicians would rather flex their muscles and decide which forms of entertainment other people can choose to watch. This is undeniable authoritarianism.

In July 2021, a viral video circulated online which captured some of the final moments of the Afghan comedian Nazar Mohammad Khasha, as he openly mocked his Taliban captors who later murdered him. Although stand-ups in the Western world are thankfully not facing the kind of oppression experienced by those in theocratic states, it should nevertheless trouble us that twelve thousand people are arrested each year in the United Kingdom for comments posted online that have been deemed offensive, and in some cases have even been imprisoned for jokes. In May 2010, Paul Chambers was found guilty of sending a joke tweet in which he said he would blow up an airport in Doncaster after it closed due to heavy snowfall. In 2012, teenager Matthew Woods was imprisoned for three months for posting jokes on Facebook about murdered children. In January 2015, Ross Loraine was arrested by police and cautioned for an offensive joke he had tweeted concerning a tragic lorry accident in Glasgow. In April 2022, Paul Bussetti from Croydon was sentenced to ten weeks in jail for sharing a video of a cardboard model of Grenfell Tower being burned on a bonfire in mimicry of a real-life tragedy that had occurred in June 2017.

Celebrities have also been criminalised for attempts at humour. In September 2016, former footballer Paul Gascoigne was found guilty in a criminal court of racially aggravated abuse, after a joke he made during a stop on his *An Evening with Gazza* tour at Wolverhampton Civic Hall. At one point during the show, he had turned to Errol Rowe, a black security guard, and said, 'Can you smile please, because I can't see you.' For this, Gascoigne was fined £1,000 and forced to pay a further £1,000 in compensation to Rowe. The joke was not even original; Barry Humphries had used the same line at an Amnesty International comedy benefit gala in 1976 while playing his alter ego, Dame Edna Everage. Gascoigne had also quipped about the 'ugliness' of footballer and third-degree burns victim Carlos Tevez, and the suicide of gay footballer Justin Fashanu. There are comics who are skilled enough to make any topic funny, irrespective of its sensitive nature. Needless to say, Gascoigne is not among them. In his summing up of the case, Judge Graham Wilkinson said that 'it is not acceptable to laugh words like this off as some form of joke'. What, then, is to stop the police demanding the extradition of popular comedians such as Dave Chappelle or Bill Burr for their routines on race, gender or sexuality? Can it be that the state is simply punishing Gascoigne for being a bad comic? If so, I dread to think what would happen if Judge Wilkinson ever visited the Edinburgh Festival Fringe. Any comedian who got a one-star review would probably be forced to undertake community service.

There is a brand of humour which relies on its sheer inappropriateness. It is why we can find ourselves laughing during funerals or other solemn occasions. The social responsibility to take the matter seriously nags at our senses and dares us to rebel. John Cleese understood this all too well when he delivered the eulogy at the funeral of his fellow *Monty Python* star Graham Chapman, and noted that his deceased friend would obviously have liked him to say: 'Good riddance to him, the freeloading bastard. I hope he fries.' The novelist Simon Raven once received a telegram from his wife which read: 'Wife and baby starving send money soonest'. He replied: 'Sorry no money: suggest eat baby'. It may sound callous to admit that the sentiment is inherently funny, but the best kind of laughter is an involuntary reflex, and to find Raven's feigned pitilessness amusing is not in any way an endorsement of cannibalism and infanticide.

As we have seen, literal-mindedness is comedy's kryptonite. Before Andrew Lawrence was cancelled, he had found himself the subject of an online petition due to the following joke: 'Given that about 80 per cent of suicides in the UK last year were committed by men, if feminists truly wanted equality, they'd kill themselves.' The subsequent petition urged the BBC to ban him from any future shows on the grounds that he was willing 'to incite others to take their own lives'.

This determination to interpret jokes literally has seen politicians condemned as well as professional comedians. When former prime minister Boris Johnson was branded a 'racist' for referring to 'flag-waving piccaninnies' and 'tribal warriors' with 'watermelon smiles', few bothered to read the offending words in their original context. The article in question was an attempt at satire, and Johnson had quite plainly been using colonial rhetoric in order to mock Tony Blair for his international saviour complex. He was similarly castigated in August 2018 for an article in which he joked about Muslim women in burqas resembling letter boxes. The *Guardian* ran an article whose headline included the claim that Johnson's quip had caused a 'surge in anti-Muslim attacks'. Many media outlets followed suit, repeating the claim that there had been a 375 per cent increase in abuse and attacks on Muslim people, statistics that were comprehensively debunked by Tom Chivers in a piece for *UnHerd*. Activists so desperately wanted it to be true that they had not looked closely at the flawed methodology. The *Guardian* published an editorial piece lambasting Johnson for his 'tasteless newspaper column joke', in spite of the fact that one of its own columnists had made the exact same joke five years before. In her satirical piece, Remona Aly had suggested methods of rehabilitating the burqa's image. 'Since the burqa eye-opening has been called a letterbox slit,' she wrote, 'and with the privatisation of the Royal Mail, seize the moment to set up an independent mobile mail service, AKA The Burqa Post'. This precedent had little impact on Cressida Dick, the head of the Metropolitan Police, who spoke to specialist officers to determine whether or not Johnson had broken the law.

If I am right – which is by no means certain – that the authoritarian impulse represents the default condition of humankind, the true 'state of nature', and that civilisation is the armour we construct against our baser instincts, then laughter is what happens when the fissures appear. It is the necessary release from the pressure of maintaining our social contract, the obligation to be civil and cooperative, which years of successful socialisation have calcified into instinct. The same principle applies, albeit in a cruder manner, to the convention of Halloween costumes that are intended to shock. It might seem puerile, but rather than donning the costume of a ghost or a vampire, many partygoers now celebrate this season of horror by dressing up as the most morally repugnant human beings in history. The more outrageous the better, and the guest who displays the worst taste sometimes wins a prize. In a much-publicised example, David Wootton dressed as Salman Abedi, the terrorist who detonated a bomb at an Ariana Grande concert at Manchester Arena in 2017, killing twenty-two people, mostly children, and injuring a further thousand. Wootton wore an Arabic headdress, a T-shirt bearing the words 'I love Ariana Grande', and carried a rucksack with 'TNT' and 'boom' written on it. This was doubtless tasteless and juvenile, but the partygoers understood the rules of the game, and Wootton later claimed to have been awarded the prize for Best Costume. Once his image was posted online, however, it became a police matter, and Wootton was quickly arrested. He pleaded guilty and faced a possible jail term of two years. He also relocated and changed his name. While we will doubtless have sympathy for anyone who found the images upsetting and grotesque, it is surely more disturbing that a Halloween costume could result in a custodial sentence. Our opinions over whether such jokes are funny or offensive are entirely subjective and beside the point. It is reasonable to be troubled by those who find humour in barbaric atrocities, but it is an undeniable infringement of civil liberties for the state to punish those who do. Our profound sympathy for the families of the victims should not blind us to what the incarceration of Wootton represents.

At the same time, it would be unwise to assume that hostility towards comedians is only originating from one particular political tribe. In June 2019, the left-wing comedian Jo Brand was investigated by police for a routine on the BBC Radio 4 show *Heresy*. She had been speaking about the trend of throwing milkshakes at right-wing political figures, and had said: 'Why bother with a milkshake when you could get some battery acid?' Ricky Gervais pointed out the inherent absurdity of this interpretation:

> That was clearly a joke. She doesn't really think that Nigel Farage should be doused in acid. Not in a million years. But within minutes on Twitter people were saying, "Oh, it's OK for a comedian to throw acid in someone's face." But she didn't throw acid in someone's face. What you've done there is you've mistaken a joke for an actual crime.

This outrage was clearly selective and underscored by political bias. If one were to take Brand's jokes literally, it would be just as easy to accuse her of incitement to murder when, in her Channel 4 television show, *A Big Slice of Jo Brand* (1996), she said that actor Jane Seymour was so talentless that she ought to be decapitated. Of course, the joke was based on King Henry VIII's penchant for executing his wives, playing on the fact that one of them was also called Jane Seymour, and fantasising about the idea that he could be resurrected in order to chop off her namesake's head. Since politics played no part in this routine, nobody complained. As I have argued, sometimes the literal-mindedness is purely opportunistic.

The notion of people being offended by jokes is as old as comedy itself, and often people react angrily if humour is not to their taste. The current manifestation of this age-old debate takes the form of a simple dichotomy: 'woke comedy' versus 'anti-woke comedy'. Over the past few years we have seen the emergence of a new comedy movement, one branded by commentators as 'anti-woke', that seeks to push back against the orthodoxies of our time. Its closest historical precedent is the 'alternative' comedians of the 1980s, who also took aim at establishment norms and were often similarly blunt in their approach. The key difference today is that there is no broad agreement about where the power in society lies, and so while 'anti-woke' comedians see themselves as anti-establishment, their critics insist that the opposite is true. Consider the example of Ricky Gervais's Netflix stand-up special,

*Armageddon* (2023), which sparked yet another debate about the supposed 'red lines' in comedy. Some accused Gervais of taking a reactionary stance, most notably because of jokes relating to migrants and disabled children. Gervais has been branded an 'anti-woke' comedian, but I doubt very much that he would see it in such reductive terms. Anyone familiar with his work will know that he has always lampooned closed systems of thought, and it just so happens that wokeness has in recent years represented the dominant iteration. There was a time when many of Gervais's critics were perfectly happy to see him take a wrecking ball to the certainties of religious faith. It would appear they take a different view when it's their own belief-system taking a battering.

Gervais's previous stand-up special *SuperNature* (2022) had likewise driven the congenitally humourless into conniptions. Predictably, *PinkNews* led the charge with a report that disapprovingly quoted the most offending lines. The effect was not dissimilar to the Dalai Lama reading aloud the contents of an erotic novel; few were likely to be aroused. 'Ricky Gervais' new Netflix special is nothing more than an anti-trans garbage fire', bawled the headline. Other activists were hastily competing to see who could denounce Gervais's show in the most histrionic terms. The Gay & Lesbian Alliance Against Defamation (GLAAD) issued a statement in which they referred to Gervais as a 'so-called comedian' and claimed that *SuperNature* is 'full of graphic, dangerous, anti-trans rants masquerading as jokes', 'anti-gay rhetoric' and assured us that Netflix would 'be held accountable' for content that is 'designed to incite hate or violence'. None of these characterisations of the show is remotely close to the truth, but they do offer us an insight into how comedy is routinely misconstrued in the strange and moiling clamour of the culture wars. Far from 'punching down', Gervais exposes the increasingly fanatical ideology of the ruling class: the sanctification of gender identity.

'My target wasn't trans folk', Gervais explained, 'but trans activist ideology. I've always confronted dogma that oppresses people and limits freedom of expression.' Many of the criticisms levelled at Gervais inevitably took the form of straw men. On the comedy website *Chortle*, Steve Bennett described Gervais's 'core demographic' as being the 'sizeable brigade who believe "you can't say anything anymore"', even though people who sincerely make this claim are vanishingly rare. Others have asserted that Gervais's fans are opposed to free speech because they criticised those who took offence. But criticism is not the same as censorship; just as Gervais's detractors are free to express their misgivings, so too are those who disagree. As Gervais puts it, 'You can joke about whatever the fuck you like. And some people won't like it and they will tell you they don't like it. And then it's up to you whether you give a fuck or not. And so on. It's a good system.' Comedians who violate popular sensibilities have always faced pushback and resentment. The problem arises when the offended parties seek to impose their tastes on everyone else. So while anyone has the right to condemn Gervais's show, the online petition that was established in the hope of pressuring Netflix to censor the offending material was a disturbing assault on freedom of expression.

A simplistic reading of 'woke' versus 'anti-woke' comedy is that the former 'punches up' while the latter 'punches down', but such rules are incoherent when applied to an inherently anarchic medium. The assumption that comics such as Gervais are exploiting their privilege as performers in order to bully their audiences possibly originates in a lack of familiarity with the contemporary comedy circuit. Whenever commentators claim that 'right-wing comedy' is racist, homophobic or sexist, they invariably cite examples of long-dead comics such as Bernard Manning. But 'right-wing comedy' is a delicate shapeshifter; as a classification it is beyond useless because it is so often applied indiscriminately, with even left-wing comedians who take aim at the woke ideology so described. YouTuber Cenk Uygur, for example, claimed that Gervais was only making his jokes about gender identity to 'get Right-wing love' and a 'lucrative special', as though Netflix's commission was in any way dependent on the topics he chose to lampoon. Gervais is not right-wing, and it is laughable to suggest that he is attempting to woo a specific political demographic. Moreover, the most determined pushback against the pseudo-religion of gender identity has come from the left; most notably feminists and gay activists, who are rightly concerned about an ideology that is so explicitly hostile towards them. Uygur's attempt at mind-reading is par for the course. Much of the criticism levelled at subversive comedians tends to take the form of cod-psychological analysis. Musician Steve Albini launched into an extended variation on the genre, in which he explained that Gervais has morphed into his 'boorish, selfish, unaware' comedy persona because 'indulging the pretence eventually becomes so comfortable that it fuses with the person underneath'. What is actually happening is that Albini is making wild speculations about a total stranger's artistic choices on the basis of his own misinterpretations. In all such cases, the sheer certainty of these amateur psychoanalysts is striking.

Gervais is the latest in a long tradition of comedians successfully puncturing the pretensions of the powerful; he fulfils a similar role to the child in Hans Christian Andersen's story, innocently observing that the emperor is naked when everyone else is too cowardly to do so. It comes down to a question of how one perceives power. We have seen how the culture war is often misconceived as a conflict between left and right, with 'woke' aligned with the former and 'anti-woke' with the latter, but we have also seen that wokeness carries with it the kind of clout that transcends the political binary. So where does the real power reside? Is it with governments that can be voted out if the public tires of them? Or is it with activists who now have significant influence in all cultural, educational, political and corporate institutions, and who cannot be dislodged by means of any democratic process? So when journalist Sarah Manavis laments the 'tedious world of anti-woke comedy' in an article for the *New Statesman*, we can be fairly sure that the criticism is political. Does Manavis sincerely believe that these performers are simply trying to attack minorities and cause as much offence as possible? This is the least charitable of all suppositions, one born out of a fundamental misunderstanding of the art of comedy. It strikes me that many of those who dismiss stand-ups as 'anti-woke' are simply berating them for taking an anti-establishment stance and for believing that those in power ought to be ridiculed rather than eulogised.

The history of comedy tells us that its practitioners will always cause offence, so why do we continue to squabble over where the red lines ought to be drawn? No matter how many times the boundary is shifted, it will still end up being crossed. Personally, I have always relished those comedians who have no clear affiliations, who take aim in all directions and unsettle as much as they entertain. Aristophanes, the father of comedy, had no qualms when it came to firing salvos indiscriminately. He took no 'sides', and therefore had no need to restrict his targets. Men and women, old and young, aristocrats and slaves, fashionable and unfashionable, mortal and immortal: nobody was spared. He could laugh at the dignity of Socrates, the dramatic power of Euripides, the might of Cleon, the propriety of Aspasia. His audiences could never relax into the experience of scoffing at others, when at any point they too could become the subject of his ridicule. Today's comedy industry is not a hospitable environment for those who might emulate the freewheeling precedent of Aristophanes. Only a couple of decades ago, it was virtually unheard of for comedy promoters to take seriously complaints from audience members claiming to be 'offended'. Now, it takes little more than a few disgruntled social media posts for venues to panic and cancel bookings. But as woke comes to an end, the backlash is palpable. Many of us have grown weary of regime comedians who act as cheerleaders for powerful ideologues and substitute agitprop for jokes. Some anti-woke comedy may lack sophistication and subtlety, but maybe that's a small price to pay to redress the balance and re-energise the art form. If you want to smash taboos, sometimes you need a sledgehammer.

## The Hate Monster

In February 2018, I set up a monthly night in London called 'Comedy Unleashed' with the promoter Andy Shaw. Our intention was not to court controversy for its own sake, but rather to create a forum in which ideas could be explored freely, and where the priority would be to be make people laugh instead of delivering a homily. We wanted to encourage innovative and free-thinking acts, as well as cultivating a comedy-literate audience who understood that the art form cannot exist without the potential to cause offence. In short, we hoped to galvanise a new alternative comedy movement that would push back against the establishment.

The deranged reactions from regime comedians continue unabated to this day. When we announced that we would be embarking on a national Comedy Unleashed tour, one comic posted a series of warnings to other acts on social media. 'If you do that tour: you're a fucking scab,' he wrote. 'Comedians need to pick a side: I'm an anarchist.' At the time, the comedian in question was presenting his own show on BBC Radio 4, so his definition of 'anarchy' seems dubious at best. Later, when we announced a tour of Ireland, the predictable hysteria ensued. Activists complained to the venues, apparently not realising that purchasing tickets was in no way compulsory. One of the owners caved to the pressure and cancelled the show. As it transpired, we were able to secure another venue with twice the seating capacity. The publicity from the cancellation ensured that we quickly sold out, so if the activists had been hoping to limit our audience, they had gravely miscalculated.

In 2023, we decided to take our Comedy Unleashed night into the lair of the mainstream entertainment industry: the Edinburgh Festival Fringe. As the largest arts festival in the world, the fringe has become a kind of trade fair where acts can showcase their talent to producers and commissioners. Unsurprisingly, this month-long affair is domi-nated by the tenets of Critical Social Justice, not solely in the programming but also in the allocation of nominations and awards. When Nica Burns, the director of the Edinburgh Comedy Awards, announced the nominees that year, she made it clear that group identity was a major priority. 'For the first time ever,' she proudly declared, 'we have a Best Comedy Show shortlist where male-identifying comedians are in the minority with representation across gender and sexuality spectrums.' This kind of turgid and humourless ideological thinking is precisely what Comedy Unleashed was set up to oppose, and so it was hardly surprising that activists within and without the industry did not take kindly to the news that we would be infiltrating their hallowed domain.

One of the performers scheduled to appear at Comedy Unleashed in Edinburgh was Graham Linehan. Although widely regarded as one of the world's most accomplished comedy writers, having creating popular television sitcoms such as *Father Ted*, *Black Books* and *The IT Crowd*, he has been unable to work in the entertainment industry since 2018. The musical adaptation of *Father Ted* was halted by the rights owners, Hat Trick Productions, who had offered Linehan a substantial sum of money to have his name removed from the project. Linehan has become a pariah for holding a set of supposedly controversial beliefs: that human beings cannot change sex; that women deserve the right to single-sex spaces and the chance to compete fairly in sports; that feminists should not have to put up with rape and death threats for stating biological facts; and that gay and autistic children ought not to be medicalised and put onto a pathway to sterilisation. For blaspheming against the holy creed of genderism – one embraced wholesale by the gatekeepers of the comedy industry – he has been pilloried and ostracised. Linehan is living proof of the existence of cancel culture and how harshly heretics are treated in the current climate.

Given that we knew our show in Edinburgh would sell out, we did not advertise Linehan in advance, preferring instead to tease the audience with the prospect of a 'surprise cancelled comedian'. With the show just a few days away, we finally announced his appearance, and within twenty-four hours the venue, Leith Arches, had posted a statement on Instagram stating that they 'DO NOT suppprt [*sic*] this comedian, or his views and he WILL NOT be allowed to perform at our venue and is CANCELLED from Thursdays [*sic*] comedy show with immediate effect'. The grandstanding did not end there. 'We are an inclusive venue,' the statement continued, 'and will not allow such views to violate our space'. The venue later deleted the post and replaced it with one that was marginally more literate. Quite how a venue can claim to be 'inclusive' when it excludes performers who do not subscribe to the ideology of its staff is unclear. The show had completely sold out, and so we needed to find an alternative venue in haste. This was unfamiliar territory. In the Before Times, the prospect of an Edinburgh fringe show being cancelled due to offended activists would have been unthinkable. The fringe has always been known for controversial performances, but whereas the protests used to come from the Christian right, they now seem to be driven by the identitarian left. Same zealots, different garb.

By the time we had found a replacement venue, the cancellation of the Comedy Unleashed show had made headlines in the national press. As a result, the board responsible for the new venue held an emergency meeting and agreed that the performance could not go ahead. This second cancellation in a matter of days meant that there was little alternative. Graham Linehan and the other comedians on the bill – Bruce Devlin, Dominic Frisby and Alistair Williams – performed on a makeshift stage outside the Scottish Parliament. Outdoor comedy gigs are never ideal, and this one had been hastily arranged in only a few hours. By this point, it was more of a protest than a comedy show, with television cameras poised to record the entire event. 'Who says the punk spirit of the Edinburgh Fringe is dead?' asked an editorial in *Private Eye*. 'While some comics got their PRs to submit jokes in advance to the *Daily Telegraph* for a "best of the Fringe" list, others held an impromptu gig in front of the Scottish Parliament, using only a soapbox and a dodgy amplifier.'

The creative conditions in Scotland were soon to deteriorate further, with the introduction of the SNP's new Hate Crime and Public Order Bill. Like some kind of elaborate trolling exercise, the government had decreed that the new laws should come into effect on April Fools' Day 2024. It even included a clause that could see citizens prosecuted for words they have uttered in the privacy of their own homes. One could not help but be reminded of the speech delivered by William Pitt the Elder in the House of Commons in March 1763:

> The poorest man may in his cottage bid defiance to all the forces of the Crown. It may be frail, its roof may shake, the wind may blow through it, the storm may enter, the rain may enter, but the King of England cannot enter. All his force dares not cross the threshold of the ruined tenement.

Another section of the Scottish law covered the 'public performance of a play'. When questioned in Parliament about this aspect of the bill, its architect Humza Yousaf claimed that it would be feasible that far-right agitators might stage a theatrical performance in order to stir up hatred. Although I have never met any neo-Nazis myself, I think it is safe to assume that they are not fans of amateur dramatics.

Comedy was not immune. The front cover of the *Herald* on 19 March 2024 bore an insidious lead headline: 'Police told to target comics under new hate crime law'. The story concerned leaked materials from recent training sessions undertaken by the Scottish police. Officers were being instructed that actors and comedians whose performances were likely to 'stir up hatred' could be breaking the law. Naturally, supporters of the government scoffed at the suggestion that anyone would be arrested for simply expressing controversial opinions or telling jokes. Yet Tony Lenehan KC, president of the Faculty of Advocates Criminal Bar Association, claimed that 'performers and writers "must trust to luck" they are not prosecuted'. In addition, the police had promised to investigate all complaints. Of course, this was a gift to activists who had already pledged to exploit the new law to see J. K. Rowling prosecuted for the 'crime' of referring to a man as male (in this case the former *Big Brother* contestant India Willoughby). Solicitor Rajan Barot replied to Rowling on X, stating that any of her posts in which Willoughby was referred to as a man would be 'amenable to prosecution in Scotland' after 1 April. 'Start deleting!' he demanded.

Of course, the Scottish police have a history of authoritarian overreach. In February 2020, a freedom of information request by *The Times* revealed that forces were keeping a database of objectionable gags posted online. 'An offensive joke may be reported by someone,' a spokesperson said, 'but not amount to any criminality, so we would log this as a hate incident'. In 2016, a tweet by Police Scotland Greater Glasgow – also on April Fools' Day – claimed that officers would be knocking on doors if citizens posted anything that was hurtful, illegal, untrue, unkind or unnecessary. 'Think before you post', the tweet intoned menacingly, 'or you may receive a visit from us this weekend'. Evidently, whoever was running the account had failed to consider that if all unnecessary posts were deleted, social media would cease to exist.

Needless to say, the introduction of the new hate crime law in Scotland did not go as planned. In the first two days, the police were inundated with around four thousand complaints of 'hate speech', approximately sixty per hour. To make matters worse, the majority of these were about Humza Yousaf, the First Minister of Scotland. The complaints related to a speech he had delivered in Parliament on 10 June 2020 which was widely interpreted as a display of anti-white racism. Yousaf had complained about the high proportion of white people in senior government positions. 'Take my portfolio, for example,' he said. 'The Lord President is white, the Lord Justice Clerk is white, every High Court judge is white, the Lord Advocate is white, the Solicitor General is white, the chief constable is white, every deputy chief constable is white, every assistant chief constable is white, the head of the Law Society is white, the head of the Faculty of

Advocates is white and every prison governor is white.' In a country with a 96 per cent white population, this seemed like a curious objection to make. It had not escaped Yousaf's critics that the word 'white' had been repeatedly snarled in a manner likely to cause offence. Like most hate speech laws throughout Europe, perception of the 'victim' is the determining factor. As such, the police were in no position to deny the sincerity of the complaints.

In readiness for the new hate crime law, the Scottish government was busy making it as easy as possible for people to snoop on their fellow citizens. It set up 'hate crime reporting centres' including libraries, a mushroom farm in East Lothian, and a sex shop in Glasgow. In addition, the police created a mascot to promote their new law, a fluffy red 'hate monster' which resembled a reject from *Sesame Street*. A video featuring the hate monster was uploaded to the Scottish police website and YouTube channel, with the following voiceover in a Glaswegian accent:

> Ye might know this thing here. It's the Hate Monster. When yer feeling insecure, when ye feel angry, he'll be there, feeding off the emotions. Getting bigger and bigger till he's weighing ye doon. He'll make ye want tae have a go at somebody: a neighbour, somebody oan the street, oan a night oot, security guy oan the door, somebody in the chippy, yer taxi driver. He'll make ye want tae vent yer anger just cause folk look or act different fae you. The Hate Monster wants ye tae feel that you need to show you're better than them. Then before ye know it, ye've committed a hate crime.

The video ended with the advice: 'Don't feed the Hate Monster'. Given this wincingly patronising tone and the cartoonish design of the character, it defies belief that it was aimed at an adult population. Many critics have noted a trend in SNP politics of treating citizens as children; the party's ingrained authoritarian streak has meant that it sees itself in a specifically parental role.

To coincide with the new hate speech law in Scotland, we organised a special Comedy Unleashed show in Edinburgh for April Fools' Day. Tickets quickly sold out, but inevitably we were to face some hurdles. Four days before the show, we received an email from the venue – a cabaret bar called Coco Boho – informing us that after 'all the findings online', the managing director had 'decided this is not acceptable for our venue to host'. One wonders what these 'findings' were; this was simply a group of comedians intending to tell jokes to a paying audience. Notwithstanding the efforts of these pettifogging authoritarians, we were able to find another venue – the Hibernian Football Supporters' Club – and the show went ahead. The Hate Monster even made an appearance; that is to say, I quickly cobbled together a script with the writer Martin Gourlay which was then performed by comedian Jonathan Kogan in a downy orange outfit. Had the police decided to intervene, it was just possible that the Hate Monster himself would be arrested under the legislation that he himself had promoted. This ultimate irony would have almost been worth the inconvenience of a night in the cells.

Benevolent rulers tolerate their clowns; tyrants do not. When King Lear demands that his Fool exercise some restraint in his brutally honest barbs, he does so in the form of a threat. 'Take heed, sirrah – the whip.' The Fool is having none of it. 'Truth's a dog must to kennel', he says. 'He must be whipped out when the Lady Brach may stand by th' fire and stink.' So while the truth-telling dog is thrown outdoors, the Lady Brach, the bitch of flattery, can warm herself by the fire, her stench permeating the entire household. We can be sure that woke has come to an end once clowns no longer fear the whip. There is little purpose to a jester who acts as a propagandist for the king. More than ever, we need the jangling bells of his coxcomb to break the earnest silence of the court.

# 10

# Truth or Illusion

---

## 'The Immortal Part of Myself'

I am at the home of a psychopath. Here at the easternmost point of the island of Capri, the ancient ruins of the Villa Jovis still cling to the summit of the mountain. This was the former residence of the Emperor Tiberius, who retired here for the last decade of his life in order to indulge in what John Milton in *Paradise Regained* (1671) described as 'his horrid lusts'. He conducted wild orgies for his nymphs and catamites. He forced children to swim between his thighs, calling them his 'little fish'. He raped two brothers and broke their legs when they complained. He tortured and murdered anyone who displeased him.

Capri is one of my favourite writing retreats, and I am fond of taking my laptop to the remotest nooks of the island so that I can work in peace. Today, a local man has directed me to Il Salto, the precipice from which countless individuals threw themselves to their deaths at the behest of this depraved emperor. Tiberius even had a runway constructed for his victims to ensure that the spectacle was as entertaining as possible. It makes me a little queasy to look down the thousand-foot sheer drop, and queasier still to imagine the men in boats who used to wait below for any survivors so they could pummel them to death with oars. That these stories are unlikely to be true is beside the point. Tiberius's reputation has done wonders for the tourist trade here on Capri. Up until relatively recently, locals would gleefully regale visitors with tales of the beast who ruled the Roman empire from this secluded spot. The historians Suetonius and Tacitus started the rumours and, with the help of later generations of sensationalists, established a tradition that was to persist for almost two millennia.

All of which serves as a reminder that reputations can be constructed and sustained on the flimsiest of foundations. Suetonius and Tacitus were writing almost a century after the emperor's death, and many of their lurid stories were doubtless echoes of those circulated by his most spiteful enemies. It has even been suggested that later historians were happy to believe the very worst of Tiberius because his time on Capri coincided with Christ's crucifixion. In any case, running away to a distant island when you're meant to be ruling an empire is bound to set tongues flapping. Maybe it's simply a matter of prurience. Who can deny that the more lascivious and outlandish acts of the Roman emperors are by far the most memorable? One thinks immediately of Caligula having sex with his siblings and appointing his horse as consul. Or Nero murdering his own mother, and taking a castrated slave for his bride, naming him after the wife he had kicked to death. For all their horror, who doesn't feel cheated when such tales turn out to be false?

Our reputations are changelings: protean shades of other people's imaginations. More often than not, they are birthed from a combination of uninformed prejudice and wishful thinking. And we should be in no doubt that in our online age, when lies are disseminated at lightning speed and casual defamation has become the activist's principal strategy, reputations are harder to heal once tarnished. I am tempted to feel pity for future historians. Quite how they will be expected to wade through endless reams of emails, texts and other digital materials – an infinitude of conflicting narratives and individual 'truths' – really is beyond me. At least when there is a dearth of primary sources it is possible to piggyback onto a firm conclusion. 'Suetonius said . . .' has a satisfactory and definitive air, but only because there are so few of his contemporary voices available to contradict him.

As the culture war rumbles on towards its next phase, and I have found myself ostracised by former friends from the Before Times, I have learned that reputation is invariably a form of fiction. Not, as Othello would have it, 'the immortal part of myself'. One such friend used to complain endlessly about a certain conservative commentator, asserting that he was a mendacious hatemonger whose every action was motivated by contempt for marginalised communities. These ideas were so frequently repeated in conversation, and confirmed by others within our circle, that I had no doubt they must be true. Imagine my confusion, then, when I eventually became well acquainted with this man, and found him to be both generous and empathetic. It's like meeting Beelzebub and finding that he has been secretly baking cupcakes for the poor.

The same sense of bewilderment has struck me whenever I have happened upon bad-faith critics attempting to summarise my views. I have been variously described as 'far right', 'bigoted', 'racist', 'sexist', and even 'homophobic'. Of course, I would not expect total strangers to know my mind but, given that my actual opinions are freely available to anyone with a search engine, it does feel odd to be so wildly mischaracterised. I am not alone in this. That false narratives can be more powerful than reality is, of course, the reason why our opponents so readily resort to distortions and smears. A colleague recently alerted me to one of the more bizarre hit pieces that has been written about me in an online gossip magazine. The strategy was at least novel: the writer had contacted former students from my time as a teacher in order to trawl for unflattering anecdotes. According to one account, I had sent a pupil out of the classroom because he dared to disagree with me about the use of metaphorical language in John Steinbeck's *Of Mice and Men* (1937). But perhaps funnier than the story itself is that the author of this article was gulled into repeating it, as though it could possibly be authentic. It is a reminder that reputations are often cultivated by those who must first suspend their critical faculties. This kind of nonsense is harmless enough, of course. It falls far short of defamation and, as drag artist RuPaul so deftly put it: 'What other people think of me is none of my business.'

For all that, more serious attacks on people's reputations can be devastating. A number of years ago, I lost a friend to cancer after he had been falsely accused of sexual assault. In his final days he told me that he had no doubt that the years of intense anxiety following the trial had exacerbated his illness. The source of his distress wasn't even so much the initial accusation, which was easily disproved in court, but rather the gossip that continued to reverberate and the loved ones who no longer picked up the phone. Plato's conviction that the just life is more important than how one is perceived or treated, a reaction to the Athenian state's execution of Socrates, means little to the scapegoated and the ostracised.

In the past, I have often made the mistake of assuming the worst of my detractors, simply because a scurrilous lie has seemed more appealing than a complicated truth. Few of us who have been dragged into the deranging ideological skirmishes of the woke era will have avoided making these mistakes, but I like to think that it is still possible to maintain a healthy scepticism when it comes to the reputations of those we barely know. No doubt it is hopelessly optimistic to assume that this approach will become the default. Our brains are hardwired to take mental shortcuts – known as heuristics – and we are generally more willing to believe the worst of others than make the effort to consider that we may have been misinformed. Worse still, the inherent appeal of scandalous and titillating tales means they will be propagated at an accelerated rate, so that even outright lies can quickly become received wisdom. We tend to accept that there is 'no smoke without fire', when more often than not it's just a few troublemakers with a dry ice machine.

So perhaps we ought to give Tiberius the benefit of the doubt. In that spirit, let us consider one of Suetonius's more flattering accounts. While living on the island of Rhodes, Tiberius remarked that he ought to visit all the sick people in the town. His servants assumed that this was some kind of decree, and the local invalids were hastily summoned. Rather than turn them away, Tiberius took the time to speak to each one and apologise for the misunderstanding. This story may not satisfy our appetite for murder and depravity, but at least it might be true.

## Smear Campaigns

Fantasies can be a source of comfort. In Edward Albee's landmark play *Who's Afraid of Virginia Woolf?* (1962), the childless married couple George and Martha weave an elaborate story – which they share between themselves and their unsuspecting houseguests – about their teenage son who is due to return home for his birthday. As the night rolls on, and improbable quantities of alcoholic drinks are imbibed, they are eventually forced to confront reality. 'Truth or illusion,' says Martha, 'you don't know the difference.' 'No', replies George, 'but we must carry on as though we did.'

As we have seen, defamation has become one of the key tactics of culture warriors of all stripes. For the authoritarian, the dissemination of falsehood is a sign of moral strength if it means the silencing of one's opponents. Looking back on these years when woke prevailed, we see an elaborate struggle between those who value truth and those who value fantasy. I have spoken to activists so wedded to their false perceptions that it seems they would renounce gravity if it might help their cause. They perceive no inherent benefit to either reality or fiction; these are simply competing narratives in a broader ideological campaign. Specifically, we repeatedly see three traits on display: the tone of pharisaic certainty even when declaring falsehoods, the conviction that it is possible to intuit the private thoughts of others, and a complete disregard for the concept of defamation.

I will focus for now on the last of these traits. Throughout this book I have argued that the culture war has largely been waged through the manipulation and misapplication of language. Many activists are explicit about their refusal to debate their ideas – for the simple reason that they would collapse under scrutiny – and one of the ways this can be achieved is to destabilise shared definitions of words. In their world, libel simply cannot exist, because the meaning of language has become a purely subjective matter. For example, the term 'racism' is generally understood to mean hatred or prejudice based on race, but for intersectional activists 'racism' is an equation: prejudice plus power. We have reached the point at which these labels are no longer taken seriously. Whenever most of us come across accusations of 'racism' on social media, the default assumption must now be that they are unfounded. This has provided succour for the far right by promoting the illusion that their views are widespread. It has also made it difficult to identify genuine racists because the very concept has been downgraded to an indiscriminate term of abuse.

Casual libel is now so commonplace that the consequences are no longer feared, even by media outlets. In March 2022, the official Twitter account of Newstalk FM, an Irish radio station with over a quarter of a million followers, made the plainly false assertion that J. K. Rowling has 'a long history of opposing rights for trans people'. In July 2020, a children's news website called *The Day* issued an apology to Rowling and pledged to make a monetary contribution to a charity of her choosing after falsely asserting that she 'harmed' people who identify as transgender. It has apparently been forgotten that damaging allegations of this kind often lead to successful lawsuits. The comedian Frankie Boyle famously won over £50,000 in damages when the *Mirror* branded him a 'racist' in 2012. In March 2022, the *Telegraph* paid out more than £40,000 to Laura Murray, a former aide to Labour leader Jeremy Corbyn, for describing her as an 'anti-Jewish racist'. In legal terms, such statements simply do not fall within the scope of 'personal opinion'.

One of the most extraordinary cases of this nature took place in April 2022, when a court in Ohio rejected an appeal by Oberlin College after members of staff participated in a smear campaign against Gibson's Bakery, falsely and repeatedly stating that the local business was run by racists. As a result, the college was ordered to pay $25 million in punitive damages and a further $6 million in legal fees to the bakery, although its two owners died before the case was resolved. In November 2016, a black student had been apprehended in the act of shoplifting two bottles of wine from the store. After the incident, students at Oberlin accused the bakery of being a 'racist establishment' with a 'long account of racial profiling', even though such claims were groundless and the thief had admitted to his crime. In what struck many as a disingenuous interview with CBS News, the college president Carmen Twillie Ambar argued that Oberlin should not be 'held liable for the speech of students', omitting the fact that college staff had also been involved in the smear campaign. Witnesses confirmed that Meredith Raimondo, the vice president and dean of students, had distributed flyers which repeated the libel, and actively participated in the protests. She even ordered the college cafeteria to stop buying products from the bakery in an effort to coerce them into dropping the shoplifting charges. Students were excused from classes to attend the protests, refreshments were provided by college officials, and photocopies of the flyers were made by Oberlin's administration office. All of which is perhaps to be expected from a college which has garnered a reputation as a bastion of wokeness. When the academic and philosopher Christina Hoff Sommers gave a talk at Oberlin, students were so upset by her opinions that they retreated *en masse* to a 'safe room' with a therapy dog.

Whenever the targets of libel fight back through the courts, they are invariably accused of attempting to curtail free speech. This is a common misapprehension, although an understandable one. Many free speech advocates oppose the very concept of libel on the grounds that it has often been exploited by powerful individuals hoping to silence their critics. But when a person is publicly defamed, and their reputation or income is damaged as a result, he or she has every right to seek recompense. Our freedom of speech is in no way violated by laws against libel, fraud, perjury, blackmail or espionage. In such instances, speech is not the crime itself but the mechanism by which it has been committed. The charge of 'racism' is one of the most potentially damaging in our current climate, and so it has become the go-to slur for those looking for a quick and easy method of discrediting their political opponents and ruining their lives. On principle, such bullies ought to be opposed, and civil action against libellous statements is one way in which this can be achieved.

The widespread ignorance of defamation laws would not be such a problem were it confined to the online realm. Unfortunately, the woke supremacy has seen this foolish disregard exhibited more and more by figures of authority in our major cultural and political institutions. The warped logic and behavioural customs of social media have somehow seeped out into the real world, undermining public discourse and the possibility of good faith discussion. It remains to be seen whether the cautionary tale of Gibson's Bakery will give activists pause before belching out their unsubstantiated allegations in the future. They have become so accustomed to getting their way that they now feel entitled to smear others at will. But while litigation is best considered a last resort, it is sometimes a necessary means by which Davids can stand up to their Goliaths.

## Digital Pitchforks

We have seen how the woke era has been dominated by various factions united by common goals, biases and prejudices. If we were to pick one phrase to describe the key shared characteristic of culture warriors on the left and the right that explains the insanity of recent years, we could do a lot worse than 'identitarian collectivism'. The illiberal left and the authoritarian right both share this habitual inclination towards collective thinking. This can be seen by the way that each of these groups displays a tendency to seek out vindication through the online declarations of the likeminded. Those of us who refuse to embrace ideology or settle into a tribe are permanently vulnerable to attack, because our individual values will never tally entirely with any preexisting framework. One of the benefits of my own stubborn and idiotic addiction to social media has been a clear confirmation that I am at least correct on this one issue. My failure to appease any given group has meant that I am routinely 'dogpiled' online, even to the extent that I find my name suddenly 'trending', and it has not escaped my attention that the swarm can emerge from any direction.

A few examples will illustrate the point. Following an article I wrote in June 2023 for the *Daily Mail* outlining my reservations about the 'Progress Pride' flag, I experienced days of trans activists calling me a 'homophobe' and Christian fundamentalists calling me a 'degenerate' and a 'sodomite'. On other occasions, I've had left-wing activists smear me as 'racist' for taking issue with Critical Race Theory, and I've had white nationalists raging against my vocal opposition to racism. I've had thousands of indistinguishable clones with pronouns in their bios declaring that I am a Nazi. I've even had one former friend write long posts on Facebook about how I'm part of a covert communist organisation that controls the government. I suppose that's marginally more feasible than being a homophobic sodomite.

Many of us will have experienced something similar on X, or Twitter as it was once known. Something about the platform has the effect of curdling the sweetest Dr Jekylls into the most repugnant of Mr Hydes. It really should be preceded with a warning: '*Lasciate ogne speranza, voi ch'intrate.*' One particularly memorable pile-on took place when a cluster of angry Twitter users started imagining that I had opposed their petition for a third series of a gay pirate television show called *Our Flag Means Death*. I had never heard of the show, and still haven't seen it, but these strangers were adamant that I was somehow opposed to its continuation. This pile-on was genuinely surreal, and it was quite amusing to be bombarded for most of the day with furious messages accompanied with Jolly Roger emojis. It just goes to show that the versions of Andrew Doyle that exist in the heads of social media users are wide and varied, and often contradictory. If only I were that complex. The boring truth is that my views are relatively uncontroversial, and I'm not by nature either combative or provocative. It would never occur to me to post abuse online about a total stranger, which is perhaps why I find it so interesting when I'm on the receiving end of it. But this instinct for curiosity is, of course, self-destructive. Instead of putting down my smartphone, I read every comment. I am transfixed by mass displays of hostility and the capacity of human beings to dispense with empathy when gathered in mobs. If an angry horde were to come to my house with torches and pitchforks, I'd be too fascinated to flee.

As our society grows out of the temporary infancy of woke, we will need to reckon with the question of how we should argue with those who are incapable of argumentation. When someone brays insults online, or mischaracterises another person's views, or generally cannot engage in good faith, the block function is the only salvation. Inevitably, blocking on social media as a free speech advocate will lead to accusations of hypocrisy from those who do not understand the concept. In a surreal moment, my blocking of abusive trolls on X was actually covered in the national press. 'Confusion as GB News presenter who champions "free speech" blocks critics', ran the headline in the *Metro*. I have never blocked anyone for polite criticism as it would defeat the purpose of maintaining a presence on a public platform but, even if I had, refusing to engage with someone is not a form of censorship. Helen Pluckrose and James Lindsay have called this 'the fallacy of demanding to be heard'. If you have ever received an unwelcome phone call and hung up, you have not impinged on the caller's rights. If you choose not to read my books, I cannot claim to have been censored. If you block someone on social media, all it means is that you are not interested in what they have to say. I have been blocked by hundreds of people online and, although this clearly reflects poorly on their taste and judgement, my freedom of speech remains intact. A good rule of thumb is to block anyone who throws insults, post threats or libel, assumes bad faith, claims to know the secret motivations of others, or believes that blocking is a threat to free speech. Applying these standards will efficiently cleanse one's timeline of the soft-witted and the banal. Most clever adages end up being attributed to Mark Twain whether he wrote them or not, and this one is no exception: 'Never wrestle with a pig; you just get dirty and the pig enjoys it.'

There is something grimly fascinating about the way in which generally cordial and level-headed people behave as soon as they are within reach of a smartphone. The metamorphosis is akin to road rage, where the most timid of grandmothers might suddenly launch into an expletive-ridden tirade against the meekest occupant of a nearby Volvo. Social media dogpiling, like all forms of collective hysteria, is often messy and difficult to elucidate. There is no clear narrative, but rather multiple threads featuring both firebrands and peacemakers, a bewildering cacophony of voices shouting over each other, seizing on any misspoken phrase and amplifying it for a fresh wave of invective and bile. It appeals to the very basest of human instincts, and no doubt the anonymity stimulates the deindividuation and herd behaviour. Everyone involved is degraded; the perpetrators as much as their targets. Social media is a wilderness of tigers at the best of times, but to be the focus of this kind of onslaught is confounding.

And when it originates from supposed 'allies', it is more confounding than ever. In February 2024, I was subjected to an intense pile-on from hundreds of gender-critical feminists: those whose cause I wholeheartedly support. This particular bombardment resulted in my decision to temporarily deactivate my account, to the glee of my critics and trans activists alike. Soon afterwards, I was contacted by gender-critical friends who explained that there was a kind of civil war opening up within the movement and that many of them were exasperated at the self-sabotaging intolerance of a small minority. We are dealing yet again with purity spirals, whereby members of any given community seek to destroy anyone who does not conform to every single aspect of their worldview, even if it means that the cause is fatally undermined. This gender-critical civil war, ongoing even now while woke is dying, is being waged by a small but intimidating minority who maintain that any slight point of disagreement is a form of heresy, that language has the capacity to shape reality, and that those found guilty of wrongspeak ought to be publicly shamed and alienated. In all of this, they are indistinguishable from the gender ideologues they claim to oppose. This civil war is, of course, a boon to the high priests of genderism and their failing campaign to reorganise society around their metaphysical beliefs. Given that the stakes are so high, not least for women, children and gay people, it might be worth considering what this in-fighting is all about and how it might be avoided as wokeness finally slumps into oblivion.

First, the context. The initial rumblings were heard after the journalist Janice Turner published an interview with Debbie Hayton, author of the memoir *Transsexual Apostate* (2024). Throughout her piece, Turner referred to Hayton with female pronouns. Turner clarified her reasoning:

> The issue of pronouns is becoming absolutist on *both* sides. Stonewall demands even bearded rapists be called 'she', GC ultras refuse to call any trans woman 'she'. I reject both positions. I never call male sex offenders she/her. But I will be courteous to those who respect women.

For many, the issue of pronouns has become a red line in the gender wars, and Turner's efforts at compromise are seen not only as wrongheaded, but traitorous. It is widely held that trans-identifying individuals must never be described as anything other than their true biological sex, and cries of 'hold the line' are often heard by those who, following Turner's statement, now proudly claim the term 'ultra' for themselves. Not only are the likes of Turner demonised for attempting to find a middle ground, but they are also told that they have been 'groomed' by the men who are insisting that other people's language must be modified in deference to their sense of self. This tactic, of suggesting that an opposing view is the result of a delusion, is common to all ideological movements. Marxist theorists have often dismissed unbelievers as suffering from 'false consciousness'. Similarly, many trans activists insist that those of us who believe that sex is immutable have been 'radicalised online'. Yet this is also the identical approach of those gender-critical campaigners who deny the individual agency of their comrades and claim they are the victims of 'grooming'. I suppose it is easier to explain away disagreement as the product of some collective fantasy rather than accept that not everyone thinks the same way as you.

The inevitable pyroclasm following Turner's piece provided the backdrop to my own interview with Hayton on my show *Free Speech Nation*. As an admitted autogynephile – a heterosexual man who presents as a woman out of an erotic attraction to himself – Hayton is something of a hate figure for many in the movement. By conducting this interview, I was deemed guilty of 'enabling' and 'promoting perversion', in spite of Hayton's gender-critical beliefs. After the interview had aired, initial feedback was cordial and productive: many feminists were pleased that I had listened to their concerns and asked questions about the use of toilets, single-sex spaces, and a schools guidance policy that Hayton had co-authored for the teachers' union NASUWT in 2017. There were also many critical comments, which I welcomed and took seriously.

The first signs of trouble occurred when one of my critics began repeatedly railing against 'the gays' in her posts. She complained that

I had used the pronoun 'her' in relation to Hayton in one of the introductory pieces to camera; as it happens, this was simply because the producer had written it that way in the autocue. I explained that I use pronouns to denote biological sex, and that I consider it irresponsible and unethical for journalists to use pronouns according to 'gender identity' in their reporting (see Chapter 6). Journalists have an obligation to the truth, and so pronouns in the media should always be used according to sex, and oxymoronic phrases such as 'her penis' are to be avoided. I also said that when it comes to personal friends who identify as the opposite sex, I have in the distant past occasionally adopted their preferred pronouns and names. I have done this to avoid causing needless distress, not to signal that I share their belief-system. It would be like bowing my head for a prayer at a friend's family meal, even if I didn't believe in their particular god. When it comes to language in one's private life, I consider this very much a matter of individual choice. Nobody has the right to compel anyone else's speech.

To provide a step-by-step account of how these online dogfights escalate is rather like outlining the plot of a particularly complicated farce. Matters began to deteriorate when one of my traducers claimed that I lacked credibility and integrity because I adhere to 'a deranged homophobic, sexist ideology', even though I have consistently and outspokenly opposed it over many years on television, radio, in public debates and in my articles and books. In the fog of social media combat, my denials were taken as evidence of my deceptive nature. From there, matters escalated at a dizzying rate. If a liar, why not a misogynist? That was the inevitable next stage. The accusation came so often that I started having to block accounts; a course of action which, in turn, was taken as proof of misogyny. Before long, the stakes had been raised from 'liar' to 'misogynist' to 'grifter'. Many of my detractors took the view that my homosexuality was the issue. One self-declared feminist confessed to being 'a raging homophobe' and wrote: 'I don't like gay men anymore. I think most of them are miso[gynist] pieces of shhh [*sic*] that mock women and platform AGPs.' Another was more direct: 'The gays are definitely to blame as well. First off, sticking a penis inside a man's asshole is unhealthy. If you can't admit this then you are part of the problem.' Another went with 'I hate men in general', and then clarified her misandry in an oddly specific way: 'Gay *men*. Straight *men*. White *men*. Black *men*. All *men*. I don't discriminate. I view you all with equal amounts of derision.' At this point, there was absolutely nothing to be gained from engaging further. The mob had developed a collective mind and purpose of its own, like ants spiralling around a discarded honey cake. As new faces joined the fray, I could see them almost instantaneously becoming assimilated, and before long they were chanting the same mantras and misconceptions.

Nor was this simply a case of anonymous trolls. One of the most vicious and unprovoked attacks came from a legal scholar with a large online following, which inevitably galvanised dozens of similar responses from her minions. Having never interacted with me before, and knowing nothing whatsoever about me, this apparently telepathic individual thought it was prudent to post the following message: 'I simply do not trust you because you lie about a man's sex to pander to his feelings and his sexual fetish. What else are you ready to do for men knowing you harm women and children?' What might I have said that could have stirred such unhinged assumptions? This unsettling combination of factual inaccuracy and unlimited self-certainty is a feature of woke discourse, but here it was emerging from the supposedly anti-woke gender-critical sphere.

It is futile to attempt to understand the online mob, or its generalised failure to distinguish between abuse and legitimate criticism. The podcaster Andrew Gold has described the experience of being targeted by hundreds of strangers all at once.

Being the subject of one of these Twitter storms makes you feel like you're drowning or putting out fires. Everything you say is taken out of context and used as further evidence of your moral impurity. In terms of evolutionary biology, if 100 people turned on you in such a way in tribal times, you'd be kicked out and would likely die. So it's hard to shake the bad vibes. I can't imagine wanting to do that to someone – wanting to extrapolate the worst possible meaning from somebody's words to see them ousted from the tribe. These people must be very sad indeed.

Perhaps the abuse itself is not the chief reason why internet pile-ons have such a psychologically destabilising effect. It seems more likely that the reason why so many people who have been subjected to co-ordinated online attacks suffer from mental health problems as a result is due to the sensation of being misrepresented on a grand scale, with no possibility of redress. We all have an innate aversion to injustice, and trying to reason with the formicating legions of cyberspace is rather like attempting to persuade the tide to retreat. My experiences had begun with one woman griping about 'the gays' and ended hours later with complete strangers on my timeline discussing why gay men are so vile, invariably misogynistic, and have a tendency towards paedophilia, the most repugnant and enduring prejudice of them all. By the time someone posted an audio recording of one of my detractors saying that she would enjoy murdering gay men, I was out.

Despite the onslaught, I should emphasise that this kind of sociopathic behaviour is far from typical in the gender-critical movement. Yes, there exists a small contingent who despise homosexuals and seek to bully and harass anyone who takes a different view. They are identitarian collectivists who take the view that it is justifiable to vilify all gay men due to the bad behaviour of a few, or to assume that any criticism of individual women is evidence of 'misogyny', or that women are saintly creatures who are incapable of dehumanising or authoritarian behaviour, even when their own conduct disproves the point. The concept of judging each individual on his or her own merits and actions, irrespective of sex, race or any other immutable characteristic, is alien to them. But this is most definitely not the norm, and the overwhelming majority of women I have encountered in this fight have been generous, compassionate and courageous in the face of threats and wholly unfounded accusations of 'hate' and 'transphobia'. It is only thanks to their hard work that we have seen a recent sea-change in public understanding of the dangers of this ideology.

Inevitably, transgender activists noticed the abuse I was receiving and were soon pirouetting with glee. One of them emailed me directly: 'I don't want to say "I told you so" but . . . ha.' Many have since boasted on social media that the attacks were karma for my stupidity in associating with this brood of reactionaries. They have shared screenshots of the worst tweets and taken this as confirmation of what they have been alleging all along: that the gender-critical movement is a front for far-right homophobes. While this conclusion is nonsense, there is certainly a dark element within gender-critical circles. One prominent feminist journalist routinely targets gay men by posting images of bundles of sticks under their social media posts. This imagery is a not-so-subtle method of calling them 'faggots' and evading online bans. When I criticised this behaviour, feminists of the more tribalistic nature argued that the problem here was not that such a high-profile figure was arbitrarily abusing gay strangers, but that I had had the temerity to point it out. Such is the brain-softening impact of identitarian collectivism.

As we enter what might be the final phase of the culture war, with gender identity ideology being challenged openly in the highest courts, we are seeing LGBTQIA+ crusaders becoming more ferocious in their rhetoric and more defamatory in their slurs. At the same time, a handful of gender-critical activists and their self-proclaimed 'allies' are assuming more extreme positions and lashing out at those they deem guilty of heresy. Purity spirals are not specific to any one cause. The impulse to defame rather than discuss is essentially authoritarian, and it is common to all political and ideological clans. This approach only serves to further entrench viewpoints and stymie discussion, particularly when the mudslingers are insisting that they are merely offering their own version of criticism. Those whose first instinct is to throw insults are not interested in edging nearer to the truth of any given matter, but are instead attempting to shame their opponents into silence, or through a process of public intimidation use them as an example to others to keep schtum. And while such people are not censoring anyone by being abusive, they are certainly employing the tactics of the playground bully to assert their own dominance. Abuse, in other words, can often be an attempt at coercion.

For further evidence of this tendency within the bullying fringe of the gender-critical movement, one need look no further than the anonymous creation of the 'Troon Index' in December 2024. 'Troon' is a derogatory term for those who consider themselves to be transgender, and this site included profiles of almost five hundred so identified. It conflated law-abiding citizens with registered sex offenders, drawing no distinction whatsoever between either group. Names and photographs were published, and those listed were referred to as 'creatures', 'perverts', 'filth', 'sex deceptionists', and other similarly degrading terms. While the creator of the website did not reveal his or her identity, the 'Troon Index' was publicised approvingly by numerous gender-critical accounts online. This was not, as some later scrabbled to claim, a project intended to safeguard women from predators – if that were the case, the list would be limited to those who have criminal convictions – but rather a patent attempt to intimidate and publicly shame those who are perceived as depraved. Dr Michael Foran, a lecturer in Law at Glasgow University, who has himself been subjected to online dogpiles from the gender-critical fringe, explained how the 'Troon Index' was an exercise in dehumanisation, defining it as 'the inferential alienation of human rights from a group, usually accompanied by a disgust response based on stereotypes of deviance, most insidious when there is a genuine underlying heightened risk associated with the group that is totalised to all members'. As he pointed out, the list was 'very likely illegal for a whole host of reasons, from defamation to criminal harassment. It's not activism. It's abuse.'

Those who know anything about the history of witch hunts will recognise the tactic. It is difficult to think of an authoritarian regime that has not at some point drawn up lists of thought criminals. Consider the proscriptions of the dictator Sulla during the Roman Republic, or Robespierre's list of 'enemies of the revolution' in the Reign of Terror, or the Soviet Union purges of 'counter-revolutionaries' under Stalin. In *The Gulag Archipelago*, Alexandr Solzhenitsyn recalls how 'lists of names prepared up above, or an initial suspicion, or a denunciation by an informer, or any anonymous denunciation, were all that was needed to bring about the arrest of the suspect, followed by the inevitable formal charge'. The Red Scare under Senator Joseph McCarthy is still within living memory and, although I do not claim that the 'Troon Index' ranks among these outrages, it is indubitably motivated by the same authoritarian impulse.

In all of this, we have seen a notable deviation from bedrock feminist principles in the name of women's rights. Feminist philosopher Dr Jane Clare Jones has observed that 'what is happening now in the gender-critical community is the steady replacement of arguments based on material sex–class analysis with a politics of "woman-identity"'. The arguments we have seen from the gender-critical fringe implying that cross-dressing ought to be criminalised, or that men should not stray from their traditional roles in society, effectively reduce the characteristic of being female from an incontestable biological fact to an identity category. In this, the gender-critical fringe is the philosophical mirror image of the genderists they are reacting against. This is bad news for progressive feminists. As J. K. Rowling has noted, 'left-wing feminists are being lumped together with people whose attitude towards gender expression is as regressive as that of hardened trans activists'. One prominent women's rights campaigner has gone so far as to argue that open expressions of disgust towards cross-dressing men is a valuable form of 'social control of toxic behaviors that are harmful to healthy community relationships', describing it as a form of 'social hygiene', an undeniably ghoulish phrase. As Jones notes:

> People seem to have forgotten that the original gender-critical point was that men who wear women's clothes, or use women's names, or even take she/her pronouns, are not, thereby, made female, because being female is a material fact distinct from all the social trappings of 'woman-identity.' Women, we said repeatedly, are not an idea one can simply identify with. Women are no more or less than adult female people. And being female is not a thing that can be attacked, and not a thing that needs to be defended. It simply is. What needs to be defended is the recognition of female people, or women, as a class in law, the organization of public services and public policy on the basis of sex, and the right of women to organize and speak politically as a sex class. That is defending women's material class interests, not defending womanhood.

Just as many 'anti-woke' commentators have embraced their own kind of identity politics, so too have some of the more reactionary elements of the gender-critical movement. When reality television celebrity Josh Seiter attempts to goad his critics by stating that 'It should be illegal to be trans', he is echoing a belief authentically held by a handful of women's rights campaigners who would like to see their rights preserved at the expense of the rights of others.

Again, the liberal system affords us the most elegant solution. It should be possible to disagree without hurling abuse or defaming one's opponents. It should be possible to challenge gender identity ideology without dehumanising everyone who identifies as trans. Gender-critical activists who routinely smear all trans people as predators or perverts are collectivists whose mentality is in tandem with that of the woke. Some campaigners, such as Let Women Speak founder Kellie-Jay Keen, have called for active discrimination in housing and employment for trans-identified people. Others have defended the creation of databases such as the 'Troon Index' on the grounds that trans rights activists have made similar lists of 'TERFs'. The idea that one form of authoritarianism justifies another is the kind of *tu quoque* fallacy that even young children soon learn to avoid. Thankfully, the overwhelming majority of gender-critical campaigners recognised this list-making for the self-discrediting strategy that it is, and the 'Troon Index' was eventually taken down.

If I was mawkish enough to suggest a moral to this story, it would be this: talk to people, but not to mobs. The fate of Cinna the poet in Shakespeare's *Julius Caesar* (c. 1599) offers a salutary lesson in the frenzy of crowds. Having been galvanised into action by Mark Antony's spectacularly manipulative speech, the plebeians riot and seek revenge against Caesar's assassins. They run into Cinna, who happens to share the same name as one of the killers. 'Tear him to pieces!' they cry. Cinna explains that he has been misidentified. He is a poet, not a conspirator, and is on his way to Caesar's funeral 'as a friend'. But to the rabid crowd, this is a trivial detail. 'Tear him for his bad verses,' they cry, 'tear him for his bad verses!' Once assimilated into a righteous mob, we surrender our individuality and ability to think. The truth becomes irrelevant. A target is a target, and really anyone will suffice to satiate our bloodlust. It's as good a reason as any to avoid becoming one of the crowd.

Authoritarianism is always reprehensible, no matter where it originates or what form it takes. It is incumbent upon us to challenge this kind of intolerance even when it emerges from those who share our views. Those gender-critical activists who have made excuses for the inexcusable behaviour of their allies have allowed tribal loyalty to overcome their values. Worse still, their dishonest and underhand tactics simply bring the cause into disrepute, needlessly providing ammunition to the gender ideologues just at the point at which they seem to be losing their culture war. No doubt members of the extreme gender-critical fringe will claim that I have no right to criticise them in this way because I am male. Unfortunately for them, I am not constrained by the rules of their collectivist cult, I have no intention of kowtowing to their increasingly unhinged demands, and I have little patience for those who attempt to browbeat dissenters into silence. These faceless cry-bullies are free to rant away in their insular little bubbles; the rest of us would be far better off ignoring their cacophonous howls.

## The Legitimation Crisis

With most of the world's information only a click away, one would have assumed that ours would be the most enlightened generation in human history. We may have lost the rote-learning skills and depth of knowledge of our grandparents, but we know where to find the facts and can do so in an instant. For all that, during the culture war, many of us have developed the habit of reading multiple accounts of any given news item, because so often reports are filtered through an ideological lens. We are accustomed to accusations of 'disinformation' aimed at those who are exposing unfashionable truths, while authentic instances of disinformation are being peddled by the accusers. White lies and misrepresentations have become the norm in a media landscape where reporters are now generally encouraged to tell us what to think about a story, rather than simply relaying the key facts and leaving us to judge for ourselves. Occasionally there is a backlash, such as when the BBC modified the quotation of a rape victim so that her attacker was not misgendered, or when CBS's Margaret Brennan claimed that the Holocaust was caused by the weaponisation of free speech. But, on the whole, this routine twisting of the truth goes unnoticed.

Christopher F. Rufo has traced what he calls the 'long march through the media' in his book *America's Cultural Revolution* (2023), citing the particular influence of members of the Frankfurt School

– most notably Herbert Marcuse – whose concerted efforts have resulted in critical theory becoming 'the house style of establishment opinion'. The consequence is self-evident: a media landscape in which the truth has become secondary to the convenient illusion. There are journalists who are sufficiently hubristic to believe that they 'can alter the structure of reality through pretense', to borrow Jordan B. Peterson's formulation. To take one example from an infinite array of options, when author and journalist Joan Smith was commissioned by the *Financial Times* to write a review of a new book about violence against women, an editor instructed her to insert a deliberate untruth to promote the tenets of genderism. She later recalled the incident in a piece for *UnHerd*:

> 'Diversity' can create conflicts for journalists. 18 months ago, the FT's literary editor invited me to review a book about violence against women. I didn't like it much, not least because it focused so much on the experience of trans-identified men. I pointed out that murders of transwomen are rare in this country, while two women a week are killed by a current or former partner in England and Wales. I received a call from the literary editor, saying that staff at the FT were unhappy with my review and wanted me to add a line saying that murders of transwomen are disproportionately high compared to their numbers. This is not true and I refused, prompting a – shall we say – robust discussion. Apparently these unnamed people felt that the word 'rare' was 'pejorative'. When I stood my ground, the paper removed the reference to trans murders, even though it was accurate.

My own brushes with misinformation (unintentional misrepresentation) and disinformation (intentional deception) from the mainstream media have been, for the most part, trivial. I am not sufficiently important to warrant full-scale smear campaigns, so I can only imagine what it must be like for those in positions of power and influence to be subject to continual mischaracterisations. On one occasion, the *Evening Standard* ran a piece claiming that my Edinburgh Fringe show in 2018 was a dismal failure with the critics. I did not appear at the festival that year, so I can hardly bear any responsibility for this fantasy show and its lamentable reviews. When I contacted the editor to point out that the *Evening Standard* had misled its readers, I was told that 'it was a mistake made in haste in the heat of the morning. But I'm afraid we won't be publishing a retraction.' Personally, I've never knowingly written lies about anyone, but perhaps I'm simply immune to the hallucinogenic effects of hot mornings.

It struck me at the time as strange that the editor would admit to a mistake and not take responsibility for it, but I have since learned that this is standard practice in media circles. My publicist speculated that the piece was designed as a hatchet job to prevent people from buying tickets for my next show but, as Hanlon's Razor has it, we should never attribute to malice that which is adequately explained by stupidity. The *Guardian* offers an additional case in point. On its website, it proudly boasts that it 'delivers fearless, investigative journalism – giving a voice to the powerless and holding power to account'. But whether its executives admit it or not, the publication has developed a reputation for extreme ideological bias. In November 2024, I found myself the subject of the *Guardian*'s tactics of disinformation. Reporting on a short course on the woke movement that I was scheduled to teach at the New College of Florida, the *Guardian* described me as a 'controversial British media personality and culture warrior'. It is of course entirely predictable that culture warriors would brand their critics as 'culture warriors', but quite how my consistent defence of liberal values is 'controversial' was not explained. The article's author, Jason Wilson, claimed that the course at the New College of Florida had been 'reinstated', which is odd given that it had never been cancelled in the first place. He also asserted that I was guilty of 'courting right-wing opinion' because I had been interviewed by Jordan Peterson and Tucker Carlson. I have also appeared on shows hosted by left-wing commentators such as Hugo Rifkind and George Galloway, but thus far I have not been accused of 'courting left-wing opinion'. Perhaps Wilson is simply unfamiliar with the concept of engaging in dialogue with people of opposing views?

But the most egregious factual inaccuracy came when Wilson, in pointing out that I have written for *Spiked*, described the magazine as 'hard-right'. *Spiked* began its existence as *Living Marxism*, and has consistently supported free speech, the values of democracy and liberal immigration policies, while vehemently opposing all forms of racism and white nationalism. Mislabelling *Spiked* as 'hard-right' is either outright dishonesty or staggering ignorance. It's what happens when journalistic standards are subordinated to propaganda. The crowning moment of Wilson's inadvertent self-satire was when he admitted, in light of my forthcoming course on the woke movement, that he had been actively searching for non-profit organisations which might qualify as members. He writes – and I am not making this up – 'The *Guardian*'s search of IRS non-profit records indicate that while there are some 20 non-profits with the word "woke" in their names, none have reported any income in their most recent filings, and most appear to be inactive.' Wilson genuinely seems to believe that one can only subscribe to an ideology if it is registered with the government and has applied for tax exemptions. This is a species of literal-mindedness so colossal that it must surely be eligible for some kind of award.

On reflection, I got off lightly. A far more egregious example of the *Guardian*'s mendacity was the controversy over the Wi Spa in Los Angeles in 2021. A video of a woman who calls herself 'CubanaAngel' on Instagram was posted online, in which she could be seen complaining to the staff about a naked man in the women's Jacuzzi area. The man in question, Darren Agee Merager, was a registered sex offender with previous convictions for indecent exposure, and it was alleged that the complainant at the Wi Spa had seen him semi-erect. 'So it's okay for a man to go into the women's section and show his penis around the other women, young little girls – underage – in your spa?' she had said to staff, who defended his right to be there on the grounds of self-identification. After the video went viral, protests outside the spa were organised by women's rights campaigners. These were quickly smeared as 'far right' and mobbed by so-called 'anti-fascist' protesters. The *Guardian*, having spent years promoting the notion that womanhood is an identity category rather than a biological reality, and having faced allegations of driving female journalists from its staff for their gender-critical views, then produced two articles in quick succession implying that CubanaAngel's complaints were a hoax. The writers claimed that the incident 'provided clear evidence of the links between anti-trans and far-right movements', while *Guardian* columnist Owen Jones called the entire incident a 'campaign of lies'. Even when it emerged that Merager had been charged for indecent exposure at the Wi Spa, the *Guardian* continued to conflate the female protesters with the far-right agitators who had turned up to exploit the situation. As Josephine Bartosch put it in her overview of the case for *The Critic*, 'For all the *Guardian*'s handwringing about #metoo, when it comes to believing the women who complained about Merager's crime, rather than "giving a voice to the powerless" they pretended his victims didn't exist. Women like CubanaAngel are ideological inconveniences.'

Since Elon Musk acquired Twitter and converted it into X, the site has seen the addition of 'community notes', by which journalists can be fact-checked in real time. Inevitably, activist publications such as the *Guardian* have been slapped with these notes on numerous occasions. For instance, when it posted a piece entitled 'England riots: how has "two-tier policing" myth become widespread?', notes were quickly added to provide links to the various articles in which the *Guardian* has asserted that 'two-tier policing' based on race and sexuality is rife. When it published an article entitled 'How many more children like Sara Sharif will be killed before smacking is banned?', the community notes quickly explained that the victim had not merely been smacked, but had suffered extreme beatings and multiple forms of torture. All such hideous acts are, of course, already illegal.

Those who were comfortable with the echo chamber that Twitter had formerly established quickly began looking for an alternative once it became clear that Musk would not be censoring their political opponents. They were deserting the site not because of limitations to their own speech, but rather that the authorities were failing to limit the speech of others. And so in November 2024 there was a mass exodus to Bluesky, a rival social media platform that resembles in style the pre-Musk Twitter. Taylor Swift fans flocked in their thousands, and former CNN anchor Don Lemon posted a lengthy statement outlining his own reasons for relocating. The official account of the Clifton Suspension Bridge and Museum posted a similar statement, which led to candlelit vigils and a mass outpouring of public grief. The *Guardian* too made its escape. 'This is something we have been considering for a while', its editorial intoned with the gravity of an Old Testament prophet. 'The US presidential election campaign served only to underline what we have considered for a long time: that X is a toxic media platform and that its owner, Elon Musk, has been able to use its influence to shape political discourse.' The *Guardian* seemed to be depicting its flounce as an act of heroism, but it struck a petulant note. This was not so much Beowulf slaying Grendel as Achilles sulking in his tent.

For many users, Bluesky offers the psychological equivalent of the 'safe space', one which led Georgetown University's McCourt School of Public Policy to establish a 'self-care suite' after Trump's victory in November 2024. Here students could isolate themselves and process their trauma by playing with Lego, drawing with crayons, and binge-ing on milk and cookies. With the digital milk and cookies of Bluesky, users can be shielded from the disorientation that occurs where plurality of opinion is permitted. Such online echo chambers are, of course, largely to blame for the escalation of political tribalism that we have seen in recent years, and also for the sense of shock that many experience when elections do not go their way. While it is true that Musk has reinstated accounts on X that post some genuinely objectionable material, this is the price one pays for an open market-place of ideas.

This desire to avoid any challenges to one's ideological certainties is becoming more widespread as the woke era reaches its terminus, and will doubtless be a major factor in this next phase of the culture war. By insulating themselves from criticism, and seeking platforms where their misrepresentations will not be flagged, the *Guardian* and its ilk are doing themselves no favours. If they are serious about their goals, they should reconsider their resolution to speak only to those who will unquestioningly cheer them on. Those who withdraw from the debate stand no chance of winning it. Patrick J. Deneen has argued that ideology always fails because once its inherent 'falsehoods become more evident, the gap grows between what the ideology claims and the lived experience of human beings under its domain'. In this, he is drawing explicitly on the historian Barbara W. Tuchman's maxim: 'When the gap between ideal and real becomes too wide, the system breaks down.' The *Guardian*'s decision to abandon X is a means by which it may retreat from the battlefield of ideas, a response to this collision of ideology and truth.

The German philosopher Jürgen Habermas coined the phrase '*legit-imationsprobleme*' – usually translated as 'legitimation crisis' – to describe the consequences of the loss of public trust in figures of authority. When journalists, academics and those in positions of political power are con-tinually caught out deceiving the public, a general sense of scepticism is the inevitable result. Even reputable academic journals are now willing to sideline inconvenient facts if they are incompatible with their woke mirage. When the *New England Journal of Medicine* argued that 'sex designations on birth certificates offer no clinical utility', few of us were taken aback. The *Journal of the Royal Society of Chemistry* went so far as to produce new guidelines to 'minimise the risk of publishing inappro-priate or otherwise offensive content'. The implication is clear: if the truth hurts, it ought to be avoided. But as Aldous Huxley observed, 'Facts do not cease to exist because they are ignored'.

It is no coincidence that, as these boys have been crying wolf, belief in wild conspiracy theories has surged. We now know that the ruling class are not to be trusted, and the beneficiaries are those who peddle alternative and often bogus narratives. While the suggestion that the Covid-19 pandemic was the result of a leak from the Wuhan Institute of Virology is now widely accepted as credible, it was not so long ago that it was dismissed by leading experts as a 'racist conspiracy theory'. When molecular biologist Alina Chan and writer Matt Ridley published a defence of this theory in their book *Viral: The Search for the Origin of Covid-19* (2021), Michael Hiltzik in the *Los Angeles Times* claimed that the authors were placing 'a conspiracy theory between hardcovers to masquerade as sober scientific inquiry'. Hiltzik's certainty was premature. In December 2024, the United States government's Select Subcommittee on the Coronavirus Pandemic released its final report confirming that the lab-leak theory was most likely true.

The legitimation crisis and the erosion of confidence in our institutions was always going to be inevitable when the lies were eventually exposed. I barely scraped a GCSE in biology, but when esteemed peer-reviewed scientific journals such as *Nature* are publishing authors who maintain that the 'idea of two sexes is simplistic' and that 'there is a wider spectrum than that', it gives the false impression that my understanding of the subject is superior to theirs. This from the *Scientific American* is perhaps even more risible: 'The inequity between male and female athletes is a result not of inherent biological differences between the sexes but of biases in how they are treated in sports.' So the reason why men run faster than women has nothing to do with muscle mass, heart size, lung capacity or longer strides, but is attributable to sexist stereotyping.

While we might assume that academics would strive for greater objectivity, there are good reasons why the opposite is often the case. Those working in higher education are particularly susceptible to groupthink. Their work is based on the notion of superior knowledge, and so egos are easily bruised when they are proven wrong. Moreover, the cleverest among us are also those who are able to rationalise and justify the most improbable of theories. Many experts appear to have forgotten that the legitimacy of their claims is grounded in evidence and research, not by waving around a doctoral certificate. The degradation of authority figures is the basis of traditional farce, but when it spills out into reality, it is no laughing matter.

In some cases, this deviation from the truth is deliberate and tactical. Consider, for instance, the phenomenon that biologist Bret Weinstein has described as 'idea laundering'. The process begins with a moral impulse among certain ideologically driven academics. Journals are founded, papers are published, classes are taught, and before long what was once the vaguest intuition is supported by a body of academic literature. Author and philosopher Peter Boghossian offers the example of 'Fat Studies', an area of study which seeks to lend credence to the view that 'the clinical concept of obesity (a medical term) is merely a story we tell ourselves about fat (a descriptive term); it's not true or false – in this particular case, it's a story that exists within a social power dynamic that unjustly ascribes authority to medical knowledge'. What begins as a fanciful theory emerges as 'knowledge' through this laundering process. It explains why a notion as nebulous as 'white fragility' is now so widely and uncritically accepted. Ideas that have little basis in reality emerge from universities as *de facto* truths, and those brave enough to challenge them are quickly and mercilessly subdued. And while most of us are happy to conform for the sake of an easy life, our trust in those institutions supposedly dedicated to the production of knowledge quickly deteriorates.

Scepticism about expertise is important: no human being is infallible or free from bias, however well qualified. Yet at the same time we rely on figures in authority with specialist insight for the practical business of living. When journalists begin to conflate truth and fiction, or when academics substitute wishful thinking for empirical knowledge, we are left unmoored from reality. For the sake of our collective sanity in a post-woke world, we need to restate the primacy of truth.

# EPILOGUE

# A Seed May Fall

In *Where the Clocks Chime Twice* (1952), the novelist Alec Waugh describes his sojourn on the island of Mahé in the Seychelles where he met an anti-communist campaigner among the expatriate community. He refers to this curious figure only as 'the Colonel's widow'. On their first meeting she expresses irritation that he has declared himself 'unpolitical' and therefore ill-suited to participate in her movement. 'That's the trouble with writers nowadays,' she says huffily. 'They won't interest themselves in the things that matter.'

The thing that matters most to the Colonel's widow is preserving this remote island in the Indian Ocean from the clutches of Moscow. Not that Mahé is teeming with communists, but she fears that the Russian government might, at any time, establish a cell for the gathering of intelligence. Her maxim is: 'If the soil is ready, then a seed may fall. We must keep the soil unfertile.' She is like a one-woman *Dad's Army*, albeit without the authentic threat of invasion, constantly on the lookout for a new crusade. She had previously attempted to save the local dogs from an epidemic of hardpad. Then she had tried to establish an orphanage. Her philanthropic ambitions were regularly thwarted in their early stages due to lack of public support. Her efforts to cleanse the island of non-existent communism were doubtless to end much the same way.

Like all romantics, the Colonel's widow is inconsistent. Waugh recalls how a guest at her house had noticed a bundle of homemade spills to light fires in the kitchen and, on closer examination, realised that they were made from the pages of a book by John Strachey written in his pro-Marxist phase. It was later discovered that the Colonel's widow had taken a number of communist works from the library, including Marx's *Das Kapital* (1867) and John Reid's *Ten Days That Shook the World* (1919). She had then claimed to have lost the items, apologised profusely, and paid for them in full. When confronted about this destruction of books, the Colonel's widow is defiant. 'When you see a poisonous snake you kill it,' she says. 'Books like that should be kept under lock and key.' Incredibly, her chief objection to communists is their propensity for censorship. She despises what she calls 'their muzzling of the artist', arguing that there could be 'no health in a country where an artist isn't free to speak out of his own heart'. Waugh raises the obvious objection: 'But aren't you yourself imposing your own censorship?' Shaking her head, she replies: 'Not when it's the voice of evil speaking.'

Waugh's anecdote seemed outlandish enough for him to tell, but most of us are now familiar with such double standards. How often have we heard the mantra 'I believe in free speech, *but . . .*', as though this statement of principle is not immediately undermined by that conjunction? And how often have we seen vocal opponents of censorship make exceptions for those who have offended their sensibilities? The Colonel's widow is indulging in collectivist thinking, that fatal tendency without which the woke culture war could never have been initiated, let alone sustained for so long. The instinct to categorise people and cling to our own 'tribe' may have an evolutionary basis, but our rational capabilities help us to understand the limitations of this approach. While identity politics has played a role in the achievement of civil liberties – with groups organising in their own interests when human rights have been denied on the basis of race, sex or sexuality – too often it is deployed as a lazy substitute for critical thought.

The same goes for those of us who classify our in-group according to affiliations of religion or politics. In all such cases, we are subordinating our human individuality to a broader cause. Identitarian collectivism accounts as much for white nationalism as it does for intersectional politics; for anyone who makes sweeping statements about men, women, homosexuals, heterosexuals, white people, black people or any other group. That is not to say that there are not trends which, in some circumstances, it is wise to observe, but once we expand our antipathy towards certain individuals to the demographic to which they belong, we make ourselves foolish. Many on the woke right, for instance, will blame women for the rise of gender ideology, on the basis that surveys invariably point to greater support among the female sex for policies based on gender self-identification. Some feminists will blame men for the rise of gender ideology, on the basis that it is only males who benefit from the erosion of women's spaces. The truth should barely need to be stated: those responsible for the rise of gender ideology are those individuals who have promoted it, be they male or female.

In a post-woke landscape, with a fresh vacuum calling to be occupied by a new dominant ideology, we would be well advised to guard against this collectivist mindset. We can observe it in 'whiteness experts', who claim that 'white people are racist' because of the existence of some racist white people, or feminists who claim that 'gay men are misogynistic', because of the existence of some misogynistic gay men; the formula can be extended indefinitely by substituting a different identity group. In all such cases, blame for the behaviour of a few is being projected onto a demographic. It is similarly fallacious to interpret criticism of individuals as an attack on the group to which they belong.

It is perfectly possible to criticise gay individuals without being homophobic, to criticise female individuals without being misogynistic, to criticise ethnic minority individuals without being racist, to criticise Jewish individuals without being antisemitic, to criticise Muslim individuals without being Islamophobic. Similarly, it is possible for those on the left to take the Democratic Party to task, or for those on the right to bewail the failures of Conservatives. The world is not so easily divided into taxonomies of good and evil, oppressor and oppressed, right and left. Too often we fall into the trap of assuming that our group is what defines us. First and foremost, we are human beings with our own particular thoughts, emotions, priorities, prejudices and agency. Let's start there.

Authoritarianism is that persistent whispering in the ears, that primordial impulse that we have somehow taught ourselves to ignore. It is the perennial temptation of human societies; no civilisation is immune to its lure. We hear its dismal tones chattering endlessly on social media, which is why our best defence might be to limit our time on the internet and the distorted funfair mirror of human nature it generates. My own entry into the culture war began on social media, and I can be sure that I would be much happier without it. Even the author of the preface to the Italian translation of my book *Free Speech and Why It Matters* has criticised me for spending too much time on Twitter ('*Andrew Doyle passa troppo tempo su Twitter, ma per fortuna ogni tanto scrive un libro*'). And while it's rather amusing to be criticised in one's own book, he was entirely correct to do so. Social media has always been a behemoth that devours too much of my life.

In my more fanciful moments, I see a premonition of the woke era in Edmund Spenser's epic poem *The Faerie Queene* (1590) through the figure of Fidessa. When we first encounter her, she is travelling with the Redcrosse Knight, a 'goodly Lady' clad in a scarlet robe with gold, pearls and jewels. Protestant readers at the time will have detected that something was amiss. Why was the knight's 'faire companion' dressed in the symbolic garb of the Whore of Babylon? She is later unveiled to reveal her true form, a 'loathly, wrinckled hag, ill fauoured, old' called Duessa, a monstrosity in human disguise.

> Her craftie head was altogether bald,
>> And as in hate of honorable eld,
>> Was ouergrowne with scurfe and filthy scald;
>> Her teeth out of her rotten gummes were feld,
>> And her sowre breath abhominably smeld;
>> Her dried dugs, like bladders lacking wind,
>> Hong downe, and filthy matter from them weld;
>> Her wrizled skin as rough, as maple rind,
> So scabby was, that would haue loathd all womankind.

No doubt in today's climate Spenser would be accused of misogynistic body-shaming, and yet, given that Duessa has the talons of an eagle and the tail of a fox, to classify her as a 'woman' is surely quite the stretch.

Like the Redcrosse Knight, we have been unwittingly flirting with the Antichrist. Only now are we recognising the subterfuge. Fidessa has always been Duessa; duplicity masquerading as faith. Woke had depicted itself as virtuous and saintly, a thing of beauty in a world of slurry. Beneath the lustre of compassion and justice, it was a divisive and reactionary movement, usurping the name of our civil rights heroes and reversing their achievements. The end of woke was always inevitable, because the triumph of social liberalism over the second half of the twentieth century successfully produced a progressive consensus that is not so readily dismantled. For all the claims of widespread hatred and division, most people in the West are reliably well meaning and believe in fair treatment for all, irrespective of the group identity to which they happen to belong. Wokeness demanded the opposite, and so it could only be sustained while its aims were broadly misapprehended. Where it claimed to nourish, it only poisoned. The scarlet robe has now been torn away; the dried dugs exposed.

As we emerge from this latest stage of the culture war, we would do well to remind ourselves that it could have been so much worse. When taken to its extremes, authoritarianism has been the stimulus for some of the most unforgivable atrocities in human history. Wokism has certainly destroyed lives – children have been mutilated, decent people have lost their careers, racism has been exacerbated, women have seen setbacks to their rights and have even been violently and sexually assaulted – but we should be grateful that Western society recognised the dangers and modified the trajectory. It is only thanks to the vigilance of those schooled in the history of humankind that its repetition has been prevented. To suggest that woke is dead is perhaps premature, given that authoritarianism never dies. Woke in its current incarnation is almost at an end, but already there are resurrectionists determined to see it return in a new guise. At the same time, we are contending with Islamists who have been emboldened by the complacency of the West, white nationalists who are revelling in the anti-woke backlash, and various other forms of nascent tyranny. As Patrick J. Deneen has cautioned, 'Some form of populist nationalist authoritarianism or military autocracy seems altogether plausible as an answer to the anger and fear of a postliberal citizenry.' We might not be able to anticipate how exactly the authoritarian instinct will next manifest, but that it will do so is an inevitability.

Our conviction that human freedom is paramount has origins that are perhaps ultimately incomprehensible to us. To defend the principle is one thing; to consider why it exists at all is quite another. Where we might seek answers, we find only questions. Is our belief in freedom essentially religious? Does it spring from a sense in which the value of the individual is connected to an inherent regard, however subconsciously felt, for the sanctity of human life? Does our faith in individual liberty, in other words, itself convey a faith in the divine? If men have no souls, no higher utility beyond the corporeal, why is depriving a man of his freedom or life any more objectionable than leashing a dog or crushing an insect? Or is it a matter of sheerest pragmatism? Is our belief in liberty a utilitarian project, a means by which we can achieve the greatest good for the greatest number? Or is it based on self-interest? Do we promote human liberty as a universal precept because it thereby protects us, as individuals, from tyranny? When we say 'slavery is abominable', do we mean 'it would be abominable for me to be enslaved'? Or is our sense of justice innate, either as the God-given *sine qua non* of the human condition, or the product of an evolutionary process that has endowed us with empathy and the capacity for love as an advantageous quality in the struggle for survival? I pose the questions as a man roaring into an endless void, with no expectation of the faintest echo of an answer.

All I can say for sure is that a life without liberty would be intolerable, and so on that basis alone I feel confident in defending its worth. While I have endlessly reflected on the origins of this conviction it is, ultimately, a matter of first principles. Even if, as the existentialists would have it, there is no purpose to life beyond that which we create for ourselves, the fact that we have not committed suicide already reveals our commitment to the condition of existence. If life is precious, then so too is the manner in which that life is lived. If we are invested in life, we are invested in liberty.

We see this in humanity's innate resistance to coercion and control. Notwithstanding the delight that many seem to take in following orders, there may also be a seemingly contradictory evolutionary basis for our tendency to react indignantly when others tell us what to do. In their analysis of the folly of 'unconscious bias' testing, sociologists Frank Dobbin and Alexandra Kalev have surveyed a wide range of studies which all reach a similar conclusion.

> We know from a large body of organizational research that people react negatively to efforts to control them. Job autonomy research finds that people resist external controls on their thoughts and behavior and perform poorly in their jobs when they lack autonomy. Self-determination research shows that when organizations frame

motivation for pursuing a goal as originating internally, commitment rises, but when they frame motivation as originating externally, rebellion increases.

It has been dispiriting to see so many find solace in the uncritical capitulation to authority. An Ipsos MORI poll for the *Economist* in July 2021 found that, even if the risk of Covid-19 was eliminated, 19 per cent of the British population would support night-time curfews, 26 per cent would wish to see casinos and clubs shut down, and 35 per cent would be in favour of travel quarantine. Yet the pushback against woke has been likewise dogged, and the primacy of individual agency appears to have prevailed. E. M. Forster sees this quality as hardwired into our disposition:

> The dictator-hero can grind down his citizens till they are all alike, but he cannot melt them into a single man. That is beyond his power. He can order them to merge, he can incite them to mass-antics, but they are obliged to be born separately, and to die separately, and, owing to these unavoidable termini, will always be running off the totalitarian rails. The memory of birth and the expectation of death always lurk within the human being, making him separate from his fellows and consequently capable of intercourse with them.

Given these two dissonant impulses in human nature, a yearning for both dependence and independence, resisting authoritarianism becomes a matter of ongoing vigilance. At time of writing, we cannot be certain that Donald Trump's administration, in its determination to strip away the excesses of the woke, will not introduce alternative policies that are similarly authoritarian. The case for liberalism, in other words, needs to be continually restated in each new era. As a mechanism for a functioning society, it requires careful maintenance. The authoritarian instinct may be a human constant but, with diligence, it can be forestalled.

The endless word games of culture warriors meant that many of us were caught off guard. We were befuddled by activists who asserted one thing and meant another. We allowed ourselves to believe that authoritarianism could be a force for good, that progress is somehow foreordained, what Martin Luther King, Jr. described as 'the strangely irrational notion that there is something in the very flow of time that will inevitably cure all ills'. In decades to come, this period of our history will seem incomprehensible, and perhaps future generations will struggle to make sense of it. Why, they might ask, were so many books and articles written in an effort to restate the obvious, to remind people that free speech is worth preserving, that segregating the population by skin colour is not a good idea, and that there are only two sexes in the human race? One may as well write a book about how a tiger might not respond positively if you chew on his tail. Ten years ago, who would have thought that Olympic athlete Sharron Davies would feel compelled to argue the point that men should not compete in the women's category? And yet for some reason her book *Unfair Play: The Battle for Women's Sports* (2023) was not only necessary, but considered somehow controversial. Richard Dawkins must have felt much the same way when he wrote *The Greatest Show on Earth: The Evidence for Evolution* (2009), in which he outlined in painstaking detail the irrefutable proof for an argument that most of us assumed had already been settled.

Our equilibrium is finally being restored. Many of those who were conned by the woke ideology will remain disorientated for years to come. Some will find it impossible to admit that they were wrong. Consider the following example offered by the author Helen Joyce in a recent interview:

> There are a lot of people who can't move on from this. And that's the people who have transitioned their own children. So those people are going to be like the Japanese soldiers who were on Pacific islands and didn't know the war was over. They've got to fight

> forever . . . A lot of people have done what is the worst thing you could do, which is to harm their children irrevocably . . . Those people will have to believe that they did the right thing for the rest of their lives, for their own sanity, and for their own self-respect.

Even faced with the evidence that 'gender-affirming' care is unsafe for children, those whose identity has been cultivated in the gender wars will find it almost impossible to accept the truth. But beyond the issue of the 'transing' of children, the white heat of political tribalism has left many unable to divorce their adopted ideology from their sense of self. As Timandra Harkness argues in her book *Technology is Not the Problem* (2024), our online 'personalisation' is underpinned by this quest for identity, a 'powerful but contradictory idea' that 'refers both to a unique, inner kernel, and an outward projection; both an essence and a performance for which we write the script'. The culture war has reduced 'left' and 'right' to identity brands, mere symbols of affiliation for members of the clan. Terms such as 'woke', 'anti-woke', 'Republican', 'Democrat', 'anti-fascist', 'MAGA', 'BLM', 'LGBTQIA+', and innumerable other designations of this kind are not simply political signifiers; they are defining aspects of people's identities. This is also why so many online disputes seem to be untethered from reason; many are following a set of rules established by their 'side', not thinking for themselves. The lure of collectivism is that it does away with nuance and makes the complexities of the world readily digestible. Ideology fills a gap in the brain. We are no longer dealing with disputants in an argument, but individuals who occupy entirely different epistemological frameworks.

This determination to hold fast to one's views, even when the evidence mounts up against them, is known as 'belief perseverance'. For the postmodernist mindset, the correlation of language and reality is a tenet of faith, and the test of one's devotion to that faith is that it remains secure even when obliterated by the facts. It is a natural form of psychological self-defence. In Plato's *Republic*, Socrates cautions against a certain type of deformed soul that 'is not angry when it is found in a state of ignorance, but wallows in it like a bestial hog'. The comforts of our shared fantasies are difficult to relinquish, particularly when we have convinced ourselves that we have been struggling for a noble purpose. This is why the staunchest defenders of wokeness will adhere to their precious beliefs like barnacles to the keel of a sinking ship. But if woke is not yet dead, it is certainly on life-support. Hubris had its moment. Nemesis looms.

The end of woke will necessitate a period of reconciliation, the building of 'golden bridges' to allow people a dignified retreat. Some will attempt to revise their own history and deny they had any part in it, while others will seek to punish the woke indefinitely. At the same time, elements of the 'anti-woke' tribe will seize this opportunity to reassert themselves. Increasingly, we will see those with no spiritual faith at all embracing Christianity as a political identity, scouring works of art for signs of 'degeneracy' and attempting to shackle creative freedom. Islamist encroachments on Western civilisation will continue to test our liberal resolve. The conflict over free speech between America and Europe will persist, with social media companies torn between the whims of two masters. Our challenge as we move into this next phase of the culture war is to resist authoritarianism in whatever guise it assumes, and to reject entirely the lure of collectivist and ideological thinking. It will not be easy. Too much bloody ink has been spilled, and too many friendships jettisoned for the sake of phantom tribal identities. A happy ending is out of the question, but perhaps we might settle for a tolerable one.

# Acknowledgements

The writing of a book is a collaborative affair. It's difficult to keep track of all the various influences and inspirations that contribute to such a laborious project. As a result, the duty to acknowledge debts of gratitude is fraught with risks, not least that the author is bound to overlook certain individuals. With that in mind, I should first say that if key names are absent from this list it is not to be taken as a snub, but rather evidence of my own inadequacies.

First and foremost, I would like to thank Andreas Campomar, Holly Blood, and their colleagues at Constable. I am indebted to my agent Matthew Hamilton for his patience and feedback. A special debt is owed, as ever, to Philip Doherty. Helen Pluckrose, one of the most inspirational defenders of liberal values, read an early draft and offered invaluable advice. I was fortunate enough to work with an excellent team at GB News on my show *Free Speech Nation*, and I am extremely grateful to everyone at the channel, both on and off screen. I'd particularly like to thank all the comedians who worked with me on *Headliners*, our chaotic nightly paper preview show.

Many other people have clarified points during the course of my writing and thinking about the culture war. These include, but are by no means limited to: Peter Boghossian, James Lindsay, Helen Joyce, Stella O'Malley, Julie Bindel, Sarah Phillimore, Dennis Kavanagh, Pamela Paresky, Kara Dansky, Tom Slater, Fraser Myers, Ella Whelan and Brendan O'Neill. I am grateful to my cousin Martin Melaugh for providing details about my grandfather's memories of the war. Thanks also to Björn Nordquist at Nopolar Publishing in Stockholm.

Most of my ideas for this book have been rehearsed in various articles, and so I would like to thank all those who have published my work, including *Spiked*, *UnHerd*, *The Spectator*, *The Daily Mail*, *The Mail on Sunday* and *The Washington Post*. I've had the pleasure of writing a monthly column as Titania McGrath for *The Critic*, which has been a much-needed outlet in these deranging years. Special thanks must go to the artist and satirist Lisa Graves. It was during one particularly long late-night back-and-forth in which Lisa suggested the name Titania McGrath. I immediately knew it was perfect. What better name for this fantasist than Shakespeare's queen of the fairies?

I am fortunate enough to have worked with various people over the past few years who have become stalwart friends. Most notably, I would like to thank Martin Gourlay, Rob Schneider, Graham Linehan, Andy Shaw, Ben Delo, Jeremy Hildreth, Samantha Sanns, Peter Wilson, Craig Adams, Roger Haines, James Dreyfus, Francis Foster, Konstantin Kisin, Genevieve Dolittle, Scott Capurro, Winston Marshall, Oli Foster, John Cleese, Lottie Gazzard, and all those rare creatures from the comedy industry who refused to make me into a pariah for the crime of defending liberal values.

I am grateful to all those individuals and organisations who have consistently challenged the ongoing threats to our freedoms. Toby Young's Free Speech Union has been one of the most important, defending numerous people from the depredations of cancel culture. In the United States, the Foundation for Individual Rights and Expression (FIRE) has done excellent work to champion the cause of free speech.

From her platform in the House of Lords, Claire Fox has been heroic in her determination to make the case for those freedoms that so many of us take for granted. Under Claire's leadership, the Academy of Ideas has flourished, and I have been privileged to be invited on numerous occasions to its annual 'Battle of Ideas'.

Organisations such as Genspect, Sex Matters, For Women Scotland, Transgender Trend, Keep Prisons Single Sex and Fair Play For Women have been fighting back against the ongoing attempts to reverse women's rights. Bev Jackson and Kate Harris of LGB Alliance and Dennis Kavanagh of the Gay Men's Network have done essential work to raise awareness of the increasing threats to gay rights caused by the rise of genderism. Alka Sehgal Cuthbert's work with Don't Divide Us has been instrumental in offering a more positive vision to counter the divisive racial policies of our time.

A final thanks to my parents for their ongoing support and for conjuring me into existence.

# Notes

## Prologue

1   **'Keeping Men Out of Women's Sports':** Zach Montague, 'Trump signs order barring transgender student-athletes from women's sports', *New York Times* (5 February 2025).

2   **funded educational institutions:** Title IX of the Education Amendments of 1972 states: 'No person in the United States shall, on the basis of sex, be excluded from participation, in be denied the benefits of, or be subjected to discrimination under any education program or activity receiving Federal financial assistance'.

2   **America and the United Kingdom:** Stephen Hawkins, Daniel Yudkin, Miriam Juan-Torres and Tim Dixon, *Hidden Tribes: A Study of America's Polarized Landscape* (New York: More in Common, 2018); Ed Hodgson and Luke Tryl, *Progressive Activists* (London: More in Common, 2025). According to the findings of this latter report, progressive activists 'make up eight to ten per cent of the UK population' (ibid., p. 9). The report's definition of 'progressive activists' aligns with conventional definitions of 'woke': 'A passionate and vocal group for whom politics is at the core of their identity, and who seek to correct the historic marginalisation of groups based on their race, gender, sexuality, wealth, and other forms of privilege. They are politically engaged, critical, opinionated, frustrated, cosmopolitan, and environmentally conscious' (ibid., p. 2).

2   **competing in women's sports:** Melissa Block, 'Americans are deeply divided on transgender rights, a poll shows', *NPR* (29 June 2022).

2   **risen to 79 per cent:** Jackson Thompson, 'NYT poll finds majority of Democrats oppose transgender athletes in women's sports', *New York Post* (19 January 2025).

2   **of the female category:** Ibid.

2   **found a unifying cause:** This trend has been mirrored in the United Kingdom. A poll by YouGov conducted in December 2024 found that there had been 'an increased scepticism towards transgender rights across the board' since the previous study two years before. Most remarkable was 'the growing resistance on transgender rights among those groups that are typically more permissive on the issue, like women and young people'. Matthew Smith, 'Where does the British public stand on transgender rights in 2024/25?', *YouGov* (11 February 2025).

2   **'Without you, there'd be no images like this':** J.K. Rowling, X (6 February 2025).

3   **'in order to return to an imagined past':** Sam Bright and Daisy Steinhardt, 'The Punditocracy and the Subversion of Progress', *Byline Times* (24 May 2022).

3    *ire of these culture warriors:* Andrew Doyle, *The New Puritans: How the Religion of Social Justice Captured the Western World* (London: Constable, 2022).

5    **'The only remedy to past discrimination is present discrimination':** Ibram X. Kendi, *How to Be an Antiracist* (London: Bodley Head, 2019), p. 19.

5    *now call 'woke' is 'anti-liberal':* The New Puritans, op. cit., p. 58.

5    *'a child from one sex to another':* See the executive orders published on the United States government's official website: 'Defending Women from Gender Ideology Extremism and Restoring Biological Truth to the Federal Government' (20 January 2025); 'Protecting Children from Chemical and Surgical Mutilation' (28 January 2025). All details of past executive orders are available on the Federal Register website.

5    *about being a 'dictator' on 'day one':* Jill Colvin and Bill Barrow, 'Trump's vow to only be a dictator on "day one" follows growing worry over his authoritarian rhetoric', *Associated Press* (8 December 2023).

6    *be echoed by any autocrat in history:* Donald J. Trump, X (15 February 2025).

6    *described as 'judicial activists':* Monica Sager and Gabe Whisnant, 'White House reacts to "constitutional crisis" claims', *Newsweek* (12 February 2025).

6    *to undermine the woke orthodoxy:* Danielle Wallace, '6 times judges blocked Trump executive orders', *Fox News* (12 February 2025); Jenna Portnoy and Salvador Rizzo, 'Federal judge blocks Trump order on health care for transgender youth', *Washington Post* (13 February 2025).

6    *traditionally divided into male and female:* 'Preventing and Combating Discrimination on the Basis of Gender Identity or Sexual Orientation' was signed by Joe Biden on 25 January 2021. The opening passage outlining the policy began as follows: 'Every person should be treated with respect and dignity and should be able to live without fear, no matter who they are or whom they love. Children should be able to learn without worrying about whether they will be denied access to the restroom, the locker room, or school sports. Adults should be able to earn a living and pursue a vocation knowing that they will not be fired, demoted, or mistreated because of whom they go home to or because how they dress does not conform to sex-based stereotypes. People should be able to access healthcare and secure a roof over their heads without being subjected to sex discrimination. All persons should receive equal treatment under the law, no matter their gender identity or sexual orientation.'

6    **'Advancing Racial Equity and Support for Underserved Communities Through the Federal Government':** Trump's executive order 'Ending Radical and Wasteful Government DEI Programs and Preferencing' was signed on 20 January 2025. Biden's executive order 'Advancing Racial Equity and Support for Underserved Communities Through the Federal Government' was signed on 25 January 2021.

6    *racial discrimination was to be jettisoned:* As Trump's executive order phrased it: 'Federal employment practices, including Federal employee performance reviews, shall reward individual initiative, skills, performance, and hard work and shall not under any circumstances consider DEI or DEIA factors, goals, policies, mandates, or requirements'. See 'Ending Radical and Wasteful Government DEI Programs and Preferencing', op. cit. DEIA stands for 'Diversity, Equity, Inclusion and Accessibility'.

6    *DEI work were scotched:* Andrea Hsu, 'Trump calls DEI programs "illegal." He plans to end them in the federal government', *NPR* (23 January 2025).

7    *'diversity, equity and inclusion efforts in the United States is changing':* Adria R Walker, 'Meta terminates its DEI programs days before Trump inauguration', *Guardian* (10 January 2025).

7    *scaled back their DEI commitments and goals:* Max Zahn, 'Meta, McDonald's: These companies are rolling back some DEI policies', *ABC News* (10 January 2025); Kate Gibson and Emmet Lyons, 'Meta ends diversity programs, joining McDonald's, Walmart and other major companies to back off DEI'; Johana Bhuiyan, 'Google defends scrapping AI pledges

NOTES

and DEI goals in all-staff meeting', *Guardian* (12 February 2025); Arriana McLymore, 'Amazon cuts reference to diversity from annual report', *Reuters* (7 February 2025).

7   **annual federal spending on DEI initiatives:** Josh Marcus, 'Elon Musk and DOGE eyeing $120 billion in cuts on federal diversity spending, says report', *Independent* (17 January 2025).

7   **support for its ideological boondoggling:** For more details of the cuts to USAID's humanitarian budget, see Gordon Brown, 'Be clear about what Trump and Musk's aid axe will do: people will face terror and starve, many will die', *Guardian* (7 February 2025).

7   **pottery classes and promotion in Morocco:** Republican senator Joni Ernst was particularly aggrieved, pointing out that 'Moroccans have been making pottery for thousands of years' and that the project 'clearly wasn't fully formed, because the translator they hired didn't even speak English'. Joni Ernst, X (3 February 2025).

7   **'provide economic empowerment opportunities':** Jack Izzo, 'USAID sent $2M to Guatemala, but not just for gender-affirming health care', *Snopes* (12 February 2025).

8   **'ethnic, religious, and sectarian groups':** Emma Colton, '"Sesame Street in Iraq": USAID's "wasteful and dangerous" spending exposed by senator', *Fox News* (5 February 2025). This figure was widely reported as $20 million in the press, although the *USA Spending* website indicates that $13 million was allocated. See Caleb McCullough, 'Claims about Politico, "DEI musical" and USAID spending distort the facts', *PolitiFact* (7 February 2025).

8   **'$8 million for making mice transgender':** 'Transcript of President Donald Trump's speech to a joint session of Congress', *Associated Press* (5 March 2025). Commentators and immunologists claimed that Trump's speechwriter had confused 'transgender' with 'transgenic', meaning in this case that the mice had been genetically engineered with human DNA for research purposes. However, as journalist Benjamin Ryan pointed out, Trump's claim was 'partly true'. The National Institutes of Health (NIH) had 'funded many studies that use mice to help them understand the safety and health impacts of providing cross-sex hormones to humans – meaning giving testosterone to females and estrogen to males'. Benjamin Ryan, 'Trump claimed the NIH spent $8 million 'making mice transgender,' which is actually partly true', *Hazard Ratio, Substack* (6 March 2025). Trump's speech was on the theme of the 'renewal of the American dream' and was delivered on 4 March 2025.

8   **'our enlightened elites':** Andrew Sullivan specifically cites the following examples: '$3.9 million to promote critical gender and queer theory in – checks notes – the western Balkans; $2.1 million to help the BBC "value the diversity of Libyan society" (is the British government funding insufficient?); $8.3 million for "USAID Education: Equity and Inclusion," and $7.9 million to teach Sri Lankan journalists how to avoid "binary-gendered language." Exposing this is fantastic – and could lead to real reform; but instantly shutting down whole agencies, freezing funding for others, laying off thousands and thousands, without any congressional approval, is the path to nowhere'. Andrew Sullivan, 'Dick Cheyney's wet dream', *The Weekly Dish, Substack* (7 February 2025).

9   **transgender ought to have access to surgery:** Shane Goldmacher, Maggie Haberman and Jonathan Swan, 'How Trump won, and how Harris lost', *New York Times* (7 November 2024).

9   **Trump among those who saw it:** Ibid.

9   **removed the pronouns from their social media profiles:** Sonam Sheth, 'AOC removes pronouns from X bio: what we know', *Newsweek* (14 November 2024); James Bickerton, 'Has Pete Buttigieg removed pronouns from his bio? What we know', *Newsweek* (31 January 2025). Ocasio-Cortez later claimed that her pronouns were removed for reasons of 'space'. Valerie Richardson, 'AOC says she dropped pronouns from X bio for space reasons, decries flap as "fake"', *Washington Times* (18 November 2024). Pronouns were also deleted from the Mayor of London Sadiq Khan's profile on X in January 2025, only to be restored following a backlash. Khan's spokesperson blamed the temporary change on a 'technical error', but did specify what kind of mysterious technical error would delete such details seemingly at random. See Shannon McGuigan and Lettice Bromovsky, 'Sadiq Khan vows to return his controversial he/him gender pronouns to his X bio as he blames a "technical error" that saw them quietly removed', *Daily Mail* (1 February 2025).

9    *from competing in female categories:* Nick Mulvenney, 'World Netball bans transgender athletes from competing at international level', *Independent* (9 April 2024); Daniel Trotta, 'US college organisation bans transgender athletes from competing in all women's sports', *Independent* (9 April 2024); Sean Ingle, 'World Athletics Council excludes transgender women from female events', *Guardian* (23 Mar 2023); Gillian R. Brassil and Jeré Longman, 'World Rugby bars transgender women, baffling players', *New York Times* (26 October 2020); Matthew Futterman, 'FINA restricts transgender women from competing at elite level', *New York Times* (19 June 2022); Sean Ingle, 'Transgender players banned from international women's cricket by ICC', *Guardian* (21 November 2023); Sean Ingle, 'British Cycling bars transgender women from competing in female category', *Guardian* (26 May 2023); Debbie Hayton, 'British Rowing sees sense on trans participation', *UnHerd* (4 August 2023).

9    *divisive LGBTQIA+ campaigns:* Bev Jackson, 'LGB Alliance will never be silenced', *Spiked* (13 July 2023).

9    *the* Telegraph *ran with the front-page headline 'Trans women are not women':* Daniel Martin, Janet Eastham and Hayley Dixon, 'Trans women are not women', *Telegraph* (16 April 2025).

9    *banned indefinitely in the United Kingdom:* Andrew Gregory, 'Puberty blockers to be banned indefinitely for under-18s across UK', *Guardian* (11 December 2024).

10   *published in April 2024 (see Chapter 7):* Dr Hilary Cass, *The Cass Review: Independent Review of Gender Identity Services for Children and Young People: Final Report* (April 2024).

10   *been steadily declining ever since:* 'America is becoming less "woke"', *Economist* (19 September 2024).

10   *the Black Lives Matter Global Network Foundation was facing bankruptcy:* Verity Bowman, 'Black Lives Matter at risk of insolvency as debt soars', *Telegraph* (24 May 2023).

10   *Cullors's relatives for security services:* Wilfred Reilly, 'A requiem for Black Lives Matter', *Spiked* (20 September 2022).

10   *paraglider used in the attack:* Tony Diver, 'Fury as Black Lives Matter group posts image of paratrooper and says it "stands with Palestine"', *Telegraph* (10 October 2023).

10   *participants changed the nature of the debate:* Helena Ivanov, 'Anti-Semitism has exploded in British universities', *Spiked* (8 July 2024).

11   *a new advertisement campaign in November 2024:* Joe Hutchison, 'Jaguar fans compare new logo rebrand to Bud Light controversy: "Where are the vehicles in this woke commercial?"', *Daily Mail* (20 November 2024).

11   *significance was in the broader reaction:* Matt Oliver, 'Jaguar sales drop by more than a quarter ahead of controversial relaunch', *Telegraph* (8 January 2025).

12   *called the 'struggle between Liberty and Authority':* John Stuart Mill, *On Liberty* (London: Everyman's Library, 1992), p. 5. Originally published in 1859.

## Chapter 1

13   *the Western world has never been more tolerant:* A recent report by the think-tank British Future found that 84 per cent of British people 'would not have any problem' with an ethnic minority prime minister, while only 9 per cent felt that it was 'very important' for someone to be white to be regarded as British. Steve Ballinger, Sunder Katwala and Heather Rolfe, *Jubilee Britain* (London: British Future, May 2022). One of the most comprehensive surveys on public attitudes to race ever conducted was the European Commission's 2019 report on *Discrimination in the European Union* (September 2019), which found that citizens of the United Kingdom are among the least racist in the world.

13   *'than even existed in 1930s Germany':* Titania McGrath, *Woke: A Guide to Social Justice* (London: Constable, 2019), p. 3.

# NOTES

14    *fluctuate depending on the pollen count:* Titania McGrath, *My First Little Book of Intersectional Activism* (London: Constable, 2020), p. 5.

14    *'successfully eliminate heterosexuality':* Ibid., p. 2.

14    *arrest people for their words and thoughts:* 'The only way we can stop fascism is if the police are allowed to arrest people for what they say and think.' *Woke*, op. cit., p. 149.

14    *'everyone thinks in exactly the same way as me':* *My First Little Book of Intersectional Activism*, op. cit., p. 158.

14    *voluntarily immersing myself in a world of lunatics:* Ken Kesey, *One Flew Over the Cuckoo's Nest* (New York: Viking Press, 1962).

14    *a particular focus on woke issues:* *Free Speech Nation* presented by Andrew Doyle was broadcast from June 2021 until December 2024 on GB News.

15    *the very thing it seeks to suppress:* In 2023, the singer Barbra Streisand filed a lawsuit against a photographer who had published an image of her Malibu home without her permission. The resultant publicity ensured that the photograph was shared widely.

15    *'I now understand how Nelson Mandela felt':* Titania McGrath, 'I now understand how Nelson Mandela felt', *Quillette* (13 December 2018).

15    *'lampooning the language of social justice is a cheap shot':* Alex Clark, 'Titania McGrath: laugh if you want, but woke's no joke', *Observer* (10 March 2019). When Clark described Titania as a 'speedy cash-in', she encapsulated perfectly one of Titania's chief failings: she routinely intuits the motives of her ideological opponents, and frames her speculations as fact. That is to say, she knows your evil intentions, even if you don't know them yourself.

15    *tended to divide along political lines:* Christopher Hart, 'Bullseye! Skewering of a woke monster is pure bliss', *Daily Mail* (18 September 2021); Rachael Healy, 'Titania McGrath: Mxnifesto review – Twitter activist misfires on all cylinders', *Guardian* (2 November 2021).

15    *the only answer that springs to mind is: 'you':* Ibid.

16    *'it probably isn't sufficiently progressive':* *My First Little Book of Intersectional Activism*, op. cit., p. 153.

16    *complained that it was inciting violence against vegans?:* Titania had posted a clip on Twitter from BBC News on 18 February 2019 in which it was reported that 'a woman who telephoned to apply for a loan was told that all vegans should be punched in the face'. She had written, 'Hey NatWest, is it your official policy to incite violence against vegans?' The official NatWest Twitter account replied: 'Hi Titania, this matter is being taken very seriously and I can assure you that this is being dealt with in line with our internal disciplinary procedures'. Titania responded: 'Not good enough. This is *not* an internal matter. This is a matter for the police. If you continue to protect this criminal, I'll be depositing my sizeable trust fund elsewhere'.

16    *to discuss the problem of transphobia?:* On 10 February 2019, Titania had posted a tweet about Kate Scottow, the mother who was arrested in front of her children and locked in a cell for seven hours for 'misgendering' a trans-identified male online. In response, Liz Wheeler had written: 'Hi Titania, my name is Liz Wheeler. I host "Tipping Point" on One America News Network. Are you interested in coming on my show to talk about this arrest & your tweet?'

16    *'There is no place for racism in my house':* Titania McGrath, X (7 November 2024).

16    *'Is this possibly real?':* Ted Cruz, X (8 November 2024).

16    *retweeted approvingly by Rokhaya Diallo:* Pierre Valentin, 'Quand la parodie du wokisme devient prophétie', *Le Point* (19 December 2021).

16    *France's most renowned social justice activist:* Rokhaya Diallo has been described as the 'visage célèbre des SJW' (famous face of social justice warriors). See Nicolas Moreau, 'Quand les justiciers progressistes prennent leur propre caricature au sérieux: l'étude du cas Rokhaya Diallo', *Atlantico* (18 January 2020).

16    *pretentious statements made in any given week:* Private Eye's error was mentioned by Charles Moore, 'Why I'm a fan of Titania McGrath', *Spectator* (9 February 2019).

17    *demean minorities while claiming to defend them:* Titania once described herself as being brave enough to stand up for the rights of the marginalised, 'even when they don't know what's best for themselves'. *My First Little Book of Intersectional Activism*, op. cit., p. 158.

18    *'It's much nicer than being an ignorant fucking twat':* Kathy Burke, Twitter (13 March 2022).

18    *would happily embrace the term:* 'They're calling you "woke" if you call out bad things, basically. If you're not racist, you're woke. If you're not homophobic, oh, you're woke. Be woke, kids. Be woke." Quoted by Isobel Lewis, 'Kathy Burke praised for "woke" rant after Amanda Holden's Paul O'Grady remark', *Independent* (1 April 2023).

18    *'woke and proud':* Quoted by Rod Garner, 'Is "woke ideology" a threat to the West?', *Church Times* (7 March 2025).

18    *'who would not want to be woke?':* Theresa May, *The Abuse of Power: Confronting Injustice in Public Life* (London: Headline, 2023), p. 65.

18    *'transgender issues that affect virtually no one':* Joyce Carol Oates, X (7 February 2025).

18    *'men identifying into their category':* Emily Crane, 'The staggering number of medals female athletes lost to trans opponents revealed in explosive UN report', *New York Post* (23 October 2024).

19    *now expected to share facilities with men:* Ministry of Justice, *A Whole System Approach for Female Offenders: Emerging Evidence* (June 2018).

19    *a racially divisive endeavour:* See *The New Puritans*, op. cit., pp. 198-201.

19    *born female but now identifies as male:* Daniel Sanderson, 'A third of Britons don't know that transgender women were born male', *Telegraph* (6 August 2023).

20    *'more popular reforms such as marriage equality':* Quoted by James Kirkup, 'The document that reveals the remarkable tactics of trans lobbyists', *Spectator* (2 December 2019).

20    *public understanding of the issues has been limited:* As Kirkup explains, the report 'offers extensive advice about the need to keep the trans-rights agenda out of the public's gaze, the report has rather less to say about the possibility that advocates might just try doing what everyone else in politics does and make a persuasive argument for their cause. Actually convincing people that this stuff is a good idea doesn't feature much in the report, which runs to 65 pages' (ibid).

20    *'they might well object to them':* Ibid.

21    *'and people who love it':* James O'Brien, Twitter (5 July 2020).

21    *presided over its worst excesses:* Ben Bradshaw, Twitter (6 July 2023).

21    *'being used as a culture-war distraction':* Joyce McMillan, 'Gender Recognition Reform Bill is being used as a culture war distraction by the Tories, who are no champions of women's rights', *Scotsman* (20 January 2023).

21    *'stop talking about it, it will finally go away':* Matthew Parris, 'War over trans lobby is manna for the right', *The Times* (2 June 2023).

21    *only explains so much:* The claim that the culture war is a fabrication simply does not withstand serious scrutiny. Critical Race Theory, for instance, was the creation of left-leaning American legal scholars such as Derrick Bell and Kimberlé Crenshaw, and certainly cannot be dismissed as a fantasy of stuffy conservatives. Conor Friedersdorf in the *Atlantic* has written contemptuously of 'trolls waging a culture war against critical race theory' in relation to those who applauded the United States government's investigation into Princeton University following its confession of 'systemic racism'. Yet surely the true culture warrior in this instance was the university's president, Christopher L. Eisgruber, who offered the

self-evidently untrue and grandstanding *mea culpa* in the first place. See Conor Friedersdorf, 'How Princeton Opened Itself to the Ultimate Troll', *Atlantic* (25 September 2020).

21    **women-only spaces and services:** Oliver Wright and Steven Swinford, 'Tory vow to end abuse of gender laws by predators', *The Times* (2 June 2024).

21    **'Conservative party seems to be fighting':** This edition of *Newsnight* aired on BBC Two on 12 June 2024.

22    **'for a narrow core voter base alone':** Tory Reform Group, X (3 June 2024).

22    **weaponisation of trans rights:** Alastair Campbell, X (3 June 2024).

22    **'the rights of half the electorate':** J.K. Rowling, X (3 June 2024).

23    **schoolchildren self-identifying as cats:** In June 2023, an audio recording went viral in which two thirteen-year-old pupils at Rye College in East Sussex could be heard being reprimanded by their teacher for refusing to accept that one of their peers could identify as a cat. After the *Telegraph* made inquiries to other schools, it was discovered that one pupil was identifying as a dinosaur, another as a horse, and one pupil was wearing a cape to lessons and demanding 'to be acknowledged as a moon'. Gordon Rayner, 'Schools let children identify as horses, dinosaurs... and a moon', *Telegraph* (19 June 2023).

23    **whether Lego is heteronormative:** In February 2025, the Science Museum in London provided a written guide for its 'Seeing Things Queerly' exhibition. A display of Lego bricks was included, with the following explanation: 'Lego bricks are often described in a gendered way. The top of the brick with sticking out pins is male, the bottom of the brick with holes to receive the pins is female, and the process of the two sides being put together is called mating. This is an example of applying heteronormative language to topics unrelated to gender, sex and reproduction. It illustrates how heteronormativity (the idea that heterosexuality and the male/female gender binary are the norm and everything that falls outside is unusual) shapes the way we speak about science, technology, and the world in general'. Frederick Attenborough, 'Science Museum attacks Lego as "heteronormative"', *Free Speech Union* (7 February 2025).

24    **'expressions of Christian faith':** Frankie Vetch, 'The Canterbury Tales given trigger warning over "expressions of Christian faith"', *Telegraph* (13 October 2024).

24    **report them for 'microaggressions':** Tom Slater, 'Beware the university campus microaggression monitors', *Spectator* (15 January 2020).

24    **should result in criminal prosecution:** James Bickerton, 'Misgendering should be a crime, according to millennials', *Newsweek* (15 July 2023).

24    **the role of the family in society:** James Davison Hunter, *Culture Wars: The Struggle to Define America* (New York: Basic Books, 1991).

25    **'capable of killing millions, perhaps billions?':** Matthew Syed, 'We need to wake up: mankind's progress could lead to our extinction', *Sunday Times* (14 May 2023).

26    **'psychologically threatening to confront':** Ibid.

26    **'they don't impose them on anybody else':** Helen Pluckrose, *The Counterweight Handbook: Principled Strategies for Surviving and Defeating Critical Social Justice – at Work, in Schools, and Beyond* (London: Swift Press, 2024), p. 2.

27    **any historical precedents that support this view:** Parris, op. cit.

28    **progressive reform was firmly established:** Quoted by Madeleine Carlisle, 'What to know about the origins of "left" and "right" in politics, from the French Revolution to the 2020 presidential race', *Time* (14 September 2019).

29    **enable such a policy:** Rowena Mason, 'Theresa May plans to let people change gender without medical checks', *Guardian* (18 October 2017).

29    **'why the Guardian won't publish this stuff?':** Julie Bindel, Twitter (24 July 2021).

29 *who was sexually assaulted by a male inmate:* Julie Bindel, '"I was sexually assaulted in a women's prison… by a fellow inmate with male genitalia": Read Amy's story and decide – can it be right to put trans sex offenders in female jails?', *Daily Mail* (23 July 2021).

29 *how to be 'a better ally':* Christopher Keelty, 'Dear White People, Your Safety Pins Are Embarrassing', *Huffington Post* (12 November 2016).

30 *'stirred up hate crimes nationwide':* Ibid.

30 *61 per cent of NHS trusts:* The scheme eventually closed down in 2024 due to lack of funding. Research by Sex Matters, a women's rights campaign group, discovered through freedom of information requests that the 'rainbow badge' scheme had been assessed by Stonewall or the LGBT Consortium, which awarded marks on the basis of ideological conformity. Higher scores were given for the deletion of terms such as 'mother', 'women' and 'female' from official policy documents and department names, encouraging staff to ask for preferred pronouns, misrepresenting the protected characteristics of the Equality Act, and the active use of the classification of 'non-binary', even though this form of self-identification has nothing to do with medical procedure and does not exist in law. See: 'What is the indelible mark left by the NHS Rainbow Badge scheme?' on the *Sex Matters* website (22 February 2024).

30 *genuine faith in genderism:* The term 'genderism' is a shorthand used by author Gareth Roberts. He defines it as 'The ideology that advocates the misty concept of gender identity, and its primacy, as opposed to the reality and importance of sex'. Gareth Roberts, *Gay Shame: The Rise of Gender Ideology and the New Homophobia* (London: Forum, 2024), p. 13.

30 *whether they were 'LGBTQ+ friendly':* Other identity categories have also been noted in Google search results, such as when restaurants are 'women-owned' or 'Asian-owned'. The journalist Steven Edginton posted his findings on this subject on X along with the comment: 'It's like a woke form of segregation'. Steven Edginton, X (1 November 2024).

31 *'No wonder the right is furious':* Gaby Hinsliff, '"Woke" isn't dead – it's entered the mainstream. No wonder the right is furious', *Guardian* (27 April 2024).

31 *misses an important qualification:* Ibid.

31 *'sensitivities around this topic and culture':* Ateh Jewel, 'This is exactly why Adele wearing Bantu knots is cultural appropriation – not cultural appreciation', *Glamour* (31 August 2020).

32 *'assign rights and set guidelines for behaviour':* Jaspreet Kaur, *Brown Girl Like Me: The Essential Guidebook and Manifesto for South Asian Girls and Women* (London: Bluebird, 2022), p. 174.

32 *'in the privacy of your own house':* Laurie Penny, *Bitch Doctrine: Essays for Dissenting Adults* (London: Bloomsbury, 2017), p. 35.

33 *'government regulation of speech platforms':* Carlos Maza, X (11 October 2024).

34 *'only legitimate way to decide who is right':* Jonathan Rauch, *Kindly Inquisitors: The New Attacks on Free Thought* (Chicago: University of Chicago Press, 1993), pp. 5-6.

34 *what became known as the 'Freedom Convoy':* 'Trudeau vows to freeze anti-mandate protesters' bank accounts', *BBC News* (15 February 2022).

34 *code for 'Heil Hitler':* Andrea Cavallier, 'Woke Canadian MP claims Freedom Convoy's "Honk Honk" catchphrase is a secret code for *heil Hitler*', *Daily Mail* (22 February 2022).

35 *will not repeat myself here:* The New Puritans, op. cit., pp. 73-97.

35 *sufficient to make the point:* For further examples of victims of cancel culture, see Andrew Doyle, *Free Speech and Why It Matters* (London: Constable, 2021), pp. 25-30 and *The New Puritans*, op. cit., pp. 217-19. In their book *The Canceling of the American Mind: Cancel Culture Undermines Trust and Threatens Us All – But There Is a Solution* (New York: Simon & Schuster, 2023), Greg Lukianoff and Rikki Schlott have shown how, in terms of sheer numbers, the witch-hunting of university staff for wrongthink in the woke era has far exceeded that of McCarthyism.

35    *reinforces demoded gender stereotypes:* 'Doctor Who writer axed over transgender tweets', *BBC News* (5 June 2019).

36    *gathering with dancers at her own home:* Rosie Kay, 'I was cancelled at my own dinner table – that's how toxic the arts world can be', *London Evening Standard* (1 February 2024).

36    *won a court case for discrimination:* Henry Bodkin, 'Gender-critical barrister wins top payout as judge issues stinging criticism of chambers', *Telegraph* (8 July 2023).

36    *figures in the publishing industry:* Josephine Bartosch, 'Inside the trans publishing purge', *UnHerd* (9 December 2021).

36    *an apology and substantial damages:* Robert Mendick, 'Damages paid to literary editor sacked over "heavy five o'clock shadow" transgender remark', *Telegraph* (7 September 2023).

37    *or compete in women's sports:* Toby Young, 'Why have Newcastle United cancelled a fan for "wrongthink"?', *Spectator* (10 February 2024).

37    *in which he was meant to be featured:* Robert Mann, 'I was stabbed in the back by Doctor Who bosses who gave in to cowardly cancel culture, rages axed star', *Sun* (19 Oct 2021).

37    *therapists treating children for gender dysphoria:* Charlotte Lytton, '"I questioned why children were being encouraged to transition – and it cost me my dream career"', *Telegraph* (13 May 2022).

37    *expelling him without a hearing:* Amelia Gentleman, 'Student psychotherapist wins apology over expulsion for gender-critical views', *Guardian* (15 August 2025).

37    *disciplinary procedure amounted to harassment:* Alexandra Topping, 'Social worker wins discrimination case over gender critical beliefs', *Guardian* (9 Jan 2024).

38    *'Make America Aim Again':* The journalist Ashley Nerbovig was one of those who posted 'Make America Aim Again' on social media. Rachel Bowman, 'Progressive Seattle journalist is slammed over warped post about Donald Trump assassination attempt', *Daily Mail* (15 July 2024).

38    *'This is what we will do':* Elon Musk, X (17 July 2024).

38    *The video went viral and she was fired:* Courtney McGinley, 'Home Depot cashier fired over Facebook comment about Trump shooting', *Newsweek* (17 July 2024).

39    *described cancel culture as 'mercy's antithesis':* Nick Cave, 'Why cancel culture destroys the creative soul', *Spectator* (31 December 2020).

39    *'Let him who is without sin cast the first stone':* John, 8:7.

39    *assassination attempt at a show in Sydney:* Bonnie McLaren, 'Jack Black axes tour over bandmate's Trump comment', *BBC News* (16 July 2024).

39    *'encourage political violence in any form':* Ibid.

40    *anti-Israel campaigning so seamlessly:* Elena Giordano, 'Greta Thunberg carried away by police at pro-Palestine demonstration, again', *Politico* (9 September 2024).

40    *'taking the knee' for Black Lives Matter:* At the NHS Tavistock paediatric gender clinic in London, staff members were urged to add a banner to their emails displaying the raised fist emblem of Black Lives Matter against a backdrop of a rainbow pride flag. Ewan Somerville, 'NHS child gender clinic drops plans to use Black Lives Matter logo on staff email signatures', *Telegraph* (5 March 2022).

40    *heteronormativity and class hierarchy:* Stuart Basden, 'Extinction Rebellion isn't about the Climate', *Medium* (10 January 2019).

40    *'environmental degradation is also considered':* Leah Thomas, 'What Is Intersectional Environmentalism? (And Why It's More Important Than Ever)', *The Good Trade* (30 October 2024).

41 **Vincent van Gogh's Sunflowers in tomato soup:** Damien Gayle, 'Just Stop Oil activists throw soup at Van Gogh's Sunflowers', *Guardian* (14 October 2022).

41 **'You had better take up religion':** Quoted in Christopher Fry's foreword to Menander, *The Bad-Tempered Man*, trans. Philip Vellacott (London: Oxford University Press, 1960), p. vii.

41 **turn to wokism in their search for meaning:** The painting was selected for its fame, but symbolically the choice seems apt for the antipathy towards humankind that appears to sustain groups such as Just Stop Oil. Van Gogh's *Sunflowers* captures a rare moment of optimism in an otherwise troubled life. In February 1888, van Gogh rented a property in Arles in the south of France, which was to be known as the 'Yellow House'. He envisaged this to be a haven for artists, and had invited Paul Gauguin to join him. His hope was to decorate the house with paintings of sunflowers, eleven of which were eventually produced (one was later destroyed in an air raid in Japan). With their bright and striking yellow tones, these paintings are infused with van Gogh's sense of hope and possibility, a stark contrast to the ominous dark violet blues of the self-portrait produced at the asylum at Saint-Rémy, a year before his suicide.

41 **'There are people who are destroying the planet!':** Carlie Porterfield, '"Mona Lisa" attacked with cake by climate change protester', *Forbes* (31 May 2022).

41 **To them, Sunflowers is just 'a painting':** Quoted by Gayle, op. cit.

42 **Bamiyan in March 2001 felt much the same way:** 'Outcry as Buddhas are destroyed', *BBC News* (12 March 2001).

42 **the grades of students from minority racial backgrounds:** Neil Johnston, 'Oxford and Cambridge to move away from 'traditional' exams to boost results of minorities', *Telegraph* (25 January 2025).

42 **'middle-class students compared with other groups':** Johnston, op. cit.

43 **disqualified from the category of 'students of color':** Robby Soave, 'School district decides Asians aren't students of color', *Reason* (16 November 2020).

43 **'US higher education colleges and universities':** Edwin Rios and Chris Stein, 'US supreme court rules against affirmative action in Harvard and UNC cases', *Guardian* (29 June 2023).

43 **another sure step on the pathway to the end of woke:** Nina Totenberg, 'Supreme Court guts affirmative action, effectively ending race-conscious admissions', *American Conservative* (29 June 2023).

44 **the United States constitution to enshrine this belief:** Ibram X. Kendi, 'Pass an Anti-Racist Constitutional Amendment', *Politico* (2019). No specific publication date is provided on the website.

44 **reference to racism as America's 'original sin':** Ibid.

44 **has been enshrined in law since 1965:** Tom Slater, 'Labour's plan to foist DEI on Britain', *Spiked* (11 February 2024).

44 **'bonanza for dodgy, activist lawyers':** Kemi Badenoch, X (5 February 2024).

45 **Joseph Goebbels and the Ku Klux Klan:** Eleni Courea, 'Race review chief Tony Sewell compared to Joseph Goebbels in social media abuse', *The Times* (2 April 2021).

45 **influence of dead white men such as Socrates, Plato and Aristotle:** Roland White, '"White, male and heteronormative": The cancelled philosophers you shouldn't quote in 2024', *Telegraph* (17 June 2024).

45 **'unknown to the structural position of whiteness':** Julie Henry, 'Geology is racist, claims university professor', *Telegraph* (16 November 2024).

45 **'from fully participating in "environmental" activities':** In response, the Welsh Conservative leader Andrew R. T. Davies said: 'This kind of outdated virtue signalling nonsense is completely out of touch with the needs of the people of Wales. Labour is stuck

on yesterday's thinking, the kind that is being roundly rejected globally. Time to turf them out'. 'New Taxpayer-Funded Welsh Government Report Claims Countryside is Racist', *Guido Fawkes* (11 November 2024).

45    *influenced by 'racist colonial legacies':* Craig Simpson, 'British countryside is a "racist and colonial" white space, wildlife charities claim', *Telegraph* (7 February 2024).

45    *ethnic minorities are troubled by the animals:* Ruth Mosalski, 'Fact check: Will dogs really be banned from the Welsh countryside?', *Wales Online* (15 November 2024).

45    *the Welsh government did not act upon this recommendation:* Ibid.

46    *wisteria specifically cited as having colonial roots:* Fraser Myers, 'Colonialist wisteria? Accusations of racism are out of control', *Telegraph* (6 October 2021).

46    *nineteenth-century rhubarb producer Joseph Myatt:* Ellie Cook, 'Now woke warriors target plants as Wisteria's "colonial roots" dubbed offensive', *Daily Express* (6 October 2021).

46    *'more racist than anywhere else – maybe, maybe not':* Helena Horton, 'British countryside is racist, says Countryfile presenter', *Telegraph* (15 October 2020).

46    *'intimidating place for BAME communities':* Nazia Parveen, 'The BAME women making the outdoors more inclusive', *Guardian* (2 December 2020).

46    *'unwelcoming to people of colour':* Faima Bakar, '"The English countryside was shaped by colonialism": Why rural Britain is unwelcoming for people of colour', *Metro* (21 September 2020).

47    *draw connections between plants and LGBTQ+ communities:* Kew Gardens was established in the mid-eighteenth century and was opened to the public in 1840. Its founders cultivated specimens from across the globe, some of which had come from Captain Cook's voyage to the South Seas. Kew is a UNESCO World Heritage Site and houses over 8.5 million items. According to its website, it has 'the largest and most diverse botanical and mycological collections in the world'.

47    *'allowing for new conversations':* Kew Gardens, X (8 September 2023).

47    *'individual plants do not neatly fit into binaries':* Kew Gardens, X (8 September 2023).

47    *'Equality, Diversity and Inclusion Delivery Plan':* The 'Equality, Diversity and Inclusion Delivery Plan' is available to download on the Kew Gardens website.

47    *oppression of the 'LGBT community':* Graham Stewart, 'Is the National Trust losing the nation's trust?', *The Critic* (14 November 2020).

48    *display their commitment to LGBT rights:* Hayley Dixon, 'National Trust asks volunteers to wear rainbow face paint and glitter for Pride', *Telegraph* (14 June 2021).

48    *decriminalisation of homosexuality:* Lucy Pasha-Robinson, 'National Trust volunteers refusing to wear gay pride lanyards in protest over "outing" former lord of the manor', *Independent* (4 August 2017).

48    *'a job that only an historian could do?':* David Starkey, 'We can't trust the National Trust's history', *The Critic* (March 2021).

49    *'understand why we find it difficult to wait':* Martin Luther King, Jr., *Letter from Birmingham Jail* (London: Penguin, 2018), pp. 8-9. Originally published in 1963.

49    *most tolerant and diverse to have ever existed:* For example, see 'Love thy neighbour? Public trust and acceptance of the people who live alongside us', *World Values Survey* (April 2023).

49    *Vivek Ramaswamy's book Woke, Inc.: Inside the Social Justice Scam (2021):* Vivek Ramaswamy, *Woke, Inc.: Inside the Social Justice Scam* (London: Swift, 2021).

49    *Western world is potentially being reversed:* In a wide-ranging analysis on his website *Reality's Last Stand*, evolutionary biologist Colin Wright has addressed the failures of DEI to

achieve its goals, and has drawn attention to a study by the Network Contagion Research Institute (NCRI) and Rutgers University which has shown that 'certain DEI practices could induce hostility, increase authoritarian tendencies, and foster agreement with extreme rhetoric'. The study reveals 'a chilling convergence' between DEI and 'authoritarian attitudes, suggesting that such training is fostering not empathy, but coercion and control'. Wright has further exposed how coverage of this study in the *New York Times* was scuppered by an unprecedented demand 'that this particular research undergo peer review – a requirement that had never been imposed on the institute's earlier findings, even on similarly sensitive topics like extremism or online hate'. At the same time, the publication of a similar story in *Bloomberg* was 'quashed outright by an editor known for public support of DEI initiatives'. Given that DEI is such a profitable industry, it should be open to public scrutiny, particularly if its results are in direct contradiction to its stated aims. Colin Wright, 'Why Was This Groundbreaking Study on DEI Silenced?', *Reality's Last Stand* (25 November 2024).

50    *'good for business and is the right thing to do':* Alexandr Wang, X (13 June 2024).

50    **good old-fashioned liberal values:** Robin DiAngelo, *White Fragility: Why It's So Hard for White People to Talk About Racism* (Boston: Beacon Press, 2018).

50    **Palmer Luckey (founder of Oculus VR) and Elon Musk:** See the responses to Alexandr Wang's post on X (13 June 2024) by Tobias Lütke, Palmer Luckey and Elon Musk.

52    *'or any other immutable characteristic':* Andrew Doyle, Twitter (10 September 2020).

52    **an accurate reflection of their own views:** In addition, a 2021 survey by the Centre for Policy Studies determined that only 37 per cent of respondents understood the definition of 'woke'. See Frank Luntz, *Britain Speaks: The New Language of Politics and Business* (London: Centre for Policy Studies, 2021).

55    **on the grounds that they were too progressive:** See the anonymous editorial 'Republicans divide and Democrats unite in the Pennsylvania primaries', *Economist* (18 May 2022).

55    *'is now being replicated on the right':* Konstantin Kisin, X (5 September 2024). See also his articles on *Substack*: 'Tucker Carlson and the woke right' (17 February 2024) and 'Thou shalt not criticise the woke right' (5 September 2024).

55    *'advocate for collective power under that heading':* James Lindsay, X (7 October 2024).

56    *'if they don't advocate for themselves no one else will':* Andrew Torba, X (17 January 2025).

56    **the disciples of Critical Social Justice to capitalise 'black':** 'Protests following the death of George Floyd, which led to discussions of policing and Confederate symbols, also prompted many news organizations to examine their own practices and staffing. The Associated Press, whose Stylebook is widely influential in the industry, announced June 19 it would make Black uppercase.' David Bauder, 'AP says it will capitalize Black but not white', *Associated Press* (20 July 2020). This decision to capitalise 'black' but not 'white' was jumpstarted in the media by the Black Lives Matter protests and riots of 2022, but drew on an existing convention within the discipline of Political Science denoting cultural groups with a shared history of slavery. Political scientist Wilfred Reilly has compared it to the capitalised 'Irish' as a 'known and specifiable' ethnic group (Twitter, 10 January 2023). Given that the new convention in the media heralded by the *Associated Press* did not make any distinctions between black Americans descended from slaves and recent migrants to the country, focusing solely on skin colour as the defining factor and choosing to leave 'white' uncapitalised, it was thereby making a specifically ideological gesture regarding the relative power of identity groups. That said, other activists took the view that both 'black' and 'white' ought to be capitalised because failing to do so would 'implicitly affirm Whiteness as the standard and norm'. Kristen Mack and John Palfrey, 'Capitalizing black and white: grammatical justice and equity', *MacArthur Foundation* (26 August 2020).

56    **given that it is 'ill-defined' and 'self-contradictory':** Connor Tomlinson, 'There is no "Woke Right"', *The Critic* (29 October 2024).

56    *'history, culture, and statehood of the peoples of the US and Europe':* Ibid.

56    *'an attempt by yesterday's Left to tone police, gatekeep, and redefine the Right'*: Ibid.

56    *akin to 'racist', 'climate denier' or 'transphobe'*: Benjamin Boyce, X (4 October 2024).

57    *'very little similarity other than loose crosstalk between them'*: Ibid.

57    **generated the most controversy**: Ariana Baio, 'White House describes Tucker Carlson's "Nazi propaganda" interview as a "sadistic insult"', *Independent* (6 September 2024).

57    **the former scenario was *'infinitely preferable in every way'***: Andrew Lapin, 'Tucker Carlson hosts "historian" who promotes Nazi falsehoods on Holocaust', *Jerusalem Post* (5 September 2024).

57    **who helmed an empire that was *'far worse than the Nazis'***: In addition, panellist Dr Onyeka Nubia criticised Churchill's *A History of the English-Speaking Peoples* (four volumes, 1956-58) for the use of terms such as 'English-Speaking Peoples' and 'Anglo-Saxon', which were deemed to be white supremacist in nature. Craig Simpson, 'Churchill College panel claims wartime PM was a white supremacist leading an empire "worse than the Nazis"', *Telegraph* (11 February 2021).

58    **was advertised as *'only open to black, Asian and ethnically diverse candidates'***: Jacinta Taylor, "BBC bans white people from applying for £18,000 trainee job on Springwatch and The One Show", *Daily Mail* (19 June 2021).

60    **and left or right affiliations**: Jordan Mossa and Peter J. O'Connor, 'The Dark Triad traits predict authoritarian political correctness and alt-right attitudes', *Heliyon* vol. 6, issue 7 (July 2020).

60    *'psychopathy, narcissism, Machiavellianism and entitlement'*: Ibid.

61    *'to control others' behavior, and draw attention to themselves'*: Zaid Jilani, 'The Woke Left v. the Alt-Right: A New Study Shows They're More Alike Than Either Side Realizes', *Quillette* (3 August 2020).

## Chapter 2

64    **consider unselfishness to be the ultimate virtue**: 'If you asked twenty good men today what they thought the highest of the virtues, nineteen of them would reply, Unselfishness. But if you asked almost any of the great Christians of old he would have replied, Love. You see what has happened? A negative term has been substituted for a positive, and this is of more than philological importance.' C. S. Lewis, *The Weight of Glory and Other Addresses* (London: William Collins, 2013), p. 25. First published as *Transposition and Other Addresses* in 1940.

67    *'will also cease because it is expedient'*: Seneca, *Epistulae Morales ad Lucilium*, IX, 9 (written circa 65 AD).

67    *'This is usually false'*: Peter Boghossian and James Lindsay, *How to Have Impossible Conversations: A Very Practical Guide* (New York: Lifelong Books, 2019), p. 26.

68    *'have had someone stop talking to them'*: Frank Luntz as quoted in 'CPS publishes landmark survey by Dr Frank Luntz on politics, economics and culture wars', Centre for Policy Studies (6 July 2021). Link to full report available on this website.

68    **such as *'Is classical music racist?'***: 'Is classical music racist?', *Classic FM* (5 July 2012).

68    *'The whiteness of* **Toy Story 4**': Stephen Galloway, 'The Whiteness of *Toy Story 4*', *Hollywood Reporter* (3 January 2020).

68    *'This new health minister thinks you can identity as a llama'*: Fraser Myers, 'This new health minister thinks you can identity as a llama', *Spiked* (11 February 2025).

68    **a right-wing talking point**: Journalist Owen Jones, for instance, has argued that there are those for whom free speech is 'nothing more than a political ploy, a ruse, a term the far right wilfully abuse to spread hatred'. Owen Jones, '"Tommy Robinson" is no martyr to freedom of speech', *Guardian* (31 May 2018).

69    *as a 'flame purification ceremony':* In September 2021, the body in charge of elementary and secondary schools in southwestern Ontario authorised the ritualistic incineration of supposedly offensive books. During the course of this 'flame purification' ceremony, almost five thousands books – including copies of *Tintin* and *Asterix* – were removed from shelves and were destroyed or recycled. Tyler Dawson, 'Book burning at Ontario francophone schools as "gesture of reconciliation" denounced', *National Post* (7 September 2021).

69    *telling them they should 'try to be less white':* Jade Bremner, 'Coca-Cola faces backlash over seminar asking staff to "be less white"', *Independent* (24 February 2021).

69    *taken seriously by the establishment:* Alex Regan, 'Calls to remove "racist" Gandhi statue in Leicester', *BBC News* (12 June 2020); Ewan Somerville, 'Imperial College told to remove bust of slavery abolitionist because he "might now be called racist"', *Telegraph* (26 October 2021).

69    *this dream King was upholding white supremacy:* Robin DiAngelo argues that individualism and colour-blindness are 'ideologies of racism'. Ibram X. Kendi claims that the principle of colour-blindness is 'a mask to hide racism'. Reni Eddi-Lodge calls it 'a childish, stunted analysis of racism' which 'starts and ends at "discriminating against a person because of the colour of their skin is bad"', without any accounting for the ways in which structural power manifests in these exchanges'. DiAngelo, op. cit., p. 89; Kendi, op. cit., p. 10; Reni Eddo-Lodge, *Why I'm No Longer Talking to White People About Race* (London: Bloomsbury Circus, 2017), p. 82.

69    *by skin colour for after-school activities:* Nicola Woolcock, 'American School in London accused of "racial indoctrination"', *The Times* (25 November 2021).

69    *teachers throughout the country would be doing the same:* Glen Owen, 'BBC sex education programme tells 9-year-olds there are "over 100 genders" and shows kids talking to adults about "bi-gender", "genderqueer" and "pansexual" identities', *Daily Mail* (23 January 2021).

69    *unable to answer the question:* During a radio interview on LBC with Keir Starmer, the host Nick Ferrari asked whether a woman could have a penis. Starmer responded: 'Uh, Nick, I'm not, er, I, I don't think we can conduct this debate with, you know, I get this, uh'. Quoted by Brendan O'Neill, 'Everyone who has a penis is a man', *Spiked* (30 March 2022).

69    *some would favour the neologism 'womxn':* Alexandra Topping, 'Wellcome Collection excoriated over use of term "womxn"', *Guardian* (10 October 2018).

69    *and 'individuals with a cervix':* Laura Parnaby, 'CEO of woke tampon brand August is slammed for repeatedly using word "menstruators" instead of "women" during Gayle King interview and brags that her brand her is proudly pro-trans', *Daily Mail* (6 July 2023); Craig Simpson, '"Women" and "girls" left out of NHS-backed periods guidance website', *Telegraph* (9 August 2022); Gisela Crespo, 'American Cancer Society now recommends cervical cancer screening start at 24, not 21', *CNN Health* (30 July 2020).

69    *where they would commit further sexual assaults?:* Nazia Parveen, 'Karen White: how "manipulative" transgender inmate attacked again', *Guardian* (11 October 2018).

69    *should be put on medication to halt puberty:* See Chapter 7 of the present volume.

69    *but that it's a spectrum?:* Colin Wright, 'On sex and gender, the New England Journal of Medicine has abandoned its scientific mission', *Quillette* (23 Dec 2020).

69    *for saying that biological sex is real?:* Sam Damshenas, 'Maya Forstater wins appeal against employment tribunal over "gender critical" views', *Gay Times* (10 June 2021).

70    *missing the entirety of the American Revolution:* Washington Irving, 'Rip Van Winkle', in *The Sketch Book of Geoffrey Crayon, Gent.* (New York: C. S. Van Winkle, 1819), pp. 59-94.

70    *due to perceived social pressures:* Timur Kuran, *Private Truths, Public Lies: The Social Consequences of Preference Falsification* (Cambridge, Massachusetts: Harvard University Press, 1995).

70    *adapt to their oppressive conditions:* Jonathan Waterlow, *It's Only a Joke Comrade!: Humour, Trust and Everyday Life under Stalin* (Oxford: 2018).

71     *they seemed to belong to two cultures at once:* Ibid., p. 5.

71     *'in the crosshatching of ideology and daily experience':* Ibid., p. 6.

72     *'For 'tis of aspics' tongues':* William Shakespeare, *Othello*, act 3, scene 3.

73     *rated around 'seven' or 'seven and a half':* Caroline Mortimer, 'Jeremy Corbyn on The Last Leg: enthusiastic about staying in the EU but won't share a platform with Cameron', *Independent* (10 June 2016).

76     *least xenophobic countries in the world:* A study by the European Union Agency for Fundamental Rights concluded that 'the UK had one of the lowest reported levels of race-related harassment and violence in the 12-country study'. Rakib Ehsan and Doug Stokes, 'Poor white men and Labour's identity trap', *The Critic* (May 2021).

76     *national referendum was some kind of 'coup':* William Keegan, 'Brexit was becoming a farce. Now it is turning into a coup', *Guardian* (11 August 2019).

76     *most of the electorate did not vote:* Roger Scruton, *Conservatism: An Invitation to the Great Tradition* (New York: All Points Books, 2017), p. 152.

77     *'and to that extent it deserves our support':* E. M. Forster, *Two Cheers For Democracy* (London: Edward Arnold, 1951), p. 79.

78     *their supporters as 'fruitcakes', 'loonies' and 'closet racists':* Simon Heffer, 'Why Cameron will regret his "fruitcakes and loonies" insult', *Daily Mail* (23 November 2012).

78     *12 per cent of the population, respectively:* Trust in Government Survey, UK: 2023, Office for National Statistics (19 January 2024).

78     *'you can have the election stolen from you':* Quoted by Susan Ferrechio, 'Stolen, rigged and illegitimate: Democrats' long history of objecting to election results', *Washington Times* (21 August 2023).

78     *'find 11,780 votes' to overturn the result:* Martin Pengelly and Richard Lescombe, '"I just want 11,780 votes"': Trump pressed Georgia to overturn Biden victory', *Guardian* (3 January 2021).

79     *many members of the public soon grew to resent:* In the aftermath of the Brexit vote, politicians on both sides of the House of Commons were again attempting to rig the system in their favour. Prime Minister Boris Johnson prorogued Parliament in an effort to constrain the powers of the legislature. Opposition MPs abused Standing Order No 24, a procedure by which emergency debates can be held, in order to make it illegal to leave the European Union without a deal. The speaker, John Bercow, surrendered all pretence of impartiality and allowed them to do so in spite of accepted protocol. This was all technically permissible, but was nonetheless the kind of constitutional sleight of hand that fatally undermined faith in Parliament.

     Similarly, although there is no requirement for MPs who defect from one party to another to trigger a by-election, in these circumstances there was no doubt a moral responsibility to do so. In defiance of what she perceived to be her party's acquiesce with Brexit, Labour MP Angela Smith joined the Liberal Democrats via the short-lived party Change UK, in spite of the fact that in her constituency of Penistone and Stocksbridge the Liberal Democrats won a mere 4.1 per cent of the vote. In Phillip Lee's Bracknell constituency, the Liberal Democrats won just 7.5 per cent, so his defection from the Tories (whose share was 58.8 per cent) was no trivial matter. 'We don't need by-elections', Lee said in an interview with Julia Hartley-Brewer (posted on the Talk TV Twitter account on 4 September 2019). 'We don't actually need General Elections at the moment.' Such sentiments were suggestive of a Parliament that had developed a fear of the public.

     At the same time, Boris Johnson had been described as 'hard right' and 'extreme' for attempting to implement the referendum result. As Fraser Nelson pointed out in the *Telegraph*, such claims simply would not pass muster with an electorate that voted in good faith to leave the European Union. See Fraser Nelson, 'Boris's agenda isn't "extreme" or "hard-Right" – and voters know it', *Telegraph* (5 September 2019).

     Moreover, claims that there was 'no mandate for a No Deal Brexit' were hardly persuasive. The referendum was a binary decision based on leaving or staying. Any subsequent referendum on the deal would only have been legitimate had it offered the option of leaving the EU on WTO terms or a deal that had been agreed by Parliament. To offer the option to remain in the EU all over again would have been to nullify the referendum that had already been held. We can only claim to be living in a democracy if our votes have meaning, and the majority of the population understands this even if our parliamentarians do not.

79 **'but upon the sovereignty of the People':** These words are taken from the letter by Tony Benn addressed to his constituents in 1975, republished in the *Spectator* on 24 May 2016.

79 **it might as well have been called How to Stop Democracy:** Nick Clegg, *How to Stop Brexit (and Make Britain Great Again)* (London: Vintage, 2017).

79 **'submit to the decisions of incompetent voters':** Jason Brennan, *Against Democracy* (Oxford: Princeton University Press, 2016), pp. 142-143.

80 **'simply to consider ways to jettison democracy':** Patrick J. Deneen, *Why Liberalism Failed* (New Haven: Yale University Press, 2019), p. 157. See also Bryan Caplan, *The Myth of the Rational Voter: Why Democracies Choose Bad Policies* (Princeton: Princeton University Press, 2007); Jeffrey Friedman, 'Democratic Incompetence in Normative and Positive Theory: Neglected Implications of "The Nature of Belief Systems in Mass Publics"', *Critical Review*, vol. 18, nos. 1-3 (January 2006), pp. i-xliii; Damon Root, *Overruled: The Long War over Control of the U.S. Supreme Court* (New York: Palgrave Macmillan, 2014).

80 **'rewrite our geopolitical and economic status':** Will Dunn, 'Why the Brexit debate will never die', *New Statesman* (31 January 2025).

80 **'divinely blessed, and is ever faithful to it':** Plato, *The Republic*, trans. A. D. Lindsay (London: Everyman's Library, 1992), p. 245. This translation originally published in 1935. *The Republic* was authored circa 375 BC.

81 **'is entitled to at least as many':** John Stuart Mill, *Thoughts on Parliamentary Reform* (London: John W. Parker and Son, 1859), pp. 25-26.

82 **'so frequently controlled elections':** Walter J. Shepard, 'Democracy in Transition', American Political Science Review vol. 29, no. 1 (February 1935), pp. 1-20. Quotation taken from p. 9.

82 **cast by black Americans would count twice:** Brandon Hasbrouck, 'The votes of black Americans should count twice', *Nation* (17 December 2020).

82 **'How do we get rid of you':** Quoted by John Nichols, 'Tony Benn and the five essential questions of democracy' *The Nation* (14 March 2014).

83 **to countenance such an eventuality:** The last serious attempt at electoral reform was the referendum on the Alternative Vote (AV) which came about due to the Conservative and Liberal Democrat coalition government that formed after the 2010 general election. It seemed like a fudge, a system of ranking candidates in order of preference that occupied a kind of middle ground between 'first past the post' and proportional representation (Nick Clegg called it a 'miserable little compromise'). Explanatory leaflets from the Electoral Commission made the AV system appear needlessly complicated. Those who were keen for reform were being asked to settle for second best. Little wonder that the voters were not persuaded.

84 **anyone who has read his famous 'fairy story':** George Orwell, *Animal Farm: A Fairy Story* (London: Secker and Warburg, 1945).

84 **Wallington and the 'Willingdon' of the book:** Some have claimed that Orwell based the 'Willingdon' of his novel on the real-life village of Willingdon in the Wealden District of East Sussex. While it is true that he spent significant parts of his childhood in this area of Eastbourne, it seems more likely that the name was simply borrowed due to its resemblance to 'Wallington'.

85 **low front door and ceilings:** The name of 'The Stores' related to its history as the local shop, and upon moving in Orwell quickly restored its original purpose. The proceeds from the shop helped him to offset the rent and that also meant that he was working from home, an obvious advantage for one who spent much of his time writing at his desk.

86 *Orwell simply wrote next to it: 'Balls':* Quoted in Julian Symons's introduction to George Orwell, *Animal Farm* (London: Everyman's Library, 1993), pp. xi-xxiii. Quotation taken from p. xv. *Animal Farm* was originally published in 1945.

86 *'the worst kind of reactionary turncoat':* Benjamin Norton 'George Orwell was a reactionary snitch who made a blacklist of leftists for the British government', *Medium* (14 December 2016).

86 *'a small child trying to bring down an elephant with a pea-shooter':* D. J. Taylor, *Orwell: The New Life* (London: Constable, 2023), p. 11. That Taylor has written two biographies would have angered Orwell. In his will, he had insisted that no biography should be written after his death. Orwell's widow, Sonia Brownell, spent the next few decades fending off would-be biographers; she even enlisted Malcolm Muggeridge as a decoy who pretended to be busy at work on the project. Taylor's first biography was *Orwell: The Life* (London: Chatto & Windus, 2003).

86 *both in terms of their flair and intellectual heft:* George Orwell, *Nineteen Eighty-Four* (London: Secker and Warburg 1949).

87 *basis of his memoir* Homage to Catalonia *(1938):* George Orwell, *Homage to Catalonia* (London: Secker and Warburg 1938).

87 *particularly among those of a postmodernist bent:* I have discussed this in *The New Puritans* (op. cit., pp. 75-76) and quoted the following passage from Orwell: 'A speaker who uses that kind of phraseology has gone some distance toward turning himself into a machine. The appropriate noises are coming out of his larynx, but his brain is not involved as it would be if he were choosing his words for himself. If the speech he is making is one that he is accustomed to make over and over again, he may be almost unconscious of what he is saying, as one is when one utters the responses in church'. George Orwell, 'Politics and the English Language' (1945), in *Essays* (London: Everyman's Library, 2002), ed. Peter Davison, pp. 954–67. Quotation taken from p. 963. See also Christopher Hitchens, *Why Orwell Matters* (New York: MJF Books, 2002), pp. 193-204, for a further analysis of how contemporary postmodernist critics fail the test of Orwell's intellectual honesty.

87 *what he described as 'ready-made phrases':* 'Politics and the English Language', op. cit., p. 964.

87 *in his extended piece on* Charles Dickens *(1940):* George Orwell, 'Charles Dickens' (1940), in *Essays*, op. cit., pp. 135-85. Quotation taken from p. 173.

88 *it seems to settle the matter for good:* George Orwell, 'Lear, Tolstoy and the Fool' (1947), in *Essays*, op. cit., pp. 1183-1200.

88 *cover many contemporary novelists and their approach to social commentary:* George Orwell, 'Inside the Whale' (1940), in *Essays*, op. cit., pp. 211-49.

88 *'keep up an attitude of the completest indifference, no matter what happens':* Ibid., p. 242.

88 *to take up arms in defence of their country:* George Orwell, 'Unpublished Response to *Authors Take Sides on the Spanish War*' (1937), in *Essays*, op. cit., p. 74. In his biography, D. J. Taylor speculates that Orwell's deep-seated revulsion towards gay men might have originated in suppressed desires of his own. 'All the same, there is a faint suspicion that in railing against "fashionable pansies" and moneyed young men who can't pronounce their "r"s, Orwell may have been protesting too much.' Taylor, op. cit., p. 444.

88 *only later revealed as a fabrication of our author's imagination:* George Orwell, 'The Moon Under Water' (1946), in *Essays*, op. cit., pp. 1026-1028.

88 *to the successful brewing of this quintessentially English drink:* George Orwell, 'A Nice Cup of Tea' (1946), in *Essays*, op. cit., pp. 990-92.

88 *to the grisly experience of 'Shooting an Elephant':* George Orwell, 'Shooting an Elephant' (1936), in *Essays*, op. cit., pp. 42-49.

89 *'drive a bayonet into a Buddhist priest's guts':* Ibid., p. 43.

89    *to obliterate a perfectly healthy human life:* George Orwell, 'A Hanging' (1931), in *Essays*, op. cit., pp. 16-20.

89    *'cutting a life short when it is in full tide':* Ibid., p. 18.

89    *one cannot help but feel repulsed:* George Orwell, 'Notes on the Way' (1940), in *Essays*, op. cit., pp. 252-59.

89    *'the dreadful thing that had happened to him':* Ibid., p. 252.

89    *describes his night in a foetid London workhouse:* George Orwell, 'The Spike (1931), in *Essays*, op. cit., pp. 8-16.

89    *got drunk in order to experience arrest and imprisonment:* George Orwell, 'Clink' (1932), in *Essays*, op. cit., pp. 21-30.

90    *an Eton-educated man romanticising the working class:* George Orwell, *Down and Out in Paris and London* (London: Victor Gollancz, 1933); George Orwell, *The Road to Wigan Pier* (London: Victor Gollancz, 1937).

90    *'the kind of person he imagined himself to be':* Taylor, op. cit., p. 450.

90    *surely this criticism could be applied to almost anyone:* Taylor draws out Orwell's many contradictions and speaks of his 'abiding inner conflict', generated by the combination of his 'intensely conservative background' and 'the radicalism of his politics', that informed his fiction from the outset (ibid., p. 403). In *Why Orwell* Matters, Christopher Hitchens makes a compelling case that during the course of his lifetime Orwell reasoned his way out of his own innate conservative prejudices. The imperialist system of Orwell's time as a police officer in Burma, the inspiration for his debut novel *Burmese Days* (London: Victor Gollancz, 1934), is one he eventually found rebarbative. For all his adoration of Rudyard Kipling, Orwell took him to task for his failure to acknowledge the exploitative nature of empire. Yet, as Taylor points out, Orwell could not help but feel some vestigial admiration for the 'personal dynamism' of British colonialists of the Raj, along with 'the achievements of a caste made up of people "who did things"'. Taylor, op. cit., p. 413.

90    *impersonating a cat at the feet of the actress Rula Lenska:* Danya Bazaraa, 'When George Galloway pretended to be a cat on Big Brother: Moment the new MP for Rochdale got down on all fours and pretended to lap up milk from actress Rula Lenska's hands', *Daily Mail* (1 March 2024).

90    *'The Penised Individual Who Raped You is a Woman':* J.K. Rowling, Twitter (12 December 2021).

91    *least of all by the political right:* Why Orwell Matters, op. cit., p. 102.

91    *conveyed in his essay 'The Lion and the Unicorn':* George Orwell, 'The Lion and the Unicorn: Socialism and the English Genius' (1941), in *Essays*, op. cit., pp. 291-348.

91    *'if not fought against, could triumph anywhere':* Why Orwell Matters, op. cit., p. 85.

91    *'unwillingness to admit that Socialism has totalitarian possibilities':* George Orwell, 'Review of *Reflections on the Revolution of Our Time* by Harold J. Laski', *Observer* (10 October 1943).

91    *'the socialism of Marxism and the managerial revolution':* Quoted by Taylor, op. cit., p. 517.

91    *'even if socialism itself had bureaucratic and authoritarian tendencies':* Why Orwell Matters, op. cit., p. 83.

92    *commander-in-chief whose relationship with the truth is erratic:* '"1984" sales soar as "alternative facts" and Trump claims echo Orwell's dystopian world', *Telegraph* (25 January 2017).

92    *'History has stopped':* George Orwell, *Nineteen Eighty-Four* (London: Everyman's Library, 1992), p. 162. Originally published in 1949.

92     *results in the outsourcing of individual agency:* George Orwell, 'Notes on Nationalism' (1945), in *Essays*, op. cit., pp. 865-84.

92     *'recognising no other duty than that of advancing its interests':* Ibid., p. 865.

92     *'is to destroy yourself as a writer':* George Orwell, 'Writers and Leviathan' (1948), in *Essays*, op. cit., pp. 1261-1268. Quotation taken from p. 1267.

93     *could be advantageous to British conservatives:* For details of this conversation see Taylor, op. cit., p. 464.

93     *'you know that it is your duty to shut up immediately':* 'For example, if you say anything damaging about British imperialism, you are playing into the hands of Dr Goebbels. If you criticize Stalin you are playing into the hands of the *Tablet* and the *Daily Telegraph*. If you criticize Chiang Kai-Shek you are playing into the hands of Wang Ching-Wei - and so on, indefinitely.' George Orwell, 'As I Please' (1944), in *Essays*, op. cit., pp. 666-69. Quotation taken from p. 668.

93     *'Pretend there are no slums?':* Ibid.

93     *'help your friends and harm your enemies':* Plato, op. cit., p. 8.

93     *rigorous in demanding to see his medical assessments:* Gloria Oladipo, 'Biden apologizes after mistakenly calling on late congresswoman', *Guardian* (4 October 2022).

94     *no authors actively seeking to improve society:* 'Inside the Whale', op. cit., p. 248.

94     *purposefully crafted in the hope of actuating real-world change:* Ibid.

94     *'but already it was impossible to say which was which':* George Orwell, *Animal Farm* (London: Everyman's Library, 1993), p. 93. Originally published in 1945.

## Chapter 3

95     *'lying quite still for almost fifteen minutes while bleeding to death':* Welles later 'developed an angry conviction that the blame was entirely Joe's for making a wrong move and impaling himself on Brutus's stationary blade'. Houseman and Welles paid his hospital bills and there was no lawsuit. John Houseman, *Run-Through* (New York: Simon and Schuster, 1972), pp. 347-48.

97     *'eating into the moral fibre of the next generation':* Ayaan Hirsi Ali, 'Why I am now a Christian', *UnHerd* (25 December 2023).

98     *it was ultimately 'imperfect':* Forster, op. cit., pp. 67-68. This quotation is taken from 'The Challenge of our Time', an essay originally published in 1946.

98     **Why Liberalism Failed (2018) and Regime Change: Towards a Postliberal Future (2023):** Patrick J. Deneen, *Regime Change: Towards a Postliberal Future* (London: Forum, 2023).

98     *'cultural norms and political habits essential to self-governance':* *Why Liberalism Failed*, op. cit., p. xxvi.

99     *too much freedom had a toxic effect on our culture:* Louise Perry, *The Case Against the Sexual Revolution: A New Guide to Sex in the 21st Century* (Cambridge: Polity Press, 2022).

99     *emphasis on justice and humanity, ultimately had the opposite effect:* Christopher Caldwell, *The Age of Entitlement: America Since the Sixties* (New York: Simon & Schuster, 2020).

100     *interpreted as a call to eliminate Jews from the state of Israel:* Edward Malnick, 'Met Police adviser led "from the river to the sea" chant', *Telegraph* (4 November 2023).

100     *the curbing of freedom of speech along religious lines:* James Jackson, 'Protesters call for Islamic state in Germany', *Telegraph* (28 April 2024).

100     *sparked a series of protests and civil unrest:* Lipika Pelham, 'Mahsa Amini: Iran responsible for "physical violence" leading to death, UN says', *BBC News* (8 March 2024).

100     **campaigned partly on the fulfilment of this pledge:** David Zimmerman, 'Senator Cotton Urges Mayorkas to Deport Foreign Nationals Who Support Hamas', *National Review* (17 October 2023); Nathan Layne, 'Trump pledges to expel immigrants who support Hamas, ban Muslims from the U.S.', *Reuters* (17 October 2023).

100     **although his decree was largely ignored:** Angela Charlton and Jeffrey Schaeffer, 'France has banned pro-Palestinian protests and vowed to protect Jews from resurgent antisemitism', *Associated Press* (12 October 2023).

100     **those who would typically defend the right to free expression:** Will Bolton, Ben Riley-Smith and Benedict Smith, 'Met Police chief urged to ban pro-Palestinian Armistice Day protests', *Telegraph* (5 November 2023).

101     **to prevent the Remembrance events being disrupted:** Daniel Martin, Robert Mendick and Will Bolton, 'Sunak orders police to stop pro-Palestinian protest disrupting Remembrance events', *Telegraph* (3 November 2023).

101     **the marches 'should be allowed to go ahead':** Jack Walters, 'Only one-in-five Brits support pro-Palestine protest on Armistice Day, new poll reveals', *GB News* (4 November 2023).

101     **cancelled out of concern for the 'safety and wellbeing' of students:** Eirian Jane Prosser, 'How Israel-Hamas war has sparked a wave of UK campus "cancel culture": Universities axe lectures and events due to "sensitivities" around Gaza - while Jewish students are "abused" and Oxford union calls for "intifada until victory" after terror attack', *Daily Mail* (25 October 2023).

101     **article from The Onion which took a pro-Palestine stance:** Michael Eisen, X (23 October 2023).

101     **while a degree of Schadenfreude is understandable, it is hardly helpful:** On Twitter (17 March 2022), Michael Eisen had asked 'has anyone, anywhere actually been cancelled?'

101     **we should claim 'the right not to tolerate the intolerant':** 'Unlimited tolerance must lead to the disappearance of tolerance. If we extend unlimited tolerance even to those who are intolerant, if we are not prepared to defend a tolerant society against the onslaught of the intolerant, then the tolerant will be destroyed, and tolerance with them. In this formulation, I do not imply, for instance, that we should always suppress the utterance of intolerant philosophies; as long as we can counter them by rational argument and keep them in check by public opinion, suppression would certainly be most unwise. But we should claim the right even to suppress them, for it may easily turn out that they are not prepared to meet us on the level of rational argument, but begin by denouncing all argument; they may forbid their followers to listen to anything as deceptive as rational argument, and teach them to answer arguments by the use of their fists. We should therefore claim, in the name of tolerance, the right not to tolerate the intolerant.' K. R. Popper, *The Open Society and Its Enemies* (London: George Routledge & Sons, 1945), vol. 1, p. 226.

102     **that satirises the death of the king's father:** *Game of Thrones*, season 1, episode 10: 'Fire and Blood' (HBO, 2011).

104     **denote the form of evangelism now known as 'wokeness':** Mark Lilla, *The Once and Future Liberal: After Identity Politics* (New York: HarperCollins, 2017), p. 12.

105     **'all social institutions and political arrangements':** John Gray, *Liberalism* (Milton Keynes: Open University Press, 1986), p. x.

105     **'in so far as these concern the interests of no person but himself':** Mill, op. cit., p. 90.

105     **'may be subjected either to social or to legal punishments':** Ibid.

107     **reject some or all of the principles outlined above:** Helen Pluckrose puts it this way: 'It seems clear to me that some who say that liberalism has failed really mean that society has failed to be liberal. This is not wordplay. It is the difference between antibiotics failing to work and an individual failing to take their antibiotics; a diet not working and an individual not sticking to their diet. If you are someone who would like to live in a genuinely liberal

society but recognise that you are not, I urge you not to give up on liberalism, but help the push to create that society.' Helen Pluckrose, 'Has liberalism failed or are we failing to be liberal?', *The Overflowings of a Liberal Brain*, Substack (29 April 2023).

107   *'That's the experiment I would like to run':* This quotation is taken from Christopher Hitchens's appearance at an event at Google headquarters in Mountain View, California on 16 August 2007. The full recording is available on YouTube.

108   *'is in reality expressing the highest respect for law':* Letter from Birmingham Jail, op. cit., p. 12.

109   *'What the hell is water?':* David Foster Wallace, 'Plain old untrendy troubles and emotions', *Guardian* (20 September 2008). This was a posthumous publication of the transcript of his commencement speech delivered at Kenyon College in Ohio in 2005.

112   *radical ideas are best served by subtlety:* Forster, op. cit., p. 342.

112   *on a bronze plaque in the pedestal's museum:* The bronze plaque was presented in 1903 by the philanthropist Georgiana Schuyler in commemoration of Emma Lazarus and installed on the pedestal's interior wall. It was later housed in the pedestal museum in July 1986.

112   *'an unabashed victory of economic and political liberalism':* Francis Fukuyama, 'The End of History', *The National Interest* (Summer 1989). The essay was later developed into a book, *The End of History and the Last Man* (New York: Free Press, 1992).

114   *'means to make use of these rights and liberties':* John Rawls, *Lectures on the History of Political Philosophy* (Cambridge: Harvard University Press, 2007), p. 12. See also John Rawls, *A Theory of Justice: Revised Edition* (Cambridge: Harvard University Press, 1999), pp. 176-80. First edition published in 1971.

114   *'solitary, poore, nasty, brutish, and short':* Thomas Hobbes, *Leviathan or The Matter, Forme and Power of a Commonwealth Ecclesiasticall and Civil* (London: Andrew Crooke, 1651), p. 62.

114   *key foundational document in the history of liberalism:* John Locke, *Second Treatise of Government* (Illinois: Harlan Davidson, 1982), ed. Richard Cox. Originally published in 1689.

115   *'an undoubted right to dominion and sovereignty':* Ibid., p. 3.

115   *for the retention of individual conscience and belief:* John Locke, *A Letter Concerning Toleration* (London: Awnsham Churchill, 1689).

115   *between individual desires and the 'general will':* Jean-Jacques Rousseau's *The Social Contract* was first published as *Du contrat social; ou Principes du droit politique* in 1762.

115   *rather than through the rigidities of formal education:* Jean-Jacques Rousseau's *Émile* was first published as *Émile, ou De l'éducation* in 1762.

115   *'And forget his youthful spring?':* William Blake, 'The School-Boy' in *Songs of Innocence and Experience* (Oxford: Oxford University Press, 1967), p. 154. Originally published in 1789.

116   *submission to the law or the impositions of oppressive hierarchies:* 'Liberalism further undermines education by replacing a definition of liberty as an education in self-government with liberty as autonomy and the absence of constraint. Ultimately it destroys liberal education, since it begins with the assumption that we are born free, rather than that we must learn to become free.' Deneen, op. cit., p. 111.

117   *he is namechecked in* **The Merry Wives of Windsor:** The line is delivered by Slender: 'I have seen Sackerson loose twenty times, and have taken him by the chain. But I warrant you, the women have so cried and shrieked at it that it passed'. *The Merry Wives of Windsor*, act 1, scene 1.

118   *these debates cannot evade these definitional quagmires: Why Liberalism Failed*, op. cit.

118   *perished before his case has even been launched:* Roger Scruton, *England: An Elegy* (London: Chatto & Windus, 2000).

118    *in which he asserts that 'liberal civilization has passed away':* John Gray, *The New Leviathans: Thoughts After Liberalism* (London: Allen Lane, 2023), p. 6.

118    *'Liberalism has failed because liberalism has succeeded':* *Why Liberalism Failed*, op. cit., p. 179.

118    *'entering and exiting an election booth':* Ibid., p. xv.

118    *its danger lies in its pretence to neutrality:* Ibid., p. 5.

119    *a common tactic that I have never found persuasive:* Richard Dawkins has addressed this fallacy of classifying atheism as 'a matter of fundamentalist faith' in *The God Delusion* (London: Bantam Press, 2006), pp. 282-86.

119    *it is an imaginary idyll that cannot be reified:* 'Utopia means nowhere or no-place. It has often been taken to mean good place, through confusion of its first syllable with the Greek *eu* as in *euphemism* or *eulogy*. As a result of this mix-up, another word, dystopia, has been invented, to mean bad place. But, strictly speaking, imaginary good places and imaginary bad places are all utopias, or nowheres.' John Carey, introduction to *The Faber Book of Utopias* (London: Faber, 1999).

119    *'human separation from and opposition to nature':* *Why Liberalism Failed*, op. cit., p. 31.

120    *but this is not the fault of liberalism:* 'Then shall we next explain why the majority [of philosophers] are necessarily rascals, and try to show, if we can, that this is not the fault of philosophy either?' Plato, op. it., p. 172.

120    *freefall will require the fail-safe of positive law:* *Why Liberalism Failed*, op. cit., p. 38.

120    *'socially destructive behaviors begin to dominate society':* Ibid., p. 39.

120    *evolutionary history or our current way of life:* Ibid., p. 78.

121    *'no one of us is sufficient for himself, but each is in need of many things':* Plato, op. cit., p. 44.

121    *'aggregation of individual opinion over common good':* *Why Liberalism Failed*, op. cit., 155.

121    *what Deneen describes as a 'liberlocratic despotism':* Ibid., p. 182.

121    *'in which extreme license coexists with extreme oppression':* Ibid., p. 42.

122    *possibly selling them on as souvenirs:* See Carol Barton, '"Ill fare the hands that heaved the stones": John Milton, a preliminary thanatography', *Milton Studies*, vol. 43 (Pennsylvania: Penn State University Press, 2004), pp. 198–260.

123    *whose worldview was grounded in reason above all else:* On 1 November 2022, I gave a talk on John Milton at Gonville and Caius College in Cambridge, where only the week before protesters had attempted to silence the journalist Helen Joyce. The master of the college had hardly helped matters, by emailing all students and staff in advance to smear her work as 'offensive, insulting and hateful'. This seems very much at odds with the college's statement on freedom of speech: 'An active speaker programme is fundamental to the academic and other activities of the College and Fellows, staff and students are encouraged to invite a wide range of speakers and to engage critically but courteously with them.' Of course, disparities between an institution's official statements and its actual behaviour are nothing new, particularly when there has been a degree of ideological capture.

123    *his intention to 'justify the ways of God to men':* John Milton, *Paradise Lost* (1667, revised 1674), in *The Complete English Poems* (London: Everyman's Library, 1992), ed. Gordon Campbell, pp. 143–441. The phrase 'justify the ways of God to men' is quoted from Book I, line 26 (p. 150).

123    *'I made him just and right, / Sufficient to have stood, though free to fall':* Book III, lines 98-99. Ibid., p. 204.

124    *'By destiny, and can no other choose?':* Book V, ll. 524-34. Ibid., p. 264.

124 *'Twinned, and from her hath no dividual being'*: Book XII, ll. 83-85. Ibid., p. 425.

125 'For all this waste of wealth and loss of blood': Ibid., p. 100.

125 *printed texts should be approved by a censor before publication:* John Milton, *Areopagitica: A speech for the liberty of unlicensed printing, to the parliament of England* (1644), in *The Complete English Poems* (London: Everyman's Library, 1992), ed. Gordon Campbell, pp. 573-618. This edition also includes the text of the Licensing Order of 14 June 1643 (pp. 619-620). The title is in direct reference to the Greek orator Isocrates (436-338 BC) who delivered a speech called the *Areopagiticus*. The Areopagus is a mound at the Acropolis in Athens, derived from the Greek for 'Hill of Ares' ('*Areios Pagos*'), which was once the seat of the judiciary.

125 *'to argue freely according to conscience, above all liberties'*: Ibid., p. 613.

126 *'any subject that is not to their palate'*: Ibid., p. 584.

126 *('quis custodiet ipsos custodes')?*: Juvenal's question is not in relation to censorship. He is lamenting the fate of husbands who fear being cuckolded by their wives. One might arrange for guards to ensure a spouse's fidelity, but then *'quis custodiet ipsos custodes.'*

126 *'the grace of infallibility and uncorruptedness?'*: *Areopagitica.*, op. cit., p. 593.

126 *'is an assumption of infallibility'*: Mill, op. cit., p. 19.

126 *'in a free and open encounter?'*: *Areopagitica*, op. cit., p. 613.

127 *'that ethereal and fifth essence, the breath of reason itself'*: Ibid., p. 579.

127 *he tells us, 'slays an immortality rather than a life'*: Ibid.

127 *he had fallen foul of the 'hate speech' laws of the Holy See:* 'There it was that I found and visited the famous Galileo, grown old, a prisoner to the Inquisition, for thinking in astronomy otherwise than the Franciscan and Dominican licensers thought.' Ibid., p. 602.

128 *'Now you got to have all three of these to have a complete life'*: Martin Luther King, Jr., 'The three dimensions of a complete life' in *Letter from Birmingham Jail* (London: Penguin Books, 2018), pp. 31-51. Quotation taken from p. 32.

129 *'no one ought to harm another in his life, health, liberty, or possessions'*: *Second Treatise of Government*, op. cit., p. 4.

129 *'ultimately forced us on a starvation diet'*: *Why Liberalism Failed*, op. cit., p. 126.

129 *'the life, character, and purpose of its individual members'*: J. A. Hobson, *The Crisis of Liberalism: New Issues of Democracy* (London: P. S. King & Son, 1909), p. 73.

130 *'self-development be adjusted to the sovereignty of social welfare'*: Ibid., p. xii.

130 *the Miltonic view of liberty as rational self-governance:* Quoted in *Why Liberalism Failed*, op. cit., p. 174.

130 *'Do what thou wilt shall be the whole of the law'*: Quoted by Tim Cummings, 'Beyond belief', *Guardian* (9 July 2004).

130 *'everything else is a mockery'*: Norman Douglas, *How About Europe? Some Footnotes on East and West* (Florence: Giuseppe Orioli, 1929), p. 145.

130 *'the very definition of right and wrong, valuable and contemptible, good and evil'*: Jordan B. Peterson, *We Who Wrestle with God: Perceptions of the Divine* (London: Allen Lane, 2024), p. 62.

131 *'falls short of no extreme of folly or shamelessness'*: Plato, op. cit., p. 256.

132 *these proclivities are 'revealed in dreams'*: Ibid., p. 257.

132 *as outlined in* **The Birth of Tragedy** *(1872):* Friedrich Nietzsche, *The Birth of Tragedy* (London: George Allen & Unwin, 1909), trans. William A. Haussmann. This first English translation was the first volume of *The Complete Works of Friedrich Nietzsche*, edited by Oscar Levy. Nietzsche's book was originally published as *Die Geburt der Tragödie aus dem Geiste der Musik* in 1872.

132 *'still flourishes in art, eroticism, astrology, and pop culture':* Camille Paglia, *Sexual Personae: Art and Decadence from Nefertiti to Emily Dickinson* (London & New Haven: Yale University Press, 1990), p. xiii.

132 *'where there is no law but sex, cruelty and metamorphosis':* Ibid., p. 4.

133 *'those eternal forces at work beneath and beyond social convention':* Ibid., p. 24.

133 *more intense and more maddening than sexual pleasure:* In Book III, Socrates asks Glaucon: 'Can you name any pleasure more excessive and more intense than sexual pleasure?' Glaucon replies: 'I cannot, nor any more maddening either'. Plato, op. cit., p. 81.

133 *'except to the two people who are indulging in it the sexual act is a comic operation':* Compton Mackenzie, *My Life and Times: Octave Five 1915 – 1923* (London: Chatto & Windus, 1966), p. 168.

133 *'freely choosing individuals, but only when set in the social context that makes them so':* *Conservatism: An Invitation to the Great Tradition*, op. cit., p. 55.

134 *'It is eating of the tree of Knowledge of Good and Evil':* Quoted by Peter Ackroyd, *Blake* (London: Sinclair-Stevenson, 1995), p. 23.

134 *school curricula as a means to sever the bridles of ideology:* *The New Puritans*, op. cit., pp. 289-95.

134 *'The more I think about it the more I believe teaching standard English is racist':* Pran Patel, Twitter (13 February 2021). The tweet was subsequently deleted.

134 *taught about the work of the rapper Stormzy instead of Mozart:* Gabriella Swerling, 'Stormzy should be taught in schools instead of Mozart to prevent exclusions, charity urges', *Telegraph* (22 May 2019).

135 *such as Critical Race Theory and gender identity ideology:* In October 2020, equalities minister Kemi Badenoch addressed Parliament to clarify the Government's position. 'We do not want teachers to teach their white pupils about white privilege and inherited racial guilt. Let me be clear that any school that teaches those elements of critical race theory as fact, or that promotes partisan political views such as defunding the police without offering a balanced treatment of opposing views, is breaking the law.' Hansard, 20 October 2020.

135 *in the United Kingdom and Barnes & Noble in the United States:* Monica Greep, 'Bedtime stories go woke! Waterstones shelves bulge with feminist fairytales, gingerbread man migrants and memoirs such as "How To Be A Better White Person" to teach children about white privilege and racism', *Daily Mail* (26 October 2021).

136 *babies as young as three months old are capable of racial prejudice?:* Sam Dorman, 'Arizona teaching material suggests babies need anti-racism guidance', *New York Post* (9 March 2021). Two studies published by the University of Toronto in April 2017 had also argued that babies display racial biases. Molly Shea, 'Your baby is a little bit racist, science says', *New York Post* (13 April 2017).

136 *obstetricians choose the sex of babies by flipping a coin:* *My First Little Book of Intersectional Activism*, op. cit., p. 96.

136 *'Maybe they got it right, maybe they got it wrong':* Theresa Thorn, *It Feels Good To Be Yourself: A Book About Gender Identity* (New York: Henry Holt & Co, 2019).

136 *every fifteen pupils identifies as transgender or non-binary:* Sanchez Manning, 'Nearly one in every 15 pupils at a leading secondary school identify as trans or non-binary – with majority declaring their gender change after lockdown last summer', *Daily Mail* (23 April 2022).

136 *'their gender identity between the ages of three and five':* Adam Kula, 'Editing out a paragraph about three-year-old transgender children is just "a first step in getting trans ideology out of schools" in Northern Ireland say campaigners', *Belfast News Letter* (20 June 2024).

136 **'He's so much happier now':** 'My toddler came out as trans at age 4. He's so much happier now', *Business Insider* (22 September 2021).

136 **'We all know who's making the lifestyle choices':** Blaire White, Twitter (21 March 2022).

137 **teaching of gender identity to children as young as three:** Georgia Edkins, 'More than 5,000 parents go to war with Welsh government over plans to teach children as young as three about "sexual attraction" and gender identity', *Daily Mail* (24 April 2022).

137 **Matt Walsh's book for children, Johnny the Walrus (2022):** Matt Walsh, *Johnny the Walrus* (Nashville: DW Books, 2022).

137 **held a meeting to discuss the 'trauma' the book had caused:** Natasha Anderson, 'Woke Amazon staffer cries in meeting to discuss the "trauma" caused by best seller children's book "Johnny the Walrus" that compares being transgender to pretending to be a walrus', *Daily Mail* (27 April 2022).

137 **in decline and that 'self-censorship is very common':** Terence Karran and Lucy Mallinson, *Academic Freedom in the U.K.: Legal and Normative Protection in a Comparative Context* (Lincoln: University and College Union, 2017).

138 **'other unconscionable behaviour from being even higher':** Ibid.

138 **'in the pursuit of knowledge and academic freedom':** Ibid.

138 **'you just never, ever tell people on the outside':** Matt Goodwin, *Bad Education: Why Our Universities Are Broken and How We Can Fix Them* (London: Bantam Press, 2025).

138 **'an increasingly monocultural higher education ecosystem':** Eric Kaufmann, 'From monoculture to counterculture: why I am leaving Birkbeck for Buckingham', *The Critic* (2 October 2023).

138 **right-wing scholars are those most likely to self-censor:** A 2020 report found that one in three Right-leaning scholars censor themselves 'for fear of consequences to [their] career'. *Academic Freedom in the UK: Protecting Viewpoint Diversity* (London: Policy Exchange, 2020).

138 **'This conference believes Julie Bindle [sic] is vile':** Julie Bindel, 'Trans activism's war on solidarity', *UnHerd* (15 October 2021).

138 **among them Linda Bellos, Selina Todd, Kathleen Stock and Jo Phoenix:** Feminist campaigner Linda Bellos was 'no-platformed' in October 2017 by the Beard Society, a feminist group at Peterhouse College, Cambridge. Selina Todd, a professor of History, was 'no-platformed' from hosting a women's rights event in March 2020 at Exeter College, Oxford; threats from activists results in her being assigned bodyguards at lectures. Kathleen Stock, a professor of Philosophy, was the subject of a campaign of harassment and abuse at the University of Sussex and resigned in October 2021. Jo Phoenix, a professor of Criminology, was the victim of what the courts described as a 'targeted campaign of harassment' by colleagues while working at the Open University in 2019. James Gillespie and Sian Griffiths, 'Linda Bellos barred in Cambridge University row', *The Times* (1 October 2017); Camilla Turner, 'Oxford college investigates after female lecturer is "no platformed" at feminist summit', *Telegraph* (3 March 2020); Jamie Phillips, 'The gender-critical academic "cancelled for thoughtcrime": Feminist professor Kathleen Stock was hounded out of work by trans activists for doubting that biological men can become women - and she's still pilloried for her views', *Daily Mail* (30 May 2023); Sonia Sodha, 'Vindictive, cowardly leaders bowed to the gender bullies and failed Jo Phoenix', *Observer* (28 January 2024).

139 **for a temper-tantrum masquerading as a crusade:** Julie Burchill, *Welcome to the Woke Trials: How #Identity Killed Progressive Politics* (London: Academica Press, 2021), p. 213.

139 **discipline their parents and send them back to school:** Richard Brome, *The Antipodes* (London: Francis Constable, 1640). The title page of this original quarto claims that the play was first performed in 1638.

139   *'a free speech event on campus, here are some resources . . .'*: Robby Soave, 'Colorado State University sign directs students "affected by a free speech event" to seek help', *Reason* (31 January 2022).

140   *as an 'abomination', a 'gulag' and a miniature 'North Korea'*: Hannah Rose Woods, 'Is Britain's Strictest Headmistress a visionary or a tyrant?', *New Statesman* (24 May 2022).

140   *characterised as 'scary' and a 'dragon woman'*: Jacob Bentley-York, 'Tough lesson: I'm Britain's strictest headteacher, I've banned corridor chat & think detention is an 'act of love' – parents hate me', *Sun* (19 February 2022).

140   *'Is Britain's Strictest Headmistress a visionary or a tyrant?'*: Woods, op cit.

140   *more serious misdemeanours are far less likely to occur:* This principle is based on the 'broken windows theory' developed by social scientists James Wilson and George Kelling, which posits that minor indications of disorder in a society lead to more serious disorder.

141   *grades that exceed those of most private schools:* Fraser Nelson, 'The "trial" of Katharine Birbalsingh is a battle for the future of Britain', *Telegraph* (18 January 2024).

141   *'And shining morning face, creeping like snail / Unwillingly to school':* William Shakespeare, *As You Like It*, act 2, scene 7.

141   *the greatest good for the greatest number it would appear to be the optimal approach:* For instance, the writer Helen Pluckrose has told me that her strict conservative education meant that her 'brain rebelled utterly' and she 'checked out'. As she puts it, her school's 'focus on order and discipline and learning only specific things in specific ways left me with the entirely false impression that education was about systems and order and rote learning' and that 'having any intellectual curiosity, interest in or passion for anything' was considered 'deeply suspicious and subversive'. My liberal defence of a conservative education is not to deny that there are some individuals for whom this system will not yield results.

142   *have dubbed this the 'Unread Library Effect':* Peter Boghossian and James Lindsay, *How to Have Impossible Conversations: A Very Practical Guide* (New York: Lifelong Books, 2019), pp. 36-37.

143   *it severed the thread of transhistorical human experience:* Compton Mackenzie, *My Life and Times: Octave Nine 1946 – 1953* (London: Chatto & Windus, 1970), p. 231.

143   *would herald 'the end of the British empire':* Ibid.

143   *would eventually lead to 'the decline and fall of western civilisation':* Compton Mackenzie, *My Life and Times: Octave Three 1900 – 1907* (London: Chatto & Windus, 1964), p. 122. Mackenzie feared that, in the future, the China orange would be far more powerful than all Lombard Street, a variation of a once common idiom that we might still comprehend today had we been better educated.

144   *'But I must dismount from my hobby-horse...':* *My Life and Times: Octave Nine 1946 – 1953*, op. cit., p. 232.

## Chapter 4

145   *a BBC sitcom which ran between 1965 and 1975:* *Till Death Us Do Part* was so popular that it spawned a sequel series, *In Sickness and In Health* (1985-1992) and the American remake *All in the Family* (1971-1979). The show's socialist author, Johnny Speight, had created the character to ridicule the follies of reactionary England after the major wave of immigration from the commonwealth in the 1960s. Like its spin-off series *Curry and Chips* (1960), in which Spike Milligan wore brown make-up to play a half-Pakistani half-Irish immigrant, *Till Death Us Do Part* was widely misinterpreted as endorsing the racist views it sought to satirise.

145   **Cleaning Up TV: From Protest to Participation (1967) by the campaigner Mary Whitehouse:** Mary Whitehouse, *Cleaning Up TV: From Protest to Participation* (London: Blandford Press, 1967).

146    *'hard to understand of juvenile delinquents towards the elderly and helpless'*: Ibid., p. 165.

146    *'held racialist views and were like the killers of Christ'*: 'Damages for Mrs Mary Whitehouse', *Glasgow Herald* (28 July 1967), p. 11.

146    *'wholly inapplicable to Mrs Whitehouse and her associates'*: Ibid.

146    *have chosen this form of protest for good reason:* Dan Sales, 'Now trans activists burn Harry Potter books: JK Rowling ridicules Australian campaigner over video showing copy of the "Goblet of Fire" being torched - as Brit women's right's protester Kellie-Jay Keen leaves Down Under after violent clashes', *Daily Mail* (27 March 2023).

146    *sets fire to the library of his master Sepulchrave, the seventy-sixth Earl of Groan:* Mervyn Peake, *Titus Groan* (London: Eyre & Spottiswoode, 1946).

147    *'if thou have any power, come down thyself and work a miracle'*: Christopher Marlowe, *Tamburlaine Part Two*, act 5, scene 1.

147    *'agitation against an ethnic or national group'*: Ellen Francis, 'Iraqi at center of Quran burnings in Sweden shot dead before court verdict', *Washington Post* (30 January 2025).

147    *the assassination may have involved a foreign power:* Jennifer Rankin, 'Sweden points to "foreign power" after Iraqi refugee on trial for Qur'an burnings shot dead', *Guardian* (30 January 2025).

147    *given a suspended sentence and fined for his role in the burnings:* Miranda Bryant, 'Man who participated in Qur'an burnings convicted of incitement in Sweden', *Guardian* (3 February 2025).

147    *'or say anything without risking offending the group that holds that belief'*: Ibid.

147    *'should be viewed as a hate crime and the offender should face consequences'*: Bushra Shaikh, X (30 January 2025).

148    *not responsible for those who break the law in response:* In August 2023, the *Guardian* published a piece that presented Momika's Koran-burning as evidence of a 'racism crisis'. One of the Swedish Muslim interviewees was quoted as saying: 'I understand you are allowed to think and feel what you want, this is a free country, but there must be boundaries. It's such a pity that it has happened so many times and Sweden doesn't seem to learn from its mistakes.' Those of us who still believe in liberal values will baulk at the suggestion – and the implied threat – in claiming that we are mistaken to support freedom of expression. Miranda Bryant, '"It's a racism crisis": call for action on Qur'an burnings in Sweden', *Guardian* (3 August 2023).

148    *'abolishing protests that involve burning texts in certain circumstances'*: Maia Davies and Danny Aeberhard, 'Man who burned Quran "shot dead in Sweden"', *BBC News* (30 January 2025).

148    *in which copies of the Koran had been destroyed:* Miranda Bryant, 'Danish MPs vote to ban desecration of religious texts after Qur'an burnings', *Guardian* (7 December 2023).

148    *'risks harming the security of Danes abroad and here at home'*: Ibid.

148    *while bystanders, including police officers, did nothing to intervene:* Alissa J. Rubin, 'Flawed Justice After a Mob Killed an Afghan Woman', *New York Times* (26 December 2015).

148    *then tied to a tree and stoned to death in Pakistan:* '10 weeks after Sialkot tragedy: 85 held for lynching man in Khanewal', *News International* (14 February 2022).

148    *that he could no longer speak or walk:* Maryam Foumani and Patrick Wintour, 'Iran to execute mentally ill man for allegedly burning Qur'an during protest', *Guardian* (19 January 2023).

148    *later died in prison under suspicious circumstances:* Nadeem Shad, 'Javad Rouhi: Iranian protester dies in jail after avoiding death sentence', *BBC News* (31 August 2023).

149   *alarmed that 'their community is so uniquely combustible':* See the podcast *Making Sense with Sam Harris*, episode 343: 'What is "Islamophobia"?' (6 December 2023).

149   *The headline said it all: 'No One Murdered Because Of This Image':* 'No One Murdered Because Of This Image', *The Onion* (13 September 2012).

149   *'Where they burn books, they will in the end burn people too':* 'Dort wo man Bücher verbrennt, verbrennt man am Ende auch Menschen'. These words are engraved onto a bronze plaque at the centre of Berlin's Bebelplatz, formerly known as the Opernplatz.

150   *'the desecration of all religious texts and the prophets of the Abrahamic religions?':* Hansard, 27 November 2024.

150   *'forms of hatred and division, including Islamophobia in all its forms':* Ibid. See also James Price, 'Why is a Labour MP calling for a blasphemy law?', *Spectator* (27 November 2024).

151   *burning the Koran in solidarity with the victim:* Pat Hurst, 'Man in court after copy of Koran burned in Manchester', *Independent* (3 February 2025).

151   *the suspect's name and date of birth were published:* Greater Manchester Police, X (3 February 2025).

151   *another man burned his Koran outside the Turkish consulate in London:* Michael Murphy, 'Man denies religious aggravation after Koran is burned', *Telegraph* (15 February 2025).

152   *during a televised interview for RTÉ in early 2015:* Pádraig Collins, 'Stephen Fry investigated by Irish police for alleged blasphemy', *Guardian* (6 May 2017).

152   *'who creates a world which is so full of injustice and pain?':* *The Meaning of Life with Gay Byrne* (1 February 2015). Available on the RTÉ YouTube channel.

153   *ultimately repealed in January 2020 after a constitutional referendum:* Roy Greenslade, 'Why Ireland must get rid of its disgraceful blasphemy law', *Guardian* (11 April 2016); Emma Graham-Harrison, 'Ireland votes to oust "medieval" blasphemy law', Guardian (27 October 2018).

153   *he was merely doing his 'civic duty':* Quoted by Collins, op. cit.

153   *was banned for two months by British Gymnastics:* Martin Ziegler, 'Olympic gymnast Louis Smith banned over video antics', *The Times* (1 November 2016).

153   *'Our faith is not to be mocked':* Dan Sales, Patrick Gysin and Jason Johnson, 'Has he got a screw Louis? Olympic ace Louis Smith accused of mocking Islam after yelling "Allahu Akbar" and pretending to pray in boozy video', *Sun* (7 October 2016).

153   *sentenced to six months in prison for his harsh criticisms of Islam:* Sabine Beppler-Spahl, 'Stabbed by an Islamist, now silenced by the state', *Spiked* (4 December 2024).

153   *'an act of right-wing extremism that needs to be censored':* Ibid.

154   *'Resist it while you can':* Christopher Hitchens in discussion with John Lennox for the Fixed Point Foundation at Samford University, Birmingham, Alabama (March 2009).

154   *the monetisation platform Patreon swiftly deleted the video:* Andrew Gold, 'I did a hate speech', *Heretics*, Substack (29 January 2025).

154   *the 'stark alternatives of cultural loyalty or state loyalty':* Riazat Butt, 'Archbishop backs sharia law for British Muslims', *Guardian* (7 February 2008).

155   *yet another vaguely defined term on the statute books:* Charles Hymas, 'Angela Rayner to set rules on Islam and free speech', *Telegraph* (3 February 2025).

155   *'a type of racism that targets expressions of Muslimness or perceived Muslimness':* Ibid.

156   *'God made Adam and Eve, not Adam and Steve':* For the concept of 'thought-terminating clichés', see Joyce, op. cit., p. 154. The phrase was used by Robert Jay Lifton in *Thought*

*Reform and the Psychology of Totalism: A Study of 'Brainwashing' in Communist China* (London: Victor Gollancz, 1961).

157    **children who are prone to violent tantrums when insulted:** Qanta Ahmed, 'The ECHR's ruling on defaming Mohammed is bad news for Muslims', *Spectator* (10 November 2018).

157    **cooperation to a country ravaged by conflict:** Salman Rushdie, *Shalimar the Clown* (London: Jonathan Cape, 2005).

157    **with 'skin the colour of rusting metal':** Ibid., p. 115.

157    **so that the locals can hear the metallic clang:** Ibid., p. 117.

158    **'who mistake tolerance for virtue and harmony for peace':** Ibid., p. 116.

158    **'bent fenders spearing upwards like horns':** Ibid., p. 119.

158    **a unified front on behalf of one of our finest writers:** Salman Rushdie, *The Satanic Verses* (London: Viking, 1988).

158    **'there is no absolute standard of free speech in any society':** Quoted by Ed Power, '"Should we be free to burn Korans?": how John le Carré and Salman Rushdie fought over free speech', *Telegraph* (16 December 2020). Rushdie was later to outline the entire spat in his memoir *Joseph Anton*, and noted that during an interview in 2008 Le Carré conceded: 'Perhaps I was wrong. If so, I was wrong for the right reasons'. Salman Rushdie, *Joseph Anton* (London: Jonathan Cape, 2012), pp. 527-31.

158    **he would have no objections to Rushdie being burned alive:** Mark Edmonds, 'Not such a cool Cat after all! Yusuf Islam (aka pop legend Cat Stevens) claimed he'd been misunderstood over his support for the deadly fatwa on Salman Rushdie. Here the furious author demands: "I want an apology!"', *Daily Mail* (2 October 2020).

159    **leaving him struggling for his life in hospital with multiple stab wounds:** Salman Rushdie, *Knife: Meditations After an Attempted Murder* (London: Penguin Random House, 2024).

159    **right to free expression because to do so 'might give offence':** Quoted by David Sanderson, 'Inside the row tearing the Royal Society of Literature apart', *The Times* (2 February 2024).

159    **'It cannot take sides in writers' controversies and issues, but must remain impartial':** Bernardine Evaristo, 'I will defend the Royal Society of Literature against all attacks. It is more alive than ever', *Guardian* (8 February 2024).

159    **'(Asking for a friend)':** Salman Rushdie, X (8 February 2024).

160    **or mount any kind of defence 'for all writers facing these social media attacks':** Quoted by Sanderson, op. cit.

160    **'to prevent this person from espousing their hateful views':** The survey was undertaken by McLaughlin and Associates and the results quoted by Greg Lukianoff and Jonathan Haidt, *The Coddling of the American Mind: How Good Intentions and Bad Ideas Are Setting Up a Generation for Failure* (London: Allen Lane, 2018), p. 86.

160    **others accused him of tempering Marlowe's play for Islamic sensibilities:** David Farr, 'Tamburlaine wasn't censored', *Guardian* (25 November 2005).

161    **causing some of the pages to be scuffed:** Elizabeth Haigh, 'Boy who "accidentally dropped a copy of the Quran at Wakefield school" receives "death threats": Teenager is left "absolutely petrified" by messages, says mother', *Daily Mail* (1 March 2023).

161    **the massacre at the offices of French satirical magazine Charlie Hebdo in 2015:** Brendan O'Neill, 'Charlie Hebdo: Combattons pour le droit d'être offensant', *Spiked* (8 January 2015).

161    **he had showed the offending images during a lesson:** Henry Samuel, 'Accomplices of student who beheaded Samuel Paty get 16 years in prison', *Telegraph* (20 December 2024).

161    *avoid punishment from her parents after being suspended for poor behaviour:* David Averre and Elena Salvoni, 'Muslim schoolgirl admits lying that her teacher was Islamophobic - which led to him being decapitated by a jihadist - because she was suspended for two days and worried her parents would be angry', *Daily Mail* (16 October 2020).

161    *blackmailed thousands of Romanian children to spy on their families and teachers:* Daniel McLaughlin, 'Ceausescu regime used children as police spies', *Guardian* (22 July 2006).

161    *cannot grasp the implications of turning informer on an innocent man:* Ian McEwan, *Atonement* (London: Jonathan Cape, 2001).

162    *the need for the school to observe its 'duty of safeguarding':* Jack Wright, 'Petition calling for suspended teacher to be reinstated after he showed students cartoon of Prophet Muhammad passes more than 50,000 signatures', *Daily Mail* (28 March 2021).

162    *criticised the school for not maintaining an 'inclusive space':* See the statement 'MCB Responds to Developments at Batley Grammar School' on the website of the Muslim Council of Britain (26 March 2020).

162    *denote the elevation of emotional 'safety' to a sacred value:* The term was popularised by Greg Lukianoff and Jonathan Haidt in their book *The Coddling of the American Mind: How Good Intentions and Bad Ideas Are Setting Up a Generation for Failure* (London: Allen Lane, 2018).

163    *that he had taken this action 'to guarantee public safety':* Tim Black, 'The sinister censorship of NatCon Brussels', *Spiked* (16 April 2024).

163    *smear rather than an accurate political description:* The Henry Jackson Society has offered the following definition: 'Far-right beliefs centre on the promotion of a separation of the races, rooted in the view there is a common, exclusively white identity threatened by the presence of an "other". The term is frequently used interchangeably with the 'extreme right' and white supremacism. In the United States, violence from activists holding these beliefs is often characterised as "religiously or ethnically motivated terrorism"'. Rakib Ehsan and Paul Stott (eds.), *Countering the Far Right: An Anthology.* (London: Henry Jackson Society, 2020).

163    *from the 'Rethinking Education' conference in September 2023:* Louise Clarence-Smith, 'Academic who criticised teaching "white privilege" in schools no-platformed from conference', *Telegraph* (22 September 2023).

164    *the problem of cancel culture and censorship by the mob:* Dame Sara Khan, *The Khan Review: Threats to Social Cohesion and Democratic Resilience*, Department for Levelling Up, Housing and Communities (25 March 2024).

164    *fulfilled their responsibility and that Khan's report contained 'inaccuracies':* Charlotte Wace, Mario Ledwith and Ian Leonard, 'How Muhammad cartoon teacher was "thrown under bus" by his school', *The Times* (30 March 2024).

164    *whose opinions happen to fall within the ever-narrowing Overton Window:* The 'Overton Window' refers to the range of opinions that are deemed socially acceptable. It is named after the inventor of the concept, Joseph P. Overton.

164    *'an independent, impartial Office for Social Cohesion and Democratic Resilience (OSCDR)':* Khan Review, op. cit.

165    *'with the possible exception of pickets relating to industrial action by school staff':* Ibid.

165    *notably the arrests of striking miners during the Thatcher years:* At the same time, when it comes to the protection of children there is a compelling argument that they should not be exposed to dangerous protests. One recalls the terrible scenes on the streets around the Holy Cross Catholic primary school in Belfast in 2001, when loyalists picketed the school. Riot police were deployed to protect the children from mobs who shouted sectarian abuse, and threw bricks, fireworks and even urine-filled balloons. On one particular day, a pipe bomb was hurled at the police, causing panic among the children when it exploded. Gareth

Gordon, 'Holy Cross dispute: The terror and the trauma recalled 20 years on', *BBC News* (8 September 2021).

166 *'It's love that makes books last. Please keep reading':* Joseph Anton, op. cit., p. 316.

167 *a new company that specialises in heterodox writing:* Andrew Doyle, *Yttrandefriheten: Och varför den spelar roll*, trans. Öyvind Vågen (Stockholm: Nopolar, 2023); Andrew Doyle, *De nya puritanerna: Hur religionen Social Rättvisa kunde fängsla västvärlden*, trans. Linnéa Macdonald (Stockholm: Nopolar, 2023); Titania McGrath, *Woke: en guide till rättvisa*, trans. Jens Ganman (Stockholm: Nopolar, 2023).

168 *rise in gang warfare between those who do not respect the rule of law:* Miriam Kuepper, 'Warfare between migrant criminal gangs has brought an 'unprecedented' wave of violence to Sweden, police admit', *Daily Mail* (13 September 2023).

168 *social trust among the forty-seven countries included in the survey:* Richard Wike and Kathleen Holzwart, 'Where trust is high, crime and corruption are low', *Pew Research Center* (15 April 2008).

168 *international foreign policy that favoured left-wing and revolutionary causes:* Ann-Sofie Dahl, 'Sweden: Once a Moral Superpower, Always a Moral Superpower?', *International Journal*, vol. 61, no. 4 (Autumn 2006), pp. 895-908; Steven Erlanger, 'Sweden was long seen as a 'moral superpower. That may be changing', *New York Times* (3 September 2018).

169 *'who don't accept Swedish values and where ethnic Swedes have had to move out':* Quoted by Perkin Amalaraj, 'Fury in Sweden at video of Syrian asylum seeker pushing a 91-year-old widow down stairs before violently mugging her as she visits husband's grave', *Daily Mail* (11 November 2024).

169 *'first-generation migrants who control the nation's illicit drug and prostitution trades':* 'According to a 2023 police report, there are believed to be 14,000 active gang members in Sweden along with a further 48,000 people with 'gang affiliation', many as young as just nine or ten. Over the first six months of this year alone, Sweden suffered a shocking 148 shootings, resulting in 20 deaths. Last year, 55 people were shot dead across 363 incidents. In 2022, there were a record 62 fatal shootings while 73 people aged between just 15-20 were arrested for suspected or attempted murder with a firearm' (ibid).

169 *highest incidence of grenade and bomb attacks in any nation not at war:* Michael Murphy, 'Europe's migrant crime wave is coming to Britain', *Telegraph* (16 May 2024).

169 *'too self-interested to heed the humanitarian clarion call':* Malcom Kyeyune, 'Sweden's cultural revolution', *UnHerd* (22 September 2021).

170 *penned an article for the* Telegraph *in which she denied that 'all cultures are equally valid':* Kemi Badenoch, 'Migrants who come to Britain must uphold its traditions, not change them', *Telegraph* (28 September 2024).

170 *'That sentiment has no place here':* Ibid.

173 *'which grows to four times for robbery, and five times for rape':* He continues: 'The problem often becomes more pronounced as more migrants (and asylum seekers in particular) arrive. Sweden's annual migration figures ballooned more than five-fold from the mid 80s to more than 160,000 by the mid-noughties, many of which came seeking asylum. During this time, the Swedish economist Tino Sanandaji notes that the foreign-origin population's "share of total registration for crime as suspects" increased from 31 to 58 per cent – and from 42 to 72 per cent for homicide. This likely underrepresents the crime share of certain groups, as immigrants from East and Southeast Asia commit negligible levels of many types of crime when compared with migrants from Menapt (Middle East, North Africa, Pakistan and Turkey).' Murphy, op. cit.

173 *three times more likely to be arrested for sexual offences, and twice as likely for all other crimes:* Michael Knowles, 'Migrants 3 times more likely to be arrested for sex crimes, landmark study reveals', *Express* (6 January 2025).

174    *gave a publicity boost to those on the far right who were sounding the alarm:* Dominic Howell, 'The fear of being seen as racist', *BBC News* (20 August 2014).

174    *'others remembered clear direction from their managers not to do so':* Quoted by Rakib Ehsan, 'Grooming gangs: the making of a national scandal', *Spiked* (17 July 2022).

174    *because they felt it would be 'too politically incorrect':* 'Telford child sex abuse inquiry: Abuse suspects disregarded over racism fears', *BBC News* (13 July 2022).

174    *she faced resistance 'because some editors feared an accusation of racism':* Julie Bindel, 'I wrote the first ever piece about the grooming gang scandal in northern English towns in 2006 – but the media didn't want to know', *Independent* (17 May 20170.

175    *inquiry into these failings were jumping 'on a bandwagon of the far right':* Daniel Martin and Charles Hymas, 'Starmer: Calls for grooming gang inquiry are "far-Right bandwagon"', *Telegraph* (6 January 2025).

175    *which makes her later policy of unchecked immigration even more bewildering:* Matthew Weaver, 'Angela Merkel: German multiculturalism has "utterly failed"', *Guardian* (17 October 2010).

175    *he was accused of 'stigmatising' a marginalised group:* Rowena Mason and Harriet Sherwood, 'Cameron "stigmatising Muslim women" with English language policy', *Guardian* (18 January 2016).

176    *'with men able to end their marriages by saying "divorce" three times':* Dominic Kennedy, 'How the UK became "western capital" for sharia courts', *The Times* (18 December 2024).

176    *'it's a woman's duty to be ready any time':* Quoted by Rosamund Urwin, 'In Sharia court women are seen as having half the worth of men', *London Evening Standard* (11 December 2015).

176    *'as well as resolving British commercial disputes in a manner consistent with Jewish law':* Rakib Ehsan, 'Sharia courts exploit Britain's rich traditions of religious freedom', *Telegraph* (20 December 2024).

177    *a whimsical tale about a future Islamic England:* G. K. Chesterton, *The Flying Inn* (London: Methuen, 1914).

177    *'for it was sketched out before the legend of the Invincible Turk was broken':* Ibid,. p. 304.

178    *but 'cared for the Cause of Dogs':* Ibid., p. 95.

178    *able to preach his creed to the gullible* bons vivants *of the upper middle-class:* 'Something like a faint smile passed over the earnest faces of the two or three most intelligent of the Simple Souls, but for the most part the Souls seemed very simple indeed, helpless looking people with limp hair and gowns like green curtains, and their dry faces were as dry as ever.' Ibid., p. 67.

178    *'and the Atlantic and Pacific are a single sea':* Ibid., p. 65.

178    *today's oft-echoed slogan of Islam as the 'religion of peace':* Ibid., p. 113.

178    *founder of the religion 'wanted to generate as much inclusivity as possible':* Vanessa Elshamy, 'Prophet Muhammed was an intersectional feminist', *Muslim Girl* (27 May 2018).

178    *'when it allows the womanhood to be present in so large numbers?':* Chesterton, op. cit., p. 69. We see this kind of laughably contorted logic developed in Ammon's extolling of the virtues of Islam over Christianity. When we first encounter him, he is speaking to crowds on the seafront about how the symbolism of his faith is already predominant in England. So while he acknowledges that there are many 'crosses' in London – Charing Cross, King's Cross, Gerrard's Cross, and so on – there are many more crescents: 'Denmark Crescent; Mornington Crescent! St. Mark's Crescent! St. George's Crescent! Grosvenor Crescent! Regent's Park Crescent! Nay, Royal Crescent! And why should we forget Pelham Crescent? Why, indeed? Everywhere, I say, homage paid to the holy symbol of the religion of the Prophet! Compare with this network and pattern of crescents, this city almost

consisting of crescents, the meagre array of crosses, which remain to attest the ephemeral superstition to which you were, for one weak moment, inclined. He even cites the names of pubs as evidence of Islamic supremacy. 'The Saracen's Head', he claims, is a corruption of 'The Saracen is Ahead', and the 'Green Dragon' was once the 'Agreeing Dragoman'. Ibid., p. 6.

179   *as it's rather easier to make, I believe it will be generally adopted'*: Ibid., p. 260.

179   *'will soon superimpose himself for your plus sign'*: Ibid., pp. 262-63.

179   *is soon to be supplanted by 'Noughts and Crescents'*: Ibid., p. 263.

180   *Ivywood replies, 'and I will make it over again'*: Ibid., p. 269.

180   *'steeping us in the atmosphere before he actually introduces . . . the institution'*: Ibid., p. 294.

180   *'merely that England had conquered India: and Turkey had conquered England'*: Ibid., p. 299.

181   *'Conquest by barbarians'*: Ibid., p. 277.

181   *did not enjoy the kind of longevity its author had envisaged:* Anthony Burgess, *The Worm and the Ring* (London: Heinemann, 1961).

181   *'waiting to be awakened and revealed by time'*: Ibid., p. 32.

182   *'And then quiet laughter in the corridor as they went off, having missed a whole period of PT'*: Ibid., pp. 42-43.

182   *'even with those who harm it, criminals, and does this quite seriously and honestly'*: Friedrich Nietzsche, *Beyond Good and Evil: Prelude to a Philosophy of the Future*, trans. Walter Kaufmann (New York: Vintage, 1966), p. 114. Originally published in 1886 as *Jenseits von Gut und Böse: Vorspiel einer Philosophie der Zukunft*.

183   *'as yet no one has suggested a practicable way out'*: George Orwell, review of *Spanish Testament* by Arthur Koestler, *Time and Tide* (5 February 1938).

183   *the codes of honour in battle would be observed by his foe:* William Shakespeare, *Troilus and Cressida*, act 5, scene 9.

184   *'to deter serious criminality and not in response to any particular threat'*: Surrey Police, X (3 December 2024).

184   *at Christmas markets was simply 'to keep you all safe'*: Manchester City Centre Police, X (8 November 2024).

185   *killing eighty-six and injuring a further four hundred and thirty-four:* Robert McLiam Wilson, 'In a deserted courtroom, the grim details of the Nice atrocity go mostly unnoticed', *Guardian* (29 October 2022).

185   *terrorist attacks are simply 'part and parcel of living in a big city'*: Gabriel Samuels, 'Sadiq Khan: London mayor says being prepared for terror attacks "part and parcel" of living in a major city', *Independent* (25 May 2017).

186   *75 per cent of MI5's counter-terrorism work is specifically related to Islamist threats:* Liam Duffy, 'MI5 must rethink Islamic terrorism', *UnHerd* (October 9, 2024).

186   *prompted shop owners to protect even low-cost goods behind locked plexiglass:* For instance, Proposition 47, passed in the state of California in 2014, determined that thefts of goods below the value of $950 are charged as misdemeanours under state law. Emily Schultheis, 'Trump hits Harris on decade-old California criminal justice policy', *Politico* (15 August 2024).

187   *'and they suffer less often from any number of social ills'*: Richard Wike and Kathleen Holzwart, 'Where Trust is High, Crime and Corruption are Low', *Pew Research Center* (15 April 2008).

187   *'there are fewer worries about crime or corrupt political leaders':* Ibid.

187   *the assault of a ninety-one-year-old woman at Sollentuna Station near Stockholm went viral:* Amalaraj, op. cit.

188   *inform migrants that raping women was unacceptable in German society:* Allan Hall, 'Cologne carnival organisers hand out leaflets telling migrants not to rape women or urinate in public in the wake of New Year sex attacks', *Daily Mail* (27 January 2016).

188   *'where I would advise people who wear a kippah or are openly gay to be more careful':* Jörg Luyken, 'Jews and gay people should hide identity in "Arab neighbourhoods", says Berlin police chief', *Telegraph* (18 November 2024).

189   *'Should he now be punished again? And this time much harder?':* Will Worley, 'Norwegian rape survivor "feels guilty" the man who assaulted him was deported', *Independent* (8 April 2016).

189   *the rapist was 'very naïve and immature when it comes to sexual matters':* Paul Bentley, 'Muslim abuser who "didn't know" that sex with a girl of 13 was illegal is spared jail', *Daily Mail* (25 January 2013).

189   *52 per cent thought that homosexuality ought to be against the law:* Frances Perraudin, 'Half of all British Muslims think homosexuality should be illegal, poll finds', *Guardian* (11 April 2016).

190   *concerns about Pakistani grooming gangs and the need for a more 'muscular' approach to integration:* Dominic Kenedy, 'Labour suspends race pioneer Trevor Phillips over Islamophobia claims', *The Times* (9 March 2020). The suspension was eventually lifted in July 2021. Haroon Siddique, 'Labour lifts Trevor Phillips' suspension for alleged Islamophobia', *Guardian* (6 July 2021).

190   *once described as 'the soft bigotry of low expectations':* Laurie Rubel and Andrea V. McCloskey, 'The "soft bigotry of low expectations" and its role in maintaining white supremacy through mathematics education', *Bank Street College of Education: Occasional Paper Series*, no. 41, (March 2019). Bush delivered the speech at an event for the National Association for the Advancement of Colored People (NAACP) in 2000.

190   *the British media to overlook or minimise evidence of rising antisemitism:* In his memoir *Hitch-22*, Christopher Hitchens raises the question of 'why it is that anti-Semitism is so tenacious and so protean and so enduring'. It is a valid question, even if his answer fails to convince. 'If you meet a devout Christian or a believing Muslim, you are meeting someone who would give everything he owned for a personal, face-to-face meeting with the blessed founder or prophet. But in the visage of the Jew, such ardent believers encounter the very figure who *did* have such a precious moment, and who spurned the opportunity and turned shrugging aside. Do you imagine for a microsecond that such a vile, churlish transgression will ever be *forgiven?*' Christopher Hitchens, *Hitch-22: A Memoir* (London: Atlantic Books, 2010), p. 379.

190   *over 5,500 antisemitic incidents recorded, three times more than the previous year:* Aamna Mohdin and Neha Gohil, 'British Jews adjusting to "new reality" after year-long surge in antisemitism', *Guardian* (2 October 2024).

191   *a banner in New York City declared 'Long live 7 October':* Nick Cater, 'Australia has succumbed to anti-Semitism', *Spiked* (20 February 2024); David Propper, 'NYC anti-Israel protesters unfurl "Long live October 7" banner as mob harasses reporter', *New York Post* (11 June 2024).

191   *to blame the massacre on the Israel Defense Forces:* 'You misspelled "IDF". Ya know the one's [sic] who killed most of the silly Ravers that day. Google Hannibal Doctrine and music festival.' Tara van Dijk, X (13 May 2024).

191   *could possibly be explained away as anything other than racial hatred:* 'Suspect who painted red hands on Paris Holocaust memorial denies racial motives', *Times of Israel* (7 August 2024).

# NOTES

191 **'He's white, he's male, he's probably cishet – he's fine':** Brendan O'Neill, *After the Pogrom: 7 October, Israel and the Crisis of Civilisation* (London: Spiked Ltd, 2024), p. 167. The term 'cishet' is a compound of 'cisgender' and 'heterosexual'.

192 **campaigning at universities in the United States had at least some sympathy for Hamas:** Deirdre Bardolf, 'Students largely sympathize with Hamas, get most war info from TikTok: shocking survey', *New York Post* (May 11, 2024).

192 **'The 7 October is about to be every fucking day for you. You ready?':** 'Campus Antisemitism Surges Amid Encampments and Related Protests at Columbia and Other U.S. Colleges', Anti-Defamation League website (22 April 2024).

193 **'Sometimes I go about and poison wells':** Christopher Marlowe, *The Jew of Malta*, act 2.

193 **murdered Christian infants to replenish their blood:** James Shapiro, *Shakespeare and the Jews* (New York: Columbia University Press, 1996), pp. 37-38.

193 **'the Jews almost every year crucify one child, to the injury and contumely of Jesus':** Quoted by Frank Felsenstein, *Anti-Semitic Stereotypes: A Paradigm of Otherness in English Popular Culture, 1660-1830* (Baltimore: John Hopkins University Press, 1995), p. 32.

193 **what he describes as the 'lowest point in human history':** Anthony Burgess, *Earthly Powers* (London: Hutchinson & Co., 1980), p. 457.

193 **but also of his psychological need to reckon with the evil he had glimpsed:** Mervyn Peake, *Titus Alone* (London: Eyre & Spottiswoode, 1959).

195 **'That last weak cough of her small, trembling head':** Mervyn Peake, 'The Consumptive. Belsen 1945', in *Peake's Progress: Selected Writings and Drawings of Mervyn Peake*, ed. Maeve Gilmore (London: Allen Lane, 1978), pp. 168-69.

## Chapter 5

197 **I have before me a copy of a rare book from 1942 called Calvary:** Peregrine, *Calvary* (London: The Bodley Head, 1942).

197 **our attention directed to the aeroplane passing over like an angel of death:** Ibid., pp. 40-41.

197 **against a backdrop of a building engulfed in flames:** Ibid., p. 43.

197 **to repel the grinding machinery and smoke that dances around him:** Ibid., p. 67.

198 **carrying a wounded compatriot through an imploding cloud of destruction:** Ibid., p. 81.

198 **her toy doll like a small smiling corpse discarded to the floor:** Ibid., p. 37.

198 **two burly men are seen hewing through the base of Christ's cross with a crosscut saw:** Ibid., p. 55.

198 **repeatedly fails to detect the early signs of totalitarianism:** Compton Mackenzie, 'The Little Man', ibid., pp. 7-28.

198 **and so leaving it too late to tackle the rising threat:** Ibid., p. 12.

198 **so that the far left and far right almost meet:** The 'horseshoe theory' was first advanced by Jean-Pierre Faye in *Théorie du récit: introduction aux langages totalitaires* (Paris: Hermann, 1972).

198 **'provide the first three letters for the Left, and T stands for Totalitarianism':** This passage does not appear in *Calvary*, but is included in an alternative version of 'The Little Man' quoted in Mackenzie's autobiography. See Compton Mackenzie, *My Life and Times: Octave Eight 1939 – 1946* (London: Chatto & Windus, 1969), p. 92.

198 **it struck him as 'black and poisonous-seeming as a tarantula':** *Calvary*, op, cit., p. 16.

199 **'lead the body of Western man along a path in which his soul must shrivel':** Ibid., p. 17.

200    *'That is about as near to a definition as this much-abused word has come'*: George Orwell, 'As I Please' (24 March 1944), in *Essays*, op. cit., pp. 570-73. Quotation taken from p. 573.

200    *as is usually done, degrade it to the level of a swearword'*: Ibid.

200    *'now no meaning except in so far as it signifies "something not desirable"'*: 'Politics and the English Language', op. cit., p. 959.

201    *'sharply diminishing what had once been untouchably private'*: Robert O. Paxton, *The Anatomy of Fascism* (New York: Alfred A. Knopf, 2004), p. 11.

201    *eventually published in 1932 as part of the* Enciclopedia Italiana: Benito Mussolini, *The Doctrine of Fascism* (New York: Howard Fertig, 2006). Originally published in 1932.

201    *when they 'coincide with those of the State', which must have 'absolute primacy'*: Ibid., p. 10.

201    *with its assumption that the class struggle can explain all aspects of human history*: Ibid.

201    *must ultimately serve as 'the conscience and the will of the mass'*: Ibid., p. 12.

202    *he insists that 'history does not travel backwards'*: Ibid., p. 25.

202    *'preserves what may be described as "the acquired facts" of history; it rejects all else'*: Ibid., p. 26.

202    *'If liberalism spells individualism,' he writes, 'Fascism spells government'*: Ibid., p. 29.

202    *seeing in 'the tendency of nations to expand' a 'manifestation of their vitality'*: Ibid., p. 31.

202    *'sets the seal of nobility on those peoples who have the courage to face it'*: Ibid., p. 19.

203    *'whispered in English to leave Hitler to him because he knew how to manage him'*: *Calvary*, op, cit., p. 10.

203    *'the funny little man would stagger and nearly fall back on the seat'*: Ibid., p. 10.

203    *to resemble 'an anxious lavatory-attendant at a railway terminus'*: Ibid., p. 11.

203    *seizes power through a wave of populism and initiates the country's descent into chaos*: Salman Rushdie, *The Golden House* (London: Jonathan Cape, 2017).

203    *'One of them is the Trump, and the other is the Joker'*: Helena Keeble, 'Rushdie and 'the Joker', *The Orbital* (26 February 2019).

204    *she said, 'it is entirely possible that we will not have the opportunity to ever cast a ballot again'*: Nikki Schwab, 'Oprah Winfrey and Megyn Kelly give chilling election warnings as they appear for Harris and Trump at rival final rallies', *Daily Mail* (5 November 2024).

204    *suggesting that Trump's political opponents would also be incarcerated*: Ryan King, 'Dem Michigan Rep. Debbie Dingell frets to CNN's Jake Tapper she'll get tossed in "internment camp" if Trump wins: "May have to visit me"', *New York Post* (29 October 2024).

204    *was remixed into dance tracks and shared more widely than any campaign statement*: Liz O'Connell, 'Donald Trump "They're eating the dogs" song takes off online', *Newsweek* (18 September 2024).

204    *embracing the 'Brat' identity bestowed upon their candidate by the popular singer Charli XCX*: Conor Murray, 'Charli XCX embraces Kamala Harris "Brat" memes: "Happy to help to prevent democracy from failing', *Forbes* (26 August 2024). The name 'Charli XCX' is apparently an abbreviation of 'kiss Charlie kiss'. Her surname in Roman numerals means 100 - 10 + 10, so one would be forgiven for assuming that she was a classical scholar making a sardonic point about the philosophical principle of eternal recurrence.

204    *'packed the Garden for a so-called pro-America rally'*: Patrick Reilly, Alexandra Steigrad and Chris Nesi, '"Shameful" MSNBC blasted for splicing Nazi rally clips into coverage of Trump's Madison Square Garden rally: "Incitement"', *New York Post* (28 October 2024).

205    *'a big rally that happened in the mid-1930s at Madison Square Garden'*: Tara Suter, 'Walz compares Trump's Madison Square Garden rally to 1939 pro-Nazi event', *The Hill* (27 October 2024).

205    *production of* Julius Caesar *in Central Park in which the titular role was portrayed as Trump*: Kate Maltby, 'Character assassination? The theatre takes on Trump', *Financial Times* (16 June 2017).

205    *along with the title 'American fascism: what it would look like'*: Michael Tomasky, 'Yes, that's right: American Fascism', *New Republic* (16 May 2024). The alternative title on the magazine's front cover was 'American fascism: what it would look like'.

206    *'that has been the foundation of Western progress for so long'*: David Lammy, 'I'm a British Lawmaker. Here's Why I'm Protesting Trump's Visit to the U.K.', *Time* (10 July 2018).

206    *saying that he was 'looking forward' to working with him in the future*: David Lammy, X (6 November 2024).

206    *'Yes, it's okay to compare Trump to Hitler. Don't let me stop you'*: Mike Godwin, 'Yes, it's okay to compare Trump to Hitler. Don't let me stop you', *Washington Post* (20 December 2023).

206    *Her answer was 'Yes, I do'*: Zeke Miller and Will Weissert, 'Harris to give her campaign's closing argument at the Ellipse, where Trump helped spark Capitol riot', *Associated Press* (24 October 2024).

206    *'a president of the United States who admires dictators and is a fascist'*: Emma Bowman, 'Harris called Trump a "fascist". Experts debate what fascism is – and isn't', *NPR* (29 October 2024).

206    *even called her a 'Marxist, communist, fascist, socialist'*: Daniel Dale, 'Vance warns calling a candidate a "fascist" can lead to violence but doesn't mention that's what Trump calls Harris', *CNN* (17 September 2024).

207    *that Hitler has been reincarnated and is running for office*: The first assassination attempt took place on 13 July 2024 at a rally near Butler, Pennsylvania. Trump was shot in the ear, and retired fire chief Corey Comperatore was killed while trying to shield his family from gunfire. The shooter, Thomas Matthew Crooks, was killed by security forces. The second assassination attempt took place on 15 September 2024 at the Trump International Golf Club in West Palm Beach, Florida. The suspect, Ryan Wesley Routh, had been seen hiding in shrubbery with a rifle and was fired upon by a member of Trump's security staff.

207    *for instance, explicitly called Brexit a 'fascist coup'*: Julie Ward, Twitter (14 June 2019).

207    *in which he revealed that he doesn't know what 'fascism' means*: Paul Mason, *How to Stop Fascism: History, Ideology, Resistance* (London: Allen Lane, 2021).

207    *in her book* Sexual Revolution: Modern Fascism and the Feminist Fightback *(2022)*: Laurie Penny, *Sexual Revolution: Modern Fascism and the Feminist Fightback* (London: Bloomsbury, 2022).

207    *represents 'one of the dominant strains of fascism in our time'*: Jules Gleeson, 'Judith Butler: "We need to rethink the category of woman"', *Guardian* (7 September 2021). Hours after this piece was published, Butler's remarks were deleted. See Julie Bindel, 'No Judith Butler, gender-critical feminists aren't "fascists"', *UnHerd* (8 September 2021).

207    *to privatise Channel 4 was 'the seedbed of fascism'*: Claudia Webbe, Twitter (4 April 2022).

208    *could be thrown in jail if he were to win the election*: Hannah Knowles, 'Trump again suggests political opponents may face prosecution, too', *Washington Post* (5 June 2024).

208    *so they are in no position to complain about 'threats to democracy'*: Elie Honig, 'Prosecutors got Trump – but they contorted the law', *Intelligencer* (31 May 2024).

210    *that happened to display pro-Trump insignia were neglected*: Cameron Henderson, 'Fema official told relief workers to skip Trump supporters' houses in wake of hurricane', *Telegraph* (9 November 2024).

210 *that was being exposed in the early part of Trump's second term:* Elon Musk, X (4 February 2025). Musk was responding the accusation by Chuck Schumer, the Minority Leader of the United States senate, that his work via DOGE (Department of Government Efficiency) amounted to a 'shadow government'. Quoted by Monica Sager and Gabe Whisnant, 'Democrats tell Trump administration to "stop the steal" with new bill', *Newsweek* (4 February 2025).

210 *'and yet are conceivably running the country':* Transcript from *Firing Line*, broadcast on 21 December 1972.

211 *and other government departments in the United Kingdom:* Steven Edginton, 'Military's 111 diversity champions "undermine combat effectiveness"', *Telegraph* (23 February 2024); Tim Sigsworth and Steven Edginton, 'Navy could make climate change courses compulsory', *Telegraph* (13 February 2024); Steven Edginton, 'Ministry of Defence has 93 diversity networks including 10 for gender issues', *Telegraph* (11 February 2024); Steven Edginton, 'Soldiers told to avoid Christian "elements" in Acts of Remembrance', *Telegraph* (10 February 2024); Steven Edginton, 'BBC staff told not to hire candidates who are "dismissive" of diversity', *Telegraph* (29 January 2024); Steven Edginton, '"Disbelief" as under-manned Royal Navy seeks to re-deploy officers to diversity and inclusion team', *Telegraph* (27 January 2024)' Steven Edginton, 'Civil servants told they should "yield power to the marginalised"', *Telegraph* (20 January 2024); Steven Edginton, 'Children wanting to transition "can ignore parents", says Civil Service diversity ambassador', *Telegraph* (13 January 2024); Steven Edginton, '"Chaos, dysfunction and woke initiatives": Inside the Home Office struggle to curb migration', *Telegraph* (13 January 2024); Steven Edginton, 'I exposed woke Whitehall – then found out what civil servants really think of me', *Telegraph* (8 January 2024); Steven Edginton, 'Civil servant given warning after "inappropriately" saying there are two sides to the trans debate', *Telegraph* (6 January 2024); Steven Edginton, 'MoJ to consider "pregnant and breastfeeding people" in equality framework', *Telegraph* (17 December 2023); Steven Edginton, 'Civil servants told to check up on colleagues who don't list pronouns', *Telegraph* (25 November 2023); Steven Edginton, 'Civil servants held meeting on Why I Don't Talk to White People About Race book', *Telegraph* (25 November 2023); Steven Edginton, 'Senior civil servant wore Black Lives Matter lanyard at official meeting', *Telegraph* (18 November 2023); Steven Edginton, 'Navy personnel told to introduce themselves with pronouns in trans guidance', *Telegraph* (30 September 2023); Steven Edginton, 'Healthcare workers invited to three-day diversity conference featuring pronouns and gender', *Telegraph* (24 September 2023); Steven Edginton, 'Gender-critical civil servants' views compared to "Nazism" in diversity meeting', *Telegraph* (23 September 2023); Steven Edginton, 'How the machinations of "The Blob" have frustrated ministers', *Telegraph* (23 September 2023); Steven Edginton, 'Civil servant revolt at "woke takeover of Whitehall"', *Telegraph* (22 September 2023); Steven Edginton, 'Thirty days of Pride and lessons on white supremacy: inside Whitehall's woke training regime', *Telegraph* (22 September 2023); Steven Edginton, 'Home Office guidelines urge protection for civil servants whose gender "may vary regularly"', *Telegraph* (25 August 2023); Theodore Dalrymple and Steven Edginton, 'Britain has become a dictatorship of virtue, led by woke-mad "public" servants', *Telegraph* (18 August 2023); Steven Edginton, 'Home Office's false claim of Polish "LGBT-free zones" causes diplomatic row', *Telegraph* (12 August 2023); Steven Edginton, 'Academic who described Suella Braverman's immigration views as "odious" to address civil servants', *Telegraph* (9 August 2023); Steven Edginton, Dominic Penna and Louise Clarence-Smith, 'Whitehall "blob" blocked me from meeting Kathleen Stock, says Boris's "free speech" minister', *Telegraph* (31 May 2023); Steven Edginton, 'Tory candidates given lessons on "white resentment" before standing for Parliament', *Telegraph* (23 January 2023); Steven Edginton, 'Treasury aims to have six per cent of staff from black backgrounds in race target', *Telegraph* (15 November 2022); Steven Edginton, 'Parents blocked from checking their child's trans sex education lessons', *Telegraph* (7 October 2022); Ewan Somerville and Steven Edginton, 'Nurse sues NHS for "forcing racist ideology" on students', *Telegraph* (1 October 2022); Steven Edginton, 'Senior Whitehall officials accused of wasting time on "woke projects"', *Telegraph* (30 July 2022); Steven Edginton, 'Britain must follow America's example and cut back the woke Blob' *Telegraph* (26 July 2022); Robert Mendick and Steven Edginton, 'Jacob Rees-Mogg scraps "absurd" Civil Service diversity training', *Telegraph* (1 July 2022); Steven Edginton and Robert Mendick, 'Civil servants imagine "Japanese gay grandfather" during diversity training', *Telegraph* (19 June 2022);

Steven Edginton and Robert Mendick, 'Welcome to woke Whitehall, where more than 100 genders are recognised', *Telegraph* (27 May 2022).

211 **'Maoist-style cultural revolution that has swept through government departments':** Steven Edginton, 'A culture of fear is helping mask the full scale of Whitehall wokery', *Telegraph* (25 September 2023).

211 **'the blob' of activists working within and against the system:** Anonymous, 'Why my Civil Service colleagues are celebrating the Rwanda ruling', *Telegraph* (15 November 2023).

211 **'overruling the instructions of ministers and thereby their democratic mandates':** Ibid.

212 **'must be reported, recorded and investigated with equal commitment':** Sir William MacPherson, *The Stephen Lawrence Inquiry Report* (February 1999), p. 376.

212 **which drew a clear distinction between a 'hate crime' and a 'hate incident':** Association of Chief Police Officers, *Hate Crime: Delivering a Quality Service – Good Practice and Tactical Guidance* (March 2005), p. 9.

213 **but people have been rigorously investigated for 'misgendering':** For instance, journalist Caroline Farrow was investigated by police for six months after she allegedly referred to a girl who identifies as male with a female pronoun. Martin Evans and Gabriella Swerling, 'Devout Catholic "who used wrong pronoun to describe transgender girl" to be interviewed by police', *Telegraph* (20 March 2019).

213 **NCHIs persisted throughout the years of Conservative rule:** In April 2021, Home Secretary Priti Patel instructed the police to stop recording non-crime hate incidents. This was following by the publication of revised guidelines in March 2023 by her successor Suella Braverman reiterating this demand. According to these guidelines, incidents should only be recorded if 'clearly motivated by intentional hostility' and posed a risk of 'causing significant harm or a criminal offence'. Quoted by Andrew Tettenborn, 'The worrying return of non-crime hate incidents', *Spectator* (29 August 2024).

213 **'We have never lived in an Orwellian society':** Quoted by Fraser Myers, 'The dreadful return of the non-crime hate incident', *Spiked* (28 August 2024). The High Court case was pursued by former police officer Harry Miller with support from the Free Speech Union. Miller had been contacted by Humberside Police in 2019 after an offended party had complained to police about a supposedly 'transphobic' poem that Miller had shared online. Miller asked why the unnamed complainant was being described as a 'victim' if no crime had been committed, and why he was being investigated in the first place. The investigating officer replied: 'We need to check your thinking'.

214 **since the policy was inaugurated, an average of sixty-five per day:** Matt Dathan, 'Police record more non-criminal hate incidents despite crackdown', *The Times* (3 September 2024).

214 **were recorded between June 2023 and June 2024:** James Beal, 'Police investigate nine-year-old for hate incident', *The Times* (15 November 2024).

214 **which for some reason was interpreted as racist:** Michael Powell and Matthew Davis, 'Man gets "racial hatred" police record – for whistling the Bob The Builder theme tune at his neighbour', *Daily Mail* (17 July 2021).

214 **and even children's playground insults:** Jake Hurfurt, 'The dog accused of a hate crime after fouling outside a home in just one of 2,500 cases probed over two years', *Daily Mail* (17 November 2018).

214 **a nine-year-old child who referred to a classmate as a 'retard':** James Beal, 'Police investigate nine-year-old for hate incident', *The Times* (15 November 2024).

214 **along with the caption 'my dog will call me a Nazi for cheese':** Sarah Phillimore, 'Post-hate policing', *The Critic* (7 February 2022).

214 **'a man who wears a wig and calls himself a proud lesbian':** Martin Beckford, 'Police record "hate incident" against trans row Tory Rachel Maclean who was forced to apologise for sharing post calling rival Green Party candidate a "man in a wig"', *Daily Mail*, 18 December 2023.

215  *in a speech at the Tory party conference:* Alan Travis, 'Amber Rudd speech on foreign workers recorded as hate incident', *Guardian* (12 Jan 2017).

215  *an online post regarding the SNP's policies on gender self-identification:* Daniel Sanderson, 'Murdo Fraser accuses Police Scotland of acting "outrageously and unlawfully" and demands the force to delete the record of the incident', *Telegraph* (25 March 2024).

215  *'I'm not sure Governments should be spending time on action plans for either':* Murdo Fraser, X (18 November 2023).

215  *being arrested early in the morning by two officers of the law:* Franz Kafka, *The Trial*, trans. Idris Parry (London: Penguin, 2000). Written circa 1914 and first published posthumously in 1925 as *Der Prozess.*

215  *'you will learn everything in good time':* Ibid., p. 2.

215  *on the morning of Remembrance Sunday in November 2024:* Allison Pearson, 'My visit from police on Remembrance Sunday is living proof of our two-tier justice system', *Telegraph* (12 November 2024).

216  *'"How am I supposed to defend myself, then?"':* Ibid.

216  *But what else are we to call it?:* 'When Christopher Hitchens visited Prague in 1988 to report on the Communist regime, he was determined to be "the first visiting writer not to make use of the name Franz Kafka". During one of Vaclav Havel's "Charter 77" committee meetings, police burst into the property with dogs and searchlights, threw Hitchens against a wall, and arrested him. When he asked for the details of the charge, he was told that he "had no need to know the reason". For all Hitchens's best intentions, the Kafka cliché was forced upon him. As he later observed: "They make you do it"'. *Free Speech and Why It Matters*, op. cit., p. 3.

217  *presumably to avoid debating the matter openly:* Poppy Wood, 'Phillipson tried to pull plug on new free speech law days after election', *Telegraph* (28 December 2024).

217  *'the Act would be burdensome on providers and on the OfS [Office for Students]':* Quoted by Nina Lloyd, 'Powers to fine universities over "free speech" breaches put on hold', *London Evening Standard* (26 July 2024).

217  *an act of political vandalism that nobody anticipated:* Even before this, Phillipson had announced that she wanted to compel free schools and academies to teach the national curriculum, and to have it rewritten by Professor Becky Francis, an academic whose intersectional activism was clear with even a cursory examination of her publication history. While head of UCL's Institute of Education, Francis had launched the Centre for Sociology of Education and Equity, which prioritises 'equity and social justice' in schools. The emphasis on 'equity' rather than equality, a keystone of intersectional thought, was telling. See Toby Young, 'The intersectional feminist rewriting the national curriculum', *Spectator* (27 July 2024).

217  *declaring that the 'era of culture wars is over':* Peter Walker, 'Era of culture wars is over, pledges new culture secretary Lisa Nandy', *Guardian* (9 July 2024).

217  *the Conservative party's pledge to limit the recording of NCHIs:* Charles Hymas, 'Hate crime measures axed by Tories over free speech fears back on agenda', *Telegraph* (27 August 2024).

217  *'threats to Jewish and Muslim communities that may escalate into violence':* Matt Dathan, 'Hate crime measures back on agenda despite fears for free speech', *The Times* (28 August 2024).

218  *'whether that's propagated online or in person, has real world consequences':* Charles Hymas, 'Police should use "common sense" when recording non-crime hate incidents, says Yvette Cooper', *Telegraph* (19 November 2024).

218  *demonstrate how even 'biased attitudes' can escalate into genocide:* Gordon Allport, *The Nature of Prejudice* (Cambridge, Massachusetts: Addison-Wesley, 1954).

219    *to physical attack, and finally to extermination:* Ibid., pp. 14-15.

219    *'The final step in the macabre progression was the ovens at Auschwitz':* Ibid., p. 15.

219    *'to Islamophobia but not to antisemitism?':* Toby Young, 'The police handle crimes against Jews strangely leniently', *Jewish Chronicle* (20 November 2024).

220    *'Cheaper that way than prison or bullets':* Sarah Phillimore, X (25 March 2024).

221    *a more generalised obsession with anti-white hatred and genocide:* Judith Moritz and Sarah Spina-Matthews, 'Teen accused of Southport murders facing terror charge', *BBC News* (29 October 2024).

221    *mosques were assailed with bottles and bricks:* Tom Slater, 'The grotesque rise of white identity politics', *Spiked* (5 August 2024).

221    *'as an expression of white male British victimhood':* Ibid.

222    *there were multiple 'missed opportunities' to intercept the killer:* A statutory public inquiry was ordered by the Home Office in 2019, and was chaired by the Hon Sir John Saunders. For the details on 'missed opportunities', see *Manchester Arena Inquiry Volume 1: Security for the Arena* (June 2021), pp. 11-28.

222    *'and would be in trouble if he got it wrong':* Ibid., p. 25.

223    *the need for stronger internet censorship:* Archie Mitchell, 'Starmer promises action to end "shockingly easy" access to knives online', *Independent* (22 January 2025). Starmer's reaction is reminiscent of G. K. Chesterton's remarks in *The Flying Inn* about 'the people who think they can solve a problem they cannot understand by abolishing everything that has contributed to it. We all know these people. If a barber has cut his customer's throat because the girl has changed her partner for a dance or donkey ride on Hampstead Heath, there are always people to protest against the mere institutions that led up to it. This would not have happened if barbers were abolished, or if cutlery were abolished, or if the objection felt by girls to imperfectly grown beards were abolished, or if the girls were abolished, or if heaths and open spaces were abolished, or if dancing were abolished, or if donkeys were abolished. But donkeys, I fear, will never be abolished.' Chesterton, op. cit., pp. 89-90.

223    *sentenced to twenty months for inciting racial hatred:* Alex Croft, 'Armchair thug jailed for Facebook posts urging rioters to attack asylum hotel', *Independent* (11 August 2024).

223    *'If that makes me racist, so be it':* Michael Deacon, 'Lucy Connolly's tweet about asylum seekers was vile. But she shouldn't be in prison', *Telegraph* (19 October 2024).

224    *'whether media messages had any effect on individuals at all':* Ralph E. Hanson, *Mass Communication: Living in a Media World* (Washington, DC: CQ Press, 2011), pp. 47–48.

224    *'interpret these messages selectively according to individual differences':* Ibid.

224    *'a very powerful message to anybody involved, either directly or online':* Damian Grammaticas and Thomas Mackintosh, 'Rioters can expect rapid sentencing, says Starmer', *BBC News* (7 August 2024).

225    *'was intended to be seriously acted upon':* Quoted by Dominic Penna, 'Johnson questions jail sentence for Tory councillor's wife who posted racist tweet', *Telegraph* (18 October 2024).

226    *and imprison citizens on the basis of what they choose to say:* In August 2024, I was invited to discuss the issue of incitement to violence on a show called *Talkback* on BBC Radio Ulster. The host William Crawley, and his guest Claire Hanna (a member of Parliament for the SDLP in Northern Ireland), both took the view that incitement to violence should be prosecuted even when there was no evidence that the words had directly caused harm. They further made the case that the criminal prosecution of Markus Meechan (aka 'Count Dankula') for a comedic video in which he taught his girlfriend's pug to react excitedly to phrases such 'gas the Jews' and 'Sieg Heil' was justified on the grounds that they did not find the joke funny (for more details see *The New Puritans*, op. cit., pp. 118-25). When the topic of discussion turned to Elon Musk and the less restrictive censorship policies on Twitter since

he acquired the platform, Hanna repeatedly asserted that Musk's views on free speech were illegitimate because he had once mistakenly shared an antisemitic conspiracy theory online. Crawley jumped to her defence, asserting that Musk was indeed guilty of spreading white supremacist content. I asked him whether the same could be said of the BBC, which likewise had promoted an antisemitic conspiracy theory – in this case that the IDF had been targeting medics at a Gaza hospital – and, like Musk, later apologised for the mistake. Crawley refused to answer. See Ariel Zilber, 'BBC forced to apologize after falsely claiming Israel "targeting" medical teams, Arabic speakers: "Blood libel"', *New York Post* (15 November 2023).

226 **no two governments are able to agree on its meaning:** Paul Coleman, *Censored: How European 'Hate Speech' Laws are Threatening Freedom of Speech*, second edition (Vienna: Kairos Publications, 2016).

226 **'the possibility of reaching a universally shared definition seems unlikely':** Ibid, p. 5.

226 **but can actually heighten bias in the workplace:** 'Current data do not allow the identification of reliably effective interventions to reduce implicit biases. As our systematic review reveals, many interventions have no effect, or may even increase implicit biases. Caution is thus advised when it comes to programs aiming at reducing biases. Much more investigation into the long-term effects of possible interventions is needed.' Frank Dobbin and Alexandra Kalev, 'Why diversity programs fail', *Harvard Business Review* (July-August 2016). Quoted in *The Counterweight Handbook*, op. cit., pp. 75-76.

227 **a 1,426 per cent increase in transphobic hate crime since 2012:** Brooke Davies, 'Map shows UK hotspots for homophobic hate crimes', *Metro* (10 June 2024).

227 **'the true scale of hate crime remains hidden':** Fraser Myers, 'The manufacturing of a hate-crime epidemic', *Spiked* (23 August 2021).

227 **'targets that see success as reducing hate crime are not appropriate':** Quoted by Brendan O'Neill, 'We are not a hateful nation', *Spectator* (6 August 2016).

227 **'a better identification of what constitutes a hate crime':** Quoted by Myers, op. cit.

228 **those who identify as trans are among the safest demographic in Europe:** Madison Smith, 'Neither marginalised, abused nor vulnerable', *The Critic* (21 October 2021).

228 **'to remember people who have lost their lives in acts of transgender violence':** City of Edinburgh Council, X (20 November 2024).

228 **an 'unmanageable risk to public safety':** Lizzie Roberts, 'Nicola Sturgeon under fire after another trans prisoner is moved to women's jail', *Telegraph* (28 January 2023).

229 **based on religion, race, ethnicity or national origin:** Kim Willsher, 'French magazine faces legal inquiry over racist slur against politician', *Guardian* (13 November 2013).

229 **'shall be liable to imprisonment of up to three years or a fine':** Quoted by Sabine Beppler-Spahl, 'Germany's unfunny attack on the freedom to mock', *Spiked* (12 April 2016).

229 **that was perceived to be homophobic:** Lois McLatchie, 'How quoting the Bible became a crime', *Spiked* (24 January 2022).

229 **leading to a potential $20,000 fine for those found guilty:** Brendan O'Neill, 'How Canada became a cauldron of authoritarianism', *Spiked* (10 March 2024).

229 **the most severe forms of hate speech legislation yet produced:** Gerard Casey, 'This is a law designed to make you afraid', *Gript* (5 November 2022).

229 **'but we're doing it for the common good':** Níall Feiritear, 'Green Party Senator feels necessity to "restrict freedoms" whilst commentator calls her "bonkers"', *Sunday World* (16 June 2023).

230 **simply for possessing offensive material:** Frederick Attenborough, 'Tougher Irish laws on hate crime come into force', *Free Speech Union* (31 December 2024).

230 **'their protected characteristics or any one of those characteristics':** Ibid.

231    *'posting anti-feminist comments online as part of "combating misogyny" on the internet'*: See the transcript of J. D. Vance's speech, *Spectator* (14 February 2025).

232    *'there is nothing America can do for you'*: Ibid.

232    *with the German defence minister Boris Pistorius huffily dismissing it as 'not acceptable'*: Emily Atkinson, 'JD Vance attacks Europe over free speech and migration', *BBC News* (15 February 2025).

233    *'expressed a lot of frustration with our teams when we didn't agree'*: Mark Sweney, 'Mark Zuckerberg says White House "pressured" Facebook to censor Covid-19 content', *Guardian* (27 Aug 2024).

233    *'if he doesn't stop disseminating lies and hate on X'*: Robert Reich, 'Elon Musk is out of control. Here is how to rein him in', *Guardian* (30 August 2024).

233    *'You know who else should be on trial for the UK's far-right riots? Elon Musk'*: Jonathan Freedland, 'You know who else should be on trial for the UK's far-right riots? Elon Musk', *Guardian* (9 August 2024).

233    *'and pull the plug on the service until this stops'*: Paul Mason, X (6 August 2024).

233    *attempting 'to stoke racial conflict and civil breakdown'*: Edward Luce, X (5 August 2024). Such a reaction was always predictable. Whistleblowers at the *Financial Times* have exposed the extent to which Luce's publication is ideologically captured, leaking its 'Diversity and Inclusion Toolkit' to writer James Esses. See Thomas O'Reilly, 'Leak: Diversity and Inclusion Policies Run Rampant at the Financial Times', *European Conservative* (21 March 2024).

233    *'there is, both inside and outside the company, an apocalyptic feel to the ordeal'*: Charlie Warzel, 'How Elon Musk could actually kill Twitter', *Atlantic* (27 October 2022).

233    *likening the platform's new ownership to the opening of the 'gates of hell'*: Lee Brown, 'Left loses mind over Elon's Twitter takeover: "Like the gates of hell opened"', *New York Post* (28 October 2022).

233    *which ran with: 'RIP Twitter, 2006-2022: Dead at the hands of Elon Musk'*: Hannah Selinger, 'RIP Twitter, 2006-2022: Dead at the hands of Elon Musk', *Independent* (4 November 2022).

234    *'a wide range of beliefs can be debated in a healthy manner, without resorting to violence'*: Elon Musk, Twitter (27 October 2022).

234    *including Vijaya Gadde, who was head of legal, policy and trust*: Sheila Dang and Greg Roumeliotis, 'Musk begins his Twitter ownership with firings, declares the "bird is freed"', *Reuters* (8 October 2022).

235    *between Twitter and the state to see certain viewpoints censored*: Tom Slater, 'The Twitter Files and the silence of the hacks', *Spiked* (5 December 2022).

235    *an article by the New York Post in the run up to the 2020 election*: Brendan O'Neill, 'Why Hunter Biden's laptop really matters', *Spiked* (23 March 2022).

235    *may have been involved in his son's various dealings with foreign businessmen*: Emma-Jo Morris and Gabrielle Fonrouge, 'Smoking-gun email reveals how Hunter Biden introduced Ukrainian businessman to VP dad', *New York Post* (14 October 2020); Emma-Jo Morris, 'Emails reveal how Hunter Biden tried to cash in big on behalf of family with Chinese firm', *New York Post* (15 October 2020).

235    *even in the form of private messages*: Facebook likewise limited the reach of the news story, claiming that it 'would be eligible for review by independent fact-checkers'. Noah Manskar, 'Twitter, Facebook censor Post over Hunter Biden exposé', *New York Post* (14 October 2020).

235    *listed tweets that had been flagged and chillingly responded: 'handled these'*: Quoted by Slater, 'The Twitter Files and the silence of the hacks', op. cit.

236    *'Government censorship of speech is intolerable in a free society'*: 'Restoring Freedom of

Speech and Ending Federal Censorship' was signed by Donald Trump on 20 January 2025.

236 **mindless drones who act on cue to commands issued on social media:** Jake Kanter and Adam Bienkov, 'UK officials now think Russia may have interfered with the Brexit vote', *Business Insider* (23 February 2017).

237 **because of its misleading editing of an interview with Kamala Harris:** Patrick Svitek and Amy B. Wang, 'Trump calls for CBS to lose broadcasting rights over Harris interview', *Washington Post* (10 October 2024).

237 **those who burn the national flag ought to be imprisoned for a year:** David Smith and Sabrina Siddiqui, 'White House dismisses Trump claim that flag burners should be imprisoned', *Guardian* (29 November 2016); Gustaf Kilander, 'Trump wants to lock up flag burners as he insists world's autocrats think Americans are "bunch of babies"', *Independent* (25 July 2024).

237 **'open up the libel laws' to make it easier to sue his critics:** Callum Borchers, 'Donald Trump vowed to "open up" libel laws to make suing the media easier. Can he do that?', *Washington Post* (26 February 2016).

237 **The Democratic Party fared no better:** In October 2024, former presidential candidate Hillary Clinton thudded her way into the debate during an interview with CNN. 'We should be, in my view, repealing something called Section 230', she argued, referring to the section of the Communications Decency Act introduced in 1996 that protects online platforms from liability for comments posted by users. Without these protections, big tech would have little choice but to implement draconian censorship measures. The consequences for free speech, in the *de facto* public square of our digital age, would be catastrophic. See Elizabeth Nolan Brown, 'Hillary Clinton wants to repeal section 230', *Reason* (7 October 2024).

237 **'hate speech' is excluded from First Amendment protections:** The debate between J. D. Vance and Tim Walz took place in New York on 1 October 2024, and was moderated by Norah O'Donnell and Margaret Brennan from CBS. Emma Camp, 'Yes, Tim Walz, you can shout "fire" in a crowded theatre', *Reason* (2 October 2024).

238 **'a major block to be able to just, you know, hammer it out of existence':** Kerry's comment was made at a World Economic Forum panel on green energy investment. James Lynch, 'John Kerry Says the First Amendment Is Getting in the Way of Online Censorship', *National Review* (29 September 2024).

238 **for leftist activists 'to call for lower legal protections for speech':** Lee Rowland, 'Free speech can be messy, but we need it', *ACLU* (9 March 2018).

238 **'keep the government from regulating the conversations that spark change in the world':** Ibid.

238 **republished their 1997 book Must We Defend Nazis?: Hate Speech, Pornography, and the New First Amendment:** Richard Delgado and Jean Stefancic, *Must We Defend Nazis?: Hate Speech, Pornography, and the New First Amendment* (New York: NYU Press, 1997).

238 **the subtitle was now Why the First Amendment Should Not Protect Hate Speech and White Supremacy:** Richard Delgado and Jean Stefancic, *Must We Defend Nazis?: Why the First Amendment Should Not Protect Hate Speech and White Supremacy* (New York: NYU Press, 2018).

238 **he wrote, 'the First Amendment is disproportionately applied to trample that dissent':** Justin Hansford, 'The First Amendment Freedom of Assembly as a Racial Project', *Yale Law Journal Forum*, vol. 127 (20 January 2018).

239 **legal scholar Mary Anne Franks took aim at 'First Amendment fundamentalism':** Mary Anne Franks, *The Cult of the Constitution: Our Deadly Devotion to Guns and Free Speech* (California: Stanford University Press, 2019).

239 **an article for the Washington Post entitled 'Why America needs a hate speech law':**

Richard Stengel, 'Why America needs a hate speech law', *Washington Post* (29 October 2019).

239    *'In an age when everyone has a megaphone, that seems like a design flaw':* I am reminded of one of the most chilling reviews for my book *Free Speech and Why It Matters* in which the reviewer exposed his own authoritarian instincts. 'Sometimes the answer to bad speech is not "more speech"', he wrote, 'it's to unplug the speaker's microphone'. Henry Mance, 'How can we move beyond the nihilistic culture wars?', *Financial Times* (30 March 2021).

239    *reacts mechanically according to decrees from above:* Herbert Marcuse, *One-Dimensional Man: Studies in the Ideology of Advanced Industrial Society* (Boston: Beacon Press, 1964).

## Chapter 6

241    *'to be mild, timorous, tractable, benign, of sure remembrance, and shamefast':* Sir Thomas Elyot, *The Boke named the Governour*, ed. Donald W. Rude (New York and London: Garland, 1992), p. 93.

242    *Prynne dismissed actresses as 'notorious whores':* William Prynne, *Histrio-Mastix* (London: Michael Sparke, 1633), p. 1045.

242    *an affront to scripture and natural law:* Ibid., p. 215.

242    *'Is like to hear on't':* John Fletcher, *Love's Cure*, act 1, scene 2.

243    *sees gender non-conformity as something to be fixed:* Hic Mvlier: Or, The Man-Woman: Being a Medicine to cure the Coltish Disease of the Staggers in the Masculine-Feminines of our Times (London: Eliot's Court Press, 1620).

243    *are described as 'an infection that emulates the plague':* Ibid.

243    *a masculine woman discuss their respective conditions:* Haec-Vir: Or, The Womanish-Man (London: Eliot's Court Press, 1620).

243    *'yet it shall be with contempt and disgrace':* Ibid.

244    *claims Dr Nicholas Matte of the Sexual Diversity Studies programme at the University of Toronto:* This quotation is taken from a debate on *The Agenda with Steve Paikin* on TVO, Ontario's public television broadcaster, between Nicholas Matte and Jordan Peterson. Broadcast on 26 October 2016.

244    *or 'gender in disguise':* Amia Srinivasan, *The Right to Sex* (London: Bloomsbury, 2021), p. xii.

244    *'that makes a person biologically male or female':* Kim Elsesser, 'The myth of biological sex', *Forbes* (15 June 2020).

245    *including the prestigious* **New England Journal of Medicine:** Wright, op. cit.

245    *historian and sexologist Thomas Laqueur has described as the 'one canonical body':* Thomas Laqueur, *Making Sex: Body and Gender from the Greeks to Freud* (Cambridge, Massachusetts: Harvard University Press, 1992), p. 62.

245    *'because their dull and sluggish heat is not sufficient to thrust them out':* Quoted by Stephen Orgel, *Impersonations: The Performance of Gender in Shakespeare's England* (Cambridge: Cambridge University Press, 1996), p. 21

245    *emerge from her body as she takes a particularly masculine stride:* Donald M. Frame, trans., *The Complete Essays of Montaigne* (California: Stanford University Press, 1943, rpt 1958), pp. 68-76.

245    *'If that is granted, all else follows':* George Orwell, *Nineteen Eighty-Four* (London: Penguin, 1987), p. 84.

246    *tracing the equation '2+2=5' in the dust on a table:* Ibid., p. 303.

246 *about pronouns was 'viewed as not aligning with our policy of inclusion':* Quoted from 'A statement from the National Multiple Sclerosis Society' on the National MS Society website (February 15, 2024). The National MS Society later issued an apology. See Bethan Sexton, 'MS Society U-turns and issues groveling apology to fired 90-year-old volunteer who they forced to step down after she asked "what pronouns meant"', *Daily Mail* (21 February 2024).

247 *'the presence of trans women in women's single-sex spaces . . .':* Katha Pollitt, 'Not everything is about gender' *The Atlantic* (25 March 2024).

248 *claims one writer for the* **Los Angeles Times:** Jen Manion, 'The rightness of the singular "they"', *Los Angeles Times* (15 December 2019).

248 *claims another on the* **Medium** *website:* Emily Roche, 'Shakespeare used the singular they, and so should you', *Medium* (3 April 2015).

248 *'just as many English speakers do now':* Anne Curzan, '"They" has been a singular pronoun for centuries. Don't let anyone tell you it's wrong', *Washington Post* (21 October 2021).

248 *"'Tis meet that some more audience than a mother – Since nature makes them partial – should o'erhear the speech":* Manion, op. cit.

249 *he is here promoting the validity of non-binary identities:* One might as well quote Cardinal Wolsey's lines from *Henry VIII* for a further example: 'The Spaniard, tied by blood and favour to her, / Must now confess, if they have any goodness, / The trial just and noble' (act 2, scene 2). Here, Wolsey is referring to the Spanish people, not an individual Spaniard. Only the most literal of minds would take this poetic device as proof that 'they' is being deployed as a singular pronoun. Incidentally, this very quotation was cited by Samuel Johnson in his definition of 'they' for his original dictionary of 1755.

249 *to be 'the master of his own thoughts':* R. H. M. Elwes (trans.), *The Chief Works of Benedict de Spinoza*, 2 vols. (London: Chiswick Press, 1883), vol. I, p. 258.

250 *happy with their biological sex need to be defined against something:* This is reminiscent of the historian John Boswell's repeated use of the term 'nongay' when speaking of heterosexual love in his book *Christianity, Social Tolerance, and Homosexuality*. His justification is less provocative insofar as the focus of his book is homosexual love, but he acknowledges that the phrase 'may startle some readers' given that it bears an implication that straight sexuality ought to be defined *against* the homosexual norm. As he points out, it 'is no less justifiable than "non-Jewish", "non-Catholic", "non-German", or "non-" anything else which comprises the focus of attention'. John Boswell, *Christianity, Social Tolerance, and Homosexuality: Gay People in Western Europe from the Beginning of the Christian Era to the Fourteenth Century* (Chicago: University of Chicago Press, 1980), p. 45.

250 *dividing humankind into 'Marxists' and 'non-Marxists':* Johns Hopkins University took a similar approach when it updated its 'LGBTQ Glossary' to define 'lesbian' as a 'non-man attracted to non-men', a revision that many have seen as evidence of the misogyny baked into gender ideology. James Gordon, 'Trust the science? Prestigious Johns Hopkins University erases women from woke new inclusive language guide that describes lesbians as "non-men attracted to non-men," – but still refers to male gays as "men"', *Daily Mail* (13 June 2023).

251 *physically assaulted at an event in Auckland, New Zealand:* Posie Parker, 'Fear and loathing in New Zealand', *Spectator* (1 April 2023).

252 *that some believe is a cipher for 'white power':* Stephen Knight, 'New Zealand News channel invents fake Kellie-Jay Keen "white supremacist" controversy', *The Knight Report, Substack* (23 March 2023).

252 *'someone intending to signal to their white supremacist supporters':* Ibid.

252 *'saw an opportunity to hijack the event for their own publicity':* Australian Jewish Association, Twitter (19 March 2023).

253 *resulting in a concussion and bruising:* Craig Kapitan and Joseph Los'e, 'Activist pleads

guilty to punching elderly woman at heated Auckland trans rights protest', *New Zealand Herald* (10 August 2023).

253 *she has remarked she could 'paper the house with them':* J. K. Rowling, Twitter (22 November 2021).

253 *have been collated on the 'Terf is a Slur' website:* The examples have been collated at terfisaslur.com by an anonymous campaigner.

254 *'I say this because talking to them absolutely will not work':* Ibid.

254 *'or transphobic speaker than it is to shout them down':* Jeff Zymeri, 'Prof suspended for post saying it's "admirable to kill a racist, homophobic, or transphobic speaker', *National Review* 27 March 2023).

255 *'punch them in the fucking face':* Miriam Kuepper, 'Fury as Transgender activist who served 30 years in jail for attempted murder tells cheering crowd at Trans Pride march "if you see a TERF, punch them in the face"', *Daily Mail* (9 July 2023).

255 *why would the crowd cheer upon hearing these words:* There is little doubt that violence, both in rhetorical and physical terms, has become commonplace within trans activist circles. Every movement has its 'bad apples', which leading figures ought to criticise wherever possible. When anti-gay campaigner Anita Bryant was hit in the face with a pie in 1977, LGB rights groups were quick to condemn the assault. This is not simply a matter of exercising sound moral judgement; it is also strategic. If a group fails to condemn the most egregious actions of its own members, those elements end up representing the group in the eye of the public, and once you have expressed sympathy with those committing acts of violence for political purposes – even if it's as harmless as throwing a pie – then you cannot complain when such tactics are used against you. Nor should anyone be surprised when the choice of missiles escalates to something more serious. Many leftist commentators dismissed the throwing of milkshakes at Nigel Farage, leader of Reform UK, as trivial, but it wasn't long before one activist threw a coffee cup and wet cement, objects that could easily have caused injury. Hannah Kane, 'Man charged after cup of wet cement chucked at Nigel Farage during Reform campaign event', *Daily Express* (12 June 2024).

255 *an image of a guillotine, and they didn't even notice:* Daniel Sanderson, '"Decapitate Terfs" signs at pro-trans rally attended by SNP politicians', *Telegraph* (22 January 2023).

256 *depicted as a large wooden horse surrounded by neo-Nazis:* The cartoon appeared in the *New Zealand Herald* on 25 March 2023.

257 *'into story telling and entertaining local children':* Stella Creasy, Twitter (26 July 2022).

257 *describing the event as 'so wholesome':* Nadia Whittome, Twitter (26 July 2022).

257 *'I don't think this is an avenue that you would want your child to explore':* Kitty Demure, video uploaded to YouTube (20 January 2020).

257 *they were connoisseurs contemplating a sculpture by Henry Moore:* I recall another drag performance where the artist on stage was smoking liberally throughout the show, blowing smoke at a pregnant woman on the front row and saying 'I hope you have a miscarriage'. It was a far cry from *RuPaul's Drag Race*.

258 *presented in large neon lettering on the upstage wall:* Russell Falcon, 'Dallas drag queen event for kids sparks outrage', *The Hill* (7 June 2022).

258 *with a large fake penis attached to his crotch:* Isabella Nikolic, 'Parents' disgust as actor in rainbow coloured monkey costume with fake penis and nipples appears at library event encouraging children to read', *Daily Mail* (12 July 2021).

258 *despite being aimed at children as young as five:* Ross Slater, 'Fury as theatre company stages naked show exploring "sexuality, sexual pleasure and queerness" aimed at children as young as five', *Daily Mail* (8 April 2022).

258 *as the website of* The Family Sex Show *suggested:* Paul Bracchi, 'How *could* this sex show

for children as young as five get £40,000 of public cash? Production urging youngsters to explore "sexual pleasure" is cancelled after more than 38,000 sign petition', *Daily Mail* (22 April 2022).

259    *and accusing the performer of 'child grooming':* Ewan Somerville, 'Protesters storm first drag queen storytime for primary school children', *Telegraph* (26 July 2022).

259    *as though the two were in any way synonymous:* Sophie Atherton and Ewan Somerville, 'Call drag queens "pantomime dames" to fool protesters, librarians told', *Telegraph* (30 July 2022).

259    *'children as young as two recognise their trans identity':* Stonewall, Twitter (22 July 2022).

259    *'we can change the world book by book!':* Kingston Libraries, Twitter (6 October 2022).

260    *as 'a clear violation of the First Amendment':* 'LGBTQ student group sues to overturn Texas A&M's unconstitutional drag ban', *FIRE* (5 March 2025).

260    *the broadcaster had broken guidelines on obscenity and indecency:* Suzanne Downing, 'Complaint filed against NBC for airing obscene content during Olympic Opening Ceremony', *Must Read Alaska* (30 July 2024).

261    *the organising committee was eventually forced into an apology:* Angela Giuffrida, 'Paris Olympics organisers apologise to Christians for unintentional Last Supper parody', *Guardian* (28 July 2024).

261    *'but at least was confined safely to bad gay pubs':* Gareth Roberts, 'Has the Olympics opening ceremony finished yet?', *Spectator* (27 July 2024).

261    *'celebrates every person's unique identity and gifts':* Steve Warren, '"This is blasphemy": Dallas church pledges allegiance to drag queens and LGBT agenda', *Christian Broadcasting Network* (20 September 2023).

262    *to use the phrase 'LGBT+' rather than 'LGBT':* Steph Spyro, 'Sir Keir Starmer's government adopts LGBT+ acronym across all departments post-election', *Daily Express* (4 November 2024).

263    *'declared she would have to consult a flow chart':* Kathleen Stock, 'One person's blasphemy is another's religious belief. You can't ban it', *The Times* (1 December 2024).

264    *but also of incontestable biological facts:* Daisy Duman, 'Transgender woman Roxanne Tickle wins discrimination case after being banned from women-only app', *Guardian* (22 August 2024).

264    *Tickle's 'gender identity' was the discriminating factor:* The ruling puts it this way: 'A necessary part of proving that action has been taken by reason of a person's gender identity, and therefore amounts to direct discrimination, is establishing that the alleged discriminator was aware of the person's gender identity. The evidence goes no further than establishing that Ms Tickle's exclusion was likely to have been a byproduct of excluding those who were perceived as being men, by the use of visual criteria that failed to distinguish between cisgender men and transgender women'.

264    *is illegal for women to organise in their own interests:* Grover had relied on the definition of 'women' in the UN's Convention on the Elimination of All Forms of Discrimination Against Women (CEDAW). As it happens, this case has not tested this definition, as the judge explained: 'I was not satisfied that the kind of gender identity discrimination alleged by Ms Tickle under s 22 would be supported as an enactment of the Convention for the Elimination of All Forms of Discrimination Against Women (1979) (CEDAW). The respondents contended that this was because CEDAW grants protections only to women, and the word "women" in CEDAW only means adults who were female sex at birth. I do not need to decide whether that is correct or not, because the way in which the term "discrimination against women" is defined in CEDAW means it refers only to discrimination that places women in a less favourable position than men. It therefore does not cover the kind of 4 discrimination that Ms Tickle alleges in this case, which is discrimination that

placed her in the same position as men.' At the very least, we can say that in the wake of this judgement the international definition of 'women' still holds firm.

266  **'I hope that others around the House will as well':** Hansard (5 November 2024).

266  **'genderqueer, gender-variant, genderless and non-binary':** Hansard (9 February 2024).

266  **'deliberately played with to combine gender-specific signals':** Quoted from the *LGBTQIA+ Wiki* website.

268  **'your relationship with your primary and secondary sex characteristics':** Quoted from an 'expert panel on sex and gender' featuring psychiatrist Jack Turban, neurobiologist Gina Rippon and philosopher Alex Byrne held by the Dartmouth Political Union (DPU) on 1 May 2024. The full discussion is available to watch on the DPU YouTube channel.

269  **as 'an essence of male or female':** *Free Speech Nation* (10 March 2024), available to watch on the GB News YouTube channel.

269  **'inexplicable self-understanding of what sex/gender one should be':** Quoted from the 'trans, gender, sexuality, & activism glossary' on Julia Serano's website.

269  **described as 'something like a sexed soul' within a discrepant body:** Helen Joyce, *Trans: When Ideology Meets Reality* (London: Oneworld, 2021). Journalist Sarah Ditum plumps instead for 'an immaterial sense of self'. Sarah Ditum, 'The taboo trans question', *UnHerd* (10 March 2022).

269  **'supposedly transcends such superficial physical indicia as gonads and genitalia':** Wright, op. cit.

269  **'within the obligatory frame of reproductive heterosexuality':** Judith Butler, *Gender Trouble: Feminism and the Subversion of Identity* (London: Routledge, 1999), p. 173. Originally published in 1990.

270  **'in relation to all those who claim to possess its correct definition':** Judith Butler, *Who's Afraid of Gender?* (New York: Farrar, Straus and Giroux, 2024), p. 243.

270  **'but also social constructs that don't actually exist':** Titania McGrath, 'Gandhi: what xe would have done', *The Critic* (November 2021).

270  **'a biological phenomenon which determines our assumed identity':** Julie Bindel, *Feminism for Women: The Real Route to Liberation* (London: Constable, 2021), p 13

270  **even young children were photographed holding placards bearing the phrase:** Benedict Smith, 'Supreme Court set to uphold law against puberty blockers for children', *Telegraph* (4 December 2024).

271  **'more harm than lobotomies and false memory syndrome combined':** J. K. Rowling, X (28 December 2024).

272  **'the matrix of the woman is nothing but the scrotum and penis of the man inverted'):** Quoted by Laqueur, op, cit., p. 62. He offers two other examples from obscure sources: 'A German doctor of no great fame pronounced, "Wo du nun dise Mutter sampt iren anhengen besichtigst, So vergleich sie sich mit allem dem Mannlichen glied, allein das diese ausserhalb das Weiblich aber inwendig ist" (Viewing the uterus along with its appendages, it corresponds in every respect to the male member except that the latter is outside and the former inside). Or "the likeness of it [the womb] is as it were a yarde reversed or turned inward, having testicles likewise," as Henry VIII's chief surgeon says in a matter-of-fact way' (ibid).

273  **objects to the concept of a 'Christian child' or a 'Muslim child':** 'The very sound of the phrase "Christian child" or "Muslim child" should grate like fingernails on a blackboard... A child is not a Christian child, not a Muslim child, but a child of Christian parents or a child of Muslim parents'. Richard Dawkins, *The God Delusion* (London: Bantam Press, 2006), pp. 338-39.

275  **'used the caution necessary to preserve such brittle bodies':** John Locke, *An Essay*

*Concerning Human Understanding* (London: Thomas Tegg, 1825), p. 94. Originally published in 1689).

275     **a group of people inexplicably 'danced themselves to death':** Rosalind Jana, 'The people who "danced themselves to death"', *BBC Culture* (13 May 2022).

275     **would involuntarily shake their hands whenever they performed writing exercises:** 'In 1893, a girls' school in Basel, Switzerland, was affected by contagious shaking and convulsions involving female students who were unable to complete in-school written assignments. Symptoms subsided after school hours, relapsing only upon re-entering school grounds. In 1904, the same school reported a similar outbreak. At Gross Tinz, Germany, between 28 June and mid-October 1892, hand tremors affected the entire body and 8/20 victims exhibited altered consciousness and amnesia. At a school in Chemnitz, Germany, in February 1906, arm and hand tremors in female elementary students appeared during their writing exercise hour. The symptoms began in two pupils but gradually spread to 21 females over 4 weeks. The pupils performed all other manual tasks normally, including gymnastics class. Electric shocks were administered to those affected, and during their writing period demanding drills in mental arithmetic were given; the symptoms ceased soon after.' Robert E. Bartholomew and Simon Wessely, 'Protean nature of mass sociogenic illness', *British Journal of Psychiatry*, vol. 180, issue 4 (April 2002), pp. 300-306.

275     **the figure had risen to more than five thousand (mostly female) patients:** Amelia Gentleman, '"Children are being used as a football": Hilary Cass on her review of gender identity services', *Guardian* (10 April 2024).

277     **'something abusive happened to you, it probably did':** Quoted by Jo Woodiwiss, 'Why do women identify themselves as victims of childhood sexual abuse?', *Guardian* (11 March 2010).

277     **'being seen in clinic were more likely to proceed to a medical pathway':** Cass, *Final Report*, op. cit., p. 31.

278     **'Non-binaries for the fucking win':** Emma Wilkes, 'Bambie Thug declares "Fuck the EBU" in post-Eurovision press interview', *NME* (12 May 2024).

279     **'something that was literally invented on Tumblr in 2011':** *Gay Shame*, op. cit., pp. 216-17.

280     **outlined in a report on the BBC News website in March 2022:** 'Pensioner arrested after dismembered body found', BBC News (14 March 2022).

280     **had 'recently identified as a woman':** Ibid.

280     **an article with the headline: 'Cat-killing woman guilty of murdering man as he walked home in Oxford':** Sammy Gecsoyler, 'Cat-killing woman guilty of murdering man as he walked home in Oxford', *Guardian* (23 February 2024). The headline was later amended to 'Cat killer guilty of murdering stranger as he walked home in Oxford' and a reference to the murderer's transgender status was added to the article.

280     **'understand what constitutes a fact, and stops deceiving its readers':** Louise Tickle, X (25 February 2024).

280     **who had directed a man to abuse a four-year-old child:** '"Predatory" woman who incited man to abuse child, 4, jailed', *BBC News* (8 December 2023).

281     **sentient readers will be aware that these crimes were committed by men:** Jordan King, 'Ex-solder exposed her penis and used wheelie bin as sex toy in public', *Metro* (12 April 2022); Matthew Dresch, 'Women jailed over cocaine-fuelled sex with dog in disgusting incident', *Mirror* (23 December 2021).

281     **just two on the basis of biological sex:** *How Police Forces in England & Wales Record Suspects' Sex in Crime & Incident Reporting*, Keep Prisons Single Sex (April 2022).

282     **wearing an unconvincing wig and calling himself 'Isla Bryson':** Jo Bartosch, 'How the "Isla Bryson" scandal exposed the trans cult', *Spiked* (24 December 2023).

282   *it arguably contributed to the fall of First Minister Nicola Sturgeon:* Susan Dalgety, 'Nicola Sturgeon may deny it, but rapist Adam Graham, aka Isla Bryson, played a part in her downfall', *Scotsman* (15 February 2023).

282   *style guides established by ideologically biased authorities:* While it is true that journalists are obliged to quote the proceedings of a court case with total fidelity – even if a criminal is being described with inaccurate pronouns – this does not mean that reports must likewise misstate the sex of the perpetrator beyond the act of quotation. In any case, most media reports are concerned with already convicted criminals, so there is no justification whatsoever for the pretence.

282   *it had only consulted with trans activist groups:* 'Guidance on researching and reporting stories involving transgender individuals', Independent Press Standards Organisation (October 2016).

282   *'the individual uses to describe themselves in your story?':* Ibid., p. 4.

282   *'Have you taken care not to publish inaccurate or misleading information?':* Ibid., p. 5.

283   *spare the feelings of rapists, paedophiles and murderers:* Journalists and editors who would like further guidance on how to accurately report the sex of criminals should read the media handbook on sex and gender published on the website of campaign group Sex Matters.

283   *were demonised both in the press and online:* Hugo Greenhalgh, 'Britain's top LGBT+ rights group draws fire over trans rights', *Reuters* (4 October 2018).

284   *'Who is benefiting from all this? The patriarchy':* Julia Llewellyn Smith, 'Sandi Toksvig: "Feisty old ladies are the backbone of society"', *Sunday Times* (6 October 2024).

284   *'sports-centre changing rooms happen in unisex facilities':* Andrew Gilligan, 'Unisex changing rooms put women in danger', *Sunday Times* (2 September 2018).

285   *and the family later sued for compensation:* Salvador Rizzo, 'Victim of school bathroom sexual assault sues Va. school district', *Washington Post* (5 October 2023).

285   *13,234 sex offenders out of 78,781 men (16.8 per cent):* These statistics are taken from evidence submitted to Parliament by Rosa Freedman, Kathleen Stock and Alice Sullivan on 9 December 2020 based on data from the Ministry of Justice.

285   *had committed at least one sexual offence:* Martin Evans, 'Almost two thirds of trans women prisoners are sex offenders', *Telegraph* (31 December 20240.

285   *in England and Wales are convicted sex offenders:* Madra Salach, 'Disability, same-sex carers, and safe spaces', *Genspect* (18 January 2023).

285   *one in every 2,750 men and one in every 243,000 women:* Ibid.

285   *'to carry out abusive and predatory behaviour':* Quoted by Mandy Rhodes, 'Predatory men have always pretended to be something else to abuse women', *Holyrood* (7 March 2022).

286   *he went on to sexually assault two inmates:* Nazia Parveen, 'Karen White: how "manipulative" transgender inmate attacked again', *Guardian* (11 October 2018).

286   *'And the SNP's bill introduces them':* Debbie Hayton, 'Scotland's Gender Recognition Act won't help trans people', *UnHerd* (3 March 2022).

286   *she had received for her gender-critical views:* Greg Heffer, 'Labour MP Rosie Duffield to skip party's conference "due to threats" amid calls for end to "factionalism" and "intolerance"', *Sky News* (19 September 2021).

287   *'out of dehumanising one of the most marginalised groups in society':* Nadia Whittome, X (28 September 2024).

287   *thereby silenced this pesky termagant for good:* Ibid.

287   *'resist calls to exclude trans women from women's spaces':* See the video clip posted by John James, X (19 June 2024).

287. **the International Boxing Association (IBA) 'conclusively' revealed XY chromosomes:** Mike Keegan, 'IBA boss who disqualified two boxers caught up in a gender row storm at the Paris Olympics brands the pair "men"', *Daily Mail* (5 August 2024).

287 **such a powerful punch and had feared for her life:** Etienne Fermie and Joshua Jones, 'Female Olympic boxer *walks out* of fight in tears after just 46 seconds against rival who previously failed gender test', *Sun* (1 Aug 2024).

288 **'the male world champion in each category lifts around 30 percent more than the female one':** Joyce, op. cit., p. 178.

288 **beat the women's national team 5–2 in a friendly game:** Will Griffee, 'From world champions to humbling defeat against Under 15s side… World Cup-winning USA women's team suffer 5-2 loss against Dallas academy boys', *Daily Mail* (7 April 2017).

288 **she 'would lose 6–0, 6–0 in five to six minutes, maybe ten minutes':** Quoted by Scott Allen, 'John McEnroe: If Serena Williams played the men's circuit, she'd rank "like 700"', *Washington Post* (25 June 2017).

289 **'See, I love smacking up Terfs in the cage who talk transphobic nonsense. It's bliss!':** Ewan Somerville, 'BBC apologises after interviewing transgender athlete who boasted of violence against women', *Telegraph* (16 July 2022).

289 **tend to be demonised, harassed and subjected to threats:** *Free Speech Nation: The Podcast*, GB News (3 July 2022).

289 **Women's Swimming and Diving Championship:** Alan Blinder, 'Lia Thomas wins an N.C.A.A. swimming title', *New York Times* (17 March 2022).

289 **the elite women's Madison at Washington's Marymoor Grand Prix:** Dominic Yeatman, 'Hulking transgender athletes take gold, silver and bronze spots on female podium at Washington cycling championship', *Daily Mail* (23 July 2024).

290 **when it comes to trans athletes 'we have a long way to go':** Megan Janetsky, 'Paris Olympics set record for number of openly LGBTQ+ athletes', *Los Angeles Times* (31 July 2024).

290 **compelled to undress in front of male colleagues who identified as female:** Ian Gallagher, 'Darlington Five bring fight for women spaces in hospitals to No 10 as they claim transgender policies are putting women at risk', *Daily Mail* (26 October 2024).

290 **lingered in the changing room 'longer than necessary':** Daisy Graham-Brown, '"You need to be re-educated": That's how a group of NHS nurses say hospital chiefs reacted when they complained that a transgender colleague – who shared their women's changing room – stared as they got undressed', *Daily Mail* (22 June 2024).

291 **they should be 'more inclusive', 'broaden their mindset' and 'be re-educated':** Ibid.

291 **in the female changing room:** Jo Bartosch, 'The NHS's cruel witch-hunt of a gender-critical nurse', *Spiked* (17 February 2025).

291 **the term 'biological sex' was a 'nebulous dog whistle':** Quoted by Daniel Sanderson, '"I'm biologically female", insists trans NHS doctor', *Telegraph* (10 February 2025). This is what Upton had to say at the tribunal about the incontestable reality of sexual dimorphism: 'Biological sex is a nebulous term and it doesn't really mean anything, because nobody can accurately or usefully define biological sex because pretty much every human I'm aware of is at least in part biological and many of them have a sex characteristic. I am quite aware of the impacts and implications of somebody's biological makeup, and as a trans person I'm quite aware of the implications of someone's biological makeup. There are very few people who don't think understanding some aspect of somebody's biology is important in some situation, but there is no agreed definition of biological sex. It's a nebulous dog whistle'. Quoted by David Walker, 'Trans Dr Beth Upton's "biologically denying" evidence leads to flurry of complaints to medical watchdog', *Scottish Daily Express* (12 February 2025).

291 **'just trying to be themselves':** Quoted by Tribunal Tweets, X (12 February 2025).

292   *'someone's trauma doesn't justify bad behaviour towards colleagues'*: Quoted by Tribunal Tweets, X (10 February 2025).

292   *reported to the police for 'intentional and gratuitous misgendering and deadnaming'*: Ben Borland, 'Scottish Express reported to the police for referring to transgender Dr Beth Upton as a man', *Scottish Daily Express* (16 February 2025).

292   *a former support counsellor at the Edinburgh Rape Crisis Centre:* Michael Foran, 'Why Roz Adams won', *The Critic* (20 May 2024).

293   *their ideology matters more than the people supposedly in their care:* During the tribunal, the details of internal communications by the 'non-binary' member of staff at the Edinburgh Rape Crisis Centre were revealed. On hearing about the establishment of Beira's Place, she had written an email on 14 December 2022 to all staff under the heading 'Bad News in Collective Care': 'Hey everyone just writing to acknowledge the really terrible news that came yesterday about JK Rowling's new Centre. It landed really heavy with me, and I wonder if it did for some of you too. I wonder if it would be useful to have a moment to get together (online ofc) to talk about it and rage about it and express whatever other feelings come up. If everyone would like that reply to this or my SLACK message and I'll set up a time. Big love to you all in the face of this total festive stinker.'

293   *or domestic violence should have access to female-only services:* Women's Services: a Sector Silenced, Sex Matters (15 January 2024).

293   *'But please also expect to be challenged on your prejudices'*: Quoted by Josephine Bartosch, 'Reframe your trauma', *The Critic* (11 August 2021).

293   *develop 'a more positive relationship with it'*: Ibid.

294   *such as 'chestfeeding' and 'birthing parent' into its professional lexicon:* 'Brighton NHS Trust introduces new trans-friendly terms', *BBC News* (10 February 2021).

294   *has referred to women as 'individuals with a cervix'*: CNN, Twitter (30 July 2020).

294   *while Kotex has settled for 'menstruators'*: Tampax, Twitter (15 September 2020); U by Kotex, Twitter (12 August 2020).

294   *rebranded vaginas as 'front holes' and 'bonus holes' respectively:* Ellie Bufkin, 'Health info provider adds "front hole" and other "inclusive" terms to safe sex guide', *The Federalist* (23 August 2018); Alex Barton, 'Vagina rebranded as "bonus hole" by cervical cancer charity', *Telegraph* (9 July 2023).

294   *women ought to be referred to as 'bipedal gestation units'*: Titania McGrath, 'Biden's brave new world', *The Critic* (January/February 2021).

294   *to produce milk 'comparable to that produced following the birth of a baby'*: Michael Searles, 'Trans-women's milk as good as breast milk, says NHS trust', *Telegraph* (18 February 2024).

294   *at University College London and a 'lactation consultant trainee'*: Charlotte Gill, 'Academic who claims trans women's milk is as good as breast milk has taxpayer funding', *Telegraph* (6 April 2024).

295   *was 'at least, if not higher, quality' than breast milk from mothers:* Ibid.

295   *'should be used during breastfeeding only if your physician considers this clearly necessary'*: Searles, op. cit.

295   *were known to perform birthing ceremonies with wooden babies:* See Rictor Norton, *Mother Clap's Molly House: Gay Subculture in England 1700-1830* (London: Gay Men's Press, 1992).

295   *their sense of gender identity ought to be prioritised over 'normal foetal outcomes'*: John Ely, 'Fury over "insane" call to let pregnant trans men take testosterone despite risk to babies – as woke, Government-funded researchers claim gender-affirming care is more important than having a "normal" kid', *Daily Mail* (19 July 2023).

296   *'not without potentially-harmful consequences for trans people'*: Ibid.

## Chapter 7

297 **'Rare cancer seen in 41 homosexuals':** Lawrence K. Altman, 'Rare cancer seen in 41 homosexuals', *New York Times* (3 July 1981).

298 **'perverts are to blame for the killer plague':** Quoted by Patrick Strudwick, 'This man spent 25 years fighting newspapers over their anti-gay reporting and finally won', *Buzzfeed* (15 June 2019).

298 **letters to the editor followed suit:** George Gale's comment in the *Express* is quoted by Terry Sanderson in his 'Mediawatch' column, *Gay Times* (October 1985). Sanderson wrote the column for almost twenty-five years, beginning in 1983, and it is a valuable historical record of the media coverage of gay issues during this period.

298 **'Bury them in a pit and pour on quicklime':** Quoted from a letter to the editor of the *Express* on 13 December 1986. See Terry Sanderson, *Mediawatch: The Treatment of Male and Female Homosexuality in the British Media*, (London: Cassell, 1995), p. v.

298 **those diagnosed with HIV 'can live a healthy, happy life just like anyone else':** 'First TV ad on HIV since "tombstones" 40 years ago set to tackle attitudes stuck in the 1980s', press release on the website of the Terrance Higgins Trust (16 October 2023).

298 **Larry Kramer's The Normal Heart (1985) that I saw in New York in 2004:** Larry Kramer, *The Normal Heart* (London: Methuen, 1986). The original production was at The Public Theater in New York in 1985.

299 **mistrusted by the gay community for its moralising implications:** Larry Kramer, *Faggots* (New York: Random House, 1978).

300 **'because they don't know what homosexual ethics would be. And neither do we':** John Boswell, *Rediscovering Gay History* (London: Gay Christian Movement, 1982), p. 12.

301 **from 59 per cent to 51 per cent in just three years:** Laurel Duggan, 'US support for same-sex marriage falls to 51 per cent', *UnHerd* (7 June 2024).

301 **which had made it legal for same-sex couples to marry:** Jo Yurcaba and Brooke Sopelsa, 'Lawmakers in 9 states propose measures to undermine same-sex marriage rights', *NBC News* (25 February 2025).

302 **dismissed the findings rather than engage with the problem they identified:** Carmen Fishwick, Sarah Marsh ad Guardian readers, 'What British Muslims really think about Channel 4's show', *Guardian* (14 April 2016).

302 **that they discriminate against men who identify as female:** Eva Kurilova, 'Australian Human Rights Commission decision prohibits female-only events for lesbians', *Reduxx* (26 September 2023).

303 **encouraging women to deceive men into sexual activity in gay saunas:** Michael Powell, 'NHS-funded clinic is promoting prostitution as a way for trans people to pay for their treatment', *Daily Mail* (12 March 2022).

303 **might know it as the 'bed trick':** Helena in *All's Well That Ends Well* tricks Bertram into having sex with her by substituting herself for Diana, the woman he believes himself to be seducing, in a bedchamber by night. A similar plot device occurs in *Measure for Measure* when the Duke tricks Angelo into sleeping with Marina instead of Isabella to satisfy their former engagement. This conceit is probably derived from Giovanni Boccaccio's *Decameron* (c. 1350), although an incestuous variation can be found in the story of Myrrha deceiving her father King Cinyras into sexual intercourse in Book X of Ovid's *Metamorphoses*.

303 **because trans men are men and trans women are women:** Quoted by Gabriella Ferlita, 'Grindr's trans-inclusive filter angers gay rights activist: "Delete your service"', *PinkNews* (8 February 2024).

304 **how he finds the sight of two men kissing 'really creepy':** Alexandra Topping, 'Nick Griffin's Question Time comments about gay men seen as "ridiculous"', *Guardian* (23 October 2009).

304 *that sexual orientation based on biological sex is a form of 'trauma'*: James Kirkup, 'Some women have penises. If you won't sleep with them you're transphobic', *Spectator* (2 July 2019).

305 *'can't resist a young furry ftm [female-to-male] cub'*: Prof. Stephen Whittle, X (20 February 2024).

305 *'disturbed and disturbing on every level'*: Bev Jackson, X (20 February 2024).

305 *who has been described as a 'hero for LGBTQ+ equality'*: Jimmy Brightwell, 'LGBT+ History Month 12/28: Stephen Whittle', University of Bath website (12 February 2021).

305 *'natural throttle of a female counterpoint is genuinely disturbed'*: Anna Slatz, X (3 November 2024).

305 *'male sexuality will naturally deviate towards the obscene'*: Anna Slatz, X (26 August 2023).

305 *throwback to the Victorian perception of women as dainty, timid and prudish*: Charlotte Hays, 'Christina Hoff Sommers speaks out on "fainting couch feminism"', *Independent Women's Forum* (3 November 2016).

305 *is achieved in a culture where victimhood equates to power*: Joanna Williams, *Women Vs Feminism: Why We All Need Liberating from the Gender Wars* (Bingley: Emerald Publishing, 2017), p. 112.

305 *'feed the idea that women are vulnerable creatures in need of protection from public life'*: Ella Whelan, *What Women Want: Fun, Freedom and an End to Feminism* (Brisbane: Connor Court, 2017), p. 60.

306 *'Women in search of romance are coming to grief at the hands of men who are after conquest'*: Germaine Greer, *On Rape* (London: Bloomsbury, 2018), p. 85.

306 *'always been opposed by other feminists'*: Helen Pluckrose, 'Homophobia in the gender critical movement?', *The Overflowings of a Liberal Brain*, Substack (1 November 2024).

306 *inherently dangerous alongside a belief in the gentle purity of female sexuality*: Ibid.

307 *'rejection of women and therefore completely objectionable'*: Michael Musto, 'Gay men can't take criticism', *Advocate* (12 March 2015).

307 *'render it unfit for human consumption'*: Quoted by Terry Sanderson in his 'Mediawatch' column, *Gay Times* (October 1986).

307 *'some of the gullible young to follow in his example?'*: Quoted by Terry Sanderson in his 'Mediawatch' column, *Gay Times* (January 1992).

307 *'For his kind, Aids is a form of suicide'*: Ibid.

307 *'He died from it'*: Ibid.

308 *'maybe being gay is an outdated concept'*: Reposted by Benjamin Ryan, X (15 June 2024).

308 *'because they couldn't be women'*: Quoted by Douglas Robertson, 'All my life I thought I was a gay man – but according to Juno Dawson in Attitude today, I'm actually a trans woman', *Independent* (24 May 2017).

308 *'How To Eat Pussy – For Gay Men'*: Davey Wavey, Twitter (13 April 2022).

308 *trans-identified males to 'sexual racists'*: Josephine Bartosch, 'Trans lobby group Stonewall brands lesbians "sexual racists" for raising concerns about being pressured into having sex with transgender women who still have male genitals', *Daily Mail* (20 November 2021).

308 *the Village of the streets that wouldn't be straight!*: Anna Alice Chapin, *Greenwich Village* (New York: Dodd, Mead and Company, 1917), p. 178.

309 The Stone Wall *which had been published that year*: Mary Casal, *The Stone Wall: An Autobiography* (Chicago: Eyncourt Press, 1930).

309 **'a coded message to lesbians that they would be welcomed there':** David Carter, *Stonewall: The Riots That Sparked the Gay Revolution* (New York: St. Martin's Press, 2004), p. 8.

310 **which on one occasion resulted in an outbreak of hepatitis:** Ibid., p. 80.

310 **it is worth setting the record straight:** Scott James, 'Queer people of colour led the L.G.B.T.Q. charge, but were denied the rewards', *New York Times* (22 June 2019).

310 **to a few transvestites and some transsexuals:** Carter, op. cit., p. 77.

310 **a fair number came from middle-class families:** Ibid., p. 262.

311 **'a riot by trans people':** 'Last night, Rachel Maddow lied brazenly about the history of the gay rights movement, specifically regarding the Stonewall Riots. In her report, she stated the following: "Hundreds of people showed up to protest the Trump administration removing all mention of trans people from the Stonewall National Memorial site, which, after all, commemorates a riot by trans people."' Joseph Jones, X (15 February 2025).

311 **'threw the first brick':** Cecilia Nowell, 'US park service erases references to trans people from Stonewall Inn website', *Guardian* (13 February 2025).

311 **the uprising requires a total disregard for the facts:** As Fred Sargeant, a participant at the Stonewall riots has noted, 'we know from Johnson himself that he wasn't at the Stonewall Inn in the early hours of 28 June 1969, when police raided the premises. Nor was he in the crowd that quickly formed to riot in the street in front of the bar. He did arrive at a later point, during that first evening of rioting, although there are no references that place him outside the Stonewall during any of the following nights of rioting'. Fred Sargeant, 'The myth of Marsha P Johnson', *Spiked* (28 January 2023).

311 **'it was trans people who fought alongside them for LGB rights':** Hansard, 4 March 2024.

312 **trans-identifying population was predominant:** Carter, op. cit., p. 110.

312 **"Hello there, fella!":** Ibid., p. 145.

312 **'We Shall Overcome':** Ibid., p. 148.

313 **'As it turned out they were waiting for paddy wagons, and they were waiting for back-up':** See *Our Heroes: Fred Sargeant* on the YouTube Channel of LGB Alliance, uploaded on 31 August 2023.

313 **'like a powerful rage bent on vendetta':** Howard Smith, 'Full moon over the Stonewall', *Village Voice* (3 July 1969), p. 1 and p. 25. Quotation taken from p. 25.

313 **We show our pubic hairs:** Carter, op. cit., p. 176.

313 **'Lily Law':** Ibid., p. 177.

314 **the Rubicon that the gay community had finally summoned the courage to cross:** Walter Troy Spencer, "Too much, my dear," *Village Voice* (10 July 1969), p. 36.

314 **'rocks through windows don't open doors':** Carter, op. cit., p. 213.

314 **'Sunday tourists traded incredulous looks, wondrous faces poked out of air-conditioned cars':** Jonathan Black, 'A happy birthday for gay liberation', *Village Voice* (2 July 1970), p. 1 and p. 58.

315 **the world's largest producer of armaments:** Carlos Turcios, 'Local Pride event features drag queens, sex toys', *Dallas Express* (10 June 2024).

315 **the animals have undergone special training to overcome their fears:** Michael Murphy, 'Spooked police horses given special training on going over the LGBT rainbow', *Telegraph* (31 March 2022).

315 **polysexual, agender, genderfluid, genderqueer, neutrois, two-spirit and many more:** In April 2024, staff at Royal Stoke Hospital were photographed holding a banner with twenty-one of these flags. And in January 2024, Network Rail unveiled its 'Pride Pillar' at London

Bridge station, which displayed a similarly garish range. Paul Brachhi, 'Its waiting list for operations is the fourth worst in the country, yet a Stoke hospital found time to hang a banner celebrating 21 genders and sexualities. No wonder patients and nurses are calling it *absolute madness*', *Daily Mail* (20 April 2024); Iwan Stone, '"Pride Pillar" unveiled by Network Rail at London Bridge station that celebrates "demisexuality" and "polyamory" that cost taxpayer £3,500 is "virtue signalling", say critics', *Daily Mail* (7 March 2024).

317   **'I'm straight and in a long-term hetero relationship':** The point was further clarified in a later interview. 'I will run to anything sparkly, rainbow, camp,' Minogue said. 'It must emanate from me. Gay people have always been the people who I'd be drawn to, who I'd want to hang out with. Everything in my world is queer and fabulous and I love it – even though I'm a straight girl.' Adam White, 'Dannii Minogue: "My queer dating show will be a time capsule for this country"', *Independent* (7 May 2024).

317   **Cuomo had effectively 'come out' as an old-fashioned heterosexual:** Randee Dawn, 'Andrew Cuomo's daughter Michaela Kennedy-Cuomo comes out as demisexual', *Today* (4 July 2021).

317   **'just noises masquerading as words, like a small child deciding to bark and demanding to be accepted as a dog':** Julie Burchill, 'Dannii Minogue and the heterosexual "queers"', *Spiked* (12 May 2024).

317   **39 per cent identified as 'LGBT':** Paul Bond, 'Nearly 40 percent of U.S. Gen Zs, 30 percent of young Christians identify as LGBTQ, poll shows', *Newsweek* (20 October 2021).

318   **we would be unwise to draw any conclusions from them:** Poll by 'ianjedi48%JAM', X (3 June 2024).

318   **and that his answer was a resounding 'No':** Fred Sargeant, X (6 June 2024).

318   **Sargeant was physically attacked by trans activists:** Sargeant was attacked after activists spotted that we can carrying a sign with the phrase 'No blackface, no womanface', implying that identifying as the opposite sex is the moral equivalent to a white person pretending to be black. Sanchez Manning, 'How trans fanatics tore Pride apart', *Telegraph* (17 June 2024).

318   **'lesbians don't like penises' and 'trans activism erases lesbians', were causing consternation:** Jo Bartosch, 'Pride Cymru and the rise of woke homophobia', *Spiked* (28 August 2022).

319   **'for helping me to bring about this change':** Yasmin Benoit, Twitter (July 1 2023).

319   **'other than an increase in her own profile?':** Stephen Knight, 'No, asexuals are not oppressed', *Spiked* (5 July 2023).

320   **trans movements in the twentieth century were completely separate:** Fred Sargeant, X (16 June 2024).

320   **'seeks reforms did not come into existence until the 1990s':** *Proceedings from the Third International Conference on Transgender Law and Employment Policy* (Houston: Phyllis Randolph Frye, 1994).

320   **'That was certainly scary. But we held our heads high':** Bev Jackson, X (28 December 2024).

320   **the anachronistic application of the initialism 'LGBT' to this period:** Ibid.

320   **'to encourage transsexuals and transvestites to make their own revolution':** Stuart Feather, *Blowing the Lid: Gay Liberation, Sexual Revolution and Radical Queens* (Winchester: Zero Books, 2014), p. 328.

320   **Louisa May Alcott, George Eliot, Dr James Barry and Radclyffe Hall:** Peyton Thomas, 'Did the mother of young adult literature identify as a man?', *New York Times* (24 December 2022); Grace Lavery, 'How to brainwash yourself', *Literary Hub* (31 May 2023); Rebecca Ortenberg, 'How History Keeps Ignoring James Barry', *Distillations Magazine* (20 October 2020); Hephzibah Anderson, 'The Well of Loneliness: the book that could corrupt a nation', *BBC Culture* (22 November 2022).

320 *particularly vulnerable to this kind of retrospective 'transing':* In *My First Little Book of Intersectional Activism*, Titania McGrath applauds this process of 'retrospective transitioning' and claims that she is 'thinking of writing a book about how the Ancient Greek philosophers were actually a group of black lesbian vegan insurrectionists'. She devotes a chapter to Abraham Lincoln. 'The great thing about deciding that Abraham was trans', she writes, 'is that we can now say in all honesty that there has been at least one female president of the United States of America. This is particularly important ever since Hillary Clinton was robbed of the presidency on the very flimsy grounds that she failed to get enough votes'. *My First Little Book of Intersectional Activism*, op. cit., p. 28.

321 *colours of different groups, including bisexuals, demisexuals and asexuals:* Arwa Mahdawi, 'What have Budweiser's "demi-sexual" drinking cups got to do with Pride?', *Guardian* (5 June 2019).

321 *they do not do the same for their outlets in the Middle East:* Stephen Daisley, 'When will companies end their embarrassing Pride hypocrisy?', *Spectator* (3 June 2022).

321 *'working to ensure the FIFA World Cup Qatar 2022 will be a celebration of unity and diversity':* FIFA, Twitter (1 June 2022).

322 *specified that sex must take precedence over identity:* Steven Swinford, 'Lavatory clampdown for trans pupils in new government guidance', *The Times* (25 April 2023).

323 *promoting a movement whose objective is the elimination of homosexuality:* Billy Bragg's continual promotion of gender identity ideology is well established. He has been described in the national press as a 'trans rights activist' and as one who 'insists that trans women are women'. He also regularly deploys the terminology of gender ideologues, such as 'cisgender' and 'cis men'. He has lambasted 'white evangelical Christians' who 'believe that gender is determined by sex at birth' and has declared 'allyship with the trans and non-binary communities'. He has criticised Donald Trump for asserting that there are 'only two genders', as well as those who hold 'traditional values' which he defines as 'arguing that sex is binary'. See Michael Deacon, 'Billy Bragg's attack on JK Rowling highlights the idiocy of woke tribalism', *Telegraph* (2 May 2024); Julie Bindel, 'Billy Bragg still doesn't understand feminism', *UnHerd* (29 April 2024); Billy Bragg, Twitter (15 November 2021); Billy Bragg, 'Why I've made my old lyrics trans-inclusive', *New Statesman* (15 November 2021); Billy Bragg, X (21 January 2025); Billy Bragg, X (9 January 2024).

323 *when teenage activists unleashed thousands of crickets into the auditorium:* Albert Tait, 'Suspected trans protesters release crickets to disrupt gay rights conference', *Telegraph* (11 October 2024).

324 *when your feelings about yourself are in constant flux:* Quoted from Bev Jackson's appearance on *Free Speech Nation* on GB News (13 October 2024).

325 *'implement a full, trans-inclusive, ban on all forms of conversion therapy':* Daniel Martin, 'Starmer to outlaw all forms of conversion therapy if Labour wins election', *Telegraph* (30 January 2024).

325 *62 per cent feel the same about 'trans conversion therapy':* Isabelle Kirk, 'Most Britons want conversion therapy banned, including that aimed at transgender people', *YouGov* (12 April 2022).

326 *fundamentalists have established programmes to address the 'problem' of homosexuality:* This was satirised in an episode of the American comedy cartoon *South Park* in which the young Butters Stotch is mistakenly assumed to be gay by his parents and dispatched to 'Camp New Grace' whose slogan is 'Pray the Gay Away'. At one point, the boys attend a presentation by Pastor Phillips, who tells them that he 'used to have unclean urges' but was healed through the power of prayer, all the while prancing around like Nathan Lane in *The Birdcage* (1996). The episode doesn't shy away from the darker side of these kinds of retreats. Suicides are shown to be common among the boys, all of which the staff are happy to shrug off. *South Park*, 'Cartman Sucks' (season 11, episode 2).

326    **'Septal stimulation for the initiation of heterosexual behavior in a homosexual male':** Charles E. Moan and Robert G. Heath, 'Septal stimulation for the initiation of heterosexual behavior in a homosexual male', *Journal of Behavior Therapy and Experimental Psychiatry*, vol. 3, iss. 1 (March 1972), pp. 23-26.

326    **injected with substances that caused him to vomit:** Matthew Baldwin and Thomas Hescott, *Outings & The Act* (London: Samuel French, 2017), pp. 21-24.

326    **the 'epidemic of corrective rape' in South Africa:** Clare Carter, 'The brutality of "corrective rape"', *New York Times* (27 July 2013).

327    **the Tavistock paediatric gender clinic were same-sex attracted:** 'When GIDS asked older adolescents about who they were attracted to, around 90 per cent of natal females reported that they were same-sex attracted or bisexual (67.6 per cent and 21.1 per cent respectively). Just 8.5 per cent were opposite-sex attracted – attracted to males. For the natal males, 80.8 per cent reported being same-sex attracted or bisexual (42.3 per cent and 38.5 per cent respectively), and 19.2 per cent opposite-sex attracted. These percentages are high, but are from those referred in 2012. GIDS say that in their most recent statistics – from 2015 – 60 per cent of natal males were same-sex attracted or bisexual (30 per cent for each). Thirty per cent were attracted to females. The remainder 'described themselves as not being attracted to either males or females, or as asexual'. For females, over half were same-sex attracted, just under 20 per cent were bisexual, and a quarter were attracted to males. GIDS make clear that these data are by no means complete. We don't know what percentage of more recent referrals have been same-sex attracted.' Hannah Barnes, *Time to Think: The Inside Story of the Collapse of the Tavistock's Gender Service for Children* (London: Swift Press, 2023), p. 217.

327    **GIDS were either homosexual or bisexual:** *Cass Review*, op. cit.

327    **whistleblowers revealed that homophobia was endemic:** Joyce, op. cit., p. 86. For more on the Tavistock Clinic see Jamie Doward, 'Gender identity clinic accused of fast-tracking young adults', *Observer* (3 November 2018).

327    **'autism, depression or other problems that might have explained their unhappiness':** Gordon Rayner, 'Tavistock clinic "ignored" link between autism and transgender children', *Telegraph* (14 February 2023).

328    **these children were under twelve and a half years old:** Leor Sapir, 'A Consensus No Longer', *City Journal* (12 August 2024).

328    **'suppress a person's sexuality or gender identity':** Dennis Kavanagh, 'The disaster of the Scottish Conversion Therapy offence in practice', *Kavanagh's Substack* (12 January 2024).

328    **gender dysphoria that in most cases will naturally resolve themselves through puberty:** Dr Hilary Cass, *The Cass Review: Independent Review of Gender Identity Services for Children and Young People – Interim Report* (February 2022), p. 63.

328    **an eleven-year-old boy treated for gender dysphoria:** Sallie Baxendale, 'The impact of suppressing puberty on neuropsychological function: A review', *Acta Paediatrica* (9 February 2024).

328    **present risks to the healthy development of bones:** 'Results consistently indicate a negative impact of long-term puberty suppression on bone mineral density, especially at the lumbar spine, which is only partially restored after sex steroid administration. Trans girls are more vulnerable than trans boys for compromised bone health.' Silvia Ciancia, Vanessa Dubois and Martine Cools, 'Impact of gender-affirming treatment on bone health in transgender and gender diverse youth', *Endocrine Connections* (28 September 2022).

328    **'conversion therapy for gay kids':** Daniel Martin, 'Kemi Badenoch: I have evidence gay young people are being told they are transgender', *Telegraph* (6 February 2024).

329    **that enable them to establish a homosexual identity:** Ibid.

329    **'Why are you like this? Go and change your gender':** Ali Hamedani, 'The gay people pushed to change their gender', *BBC News* (5 November 2014).

329   *oblivious to the anti-gay reasoning behind the decision:* PinkNews, Twitter (12 January 2020).

330   *thwarted by a lack of cooperation from the adult gender services':* Ibid., p. 20.

330   *'the families, carers and clinicians doing their best to support them':* Stonewall, X (10 April 2024).

330   *'The absolute fucking nerve of these people':* James Dreyfus, X (10 April 2024).

331   *'we're not medical experts, we don't advocate for any pathway':* See the interview from *Sky News* posted on X by John James (10 April 2024).

331   *to strip LGB Alliance of its charitable status:* Amelia Gentleman, 'Trans children's charity Mermaids fails to have charitable status stripped from LGB Alliance', *Guardian* (6 July 2023).

331   *(GIDS) at the Tavistock Clinic:* Hayley Dixon, 'Trans lobby group Mermaids helped NHS plan treatment for children', *Telegraph* (27 May 2023).

331   *there was 'no evidence of misconduct', it had been 'mismanaged':* James Melley, 'Trans charity Mermaids was mismanaged, regulator says', *BBC News* (24 October 2024).

331   *which can result in broken ribs and breathing difficulties:* Hayley Dixon, 'Trans charity Mermaids giving breast binders to children behind parents' backs', *Telegraph* (25 September 2022). It was also discovered that Mermaids had appointed a trustee who had attended a conference which had been arranged by an organisation calling for paedophiles to be able to live in 'truth and dignity'.

331   *to Thailand on his birthday to have castration surgery:* Writer and television producer Malcolm Clark has described Susie Green as 'one of the most controversial social justice activists in the UK'. He writes: 'She has often been criticised for promoting the notion that children as young as two can signal their trans identity. She claims to have become convinced her own son Jack was really a girl before he could properly walk. "As a toddler," Green has explained, "he always headed for the dolls in toy shops". He also "loathed having his hair cut", she says, to dispel any lingering doubts. So confident was Green of her son's transgender status she flew Jack to Thailand in 2009 to have him castrated. This would have been a criminal offence if it had been conducted in the UK. This kind of "sex change surgery" can only be conducted on over 18s in this country (Jack was 16 at the time). The same rule now applies in Thailand too.' Malcolm Clark, 'The Susie Green light', *The Critic* (24 December 2024).

331   *'Only a small proportion of cases will result in a transsexual outcome':* Quoted in 'A History of Affirmation', *Bayswater Support Group* website (24 May 2021).

332   *'people afraid even of listening to another view':* Rachel Cooke, 'Tavistock trust whistleblower David Bell: "I believed I was doing the right thing"', *Observer* (2 May 2021).

332   *those who have objected to the rise of this ideology:* Julie Bindel, 'Why I sued PinkNews', *UnHerd* (20 November 2021).

332   *Cass is neither deliverable nor desirable:* 'Cass Review Delivers Controversial Verdict on NHS Trans Healthcare', *Novara Media* (10 April 2024). The podcast is available on YouTube.

332   *so why had we been blocking the cure?:* Helen Joyce points out that research shows around 80 per cent of children eventually become reconciled with their biological sex, either before or in the early stages of puberty, if they 'are permitted to express themselves how they wish but not encouraged to believe that they are members of the opposite sex'. Joyce, op. cit., p. 33.

333   *'Don't feel bad about it':* O. S. Warren, 'How to Navigate Britain's Broken Trans Healthcare System', *Novara Media* (3 December 2021).

333   *'they've been abused, because it's so high stakes at that point':* John Ely, 'Children were being "coached" on what to say to NHS doctors to get puberty blockers, author of bombshell report into trans care reveals', *Daily Mail* (10 April 2024).

333     *'developmental rigour':* Cass Review, op. cit., p. 6.

334     **Hormonal Experiments on Children, Adolescents, and Vulnerable Adults:** Mia Hughes, *The WPATH Files: Pseudoscientific Surgical and Hormonal Experiments on Children, Adolescents, and Vulnerable Adults* (Albany: Environmental Progress, 2024). The report was published on 4 March 2024.

334     *'they didn't really understand that they are going to have facial hair, right?':* Ibid., pp. 185-86.

335     *'people who haven't even had biology in high school yet':* Ibid., p. 184.

335     *'but we're doing the same thing to our children':* Quoted by Yasmin Zenith, 'The dissenting doctor', *The Critic* (July 2023).

335     *'the "right thing to do?"':* Mia Hughes, *WPATH Files Excerpts: Exposing the Realities of Gender Medicine* (Albany: Environmental Progress, 2024), p. 3.

335     *'phallus-preserving vaginoplasties, and nullification procedures':* Ibid., p. 5.

335     *(removal of the testicles):* Ibid., p. 3.

335     *'it's there, and I don't think any of that surprises us':* Ibid.

336     *'but at the end of the day it is a risk/benefit decision':* Ibid., p. 8.

336     *as the first line of treatment for gender-dysphoric youth:* 'Youth gender transition is pushed without evidence', *Wall Street Journal* (13 July 2023).

336     *blockers reduced the risk of suicidal ideation:* In March 2025, a study of more than 107,000 patients suffering from gender dysphoria was published in the *Oxford Academic Journal of Sexual Medicine*. It concluded that 'those who undergo transgender surgeries, are at greater risk for mental health problems, including depression, suicidal ideation, anxiety, and others'. Thomas Stevenson, 'Transgender surgeries associated with increased risk of suicidal ideation, depression: Oxford Academic study', *Post Millennial* (1 March 2025).

336     *gender dysphoria between 1996 and 2019:* Mary Harrington, 'New study: trans youth not at elevated risk of suicide', *UnHerd* (19 February 2024).

336     *'Do you want a happy little girl or a dead little boy?':* DeShanna Neal, '"Do You Want a Happy Little Girl or a Dead Little Boy?": My Choice as a Mother', *Vice* (13 April 2017).

337     *'suggests that gender medicine does not fall into this category':* The WPATH Files, op. cit., p. 3.

337     *gender identity that requires surgical actualisation:* Mike Wade, 'Health chiefs apologise over claim that eunuch should be gender identity', *The Times* (16 June 2022).

337     *'to eliminate masculine physical features, masculine genitals, or genital functioning':* 'Standards of Care for the Health of Transgender and Gender Diverse People, Version 8', *International Journal of Transgender Health*, vol. 23, no. 1, p. 88.

337     *'that meet the needs of eunuch individuals':* Ibid., p. 89.

337     *website called the 'Eunuch Archives':* Daniel Sanderson, '"Eunuch" should be a gender, according to Scottish NHS', *Telegraph* (15 June 2022); Daniel Sanderson, 'Gender identity clinics across Scotland secretly use extreme guidelines from controversial trans group', *Telegraph* (27 October 2022).

337     *this site depicted fantasies about the castration of children:* Genevieve Gluck, 'Top trans medical association collaborated with castration, child abuse fetishists', *Reduxx* (17 May 2022).

337     *'depictions of children with stunted puberty being raped by doctors':* Ibid.

337     *'"freezing" them in a childlike state':* Ibid.

338     *'access stories specifically featuring children':* Ibid.

338    *filibustering about ferrets in order to prevent the discussion:* Alexandra Rogers, 'Liz Truss "furious" after MPs accused of blocking transgender reform bill', *Sky News* (15 March 2024).

339    *children as young as eight should be able to transition – has already decried its contents:* Greg Heffer, 'Green MSP Maggie Chapman claims Scotland "should be exploring" options for *eight-year-olds* to legally change their gender and suggests people "don't know what biological sex they are until they've had their chromosomes tested"', *Daily Mail* (17 January 2023).

339    *'the age of accessing gender-affirming care to 25':* Maggie Chapman MSP, X (10 April 2024).

339    *'a potentially vulnerable stage in their journey':* Cass Review, op. cit., p. 42.

339    *the new Health Secretary Wes Streeting in December:* Wes Streeting made the announcement in Parliament on 11 December 2024. 'The Cass review made it clear that there is not enough evidence about the long-term effects of using puberty blockers to treat gender incongruence to know whether they are safe or beneficial. That evidence should have been established before they were ever prescribed for that purpose. It is a scandal that medicine was given to vulnerable young children, without proof that it was safe or effective, or that it had gone through the rigorous safeguards of a clinical trial' (Hansard).

340    *'remove the clinical expertise from medical decision making':* Ibid.

340    *'Does he understand that this is, at heart, discriminatory?:* Ibid.

340    *'why we should listen to clinicians, not politicians':* Ibid.

340    *those who have tried to warn people of the dangers over the last decade:* James O'Brien, X (10 April 2024).

## Chapter 8

341    *Whitehouse sued and was awarded £500 in damages:* Cleaning Up TV, op. cit., p. 49.

342    *the scant attire of Sylvester Stallone's anti-hero:* This episode of *Daytime*, produced by Thames Television, aired on 10 September 1985.

342    *two thugs were on their way from London to attack her:* Cleaning Up TV, op. cit., p. 64.

342    *'who have invented this new term "hate speech"':* Andrew Doyle, 'Ricky Gervais: why I'll never apologise for my jokes', *Spectator* (21 December 2019).

343    *'The Urgency of Intersectionality':* Andrew Doyle, 'Now that BLM has gone mainstream our children are being brainwashed by a divisive new dogma that I fear will stoke, not heal, racial tensions', *Daily Mail* (12 September 2020).

343    *'to use the BBC as a vehicle for their own propaganda':* Cleaning Up TV, op. cit., p. 166.

344    *there are 'over 100 gender identities':* Glen Owen, 'BBC sex education programme tells 9-year-olds there are "over 100 genders" and shows kids talking to adults about "bi-gender", "genderqueer" and "pansexual" identities', *Daily Mail* (23 January 2021).

344    *'University of Essex campus cat honoured with statue':* Mariam Issimdar, 'University of Essex campus cat honoured with statue', *BBC News* (5 March 2024).

344    *'Recycling bins shake-up for Highland households':* 'Recycling bins shake-up for Highland households', *BBC News* (5 March 2024).

344    *'Winchester park-and-ride buses to run on vegetable oil':* Charlotte Andrews, 'Winchester park-and-ride buses to run on vegetable oil', *BBC News* (5 March 2024).

344    *'More beavers released in Cairngorms National Park':* 'More beavers released in Cairngorms National Park', *BBC News* (5 March 2024).

344    *the BBC failed to cover the story:* Victor Nava, 'Biden admin official pressured medical experts to nix age limit guidelines for transgender surgery', *New York Post* (26 June 2024).

344 **specialist knowledge of 'gender-affirming care':** *Free Speech Nation* (10 March 2024), available to watch on the GB News YouTube channel.

345 **the charity didn't have 'any real influence' at all:** Quoted by Gabriella Swerling, 'Being gender critical does not mean you are transphobic, admits Stonewall boss', *Telegraph* (18 November 2021).

345 **Dissenting voices have been marginalised, castigated, cancelled, silenced:** Charlie Walsham, 'How did the BBC get the trans debate so wrong?', *Spectator* (12 April 2024).

345 **BBC employees were trying to identify him and get him fired:** Charlie Walsham, 'Why are BBC staff trying to get me fired?', *Spectator* (5 May 2024).

347 **I cried to dream again:** William Shakespeare, *The Tempest*, act 3, scene 2.

347 **'it represents all that is good and noble and disinterested':** Eric Gill, quoted in the *Illustrated London News* (8 March 1941).

347 **'it ought to be the BBC's':** Ibid.

348 **desecrating an image of God and his son:** It was only after the publication of *Eric Gill* (London: Faber and Faber, 1989), a biography by Fiona MacCarthy, almost five decades after the artist's death, that there were widespread calls for his artwork to be removed from public spaces. Apparently Gill had admitted in his diaries to sexually abusing his daughters, committing incest with his sisters, and experimenting sexually with the family dog. The first attack on the statue took place in January 2022. See Andrew Doyle, 'We are living through a frenzy of conformity', *Spectator* (20 June 2020).

348 **'Mr French is much better looking, though, and his legs really aren't a bit like that':** R. W. Hallows's comments are quoted in the *Sunday Mirror* on 12 November 1933.

348 **may tread the path of wisdom and uprightness:** *Cleaning Up TV*, op. cit., p. 2.

348 **she called for its ideology to be replaced with hers:** Ibid., p. 15.

349 **bring Him back to the heart of our family and national life:** Ibid., p. 23. Later version of the manifesto modified the first point so that it referred instead to the 'men and women of Britain'.

349 **Ethan, who wants to dress up as a teddy bear for sexual gratification:** Katie Hind, 'BBC's Doctors explores "furry" culture: Daytime soap shows how teenager who "dresses up as a teddy bear" is thrown out by his grandfather who calls him "perverted" before they later reconcile', *Daily Mail* (24 November 2023).

350 **'likely to affront the good taste of the country':** Ibid., p. 20.

350 **BBC's General Advisory Council in the 1960s, as the 'new populists':** Ibid., p. 143.

350 **she mused sardonically:** Ibid., p. 124. *Fable* was broadcast as part of *The Wednesday Play* series on BBC One on 27 January 1965.

351 **'on the thousands of homosexuals who must have seen it?:** 'Was it at least part of the idea behind this play to move people to compassion so that they hastened to change the law and legalize sodomy? We need to understand the human tragedy of situations like these. But when the emphasis is on one aspect only it becomes suspect. There are thousands of men with homosexual tendencies who have found creative outlet for their sexual energies and understand what self-discipline and faith can do for them. Why should these not become the theme of a Wednesday play?' Ibid., p. 167. *Horror of Darkness* was broadcast as part of *The Wednesday Play* series on BBC One on 10 March 1965.

351 **'all broadcasting is propaganda: the question is for what?':** Ibid., p. 69 and p. 187.

351 **a great deal of influence in the Critical Social Justice movement:** I have pointed out elsewhere that although Michel Foucault is continually cited by the woke, the Frankfurt School is overlooked. Yet the theories of the likes of Max Horkheimer, Theodor Adorno, Erich Fromm, Herbert Marcuse, *et al.* linger in the ideology of Critical Social Justice. I have

offered the example of Marcuse's 1965 essay on 'repressive tolerance' as a kind of blueprint for woke activism, 'calling as it does for militant disobedience and an intolerance of the intolerant'. See *The New Puritans*, op. cit., pp. 91-97.

351 **'people who make freedom a fetish are dangerous':** *Cleaning Up TV*, op. cit., p. 118.

351 **Cleaning Up TV is entitled 'Fetish of Freedom':** Ibid., pp. 118-32.

352 **'as though debate is itself an innocuous, neutral act':** Nadia Whittome, 'The only way to avoid hysteria about trans rights is to ground the debate in real life experiences', *Independent* (23 July 2020).

352 **she took a different line on artistic freedom:** 'The suppression of viewpoints and the elimination of controversy would be indefensible.' *Cleaning Up TV*, op. cit., p. 151.

352 **when the smirk goes they can look very nasty indeed:** Mary Whitehouse, *Whatever Happened to Sex?* (Hove: Wayland Publishers Limited, 1977), p. 118.

352 **the opportunity nor the power to exercise such control:** *Cleaning Up TV*, op. cit., p. 149.

353 **television programmes ought therefore to promote her favoured values:** Ibid., p. 162.

353 **'exciting drama and discussion':** Ibid., p. 52.

353 **'the deepest needs and fullest potential of the human personality':** Ibid., p. 85.

353 **'loyally maintained monogamous marriages':** Ibid.

354 **various works lamenting the moral shortcomings of the artists:** In *The New Puritans*, I offer a particularly egregious example in the form of an exhibition at the Tate Britain of William Hogarth's works. The curators sought to highlight the 'sexual violence and slavery' of the exhibits, with one comment on a self-portrait that claimed the chair featured in the image was probably constructed from 'timber shipped from the colonies'. Bizarrely, it asks whether the chair in question could 'stand in for all those unnamed black and brown people enabling the society that supports his vigorous creativity?' *The New Puritans*, op. cit., p. 237.

354 **to reflect the common usage of words:** See ibid., pp. 139-41.

354 **Material Girls (2021) by Kathleen Stock:** Abigail Shrier, *Irreversible Damage: Teenage Girls and the Transgender Craze* (London: Swift Press, 2020); Helen Joyce, *Trans: When Ideology Meets Reality* (London: Oneworld, 2021); Kathleen Stock, *Material Girls: Why Reality Matters for Feminism* (London: Fleet, 2021).

355 **Adolf Hitler's Mein Kampf (1925):** Craig Simpson, 'Gender-critical books "treated like Mein Kampf" by public library', *Telegraph* (28 October 2023).

355 **'go back to hiding this cunt's books in the storeroom':** 'Hi Waterstones. Can you confirm if members of your staff are allowed to hide books from customers? And then boast publicly about it? Have you become a not-for-profit company? If so perhaps customers should know.' Douglas Murray, X (29 February 2024). The post was accompanied by a link to screenshots from the member of staff declaring that she had hidden books by Douglas Murray and Graham Linehan.

355 **without devious little pink-haired gremlins getting in the way:** Waterstones seems to have a particular problem in this regard. In July 2023, the *Daily Mail* reported that 'a swathe of customers' had complained that they were unable to find works by gender-critical feminists on the shelves, even when the customer service department had confirmed that they were in stock. 'Waterstones run their branches as mini dictatorships', wrote one user on X. 'Couldn't buy Andrew Doyle's book where I was staying at the time because he'd "offended" the local Uni wokies in a speech and they didn't stock it'. While the free speech of authors is unaffected by these capers, it does remind us just how far the tentacles of this ideology have unfurled. One would have hoped that an activity as simple as buying a book would not involve a scrimmage with the acolytes of this joyless cult. See Arthur Parashar and George Iddenden, 'Waterstones customers accuse bookshop of "censorship" amid claims they can't

find works by Sharron Davies and other gender critical feminists including Helen Joyce on shelves', *Daily Mail* (17 July 2023).

355    **to protect the mental health of students:** Tiffany Crawford, 'Surrey schools pull To Kill a Mockingbird and other books from recommended reading curriculum', *Vancouver Sun* (29 February 2024).

355    **Part-Time Indian (2007) by Sherman Alexie:** John Steinbeck, *Of Mice and Men* (New York: Covici Friede, 1937); Harper Lee, *To Kill a Mockingbird* (Pennsylvania: J. B. Lippincott & Co., 1960); John Ball, *In the Heat of the Night* (New York: Harper & Row, 1965); Sherman Alexie, *The Absolutely True Diary of a Part-Time Indian* (New York: Little, Brown, 2007).

356    **discover what it is your elders don't want you to know:** Stephen King, 'The book-banners: adventure in censorship is stranger than fiction', *Bangor Daily News* (20 March 1992).

356    **'we should expel poetry from the city':** Plato, op. cit., p. 296.

356    **'a form of amusement and not a serious occupation':** Ibid, p. 290.

357    **But we shall have to throw away most of the stories they tell now:** Ibid., p. 54.

357    **Mary Whitehouse's guiding principle:** Ibid., p. 56.

358    **at the Seven Dials Playhouse in London:** While comedy tends to fare badly with the passage of time, relatively recent productions of Joe Orton's farces have proven hugely successful. The 50th anniversary production of *Loot* at the Park Theatre in London in 2017 was one of the best I have seen, and was enhanced immeasurably by a live actor playing the corpse that is stripped naked and bundled about the stage in the escalating mania. It was quite the contrast to the 2012 production of *What the Butler Saw* at the Vaudeville Theatre in London, whose fatal misstep was to allow the characters to find their own lines funny. If Orton's farces aren't played straight, they simply don't work.

358    **Orton's targets might be in the context of today's culture wars:** That Orton's appeal has endured is, of course, partly due to the mystery surrounding his gruesome death. In 1967, Orton was beaten to death with a hammer by his lover and mentor Kenneth Halliwell in their small Islington flat. In his suicide note, Halliwell wrote: 'If you read his diary all will be explained. KH. P.S. Especially the latter part'. Yet the final pages were missing. Some believe that Orton's agent Peggy Ramsay took the diary from the murder scene and may have removed the final section, possibly to protect someone's identity. Friends of Orton have testified that he was having an affair and was on the brink of leaving Halliwell, but the man in question has never been named. The theatre critic Michael Thornton was informed by police that he was mentioned in those final pages, and that they had been withheld because they 'contained sensitive information about persons still living'. If true, this would scupper the theory that Ramsay censored the document, and would suggest that the solution lies buried in police archives. Of course, Orton's promiscuity may have been the catalyst to Halliwell's mania. Orton would leave his diary around the flat in the knowledge that his lover would read his accounts of sexual exploits with strangers. This is also why the reliability of the diaries cannot be trusted. See Michael Thornton, 'Why I blame myself for the murder of Sixties playwright Joe Orton', *Daily Mail* (4 April 2009).

358    **this country will shortly strike back!:** John Lahr (ed.), *The Orton Diaries* (New York: Harper & Row, 1986), p. 281.

359    **'This truly horrible play shouldn't contaminate our streets.':** Ibid., p. 287.

361    **than exposing the follies of the powerful:** Gwilym Mumford, 'The problem with The Problem with Jon Stewart', *Guardian* (19 November 2021).

362    **ideological goals over the pursuit of truth and knowledge:** Jennifer Schuessler, 'Hoaxers slip breastaurants and dog-park sex into journals' *New York Times* (4 October 2018).

362    **during lessons as a form of reparation for slavery:** By the time the hoaxers were discovered, this article was at the 'revise and resubmit' stage of the process. Helen Pluckrose tells me that one reviewer had said that 'they'd like to see it in classrooms'.

362 *'old whore society really lifted up her skirts and the stench was pretty foul':* Lahr, op. cit., p. 28.

363 *'they'll be screaming hysterics in next to no time':* Ibid., p. 125.

363 *a play about defending homeland and Englishness seems ill-judged:* Andrew Dickson, 'Is Jerusalem still the play of the century? Top playwrights give their verdicts', *Guardian* (4 April 2022).

364 *to rescue the arts from this self-constructed oubliette:* According to its website, the three key mission statements of Freedom in the Arts are: (i) 'to protect freedom of speech and to offer artists all levels of support to protect their rights', (ii) 'to protect freedom of expression and make sure that the arts are the place where difficult ideas can be addressed, explored and discussed', and (iii) 'to uphold the mission of institutions that serve the arts and the public, to make sure they maintain impartiality and are non-ideologically driven'.

364 *'Cheaters, idle, infamous, base, prophane, and godlesse persons':* Prynne, op. cit., p. 145.

365 *'saw through everybody equally':* A. L. Rowse, *William Shakespeare: A Biography* (New York: Harper & Row, 1963), p. 90.

366 *'Shakespeare's plays through the lens of race and social justice':* Quoted by Chris Hastings, 'Now they claim that Macbeth promotes white supremacy!', *Scottish Mail on Sunday* (3 September 2023).

366 *Queen Elizabeth I could have been 'non-binary' for similar reasons:* Oliver Price, 'Shakespeare's Globe Theatre academic says Elizabeth I may have been non-binary in essay calling Virgin Queen "them" after row over transgender Joan Of Arc play', *Daily Mail* (13 August 2022).

366 *'their male monarchical role at different points':* Ibid.

366 *disability-blind production' of Hamlet (c. 1600):* Quoted by Ella Whelan, 'Identity politics is ruining Shakespeare', *Spiked* (25 May 2018).

366 *'To leave or not to leave: that is the question':* Ibid.

367 *Never has tragedy been so tedious:* Not all modern productions of Shakespeare have been so dismal. I was fortunate enough to see the site-specific production of *Macbeth* at Dock X in London in March 2024. As much as I admire its stars, Ralph Fiennes and Indira Varma, my expectations were naturally low. On making our way into the auditorium, the audience passed through a kind of warzone, complete with the rubble of fallen buildings and a burned-out car. Any sense of an immersive experience was impossible with so many punters taking selfies next to the car while carrying their plastic beakers of wine. Gimmicks aside, once we were fifteen minutes into the show I felt a sense of relief. This was actually Shakespeare's play; updated to a modern setting, to be sure, but otherwise intact. There were some textual modifications here and there: Duncan's entrance was postponed so that the Captain's account of the battle could be delivered as a soliloquy, and the scenes with the Porter and Hecate were removed. Something is always lost in such interventions, but these are minor grumbles, and at least we weren't subjected to moralistic hectoring disguised as drama. This production may not have soared to the heights of which Shakespeare's masterpiece is capable – and I had reservations about the choice to present Macbeth as an awkward and weatherworn veteran – but it was a fairly solid effort. And all it took was for the director to have faith in the text and the immense power of Shakespeare's words. The show worked precisely because it didn't attempt to reconfigure Shakespeare as a prophet of intersectional monomania.

367 *'in tandem with a global white cultural supremacy':* Arthur L. Little, Jr., *White People in Shakespeare: Essays on Race, Culture and the Elite* (London: Bloomsbury, 2023).

367 *'or deemphasized to make room for modern, diverse, and inclusive voices':* Amanda MacGregor, 'To Teach or Not To Teach: Is Shakespeare Still Relevant to Today's Students?', *School Library Journal* (4 January 2021).

367 *'create a more inclusive museum experience':* Craig Simpson, 'Shakespeare's birthplace to be decolonised after "white supremacy" fears', *Telegraph* (16 March 2025).

367   *'language or depictions that are racist, sexist, homophobic, or otherwise harmful'*: Ibid.

368   *'descriptions of race, class and ability which we would find unacceptable today'*: Craig Simpson, 'Virginia Woolf's "unacceptable views" explained via QR code on her statue', *Telegraph* (25 June 2024).

368   *'when a gale is blowing the lower branches of a tree can touch the top ones'*: I have only Alec Waugh's word for it that this simile is Turgenev's invention; I have been unable to locate the phrase for myself. Still, it describes so perfectly the scenario under discussion that it would be remiss not to quote it simply because of concerns over its precise source. Alec Waugh, *Where the Clocks Chime Twice* (London: Cassell & Co. Ltd, 1952), p. 112.

368   **P. G. Wodehouse, Ian Fleming, Agatha Christie and Roald Dahl:** Simon Evans, 'How dare they rewrite PG Wodehouse?', *Spiked* (17 April 2023); Armani Syed, 'The trouble with the rewrites to the James Bond books', *Time* (27 February 2023); Rachel Hall, 'Agatha Christie novels reworked to remove potentially offensive language', *Guardian* (26 March 2023); Hayden Vernon, 'Roald Dahl books rewritten to remove language deemed offensive', *Guardian* (18 February 2023).

368   *'wear wigs and there is certainly nothing wrong with that'*: Quoted by Ed Cumming, Abigail Buchanan, Genevieve Holl-Allen and Benedict Smith, 'The rewriting of Roald Dahl', *Telegraph* (24 February 2023).

368   *'his' became 'its'*: Ibid.

368   *'we could round them all up and put them in the meat-grinder'*: Ibid.

369   **but are readers genuinely all that corruptible?:** Ian Fleming, *The Spy Who Loved Me* (New York: Viking Press, 1962), p. 188.

369   **Tom Brown's School Days (1857) by Thomas Hughes:** George MacDonald Fraser, *Flashman* (London: Barrie & Jenkins, 1969); Thomas Hughes, *Tom Brown's School Days* (London: Macmillan, 1857).

369   **And dying thus around us every day:** Charles Dickens, *Bleak House* (London: Macmillan, 1895), p. 602. Originally serialised between 1852 and 1853.

370   **Woolf writes: 'Down among the bushes she worked like a nigger':** Virginia Woolf, *Between the Acts* (New York: Harcourt, Brace & World, Inc., 1941), p. 150.

370   **The obtrusiveness of the fellow is also Nigger-like:** Letter from Karl Marx to Frederick Engels (30 July 1862). Saul K. Padover (trans.), *The Letters of Karl Marx* (New Jersey: Prentice-Hall, 1979), pp. 466-68.

371   *'The past is a foreign country: they do things differently there'*: L. P. Hartley, *The Go-Between* (London: Hamish Hamilton, 1953).

372   **O so lovely! O so soft, sweet, soft!:** James Joyce, Ulysses (London: Egoist Press, 1922), p. 350.

372   *'But it is damn well worth it'*: Quoted by Adam Thirlwell, 'It's Still a Scandal!', *New York Review of Books* (23 April 2015).

372   **right-leaning readership due to its graphic depictions of sex and violence:** Bret Easton Ellis, *The Shards* (New York: Alfred A. Knopf, 2023).

372   *'rebelling against the prevailing culture'*: Nick Dixon, 'Why I still love Bret Easton Ellis', *Substack* (22 September 2024).

372   *'the philistinism sometimes associated with the right'*: Ibid.

373   **which marked for destruction over four thousand 'obscene' works:** Alan Travis, *Bound and Gagged: A Secret History of Obscenity in Britain* (London: Profile, 2000).

373   *'The argument is circular'*: Anthony Burgess, *Obscenity & The Arts* (Manchester: Pariah Press, 2018), p. 59.

373   **while pointing at the buttons on his fly:** *My Life and Times: Octave Five 1915 – 1923*, op. cit., p. 165.

373    *a sign that the marriage was 'imperfect'*: Ibid., pp. 167-68.

373    *'make the sex relations valid and precious'*: Ibid.

374    *where the phallus rose thick and arching, it was gold-red, vivid in a little cloud:* D. H. Lawrence, *Lady Chatterley's Lover* (New York: Bantam Books, 1973), p. 226. Originally published in 1928.

374    *could not possibly have been further from Lawrence's intention:* The phrase 'dirt for dirt's sake' had also been used by the judge in the obscenity trial of Alan Ginsberg's poem 'Howl' (1956). Virginia Heffernan, 'Lawrence Ferlinghetti's life contains a lesson for cancel culture', *Los Angeles Times* (26 February 2021).

374    *'wish your wife or your servants to read'*: Quoted by Mark Brown, 'Judge's copy of Lady Chatterley's Lover temporarily barred from leaving UK', *Guardian* (13 May 2019).

374    *Rabelais's description of Pope Calixtus as a 'cunt barber' is anyone's guess:* Donald M. Frame (trans.), *The Complete Works of François Rabelais* (Berkeley: University of California Press, 1991), p. 233. *The Five Books of the Lives and Deeds of Gargantua and Pantagruel* were originally published between c. 1532 and c. 1564.

375    *as blood seeped from her crotch…:* Hubert Selby, Jr., *Last Exit to Brooklyn* (New York: Grove Press, 1964), pp. 113-14.

375    *'by the deliberately gratuitous line 'and thus makes she her great P's'*: See Eric Partridge, *Shakespeare's Bawdy*, third edition (London: Routledge, 1968), pp. 160-61. Originally published in 1947. Patridge references an article by the writer David Garnett, who had made this point as early as 1933. Garnett laments the exclusion of 'obscene' words from the *Oxford English Dictionary* by its original Victorian lexicographers. 'A word on which Hamlet is pleased to pun when addressing Ophelia and which even so virtuous a character as Malvolio begins to spell aloud in the theatre has, I feel, a place in English literature. My objection is not really a practical one, since there is not much likelihood of these words dying out. But the Oxford lexicographers will have to face the problem sooner or later, since some of these words which were filthily indecent in 1880 are passing into the vocabularies of respectable people, and are losing their obscene character. The more this happens the healthier both the language and the minds of the people who use it will become. The Oxford Dictionary is a bit too genteel.' David Garnett, 'Current literature', *New Statesman and Nation*, vol. 6, iss. 147 (16 December 1933), p. 812.

376    *No thing:* William Shakespeare, *Hamlet*, act 3, scene 2.

376    *'or make morally bad, a significant proportion of the likely audience'*: Quoted by Sarah Cleary, '"Maggot maladies": origins of horror as a culturally proscribed entertainment', Kevin Corstorphine and Laura R. Kremmel (eds.), in *The Palgrave Handbook to Horror Literature* (London: Palgrave Macmillan, 2018), pp. 391-406. Quotation taken from p. 392.

377    *'things we don't like'*: Christopher Hooton, 'A long list of sex acts just got banned in UK porn', *Independent* (2 December 2014).

377    *and ejaculate violently like wild stallions?:* Ezekiel, 23:20.

377    *'I will give you proofs of my virility'*: Charles Stuttaford, *The Poems of Gaius Valerius Catullus* (London: G. Bell & Sons, 1912), p. 27.

377    *'either in jest or in anger'*: Ibid., pp. vii-viii.

377    *F. W. Cornish substitutes the entire line for an ellipsis:* F. W. Cornish, *The Poems of Gaius Valerius Catullus* (London: William Heinemann, 1921), p. 23.

377    *from old comedy shows without alerting the viewer:* For instance, the sixth episode of the first series of *Fawlty Towers* (1975) entitled 'The Germans' is quietly censored in its current form on the BBC iPlayer streaming service. A scene featuring a conversation between Basil Fawlty (played by John Cleese) and Major Gowen (played by Ballard Berkeley) has been deleted due to the Major's anecdote about taking a woman on a date to a cricket match. He says: 'The strange thing was that throughout the morning, she kept referring to the Indians as "niggers". No, no, I said. Niggers are the West Indians. These people are wogs. "No, no,"

she said, "all cricketers are niggers"'. After the entire episode was removed from UKTV's streaming site due to its 'racial slurs' and 'outdated language', Cleese explained, with infinite patience: 'One of the things I've learned in the last 180 years is that people have very different senses of humour. Some of them understand that if you put nonsense words into the mouth of someone you want to make fun of, you're not broadcasting their views, you're making fun of them. The Major was an old fossil left over from decades before. We were not supporting his views, we were making fun of them. If they can't see that, if people are too stupid to see that, what can one say?' Quoted by Ellie Harrison, 'Fawlty Towers: John Cleese hits back at "stupid" decision to remove episode from UKTV', *Independent* (12 June 2020).

378    *'be relied upon to keep their filth in its proper place'*: Mark Holloway, *Norman Douglas: A Biography* (London: Secker & Warburg, 1976), p. 368.

378    *And spat them all over her chest:* Norman Douglas, *Some Limericks* (Florence: Pino Orioli, 1928), p. 33.

378    *written this work for the 'Dirty-Minded Elect':* Holloway, op. cit.

379    *'as a matter of fact had literally gone to pieces after his arrest':* Compton Mackenzie, *My Life and Times: Octave Six 1923 – 1930* (London: Chatto & Windus, 1967), p. 164.

380    *Review of a production of Frankenstein in the* **Manchester Guardian:** Ibid., p. 206-07.

381    *because it is more inclusive (infraction level 2):* Kate Clanchy, 'How sensitivity readers corrupt literature', *UnHerd* (18 February 2022).

381    *'paragraphs, sub-sections and even entire chapters should be revised':* Ibid.

382    *'Charlie Hebdo beheads Theresa May and mocks London Bridge terror victims':* Jen Mills, 'Charlie Hebdo beheads Theresa May and mocks London Bridge terror victims', *Metro* (9 June 2017).

382    **Charlie Hebdo** *in the wake of the horrific massacre by Islamist philistines:* Jeffrey Goldberg, 'The Dangerous Myths About *Charlie Hebdo*', *The Atlantic* (5 May 2015).

382    *'that is already marginalized, embattled and victimized':* Quoted by Alan Yuhas, 'Two dozen writers join Charlie Hebdo PEN award protest', *Guardian* (29 April 2015).

382    *'But they're not going to sell those cars':* David Blackmon, 'What Trump actually means by a "bloodbath" if he's not elected', *Telegraph* (18 March 2024).

382    *ran one typical headline in the* **Independent:** Lucy Leeson, 'Donald Trump warns of a "bloodbath" in US if he isn't elected as president again', *Independent* (17 March 2024).

383    *ran another in* **Politico:** Myah Ward, 'Trump says country faces 'bloodbath' if Biden wins in November', *Politico* (16 March 2024).

383    *"'let's send 10,000 troops right into the mouth of the enemy'":* Becket Adams, 'No, Trump did not threaten Liz Cheney with a firing squad', *The Hill* (3 November 2024).

383    *once occupied by Barack and Michelle Obama:* Andrew Doyle, 'Trump isn't clever enough for urinary Dadaism', *Spiked* (13 January 2017).

384    *Rowland had 'called for' the vessels to be sunk:* Jenifer Rankin, 'Brexit party MEP called for EU fishing vessels to be "sunk like Belgrano"', *Guardian* (12 July 2019).

384    *'called for the Royal Navy to sink EU fishing vessels':* Jon Stone, 'Brexit Party MEP says Royal Navy should attack EU fishing boats', *Independent* (12 July 2019).

384    *'calling for fishermen from another nation to die in our waters':* Quoted by Jennifer Rankin, 'Brexit party MEP called for EU fishing vessels to be "sunk like Belgrano"', *Guardian* (12 July 2019).

384    *Trump's most powerful ally had just publicly endorsed Hitler live at his inauguration:* Martin Pengelly, 'Elon Musk appears to make back-to-back fascist salutes at inauguration rally', *Guardian* (20 January 2025).

384 **perhaps even the benefit of the doubt, and take a breath:** Anti-Defamation League, X (20 January 2025).

385 **'sure looked like a "Sieg heil" to me':** Rex Huppke, 'Elon Musk's "odd-looking" salute sure looked like a "Sieg heil" to me', *USA Today* (20 January 2025).

385 **this hateful gesture for what it is: antisemitism:** Sarah Fortinsky, 'Nadler condemns "what appears to be a Heil Hitler salute" from Musk', *The Hill* (20 January 2025).

386 **'if you're not good I'll throw you out of the port-hole':** *My Life and Times: Octave Eight 1939 – 1946*, op. cit., p. 271.

386 **'the right way to deal with bad behaviour':** Ibid.

## Chapter 9

388 **'which often meant striking out on your own':** Ross Simonini, 'Bridget Phetasy wants you to kill your hypochondria before it kills you', *The Believer* (2 June 2021).

388 **'which colours should be on a colour chart':** John Cleese, X (25 October 2024).

388 **'do it differently because it's a different time':** James Grant, 'Computer says no! Little Britain will return to TV for the first time in 12 years but David Walliams and Matt Lucas say they'll have to do things differently for today's "woke" viewers', *Daily Mail* (21 January 2020). Some of the offensive caricatures include the fat women Bubbles and Desiree, the cross-dressing men Emily and Florence who claim to be 'ladies', the mail-order bride Ting Tong, and Daffyd (the 'only gay in the village').

388 **always watchful for potential future transgressions:** In the early days of *Little Britain*, commentators for the *Guardian* and the *Independent* would often cite the character of Vicky Pollard – the tracksuit-clad teenage mother who swapped her baby for a Westlife CD – as an example of how Lucas and Walliams were 'punching down' at the oppressed. Owen Jones criticised what he perceived to be *Little Britain*'s damaging stereotypes in his book *Chavs*. Yet many of the leftists who took umbrage at such characterisations at the time are the same who now routinely demonise the working class in the name of progress. In today's context, Vicky Pollard could work well as a satire of the kind of attitudes held by prominent left-wing columnists who dismiss working class people as 'gammons'. For all their pretence that the slur was aimed at affluent Little Englanders, in practice it was mostly reserved for white Brexit voters on the very lowest incomes. In trendy metropolitan circles, it became de rigueur to deride the working class as stupid and suggestible creatures, fuelled by race hatred, who can't stop themselves from voting the wrong way. If Vicky Pollard ever did return to our television screens, we might well expect to see her gloating about Brexit to her gammony friends. See Owen Jones, *Chavs* (London: Verso, 2011), pp. 127-29.

389 **to 'clean up their act':** Zoe Williams, 'Little Britain is coming back. But was it ever really funny?', *Guardian* (22 January 2020); Barbara Ellen, 'Can Little Britain stagger out of the gutter this time? We can only hope', *Guardian* (25 January 2020).

389 **'leaving behind an era we should all be ashamed of':** Chloe Laws, 'Finally Little Britain has been pulled from iPlayer and Netflix because it has no place in 2020', *Glamour* (10 June 2020).

389 **a phenomenon that is fatally counter-productive to the craft:** I have lost count of the number of occasions when I have had to explain that my jokes ought not to be taken at face value. Back in 2019, I posted a screenshot of an extremely improbable result from 'The Political Compass', a website that measures an individual's political temperament against economic (left-right) and social (authoritarian-libertarian) axes. It wasn't my result at all, but that of an extreme far-right tyrant. I added the caption: 'Turns out I'm more left-wing than I thought…' Within two hours, my silly joke had been quoted back to me as evidence of my right-wing beliefs.

389 **'is not acceptable and does not align with our values':** Quoted by Oliver Norton, 'No laughing matter: controversial comedian's Edinburgh Fringe show axed after he "got penis out on stage" & made "indefensible" comments', *Sun* (13 August 2022).

NOTES

389 *He's also one of the best showmen on the Edinburgh Fringe:* Andrew Doyle, review of *Jerry Sadowitz: Comedian, Magician, Psychopath II*, ScotsGay, issue 83 (August 2008), p. 18.

390 *But when it comes to performers like Sadowitz, context is everything:* Anyone who has undertaken the least research into Sadowitz will know what they are in for. The Pleasance was certainly aware of his style and content – and his tendency to expose his penis – well in advance of the festival. Sadowitz had even posted a promo video in which he referred to himself in the third person, saying: 'He's gonna be funny. He's gonna be rude. He's gonna do magic tricks. He's gonna do impressions. He's gonna get his dick out. He's gonna do every fucking thing.' In another promo, Sadowitz said: 'I might just do card tricks and say nothing for a whole hour or I might just do the usual "screaming fascist" schtick. Or both. Patrons may wish to drink alcohol pre-show to avoid boredom, embarrassment and guilt.' His cancelled show was entitled *Not For Anyone*. When I reviewed his show in 2008, it was called *Comedian, Magician, Psychopath II*. One can hardly accuse Sadowitz of false advertising; it's not as though he was masquerading as a Pam Ayres tribute act.

390 *how little it understands about the essential theatricality of stand-up:* 'Edinburgh Fringe: Jerry Sadowitz show cancelled by venue bosses', *BBC News* (13 August 2022).

390 *And they have a style book:* Kate Copstick, 'This is a frightened Fringe. And that is unacceptable', *Scotsman* (19 August 2022).

391 *'to challenge or to embed power?':* Jolyon Maugham, Twitter (14 August 2022). Maugham was responding to an article by Kenan Malik, 'Where Salman Rushdie defied those who would silence him, today too many fear causing offence', *Guardian* (14 August 2022).

391 *Jews don't count:* David Baddiel, *Jews Don't Count: How Identity Politics Failed One Particular Identity* (London: TLS Books, 2021).

391 *'encourage street harassment, rape culture and normalises misogyny':* 'You are not "pushing at boundaries"', *Chortle* (10 Nov 2014). The tipping point for the cancellation of Daniel O'Reilly appeared to be a video clip of a joke told at a gig on 16 October 2014 at the Scala in London. In an ad-libbed moment, O'Reilly had referred to a critic who had described his brand of comedy as a 'rapist's almanac'. He had said: 'My show is a rapist's go-to guide? I filmed six episodes, half-hour-each episodes, right. If it was a fucking guide to rape I would have done one five-minute episode going, "Oi, Oi! I'm Dapper Laughs. Go down the shop, get some rope, bit of duct tape, rape the bitch, well done, see you later!"'. A female audience member had then interjected with: 'Dapper, don't worry about that. My friend Lucy loves you, she's gagging for a rape'. O'Reilly repeated the heckle in the form of a question – 'What's that? She's gagging for a rape?' – and it was this phrase that was presented in the media as evidence that he was a 'pro-rape comedian'. Live comedy events are never well represented by being quoted out of context. Quoted by Tom Slater, 'Dapper Laughs: "There's nothing wrong with lads being lads"', *Spiked* (7 October 2015).

391 *'be satirical or write jokes was easy to destroy':* O'Reilly continued: 'Some of those comedians who signed the open letter to cancel me or wrote hit pieces against me, even comedians I admired, later faced their own cancel scandals. I could've hit back, but I don't. I own my screw-ups, truly believe in comedy and free speech, and think we should learn, not burn, from our mistakes.' Daniel O'Reilly, X (1 March 2025).

392 *co-written by the trans person he was dating at the time:* Leo Kearse, 'Cancel culture is a grave threat to comedy', *Spiked* (15 July 2021).

392 *to overturn the result of the Brexit referendum:* Alistair Williams later remarked: 'Because I am a comedian that supports Brexit you can no longer find me on the comedy club circuit'. Quoted by Patrick O'Flynn, 'Nish Kumar and the anti-Brexit comedy club', *Spectator* (3 December 2019).

392 *her material made them feel 'unsafe':* See Andrew Doyle's interview with Mary Bourke on *Free Speech Nation* (6 February 2022), available on the GB News YouTube channel.

392 *cancelled for pointing out that men cannot get pregnant:* See Andrew Doyle's interview with Raurie Williams on *Free Speech Nation* (23 April 2023), available on the GB News YouTube channel.

392    *in defence of women's single-sex spaces:* Lee Garrett, 'Leicester Comedy Festival show axed over performer's trans rights remarks', *Leicester Mercury* (16 February 2023).

392    *censor his material on Israel and Palestine:* See my interview with Lewis Schaffer and Scott Capurro on *Free Speech Nation* (3 March 2024), available to watch on the GB News YouTube channel.

392    *which must have come as a surprise to his husband:* Claire Smith, 'Scott Capurro reported to police for "homophobia"', *Entertainment Now* (1 May 2024). His account is quoted in the article: 'I was playing a club in London and I was informed there had been a hate crime reported about me. The club didn't know what to do. Apparently someone called in and told the police in Islington that I'm homophobic. I don't know what to do about this except ignore it. It's not enough that I have had sex with over 2,000 men in the last 20 years. And I'm married to a guy. And I come from San Francisco'.

392    *was cancelled following a 'public outcry':* James Walker, 'Roy "Chubby" Brown show cancelled by Highland venue', *The National* (4 July 2023).

392    *'the language and material associated with this individual's show':* Ibid.

393    *the UEFA European Football Championship in July 2021:* James Robinson, 'Comedian Andrew Lawrence's shows are cancelled after he posted racist "jokes" on Twitter about England's black players missing penalties in the Euros 2020 final', *Daily Mail* (12 July 2021).

394    *sentenced to four months in a workhouse:* Ronald L. Collins, '"Your words are offensive!" – "Pardon me?" – The 20th anniversary of Lenny Bruce's posthumous pardon', *FIRE* (20 December 2023).

394    *'you can't say "fuck the government"':* Quoted by Rob Schneider, *You Can Do It! Speak Your Mind, America* (New York: Center Street, 2024), p. 110.

395    *'for other people's interpretations of what they said':* Ibid., p. 75.

395    *jokes of this kind that appear on streaming services:* Jedidajah Otte, 'New laws would hold Netflix to account after "shocking" Jimmy Carr joke', *Guardian* (5 February 2022).

395    *'which don't tackle harmful content on their platforms':* Jacob Stolworthy, 'Jimmy Carr: Boris Johnson calls comedian's Holocaust joke "deeply disturbing"', *Independent* (7 February 2022).

395    *'his applauding audience':* Steerpike, 'SNP councillor: "Prosecute Jimmy Carr's audience"', *Spectator* (7 February 2022).

396    *because no one ever wants to talk about the positives:* Nadia Khomami, 'Jimmy Carr condemned for "abhorrent" Holocaust joke about Roma people', *Guardian* (4 February 2022).

396    *described the joke as 'not comedy':* Quoted by Chris Matthews, Stewart Carr and Katie Feehan, '"The joke that ends my career is already out there": Jimmy Carr says he will be *cancelled* over Holocaust joke about gypsies being murdered by the Nazis after David Baddiel slams it "racist" and "inhumane"', *Daily Mail* (6 February 2022); Abbey White, 'Jimmy Carr Netflix special holocaust remarks condemned by U.K. culture secretary, anti-hate groups', *Hollywood Reporter* (5 February 2022).

397    *his Taliban captors who later murdered him:* Alex Horton and Ezzatullah Mehrdad, 'After "comedian" is killed by Taliban, videos of his treatment spark outrage across Afghanistan', *Washington Post* (28 July 2021).

397    *in some cases have even been imprisoned for jokes:* Charlie Parker, Yennah Smart and George Willoughby, 'Police make 30 arrests a day for offensive online messages', *Times* (4 April 2025).

397    *it closed due to heavy snowfall:* The conviction was later overturned by the High Court in London. Owen Bowcott, 'Twitter joke trial: Paul Chambers wins high court appeal against conviction', *Guardian* (27 July 2012).

397    *jokes on Facebook about murdered children:* Steven Morris and Dan Sabbagh, 'April Jones: Matthew Woods jailed over explicit Facebook comments', *Guardian* (8 October 2012).

397   *a tragic lorry accident in Glasgow:* Chris Clements, 'Glasgow bin lorry tragedy: Sick web troll who posted offensive tweet hours after crash escapes with just a caution', *Daily Record* (27 January 2015).

397   *a real-life tragedy that had occurred in June 2017:* Ryan Hooper, 'Paul Bussetti: Man who made "abhorrent" video of Grenfell Tower effigy on bonfire spared jail', *Independent* (20 April 2022).

397   **An Evening with Gazza *tour at* Wolverhampton Civic Hall:** 'Paul Gascoigne guilty over racist comment', *BBC News* (19 September 2016).

398   *'it is not acceptable to laugh words like this off as some form of joke':* Ibid.

398   *'Sorry no money: suggest eat baby':* Quoted by Tim Dawson, 'I miss the Simon Ravens', *The Critic* (19 June 2022).

398   *'if feminists truly wanted equality, they'd kill themselves':* Adam Boult, 'BBC urged to ban right-wing comedian Andrew Lawrence', *Telegraph* (17 December 2015).

399   **read the offending words in their original context:** Boris Johnson, 'If Blair's so good at running the Congo, let him stay there', *Telegraph* (10 January 2002).

399   **Muslim women in burkas resembling letter boxes:** Boris Johnson, 'Denmark has got it wrong. Yes, the burka is oppressive and ridiculous – but that's still no reason to ban it', *Telegraph* (5 August 2018).

399   *'surge in anti-Muslim attacks':* Nazia Parveen, 'Boris Johnson's burqa comments "led to surge in anti-Muslim attacks"', *Guardian* (1 September 2019).

399   **Tom Chivers in a piece for UnHerd:** Tom Chivers, 'Don't blame Boris for hate crime', *UnHerd* (3 September 2019).

399   **had made the exact same joke five years before:** 'The Guardian view on Boris Johnson: it's about him not the burqa', *Guardian* (7 August 2018).

399   *'an independent mobile mail service, AKA The Burqa Post':* Remona Aly, 'Nine uses for a burqa... that don't involve bashing them', *Guardian* (6 November 2013).

399   **to determine whether or not Johnson had broken the law:** Kate Ferguson, 'Met Commissioner Cressida Dick asked her officers to probe Boris Johnson's burqas comments – but was told he did *not* break hate crime laws in comparing them to letterboxes', *Daily Mail* (9 August 2018).

400   **and carried a rucksack with 'TNT' and 'boom' written on it:** Emily Jane Davies, 'Prankster who dressed up as Manchester Arena bomber Salman Abedi for Halloween faces being sent to prison', *Daily Mail* (15 September 2024).

400   *a routine on the BBC Radio 4 show* **Heresy:** Simon Murphy, 'Police investigate Jo Brand's battery acid remark', *Guardian* (13 June 2019).

401   **you've mistaken a joke for an actual crime:** 'Ricky Gervais: why I'll never apologise for my jokes', op. cit.

402   **that disapprovingly quoted the most offending lines:** Josh Milton, 'Ricky Gervais' new Netflix special is nothing more than an anti-trans garbage fire', *PinkNews* (24 May 2022).

402   *'designed to incite hate or violence':* GLAAD, Twitter (24 May 2022).

403   *'that oppresses people and limits freedom of expression':* Quoted by Dominic Maxwell, 'Does Ricky Gervais want to be cancelled?', *The Times* (26 May 2022).

403   **who sincerely make this claim are vanishingly rare:** Steve Bennett, review of *Ricky Gervais: SuperNature, Chortle* (24 May 2022).

403   *'It's a good system':* Ricky Gervais, Twitter (14 September 2019).

403   **a disturbing assault on freedom of expression:** Bruce Haring, 'Ricky Gervais responds to petition asking for joke removal from Netflix "Armageddon" special', *Deadline* (21 December 2023).

404    *the topics he chose to lampoon:* Cenk Uygur, Twitter (24 May 2022).

404    *'becomes so comfortable that it fuses with the person underneath':* Steve Albini, Twitter (24 May 2022).

404    *we can be fairly sure that the criticism is political:* Sarah Manavis, 'The tedious world of anti-woke comedy', *New Statesman* (28 September 2023).

406    *'Comedians need to pick a side: I'm an anarchist':* Andrew O'Neill, Twitter (27 July 2022).

407    *'with representation across gender and sexuality spectrums':* Phyllis Stephen, 'Edinburgh Comedy Awards 2024 – the shortlists…', *Edinburgh Reporter* (21 August 2024).

407    *at Comedy Unleashed in Edinburgh was Graham Linehan:* The other comedians on the bill were Bruce Devlin, Mary Bourke, Dominic Frisby and Alistair Williams.

407    *to have his name removed from the project:* Graham Linehan, *Tough Crowd: How I Made and Lost a Career in Comedy* (London: Eye Books, 2023), pp. 240-52.

408    *'from Thursdays [sic] comedy show with immediate effect':* Leith Arches, Instagram (15 August 2023).

408    *Comedy Unleashed show had made headlines in the national press:* 'Father Ted writer Graham Linehan comedy show cancelled over gender views', *BBC News* (16 August 2023).

408    *performed on a makeshift stage outside the Scottish Parliament:* Severin Carrell, 'Graham Linehan show staged outside Scottish Parliament after second venue cancels', *Guardian* (17 August 2023); Oliver Price and Tash Mosheim, 'Graham Linehan arrives to defiantly perform outside the Scottish Parliament after outrage at two Edinburgh festival venues that cancelled him for his gender critical views', *Daily Mail* (17 August 2023); Katharine Hay, 'Graham Linehan stages gig outside the Scottish Parliament after venues cancel', *Scotsman* (17 August 2023); Suzanne Moore, 'Banning free speech in the name of inclusivity and diversity is the Fringe's sickest joke', *Telegraph* (18 August 2023); Andrew Doyle, 'What a joke! The woke activists who stopped an Edinburgh Fringe show by my brilliant friend and Father Ted creator Graham Linehan prove cancel culture *does* exist', *Daily Mail* (16 August 2023).

409    *come into effect on April Fools' Day 2024:* For further details about the Hate Crime and Public Order (Scotland) Bill, see *The New Puritans*, op. cit., pp. 106-10.

409    *words they have uttered in the privacy of their own homes:* Mick Hume, 'Sending the Thought Polis into Scottish homes', *Spiked* (29 October 2020).

409    *the 'public performance of a play':* Daniel Sanderson, 'Actors face prosecution for "abusive" speech in SNP hate crime crackdown', *Telegraph* (19 March 2024).

409    *'performers and writers "must trust to luck" they are not prosecuted':* 'Hate crimes: Police will not "target performers"', *BBC News* (19 March 2024).

410    *'Start deleting!' he demanded:* Rajan Barot, X (17 March 2024).

410    *database of objectionable gags posted online:* Charlie Parker, 'Offensive jokes logged in "non-crime" databases', *The Times* (19 February 2020).

410    *'or you may receive a visit from us this weekend':* Police Scotland Greater Glasgow, Twitter (1 April 2016).

410    *complaints of 'hate speech', approximately sixty per hour:* Eiran Jane Prosser, '"More complaints" were made about First Minister Humza Yousaf and his 2020 speech about "often being the only non-white person in the room" than JK Rowling under new Scots hate crime law – as police receive nearly 4,000 reports in first two days', *Daily Mail* (3 April 2024).

411    *'and every prison governor is white':* Ibid.

411    *and a sex shop in Glasgow:* John Boothman, 'Victims urged to report hate crimes at a sex shop and caravan park', *The Times* (13 March 2024).

411　*which resembled a reject from Sesame Street:* Graham Grant, 'Police face ridicule over "ludicrous" Hate Monster campaign', *Daily Mail* (14 March 2024).

411　*Then before ye know it, ye've committed a hate crime:* The video continues: 'Disnae make ye feel better though, does it? Mibbae for a minute, but then ye just feel worse, don't ye? Cause the hate just hangs aboot like a bad smell. But it disnae need to be like this. You're better than that, an you know it. You've got aw this energy so dae something positive wae it. The Hate Monster disnae like that. In fact he *hates* it. Go on; be good tae yourself. Don't feed the Hate Monster.' The video was uploaded on 25 April 2023 on the Police Scotland YouTube channel.

412　*Jonathan Kogan in a downy orange outfit:* The voice of the Hate Monster was performed by Martin Gourlay from the back of the room through a microphone. The full performance can be seen on the Comedy Unleashed YouTube Channel.

412　*'He must be whipped out when the Lady Brach may stand by th' fire and stink':* William Shakespeare, *King Lear*, act 1, scene 4.

## Chapter 10

413　*described as 'his horrid lusts':* The relevant quotation is taken from Book IV: 'This emperour hath no son, and now is old, / Old and lascivious, and from Rome retired / To Capreæ, an island small, but strong, / On the Campanian shore, with purpose there / His horrid lusts in private to enjoy'. John Milton, Paradise Regained (London: F. C. and J. Rivington, et al.), p. 72. Originally published in 1671.

415　*'the immortal part of myself':* William Shakespeare, *Othello*, act 2, scene 3.

416　*'What other people think of me is none of my business':* RuPaul, Twitter (2 March 2011).

416　*I lost a friend to cancer after he had been falsely accused of sexual assault:* Andrew Doyle, 'RIP Simon Warr', *Spiked* (24 February 2020).

417　*'No', replies George, 'but we must carry on as though we did':* Edward Albee, *Who's Afraid of Virginia Woolf?*, in *The Collected Plays of Edward Albee: Volume 1* (London: Overlook Duckworth, 2004), pp. 149-311. Quotation taken from p. 285.

418　*'a long history of opposing rights for trans people':* Newstalk FM, Twitter (26 March 2022). The tweet was eventually deleted.

418　*she 'harmed' people who identify as transgender:* Katie Weston, 'Children's news website The Day apologises to JK Rowling after the Harry Potter author threatened legal action over article claiming she had "harmed" transgender people', *Daily Mail* (24 July 2020).

418　*when the Mirror branded him a 'racist' in 2012:* 'Boyle wins £54,650 in "racism" libel case', *BBC News* (22 October 2012).

419　*simply do not fall within the scope of 'personal opinion':* Haroon Siddique, 'Telegraph apologises for claim former Corbyn aide was "anti-Jewish racist"', *Guardian* (17 Mar 2022).

419　*although its two owners died before the case was resolved:* Thomas M. Boyd, 'Oberlin College Loses Its Appeal', *Wall Street Journal* (1 April 2022).

419　*that college staff had also been involved in the smear campaign:* 'Oberlin College president responds to $44 million defamation lawsuit', *CBS News* YouTube channel (26 June 2019).

419　*that they retreated en masse to a 'safe room' with a therapy dog:* Sean Illing, '"Amoral masculinity": a theory for understanding Trump from feminist contrarian Christina Hoff Sommers', *Vox* (2 November 2016).

420　*against libellous statements is one way in which this can be achieved:* Dr Jane Clare Jones has outlined a now common libellous strategy by the bullying fringe of the gender-critical movement. Typically, this tactic is aimed at other gender-critical individuals who have the audacity to veer even slightly from the approved set of opinions. The trick is to brand such heretics as a 'safeguarding risk' in order to smear them and discredit their views. Jones explains it as follows: 'It's become like a magic talisman claim to justify any abusiveness. And anyone who resists their abusive authoritarianism is immediately relegated to those who don't care about safeguarding. Ergo, a danger to children. Ergo, a pedophile apologist, Ergo, check their hard-drive. My mother is a child protection specialist. You don't use claims about safeguarding as a weapon like this if you genuinely care about children's well being. Just like you don't use accusations of rape or rape apologia as a weapon if you care about rape, or challenging rape.' Many feminists and gay men have been targeted in this way. It is no coincidence that gay people are particularly vulnerable to the accusation; the conflation of homosexuality and child abuse is the most long-established of all homophobic tropes. Dr Jane Clare Jones, X (10 December 2024).

421    *calling me a 'degenerate' and a 'sodomite'*: Andrew Doyle, 'When I was growing up, Pride's rainbow flag was a shining beacon of tolerance. But these ugly new versions are divisive, dangerous – and deeply homophobic', *Daily Mail* (24 June 2023).

421    **'Lasciate ogne speranza, voi ch'intrate'**: Dante, *Inferno*, canto III, line 9.

422    *'"free speech" blocks critics', ran the headline in the Metro*: Pierra Willix, 'Confusion as GB News presenter who champions 'free speech' blocks critics', *Metro* (27 December 2023).

422    *'the fallacy of demanding to be heard'*: Helen Pluckrose and James Lindsay, 'Freedom of speech and the fallacy of demanding to be heard', *New Discourses* (22 January 2020).

423    *'Never wrestle with a pig; you just get dirty and the pig enjoys it'*: In the midst of online pile-ons, I have been known to block the most sociopathic offenders and all of their followers. This instantaneously has the effect of curbing the swarm; a clipping of the winged monkeys, if you will. For some reason, there is usually a pile-on around Christmas time, perhaps due to a combination of boredom and cheap sherry. At time of writing, I am being assailed by various online missiles from a tribe proudly displaying United States flags and 'MAGA' hashtags that apparently perceives me to be a left-wing degenerate. I had made the mistake of commenting on the way in which there has been a notable escalation of antagonism towards gay men from conservatives who are failing to distinguish between the 'LGB' and the excesses of the 'TQ+'. The hundreds of responses I have received reveal that I have clearly failed their purity test. 'Have you tried not being a fag?', one writes. 'Sorry you have the AIDs dude', says another. My favourite: 'Homosexuality is a sexual perversion, normal sexuality is not. Huge difference. Stop deceiving people like Satan does'. Wasn't it Queen Gertrude in *Hamlet* (c.1600) who made the famous remark about a certain lady protesting too much?

424    *author of the memoir* **Transsexual Apostate** *(2024)*: Janice Turner, 'Debbie Hayton: the trans woman taking on the trans activists', *The Times* (5 February 2024); Debbie Hayton, *Transsexual Apostate: My Journey Back to Reality* (London: Swift Press, 2024).

424    *But I will be courteous to those who respect women*: Janice Turner, X (3 February 2024).

426    *a course of action which, in turn, was taken as proof of misogyny*: The accusations of misogyny were particularly bizarre given that over the past few years I have covered the rising threats to women's rights on my show with a tenacity that has been notably absent in other media outlets. Every week on my show I have invited women to appear, including Helen Joyce, Maya Forstater, Jo Phoenix, Julie Bindel, Alka Sehgal Cuthbert, Milli Hill, Kellie-Jay Keen, Dr Jane Clare Jones, Jo Bartosch, Mara Yamauchi, Lisa Keogh, Holly Lawford-Smith, Sarah Phillimore, Nadine Strossen, Carol Decker, Kate Coleman, Joan Smith, Baroness Claire Fox, Rosie Kay, Marion Calder, Emma Hilton, Stella O'Malley, Judy Glenney, Moira Deeming, Yasmine Mohammed, Kara Danksy, Sall Grover, Denise Fahmy, Ayaan Hirsi Ali and Sharron Davies. If my critics are correct, and I am indeed a rabid misogynist, surely I at least deserve some credit for going to such elaborate lengths to disguise it?

427    *'What else are you ready to do for men knowing you harm women and children?'*: Allesandra Asteriti, X (5 February 2024).

428    *These people must be very sad indeed*: Andrew Gold, 'Why I didn't ask Peter Tatchell about paedophilia condoning', *Heretics*, *Substack* (17 September 2024).

# NOTES

429    *not-so-subtle method of calling them 'faggots' and evading online bans:* For screenshots and analysis, see 'Homophobia in the Gender Critical Movement?', op. cit.

430    *Abuse, in other words, can often be an attempt at coercion:* The writer and psychotherapist Stella O'Malley has also been on the receiving end of intense vitriol from this small unrepresentative faction. She has recently decried the 'lunatic fringe of the GC movement' who 'have become what they first sought to fight against'. As she writes: 'There have been way too many people who had important perspectives to offer and who were mercilessly bullied - and sometimes shamed into silence. I think of Jane Clare Jones, Jenny Watson, Laura Becker, Shannon Thrace, Ali Ceesay, Janice Turner, Sarah Phillimore, Exulansic, Helen Pluckrose, Christina Buttons, Colin Wright, Andrew Gold, Fionne Orlander, Debbie Hayton, Miranda Yardley, Kristina Harrison, Buck Angel, Claire Graham, Graham Linehan, James Esses, Benjamin Boyce, Clive Simpson, Mike Bailey, Phil Illy, James Cantor, Ken Zucker, Ray Blanchard, Billboard Chris, Genspect, LGB Alliance, Kathleen Stock, Julie Bindel, Women's Place UK, Judith Green, Labour Women's Declaration, Fair Play for Women, Aaron Tyrrell, Aaron Kimberly, GD Alliance, Corinna Cohn, and, of course, myself and hundreds more that I've missed or forgotten about.' O'Malley notes that while she doesn't agree with all these individuals on every point, 'bullying is always wrong'. Stella O'Malley, X (10 December 2024).

430    *'associated with the group that is totalised to all members':* Dr Michael Foran, X (9 December 2024). For details of Foran's experiences of online abuse, see Roddy Dunlop KC, 'In defence of Michael Foran', *The Critic* (25 October 2024).

431    *'It's not activism. It's abuse':* Dr Michael Foran, X (10 December 2024).

431    *'followed by the inevitable formal charge':* Aleksandr Solzhenitsyn, *The Gulag Archipelago 1918–56: An Experiment in Literary Investigation*, trans. Thomas P. Whitney and Harry Willetts (London: Vintage, 2018), p. 68. Originally published in 1973.

431    *'based on material sex–class analysis with a politics of "woman-identity"':* Jane Clare Jones, 'Feminism is not identity politics', *Gender-Critical Disputes* (February 2023), pp. 15-30. Quotation taken from p. 21.

431    *'as regressive as that of hardened trans activists':* J. K. Rowling, X (19 December 2024).

432    *a form of 'social hygiene', an undeniably ghoulish phrase:* Amy E. Sousa, X (22 January 2024)

432    *not defending womanhood:* Jones, op. cit., p. 21.

432    *the more reactionary elements of the gender-critical movement:* Of course, those who perceive the world in collectivist terms are easily stumped when faced with dissent from their own 'group'. This is why so many who have complained about my criticism of the 'Troon Index' are flummoxed when the identical points are made by women. To give one example, a gender-critical extremist took to X to berate me for daring to oppose this authoritarian list-making. She wrote: 'You don't have children and you don't get stalked by hulking blokes dressed as women. We women do, and a simple list is helpful to close information gaps. This approach has also been used for dangerous men on dating apps. You can bleat all you want but methinks it's suspicious'. All the tropes were present and correct: the intimation that I am a safeguarding risk, the identitarian obsession, the conviction that only women and parents are permitted to hold an opinion on these subjects. Soon after, barrister Sarah Phillimore weighed in: 'I have a child. Am I allowed to say I think you are dangerous?' The gender-critical troll was, of course, stumped. She had earlier declared that any woman who disagreed with her was a 'dick panderer', but she lacked the courage to repeat the slur when directly challenged. Like most trans rights activists, these extreme outliers in the gender-critical movement are so immersed in the politics of identity that they are impervious to reason. This assumption - that women who take a different view cannot think for themselves and are merely seeking to flatter men - is about as misogynistic as it gets.

432    *rights preserved at the expense of the rights of others:* Josh Seiter, X (23 October 2024).

432 **and employment for trans-identified people:** 'If you work in a shop, if you own a small business, if you own a funeral home, or if you own a salon that has mostly female clients, if not all female clients, or whatever, if you own a hairdressing salon, if you own a beautician's, I want you to be able to discriminate as much as you like against a man who calls himself a woman who wants to work. In fact, I would advise you to also not employ anybody who claims to have body dysmorphia so much so they cut their own breasts off. Because I don't know anybody who works with somebody who calls themselves trans who doesn't find that person lazy, entitled, and difficult to work with. Because actually, those people are not employees, they are activists first. Okay? So let me just be really clear. I don't care. If I owned a house, there is no way I would rent my house to somebody who called themselves trans. I just wouldn't. Because I know that they will use everything in their power to probably not pay rent. So, you lovely people, you can talk about your trans rights if you want, you can talk about not discriminating, you can talk about how you want everyone to wear what they like, and call themselves what they like, and all this stuff. And I'm just going to tell you, I don't feel that way. You know, I think wear what you like, but accept the consequences that you won't be accepted by the majority of people who will think you're weird.' Video of Kellie-Jay Keen, uploaded by Harvey Jeni, X (24 May 2024).

433 **the 'Troon Index' was eventually taken down:** 'If you are making lists of evil troons for "safeguarding" purposes – or is that "social hygiene" as one GC said? – can you just do us all a favour and stop pretending to be so very outraged about why people are increasingly horrified by you, and some of us tried to raise the alarm about how your rhetoric could go to bad places really fast.' Dr Jane Clare Jones, X (10 December 2024).

433 **'Tear him to pieces!' they cry:** William Shakespeare, *Julius Caesar*, act 3, scene 3.

434 **a rape victim so that her attacker was not misgendered:** Jake Kanter, 'BBC "altered gender in trans rape claim"', *The Times* (31 May 2022).

434 **the weaponisation of free speech:** During an interview with secretary of state Marco Rubio on the CBS show *Face the Nation*, Margaret Brennan described Germany as 'a country where free speech was weaponised to conduct a genocide'. Quoted by Paul du Quenoy, 'Margaret Brennan's CBS humiliation exposed everything that's wrong with the Left-wing media', *Telegraph* (18 February 2025).

435 **'the house style of establishment opinion':** Christopher R. Rufo, *America's Cultural Revolution: How the Radical Left Conquered Everything* (New York: Broadside Books, 2023), p. 55.

435 **to borrow Jordan B. Peterson's formulation:** Jordan B. Peterson, *Beyond Order: 12 More Rules for Life* (London: Penguin Random House, 2021), p. 345.

435 **the reference to trans murders, even though it was accurate:** Joan Smith, 'The Financial Times is ticking boxes to win over female readers', *UnHerd* (12 September 2023).

436 **my Edinburgh Fringe show in 2018 was a dismal failure with the critics:** The Londoner, 'Boris Johnson is being busy behind the scenes', *London Evening Standard* (11 June 2019).

436 **'controversial British media personality and culture warrior':** Jason Wilson, 'Florida liberal arts college reinstates "wokeness" course amid furore', *Guardian* (14 November 2024).

437 **'their most recent filings, and most appear to be inactive':** Ibid.

437 **a naked man in the women's Jacuzzi area:** For an overview of this story, see Josephine Bartosch, 'Wheesht Spa', *The Critic* (6 September 2021).

438 **that implied CubanaAngel's complaints were a hoax:** Suzanne Moore, 'Why I had to leave The Guardian', *UnHerd* (29 December 2020).

438 **Owen Jones called the entire incident a 'campaign of lies':** Sam Levin and Lois Beckett, '"A nightmare scenario": how an anti-trans Instagram post led to violence in the streets', *Guardian* (28 July 2021); Owen Jones, Twitter (29 July 2021).

438 **'Women like CubanaAngel are ideological inconveniences':** 'Wheesht Spa', op. cit.

NOTES

438   *'two-tier policing' based on race and sexuality is rife:* Archie Bland and Vikram Dodd, 'England riots: how has "two-tier policing" myth become widespread?', *Guardian* (6 August 2024).

438   *but had suffered extreme beatings and multiple forms of torture:* Catherine Bennett, 'How many more children like Sara Sharif will be killed before smacking is banned?', *Guardian* (19 October 2024). Following the community notes, the headline was changed on 21 October to 'A society that abhors child cruelty should not tolerate any physical punishment of children'.

439   *a lengthy statement outlining his own reasons for relocating:* Vittoria Elliott, 'Taylor Swift fans are leaving X for Bluesky after Trump's election', *Wired* (8 November 2024); Mike Bedigan, 'Don Lemon highlights alarming change to X's terms of service as he leaves the platform', *Independent* (13 November 2024).

439   *and a mass outpouring of public grief:* Clifton Suspension Bridge, X (11 November 2024).

439   *'Elon Musk, has been able to use its influence to shape political discourse':* 'Why the Guardian is no longer posting on X', *Guardian* (13 November 2024).

439   *'self-care suite' after Trump's victory in November 2024:* Melissa Koeing and Alyssa Guzman, 'Ivy league students offered crayons, Legos and cookies with milk to cope with Trump's election win', *Daily Mail* (7 November 2024).

440   *'and the lived experience of human beings under its domain':* Deneen, op. cit., p. 6.

440   *'between ideal and real becomes too wide, the system breaks down':* Barbara W. Tuchman, *A Distant Mirror: The Calamitous 14th Century* (New York: Ballantine Books, 1978), pp. xix-xx.

440   *'Facts do not cease to exist because they are ignored':* Aldous Huxley, *Proper Studies* (London: Chatto & Windus, 1929). p. 205. Originally published in 1927.

441   *leading experts as a 'racist conspiracy theory':* Throughout the pandemic we saw experts silenced or marginalised if they offered views that deviated from the accepted narrative. An interview featuring Professor Karol Sikora for *UnHerd* was taken offline after he suggested that the virus was likely to 'burn out' and that levels of public immunity had been misjudged; apparently this former advisor to the WHO was not entitled to an opinion. Freddie Sayers, 'Banned by YouTube: Professor Karol Sikora discusses Covid-19', *UnHerd* (21 May 2020). Meanwhile, experts who peddle 'accepted' narratives have been at liberty to indulge in blatant untruths that we have been expected to take on trust. In June 2020, more than 1,200 medical practitioners signed a letter arguing that existing restrictions put in place to curb the spread of coronavirus ought not to apply to Black Lives Matter demonstrations. On 2 June 2020, the epidemiologist Jennifer Nuzzo wrote on Twitter: 'We should always evaluate the risks and benefits of efforts to control the virus. In this moment the public health risks of not protesting to demand an end to systemic racism greatly exceed the harms of the virus'. Were we really meant to believe that the virus would simply time off so long as the protesters' cause was just?

441   *'to masquerade as sober scientific inquiry':* Michael Hiltzik, 'These authors wanted to push the COVID-19 lab-leak theory. Instead they exposed its weaknesses', *Los Angeles Times* (15 November 2021).

441   *that the lab-leak theory was most likely true:* Cassidy Morrison, 'House committee reveals where it believes COVID originated from after years-long investigation', *Daily Mail* (2 December 2024).

441   *that my understanding of the subject is superior to theirs:* Claire Ainsworth, 'The idea of two sexes is simplistic. Biologists now think there is a wider spectrum than that', *Nature*, vol. 518 (February 2015), pp. 288-91.

441   *'but of biases in how they are treated in sports':* Cara Ocobock and Sarah Lacy, 'The theory that men evolved to hunt and women evolved to gather is wrong', *Scientific American* (1 November 2023).

442     *Bret Weinstein has described as 'idea laundering':* See Rod Dreher, 'Idea laundering', *American Conservative* (26 November 2019).

442     *that unjustly ascribes authority to medical knowledge:* Peter Boghossian, '"Idea Laundering" in Academia', *Wall Street Journal* (24 November 2019).

## Epilogue

443     *this curious figure only as 'the Colonel's widow':* Waugh, op. cit., pp. 176-188.

443     *'They won't interest themselves in the things that matter':* Ibid., p. 176.

443     *'We must keep the soil unfertile':* Ibid., p. 177.

444     *'Books like that should be kept under lock and key':* Ibid., p. 187.

444     *'Not when it's the voice of evil speaking':* Ibid., p. 188.

445     *the female sex for policies based on gender self-identification:* For example, a study at the University of Turku, published in the *Scandinavian Journal of Psychology*, found that of the nearly 6,000 respondents women were far more likely to support 'woke' causes. 'Overall, the study sample rejected critical social justice propositions, with strong rejection from men. Women expressed more than twice as much support for the propositions'. Oskari Lahtinen, 'Construction and validation of a scale for assessing critical social justice attitudes', *Scandinavian Journal of Psychology* (14 March 2024).

446     *'ma per fortuna ogni tanto scrive un libro':* Davide Piacenza, preface to Andrew Doyle, *Libertà di parola: Sul totalitarismo dei buoni*, trans. Antonio Tozzi (Prato: Piano B, 2022). English version published in 2021.

446     *in a scarlet robe with gold, pearls and jewels:* Edmund Spenser, *The Faerie Queene*, ed. A. C. Hamilton (London: Longman, 1977), p. 47. Originally published in 1590. The introduction to Duessa in disguise takes place in book I, canto ii, verse 13.

447     *So scabby was, that would haue loathd all womankind:* Ibid., p. 117 (book I, canto viii, verse 47).

448     *'an answer to the anger and fear of a postliberal citizenry':* Why Liberalism Failed, op. cit., p. 181.

450     *when they frame motivation as originating externally, rebellion increases:* Frank Dobbin and Alexandra Kalev, 'Why diversity programs fail', *Harvard Business Review* (July-August 2016). Quoted in *The Counterweight Handbook*, op. cit., p. 84.

450     *35 per cent would be in favour of travel quarantine:* 'Some Britons crave permanent pandemic lockdown', *The Economist* (10 July 2021).

450     *from his fellows and consequently capable of intercourse with them:* Forster, op. cit., p. 85.

450     *will not introduce alternative policies that are similarly authoritarian:* At time of writing, many commentators fear that Trump is leaning towards the solution advocated by the woke, which is to use the force of law to silence and prohibit rebarbative viewpoints. On 4 March 2025, Trump posted the following on Truth Social: 'All Federal Funding will *stop* for any College, School, or University that allows illegal protests. Agitators will be imprisoned/or permanently sent back to the country from which they came. American students will be permanently expelled or, depending on on [*sic*] the crime, arrested. *No masks!* Thank you for your attention to this matter'. If by 'illegal protests' he means illegal conduct that arise during protests – such as harassment, violence and threats – then few will complain. But if he means that peaceful protesters should have their rights restricted due to the poor conduct of a minority within their ranks, then we are right to be wary. Is the phrase *'No masks!'* simply an expression of Trump's disdain for those who choose to remain anonymous while demonstrating, or a suggestion that he will seek to prohibit this right? If the latter, it would endanger those whose cause is so controversial that their identities must be protected.

451    *'very flow of time that will inevitably cure all ills':* Letter from Birmingham Jail, op. cit., pp. 15-16.

451    **was not only necessary, but considered somehow controversial:** Sharron Davies and Craig Lord, *Unfair Play: The Battle for Women's Sports* (London: Swift Press, 2023).

451    **an argument that most of us assumed had already been settled:** Richard Dawkins, *The Greatest Show on Earth: The Evidence for Evolution* (London: Bantam Press, 2009).

452    **for their own sanity, and for their own self-respect:** Quoted by Jonathon Van Maren, 'Transgender Movement's Last Defenders: Parents Who "Transitioned" Their Children', *European Conservative* (16 August 2023). The quotation is taken from Helen Joyce's interview on Peter Boghossian's YouTube channel, uploaded on 3 July 2023.

452    *'both an essence and a performance for which we write the script':* Timandra Harkness, *Technology Is Not the Problem: The Ultimate History of Our Relationship With Technology and How It Has Shaped Our World Today, From Smartphones to AI* (London: HarperCollins, 2024).

452    **against them, is known as 'belief perseverance':** The concept of 'belief perseverance' was popularised in an article by Lee Ross, Mark R. Lepper and Michael Hubbard, 'Perseverance in self-perception and social perception: biased attributional processes in the debriefing paradigm', *Journal of Personality and Social Psychology*, vol. 32, no. 5 (1975), pp. 880-92. The researchers ran two experiments on more than 200 participants which ultimately demonstrated that 'self-perceptions and social perceptions may persevere after the initial basis for such perceptions has been completely discredited'.

453    *'but wallows in it like a bestial hog':* Plato, op. cit., p. 220.

# Index

INDEX